D1593718

MYTH AND MEANING
IN
EARLY TAOISM

HERMENEUTICS
Studies in the History of Religions

GENERAL EDITOR
Kees W. Bolle
UCLA

MYTH AND MEANING
IN
EARLY TAOISM
The Theme of Chaos
(hun-tun)

N. J. GIRARDOT

UNIVERSITY OF CALIFORNIA PRESS

Berkeley   Los Angeles   London

Parts of chapters 2, 3, and 4 originally appeared in a much altered form in *History of Religions* 16 (1977): 294–324, *Journal of Chinese Philosophy* 5 (1978): 21–69, and *Philosophy East and West* 28 (1978): 299–321.

The inverted bottle-gourd visage on the jacket is the traditional Peking Opera mask of Liu T'ang, known as the "Redhaired Devil."

The lines from *Sphere, The Form of a Motion*, by A. R. Ammons, with permission of W. W. Norton & Company, Inc. COPYRIGHT © 1974 by A. R. Ammons

UNIVERSITY OF CALIFORNIA PRESS
Berkeley and Los Angeles, California

UNIVERSITY OF CALIFORNIA PRESS, LTD.
London, England

Library of Congress Cataloging in Publication Data

Girardot, N. J.
  Myth and meaning in early Taoism.

  Bibliography: p. 401
  Includes index.
  1. Taoism.   I. Title.
BL1920.G56   299'.51424   81-21964
ISBN 0-520-04330-8   AACR2

PRINTED IN THE UNITED STATES OF AMERICA

1 2 3 4 5 6 7 8 9

TO
MY GOURDKIN AND ANCESTRAL TRIAD:

Kay, who discerns,
David, who descries,
And Jacob, who wriggles.

CONTENTS

Hun-tun. The Two and the Three. Struggle and Conflict in
Chinese Dualism. Comparative Considerations: The Dayak
Tertium Quid.

ABBREVIATIONS

CCT   *Concordance to the Chuang Tzu (Chuang Tzu Yin Te)*

Chan   Chan Wing-tsit, *The Way of Lao Tzu*

DL   Granet, Marcel, *Danses et légendes de la Chine ancienne*

Graham   Graham, A. C., *Book of Lieh-tzu*

HNTCS   *Huai Nan Tzu Chu Shih*

LC   Eberhard, Wolfram, *The Local Cultures of South and East China*

LTCK   Chiang Hsi-ch'ang, *Lao Tzu Chiao Ku*

LTCS   Yang Pai-ling, comp., *Lieh Tzu Chi Shih*

Morgan   Morgan, E., *Tao, The Great Luminant*

SCC   Needham, Joseph, *Science and Civilisation in China*

Watson   Watson, Burton, *The Complete Works of Chuang Tzu*

PREFACE

LONG, LONG AGO in a far distant galaxy I wrote a dissertation that, like all such initiatory works, contained a small nascent germ of cogency hidden amid a pulpy mass of fatuity. Undoubtedly fatuity persists, but this is not that work. "I have learned many things, just by writing," St. Augustine once wrote; and I would like to think that the rewriting of that cosmogonically inchoate work has led to a more insightful and demonstrable thesis. At the very least it has given birth to an empty gourd that, along with the "people without anuses," may constitute more than anyone ever cared to know about such preposterous subjects. In any event, some sort of "ordered-chaos" has emerged and as Chuang Tzu knew so well, other interpretations are always possible.

Ritual reciprocity requires that I render homage to those who helped along the way and, as a historian of religions, I could hardly do otherwise. The first in my litany of respected elders, and the one who set me upon this aimless path, is of course that slightly mad and very maddening sage, Chuang Tzu, who introduced me to Mr. Hun-tun. Others who were involved during the incubation of my chaos fixation were my teachers and scholarly mentors at the University of Chicago—Mircea Eliade, Charles Long, Joseph Kitagawa, and Anthony Yu. All of them had the patient and cautioning foresight to see that there was something there at the beginning.

Most important for me, and yet most difficult because his influence runs so deeply through my work, is to acknowledge my special debt of gratitude to Professor Eliade. It was *in illo tempore* that his written muse first brought me from the study of medicine to Chicago to ponder religions, China, myths, alchemy, chaos, Snow White, and squirrels. Passionately curious and enthusiastic with respect to peculiar ideas, obscure books, and ridiculous student queries, boundlessly devoted to the liberation that comes from bibliographical research, and warmly gracious, humble, and supportive to those who sought his counsel or simply wanted to talk about odd and sundry matters. Professor Eliade's great virtue was to synthesize the best of a Taoist spirit and a Confucian pedagogy. I learned from him the humanistic significance, daemonic excitement, and scholarly toil of a history of religions that respects the strange contradictory meanings of religion in human life. Most of all I learned through him that religions often find their meaning in the interstices of the unexpected.

Others who have given valuable assistance, advice, criticism, and encouragement include Professors Laurence Thompson, Anna Seidel, Ellen Marie Chen, Nathan Sivin, Michael Saso, Tsai Yuan-huang, Kees Bolle, and Joseph Needham. Professors Charles Heiser, David Yu, and Isabelle Robinet took the extra time and trouble to read and comment on various drafts of some of the chapters. Having rescued me from many a blunder, Professors Heiser and Robinet have been extraordinarily helpful in this regard. For their concern and inspiration at timely moments during the long preparation of this work, I would also like to thank two Stanford graduate students, Edward Shaughnessy and Sun Lung-kee. To all of these colleagues I extend my thanks. Needless to say, responsibility for any remaining factual inaccuracies and scholarly ignorance is wholly mine. Concerning any interpretive foolishness and bias I have perpetrated, I am reminded of Eugene Genovese who, on a similiar prefatory occasion, remarked that "the usual disclaimer is unnecessary since no one in their right mind is likely to hold them responsible" (quoted in Peter Passell and Leonard Ross, *The Best* [New York: Farrar, Strauss, and Giroux, 1974], p. 9).

The tediously convoluted physical preparation of the several manuscripts that went into the final version of this book was aided and abetted by many different hands, but I would particularly like to acknowledge the assistance of three of my students at various institutions: Fritz West at Notre Dame, Shawn Rosenheim at Oberlin College, and Angelo Spinosa at Lehigh University. In this regard, also, I wish to thank my eleventh-hour typists—Gerry Dettra, Rhonda Dalla Palu, and Nancy and Kyle Sutton—who were able to instill typographic order into an incredibly motley manuscript. Anne Reese of the Lehigh University Publications Office is to be specially acknowledged for the handsome artistic execution of the title page's gourd design and for drawing the various figures. The preparation of the final typescript for publication was financially supported by the Committee on Unsponsored Research at Lehigh University, for which I am most appreciative.

Three others require special mention and recognition at this point. The first of these is my mother, Ruth M. Girardot, whose blithe spirit materialized at a crucial point during the last frenzied weeks of revising the final version of the manuscript. I would also like to thank my editor at the University of California Press, John Miles, who had the forbearance to wait out graciously the protracted culmination of this work. Lastly I would like to acknowledge the memory of a courtly and wise scholar-*hsien*, Holmes Welch, who died as I was completing this book. Despite personal troubles and difficulties that encumbered his last years, he was someone who embodied the principle that *wu-wei* is not without conscientious effort. I will always treasure my acquaintance with him and his care and concern for the foibles of a younger scholar.

One final caveat is in order. If at times I have seemed to be too completely empathetic with the Taoist metaphorical universe, I have been so advisedly in order to present the early Taoist symbolic counterpoint to the Confucian perspective. Anyone familiar with China, however, is aware of the fact that the wisdom of Chinese tradition is always to seek out the harmony of all cultural antinomies. As Chuang Tzu playfully respected the sagacity of his logical facsimile, Hui Shih, so also in the *Chuang Tzu* is Confucius capable of a partial Taoist metamorphosis. The lesson of the cicada and the dove works both ways, and Taoists in Chinese history also sought out a meaningful Confucian transformation. Confucian gentlemen need not always be boring.

N. J. G.

July, 1981
Lehigh University
Bethlehem, Pennsylvania

HUMPTY DUMPTY

An ancient immortal has said that . . . Hun-tun
is round and whole but its meaning is difficult to
make known.
>   —*Hsien Hsüeh Tz'u Tien*

. . . far from the scaffolding of the

human imagination, old (presumed) Chaos
stirred in himself, spirals (cellular whirlwinds),
upward swoops of bending aspiration, colli-
sions high with potentials of linkage, dissolv-
ings and

meldings lengthy and free—these "motions"
brought particles into progression often: if
the progressions often failed into tatter-
demalions, do-funnies, whatchamacallits, and
thingumabobs,

there was time enough in the slow motions of
landforms, oceans, of moon and sun for Chaos
to undo and recommence: certain weaves
caught on to random hooks and came into
separation and

identity: and found ways to cause the causes of
origin to recur with increasing frequency: one
must be careful not to bestow intention where
there may have been no more (much) than
jostling

possibility: keep jiggling the innumerable
elements and even integrations can fall out of
disintegrations: in any case, physicochemical
phenomena account sufficiently for the

output up to now: but all movements are religious: inside where motions making up and
rising turn about and proceed, node and come to
pass, prayer is the working in the currents . . .
>   —A. R. Ammons, *Sphere*

INTRODUCTION
ORDERING CHAOS
COMPARATIVELY

It is a queer enterprise—this attempt to determine the nature of something consisting of
phantomic phases.
—V. Nabokov. *Ada*

Myth can only be understood mythically.
—Jean Rudhart

ORDER AND SILENCE

In his discourse on the meaning of "order" in the human sciences Michel
Foucault starts with an amused and perplexed reflection on a " 'certain
Chinese encyclopaedia' in which it is written that 'animals are divided into:
(a) belonging to the Emperor, (b) embalmed, (c) tame, (d) sucking pigs, (e)
sirens, (f) fabulous, (g) stray dogs, (h) included in the present classification, (i)
frenzied, (j) innumerable, (k) drawn with a very fine camelhair brush, (l) *et
cetera*, (m) having just broken the water pitcher, (n) that from a long way off
look like flies.' "[1]

Foucault is quoting from one of Jorge Borges's fantastic literary universes
wherein the "Chinese" encyclopedia in question is more imaginative than
actual. Nevertheless, for both the social historian, Foucault, and the literary
artist, Borges, this quotation does set out the overall problem of the cultural
relativity of the idea and experience of order. This is an issue that is most
directly raised by the comparative confrontation of differing cultural orders,
especially in reference to the seemingly impossible order, the exotic chaos of
order, of a Chinese system of thought outside the conventions and codes

1

defining the Western perception and definition of the cosmos. The problem with either the imaginary or traditional "Chinese" conception of order is that it appears to be the antithesis of order in any meaningful or ordinary sense. The difficulty is, as Foucault remarks, "the stark impossibility of thinking *that*."[2] Confronting the fabulous absurdity of another culture's ordering of the "wild profusion of existing things" threatens our commonplace distinction between order and chaos.[3]

The fundamental question for Foucault is that "in every culture, between the use of what one might call the ordering codes and reflections upon order itself, there is the pure experience of order and of its modes of being."[4] This is at heart the very same problem addressed by all philosophies and all religions; and for the discussion at hand, this aptly poses the question of chaos and order, or the meaning of the Tao, for the early Taoist texts. The real problem is that the pure experience of order, the "inner law" or "hidden network" of our experience of life and self, is that "which has no existence except in the grid created by a glance, an examination, a language."[5] As the Taoist texts assert of the hidden Tao, the "Tao not spoken," it "is only in the blank spaces of this grid that order manifests itself in depth as though already there, waiting in silence for the moment of its expression."[6] "The West," to use the words of the poet Octavio Paz, "teaches us that being is dissolved into meaning, and the East that meaning is dissolved into something which is neither being nor non-being: In a The Same which no language except the language of silence names."[7]

The issue of the different human ways of perceiving order is also the problem of the various meanings of the Tao in Chinese tradition.[8] Part of the perverse genius of the early Taoists was to question the cosmological determinism of the ordinary Chinese cultural grid imposed by an Emperor's glance, Confucian ethics, or the Chinese language. The early Taoist vision sought to return to an experience of a deeper and more primitive life-order hidden by conventional language and culture and yet "waiting in silence for the moment of its expression." To know and experience the hidden order of the Tao was to know that it was not just the ordinary, civilized, or cosmic order. Tao is somehow and in some way "that something which is neither being nor non-being."

The oddity of early Taoist thought was its strange solicitude for chaos, its mystically austere passion for confusion. "The sage," the *Chuang Tzu* says, "steers by the torch of chaos and doubt [*ku i*]."[9] The Taoists affirmed that the silent, hidden, or real order of Tao embraced both chaos and cosmos, non-being and being, nature and culture. Grinning like obscene Cheshire Cats, the early Taoist sages anarchistically, yet not nihilistically, alleged that it is the de-natured order of the civilized cosmos that constitutes a destructive limitation and "fall" from the original and ongoing source of the creation of the world, man, and culture. The dilemma of the relativity of all orders, which is itself an Order, is for the early Taoists above all related to the mythological idea of a self-activated (*tzu-jan*) order of creation and nature. The secret of life, the mystical secret of salvation, is to return to the primitive chaos-order or "chaos-mos" of the Tao.[10] In early Taoism chaos, cosmos, becoming, time, and Tao are synonymous for that which is without an Orderer but is the "sum of all orders."[11] It is the nature of human life to be spontaneously *et cetera*.

CHAOS AND COSMOS

The difficulty with the early Taoist nostalgia for the primal spontaneity and saving power of chaos, the "stark impossibility of thinking *that*," is the overwhelming cultural compulsion to distinguish cosmos and chaos respectively in terms of absolute order and disorder, meaning and nonsense.[12] In many archaic traditions this kind of dichotomy is apparently sanctioned by the mythical imagery of a primordial battle between the forces of chaotic disorder and the triumphant powers of the sacred order of cosmos.[13] The mythic chaos, however, is never just equivalent to nothingness, profanity, neutrality, unreality, nonbeing, death, or absolute disorder.[14] Despite the fact that chaos constantly threatens the cosmic order, frequently becoming synonymous with the demonic, a comparative assessment of creation mythology generally affirms that the cosmos originally came from, and continually depends on, the chaos of the creation time.[15] The logic of myth claims that there is always, no matter how it is disguised, qualified, or suppressed, a "hidden connection" or "inner law" linking chaos and cosmos, nature and culture. Chaos, in other words, is Paz's inherently ambivalent "The Same" that stands between all dualities.

Jonathan Smith remarks that "chaos is never, in myths, finally overcome. It remains as a creative challenge, as a source of possibility and vitality over against, yet inextricably related to, order and the Sacred."[16] Even in those elite civilizational and literary mythologies that emphasize a seemingly decisive battle between chaos and cosmos, dragon and hero, monster and God, the chaos figures are in the final analysis "depicted as the very source of creative power."[17] The abiding creative power of the primordial chaos that is hidden within the measured order of the civilized cosmos is, for example, displayed by the inevitable and necessary return to chaos seen in the worldwide myth-ritual scenarios of the New Year and other important seasonal times of licensed folly.[18] Moreover, in mythologies from "primitive" or noncivilizational cultures (to some degree, also, in relation to the peasant/folk/barbarian/outsider dimension within early archaic civilizations) where the incongruities and anxieties of human life are more pronounced, there is sometimes reason to speak of a kind of "divine Chaos."[19] Mythologies of this type ultimately "insist on the interdependence of being and not-being, and it is the inexplicable transcendent unity of these two that they recognize in wonder and awe as absolute and call *Holy*."[20] "*Holy*," it should be added, because chaos is that which makes the parts of phenomenal existence temporarily "whole" again.

In contrast to the elite-lore of ancient civilizations that sought to control the image and power of chaos in human life by making myth into an institutionalized religious and literary form (i.e., the "classics"), the myth telling of "primitive" cultures and the continuing oral tradition of folkloristic story telling within an early civilizational context tend more readily to remember chaos as the principle that finally re-members and refreshes all existing forms of life. This is a bit like the difference between the "primitivity" of oral discourse that is always to some degree openended and ambiguous and the civility of written expression that freezes thought and sentiment into a single mold.

There may, in fact, be some covert connection here since the cultural passage from early nonliterate, neolithic traditions (i.e., "Developed Village Farming Efficiency" cultures)[21] to hierarchical, urban civilizations suggests, to borrow from both Octavio Paz and Claude Lévi-Strauss, that the civilized rite of writing was fundamentally the property of a religious/political "minority and was not used so much for communicating knowledge as for dominating and enslaving men."[22] From this point of view, writing and civilizations represent a "fall" from a more primitive state that respected the prestige of oral dialogue in the affairs of men. While ceremonially drawing men together into a single hierarchically centered order of the city-state, written expression at the same time breaks the harmonious intercourse among men as, perhaps, official literary versions of earlier, more primitive and oral myths tend to sever and hide the originally intimate connection between chaos and cosmos. Writing clears up the confusion of verbal expression only by sacrificing the mutuality and nuance of speech to the precision and power of abstract conceptualization. Writing, like all civilizational technologies, speaks and controls but does not listen: it suppresses dialogue.[23]

The English words *chaos* and *cosmos* derive, of course, from Greek terms that were originally associated with mythological images and themes. It is instructive in this sense to note that the earliest Greek uses of *chaos* carried little of the later extreme negative connotations of absolute disorder or meaningless nonbeing, interpretations that were in part due to the theological exclusivity found in the Biblical ideas of "genesis" and the antagonistic dualism of early

Zoroastrian tradition and some forms of Hellenistic gnosticism.[24] Even in Hesiod's synthetic literary rendition of earlier, more primitive mythologies (ca. eighth to seventh centuries B.C.), the cosmogonic scheme found in the first part of the *Theogony*—a scheme that is the structural basis for the other two sections telling the stories of Ouranos and Zeus as well as constituting the basis for the New Year's festival—presents *chaos* primarily as the "yawning gap" or the "empty separation" between heaven and earth during the beginning time.[25] In like manner the word *beginning* comes from the Old Norse *gina* (cf. Saxo-Grammaticus' *Ginnunga-gap*) and the Old English *on-ginnan*, which mean "to gape" or "to yawn." The Old Norse and Old English are in turn etymologically related to the Greek *chaos*.[26]

In Hesiod it is also the case that the primordial yawn of chaos, the toothless gaping emptiness of the beginning, is not an absolute nothingness or confusion but the fertile space of the center that established the dual cosmic form of heaven and earth and is filled with the power of Eros (= light), the personified third term of mutual attraction and reunion.[27] Chaos as grinning gulf, the yawning dawn of creation, is therefore the very basis of a cosmogonic process that manifests itself in the gestalt of a trinitarian form—a formless form that because of its emptiness mysteriously links the uncreated one and the created two into a meaningful whole.

If chaos is not in its mythological origins to be equated with the absence of all order, so also is cosmos not to be related entirely with the idea of order. *Kosmos* connotes basically the image of the "ornamentation" or "cosmetic" camouflage of chaos's stupid monkey-grin.[28] Cosmos is the cultivated *persona* of chaos. While acquiring the general meaning of a world system or universal order, cosmos suggests a special kind of "unnatural" or cultural order that can be etymologically related to the various words of decorum, decoration, polite, police, cosmetic, costume, and custom.[29] Cosmos is not necessarily associated with the creation of the world, order, nature, or culture per se but with the establishment of a measured, ranked, or ruling cultural order which masks a prior, more primitive kind of order (cf. in the New Testament 1 Cor. 1:21). In this sense of the word, the cosmos, cosmic order, or cosmological description of the world is especially related to the aristocratic codes of ritual propriety, status, decorum, merit, and "face" found within the context of a civilizational tradition. The acceptance of "civil" order as the definitive and true meaning of all order, as well as the basis for the very structures of reality, is to efface the intrinsic mythological connection between the wild and polite orders of chaos and cosmos, nature and culture.[30]

The gulf spontaneously created by the primal grin of formless matter is the empty source of the light and sound of created nature and human culture. It is not, however, polite to grin with a gaping mouth at a formal banquet. Civility and proper table manners require the control of one's bodily functions, one's inner organic demons of formless sound and gas, along with one's sense of humor, by maintaining the propriety of a stiff upper lip and only speaking when spoken to.[31] Even though there are times when a gentleman may feel a sudden urge to scratch and yawn, the ritual rule of civilized decorum rests on the idea that it is the appearance of cool control that counts. Taoists, as I will try to show, tend to grin somewhat idiotically while slurping their soup. This has its own kind of crazy logic and yeasty propriety.

DOUBTS AND DEFINITIONS

The crazy logic which links chaos and cosmos suggests that one of the basic findings of this study is that early Taoist thought is most adequately understood in terms of its relation to a mythological theme of creation, fall, and "salvational" return. Since in the pages that follow I will demonstrate as critically as possible the labyrinthian implications and structural coherence of the mythological cast of Taoist thought, I want in this introduction to set out in a synoptic way some of my general operating presuppositions.

The first issue to address is my methodological assumption that it is valid and necessary to consider the texts of early, classical, philosophical, or mystical Taoism as essentially and properly "religious" in nature. Most simply and without engaging in an elaborate defense of my point of view, this means that the philosophy of the early texts represents a system of symbolic thought and action that is "focused on salvation" and is interpretively grounded in mythical or cosmological "formulations of a general order of existence."[32] To define religion in this way is not to invoke an idea of salvation with a specific, once-and-for-all Christian flavor of savior, permanent eschatological redemption, or transcendental immortality. But from a broader and more anthropological perspective, it is to say that religion as a cultural system of symbols is concerned with a means of transforming, temporally or permanently, some "significant ill" that is seen to be part of the cosmological or existential order of human life.[33] Death is not always the most important of these "ills" and, more significantly and primitively, death may be interpreted as only one phase of the total process of human life in time.[34] The overall interpretation of human existence constitutes the "meaning context" for the particular idea of "salvation" since for many traditions, and China and the early Taoist tradition provide an exemplary case, existence, the organic round of life and death, is understood as a "rite of passage" that constantly involves moments of growth and regression, security and danger.

The salvational problem of life interpreted as a process of interrelated positive and negative changes is one that is focused on the relational ambiguities of knowledge, suffering, and justice in the affairs of men and women in culture.[35] Religion exists as a kind of sum of all other cultural systems to say that these ambiguities, the felt chaos of life, has meaning because it is interpretable. It is part of a larger fictional story—the myth—or the permanent cosmological structures of reality. That the mythic story and "formulations of a general order of existence" feel real, or are *made* real, is by virtue of the cultural fact that the ideal fiction of myth becomes an existential fact in the ritual embodiment of the story, structure, and meaning of life.[36] Ritual "salvation" in this sense is never final or finished. It always involves to some degree, either narratively or structurally, the dramatized repetition or retelling of the ultimate stories of why things are the way they are. Salvation is cosmologically grounded and infinitely repeatable. "Myths," as Victor Turner says, "treat of origins but derive from transitions."[37]

Salvation refers to "deliverance possessing cosmic implications," and religion, as "behavior focused on salvation," is concerned with healing human life in relation to the culturally perceived meaning and structure of the world.[38] Putting aside the issue of specific forms of religious expression within a civilizational context, religion—generically, culturally, and primitively—is a system of symbols that tells a story (through myths and rituals, cosmological classification and thought, sacred biographies, exemplary histories, theological and ethical doctrines, the theory and form of meditation and mysticism, etc.) of the "fall" (or multiple "falls" and anxieties) of ordinary human existence and, at the same time, provides a means of periodically recovering in this lifetime a condition of original wholeness, health, or holiness—terms that are all etymologically related to the primitive meaning of the word "salvation."

In consideration of the role of myth, and its cultural permutations, as the foundational symbolic form or "ideal structure" for expressing a religious interpretation of human life, it behooves me to clarify my working definition of myth as a specific kind of linguistic communication. Torn between claims of romantic spookiness and rationalist nonreferential banality, the modern scholarly discussion of the meaning and nature of myth has itself taken on mythic proportions and, for that reason, I would like to proceed as straightforwardly and heuristically as possible.

Perhaps the easiest route to follow is to say in agreement with the classicist Walter Burkert that myth most generally "within the class of traditional tales, is nonfactual story telling."[39] To fill out the terse accuracy of this definition, it can also be said that, whether as oral or written stories within early cultures, myths are ordinarily held to be religiously significant, traditional tales because they must be constantly repeated, retold, and reactivated in the course of human life.[40] The world of repetition affirmed by myth is "le monde de la *création continuée*."[41] Myths in this sense are distinguished from other kinds of traditional stories because they define and validate the existing cultural tradition. Myths, says Burkert, are "serious" traditional tales that are applied "to something of collective importance."[42]

It is necessary to remember myths in different ways because they account for a culture's most fundamental "formulations of a general order of existence" by relating present life to some ideal past (i.e., the characters are somehow suprahuman and the setting is some beginning period before the time of ordinary human existence). Mythic tales always tell of some kind of "once upon a time" origin that is an explanation for the problematics of human existence and functions as a model for current life.[43] Mythic tales in either nonliterate cultures or in archaic civilizations tell those cultures' most basic stories of the religious meaning or storied nature of tradition.

In this way, as well, myth is an ideal and nonfactual story form in that it does not directly refer to reality but *gives* tense and narrative meaning to the temporal flux of experienced reality. While natural forms of life may involve a narrative element as perceived by cultures, the "form of the tale is not produced by reality" but by language or the symbolic capacity of men.[44] A tale's character of linearity is, then, a result of the linguistic narrativity of human discourse. There is "no isomorphism between reality and tale" but it may be said that it is in the nature of language and symbol to interpret reality *as if* there were analogies between natural and cultural life.[45]

Reality does not "automatically yield a tale" since language always represents a "selection, condensation, structuralization" of perceived reality.[46] Myth says that the world *is like* a story. But the human use of language does automatically tend toward a tale-ordering of reality; and because of the historical focus of cultural interests, certain natural objects might be said to be especially tale-responsive. Myth is the traditional storied use of language for purposes of finding and making sense of the world. Narratively analogical and interpretive, myth in the history of culture represents the first use of a comparative method for understanding the meaning of human experience.

The meaning of a myth, its "structure of sense," depends on the Proppian formalities of its narrative "functions" but is also affected by its particular, historically and culturally bound, analogical symbolic content.[47] Contrary to the Lévi-Straussian position, it is necessary to take into account the specific kinds of symbols, and thematically related sets of symbols, within the context of cultural history in order to arrive at a meaningful interpretation. To do otherwise is to seek only abstract decipherment and not understanding.[48]

By their nature as a "primitive" form of interpretation, myths are subject to endless linguistic transformations in cultural history. It may be said, however, that myths do not die. They go underground and resurface as "mythic themes" in nonmythological literary forms.[49] "Mythic themes" in this sense represent interpretive literary abstractions of traditional mythological tales. Avoiding any Jungian metapsychological implications, mythic themes are "archetypal" or "paradigmatic" when they are found to be a "recognizable unit of recurrence whose variation and transformation may provide an aid in the interpretation of the specific works of a given tradition."[50]

For purposes of this study, therefore, a mythic theme will be taken to mean the detectable presence in written texts of recurrent symbolic images, or particular paradigmatic clusters of related images, that both summarize a central mythological idea and condense in an ideal-typical way the basic structure or logic of a set of myths, not all of which necessarily have the same historical or cultural background. Thematic exegesis will consequently pay attention to both the structural character of themes (the sequence and relation of images) and the particular symbolic content of an image or thematic ensemble of images (that, for example, the text employs an image of, say, a "gourd" rather than something else). The salient point here is that a theme qualifies as a "mythic theme" when both its symbolic content and its structural logic can comparatively be shown to refer back to identifiable mythological prototypes.

Besides the definitional issues of religion, myth, and mythic theme, there is also the problem of the seemingly illusory existence of a Taoist "tradition" in Chinese history. From the standpoint of Chinese social history "early Taoism" (what is traditionally called in Chinese, *Tao-chia*) appears to be only a bibliographical category for a set of miscellaneous and anonymous textual compilations.[51] The texts in question include especially the Eastern Chou/Pre-Han (ca. seventh to second centuries B.C.) *Lao Tzu*, or *Tao Te Ching*, and the *Chuang Tzu* along with, to some degree, the Han period (second century B.C. to second century A.D.) syncretistic works known as the *Huai Nan Tzu* and *Lieh Tzu*. These materials clearly do not constitute a wholly self-conscious school of thought or an organized social movement; but I would maintain in concert with several other scholars that the texts, however unconsciously or "structurally" at times, do display a generally consistent inner logic, a "central idea," or a mythically grounded pattern of religious convictions and procedures.[52] Based on my analysis of these texts, I feel that it is possible to trace out a thematic trajectory of salvational intent that can be taken as the basis for meaningfully referring to a Taoist "tradition" that embraces the early texts and certain aspects of the later, socially identifiable movements of *Tao-chia*.[53]

I use the term *trajectory* since the religious vision I will set out is never static or final and has undergone phases of reinterpretation. What I am suggesting is that despite important differences relevant to varying historical and sociological situations, there is finally a transformable, yet coherent, structure that informs the religious meaning to be found in all of the early texts. In a quite altered yet related way, this same underlying thematic structure may also be found behind much of the esoteric theory and practice of organized Taoism emerging out of the post-Han Way of the Celestial Master (Chang Tao-ling). The early Taoists' unqualified solicitude for chaos will, however, be reinterpreted somewhat schizophrenically in relation to a popular and private understanding of the Taoist religion.[54]

It is possible to be more precise as to the nature and shape of the thematic structure I am referring to and to suggest why it is foundational for the religious intentionality of the early Taoist texts. I will show that the early texts all manifest a set of multivalent symbolic images that is rooted in a particular mythological narration of the beginning (*arché*—creation of the world, man, and culture), middle-reversal-fall (*peripéteia*—the "dis-ease" of civilizational existence), and end (*lýsis*—an end that is a return to the beginning). Burkert notes that this classic tripartite definition of narrative *mythos* "comes remarkably close" to Vladimir Propp's fixed sequence of motifemes[55] and, I would add, to Arnold Van Gennep's structure for initiatory "rites of passage."[56] This mythic structure provides an understanding of the early Taoist interpretation of the "significant ill" of ordinary human life and its soteriological solution. In this exemplary and thematic sense, which is found throughout the various texts and different historical periods, the mythic model or structure can be called "paradigmatic" or "archetypal" for the theory and practice of early Taoist mysticism.

The structure that I will demonstrate as the paradigmatic basis for the unity of early Taoist mysticism can be given a name. Thus, the texts can be shown to harbor the presence of a certain ideal-typology of cosmogonic myth. I emphasize a typologically thematic rather than the actual narrative presence of myth, since the structure in question is clearly an abstract literary and philosophical ensemble of individual mythic images and themes coming from the debris of different oral/folk mythological traditions. The best name or label for this typology, indeed the Chinese and Taoist name found over and over again in the ancient sources, is *hun-tun* (along with its phonetic variants). This term is ordinarily translated as "chaos" and derives from ancient cosmogonic and anthropogonic myths involving the primary symbolic images of a cosmic egg-gourd (as well as the interrelated images of an ancestral animal deity, culture hero, cosmic giant, primordial couple, mass of flesh, etc.) as the original chaos condition/figure of the creation or flood time. That this is the best, or most mythologically and thematically proper, label for the inner structure and logic of the early Taoist religious vision is indicated by the fact that a *hun-tun* myth of primordial chaos was certainly present in China by the time of the Eastern Chou and is a key technical term in all of the early texts.

The word *hun-tun* in its Taoist use is, above all, an excellent example of what Lewis Carroll's Humpty Dumpty called a "portmanteau" word—that is, a word "packed up" with several meanings.[57] Unpacking these meanings and reconstructing the thematic order of their relationship can, therefore, tell something of the story and intent of the wayfarer. Indeed, the specific conceptual content of *hun-tun* as a word is not so important as the fact that it serves as a symbol for an underlying mythological form, theme, system, structure, pattern, or shape in the texts. In this way it is helpful to remember that Humpty Dumpty also affirmed that his reduplicated name, like *hun-tun*, means nothing but the "shape I am."[58] Being shaped like a large egg, both Humpty Dumpty and *hun-tun* (especially Hun-tun in the *Chuang Tzu*) refer primarily to the mythic theme of the creation, tottering, and eventual fall of the cosmic egg. The same is true for James Joyce's Tim Finnegan, the Irish hod carrier, whose drunken fall echoes the cosmic egg theme of Humpty Dumpty and suggests the "fall of Lucifer and the fall of man."[59] Curiously, the fall in *Finnegans Wake* is symbolized by Joyce's ten hundred-letter thunderclaps that phonetically and thematically "pack up" both Humpty Dumpty and Hun-tun: "bothall-choractorschumminaroundgansumminarumdrumstrumtruminahumpatadump-waultopoofoolooderamaunstrunup."[60]

"PHANTOMIC PHASES": THE QUESTION OF CHINESE MYTH

I have stressed that this study is primarily directed toward an unveiling of the latent mythic structure of Taoist thought and practice and that this structure, this hidden order, is the basis for speaking of the religious meaning or soteriological intent of the early texts. My concern for the mythological context of early Chinese tradition is admittedly fraught with problems. The role of myth in early Chinese literature, for example, is somewhat like the "curious incident of the dog in the night-time" from the *Memoirs of Sherlock Holmes*:

> "Is there any point to which you would wish to draw my attention?" [asked the Inspector]

"To the curious incident of the dog in the night-time."
"The dog did nothing in the night-time."
"That was the curious incident," remarked Sherlock Holmes.[61]

The point here is that in comparison with other ancient civilizational traditions, early China seems to be singularly lacking in any complete or coherent mythological narratives, especially creation myths. Myth curiously seems *to do nothing* in early Chinese tradition. This all-too-common observation has led some scholars to claim that it is particularly the absence of cosmogonic myth that gives rise to the "cosmological gulf" between Chinese and Western traditions.[62] In nineteenth-century scholarship the apparent unconcern for cosmogonic thought and mythological expression even seemed to make ancient China a welcome anomaly in the history of world civilizations since there was never any superstitious "deification of sensuality."[63] In sympathy with the Confucian humanistic admonition to keep the spirits at a distance, the absence of myth seemed to insure that ancient China was "singularly pure" when contrasted with all other archaic civilizations caught up in the superstitious throes of religion and myth.[64]

There is no doubt that there are significant differences in the ancient Chinese world view in comparison with other traditions, but the notion that the cosmological gulf consists in the nonexistence of myth, creation myth, or mythological thought is an issue that deserves to be put to rest with all possible dispatch. It is not the absence of creation mythology that accounts for the cosmological differences but the manner and nature of the Chinese interpretation of traditional mythological creation tales. The real "gulf" has to do with how different early civilizations fathomed the mythological gap of chaos.[65]

The work of Chang Kwang-chih and others shows that during the Eastern Chou period there was a rich traditional mythological lore that affected all levels of early Chinese civilization.[66] There is also sufficient evidence to argue for the presence of mythological systems of "cosmogonic formations and construction" that influenced all the major ancient text traditions or "schools."[67] Moreover amid the congeries of mythology reconstructed by Chang, there is finally the central cosmogonic theme that in the beginning the "cosmos was . . . a chaos [*hun-tun*], which was dark and without bounds and structure."[68]

Chang goes further to classify the ancient creation themes into the functional categories of either the "separation" or the "transformation" of the original *hun-tun* condition or thing.[69] The separation thesis follows the principle of multiplication ("the Chaos was One, which was divided into two elements") such as in chapter 42 of the *Tao Te Ching* and as is "unquestionably implied in

Chuang Tzu and T'ien Wen of *Ch'u Tz'u*.''[70] While this theme is already philosophized in most of the texts, there are clear traces of its connection with the widespread cosmic egg-gourd and primordial couple myths. The other transformation theme states that ''certain natural elements were transformed out of the bodily parts of mythical creatures'' and is seen in texts like the *Shan Hai Ching* that speak of such creation deities as Chu-lung, Nü-wa, and Chu-yin.[71] Chu-yin, for example, is the snakelike deity of Chung Mountain who does not ''drink, eat, or breathe.''[72]

Chang notes that the transformation theme typologically prefigures the later, more elaborate cosmic giant mythology of. P'an-ku (as well as the animal ancestor and ''mass of flesh'' themes); and, I would add that the description of the chaos monster, Chu-yin, is also analogous to the condition of the *Chuang Tzu*'s Emperor Hun-tun who is bored with seven openings in order to ''see, hear, eat, and breathe'' or the *Shan Hai Ching*'s description of Hun-tun as a mythic creature who is without face and eyes.[73]

Chang's cosmogonic categories of ''separation'' and ''transformation'' originally represented different independent mythological traditions, but in the texts of the Chou and Han they were creatively rearticulated into a common mythological pattern of meaning. This kind of interpretive coalescence of originally different mythic themes will be especially important in coming to grips with the mythological background for the coherent structure of cosmogonic intentionality found in the early Taoist texts. As Chang says, it is necessary to examine the dynamics of the functional interaction of the various independent mythic units since there are always sociological and ideological ''reasons'' allowing for their coalescence.[74]

These last comments call for some clarification since, despite the deductive and reconstructed presence of originally coherent myths and the necessary assumption of an unrecorded oral tradition of living mythological fabulation in the ancient period, it still must be admitted that the earliest written sources, including the Taoist materials, do not preserve integral mythological tales. Ancient Chinese literature is basically nonnarrative in any overt sense and is not informed by mythic themes in the dramatic and epic way of many other ancient literatures.[75]

While the *Chuang Tzu*'s parabolic style demonstrates the early literary use of mythologically based story fragments, the *Lao Tzu* or *Tao Te Ching* is totally devoid of any narrative element or even of any proper names. There is some vague, unprovable possibility that the *Tao Te Ching* may have been a kind of ''prompt book'' for a more narrative oral tradition of mystical teachings and techniques, but the demonstrable fact is that the text as it stands is only an unusually terse collection of semipoetic epigrams. It is simply the case that the earliest Taoist texts do not record or tell coherent myths or even follow an overall narrative form. Granting these realities, it can nevertheless be said that early Taoist thought and expression is "mythic" in its meaning because of its paradigmatic use of mythic themes. The "structure of sense" in the Taoist texts is based on a creative literary and religious reinterpretation of mythological images and themes. It is in this way that Taoist metaphysics might be thought of as a kind of nonnarrative "mythologie seconde."[76]

If actual mythological tales in nonliterate cultures may be thought of as a first or "primitive" use of a comparative method for interpreting the world, then early Chinese written literature of all ideological persuasions might similarly be said to represent the first wholly "structural" reinterpretation of traditional oral and folkloric mythological stories. Traditional narrative myths have been reduced in Chinese literature to an inner "logical" code of binary classification and the resolution of a centering synthesis. It is this inner thematic code that makes early Chinese literature, whether the Classics or the Taoist texts, structurally mythic if not mythological in terms of overt characters or narrative form.

In an insightful analysis Andrew Plaks has essentially argued for this kind of structural understanding of the role of myth in Chinese literature. For Plaks, Chinese literature is not built on mythological or narrative forms but on the more formal, immediately structural, cosmological-classificatory implications of an archetypal, ritual-like "logic." Because it is ritualistically archetypal, Chinese literature neglects the usual Western literary interest in the dramatic mythological detail of narrative form and action.[77]

It should already be obvious that I generally agree with Plaks' interpretation, but at the same time I think that Plaks makes too much of a polar distinction between ritual/spatial formality (a nonnarrative "structural" logic) and mythological/temporal narrativity. More accurately it may be said that the inner logical form and outer thematic content, like space and time, come together in an ideal "narrative" structure that embraces both myth and ritual. In its most basic sense this is the *mythos* structure of *arché*, *peripéteia*, and *lýsis* or beginning, middle, and end. Interpreted religiously, it is creation, fall, and return. Interpreted ritually, it is the initiatory pattern of withdrawal, transition, and reincorporation. Interpreted cosmologically, it is the numerical code of "one, two, and three." And interpreted mystically and alchemically, it is the internalized pattern of *solve et coagula* that collapses all distinctions of space and time, ritual and myth, body and spirit, microcosm and macrocosm, end and beginning.

The Chinese twist that is given to this archetypal plot is that creation, as well as cosmological and soteriological meaning, do not ordinarily involve the epic idea of a final and permanent conquest of some existential chaotic foe. Above all, in Taoist literature where there is less attention to boring civilizational knights and gentlemen, the quest for a meaningfully authentic life in the mystical sense is not a hero's prize. A Taoist does not conquer life to *win* salvation but *yields* to the eternal return of things. As the idea of creation is not a once-and-for-all heroic act of a Creator outside of time and space, so also is the soteriological meaning of early Taoism directly related to the eternity of spontaneous self-creation and return. Lacking the narrative sweep and epic pathos of other ancient religious literatures, the early Taoist texts more modestly claim that the "salvation" of man and society is a matter of the resynchronization of human periodicity with the cycles of cosmic time. This has a very "primitive" ring to it.

COMPARATIVE ORDER: "A QUEER ENTERPRISE"

As an interpretation of the Taoist second-order interpretation of original mythological interpretations, my method is fated to be a queerly proleptical enterprise. Comparative analysis, however, does not mean that a Frazerian, Tylorian, Jungian, or Hentzian mania for ethnographic "scrap-collecting" need be the ruling principle.[78] In place of stalking the elusive archetypes of the collective unconscious or ranging hither and yon in varicolored gardens of symbol, the conviction basic to the method employed here is that meaningful comparison can never disregard the ecological, cultural, and historical contexts of the texts, symbols, themes, and myths it is investigating.

With this in mind my procedure will involve a "controlled comparison" of themes and myths at three interrelated levels.[79] First and most crucial is the comparative determination of thematic constellations of homologous images that are internal to the texts in question. This is complemented by a second stage of exegesis in which the thematic assemblage is compared typologically with actual mythological and folkloric materials coming from *closely related* historical, cultural, and linguistic units. While particular images and themes may be related only in the creative imagination of the author or authors, the second phase of typological analysis does have some reference to possible historical and cultural origins, albeit rarely conclusively. Finally, I will allow myself the wary and speculative indulgence of some cross-cultural comparison of the various images, themes, and myths in the interest of suggesting some of the general significance of the Taoist vision in relation to the history of world religions. While the third strictly speculative step has a legitimate role to play in understanding the overall "structure of sense" perceived in the documents, the testing of the hypothesis—its falsification, revision, or verification—rests entirely on the critical accuracy and cogency of the first two culturally and historically delimited steps.

Fundamental to my approach is that the interpretation of ancient texts is best accomplished by a comparative method that starts with a descriptive juxtaposition of concrete images and themes and only secondarily works outward to a more abstract analytical edifice. The ordering of these steps is not always or necessarily sequential and perhaps the best image for this type of comparison is one of an ever widening and overlapping spiral that starts with, remains linked to, and constantly circles around the original textual deposit of particular images and themes. This is a method that partakes of the storied redundancy of myth. In history, cultures, and texts, images give rise to other images, themes to other themes, myths to other myths. Meaning, therefore, is contextually determined in relation to the different interconnected systems of multiple symbols, themes, and myths. Interpretations give rise to other interpretations. "Everything in human representations, or at least everything that is essential," says George Dumézil, is "system."[80]

As a final and related methodological point, I want to emphasize that this study will only indirectly be concerned with specialized sinological problems of philology and history, although I will try to draw out such issues where they are relevant. As a historian of religions, I have assumed the liberty of keeping the hermeneutical issue paramount; and, consequently, I am finally concerned with a more synthetic and interpretive perspective appropriate to the religious intentionality of the early Taoist texts. There is no doubt that there is a certain risk in such an approach, a risk that calls for a final assessment and critical evaluation in terms of the more minute philological and historical issues. On the other hand, interpretive integrations of previously isolated facts also reflect back on, and can help to refine critically, those same philological and historical problems.

The risks involved in my hermeneutical invasion of sinological territory might be said to be justified by the need to reinstate the legitimacy of the methodological spirit, if not always the specific results, of the great French tradition of Marcel Granet and Henri Maspero who, while working with immense technical expertise and the best available scholarly resources, sought to draw out a comparative sociological context of meaning from their Chinese sources that went beyond the narrow boundaries of philological exegesis.[81] Respect must always be paid to the ultimate authority of the text and one must take into account the best philological and historical determinations of that text; but at the same time, the ancient traditional documents of China can also be shown to speak a symbolic language more broadly communicative and universally meaningful than indicated by the specialized issues of philology and history.[82] The task of interpretation should be to evaluate the evidence in that double sense of critically adhering to the cultural, philological, and historical integrity of the documents while being sensitive to wider comparative possibilities of synthetic understanding. This obviously calls for a certain amount of reasoned, or even imaginative, speculation; but if there has been a conscientious attempt to ground the supposition in the concrete content of the sources, then there is no need to fear that the results must necessarily dwell within the realm of numinous humbug.

The irony of the relative neglect of a structural methodology among sinologists is that through George Dumézil and Claude Lévi-Strauss directly, and through Mircea Eliade more indirectly, Granet's method and work can be said to have influenced three of the most important subspecies of structural comparison in contemporary scholarship.[83] After a long hiatus it has been the contemporary rediscovery of structuralism through the mediation of Granet and other early twentieth-century figures that has advanced the theoretical sophistication and cultural understanding of many disciplines. This is especially true in relation to the cultural history of Indo-European traditions (Dumézil), the general history of world religions (Eliade), and social anthropology (Lévi-Strauss). Regardless of the adequacy of each of these different forms of structural comparison, it is a revealing comment on the methodological poverty of sinology that Granet's work and interpretive agenda is still largely spurned in the area of Chinese studies.[84]

But the proof of any methodology is to be found only in the textual and cultural pudding under examination. In view of the focus of this study, it is perhaps more appropriate to say that the significance of the *hun-tun* theme in Chinese and Taoist tradition may be comparatively found floating in a bowl of wonton soup! What I mean by this suitably enigmatic remark will become evident in the following pages and it is best that I conclude these introductory comments by taking to heart what Edmund Leach once said in a rare moment of methodological humility. Thus, all that either of us has attemped to do in our quite different studies is ''to show that the component elements'' in some very familiar materials ''are, in fact, ordered in a pattern of which many have not been previously aware.''[85]

PART ONE

SAT ON A WALL

PRELIMINARY MEANDERS

What manner of things are the darkness and light? How did the yin and yang commingle? How do they originate things, and how change them?

What means are there to examine what it was before heaven above and earth below had taken shape? How is it possible to probe into that age when the light and darkness were still undivided? And how do we know of the chaos of insubstantial form?

—*Ch'u Tz'u*
(T'ien Wen, trans. D. Hawkes)

Putting aside the God of Goodness . . . and taking first the God of Creation—or to give him his chief philosophical *raison d'être*, the First Cause—we see that a supernatural or divine origin is the logical consequence of the assumption that one thing leads to another, and that this series must have had a first term; that, if you like, though chickens and eggs may alternate back through the millennia, ultimately, we arrive at something which, while perhaps no longer resembling either a chicken or an egg, is nevertheless the first term of that series and can itself only be attributed to a First Cause—or to give it its theological soubriquet, God. How well founded is such an assumption? Could it be, for instance, that chickens and eggs have been succeeding each other in one form or another literally for ever?

—Tom Stoppard, *Jumpers*

1

SOUP, SYMBOL, AND SALVATION: THE CHAOS THEME IN CHINESE AND TAOIST TRADITION

> How pleasant were our bodies in the days of
> Chaos [*hun-tun*].
> Needing neither to eat or piss!
> Who came along with his drill,
> And bored us full of these nine holes?
> Morning after morning we must dress and eat
> Year after year, fret over taxes.
> A thousand of us scrambling for a penny,
> We knock our heads together and yell for dear
> life.
> —Han Shan (trans. Burton Watson)

THE LONGING FOR the lost time of an unfrenzied paradise—paradoxically the time of "chaos" or *hun-tun*—expressed in this T'ang dynasty poem finds its source in the *Chuang Tzu*, which tells the tale of the mythological Emperor of the Center called Hun-tun who dies after seven days when he is given the holes of sense, alimentation, evacuation, and sexuality that constitute human nature.[1] This deadly plastic surgery is accomplished by two well-meaning but boring guests who share in the simple hospitality of the Central Kingdom and disasterously decide to pay back (*pao*ᵃ) Emperor Hun-tun's kindness. But the discovery of the *locus classicus* for this poem's imagery only suggests one facet of the meaning of the chaos theme in Chinese tradition.

It will be my primary focus to show that the story of Emperor Hun-tun and the mythological theory of creation that it embodies lie at the very heart of the metaphysical and soteriological convictions found in the early Taoist texts. The elucidation of the semantics of the *hun-tun* theme of chaos will prove, however, to be an extremely difficult and convoluted task since it is something that overflows the boundaries of classical Taoism and displays an amazing, although at times hidden and degraded, resonance throughout diverse areas of Chinese cosmological, intellectual, religious, political, and artistic heritage. In many ways the mythological theme of *hun-tun* is integral to the overall story and ethos of Chinese cultural history. Both Taoists and Confucians, as well as *yin* and *yang*, finally come together in the Central Kingdom of Emperor Hun-tun. "Hun-tun" is not so much a word but a way, or ways, of viewing the world.

To cite only a few meandering examples of the ubiquity of the *hun-tun* theme, it is worth noting that, aside from its usage as a poetic illusion, it is found in such popular folk novels as the *Hsi Yu Chi* and *Feng Shen Yen I*, which open with titular passages invoking the creation mythology of the primal chaos.[2] Within other realms of Chinese artistic endeavor and theory, the *hun-tun* theme and the cosmogonic model found in chapter 42 of the *Tao Te Ching* have some important affinity with the famous "one-stroke" method of painting devised by the seventeenth-century artist Shih-t'ao.[3] The pervasive utopian ideas of the *t'ai-p'ing* and *ta-t'ung*[a] (the times of "great peace" and "great unity") can also be related to the notion of the *hun-tun* time as a golden age and are shared in different ways by both early Confucians and early Taoists.[4]

Politically in the ancient Han and pre-Han period, the death of Emperor Hun-tun, or the ritual shooting of arrows at a blood-filled sack known as a *hun-tun*, was symbolically associated in the Classics with the banishment of a king's wicked sons and ministers, a marriage alliance of differing political factions, the military suppression of barbarian tribes, the overthrow of an evil king/usurper, or the change of a dynasty/feudal kingdom.[5] Even in the ideologies of late sectarian, Chinese Buddhist secret societies (e.g., the White Lotus) it is possible to see an underlying connection with the archaic mythology of *hun-tun*.[6] As miniature and multiple regressions to a "chaotic" or primitive condition, any sort of "revolutionary" change or new creation (seasonal, social, political, religious) is in Chinese history often affiliated with the enigmatic Emperor of the Center.

In his erudite textual analysis Lo Meng-ts'e extensively documents the fact that, besides the early Taoist materials, ancient works like the classical *I Ching*, the legalist *Hsun Tzu* and *Han Fei Tzu*, and the Confucian *Mencius* all indicate a familiarity with the cosmological meaning of *hun-tun* through their use of such expressions as "above shape and form" (*hsing erh shang*), "purity" (*ch'un*), "being alone" (*tu-li*), "superior man" (*chün-tzu*), "great man" (*ta-jen*), "mind" (*hsin*), "nature" (*hsing*), and "funerary image" (*hsiang-jen* or *yung-jen*).[7] Lo, furthermore, argues that the creation mythology of *hun-tun* must be seen as the basis for much of early Chinese cosmological speculation of whatever particular "school." Given *hun-tun*'s connection with the foundations of the overall Chinese world view and ethos, it is not surprising that in a broad philosophical sense stretching from the earliest times of the *I Ching* and *Lao Tzu*, down to, and including, Neo-Confucianism, *hun-tun* can be shown to provide an important context for understanding such key terms as *chüeh-tui* ("absolute"), *ta-ch'üan* ("self-sufficient"), and especially *ta-hsiang* ("great form" or "ultimate reality").[8]

Another linkage that brings out some of *hun-tun*'s relation with ancient cosmogonic myth (especially of the cosmic egg variety) is the Han dynasty astronomical theory known as the Hun-t'ien[a] system. In the Hun-t'ien[a] cosmology the universe was shaped like an egg with the heavens as a sphere enclosing the earth—"Heaven is like a hen's egg and earth like the yellow in the egg, suspended lonely in the midst of heaven."[9] It is said that the ancient astronomer Chang Heng (A.D. 78–139), who perfected the uranosphere and armillary sphere (called *hun-t'i* and *hun-i*[a]) and upheld the Hun-t'ien[a] system, fathomed "heaven and earth and with his constructions he imitated creation."[10]

More prosaically, the *hun-tun* theme is found in traditional references to the *hun-t'ang*, or bathhouse with a dome-shaped cupola, which has possible associations with the meditation chamber (*ching-shih*) in esoteric sectarian Taoism where bathing was performed for physical and spiritual purification.[11] The reference to the characteristic form of the *hun-t'ang* having a "dome-shaped" ceiling suggests the more expansive and ancient cosmological symbolism of the *axis mundi* mountain, K'un-lun, which like Mt. Meru in Buddhist tradition, became a frequent religious and literary allusion as well as the mythical architectural archetype for many ancient Chinese religious structures in their reproduction of K'un-lun's bipartite cosmic form, its rounded mound, four windows, gardens, and pools.[12]

THE WORD, RITE, AND FABLE OF HUN-TUN

The idea of the cosmic mountain, K'un-lun, as an analogue for *hun-tun* both in form and sound suggests that within the context of early Taoism, and even more broadly within the Chinese folk tradition (especially in terms of what I will call the "southern" cultural complex), the mythological theme of the primal chaos time, condition, or "thing" can be shown to embrace and support a whole cluster of homologous motifs—for example, the image of a watery, fluid, or embryonic state; a primordial whirlpool or abyss; the idea of the deluge; the symbolism of darkness, void, emptiness, and nothingness; the notion of a primal matter or "mass of flesh" that is uncarved and anusless ("needing neither to eat or piss"); the sexual imagery of a feminine womblike condition, the incestuous reunion of a primordial couple, or the idea of the hermaphroditic bisexuality of an animal ancestor or cosmic giant. In addition to these images, there is a whole series of *imago mundi* associations concerning the perfectly balanced cosmological form of the paradise condition of *hun-tun*, particularly the "monde a part" motif connected with the symbolism of the calabash gourd (*hu-lu*, etc.), egg, cocoon (*chien*), empty grotto-cave (*tung* or *k'uo-lu*), split or doubled tree (*k'ung-t'ung*), land of the dead, garden, hermitage or retreat house, meditation chamber (such as the above mentioned *ching-shih*), sack (*nang*), or vase (*hu-lu*, etc.).

The homophonic permutation of *hun-tun* and *k'un-lun* intimates that another reason for seeing *hun-tun* as a primary structure of cosmological and religious meaning is that many of the associated images and motifs listed above, along with a group of important technical terms in the theory and practice of early and later Taoist meditation, are not only thematically related but are also phonetic variants of the binominal expression *hun-tun* (archaic pronunciation: **g'wen/ yuen-*d'wen/d'uen*)—for example, such phonetically reduplicated compound words as *hun-lun, hun-hun, k'un-lun, k'ung-t'ung, hsüan-t'ung, hung-t'ung, tung-t'ung*, and *hu-lu*. The relative phonetic poverty and consequent rhyming propensity of the Chinese language necessarily instills caution with respect to this point; but there is no doubt that, linguistically speaking, the double phonemic term *hun-tun* is a rather special Chinese word. As a peculiar "double-name," *hun-tun* may even reveal certain linguistic traits, some of which may not be originally of the Sino-Tibetan family of languages, that are clues to its cultural and linguistic origins.

The etymological documentation and possible cultural and mythological significance of this curious linguistic point will be discussed throughout this work; but as a foretaste of the unexpected yet strangely appropriate semiotic concoction that emerges, I would like here to take note of Rolf Stein's tentative meditation on the "word-family" that blends gourds, grottos, mountains, the cosmogonic chaos, and the mystic experience:

The calabash $hu^{f,g}$ is also called *hu-lu*. It depicts a complete world, mysterious, and closed in upon itself. *Men hu-lu* signifies: "a closed gourd, a mystery" [and] is made of two superimposed spheres. One can compare the series: hu^c "round, complete"; *hu-lun* "complete, entire"; hu^d "troubled vision, crepuscular"; hu^e "obscure, abstruse." A close graphic variant of hu^h is $k'un^a$ meaning "a passage between two walls of a mansion, women's chamber (i.e., a hidden retreat or retired, obscure)." *K'un-ao* designates a "place profoundly hidden. . . ." The series signifying "obscure, troubled" includes the words *hun* or *k'un*. Doubled, they give *hun-lun*, an expression which designates also chaos (troubled waters), closed up like an egg, and the condition of unconsciousness (*wu suo chih chih mao*). Chaos [or *hun-tun*] is an obscure leather bottle [i.e., sack made of skins] which sees nothing. The leather sack is a receptacle for wine like the calabash. The calabash *hu-lu* or the vase $hu^{f,g}$ is a mountain in the eastern ocean and an abode of the immortals. An identical abode is found in the western ocean; it is K'un-lun. K'un-lun has two tiers: an upright cone matched with a reversed cone. The calabash *hu-lu* is composed of two superimposed spheres. K'un-lun is also in the human head. There are in its most secret parts a "chamber like a grotto" (*tung-fang*, a term which also designates the nuptial chamber!) and "nirvana" (*ni-wan*). In order to penetrate into it by mystical meditation one enters into a "chaotic" state (hun^d) which resembles the primordial condition, paradise, the "unconsciousness" of the uncreated world.[13]

How all of these sundry words and images may be thought of as the ten thousand seeds from a single cucurbitic vessel remains to be seen. But along with Stein's perplexing gloss and with respect to the "doubled" nature of these words, Lo Meng-ts'e has drawn attention to the fact that from a philological perspective the expression *hun-tun* is a good example of a "rhyming compound" (*tieh-yun*) or "reduplicated word" (*tieh-tzu*) that was anciently used for its auditory or visual effect (like the English expression "long, long, ago" or for that matter, cucurbit, cucumber, a cuculiform and cucullated monk, or Humpty Dumpty!). Lo maintains that reduplicated words like *hun-tun*, and its related vocabulary, "suggest cyclic movement and transformation" by their very sound and shape.[14] Ritually mumbling the sounds of "hun-tun" might, therefore, be said to have a kind of incantatory significance that both phonetically and morphologically invokes the mythological and ontological idea of the Tao as the *creatio continua* process of infinitely repeated moments of change and new creation. As Lewis Carroll's Humpty Dumpty says, it's his shape that counts.

Whether or not it is really possible to think of *hun-tun* as an ancient mantric invocation is not entirely demonstrable. Neither is it terribly momentous for the general survey of Chinese chaos lore intended in this chapter. My random collation of form, sound, and meaning does, however, bring out the ritual functionality of the *hun-tun* theme and some of its correlated symbolic paraphernalia. Again, within a ritual context, the cosmological *hun-tun* and *hu-lu* gourd are found to be linked, especially as they are both popularly associated with practices of warding off evil influences at crucial transitional times in the cosmic and social round of life.[15]

In traditional China, for example, *hu-lu* gourds, or imitation paper calabash amulets, were commonly hung up as protective charms during the "dangerous" fifth lunar month (the summer solstice, midsummer, or dragon boat time) and were also ritually used during the festivities of the seventh month (a "harvest" or Halloween-type festival period associated with the return of the dead).[16] A contemporary and Westernized transformation of this may be seen in modern-day Taiwan where at the time of the winter solstice of the eleventh month (cosmologically equivalent to the summer solstice of the fifth month), and in preparation for the yearly resurrection of life and society at the New Year, it is a custom for some to decorate a Christmas tree with small wooden *hu-lu* gourds, which are said to bring good luck.[17]

Moreover, the ancient practice of warding off the evil influence of the "five poisonous animals" (snake, centipede, scorpion, lizard, and toad—all ambivalent "chaos" creatures outside the normal order of life) during the fifth month made use of dismembered dogs in the Han, or later, the popular talismanic prints of the "Chang T'ien-shih, the 'Heavenly Master Chang,' who kills the animals with his magic sword or his 'chaotic box.' "[18] In the post-Han legends of Chang as the "Taoist pope" and founder of sectarian Taoism, this chaotic or *hun-tun* box is identified as a bottle gourd.[19] Like Pandora's fabled container, the chaos-box was ritually fickle, responsible for either releasing or controlling demons. There are finally many other literary examples of the exorcistic function of *hun-tun* and *hu-lu* in the popular romances of *Hsi Yu Chi* and *Feng Shen Yen I*.[20]

In Japan, also, the *netsuke* tradition of protective amulets was particularly linked to calabash symbolism and, even more quaintly, it is still the tradition that a small calabash image is embossed on every pair of *geta* sandals to ward off stumbling.[21] Another Japanese instance of the same sort of symbolism concerns the popular religious prints known as the "Catfish pictures" (*namazu-e*), which appeared in 1855 after the last great earthquake in Edo (now Tokyo). In these talismanic prints the earthquake or chaos creature is depicted as a gigantic catfish (or dragon) that is subdued by an animal (monkey), wonder-child, or warrior-hero using a sword or bottle-gourd (J. *hyotan* = C.

hu-lu).[22] I need only mention in passing that there is a curious reappearance of the Catfish tradition in the popular Godzilla cycle of films which arose after the nuclear chaos unleashed upon Japan. In fact, the symbolic details in the evolution of Godzilla filmic poplore parallel in a quite surprising way the traditional Japanese and Chinese mythological and folkloric themes of the combat with an ambivalent chaos creature (some of the films, like *Mothra*, directly recalling the ancient motifs of the cosmic egg-gourd-cocoon[23]) that is usually tamed, after the failure of the forces of the civilizational order, through the special and indirect agency of children.

One common rationalized and scholastic Chinese explanation for these associations is that a hu^h (as a pot, jug, gourd, etc.; a container) can be pronounced as, or punned with, fu^b, meaning a magic spell, talisman, or charm: "hence," the figure of a pot or gourd "denotes a charm" and "in places where 'hu' is not pronounced 'fu' the pun is still maintained by confusing it with another hu^l, to protect, to guard."[24] That the "hence" in this kind of explanation is an oversimplification needs no special comment and is somewhat like saying that the presence of eggs at Easter is because Jesus liked eggs as a boy or that in English egg rhymes with keg. I have already shown that there are important linguistic and etymological factors to take into account when coming to grips with Chinese gourds and chaos; but the ritual function and symbolic meaning of the relation between gourds and the cosmogonic chaos, eggs and resurrection, in both Chinese and Western tradition is more profoundly a matter of how they draw upon a mythically grounded "pagan" (in the sense of rural or folk; as distinct from the civilized order of rational explanations) cosmological system of thought and imagination.

To continue with this "rhetoric of association," which, while ultimately specious as a comparative method, does allow for the cataloging of some traits that are similar in some superficial way,[25] I want to point out that my reference to eggs in relation to the mythological implications of gourds and chaos was not mere whimsy on my part. The ritual use of eggs (i.e., their decoration or passage from the wild to ornamental order, their prognosticative role in games of chance, and their consumption after a culinary transformation from the raw, fluid state to the "hard-boiled" condition) during the Christianized New Year festivities of Easter is not restricted to Western tradition. As J. J. M. de Groot shows in his study of south Chinese folk practices, the ritual or oracular use of eggs is clearly related in China to ancient cosmogonic themes concerning the yearly regeneration of the world, man, and society.[26]

There is no probable or necessary historical or diffusionist explanation for the parallels between the Occidental and Oriental practices, nor does the

Chinese word for egg rhyme with any Indo-European ovoid term; but more significant for my purposes is that in both cases, and even if cosmogonic stories are no longer explicitly told or remembered, eggs, cocoons, gourds, chaos, and creation have meaning because they are fabled in nature and culture. The actions performed with eggs, gourds, and chaotic boxes are calendrically and narratively storied in their symbolic structure and intentionality. Although the actual story/explanation told may be drastically transformed, reinterpreted, rationalized, or historicized (e.g., the biographical "histories" of Jesus, Chang Tao-ling, Lao Tzu, or the wicked rebel Hun-tun; that it is a matter of "superstition" or simple punning), the underlying symbolic logic can often be found to preserve covertly the more "primitive" meaning of the cosmogonic and anthropogonic foundations of human existence.

With regard to the history of Taoism this same kind of fabled relationship is indicated by the fact that, like Chang Tao-ling's "chaotic box" and his exemplary role for all later effective liturgical performances, the Taoist priest's power to expel demons is dependent on his identification in ritual meditation with the cosmogonic *hun-tun* condition of the "prior heavens." Malevolent spirits reside in the world of the "posterior heavens" and are manipulated by an adept who has returned to the very origins of creation and transformation. Taoist exorcism is in this way expressly understood within a cosmogonic frame of meaning.[27] As is always the case with the mythological "chaos," there is a profound ambivalence with respect to the priest's identification with *hun-tun* since, as I will show in the last chapter, popular liturgical Taoism has significantly altered the old unqualified solicitude for Emperor Hun-tun seen in the classical texts to the point where *hun-tun* is both the basis for the demons expelled in public ritual and at the same time, the esoteric source of the priest's personal power over the demonic.[28]

I would like to mention that the duplex term, *hun-tun*, also connotes the ideas of sexuality, intercourse, and the ritual of marriage so that, for example, *tun-lun* refers to sexual intercourse and *hun*[a,b] can mean "to marry."[29] These linguistic and ritual linkages are rooted in the ancient cosmological system of dualistic thought as is witnessed in the Han dynasty text known as the *Po Hu T'ung*. This work asks:

> What do (the words) *hun-yin* mean? *Hun* means that the rites (of meeting the bride) are performed at dusk *hun*[a]. Therefore, it is spoken of as *hun*[a]. *Yin* means that the woman becomes his wife by following her husband. Therefore it is spoken of as *yin*. . . . Why are the rites performed at dusk? In order to indicate that the *yang* descends to the *yin*.[30]

This passage concludes by saying that dusk is "the time that the *yin* and *yang* intermingle.''[31] It is a time in the diurnal cycle, nested amid the larger seasonal round, that represents a return to the twilight condition of *hun-tun*.

Since gourds have continually sprung up whenever *hun-tun* is present, it should not be thought entirely irrelevant to remark that in the ancient ritual of marriage mentioned in the *Li Chi*, the ceremony involved the use of a wedding cup made of a bottle gourd, which was divided between bride and groom.[32] A later traditional activity, which perhaps in some convoluted way rehearses the ritual and mythological scenario of *hun-tun* and gourds, is that ''in some provinces a very old custom prevails'' where *hun-tun* dumplings must be ''confectioned by any new bride who has married into the family during the year.''[33]

SOUP, SYMBOL, AND SACRIFICE

Although one learns in the history of religions that what is least serious conventionally may be a most sacred matter religiously, it seems at first glance wholly frivolous to mention that *hun-tun* also appears today on the tables of American Chinese restaurants in the form of a steaming bowl of wonton soup. The hidden cultural logic behind this strange juxtaposition of soup and symbol will be developed throughout this book. But as a ritual whetting of one's hermeneutical appetite, I would like to indicate that even a preliminary examination of the issue suggests that the hopelessly mixed and minced ingredients of wonton soup and the *hun-tun* theme finally come together in a harmonious cultural blend. The *Tso Chuan*, after all, remarks that harmony may be illustrated by soup:

> Harmony may be illustrated by soup [*keng*]. You have the water and fire, vinegar, pickle, salt, and plums, with which to cook fish and meat. It is made to boil by the firewood, and then the cook mixes the ingredients, harmoniously equalizing the several flavors, so as to supply whatever is deficient and carry off whatever is in excess. Then the master eats it, and his mind is made equable.[34]

The ancient Chinese social etiquette of eating, the use of certain vessels in relation to particular types of food, and the special harmonizing role of a soup, stew, dumplings, or kind of ''humble pie'' composed of an undifferentiated mixture of foods may, in fact, have some connection with the mythological theory of life implied by the *hun-tun* theme and wonton soup.[35] But before the mind is made equable, before some order is found in chaos, and before some dumplings are fished from the broth, it is necessary to consider the apparent haphazardness of the recipe.

From the broadest perspective, it may be said that wonton soup within the civilizational world symbolically imitates the harmonizing role of *hun-tun* in the creation of the world and human culture. The tensions of cosmological and cultural duality find resolution in the raw chaos of *hun-tun* and the cooked broth of wonton. Most superficially and simplistically this kind of linkage is suggested by the linguistic detail that "wonton" is only the Cantonese dialectical pronunciation of the Chinese characters *hun-tun* (with the "eat" radical replacing "water"). Linguistic congruence is accompanied by the mimicking of form since the macrocosmic, chaotic, fleshy mass of the creation or deluge time finds its culinary microanalogue in the existence of a wonton as an amorphous, doughy sack filled with minced ingredients. Wonton dumplings, lumpy and wrinkled, contain the basic elements for life. They float across a primordial sea waiting for their sacrificial and consumptive contribution to the continuation of the human world of alimentation.

While these similarities make it possible to think of the *hun-tun* theme as a kind of "cosmic raviolo or dumpling" cosmogony,[36] it is really misleading, and slightly silly, to proceed with this kind of imaginative rhapsody. More important is to consider some of the facts of the Chinese cultural imagination. Parallelisms of language and form are interesting but in themselves prove nothing at all with respect to either Chinese tradition or dumplings. They may, however, be clues to a more propitious and culturally meaningful fit. The question is whether there is a larger system or structure of symbolism in Chinese tradition that gives rise to, and validates, the meaningfulness of such associations. The question is what came first: wonton dumplings or the Cosmic Raviolo?

Like the relation between cocks and men in Bali, or gourds and exorcism in China, the connection between dumplings and chaos, eating and creating, is to be found in the "formulations of a general order of existence" that undergird and control the Chinese interpretation of life.[37] Within the context of traditional China, it is finally a question of attending to the symbolic systems of ancient myth and ritual that express and impress those formulations.

A common Peking proverb relating to the Chinese New Year's festival period states that hun-tun or wonton dumplings are to be eaten "at the winter solstice; at the summer solstice noodles."[38] To eat wonton, therefore, was traditionally in China an interpreted and interpretive act, an act charged with ritual and cosmological significance. The Chinese eleventh month festival at the time of the winter solstice (*tung-chih*, a period beginning at the solstice, approximately December 22 in the Gregorian calendar, and lasting twelve days), and roughly comparable to the Teutonic Yuletide or Christmas season, marks the end of the agricultural and astronomical year when the sun (or cosmological principle of *yang*) has reached the end of its downward cycle and entered a threshold period of rebirth. The solstice itself is the time when the *yin* and *yang* are at a transitional phase in preparation for the ascendancy of the *yang*. Like other moments of cosmological and sociological alternation during the year, the solstice is a time betwixt and between the conventional order of life. Cosmologically the solar solstice marks one of the multiple yearly reversions to a cosmogonic time when the order and interaction of the dual principles were established. In this way *tung-chih* represents a return to the time of a first or undifferentiated chaos condition in anticipation of the rebirth of the human order in the first month. As a ritual time "before" the creation of the normal human world, this was a socially and religiously dangerous period, as is indicated by the Han dynasty practices of the "Great Exorcism" (Ta No) that involved the licensed folly of masked "animal" dances.[39]

Soup and dumplings as symbols participated, albeit largely unconsciously and "superstitiously" in later popular tradition, in the Chinese calendrical drama of the yearly regeneration of human existence. Inasmuch as the Chinese world view most generally stresses the dynamic quality of cosmic and human life as the rhythmic "great transformation" of the Tao, and if ritual may be said to be the symbolic vehicle that translates the mythic theory of the creation of Being into the concrete action of Becoming,[40] then the ritual consumption of wonton represents a miniature *creatio continua*. It acts out and embodies, makes flesh, the calendrical ontology of the sacrificial creation of nature and culture.

Taking some liberties with Lévi-Strauss' reflections on the "raw and the cooked," it may be said that the human preparation of food through the transforming agencies of fire and culinary ritual is a reenactment of the primal passage from the natural order to the cultural order.[41] Just eating is not to be human. It is the symbolic or cognitive context of eating, the storied and ritual nature of the sacrificial sharing and mutual exchange of cooked food with others (animals, men and women, dead ancestors, gods) that is quintessentially an act of human culture. Food comes "between" the relations of men in time and, as a third term between existing dualities, potentially has the power to unite or to separate.

The culinary art is directly expressive of deeper codes of cultural meaning and the use of such things as special foods, techniques of preparation, styles of eating, and types of vessels and utensils may, therefore, be expected to be structured on the most fundamental mythic models of life that account for the origins of eating and relating, as well as the creation of the world, culture, and civilization. To cook and devour is to kill what is natural, but from this death comes human life. The fabled context for this most basic of existential scenarios is that which in China is mythically expressed in the deluge legends of a *hun-tun* hunk of meat or anusless "lump of flesh" that is chopped up to produce the food and men of the world. It is also the story of the self-sacrifice of the cosmic giant, P'an-ku, who is born from the primordial gourd/egg/cocoon of *hun-tun* and dismembers his body to create a peopled and fruited world.[42]

In view of these mythic models that in traditional cultures account for the structure and quality of human life, the symbolic forms of Chinese eating will be most adequately understood within a cosmological or mythological frame of meaning. In ancient China, in fact, it is especially the sacrificial use of certain foods and vessels that has a particular symbolic correlation with the most important phases in the yearly creation, growth, death, and recreation of the cosmic and social worlds.[43] These yearly transitional nodes (such as the times of the solstice, equinox, full moon, and "Twenty-four Solar Nodes," as well as the extended periodicity of the Sexagenary cycle of stems and branches) cosmologically represent those dialectical moments of interchange, reversal, and reunion in the interlocking dance of the forces of *yin* and *yang*.[44] Mythically they are a mimesis of the time when the existence and movement of the two deities of *yin* and *yang*, heaven and earth, were established and when the "two" harmoniously came together in the central kingdom of Hun-tun in surgical or culinary preparation for the sacrificial creation of the human world.

While wonton dumplings and soup cannot be documented before the T'ang dynasty (A.D. 618–907),[45] it is precisely at nodal times in the seasonal and social periodicity of life (or any other significant change: religious, political, military, etc.) that *hun-tun*, sacrificial, "mixed-up," or "third term" foods like dumplings, soups, stews, noodles, or meat pies (cf. in the West the lore of the umble or humble pie referring to a mixed meat dish made from the lowly parts of an animal—the noodled intestines, etc.—and associated with the fare of the humble or peasant classes) were ritually, sacrificially, and exorcistically employed to insure the continuing harmony of the "low" and "high."

Chang Kwang-chih has recently established that in ancient China there was a semiotic system of culinary classification that takes the shape of a kind of triad that "logically" balances and harmonizes the dualities of the conventional cosmological and ritual order (see fig. 1).[46] The most salient outcome of Chang's discussion is that "barbarian," "unsophisticated," or minced and mixed "dishes" (*ts'ai*, anciently known as *shan*[a]) like stews and soups (*keng*) were of special importance in centering the more ordinary dualistic classification of those things drunk (water, wines: *yin*[c]) and grain foods eaten (the "five" cereal products of the earth: *shih*[a] or *fan*[a]). In the Han period and earlier, for example, the Grand Stew or Ta-keng was a "thick liquid dish with chunks of meat or vegetables or both" and, as a sacrificial offering or dish for guests, "would always be unseasoned in order to honor its simplicity."[47] *Keng* soups are structurally ambivalent and harmonizing because they are solid foods that are drunk (*yin—shih* or, perhaps, *hun—tun*). They bring low and high, *yin* and *yang*, and the five elements together at a single rustic setting where the honored dish was ritually prepared, so says the *Li Chi*, by excavating a central hollow in the ground "in the form of a jar."[48] Chang notes that this section in the *Li Chi* was long suspected by scholars of being close to folk-peasant and Taoist conceptions.[49]

Because of the remarkable preservation of foodstuffs from the recently discovered Ma-wang-tui tombs it is now almost possible to taste the mythological flavor of these "third term" dishes that insured a successful passage from the unseasoned chaos time back to the seasoned order of civilization.[50] Given the ancient symbolic system of thought that is apparent here, and its probable foundations in mythological tradition, it is more than poetic license on my part to suggest that the ritual consumption of a *keng*, like the later significance of wonton soup at the winter solstice, was an act that "returned" the hierarchical order to a more humble time when a simple "mess" like bouillabaisse was the primary sacrificial gift of the gods to man.

Needless to say, one of the chaos foods or *keng* stews uncovered in Ma-wang-tui Tomb No. 1 was made of a minced meat/vegetable mixture of chicken and gourds.[51] Based on what I have already laid out for sampling, the strange mythological logic unfolding would seem to have required this kind of motley combination. Moreover, as Chang remarks, mixed stew or soup dishes in the Chou period were ritually to be served only on "rude" vessels (*pien*[c] and *tou*) made of earthenware or bottle gourds (in the Han, the nine *ting* or tripod cauldrons were substituted).[52] The *Li Chi* says that "at the (Great) border sacrifice" these vessels for mixed dishes "emblem the natural (productive power of) heaven and earth. . . . The things in the *pien*[c] and *tou* were from both the water and the land."[53]

The most plausible inference is that there was a fabled basis for the ritual semantics of food in ancient China. In other words, the ritual use of certain special foods and vessels symbolically united the cosmological polarities of heaven and earth, *yin* and *yang*, in a way that presupposes some ancient story of creation that typologically retold the tale of how the "two" once met harmoniously in the central kingdom of Emperor Hun-tun. Emperor Hun-tun, it might be said, had the good grace to treat his guests with a "good soup" (taking *shan*[a] as a play on Hun-tun's *shan*[b], his goodness, kindness, or gift-giving virtue). But it was because Hun-tun was "paid back" (*pao*[a]) not in kind but with the false prestige of "face" that he dies. The two guests of the north and south desired to help Hun-tun when he only wanted selflessly to give of himself. The story from the Taoist standpoint hinges on the idea that it was a mistaken understanding of ritual reciprocity that led to the sacrifice of primitivity in order to create civility.[54]

Chang is more prudent but comes to essentially similar speculative conclusions since the archaic semiotics of food in China seem to suggest not only the central role of minced foods but also that the stew of Chinese tradition is basically made of a historical and sociological "mixture of two classes, or ethnic traditions."[55] Like the "primitive," "folk," or "barbarian" concerns in early Taoism and the "civilizational" convictions of Confucianism, the symbolism of food in ancient China seems to refer cryptically to the process of cultural development from an egalitarian, neolithic, "primitive" situation to a hierarchical, "civilized-peasant" situation since, "interestingly, the food that is considered the major partner of the pair (i.e., the [civilized] grain) is the much more recent invention, and it is also the invention that is identified with the Chinese as opposed to the barbarian."[56]

One other specific example of these connections that ties together the symbolic logic of a "*hun-tun* time" soup with sacrificial exorcism and the nodal period of the fifth month is the ancient and traditional south Chinese practice of eating an owl (variously *ch'ih*, *hsiao*, or *ch'ih-hsiao*) broth on the fifth or fifteenth day of the fifth month.[57] There is some ambivalence in the Chinese symbolism of the owl, but generally it was a *hun-tun* creature linked with darkness, the moon, drummaking, metallurgy, thunder, and eclipses of the sun. In contrast with the raven, the owl was the adversary of the sun—a predatory demon who devours light and therefore must be devoured. The constantly repeated death of chaos is the life of man and human culture. As with the wicked Hun-tun in the *Tso Chuan*, the owl was "unfilial" and outside the normal social order.[58] It represented the primitive forces of the animal, barbarian, or noncivilized world.

The fifth moon period, it will be recalled, was the insecure time of the summer solstice that required exorcistic rites and sacrifice (a human sacrifice as suggested by the dragon boat races at this time?[59]) to overcome the risk of drought, a permanent heat, or the related dangers of disease and ill health due to noxious powers unleashed at this transitional time (e.g., the dangers of *ku*[e] poison made from the five poisonous animals. Cf. The above reference to Chang Tao-ling and his "chaotic" gourd box).[60] This was a time when it was

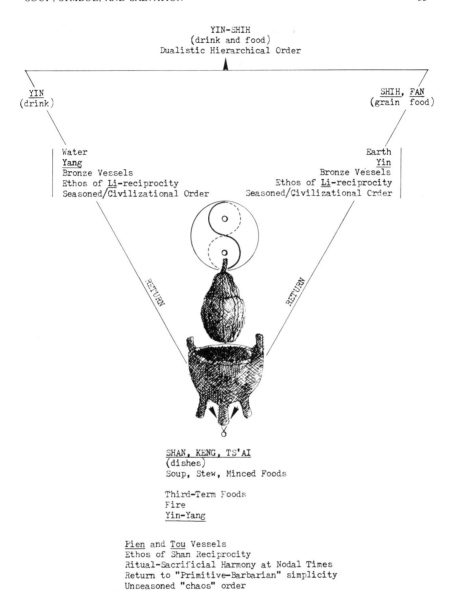

YIN-SHIH
(drink and food)
Dualistic Hierarchical Order

YIN
(drink)

SHIH, FAN
(grain food)

Water
Yang
Bronze Vessels
Ethos of Li-reciprocity
Seasoned/Civilizational Order

Earth
Yin
Bronze Vessels
Ethos of Li-reciprocity
Seasoned/Civilizational Order

RETURN

RETURN

SHAN, KENG, TS'AI
(dishes)
Soup, Stew, Minced Foods

Third-Term Foods
Fire
Yin-Yang

Pien and Tou Vessels
Ethos of Shan Reciprocity
Ritual-Sacrificial Harmony at Nodal Times
Return to "Primitive-Barbarian" simplicity
Unseasoned "chaos" order

Figure 1. Ancient Chinese Culinary Triad Synchronic Code

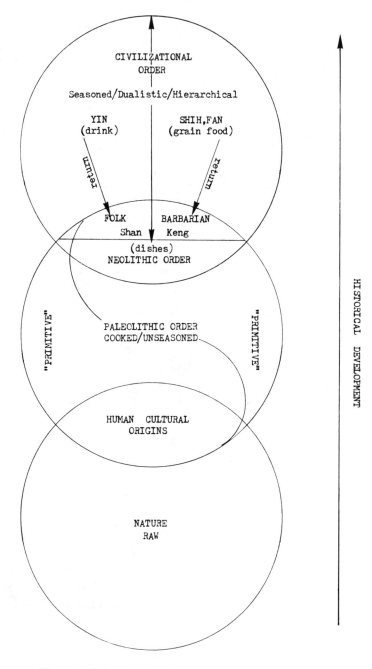

Figure 2. Culinary Triad Diachronic Dimension

wise not only to consume soups like an owl or toad broth and to suspend *hu-lu* talismans but also to hang small medicine bags of mugwort (*artemisia*) above doors to prevent any malevolent invasion of disease-bearing demons.[61] Again the structural ambiguity of these prophylactic practices is noteworthy since a "chaos" object is simultaneously the source of the danger and the protective or healing agent.

Granet asserts that these perplexing activities seem to be linked with ancient myth and ritual traditions of ritual combat (the term *hsiao* in *ch'ih-hsiao*, for example, alternately means "to kill" and "to stake out a head on a pole").[62] Thus the culinary and exorcistic practices involving a stew of chopped flesh were perhaps within the ancient feudal order connected with scapegoatlike rituals of actually, or symbolically, "putting on the skin" and consuming certain parts (especially the head and internal organs) of the ancestral "totem" animal, a sacrificial human victim, or a defeated opponent.

Most broadly the theme of ritual combat and the sacrificial devouring of the owl as the symbol of chaos at nodal seasonal moments suggests the mythological scenario of the creative struggle between the chaos dragon and culture hero (Python and Apollo, Typhon and Zeus, Tiamat and Marduk, Kung-kung and Yü, etc.).[63] In China this kind of combat myth and the siding with the triumphant ancestral culture hero (or sage king) is found within the context of the classical corpus of texts that maintain the orthodox, hierarchical, aristocratic, or civilizational interpretation of myth.

In the worst sense the just-completed exercise can quickly degenerate into an indigestible Frazerian litany of meaningless exotica. Indeed, other fragmented examples of the *hun-tun* theme in Chinese tradition could be multiplied almost indefinitely. Musing on the origin and significance of eating wonton dumplings, Joseph Needham quotes from a thirteenth-century Chinese work that comments on a tradition of frying these dumplings with mugwort.[64] This, it is said, has the effect of enhancing the pharmacological and apotropaic powers of the dumplings and "must be connected with the ancient ideas of *hun-tun*."[65] Comparing these comments with the above discussion shows how truly perspicacious Needham's hunch really was!

Chaos, gourds, exorcism, soup, dumplings, sex, owls, and sacrifice would seem to make strange bedpartners, but in Chinese tradition these are all elements of a consummated marriage rite that was made in heaven. My overlong digression on soup has served a purpose inasmuch as it strongly points to the existence of a cosmological system or fabled logic that stands behind and gives cultural and historical depth to such apparently ridiculous associations. It will be my task in the rest of this study to avoid further encyclopedic listing of such jumbled information and work toward a more complete elucidation of the mythological system of thought that gives meaning to the contradictory Chinese affair with Emperor Hun-tun. The meaning is in the melange.

The theme of *hun-tun* drifts through Chinese history in a bark made of an empty gourd shell and reveals itself in all manner of interesting and sometimes bizarre ways. Released from its protective cocoon, it floats like a butterfly in furthering the sexual propagation of the vegetal kingdom and within the cultural realm it kills, and is killed, like an owl. It harmonizes, heals, and saves like a good chicken and gourd soup.

In the ancient period *hun-tun* names a cosmogonic and cosmological system of symbols that is shared and drawn upon in different ways by all of the early "schools" and textual traditions—whether Confucian, Legalist, Mohist, or Taoist. The issue to be investigated in this study concerns the distinctive positive affinity for Emperor Hun-tun to be found in the early Taoist texts. That there was a unique Taoist nostalgia and affection for Hun-tun is not a new insight, as is evidenced by the work of Marcel Granet, Wolfram Eberhard, Rolf Stein, Hou Wai-lu, Eduard Erkes, Toshihiko Izutsu, Yoshioka Yoshitoyo, Chang Kwang-chih, Lo Meng-ts'e, and Joseph Needham.[66] Employing different methodologies and in reference to various sinological agendas, all of these scholars have recognized that there is something peculiarly important about the shape of early Taoist thought in relation to the shapeless mythological Hun-tun. All of them have seen parts of an immensely confusing cultural conundrum and all, to different degrees, have been helpful in guiding my own study.

My intention is not just to reassemble this earlier work into some sort of hermeneutical critical mass but also to look at the evidence afresh from the comparative standpoint of the history of religions. My concern is to see how the theme of *hun-tun* functions as a paradigm of religious meaning and practice in the early Taoist texts. Given the admittedly mystic cast of early Taoist thought, and aside from some notable exceptions like Granet, Maspero, and Waley, it is surprisingly the case that it is exactly the "religious" nature of the classical Taoist texts that has been so neglected. There are many historical, cross-cultural, methodological, and scholarly reasons for this state of affairs but it serves no purpose to rehearse that legacy of benign neglect here.[67] Most would agree that, at the very least, what is expressed in the early Taoist texts is clearly not only an exercise in abstract philosophical thought but, as with all of Chinese reflection, is a "way," a message and method, of rectifying, improving, harmonizing, healing, or "saving" the human condition. Religion, it would seem accurate to say, exists in culture to claim that there is a "third term" beneath the undulating surface of things. It is a cultural system that interprets all other cultural interpretations of life.

The most important result of this study is to demonstrate that it is the cosmogonic fable of *hun-tun* that defines the religious vision of early Taoist mysticism. It is the Taoist mystical interpretation of the mythological meaning of *hun-tun* that symbolically articulates both the problem of, and soteriological solution to, the Taoist understanding of human existence. But if it is the case that the fabled theme of *hun-tun* is typologically foundational for the early Chinese "formulations of a general order of existence," then it can be said that an appreciation of the mythological structure of *hun-tun* will also help to evaluate and distinguish the kind of "religiousness" or "salvational convictions" expressed in the other "ways" of interpreting life. In the most general sense it can be said that the "religious" or salvational concerns of all forms of Chinese tradition, especially the *yin* and *yang* of early Taoism and Confucianism, always involve the primarily existential questions of how to *live in relation*: with nature, with oneself, with other men and women both alive and dead, with superiors and inferiors, to name a few. It is always a "ritual" issue that is *in time*: how to eat, how to excrete, or most fundamentally, how to *become* fully and authentically human in a world that is in process. The question is always, again for both Taoism and Confucianism, premised on the fabled notion of "something" lost, broken, or hidden, some significant ill or imbalance, that needs to be repaired or healed—over and over again. "Salvation" from this point of view is not, and cannot be, once and for all. Salvation is temporary and temporal, although it may be possible as a man or ancestor to extend the moments of the Tao's pendulation and live a "long time."

Starting with the same mixture of cultural fables, sharing the same codes of reference, and asking the same questions of the meaning of human existence, the difference between early Taoism and early Confucianism is finally a matter of their respective interpretations and answers to those fables and questions. Keeping to the middle, the code remains the same. Symbolically it is a matter of their ritual fellowship with Emperor Hun-tun, of knowing and deciding how to act in his presence. Superficially it is a matter of being friends or foes of the Emperor of the Center. But this kind of simple, uncentered dichotomy fails to take into account the crucial synthetic ambivalence of the mythological idea of *hun-tun* and to some extent explains why the overall history of Chinese tradition witnesses a series of changes, reversals, and convergences in the Taoist and Confucian interpretations of *hun-tun*.

Attraction and repulsion are the twin emotions in any affair with Hun-tun, although in the overlapping histories of Taoism and Confucianism one or the other mood may predominate at one time or another. In the archaic period when the antipodes of the Chinese cultural spirit are created, and when the intellectual, social, and political gulf between the "two" is most pronounced, the relative emotions of a Taoist love and a Confucian fear for Emperor Hun-tun will be in a condition of stark relief. Loving Hun-tun in later Taoist sectarian tradition, however, will be a private matter, not an issue for public debate.

In the ancient tradition that is the concern of this book, the crux of the meaning of human life really is a question of why, when, and how one eats one's soup, seasoned or unseasoned. It is simultaneously a religious, political, social, and personal issue as to the kind of Tao and ritual path that is most meaningful for man to follow. It is a question of how far back one has to travel to find the truth of human nature. In this way it concerns the early Taoist and early Confucian, or folk and elite, disagreement over the mythological or historical interpretation of the "golden age" at the beginnings of time.

Early Taoism, while at times polemically sounding so, cannot be thought of as a nihilistic tradition that seeks to dissolve man and society permanently back into the seamless unconsciousness of nature. It is not antihuman, antisocial, or even antiritual. It is a question of interpretation: that is, the kind of human nature, society, and ritual that is felt to be most meaningful in relation to the ultimate structures of existence. As I will show throughout this work, it is an issue of deciding what is the "primitive" basis of individual and social life; what way of living and thinking most adequately fosters the well-being and maturation of men and women in relation to the existing worlds of nature and culture. The problem of the fall for early Taoism is the existential fact of being born into a world already predetermined as "civilizational." This recalls Han Shan's poetic lament:

> Morning after morning we must dress and eat
> Year after year, fret over taxes.
> A thousand of us scrambling for a penny,
> We knock our heads together and yell for dear life.

In distinction to earlier forms of cultural life, civilizations seek to suppress and control the "primitive" mythological ambivalence of the chaos principle in individual and social life by claiming that the hierarchical ritual order of the ruling class is the original, one, and only right/rite order. In this way early Taoism is politically anarchistic but not ontologically nihilistic. Early Taoism does not negate the historicity of man but does reject the value of a wholly historical interpretation of the meaning of man.[68]

Chang shows that creation myths related to the theme of *hun-tun* were common to Chinese thought by the time of the Eastern Chou period, but there is an important difference in the way these myths were transformed and interpreted by early Confucians and Taoists. In the Confucian tradition with its golden age idea attached to the genealogical lore of the sage kings and civilizational heroes, the " 'essential' was not fixed at the Creation of the World but after it," at the time of the aristocratic ordering of human civilization.[69] A kind of mythical time and mythical logic "is still involved, but it is no longer the 'first' time, what we may call the 'cosmogonic' time. The 'essential' is no longer bound up with an ontology (how the World—the real—came into being) but with a History."[70] "Salvation" within a Confucian interpretive frame is a matter of going back to the beginning of civilizational history to find models of action for the present.

In relative distinction to this historicized interpretation of myth—relative in view of the role of the *I Ching* in classical Confucian thought, though the *I* is more synchronically cosmological than cosmogonic—the early Taoist texts tend to preserve much more of a "primitive" mythological theory of meaning that focused on cosmogonic and anthropogonic origins. Wolfgang Bauer, noting this same kind of difference, remarks that the Confucians, "while intensively searching the past for models,"

> never went beyond the bounds of historicity which coincides with the rise of [civilized] human society. The time of the sage kings constituted an absolute limit for them. It was they who had taught men to distinguish themselves from "four-legged creatures and birds." For them, the "world" was actually identical with the "realm" (*t'ien-hsia*), and the creation of this world by the culture-bearing sages—an event of infinitely greater significance than the creation of the universe to which they gave no thought—was the first and also the most decisive historical event. The idea of turning one's back on this world, either temporally by an attempt to return to the period predating the inception of civilization, or spatially by an escape into the wilderness, not only seemed barbaric to them but was simply unimaginable.[71]

But it is "precisely" at this point that "the reflections of the Taoists set in."[72] It is also precisely in this way that the ontological and religious implications of the mythological *hun-tun* theme are important for the internalized mystical reversal of the cosmogony sought by the Taoists in meditation. "Salvation" here means going back to the undifferentiated beginnings in order to recreate microcosmically the world, man, and a more balanced human society.

Even though the early Taoists certainly express an analysis of the fall that is Rousseauian, their vision of paradise is finally more congruent with prehistoric reality than Rousseau's. Instead of Rousseau's model of some imaginary paleolithic hunting society, early Taoism asserts that the time of the "great equality" (*ta-t'ung*) was more accurately an idealized neolithic culture— "before the invention of writing, metallurgy and the birth of urban civilization with its debased masses and its monarchs and its bloodthirsty priests"—that came closest to the idea of a golden age.[73] This, however, polarizes the ancient Chinese understanding of the golden age and it is the harmonizing wisdom of *hun-tun* and the history of Chinese tradition to affirm that "the real Golden Age is not in nature or in history but in between them: in that instant when men establish their group with a pact which simultaneously unites them among themselves and unites the group with the natural world."[74]

One way to summarize this discussion, a discussion that will prove to be exceedingly complex in its philological and symbolic embodiment in the earliest texts, is to say that early Taoism expresses an idea of "salvation" that is not concerned with a doctrine of immortality or escaping the world of time and space. As eating, exorcism, and sacrifice may be thought of as miniature and multiple ritual "salvations" of life, early Taoist mysticism is also addressed in a similar manner to the existential and cosmological problem of the sickness and entropy of ordinary human life—that the civilized life of man is destructively out of harmony with the organic and communal life-rhythm of the Tao. The real problem of salvation, then, is the problem of a human time or cultural order that is broken from the spontaneous ritual freedom of sacrificing everything to someone else. No purely transcendental solution is possible here since all (the uncreated and the created, the one and the many) is contained within the "emptiness" of the original undifferentiated chaos of the cosmic egg, gourd, or dumpling.

The best way to characterize the Taoist idea of salvation is to see it as being fundamentally "medicinal" in intention and structure. The medicinal implications are clear in that, as Fung Yu-lan has recently written, one of the central ideas of early Taoism, and the basis for its connection with later Taoism, is the concern for *yang-sheng*—not immortality, but psychic and bodily health through "life preservation and nourishment."[75] It can almost be said that the whole thrust of Taoism has always been in terms of healing methods that seek to reestablish the original balanced wholeness of human nature and society. Salvation for Taoism is primarily a healing return to the beginning, a quest for the salve or elixir of life.

There is an intrinsic connection between this medicinal understanding of salvation and what may be called the overall "alchemical" cast of Taoist thought and practice.[76] Most generally what I mean by this is that alchemy as an esoteric and religious science is most aptly described as the traditional method for microcosmically recapitulating, manipulating, and accelerating the creative processes of temporal transformation. Alchemy is fundamentally a cosmological obstetrics of time that is primarily concerned with the temporal refinement of base matter and the healing reidentification of man with the greater life of the universe.[77] The return from a condition of fallen dispersion to an original harmony, *solve et coagula*, is the cornerstone of alchemical doctrine and practice and, in Chinese tradition, is directly structured on the Taoist metaphysics of *hun-tun*.

It can be said that the mystical return to an experience of primal unity implies a necessary cosmological interrelation of body and spirit, the reunion or marriage of *yin* and *yang*, the coexistence and copenetration of the one and the two, nonbeing and being, the uncreated and the created, egg and chicken. All of this in the early Taoist texts is rooted metaphysically in the cosmogonic mystery of the third term or central gap—the "betwixt and between"—of chaos. This is a trinitarian formula of liminal order, the alchemical paradox of *mysterium coniunctionis*. The dynamic chaotic order, or chaosmos, of the Tao is the harmony of the creation time, the "concordant discord" of the beginnings. Creation bears the impress of trinity, for "if it is true that two is the number that implies opposition and discord, three is the number of reconciliation and concord," or as the *Tao Te Ching* says (chap. 42): "Tao gave birth to the one, the one to the two, the two to the three."[78] Truth is three, not one.

In short, the thematic structure of the *hun-tun* cosmogony gives form and meaning to the overall soteriological mode of being a Taoist. It is the basis for early Taoism's mystical interpretation of that unique experience of knowing and living the Tao—being a "spirit man," "true man," "perfect man," or, even to some degree, attaining the "physical immortality" of a *hsien*[a]. To paraphrase chapter 21 of the *Tao Te Ching*, it is "by this" archaic foundation in the creation mythology of *hun-tun* that the truth of the Tao is discovered. The Taoist "knows the ways of things at the beginning."[79]

PART TWO

HUMPTY DUMPTY HAD A GREAT FALL

TEXTUAL ANALYSIS

Going back to the Beginning and
pursuing to the End, one understands the explanation of death
and life.

—Chou Tun-i, *T'ai Chi T'u Shuo*
(trans. W. T. Chan)

Les nombres n'ont pas pour fonc-
tion d'exprimer des grandeurs: ils
servent à ajuster les dimensions
concrètes aux proportions de
l'univers.

—M. Granet, *La Pensée chinois*

2

'BEGINNING AND RETURN' IN THE *TAO TE CHING*

> Hold on to the Tao of old in order to master the
> things of the present.
> From this one may know the primeval begin-
> ning (of the universe).
> This is called the bond of Tao.
>
> —*Tao Te Ching*, Chapter 14
> (trans. W. T. Chan)

T HE FIRST AND most obvious test case concerning the significance of the *hun-tun* theme should involve a critical examination of the *Tao Te Ching* or *Lao Tzu*.[1] Although the relative historical priority of the *Tao Te Ching* and the first seven chapters of the *Chuang Tzu* is still not satisfactorily resolved, the *Tao Te Ching* is traditionally considered to be the starting point for any discussion of Taoism. In terms of dating, it is sufficient to recognize that the *Tao Te Ching* and the "inner" chapters of the *Chuang Tzu* are the earliest documents (i.e., Eastern Chou, 770–221 B.C.) associated with what *Ssu-ma T'an* (ca. 110 B.C.) in the Han dynasty called the "Tao-te School" (*tao-te chia*).[2] The other chapters of the *Chuang Tzu*, the *Huai Nan Tzu*, and the *Lieh Tzu*, while containing some pre-Han material, are later, dating variously to the Ch'in (parts of the *Chuang Tzu*), Former Han (especially the *Huai Nan Tzu* and parts of the *Chuang Tzu* and *Lieh Tzu*), and, in the case of some sections of the *Lieh Tzu*, to as late as A.D. 300.

To propose yet another look at the *Tao Te Ching* may seem superfluous since this book of only 5,000-odd characters is the most translated of all Oriental works and has been subjected to innumerable interpretations from the various standpoints of Chinese, Japanese, and Western scholarship. In the context of traditional Chinese exegesis there are the works of Paul Lin and Ariane Rump on Wang Pi's classic commentary (Lin's work includes a comparison with the recently discovered Ma-wang-tui texts) and Isabelle Robinet's valuable analysis of later Taoist commentary.[3] More recently, Fung Yu-lan has put forth a Marxist interpretation of the work and Chang Chung-yuan has suggested that Lao Tzu seems to be most fully understood within a Heideggerian framework.[4] Chang, with some temerity, even felt it possible to claim that "Heidegger is the only Western philosopher who not only intellectually understands Tao, but has intuitively experienced the essence of it all as well."[5] Chang, like Fung, does provide us with a very sensitive and interesting interpretive translation of the text, but it seems at least partially presumptuous to assert that the philosophical conundrums of Heidegger or the materialistic determinism of Marx fully clarify the mystical obscurities of the *Tao Te Ching*.

As another way to approach this magnificently recalcitrant and enigmatic text, I would like to start with E. M. Chen's observation that a basic failure on the part of many scholars is their assumption that "Taoism like Confucianism expounds a man-centered or ruler-centered (since the ruler is the model of his people, he is man *par excellence*) universe."[6] Chen continues, "But the *Tao Te Ching* does not expound a man-centered universe, it teaches naturalism (chap. 25)."[7] This is to say that an ontology rooted in a specific cosmological vision is central to the *Tao Te Ching*. An understanding of the Tao in the *Tao Te Ching* should start with a consideration of it as the "Beginning"—as a cosmological first principle, origin, or primordial ground and source of being. My initial task in this chapter, therefore, will be to examine the idea of the Tao in a cosmological context of meaning, especially as it alludes to a mythological story of creation.

It is not really so much an issue of two separate and antagonistic "hermeneutic versions of Lao Tzu's cosmological thinking"—that of a cosmogonic "*sub specie temporis* (in the literal sense)" where "Tao as Origin is taken to mean the real natural cause of the existence of all things (in the time process)" versus *sub specie aeternitatis* where "no actual process of natural causation or evolution" is involved.[8] A cosmological and/or cosmogonic understanding of Tao—*sub specie temporis*—need not be taken "in the literal sense" and certainly does not exclude a more universal symbolic meaning. This view, in other words, betrays a rather narrow appreciation of the nature of creation myth since cosmogony need not necessarily imply a "creator" and may be essentially linked to the idea of cyclic or embryological growth. Indeed, the creation theme suggested by the *Tao Te Ching* seems best classified under the general thematic typology of a chaos or world-egg mythology wherein creation is self-contained and self-generated—the "idea of an organic process or birth."[9] Recalling Tom Stoppard's dissertation on the subject, the early Taoist texts tend to put forth the notion "that chickens and eggs have been succeeding each other in one form or another literally for ever."[10]

As a second level of analysis I will show that the mythological vision of Tao as the "Beginning" is thematically supportive of some of the overall individual, social, and ethical issues found in the text. Tao as the Beginning is an enduring and sustaining presence in the world; and, even though it is hidden or lost to man, it is possible to return to an identification with the source of all meaning and life. Tao, as the source and ground of nature, constantly "returns" (see chap. 40) to the conditions of the Beginning in the sense of a periodic reiteration of the cosmogony. This *creatio continua* of many constant interrelated "transitional moments" (lunar, solar, seasonal, diurnal, bodily, psychic, etc.) is the essential life principle of the Tao in the world. The renewal of man and society depends on an emulation of this "way." The continual rhythm of "beginning and return" is both the macrocosmic life of Tao in nature and the microcosmic true life of man. To rediscover and reestablish in the individual and society the "primeval beginning" is, therefore, the "bond of Tao."

TAO AS THE "BEGINNING"

1. *Chapter 25: "Something Chaotic Yet Complete"*

The first passage that must be critically examined for clues of an archaic creation mythology and the theme of chaos is found in chapter 25. The relevant section of this chapter is the following:

> There was something chaotic yet complete [*yu wu hun ch'eng*],
> Which existed before the creation [*sheng*[a]] of heaven and earth.
> Without sound and formless [*chi hsi liao hsi*],
> It stands alone [*tu*] and does not change.
> It pervades all [*t'ung hsing*] and is free from danger [*pu tai*];
> It can be regarded then as the mother of the world [*t'ien-hsia mu*].
> I do not know its proper name but will call it Tao.
> If forced to give it a name, I shall call it great.
> Great means "moving away" [*shih*[b]].

"Moving away" means "far away" [*yüan*[a]],
And "far away" means [ultimately] to return [*fan*[b]].[11]

The passage quoted presents a description of the Tao as a cosmic first principle put forth within a cosmogonic framework. In fact, the first two verses of this chapter indicate a creation mythology concerning the separation of the dual cosmological units of heaven and earth from a primordial chaos. There is, for example, an echo of this mythological scenario found in chapter 6 of the *Chuang Tzu* where it is said that the Tao is "without action and without shape [*wu-wei wu-hsing*]":

> Before there was a heaven and earth, it [*Tao*] unquestionably existed. It "gave spirit and life" [*shen*[a]] to all the spirits and gods [*kuei shen ti*] and gave birth to heaven and earth. It existed before the Supreme Ultimate [*t'ai-chi*], and yet you cannot call it lofty.[12]

The focus of concern in both the *Tao Te Ching* and the *Chuang Tzu* is basically with what precedes the creation of duality in the world. Most important is the technical equation of Tao with *hun*[d], or the mysterious condition of the Tao as the primordial source, principle, or "thing [*wu*[a]]" responsible for, and controlling, the bio-cosmic "birth" or "creation" of the ordinary phenomenal world.[13] We have, then, a description of a precosmic stage in the overall creative life process of the universe, a stage where there was not yet a separate existence of the phenomenal world. It was a stage that was a perfect, total, or complete (*ch'eng*) fusion of all things. It was the stage or condition of cosmic totality referred to here as that which is *hun-ch'eng*; or as the Neo-Confucian, Shao Po-wen (A.D. 1057–1134), says, the "chaotically complete [*hun-ch'eng*] one body" at the creation time was "called *t'ai-chi*."[14]

In Western scholarship as early as 1891 C. de Harlez remarked that *hun*[d] "is generally rendered 'chaos, chaotic.' But the choice of this term is unfortunate. The chaos of modern philosophy is one thing. The *hvan* [*hun*[d]] of Lao-tzu is something else again. The first veritably deserves the name; it is but a matter confused and mixed without order. But this is certainly not at all the case with Lao's *hvan* which is none other than the Tao or the supreme reason for all things."[15] De Harlez also notes that Wang Pi explained *hun*[d] as " 'that which one cannot succeed in understanding.' And the word (*ch'eng*) which follows as the second part of a composite word equivalent to 'chaotic,' he attributes the independent sense of 'complete, perfect,' and explains it as signifying that from which all things draw their completion.' "[16] Recognizing its mythological underpinnings, E. Erkes points out that *hun-ch'eng* may betray a textual corruption or interpolation for the term *hun-tun*, which is the "Chaos Urheberin" or "Primal Chaos-Creatress." Erkes attempts to show a connection with a cosmic egg cosmogony and feels that the first verses of chapter 25 should therefore read: "There was a Thing that laid the cosmic egg and preceded the birth of Heaven and Earth."[17]

Chiang Hsi-ch'ang shows that Tao is specifically linked to the term *hun*[d] (and by implication, *hun-tun*) in the *Tao Te Ching*.[18] In his commentary on chapter 20 where the Taoist sage is described as having the "mind of an idiot (*yü*[b])" and the condition of "chaos and dullness [*tun-tun* . . . *hun-hun*]," Chiang quotes Ssu-ma Kuang as saying this refers to the condition of the mythological Hun-tun as seen in the *Chuang Tzu*. Chiang also notes that the reference to the sage ruler having his mind "chaotically unified [*hun ch'i hsin*]" found in chapter 49 can be connected thematically to the *tun-tun hun-hun* passage of chapter 20. Moreover, the homophonic identification of *hun*[a] found in chapter 20 with *hun*[d] is also supported by semantic analogies. *Hun*[a] is, for example, related to *hun*[b] and suggests the idea of "stupidity, confused, or dull." Many of these terms linked to the idea of *hun-tun* consequently suggest the important theme of the *wu-chih* or "no knowledge" (cf. *Tao Te Ching*, chap. 3) condition of the Taoist.[19]

There is additional internal evidence in this chapter, as well as corroborating testimony from other texts, that indicates the mythological context of the passage. In this chapter and in several other chapters (cf. chaps. 1, 20, 52, and 59), the Tao is called the "mother" (*mu*) of the world, which is reflective of numerous mythologies where creation involves a cosmic ancestral giant, animal, or Great Mother that spawns a male and a female offspring who in turn incestuously engender the human world.[20] Another frequent mythological form of this idea of the Tao's motherhood, and one that appears close to the intention of the Taoist texts, is the idea of a primal ancestral bird, snake, or fish that lays a cosmic egg that subsequently splits open, giving rise to the dual principles of the cosmos.[21]

Many of these ideas are reiterated in chapter 1, which, along with chapter 25, is one of the most important presentations of the Tao in a cosmological framework. It is said there that:

> The Tao that can be spoken of is not the eternal/constant Tao
> [*ch'ang-tao*].
> The name that can be named [*ming*] is not the eternal name.
> The nameless [*wu-ming*] is the origin of heaven and earth.
> The named [*yu-ming*[a]] is the mother of the Ten Thousand Things
> [the phenomenal world].[22]

Here there is a seemingly technical use of the expressions of *wu-ming* and *yu-ming*[a] (or *wu*[b] and *yu*[a]) that, as developed later in the commentary of Wang

Pi, refer respectively to the metaphysical notions of "nonbeing" and "being."[23] But regardless of the philosophical specificity of these terms in the *Tao Te Ching*, there is still a strong attachment to a mythological theme concerning the Tao as the origin of heaven and earth and the source of the phenomenal world. What is confusing in the isolation of this chapter is that the period before the creation of the profane cosmos (the "Ten Thousand Things") includes a number of creative stages—stages or phases that are still generally a part of that which in chapter 25 is whole or "chaotically complete." That which is the primordial Tao is both nameless and formless yet can be named with a series of mythologically significant terms like "mother," "chaos," or "ancestor" (chap. 4), as well as other more abstract metaphysical terminology like "nothingness" (wu^b), "great" (ta), "empty" ($hsü^a$), and "one" (i^a).

The "named" as mother of the Ten Thousand Things and the "nameless" as the origin of the duality of heaven and earth are still to be considered as part of the original "chaotic" process of creation at the beginning. Heaven and earth have been given a preliminary cosmological shape or form, but there is a harmonious connection or fusion between the two. They are still part of that "one thing" of chaotic wholeness before the creation of the world. This is indicated by what follows in the remaining verses from chapter 1:

> These [wu^b and yu^a] proceed from the same source [$t'ung^a$], yet have
> different names.
> Both together [$t'ung^a$, the unity of wu^b and yu^a] are called the
> dark [$hsüan$].
> Dark and even darker,
> It is the gate of all hidden-wonders [$miao$].[24]

The original condition of the "dark" ($hsüan$), the source of both wu^b and yu^a, displays an internal self-generated life of creative movement. It should be pointed out that the image of "darkness" in the history of religions is especially connected with the mythological symbolism of chaos, as well as with such analogous feminine symbols as the moon, water, caves, and death.[25] Moreover, this kind of mythological linkage in the *Tao Te Ching* is also suggested by the image of the "dark female" ($hsüan-p'in$) that is cosmologically said to be the "root of heaven and earth" (chap. 6).[26]

The true mystery of primordial life is its clouded fusion, totality, or fluid unity of all separate things—the condition that is here also referred to as $t'ung^a$. This important term of $t'ung^a$, which in later tradition is the basis for the Chinese idea of the paradise time ($ta-t'ung^{a,b}$), is related in the *Chuang Tzu* (chapter 12) to the Taoist's goal of identifying himself with the condition of the creation time: "Being identical [$t'ung^a$], you will be empty [$hsü^a$]; being empty, you will be a great [*ta*]. You may join [*ho*] in the cheeping and chirping and, when you have joined in the cheeping and chirping, you may join with heaven and earth.''[27] The terminology of *t'ung*[a], *hsü*[a], *ho*, and *ta* is frequently related to a cosmogonic context of meaning in the *Chuang Tzu*; but even more interesting is the fact that this passage opens with an explicit reference to the creation time similar to those seen in chapters 1, 25, and 42 of the *Tao Te Ching*: "In the Great Beginning [*t'ai-ch'u*], there was nothing [*wu*[b]]. There was no being and no names. Out of it arose one, but it had no form [*wei-hsing*].''[28] This passage characteristically concludes with a description of the unique condition of reunification (*ho* or *t'ung*[a]) with the Tao in terms that are parallel to the reference in the *Tao Te Ching* to the condition of *hsüan-t'ung*[a,b]. Indeed, in the final verses of this passage from chapter 12 of the *Chuang Tzu*, the emphatic and reduplicated use of the terminology evokes the sound and mystery of the *hun-tun* condition. It reads: "Your reunification, how chaotic [*ho hun-hun*]! As if you were stupid [*yü*[b]]! As if you were chaotically demented [*hun*[b]]! This is called the Dark Virtue [*hsüan-te*] whereby you are reunified with the Great Unity [*ta-shun*].''[29]

In reference to the term *hsüan-t'ung*[a,b] and its relation to the creation theme of chaos, it is necessary to examine chapters 15 and 56 of the *Tao Te Ching*. Chapter 15 opens with a description of the paradise time when men were in perfect harmony with the Tao: "In ancient times those who were masters of the Tao were mysterious [*wei miao*] and profoundly [or darkly] penetrating [*hsüan-t'ung*[a]].''[30] Here the term *hsüan-t'ung*[a], as well as the quality of *wei miao*, refers to the unique experiential condition of being one with the Tao. That this interpretation is not unwarranted is indicated by a corresponding reference in chapter 56 where it is stated that to know the Tao one must:

> Close the mouth,
> Shut the doors,
> Blunt the sharpness;
> Untie the tangles,
> Blend [*ho*] the light,
> and unify [*t'ung*[a]] with the dusty world.
> This is called *hsüan-t'ung*[b].[31]

The motif of "closing and shutting" the sense organs in order to return to an identification with the Tao is especially reminiscent of the famous *hun-tun* passage in chapter 7 of the *Chuang Tzu* where it is suggested that the primordial condition of perfect unity was lost when Emperor Hun-tun was bored with the holes of face.[32] The implication there, as well as in this passage from the *Tao Te Ching*, is that the Taoist seeks to reverse that original event and reattain the paradise condition of *hun-tun, hun-ch'eng*, or *hsüan-t'ung*[a,b]. Ch'en Ming-chia feels that the use of the term *hsüan* is related to the pronunciation and use of *hun*[d] and that the technical expression of *hsüan-t'ung*[b] for the mystic experience of identification with the Tao is primarily suggestive of the mythological theme of chaos.[33]

The semantic and phonetic identification of *t'ung*[a] with *t'ung*[b], and also with the cosmogonic theme of *hun-tun* or *hun-ch'eng*, is further demonstrated by other passages in the *Chuang Tzu* (chap. 10) where *t'ung*[a] is used in the sense of the paradise time of cosmic harmony.[34] Correspondingly, the *Huai Nan Tzu* makes use of these same technical identifications so that in chapter 10 the paradise time before the creation of the profane world is referred to as either *tung-t'ung* or *hsüan-t'ung*[b]; and in chapter 14 it is said: "The mysterious unity [*tung-t'ung*] of heaven and earth chaotically [*hun-tun*] constitutes [the condition] of the uncarved block [*p'u*[a]]. It has not created, yet is complete [*ch'eng*] with things. It is called the primal one [*t'ai-i*[a]]."[35]

An additional perspective is provided by the recently discovered Ma-wang-tui "silk manuscript" text known as the *Tao Yüan*. This is a very short text (464 characters) apparently of the Former Han dynasty Huang-Lao tradition of Taoism. Its importance is that it stresses the cosmogonic significance of the Tao as the "origin" (*yüan*[b]) of the world and, in this sense, reads almost like a direct commentary on chapter 25 (and 42), although the precise *hun-tun* terminology is not used. In almost a paraphrase of chapter 25, this text opens with lines that expand on the chaos condition (*hun-ch'eng*) of the primal unity (*t'ung*[a]):

> In the beginning of the ancient past,
> All things were fused and were identical
>   with the great vacuity [*t'ung-t'ung ta-hsü*].
> Vacuous, and blended as one,
> Resting in the [condition of] one eternally.
> Moist and chaotic [*shih-shih meng-meng*],
> There is no distinction of dark and light. . . .
> From the ancient times it [*Tao*] had no form,
> It penetrated greatly but was nameless
>   [*ta-t'ung wei-ming*].[36]

To return now to the examination of chapter 25, I only want to remark on a few other descriptive factors found in this chapter and repeated in a technical sense throughout many other passages. Hence, there are a number of terms used in an exclamatory manner suggestive of some of the particular attributes of the Tao as that which is *hun-ch'eng*. It is declared to be "without sound and form [*chi . . . liao . . .*]," "pervades all [*t'ung hsing*] and does not tire [*pu tai*]," and "stands alone [*tu*]." These are all expressions used to refer to the special condition of the Tao during the creation time, its "darkness" and "hidden-ness" (*hsüan* and *miao*).

Here and also in chapter 1, there is reference to the fact that Tao is a living thing—it moves, changes, pervades, gives birth yet paradoxically remains whole by constantly regenerating itself without alteration, without consumption or exhaustion. There is an internal temporal process that is a manifestation of a cyclic pattern of creative activity or life-giving force. The Tao in its original condition of chaotic fusion "goes out" (*shih*[b] or *ch'u* in chapter 2), giving birth to all phenomenal things and finally reaching an apogee of movement (*yüan*[a] or *chiao*[a] in chapter 1), it reverses itself and "returns" (*fan*[b]) to the condition that was present at the beginning (the condition of *hun-ch'eng, hsüan-t'ung,* or *hun-tun*).[37]

The basic theme of *creatio continua* ("Heaven's Constancy") that links many of the important cosmological terms (*t'ai-i*[a], *pien*[b], *hua*[a], *ch'eng, ho, fu*[a], *ch'ang,* etc.) with *hun-tun* is further emphasized in the quasi-Taoist work of the third century B.C. known as the *Lü Shih Ch'un Ch'iu.* In this text it is said that:

> Great Unity [*t'ai-i*[a]] gives forth [*ch'u*] two
>   principles [heaven and earth];
> [And] these two principles give rise to *yin* and *yang.*
> The *yin* and *yang* are transformed [*pien hua*] further,
> One going up and the other down.
> [At first] united [*ho*] and yet complete [*ch'eng*]
>   in a state of chaos [*hun-hun tun-tun*];
> [Constantly] separating [*li*] and then returning
>   to unity [*fu ho*].
> Uniting and then returning to separation.
> This is called Heaven's Constancy [*t'ien-ch'ang*]. . . .
> All the Ten Thousand Things are that which were
>   created from the Great Unity;
> And are transformed by *yin* and *yang.*[38]

The law of cyclic return is that which is ultimately characteristic of the Tao's creative activity and enduring presence in the world. It is the mode of creative function established by the harmonious interaction of duality during the period of the *hun-tun* time (as will be seen in the discussion of chapter 42). As chapter 40 (and suggested in chaps. 14, 16, 28, 30, 52, as well as 25) says:

> Returning [*fan*[b]] is the movement of the Tao.
> . . . .
> The Ten Thousand Things of the World are born

from that which has being [yu^a].
That which has being is born from that which
is nonbeing [wu^b].[39]

As a final observation that relates the cosmogonic scenario of *hun-ch'eng* to other important Taoist terminology, it is instructive to consider the last four lines of chapter 25: "Man patterns himself on earth,/Earth patterns itself on heaven,/Heaven patterns itself on Tao;/And Tao is spontaneously patterned of itself [*tao chih tzu-jan*]."[40] One of the most characteristic descriptions of the "life" of the Tao is that it is completely self-generated and returning in on itself, going out and coming back in a completely spontaneous and creative way. Its basic rule and pattern of life is its utter self-contained freedom of movement, its *tzu-jan*, which constitutes in Taoism one of the most important technical terms for the perfect freedom of pure spontaneity and naturalness attained through an identification with the Tao. To be *tzu-jan* is to have the wholeness and freedom that was present at the beginning, to be completely "self-so" in that all actions and thoughts are generated internally and spontaneously in harmony with the organic law of cosmic life itself. The important idea of *wu-wei* represents the individual Taoist's identification with, and emulation of, the cosmic life of spontaneity and naturalness (*tzu-jan*) of the Tao. And the return to the condition of *hun-tun* implies a certain kind of conduct that emulates the unique life-order and freedom of the Tao—its *tzu-jan*.[41]

To summarize some of what can be ascertained from this chapter, I should recall first of all that the Tao is expressly described within a cosmogonic context of meaning that is associated with a number of analogous, and mythologically suggestive, themes. The primary descriptive reference for the Tao in this cosmogonic sense is the term *hun*[d] (*hun-ch'eng* or *hun-tun*), which is a primordial condition of totality or unity (*t'ung*[a]). It can also be called the mother (*mu*), the great (*ta*), the dark (*hsüan*), or the eternal/constant (*ch'ang*). It operates spontaneously (*tzu-jan*) and continuously to give birth and life to all things.

2. *Chapter 42: The "Great Form" of One, Two and Three*

Chapter 42 opens with an incredibly terse and numerically coded account of the Tao in relation to the process of creation:

The Tao gave birth to the one.
The one gave birth to the two.
The two gave birth to the three,
And the three gave birth to the Ten Thousand Things.

> The Ten Thousand Things carry *yin*,
> And embrace *yang*;
> And achieve harmony by the mixing of *ch'i*
> [*ch'ung ch'i i wei ho*]^{42}

While the precise terminology of *hun-tun* is not present,[43] scholars have often called attention to the fact that in this chapter there is "a conception of origins still very close to mythology: the Heaven and Earth are conceived as the Father and Mother of creatures. The One is clearly an abstract designation of Chaos which is itself generally described as an undifferentiated unitary condition of the 'primordial breath'."[44] In Chapter 42, in other words, mythological images have been reduced to numerical cyphers but, possibly as Lévi-Strauss would have it, content has revealed its deep structure of binary opposition and a mythological "logic" of resolution. One and two are resolved by a third term of synthesis that suggests a certain kind of mythological intentionality.

An initial problem in dealing with this passage is that there appear to be several corruptions and possible anachronisms. The terms *yin* and *yang*, for example, did not come into technical use until a somewhat later period. Moreover, the first verse is possibly garbled because of the reference to the "Tao giving birth to the one." Throughout the rest of the *Tao Te Ching* the Tao is ordinarily identified with the one (cf. chapters 10, 14, 22, 39).[45] Also relevant, although by no means decisive, is that the *Huai Nan Tzu*, in quoting this passage, omits the opening verse.[46]

Despite these considerations, it is important to recognize that there is a long Chinese tradition of commentary concerning this passage and that it is very often seen to be the very crux of early Taoist ideology and cosmology.[47] Furthermore, the cosmological theory found in this chapter is "common to nearly all Chinese philosophical schools" including the early cosmological speculations of the *I Ching* down to Chu Hsi and the formulations of Neo-Confucianism.[48] What is more important here, however, is not that this theory, which is already abstract and philosophical in nature, forms a backdrop for nearly all of early Chinese cosmological thought but that it is used by the Taoists, both in the early texts and in the *Tao Tsang*, in a specific context of interpretation and application. It is especially in the Taoist tradition that the mythological and religiously relevant character of this passage is preserved and emphasized.[49]

By way of a preliminary analysis, the puzzling issue of the meaning of the "one, two, and three" must be addressed. This is more difficult than it might seem since traditional commentarial opinion holds that the "one" refers to the Tao or the *t'ai-shih* (the "Great Beginning"), the "two" to the heaven and earth (or *yin* and *yang*, *wu*[b] and *yu*[a]), and the "three" to the basic triad of heaven, earth, and man.[50] In the light of later Chinese philosophical speculation these identifications are generally understandable and meaningful. In fact, they already indicate a certain indebtedness to mythological thought. But an approach more in harmony with the mystical "naturalism" of the *Tao Te Ching* suggests an even broader range of archaic mythological associations and images, especially in relation to the meaning of the ideas of "one" and "three."

Based on the cosmological context found throughout the *Tao Te Ching*, the idea of the "one" can be identified with the chaotic condition at the beginning that is variously called *hun-ch'eng, ch'ang-Tao*, "mother," or what the *Chuang Tzu* refers to as the "great unity" (*ta-t'ung*[a]). It is that which gave birth to the separate dual principles classically called either heaven and earth or *yin* and *yang*. In fact, the theme of "one" is specifically linked to the term *hun*[d] in chapter 14 of the *Tao Te Ching* where it is said that the "three things" of the mysterious Tao (its "dimness [*i*[c]]", and its "soundless [*hsi*[c]]", and "formless [*wei*[a]]" qualities) are "chaotically fused into the one [*hun erh wei i*]."[51] Chiang Hsi-ch'ang comments on this passage to the effect that the reference to the chaotic "oneness" of the Tao goes back to the cosmogonic theme of the great beginning (the *t'ai-ch'u*). This was the creation time before heaven and earth were separated, the period when there was only an undifferentiated condition of wholeness (*t'ung*[a]) without any particular sound, form, or substance.

Throughout the *Tao Te Ching*, this is known as the "great form" (*ta-hsiang*) of the "hidden" Tao, which is without any name (*wu-ming*) or shape (*wu-hsing*)—the amorphous, faceless condition of the mythological Emperor Hun-tun in chapter 7 of the *Chuang Tzu*.[52] According to the passage from chapter 41 that immediately precedes the creation scenario from chapter 42;

> Great form has no shape.
> Tao is hidden and nameless.
> Yet it is Tao alone that skillfully
>   provides for all and brings them to
>   perfection.[53]

Another technical use of the idea of "one" is found in the expression *pao-i*[a]—"embracing the one" or to return to an identity with the Tao as the source of life. The term *pao-i*[a] is found in chapter 10 where it has the initiatory connotation of returning to the condition of the child. In chapter 19 there is found the similar term of *pao-p'u*, and in chapter 39 the related term *te-i*. In chapter 22, it is said that the "sage embraces the one" (*pao-i*[a]) and in this case it indicates the condition of being identified with the Tao.[54]

This interpretation of "one" is in keeping with the traditional understanding, but the real problem is to decide the nature of the "three" or the "third term" that is said to give rise to the phenomenal universe of the Ten Thousand Things.[55] In distinction to the orthodox interpretation of this as "man" (man-king-emperor being the mediating factor between the hierarchical structure of the universe constituted by heaven and earth or the dual principles of *yin* and *yang*)', the early Taoists maintained a less humanistically inclined and more ultimately cosmocentric interpretation.[56] Consequently, in this passage from chapter 42, it is probably wrong to attribute any particularly human characteristic to the idea of the "three."[57]

Granting that in the sequence of creation presented here it is not until after the creation of the "three" that there is the final creation of the phenomenal world, it would seem legitimate to consider the state of the "three" as a phase of creation still in some manner partaking of the original condition of primordial unity represented by the "one." The implication is that throughout the cosmogonic process of movement from one to two to three there is a paradise condition that returns to and duplicates the harmony of absolute unity. In a mythological sense the one, two, and three are all part of a precosmological period of development best designated by the idea of *hun-ch'eng* or *hun-tun*. The passage from three to the Ten Thousand Things represents a moment of rupture with, or fall from, the creation time. With the transition from the condition of three the paradise condition of unity is ended and the human world is created.

During the period of the "three" there is still the "chaos" condition of *hun-tun*, but it is a condition that has its own internal principles of organization, change, order, and life. "Three" in this sense is the "paradise form" or "great form" (*ta-hsiang*, chap. 41) of cosmological unity that possesses the principles of duality in harmonious union and communication. There are "two" things present, but these two are mysteriously balanced by a third term that unites them perfectly. This condition of the three can at the same time be associated with the undifferentiated or embryonic condition of wholeness at the beginning, the time of "one" or *hun-ch'eng*, since in chapter 25 *hun*[d] is related to the time before the birth of heaven and earth and in chapter 14 it is the union of the "three." Here it is necessary to speak of the paradoxical idea of an "ordered chaos" since the idea of *hun*[d] (*hun-ch'eng* potentially or *hun-tun* in actuality) is not presented as an absolute chaos, disorder, or confusion. Rather, as seems to be manifest in these passages, there is a harmonious "order" of life and time inherent in the Taoist idea of the "chaos" period of creation.

Aside from the general associations with the theme of the chaos time of the Tao, the idea of the "three" or the "third term" can also be related to the idea of *ch'i*[a]—the mysterious life breath, ether-mist, fluidlike vapour, matter-energy, life force—that is said to pervade all things and constitute the connective matrix of microcosmic-macrocosmic solidarity.[58] This is suggested by the rest of the passage from chapter 42 that says that the working of the phenomenal universe is a cyclic interaction of the dual principles of *yin* and *yang* and that their interaction is achieved through a return to the mediation (blending, mixing—*ch'ung*[a]) of the *ch'i*[a]. *Ch'i*[a] is the active force or power of the empty center that links the "two" into a form that is equivalent to the original state of unity.

It can also be noted that the term *ch'ung*[a] is especially evocative of the chaotic watery void or "emptiness" (cf. chaps. 3, 4, 5) at the beginning of time. *Ch'ung*[a] connotes the idea of a "watery, bubbling" condition, "to clash or dash against," an "empty void" (such as the compound *ch'ung-hsü*), or "blended and complaisant" (i.e., the compound *ch'ung-ning* meaning "melted and congealed, blended together"). The terms *ch'ung*[a], *hsü*[a], and *ning*[a] are all specifically linked to the *hun-tun* theme in the early Taoist texts. Chapter 7 of the *Chuang Tzu*, for example, refers to the *t'ai-ch'ung*, which is said to be a particular stage of the process of returning to an identification with the Tao. In chapter 4 of the *Tao Te Ching, ch'ung*[a] (in the sense of an empty container) is used in relation to the terms *yüan*[c] ("bottomless pool") and *chan* ("deep" or "clear as water") and suggests an allusion to the watery, chaotic condition of the primordial Tao or the "ancestor [origin]" of the Ten Thousand Things (see below). Furthermore, terms like *hun-yüan, hun-lun,* and *hun-hun*[c] suggest the revolving motion of flowing water (especially in the sense of a whirlpool) or the turning of a wheel (cf. *yun*).[59]

In a comparative context there is a suggestion here that corresponds to some of the early Greek cosmogonies whereby the original seed, egg, or substance of creation experiences an internal precosmic process of organization and change—especially the motif of "swelling" to a point where its center is a "hollow" or "empty gap" infused with the invisible breath (*pneuma*) that is the source and basis of life.[60] Then comes the moment in the process when the cosmic embryo, sack, seed, gourd, or egg shapes itself into two constituent dual principles of the world and a perfect cosmos is formed. For the *Tao Te Ching* this perfect cosmos is the paradise condition of the "three" that still reflects the condition at the absolute beginning of creation. The "two" are separated by a chaotic void or hollow emptiness, but this void is alive with the invisible life-force of *ch'i*^a. This is a paradise condition of total harmony cyclically ordering the interaction and synthesis of the dual principles through a continual process of going out (expansion, swelling, rising) and returning (contraction, coagulation, lowering) mediated by the "emptiness" of the center, that third term or primordial principle (frequently called the *yüan-ch'i* or *hun-yüan* in later Taoist texts) that constantly connects all phenomenal forms, images, things with the Mother.[61] It is the empty gap of the center that allows for the original movement, sound, or flow of the life-principle.

The mythological underpinning of this passage and its technical association with the theme of *hun-tun* is brought out in chapter 7 of the *Huai Nan Tzu*, which offers an explicit reworking of the creation sequence of one, two, and three.[62] This chapter is really the earliest Chinese commentary on the creation paradigm presented by chapter 42 of the *Tao Te Ching*, and it is significant that it opens with the following cosmogonic refrain: "In the primeval period, before the time of heaven and earth, there was neither shape or form [*wu-hsing*]." These introductory verses are then followed with characteristically reduplicated terminology referring to the idea of the *hun-ch'eng* or *hun-tun* condition of unity before the appearance of the "two." The terms used are "*yao-yao ming-ming . . . mang wen mo min*," which are suggestive of the darkness, obscurity, and formlessness of this stage of the creation process.

That these terms may be identified with the theme of *hun-tun* is asserted by the next verse where this stage (or mythological god) of the creation time is called "*hung meng hung tung*." Aside from the possible homophonic identification of *hung-tung* with *hun-tun*, the use of the expression *hung-meng* is also mythologically relevant since it refers to a figure or deity that was identified with the mythic figure of Hun-tun.[63] The *Chuang Tzu*, for example, has a passage that expressly connects a certain Hung-meng with the theme of *hun-tun*.[64] More important, however, is that all of these terms for "chaos" are rooted in a congruent cosmogonic narrative related to the numerological sequence found in the *Tao Te Ching*.

A rather enigmatic verse follows the above lines saying that "no one knows its opening(s) [or gates]" (cf. *Chuang Tzu*, chap. 25), which might be taken as a mythic allusion to a condition resembling a closed, egglike unity internally harboring all of the fertile stirrings and sounds of creation. This passage continues by saying that "two spirits" (*erh shen*) were born but these "two" are still "one" by virtue of the fact that they are "born chaotically blended [*hun sheng*]."[65] There is now a "center" present that orders the "two" back into a condition that is equivalent with the "one" and gives a preliminary organization to the heaven and earth. In other words, the condition of "three" spoken of in the *Tao Te Ching* has been established as the paradise condition of the harmonious unity of the one and the two.

There is some repetitious garbling in the next few verses but the meaning seems relatively clear. Thus, the passage goes on to say that the two spirits that were previously a chaotic oneness now "separated and became *yin* and *yang* [*pieh wei yin-yang*]." These two opposite principles (the "hard and the soft") through their alternate separation and fusion then produced the Ten Thousand Things of the phenomenal world. As in chapter 42 of the *Tao Te Ching*, the condition of the three is necessary in order to give birth to the phenomenal world. This world was still a part of the paradise time since everything in it naturally reflected the oneness of the two things working together through the dialectical mediation of the *ch'i*[a].

The microcosm and macrocosm of reality were one solidarity and man's body reflects the sacred "order" of the universe: "the head is round, the shape of heaven, and the feet are square, the shape of earth." Man is linked with the source of life at the beginning of time since "heaven is his father and earth is his mother." It is at this point in the cosmogonic narrative that, in distinction to the *Tao Te Ching*, "man" can be equated with the idea of "three." Man's life is the creative product of the synthesis of "two" things and human nature basically reflects the threeness of the creation time since there must always be a blending of the two, or a return to the beginning, to maintain the fullness of life. Paraphrasing chapter 42 of the *Tao Te Ching*, this passage continues by saying that as the "two spirits" were originally blended and harmonized during the chaos time, so also do "the Ten Thousand Things bear *yin* and embrace *yang*. And the mixing [*ch'ung*[a]] of the *ch'i*[a] causes harmonious unity [*ho*]." This is the *creatio continua* principle of "Heaven's Constancy" (see *Tao Te Ching*, chap. 14).

Life itself is based on the alternation and commingling of the dualities through the circulation of the third term of *ch'i*[a]. This is the ruling principle or "bond" (*kang* and *chi*[a] of the Tao—see *Tao Te Ching*, chap. 14) that binds the sage to the sacred time of the beginning. The Tao is that which "dwells" always in the order of *hun-tun*, that realm of "empty nothingness" at the center of all things. The Tao, then, is the root of life, the original seed or egg of all creation, and all creative processes are a replication of the cosmogony. Embryological development inside the womb is but a miniature recreation of the world. This is indicated by the fact that after invoking the *Tao Te Ching's* creation paradigm of one, two, three, the *Huai Nan Tzu* goes on to discuss the "ten stages" of embryological development leading to birth, stating that in the seventh month the fetus is complete and whole. As will be shown in the next chapter, creation is completed in seven (or nine) stages of "boring" in the *Chuang Tzu's* story of Emperor Hun-tun.

For the *Huai Nan Tzu* the art of the Tao is specifically related to the art of nourishing or prolonging life, which seems to imply a reversal of the ordinary life current back to the original germ plasm of life, a *regressus ad uterum* that is a recapitulation of the cosmogony. Once the return to the absolute beginnings is accomplished, the Taoist can again experience the development of the one to the two to the three, or reach, in a sense, that seventh stage of fetal perfection where all is internally "complete" (*ch'eng*, or more accurately, *hun-ch'eng*). This symbolism has a bearing on the root meaning of other important Taoist expressions such as *pao-i*[a] ("to embrace the one") since the etymological associations for the term *pao*[b] are closely related to the idea of an enfolding, motherly embrace, or a womb/gourd/cocoon-like enclosure.

Based on the more mythologically detailed perspective gained from the *Huai Nan Tzu*, the creation scenario in chapter 42 of the *Tao Te Ching* might not be as corrupt as Duyvendak and others would have it, since the phases of Tao, one, two, and three indicate a particular type of cosmogonic narrative emphasizing a series of interrelated stages in the precosmic development of chaos.[66] Even though the *Huai Nan Tzu* leaves out the verse "the Tao gives birth to the one," it had already established with abundant mythological imagery that there was an "uncreated" stage before "one" appeared. Tao, one, two, and three are, however, all part of the overall centering process of the cosmogonic chaos-order. In this mythological sense, it may be said that the " 'one' is born of Tao (chap. 42). . . . As the origin and seed of all things, 'one' still pertains to the dark, it is not yet born, thus it is even weaker than the infant."[67]

The Tao is that absolute mystery of the beginning, the "hidden Tao without name," "great form" (see chap. 41), or great "ancestor" (see chap. 4) that initiates the ordering process of creation. There is an internal development, imagined as a kind of germination process, producing a new state or level or organization that is depicted as a swelling or hollowing out of the original prime matter. This is simultaneously the stages of "one" and "three" (undifferentiated and ordered-chaos), which may be more readily named and numbered since there is now some organized dark form, some vague shape present.

Mythologically speaking, the overall sequence of Tao to three can be named as *hun-ch'eng* or *hun-tun*. *Hun-tun* is a mythological symbol of the paradisical creation time (the time of Tao, one, two, three before the creation of the profane human world, before the "fall") having primarily feminine characteristics in the *Tao Te Ching*. It is "chaotically whole," and as "one" it is identified with the Tao as the primordial source and ground of all life. As "three" it displays an organic "order" and internal process of gestation, which is manifested by the creative power of its "emptiness" or "nothingness."

As a final observation on chapter 42, I want to note that in a mythological sense *hun-tun* must be identified both with the symbolism of a female creatress (Hun-tun as the "Divine Bird" in the *Shan Hai Ching*?) and, at the same time, with her spawn (i.e., the analogous symbolism of embryo, egg, seed, gourd, drum, cocoon, sack, bellows, etc.).[68] In this way, Erkes's interpretation of chapter 42 as really meaning "the primal female laid the cosmic egg" is not entirely correct when applied to the overall implications of the *hun-tun* theme in the early Taoist texts.[69] To be sure, some primitive mythologies do require the existence of a primal mother or creature that gives birth to the cosmic egg; but this is not always the case, or even the most typical case, with cosmic egg mythologies when incorporated into mystical thought.[70] More commonly, cosmic egg myths answer the classic puzzle of the "chicken and egg" in favor of the priority of the egg and, in a very general way, this might also be said to be the answer given by early Taoism (especially in the *Chuang Tzu* and later texts) in its espousal of the *hun-tun* theme. The imagery of "mother," "dark female," "divine bird," "primal ancestor," and also the primordial couple, primal giant, and "mass of flesh" imagery, is all relevant to the development of early Taoist thought; but the essential mystical intentionality seems to favor the idea of creation always lacking any creator separate from the creation. It is better, then, to see the idea of "chicken" as inherent in the primordial "nothingness" of the egg. Or, perhaps in keeping with the *creatio continua* idea and Stoppard's observation, it is really the case of chickens and eggs "succeeding each other in one form or another literally for ever." This is the mystery of the "three," that "great form without shape" (chap. 41).

3. Chapters 14, 21, and 4: The "Great Ancestor"

I have already partially discussed the significance of chapter 14 as it helps to elucidate chapter 42, but it is necessary to examine this chapter more closely. As noted above, the basic three qualities of Tao, its mystery of being both before and in the world, are listed as i^c, hsi^c, wei^a—dimness, soundlessness, and formlessness.[71] This is a descriptive refrain also echoed by chapters 21 and 35. Furthermore, these three attributes that deny any ultimate accessibility to sense knowledge (via the "bored" sense apertures of the face) must be considered as an aspect of the Tao's strange unity: "These three things [i^c, hsi^c, wei^a] cannot be known further, therefore they are chaotically fused into the one [*hun erh wei i*]."[72]

Chapter 14 continues with an enumeration of other attributes of the Tao. The chaotic oneness of the Tao is the reason for its paradoxical mode of being and its blending of all opposites—its movement "in going up is not bright" and its "going down is not dark." Its life force is manifested in a continual bio-cosmic process giving birth to numberless life-forms, yet it cannot be equated with any particular phenomenal form. After going out into the phenomenal world it then returns to the original condition of chaotic formlessness that harbors all forms with a seedlike latency—it "returns to nothingness [*fu-kuei yü wu wu*]." This condition of the Tao at the beginning can be called that which is paradoxically "form without form" and "image without image."

This condition can finally be called *hu-huang*, a phrase with a dictionary meaning of something like "vague and elusive"; but it can also be taken as an alternate rendering of the idea and sound of *hun-tun*, the undifferentiated chaos.[73] This is brought out in the *Huai Nan Tzu* and later sectarian texts such as the *Lao Tzu Pien Hua Ching* (The Book of the Transformations of Lao Tzu) where the cosmogonic description of the birth of the divine Lao Tzu (Lao Chün) starts with the primordial condition of *huang-hu*: "Undifferentiated [*huang-hu*]! (From it) the heavenly and the earthly are created [*pien hua*]."[74] Even more significant, and in fact the *locus classicus* for later Taoist texts, is that chapter 21 of the *Tao Te Ching* describes the primordial Tao using the emphatic exclamatory expression of *hu-huang*:

> That thing which is the Tao is chaotic [. . . *huang* . . . *hu*].
> Chaotic! [*hu* . . . *huang* . . .] Yet within it are forms.
> Chaotic! [*huang* . . . *hu* . . .] Yet within it are things.
> Chaotic! [*miao* . . . *ming* . . .] Yet within it is the life force.
> This life force is truly real; in it is the truth (of all things).[75]

A translation of *hu-huang* (or *huang-hu*) and *miao-ming* as "chaotic" or "undifferentiated" is justified by their specific relation to the cosmogonic theme of chaos seen throughout the *Tao Te Ching*.[76] This relationship is suggested both by their semantic connotations and by the exclamatory and reduplicated manner in which these terms are used in the *Tao Te Ching*. For example, the ejaculatory use of *hu-huang* is related to the precise manner in which the *hun-tun* theme itself is presented in chapter 20 (see below). Even more pertinent, however, is the fact that there appears to be a series of phonetically related word-families associated with the very sound of *hun-tun* (and its emphatic reduplication) that recalls some mythological idea concerning the sounds (thunder and lightning?) of the creation or deluge time.[77] Therefore, it is necessary to pay close attention not only to the meaning of individual characters but also to their context, mode of expression, and especially the sound quality indicated.

As a final reference to the *Tao Te Ching*'s constant reiteration of a particular cosmogonic scenario, I want to consider briefly chapter 4. In general, chapter 4 expands on the idea of the Tao's "emptiness" and ends with a suggestion that the symbolism is rooted in a mythological context. It is stated that:

> The Tao is empty [*ch'ung*ᵃ],
> Which in spite of being used is never exhausted.
> How much like a bottomless pool [*yüan*ᶜ]!
> As if it was the ancestor [origin, *tsung*ᶜ] of the Ten Thousand Things!
> . . . .
> How fathomless [*chan*]!
> As if it will exist forever!
> I do not know where it came from;
> It seems to have existed before the Emperor [s/Lord? *ti*ᵃ].⁷⁸

These lines use the already encountered image of *ch'ung*ᵃ (chap. 42), which in parallel relation with the terms *yüan*ᶜ and *chan* recollects an allusion to the watery chaotic condition of the primordial Tao. The "emptiness" of the Tao, then, connotes the image of a matrix or "magic vessel" of water, air, vapor, or mist pregnant with all life forms.⁷⁹

These only tenuously suggestive metaphors are also directly related to a mythological context. Thus, the passage concludes with the statement that the Tao is "the ancestor of the Ten Thousand Things." The use of *tsung*ᶜ for "ancestor" or "progenitor" allows for a mythological personification of the more usual abstract symbolism of the Tao as the "source" or "origin" of creation, and fits closely with the cosmogonic idea presented in chapters 25 and 42. This possibility is strengthened by the final verses of this chapter, which are parallel to the opening lines and conclude with the couplet: "I do not know where it (Tao) came from [*tzu*—a literal translation would be something like "whose son it is"]; it seems [or "its image"?—*hsiang*] to have existed before the Emperor(s)." Some Chinese commentaries maintain that *ti*ᵃ for "emperor" or "lord" refers to Shang Ti the "Emperor on High" who along with T'ien (Lord Heaven) was a High God or Great Ancestor deity of the Chou.⁸⁰ Waley, however, is of the opinion that *ti*ᵃ has reference to Huang Ti, the Yellow Emperor, one of the legendary Sage Emperors "who separated Earth from Heaven and . . . destroyed the Primal Unity."⁸¹ Duyvendak agrees that *ti*ᵃ is "to be understood in a mythological sense" but more cautiously feels that "the author merely wishes to express the idea that the Way is antecedent to everything."⁸²

There is no final solution to this problem of identification. But agreement on the precise meaning of *ti*[a] is not really crucial to an understanding of the passage since it is clear that a reference is being made to the same mythological sequence found in chapters 25 and 42.[83] That "something" that was before the creation of heaven and earth, before the *ti*[a], was the shapeless *hun-ch'eng* (chap. 25), Tao or One (chap. 42) and is here given more mythological definition in the sense of its ancestral quality as a mythological personage. Chiang comments that that which is the ultimate ancestor (*tsung*[c]), or before the *ti*[a], is *wu-ming, wu-hsing*—"without name and shape."[84] There would, therefore, seem to be a distinction between the precosmic "ancestor" (which is "shapeless" or with a gourd or animal form like *hun-tun*?) and the later, human-shaped culture heroes (the *ti*[a]). The mythological nature of this is made more convincing when we examine the *Huai Nan Tzu* where it is stated that (chap. 1): "that which has no form [*wu-hsing*] is the great ancestor [*tsung*[c]] of things."[85]

To conclude my discussion of Tao as the "beginning" and to show how this constitutes the basis for the mystical idea of "returning to the beginning," it is noteworthy that, as chapter 14 equates the "bond of Tao" with "knowing the primeval beginning,"[86] so also does chapter 21 close by saying that because of the Tao still present in life, man is able to return to the sacred conditions of the beginning:

> From the time of old until now, its name (manifestations) ever remains.
> By which we may see the beginning of all things.
> How do I know that the beginning of all things are so?
> Through this (Tao).[87]

TAO AND "RETURN"

The soteriological implications of the doctrine of "return" involve the twin concerns of society and the individual. It is imperative to consider both of these dimensions, but it should also be emphasized that it is not really possible to separate the one from the other in the *Tao Te Ching*. Creel's discussion of the "purposive" character of the text is, in this way, very apt in stressing the *Tao Te Ching*'s focus on the reformation of society through the formative influence of a sage king—"I have no desires and the people of themselves become simple" (chap. 57).[88] The text to a great extent does seem to be addressed primarily to the king as the means to achieve a societal return to the "Tao of old" (chap. 14). This does not necessarily mean that personal methods of return are absent since, on the one hand, the method of becoming a sage king basically embodies the idea of a mystical return open to all men and, on the other hand, the efforts of the individual fundamentally represent an emulation of the sage king as a model of personal renewal. As will be seen in subsequent chapters, these implications are primarily developed within the inner chapters of the *Chuang Tzu*, as well as within parts of the *Huai Nan Tzu* and *Lieh Tzu*.

The idea of "model emulation" is a crucial factor throughout Chinese tradition and in the case of the *Tao Te Ching* involves a cluster of congruent models structured on the cosmogonic paradigm of the Tao's beginning and constant return.[89] In this way the sage king's personal embodiment of the life of the Tao, as manifested through his inner "power" of *te*[a], is the virtue that allows for a condition that resembles the paradise time and, at the same time, constitutes a model for any individual seeking a way back to the "primeval beginning."

1. *Paradise Lost and Recovered*

Chapter 80 of the *Tao Te Ching* provides the classic description of the Taoist utopian vision, a vision that is embroidered throughout the tradition. As Bauer so masterfully shows, this is by no means a static ideal and involves colorations and transformations of meaning in later history that are as much Confucian and Buddhist as Taoist.[90] It is not my intention to discuss these developments but only to indicate how in the early Taoist tradition the symbolism and mystical meaning of returning to paradise have their foundation in the broader mythological theme of *hun-tun*.

The utopia envisioned in chapter 80 is as follows:

> Let there be a small country with few people.
> Let there be ten times and a hundred times
>   as many utensils
> But let them not be used.
> Let the people value their lives highly and
>   not migrate far.
> Even if there are ships and carriages, none
>   will ride in them.
> Even if there are arrows and weapons, none
>   will display them.
> Let the people again knot cords and use them
>   (in place of writing).
> Let them relish their food, beautify their clothing,
>   be content with their homes, and delight in
>   their customs.

> Though neighboring communities overlook one another
> and the crowing of cocks and barking of dogs
> can be heard,
> Yet the people there may grow old and die without
> ever visiting one another.[91]

The description presented here is basically one of a kind of idealized, primitive agricultural community, or as Needham would have it (following Hou Wai-lu), a nostalgia for a prefeudal or neolithic communal society.[92] Although the precise *hun-tun* terminology is not employed, in other texts such as the *Chuang Tzu* and *Huai Nan Tzu* this same image of a perfect society is expressly linked to the vocabulary of *hun-tun*.[93]

As with chapter 42, it is most important to see the general structural connections of the paradise theme with an underlying cosmogonic scenario. Hence, the basic intentionality of these utopian passages is that the conditions described represent the time *before* the coming of civilization initiated by the Confucian sage heroes. There is also the implication that this primitive time is analogous to the creation time of harmony before the fall into the dispersed condition of the Ten Thousand Things—that is, before the passage from "three" to "ten thousand" in chapter 42 or before the "death" of Emperor Hun-tun in chapter 7 of the *Chuang Tzu*.

The essential basis for the Taoist utopian and mystical primitivism is the notion of the fall or paradise lost. There was a time of perfect harmony in the distant past when the Tao was immediately and naturally present to men, but something happened to destroy the primal unity. The causality of why and how there was a fall from paradise is never made completely clear, and there is even the suggestion that such a fall was an inevitable event. According to the principle of Tao's *creatio continua* there will always be a cyclic interplay between creation and destruction, beginning and return, or the rise and fall of *yin* and *yang*. So also will Tao at some times be more manifest and at some times more hidden to man. The great fault or hypocrisy is to crystallize the belief that the Tao expresses itself in a unidirectional or historical way so that, for example, "civilization" is a permanent and superior replacement of the earlier more primitive and natural conditions of life.

In some Chinese texts there are echoes of a sin or ritual fault among men that caused the fall;[94] but the idea of a kind of original sin or mistake is never taken to the extent of indicating a permanent and universal internal corruption of human nature. The universality of the condition of fallenness among all subsequent men is more sociological than ontological since it is primarily due to the conditions of feudal civilization forced upon men by the "great hypocrisy" of the ancient sage heroes. Man ever since the time of the culture heroes almost necessarily develops a "machine heart" because the artificial and purely decorative principles of civilization cover up the standards of primitive natural- ness and spontaneity.[95]

Much of this doctrine of the fall, seen throughout early Taoism, is found in chapter 18 of the *Tao Te Ching*:

> When the great Tao declined,
> The doctrine of humanity and righteousness arose [*jen i*].
> When knowledge and wisdom appeared,
> There emerged great hypocrisy.
> When the six family relationships are not in harmony,
> There will be the advocacy of filial piety [*hsiao*]
>   and deep love [*tz'u*] to children.
> When a country is in disorder [*luan*[a]],
> There will be the praise of loyal ministers.[96]

Similar sentiments concerning the fall are implied in chapters 32, 38, and 57. Throughout these and other chapters the hypocrisy that comes with civiliza- tion is primarily related to the idea of the Confucian sages who sought perma- nently to order the world with the hierarchical values of righteousness and benevolence. The Taoist sage, on the other hand, is one who renounces these false principles and returns to the state of the "infant," "nonultimate" (*wu- chi*), or "uncarved block" (*p'u*[a]), (chap. 28)—or what can more generally be related to the condition of *hun-tun*. Most of all, the "great ruler does not cut up" (chap. 28) or bore away the naturalness of things.

The best description of the "returned" condition of the sage king in relation to the *hun-tun* theme is found in chapters 49 and 58. In chapter 49 the natural virtues, the *te*[a], of the sage king are described in this way:

> The sage has no fixed (personal) ideas.
> He regards the people's ideas as his own.
> I [i.e., the sage] treat those who are good
>   with goodness,
> And I also treat those who are not good with
>   goodness [*shan*[b]].
> Thus goodness is attained [*te*[a,b]].
> I am honest to those who are honest,
> And I am also honest to those who are not honest.
> Thus honesty is attained [*te*[a,b]].[97]

The sage king's feelings are not his own because he is no longer just himself but in direct accord with the cosmic life of the Tao. Furthermore, what the sage "gets" (*te*[b]) from this identification is an inner "virtue" (*te*[a]) that spreads to all others in the world. Directly taking up the *hun-tun* theme, the next verses of chapter 49 state that "the sage in the world is 'shut up' [*hsi-hsi*, or "self-effacing"]; and for the world his mind is chaotically unified [*hun ch'i hsin*]."[98]

Chapter 58 resonates with a similar theme in that the government of the sage is described as "nondiscriminating and dull [*men-men*]." Because of this quality, the "people are simple and content [*ch'un-ch'un*]."[99] It may well be that as with the syntax and semantic connotations of the technical term *hu-huang* in chapters 14 and 21, the reduplicated terms *men-men* and *ch'un-ch'un* also basically evoke the sound and symbol of *hun-tun*. That such a linkage is not only due to poetic license is at least strongly suggested by an analogous passage in chapter 20 that describes the sage as "*hun-hun . . . men-men*" (see below). These terms have a range of meaning that includes such ideas as "dullness," "stupidity," "confusion," "concealed," or "blind"; and in chapter 20 they clearly refer to the unique mental state of "chaos" attained by the Taoist sage. As I will show in more detail in the analysis of the *Chuang Tzu*, the use of the expression *men-men* would seem to indicate a condition of being "sealed up," "shut up," or "blind"—that "faceless" (*wu mien mu*), "heartless" (*wu hsin ch'iao*), or closed embryonic condition of Emperor Hun-tun.

2. *The Mystic Return of the Individual*

Because of the references to the unique chaotic condition of the sage king found in chapters 49, 58, and 20 it should be apparent that the symbolism of return potentially applies to any man. This is the point at which it is possible to speak of the *hun-tun* theme as informing the whole content and form of early Taoist mysticism, especially as Taoist mysticism must be seen to call for an individual's initiatory return to the beginnings as the prelude to a new life. The significance of initiation as a symbolic structure in Taoist mysticism will be examined in more detail for the *Chuang Tzu*, but here I would like to lay the foundation for that discussion by showing how the imagery of the sage's unique psycho-mental condition (his way of "knowing" and "being" in the world) is modeled on the chaos cosmogony.

The Taoist sage is different from other ordinary men because of his "stupidity" (chap. 20) that comes from having identified himself with the cosmic Tao. This stupidity, however, is only by way of contrast to the fallen condition of men who value "rational" ways (= the civilized ways of sense discrimination, *chih*) of knowing the world. To really know the world involves a mystic journey back to an individual's fetal origins where one's human face becomes the nonindividualized face of all men or ultimately the no-face of Hun-tun. Because of this, the sage is "no (ordinary) man" and has "no personal feelings."

As seen in my earlier analysis of chapters 25 and 42, one of the foremost technical terms for the Taoist's unique experiential condition of mystic "enlightenment" (*ming*[d]) is the expression *hsüan-t'ung*[a,b].

To establish the relevance of these observations it is necessary to reexamine chapters 15 and 20. Chapter 15 describes the man who has "returned to the root" (cf. chap. 16) and opens with a description of the paradise time:

> In ancient times those who were masters [or rulers] of Tao
> were mysterious [*wei miao*] and profoundly [or darkly]
> penetrating [*hsüan-t'ung*[a]];
> [They] are too profound to be understood [today].[100]

It is important to note that the men of Tao who lived in the paradise time are said to possess the preternatural attributes of *wei miao* (a term that is found in a cosmogonic context in the *Tao Te Ching* to describe the primordial Tao; see chap. 1) and the special quality of *hsüan-t'ung*[a], which, as already noted, can probably be taken as a variant term for *hun-tun*.

That the condition of *hsüan-t'ung*[a,b] is an experiental condition that microcosmically emulates the conditions of the creation time is more directly asserted in the following verses. Although the author says that the attributes of the ancient time can only be described vaguely, attention must be paid to the particular terminology used:

> Cautious! like crossing a frozen stream in the winter,
> Timid! like one fearing danger on all sides,
> Reserved! like one visiting,
> Supple and fluid! like ice about to melt.
> Genuine and sincere [*tun*[b]]! like a piece of uncarved wood [*p'u*[a]],
> Receptive [*k'uang*[a]]! like a valley,
> Chaotic [*hun*[d]]! like turbid waters [*chuo*].[101]

This passage speaks of seven qualities of a man of Tao. He is "cautious," "timid," "reserved," and "supple." With the fifth to seventh qualities there is a series of significant terms (*tun*[b], *k'uang*[a], *hun*[d]) that points to the mythological theme under discussion.[102] The Taoist has returned to the Tao by achieving the *hun-tun* condition. He has reversed the creation process to go back to the ultimate beginnings where things are "*tun . . . hun*."

While Chan is routinely skeptical that this sevenfold description might suggest seven stages of a progressively profound mystical experience of union with the Tao,[103] it is my contention that such an interpretation is probably the most accurate way to understand the passage. Supportive of this kind of interpretation is the whole mythological structure of meaning I have been outlining or, more specifically, that in return to the Tao, a man reverses the seven stages of destructive drilling administered to Emperor Hun-tun in the creation time. As will be seen in more detail for the *Chuang Tzu*, a Taoist reverses the creation to become a Mr. Hun-tun whose sense organs are "shut up": "Close the mouth. Shut the doors" (chaps. 52 and 56). He has, in a sense, accomplished a passage from the ordinary fallen condition of the Ten Thousand Things back to the paradise condition of "three."

From a comparative perspective, and this was something noted generally by Maspero,[104] mysticism commonly involves the idea of stages, levels, or degrees of mystic experience and knowledge and, in all traditions, the first stage involves concentration techniques of sense deprivation or "shutting up." This is a way of turning the mind in on itself whereby the journey back to the beginning may be accomplished. Texts like the *Chuang Tzu, Huai Nan Tzu*, and *Lieh Tzu* also support the idea that the mystic path of Taoism involves seven (or, alternately, three, five, or nine) stages of progressively deeper experience. That this can be seen as an exemplification of the initiatory symbolism of a mystical "rebirth" through an inner reiteration of the creation process will be discussed extensively in the chapter on the *Chuang Tzu*. Let me only remark here in relation to chapter 15 of the *Tao Te Ching* that one of the more famous of the passages from the inner chapters of the *Chuang Tzu* (chap. 7; also found in the *Lieh Tzu*) specifically describes the stepwise mystic return of the Taoist master Hu Tzu (literally Master Gourd or Gourd Master) to the time of the beginning: "I [Hu Tzu] appeared to him as Not Yet Emerged from My Source. I came at him empty, wriggling and turning, not knowing anything about 'who' or 'what,' now dipping and bending, now flowing in waves."[105]

As with the identification of the beginning with the imagery of water and amniotic fluids in the *Chuang Tzu*, it is noteworthy that the last culminating verse in the passage from chapter 15 of the *Tao Te Ching* relates the condition of *hun*[d] to the turbid quality of a muddy pool of water. The quality and condition symbolized by water is a well-known motif in Taoism, and there is no need to recount the various ways in which water is used symbolically in the *Tao Te Ching*. More relevant is the suggestion here, and elsewhere, that such terms as *chuo* and others like *yüan*[c] seen in chapter 4 are connected to the *hun-tun* condition at the beginning, which was often mythologically imagined as a watery abyss, whirlpool, or primordial ocean pregnant with all of the images and forms of the phenomenal world. As I will show, there is also an important linkage of this symbolism of a cosmogonic watery condition with the chaotic waters of a mythological flood or deluge.

Chapter 20 is another telling corroboration of the interpretation offered for chapter 15. This chapter also presents what is essentially a description of the individual Taoist's unique mystic identification with the Tao and employs the emphatic and reduplicated *hun-tun* terminology. In chapter 20 it is said:

> I am alone [i.e., the man of Tao] and inert [*tu p'o*],
>   showing no sign,
> Like an infant that has not yet smiled.
> Forlorn [*lei-lei*]! like one without a home
>   to return to.
> . . . .
> I have the mind of an idiot [*yü-jen chih hsin*],
> So chaotic and dull [*tun-tun*]!
> Ordinary men are bright and intelligent.
> I alone [*tu*] am chaotically dull [*hun-hun*ª]!
> Ordinary men are farsighted.
> I alone [*tu*] am blindly chaotic [*men-men*]!
> . . . .
> Most men follow the groove,
> I alone [*tu*] am stubborn and boorish!
> I alone [*tu*] differ from other men,
> Because I value feeding from the Mother [*shih mu*].[106]

These verses refer to the special condition a Taoist is hoping to attain by his embracing of the Tao or, as it is put here, by his feeding from the primal Mother of all things. Also evident is the fact that in going against the grain of the ordinary world, the Taoist is essentially recapitulating the process of creation and striving to experience the condition of chaotic wholeness that existed at the beginning. To these verses there is an explicit contrast between the profane condition of the common man and the Taoist's experience of cosmic primordiality. All of the ordinary qualities of the common man are consequently reversed in a symbolic sense indicative of the unique mode of being achieved when one has managed to return to the chaos time. The cosmological foundation of the symbolism is suggested in a number of ways, but I should point out the overall cosmogonic context for understanding the Tao as that something that stood "alone" (*tu*, cf. chap. 25) and "chaotically whole" before the creation of the world.

Again, the exclamatory and reduplicated use of terms indicates the specific theme of *hun-tun*. Furthermore, in the first two verses quoted, there is a reference to an important additional motif concerning the need for a return to the beginning. It is said that the Taoist is like an infant that has not yet smiled or given sign of ordinary human consciousness. The idea of returning to a childlike condition, or even to the condition in the womb, is a frequent motif in mysticism and is prominent in the *Tao Te Ching* (see chap. 55), as well as in the Taoist tradition in general. This motif is clearly to be associated with that whole cluster of ideas already extracted concerning *pao-i*[a], or with the idea of returning to the Mother.

There is another important association that is at least hinted at in these lines—that is, the idea of *p'o*[a] or "inertness." This term and a number of other frequent substitutions found in extant versions of the *Tao Te Ching* indicate that the Taoist's condition is deathlike; he has experienced an initiatory death to the ordinary world. His condition resembles the faceless, inert condition of the dead whose spirit has merged with the chaotic matrix of fertility present in the earth.[107]

What follows these lines is the exclamation of *lei-lei*, which has a dictionary meaning of "forlorn, lazy, tired out, exhausted" but also seems to be related to the notion of the unique solitariness of the Taoist expressed by the repeated use of *tu* throughout these parallel verses. Even more interesting is that this ejaculatory and reduplicated use of the term *lei*[a] may be important for its etymological associations. *Lei*[a], for example, is related to the word-family of *lei*[b], referring to thunder or the beating of a drum. The important mythological and ritual associations attached to thunder and drumming at various religiously significantly periods of seasonal change and transition will be treated below, and it is only necessary here to be reminded again of the curious importance of the very sounds of the various technical expressions used to indicate the experience of returning to the Tao.

The other terms used here (*tun, hun, men*) have already been discussed in reference to chapters 49 and 58, so I would like only to comment on the verse that describes the Taoist as having the "mind of an idiot (*yü-jen chih hsin*)" which is "chaotic and dull (*tun-tun*)." This verse stresses the motif of the sage's sacred madness or stupidity (cf. also the terms *k'uang*[a] and *men* mentioned above). The *Chuang Tzu*, for example, says that the "sage is an idiot" (chap. 2, *sheng-jen yü tun*), and in a commentary on these passages Ssu-ma Kuang states that *tun*[b] refers specifically to the condition of the mythological *hun-tun*.[108]

To conclude my examination of the *Tao Te Ching*, let me draw attention to the final lines of chapter 20, which reiterate the overall theme I have been investigating. The Taoist attains a condition of wholeness by returning to the source of all life. His identification with the "Mother" of creation provides him sustenance. By "obtaining" (*te*[b], "getting" or "embracing") the One, the Mother, he has *te*[a] and reattains the full intensity and spontaneity (*tzu-jan*) of life that existed at the beginning of the world. By sucking the breast (*shih*[c] or *te*[b]) of the Cosmic Mother, he is drinking the sap of the universe, reestablishing the intimate closed communication with the wellsprings of life that exist in the umbilical condition in the womb and in the condition of death. The common initiatory motif of *regressus ad uterum* is reflected in these lines, and it is a theme given meaning by its relation to images derived from creation mythology.

The return to the chaos condition, however, is not presented as an absolute end but as a method of constantly starting over again in the world. Returning to the beginning is not just to maintain, once and for all, the fetal or precosmic condition but to be reborn into the human world. Because of his periodic journeys back in time as an emulation of the cyclic regeneration of the Tao, the Taoist remains fresh and whole. The sage lives creatively in the world by knowing the secret of creation.

3

BORED TO DEATH: THE "ARTS OF MR. HUN-TUN" IN THE *CHUANG TZU*

Confucius said . . . "As for the arts of Mr. Hun-tun, you and I need not bother to find out about them."
—*Chuang Tzu*, chapter 12
(trans. Burton Watson)

T HE *Chuang Tzu* presents the clearest evocation of the religious significance of the chaos theme. In many respects, the *Chuang Tzu*'s Emperor Hun-tun parable, which will be discussed at length in this chapter, constitutes the most explicit example of the mythological foundations of the overall theme and, along with the creation sequence found in chapter 42 of the *Tao Te Ching*, functions as a basic symbolic bench mark for the later tradition. This one brief story, however, must be seen in contextual relation to the whole *Chuang Tzu* since it is echoed throughout the inner chapters and, at the same time, represents a principle of general thematic unity for many of the other historically diverse chapters.

It is well known that the *Chuang Tzu* is a composite text traditionally divided into the *nei-p'ien* (inner chapters, 1−7), the *wai-p'ien* (outer chapters, 8−22), and the *tsa-p'ien* (miscellaneous chapters, 23−33).[1] Moreover, the "outer" and "miscellaneous" chapters are themselves sometimes no more than collections of fragmentary material dating to different historical periods and representing the work of different authors. Some of these chapters clearly date to the

Ch'in and Han dynasties and represent syncretistic blendings of Taoist, Confucian, Mohist, and Legalist thought.[2]

A. C. Graham has recently attempted to refine these differences by applying form-critical tests to the various parts of the *Chuang Tzu*.[3] In this way he finds it possible to distinguish at least three separate strains of thought in the later chapters:

1. The "Primitivist Document" (primarily chaps. 8 through 10 and parts of chaps. 11 and 12): this is basically pre-Han material of common authorship that emphasizes the social and political vision of a primitive utopia and has affinities with the *Tao Te Ching*.

2. The "Individualist Document" (primarily chaps. 28, 29, and 31): this composite document is more of the school of Yang Chu than of the Taoist tradition.

3. The "Syncretist Document" (the introductory parts of chaps. 12, 13, 14, and most of chap. 33): this is a Han document blending Taoist, Confucian, and Legalist thought.

While Graham has started to make a convincing case for the separation of these different layers, it is is still premature to rely on the validity of such explicit distinctions. It is only worthwhile to point out that, along with the first seven chapters, most of the material discussed here falls into the "Taoist" categories of the Primitivist and Syncretist documents. As will be seen in the following chapter, the Primitivist document is especially important for linking the *Chuang Tzu*'s theme of paradise lost with the *Tao Te Ching*. It is not my intention to dispute the real differences in the *Chuang Tzu* since the case for a general thematic unity does not imply rigid ideological consistency. My procedure in this chapter will consequently pay particular attention to the historical and ideological integrity of the first seven chapters of *Chuang Tzu* but will also allow for some comparative use of materials coming from other chapters.

There are several other preliminary issues that should be raised before going to the analysis of the text. The first of these concerns the very real tonal differences between the *Tao Te Ching* and the *Chuang Tzu*. Chapter 2 of the *Chuang Tzu*, perhaps the most important of the inner chapters, appears, for instance, to condemn, or even mock, any sort of cosmological theory of origins:

> The one and what I said about it make two, and two and the original make three. If we go on this way, then even the cleverest mathematician can't tell where we'll end, much less an ordinary man. If by moving from nonbeing to being we get to three, how far will we get if we move from being to being? Better not to move, but to let things be![4]

This passage almost seems to be satirizing the cosmogonic theory of one-two-three seen in chapter 42 of the *Tao Te Ching*. The *Chuang Tzu* characteristically uses strong, if at times whimsical, language; but it is exactly the improper use of language, or the *talking about* creation, that is being condemned. These lines are not so much a dismissal of a particular cosmogonic vision but primarily an expression of the repugnance Chuang Tzu has for contrived intellectual "disputations [*pien*ᵃ]." For the *Chuang Tzu* all such controversies are only hollow linguistic games. In the first seven chapters of the *Chuang Tzu* there is a refusal to talk theoretically about what can only be experienced—"better . . . to let things be!"

This epistemological concern that leads the *Chuang Tzu* to reject the dialectical sport of disputation so characteristic of the rival schools of the late Chou period (ca. fourth to third centuries B.C.) is especially emphasized in the first seven chapters but is also something of a general Taoist trait. The Primitivist document can, therefore, be distinguished from the Individualist document on this basis.[5] Similarly, the *Tao Te Ching* constantly rejects the use of cunning or intellectual disputation.[6] Both the *Chuang Tzu* and the *Tao Te Ching* agree that the "sage is an idiot" (*Chuang Tzu*, chap. 2 and *Tao Te Ching*, chap. 20) who steers by the "torch of chaos and doubt" (*Chuang Tzu*, chap. 2).

Another apparent difference between the *Tao Te Ching* and the *Chuang Tzu* concerns the philosophical continuity of the Taoist vision. Munro has correctly pointed out that in the *Tao Te Ching* the cosmogonic imagery of the Tao as a "mother," "dark female," or Primal Creatress who gives biological "birth" (*sheng*ᵃ) to the world is replaced in the *Chuang Tzu* with the more abstract philosophical idea of the Tao as a principle of endless change. As Munro says, "in the *Chuang Tzu* 'transformation' (*hua*ᵃ) replaced 'production' (*sheng*ᵃ)."[7] This, in fact, is indicated by what is probably the most famous parable in the Taoist tradition:

> Once Chuang Chou dreamt he was a butterfly, a butterfly flitting and fluttering around, happy with himself and doing as he pleased. He didn't know he was Chuang Chou. Suddenly he woke up and there he was, solid and unmistakable Chuang Chou. But he didn't know if he was Chuang Chou who had dreamt he was a butterfly, or a butterfly dreaming he was Chuang Chou. Between Chuang Chou and a butterfly there must be some distinction! This is called the Transformation of Things [*wu hua*].[8]

The equation of the Tao with the "Transformation of Things" emphasizes the constant return of all life to the "shut up" condition of the cocoon, which is the larval source for all changes, whether of the butterfly or of Chuang Chou. The *Lieh Tzu* in a similar fashion speaks of a kind of quasi-evolutionary theory of constant cyclic transformation and metamorphosis: "man in due course returns to the germ [*chi*^b]. All the myriad things come out of germs and go back to germs" (*Lieh Tzu*, chap. 1; cf. *Chuang Tzu*, chap. 18).[9] Even the late sectarian texts of the *Tao Tsang*, especially the hagiographical accounts of Lao Tzu (Lao Chün), basically tell of an endless incarnational process of "transformation" (*pien hua*) that involves a periodic return to the shapeless origin of all shapes and forms.[10]

There is no doubt that there is a shift toward the usage of certain technical terms that stress the idea of an endless creation, "transformation," or "butterfly way" over the idea of a single original birth. Such a shift does not completely alter the underlying mythological logic since the *creatio continua* idea is also present in the *Tao Te Ching*.[11] The mystery of the Tao is that it involves an endless series of miniature "creations," or returns to the chaos condition, which accounts for both the seamless unity and boundless multiplicity of life. "Transformation" as the continuing process of creation follows the model of the "great form" of the beginning. The *Chuang Tzu* in this sense stresses cosmology over cosmogony, but it is a cosmological perspective that clearly is structured on the *hun-tun* theme of creation.

Such considerations do not mean that there are not important differences in emphasis and attitude in the *Chuang Tzu*. The inner chapters of the *Chuang Tzu* do not, for instance, share the *Tao Te Ching*'s "purposive" concern for a government of the sage king but focus more contemplatively on the survival of the individual. Thus the *Tao Te Ching*'s principle of *wu-wei* is politically motivated but in the *Chuang Tzu* tends to be replaced by the more individualistic idea of "uselessness," which "refers mainly to cultivating simplicity and living one's life in conformity with the natural process."[12] The first seven chapters of the *Chuang Tzu* in this way manifest little hope for a collective return to the golden age through political reforms brought about by the "nonstriving" of a sage king. The idea of a "return" becomes an affair of the heart potentially open to all men in the face of a hopelessly degenerate political situation. This does not so much contradict the *Tao Te Ching* but rather internalizes and universalizes the mystical and initiatory implications of becoming a sage king. Moreover the Primitivist chapters in the *Chuang Tzu* reveal a continuity with the political concerns of the *Tao Te Ching*. The important issue is that finally individual mysticism and socio-political criticism are intertwined and share a common source in the mythological theme of returning to the *hun-tun* condition. In this chapter I will examine the mystic arts of "Mr. Hun-tun" as a kind of internal initiation pertinent to the individual, and in the following chapter I will focus on the theme of "paradise lost," which has both mystic and social significance for the *Chuang Tzu*.

The necessary starting point for a discussion of the cosmogonic theme of chaos in the *Chuang Tzu* is the famous story of Emperor Hun-tun found at the end of chapter 7. The mythological basis of this passage has been noted by a number of commentators;[13] and, consequently, it is important to examine closely the story of "Emperor Hun-tun of the Center" for the light it may bring to an overall understanding of the theme of "returning to the beginning." The passage says:

> The Emperor of the South was called Shu. The Emperor of the North was called Hu. And the Emperor of the Center was called Hun-tun. Shu and Hu at times mutually came together and met in Hun-tun's territory. Hun-tun treated them very generously [*tai chih shen shan*]. Shu and Hu, then, discussed how they could reciprocate [*pao*ª] Hun-tun's virtue [*te*ª] saying: "Men all have seven openings [*ch'i ch'iao*] in order to see, hear, eat, and breathe. He alone [*tu*] doesn't have any. Let's try boring [*tso*] him some." Each day they bored one hole, and on the seventh day Hun-tun died.[14]

Needham points to the socio-political implications of this passage in the sense that *hun-tun* refers primarily to the golden age idea of returning to "the pure primitive solidarity" of the ancient tribal communities that existed before the coming of feudalism (this was the mythic paradise time of *hun-tun* or *shun-p'u*). Wary of a religio-mystical interpretation, Needham prefers to see that "the boring of the holes symbolizes the diferentiation of classes, the institution of private property, and the setting up of feudalism."[15] He goes on to relate this to chapter 56 of the *Tao Te Ching* concerning the closing up of the holes of sense knowledge: " 'Block up the "apertures"/Close the "doors" (which Change and Uncertainty [*hu*ᵇ and *shu*ª] made in Primitivity [*hun-tun*]).' "[16] Needham offers the ingenious interpretation that this refers to the Taoist concern for dissolving feudal class distinctions. For Needham, then, this passage expresses the "original meaning" of early Taoism, which was socio-politically motivated and condemned the Confucian emphasis on "differentiation into classes" (the idea of *fen* or *tso*).[17]

Needham's theory is most suggestive but is too narrowly predisposed toward making Taoist thought into a socio-political ideology. In fact, Needham criticizes Waley for his mystical interpretation but fails to acknowledge that Waley expressly sees this passage as including both an individualistic mystical concern and a nostalgia for a collective return to the paradise time.[18] It is really neither necessary nor methodologically defensible to say that the socio-political concern was the "original meaning" of Taoism and that once this meaning was lost, or felt to be impossible in the face of the Confucian ideological hegemony, a secondary mystical interpretation would develop. Rather than being "natural and inevitable" as Needham would have it,[19] it is at least as probable that individualistic mystical and socio-political implications were both intertwined from the beginning—as, indeed, Waley seems to imply.

Another approach to the meaning of this passage, and one that supports Waley's claim for a religio-mystical as well as a political meaning, is that offered by Izutsu. Based on a comparison with a passage from the *Shan Hai Ching* where Hun-tun is described as a "faceless" (*wu mien mu*) "Divine Bird" (*shen-niao*) whose body is like a "yellow sack" (*huang-nang*), Izutsu finds early Taoism as primarily revealing a shamanisic structure.[20] Izutsu seizes upon the *Shan Hai Ching*'s reference to the monster bird Hun-tun's "singing and dancing" as being suggestive of the common shamanic practice of inducing an ecstatic trance state through the use of ritual dancing and chanting. As Izutsu says, it is significant that "the monster is said to be a bird, which is most probably an indication that the shamanistic dancing here in question was some kind of feather dance in which the shaman was ritually ornamented with a feathered headdress."[21]

Throughout the early Taoist texts there are a number of specific characteristics suggestive of shamanism and especially the Ch'u tradition.[22] One clear example of this that ties together the *Chuang Tzu*'s motif of a mystic wandering or journey (*yu*[b]) with shamanism and a cosmogonic scenario is the famous Han dynasty poem "Yüan Yu" (The Far-Off Journey) found in the *Ch'u Tz'u*. In this poem, which David Hawkes describes as a "Taoist answer" to the pessimism of "Li Sao" (On Encountering Sorrow),[23] the metaphor of a heavenly journey is used to portray the adept's successful training in Taoist mysticism and yogalike techniques. Most remarkable is that the spatial metaphor of the journey away from home—which has many shamanic overtones of the Ch'u tradition—is equivalent to a return to the creation time. The mystic's journey is consequently accomplished in stages that lead ultimately to the "Great Abyss" where the senses perceive "nothing": "Transcending Inaction [*wu-wei*], I came to Purity,/And entered the neighbourhood of the Great Beginning [*t'ai-ch'u*]."[24]

Despite the significance of such parallels, it is questionable to offer the notion of "shamanism" or the southern "spirit of Ch'u" as the basis for all of early Taoist religious thought and practice or to say, as Izutsu does, that Taoism is simply the elevation of early Chinese shamanism onto a philosophical and mystical plane. One obvious difficulty with this kind of perspective is that shamanism is an extremely complex and variable phenomenon that cannot be indiscriminately seen as a monolithic religious structure. This is precisely the case for China since it is clear that there was never simply "shamanism" in the early periods of Chinese cultural development but rather a complex assortment of differing cultural and religious institutions only some of which may be loosely categorized as different types of shamanism.[25]

The *hun-tun* story in the *Chuang Tzu*, then, cannot just be called a "shamanistic myth."[26] More important is to realize that the shamanic idea of the celestial journey or the ecstatic identification of man and animal is linked to cosmogonic and initiatory symbolism. The religious and symbolic significance of shamanism results from the broader consideration that the shaman "was already charged with a mythology."[27] Some of the mythological elements of the *hun-tun* story were quite clearly related to a shamanic context of meaning; but even more fundamentally this theme suggests a deeper and more universal level of religious meaning.

INITIATION AND MEANING

After a consideration of Needham and Izutsu it is helpful to examine Granet's analysis of this passage since it emphasizes the initiatory significance of the face-giving operation. While Granet is primarily concerned with discovering the basic social institutions behind ritual action from a Durkheimian perspective, his analysis of the initiatory motif of "boring" as a surgical operation (suggesting the physical ordeals of puberty rites) evokes a symbolic pattern that would seem to be related to an overall cosmogonic scenario—especially the idea of the creation of the human world (the world of "face") through the death of a primordial deity.[28] It is probable that this motif can be related to the later and more explicit cosmogony of P'an-ku, the primordial giant born from the cosmic egg of *hun-tun*, who creates the human world through his ritual dismemberment and death. From a comparative perspective, I will show in a later chapter that the mythic theme of the creative boring and death of Emperor Hun-tun, as well as the self-sacrifice of P'an-ku, is typologically linked to the widespread egg and gourd myths, legends of the "people without anuses," and the deluge tales of an anthropogonic "mass of flesh."[29]

Granet stresses the significance and prestige of becoming completely "human" or "civilized" by having the seven openings of sense knowledge that give one a "face" and then makes the valid point that, as in many primitive initiations, death is but the necessary prelude to a new creation or rebirth—in this case, being born into the fully human world of culture and society.[30] Granet also goes on to make an interesting comparison with ancient Chinese burial practices where it was the custom to plug up all the external sense openings. He states that the purpose behind this act of the ritual closure of the corpse (in the sense of apotropaic magic) was to protect the world of the living and make sure the principle of death and decay was contained. From this observation, he implies that the Taoist sage is striving for exactly the reverse of the funeral condition—that is, to attain that state where all the seven openings of the exterior face and the seven internal openings of the heart "are open and function freely."[31] What is at issue is that the practice of plugging the orifices of the dead is not necessarily to be seen as protective magic or as implying that the dead have achieved an inferior position in relation to the living.[32] Another way of viewing this would be to see that the dead ancestors have attained a wholly new condition of life, a reidentification with the cosmic matrix of the earth. The symbolism of "closure" for the early Taoists may also indicate the attainment of a new and more powerful mode of being, a return to a closed embryonic state close to the sources of universal life and fertility.[33]

It seems most probable that this ambivalence over the evaluation of the symbolism of death represents an important distinction between the early and later Taoist tradition—especially after the rise of the "immortality" or *hsien* cult where death was seen as something to escape from.[34] For early Taoism, and especially in the *Chuang Tzu*, death was "ecstatically accepted" and had positive connotations as a symbolization of the return to the chaotic oneness that existed during the creation time. As will be demonstrated in this chapter, early Taoism is primarily concerned with the initiatory symbolism of death as a necessary prelude to rebirth. This symbolically involves a reversal of the death of Hun-tun and a *closing up* of the openings of "face" and "heart." The Taoist must reverse the creation and fall of man and return to the condition of the Beginning: the condition of the closed serenity of the fetus in the womb, the condition of the dead ancestors, the larval condition of the cocoon, or the chaos condition.

There is a certain degree of ambiguity concerning this point. While the *hun-tun* theme in early Taoism generally stresses the sacredness of the "face-less" condition there are passages in some of the miscellaneous chapters of the *Chuang Tzu*, and the *Lieh Tzu*, that seem to point to the opposite condition (i.e., the desirability of unobstructed "holes").[35] Chapter 21 of the *Chuang Tzu*, for example, says:

The Tao does not want to be obstructed, for if there is obstruction, there is choking; if the choking does not cease, there is disorder; and disorder harms the life of all creatures. . . . Heaven opens up the passages and supplies them day and night without stop. But man on the contrary blocks up the holes. The belly is a many-storied vault; and the mind has its Heavenly wandering. . . . If the mind does not have its Heavenly wanderings, then the six drilled [tso] openings will defeat each other.[36]

It seems, however, that such passages refer to preliminary breathing techniques that lead to the unique condition of *hun-tun* as the experiental culmination of different stages of meditation. In this sense, the removal of "obstructions" to correct breathing is necessary for the ultimate goal of chaotic "closure."

It is also worth noting that in an earlier work, Granet is more equivocal in his interpretation of Hun-tun's death: "Chuang Tzu professes that a change of nature, even for the better, is bad. Hun-tun, once he has been operated on, ceases to be. He ceases to be himself."[37] The emphasis in the *Chuang Tzu* is on the fact that a man must rediscover how to "be himself." For the Taoists the acceptance of "face" as a sufficient definition of human nature is only self-deception. In early Taoism true life comes from a reversal of the more ordinary socially sanctioned ideals of righteousness and benevolence.

In China of the late Chou period there is no longer any integral tribal or clan unit, and initiation is absent as a specific ritual institution; but it may be said that the societal values of puberty initiation—having face, respectability, and a socially defined existence—continue in a nondramatic, secular, or moralistic way in Confucianism.[38] In Confucianism the "face" or "name" one has is no longer only religiously related to membership in the community of ancestors but is more humanistically linked to becoming a complete human being—a mode of being that is defined by the ethical-moral principles of ritualized social interaction. It is a matter of being educated and civilized in the ways of the sage kings. But for early Taoism the acceptance of the condition of having face is the basis for the "fall" of man from paradise. A Taoist must "die" not to become simply a man but to return to the prehuman or paradise world of the Emperor Hun-tun. The implication is that the Taoist must learn the arts of "no-face."

One of the fundamental problems raised by these considerations is that both having face and having no-face symbolically involve initiatory aspects; and the difference between the two may possibly be seen comparatively in terms of the different types of initiation found in a primitive context. Thus, the Confucian notion of "face" corresponds most generally to the collective rites of puberty initiation whereby a child becomes a complete member of a particular socio-cultural unit. His sacrality or his very existence as a human being is defined in terms of the culture or civility shared by all the members of the collective group.[39]

In distinction to this mode of initiation there are often other types of initiation in precivilizational cultures that emphasize the possibility of membership in a religious elite (secret societies) or an intensely private and personal initiation to a position of religious leadership and unique religious power (such as the type of initiation associated with shamanism or, analogously in high cultures, to the vocation of the mystic). The implication behind these different types of initiation is that there are degrees or levels of sacrality beyond the ordinary sacrality shared by all members of the society who have undergone the collective puberty rites. There are seen to be other modes of existence more meaningful and intense than the socially defined "face" of human respectability.[40]

Although no longer present as separate ritual institutions, the different forms of initiatory structure and intention continue within the traditional civilizational context of China. In this way Confucianism and Taoism both incorporate an initiatory structure—Confucianism stressing the final equilibrium of the ordinary social order and Taoism emphasizing, more individualistically and mystically, a return to a liminal order. The real problem in discussing Taoism within the context of initiation is that generally in anthropology the function of initiation is related to a process of socialization and the reinforcement of social reciprocity. But it should be recalled that initiation may also have a function that is not directed toward making the initiate a better member of society. Even with regard to puberty rites, there is a suggestion that they are also a way of teaching a man the importance of self-reliance when society fails. As E. M. Mendelson says, "the importance of initiation, in its broadest aspect, lies in that it offers a way out of reciprocity."[41] In particular reference to Taoism it may therefore be possible to say:

> If, in the initiations of simple societies, the stress is usually laid on gaining socially valuable powers, this is not necessarily so in the higher forms of initiation where total power, total knowledge or any other form of completeness will enable the successful candidate to be entirely himself, living in perhaps, but not dependent upon society.[42]

Despite my qualifications of Granet's interpretation, his approach is at least conducive to preserving the overall mythological and symbolic complexity of the Hun-tun story. Hence, Granet's overall perspective incorporates some of the shamanistic details of the Hun-tun passage from the *Shan Hai Ching* passed over by Izutsu: Hun-tun as a divine or monster "bird" shaped like a "yellow sack'' lives on Heaven Mountain, which produces "gold, jade, and blue sulphide.''[43] These details, along with the other factors pointed out by Izutsu, suggest a whole set of associations having to do with what Granet postulates as the magical and initiatory practices of ancient metallurgical guilds in China.[44] Granet, therefore, goes on to speak specifically of symbolic "totem" animals such as the owl and various magical apparatus such as the bellows, sack, and drum that were apparently connected with a corpus or myth and rite surrounding the figures of the Yellow Emperor and Hun-tun.[45]

Such a highly speculative hypothesis is only on the periphery of my concerns, and in consideration of Granet's totemic interpretation it is well to be reminded of his method of evaluating the meaning of religious phenomena and symbolism only in relation to his hypothetical reconstruction of ancient Chinese social institutions. Granet, consequently, approaches the interpretation of the *hun-tun* passage in the *Chuang Tzu* as being reflective of an initiatory rite illustrative of the archaic social institution of "potlatch," which he thinks was present in early China as a mechanism of transmitting and augmenting religio-social prestige and power, particularly among various metallurgical secret societies. Granet focuses upon the use of the term *pao*[a] meaning "to pay back," which he interprets as "the exchange of gifts: a mythic surgical operation (initiation? second birth, which gives face, respectability) which compensates for [Hun-tun's] good reception.''[46]

Waley agrees that the *hun-tun* story in the *Chuang Tzu* is "no doubt an adaptation of a very ancient myth" and goes on to say that comparatively "we can indeed get some idea of the sort of primitive myth which Chuang Tzu is here refining and interpreting" by relating it, for example, to various primitive Australian myths of creation.[47] Nevertheless, Waley criticizes Granet for his "strange interpretation" that "reads like a parody of what is called the 'sociological approach,' a method which M. Granet has himself turned to such good account.''[48]

For Waley the meaning of this passage must be seen in relation to a more general understanding of the nature of early Taoist mysticism. Whereas in the *Tao Te Ching* there is a need to return to the beginning, there is also in the *Chuang Tzu* the goal of repossessing "man's true treasure" that

is his Inward Vision (*ming*[d]), generalized perception that can come into play only when the distinction between "inside" and "outside," between "self" and "things," between "this" and "that" has been entirely obliterated. Chuang Tzu's symbol for this state of pure consciousness which sees without looking, hears without listening, knows without thinking, is the god Hun-tun ("Chaos").[49]

Izutsu states this same kind of interpretation in more abstract philosophical terms: there is a fundamental distinction between a Confucian "essentialist" philosophy concerned with class, name, and face and a Taoist "existentialism" that seeks a direct intuitive knowledge and experience of the world. Izutsu says that Hu and Shu might symbolize the "precariousness of human existence" and their meeting with Hun-tun would seem

> to symbolize the human intellect stepping into the domain of the supra-sensible world of "undifferentiation," the Absolute, and finding a momentary felicity there—the ecstasy of a mystical intuition of Being, which regrettably, lasts but for a short time. Encouraged by this experience, the human intellect, or Reason, tries to bore holes in the Absolute, that is to say, tries to mark distinctions and bring out to actuality all the forms that have remained latent in the original undifferentiation. The result of "boring" is nothing but the philosophy of Names as represented by Confucius and his school, an essentialist philosophy where all things are clearly marked, delineated, and sharply distinguished from one another on the ontological level of Essences. But the moment orifices were bored in Hun Tun's face, he died. This means that the Absolute can be brought into the grasp of reason by "essential" distinctions being made in the reality of the Absolute, and becomes thereby something understandable; but this very act of intellectual grasp destroys the Absolute itself.[50]

Izutsu's analysis is perhaps more abstractly epistemological and existential than intended by Chuang Tzu; but, together with Waley's interpretation, it can be said that they are generally correct in emphasizing a mystical frame of reference. While Izutsu suggests some of the importance of an underlying mythological context of meaning, especially as colored by his enthusiasm for a shamanistic solution to the riddles of early Taoist thought, both Waley and Izutsu fail to develop the full range of interlocking symbolism and myth that links this story with the overall religious intentionality in the early Taoist texts. It is finally the case that Granet, more so than Needham, Izutsu, or Waley, does offer some important clues for a fuller appreciation of the mythological underpinnings of the passage. Setting aside the problem of an early institution of potlatch in China, Granet's general thesis concerning the initiatory significance of the story and its relationship with totemic practices has considerable merit.[51] In fact the structure unfolded by Granet could very well be shown to be analogous to the initiatory ritualizations of the Australian myths noted by Waley or the initiatory symbolism associated with shamanism. Granet's emphasis on initiation ultimately lends itself to the uncovering of a related mythological structure of meaning.

In the history of religions, initiation as a ritual structure clearly reflects social institutions and also commonly involves the reenactment of a mythological creation scenario.[52] The mythological story of creation provides the theory or model for what is dramatized in initiatory ritual; or as Victor Turner says, "myths treat of origins but derive from transitions."[53] From the perspective of Turner's elaboration on Van Gennep's classic analysis of the tripartite structure of initiation, any important transitional moment in life requires a rehearsal of the first creation and involves a return to a liminal condition symbolically equivalent to the return to the cosmogonic chaos. To accomplish a successful transition or passage depends on a regression to what is "betwixt and between" the fixed order of life.[54]

BORED TO DEATH: SYMBOL AND MYTH IN THE EMPEROR HUN-TUN TALE

To establish the interrelationship of creation and initiatory symbolism, and especially to show the relevance of the cosmogonic sequence found in chapters 25 and 42 of the *Tao Te Ching*, the Emperor Hun-tun story must be examined carefully with reference to four major stages of plot found in the narrative: 1) the condition of "two" and "three" before the fall, 2) the fatal decision to reciprocate Hun-tun's kindness, 3) the face-giving operation, and 4) the death of the Emperor of the Center.

1. *Two and Three*

The verses up to the point of the decision to drill openings in Hun-tun may be said to be illustrative of what the *Tao Te Ching* in chapter 42 referred to as the cosmogonic condition of the "two" and "three" before the creation of the phenomenal world of the Ten Thousand Things. Hu and Shu as the two emperors of the North and South are equivalent to the dual principles (heaven and earth, *yin* and *yang*) or twin deities established as part of the process of creation, the initial passage from "one" to "two."

Granet provides an interpretation of the terms *hu*[b] and *shu*[a] that indicates something of the archaic ritual and mythological context. *Hu*[b] and *shu*[a] ordinarily have the dictionary meaning of "suddenness" or "quickness" but etymologically appear to be linked to the images of lightning and thunder, or analogously, flaming arrows.[55] In many primitive religions, and it would appear also for ancient China, the cosmic events of thunder and lightning were religiously potent signs of seasonal transition or a return to the chaos time. Thunder and lightning in China were traditionally interpreted as manifestations of the clash, union, and reversal of the cosmic *yin* and *yang* principles: "when the Yin and the Yang keep precisely to their proper positions, then there is quiet and peace. But if (the balance) leans to one side, then there is wind, if they clash there is thunder, if they cross each other's path there is lightning, if they are in confusion there is fog and clouds, if they are at harmony there is rain."[56] Lightning and thunder deities in China are also frequently related to a type of "thunder-egg" creation (or deluge) myth and are, therefore, the agents of the creative rupture of the sky (or the shell of the cosmic egg), which brings rain and regeneration to the world.[57] Especially within the calendrical mode of existence that would be part of an archaic agricultural world-view, moments of cosmic rebirth and refertilization of the earth were signaled by the sound and light of creation—the drumming thunder and lightning arrows of the mythical combat of gods and creatures of the precosmic chaos time.

The "two" deities of Hu and Shu are presented in a trinitarian sense through the addition of the third term necessary for creative synthesis—personified as the mythical Emperor of the "Center," Hun-tun. The cosmogonic condition of the "three" is that which harmonizes the polarities into the perfect paradise form of the beginning and reduplicates the absolute primordiality of the "one." Therefore, as in the more abstract scenario seen in the *Tao Te Ching*, this story in the *Chuang Tzu* may be said to recount the idea of the "three" in the more mythically relevant terms of the "meeting" of Hu and Shu in the central kingdom of Hun-tun, a meeting that takes place during the sacred history of the paradise age before the creative rupture ("death" of Hun-tun) establishes the civilized human world.

Here is raised one of the basic paradoxes in discussing the mythological significance of *hun-tun* under the idea of the formless and shapeless "chaos," since the implication is always that *hun-tun* as a cosmogonic condition, period, or being does harbor a mysterious "order" or potential cosmic "form." This "chaos form" may be considered the true meaning of the cosmos as it originally existed as a paradise world of complete harmony. The creation of the profane human world (the world of "face" and civilization) is only a secondary creation and partial loss of the originally sacred conditions of the *hun-tun* time of the beginning. The symbolism associated with this chaos or paradise time (and its particular form of "three") will constitute an important motif throughout Taoist tradition, especially in relation to the *axis mundi* symbolism of the Chinese cosmic mountain idea of K'un-lun (or K'ung-t'ung) and the rich symbolism of the double calabash gourd, *hu-lu*.[58] All of this symbolism and terminology may be understood as being equivalent to the mythic chaos condition of "three," the perfect "order" of totality established during the sacred history of the creation time.

This symbolism will be taken up later. For the discussion at hand it is necessary only to set forth some of the mythological bases for the elaborations of Taoist symbolism and iconography. With this in mind, it is helpful to take up again the mythologically rooted symbolism of Hu and Shu as gods of lightning and thunder. There are important mythological associations to be made with the traditional Chinese idea of the dragon or serpent, which was linked with the ideas of thunder, lightning, the mist (*ch'i*[a]) of clouds, and the bringing of fertilizing rains to the earth.[59] There is no need to repeat the common primitive mythologies involving the combat theme of a chaos beast imagined as a cosmic dragon, snake, bird, fish or some other beast (especially the dog); but it should be noted that these Chinese mythic materials present themes and associations generally, and at times specifically, comparable to other cosmogonic narratives involving a chaos monster of the creation time.[60] As I will show in the analysis of the *Huai Nan Tzu, hun-tun*, along with the *Shan Hai Ching*'s identification of it as a "Divine" or "Monster Bird," is also linked to the term *k'un*[b], which suggests the progeny of some primordial creature.[61]

Further documentation of the symbolic connections of the *hun-tun* theme, the terms *hu*[b] and *shu*[a], and the dragon motif is provided by the "T'ien Wen" chapter of the *Ch'u Tz'u* where Shu-Hu (as a single mythic creature) is associated with "the great serpent with nine heads."[62] The entire passage from the *Ch'u Tz'u* is worth recounting since it generally appears to be asking about the nature of the lost paradise time and makes use of a jumble of mythic fragments associated with the idea of the central "chaos" land of K'un-lun or Hun-tun as that fabulous realm where all normal values are reversed. It enigmatically asks:

> Where is K'un-lun with its Hanging Garden? How many miles high are its ninefold walls? Who goes through the gates in its four sides? When the north-east one opens, what wind is it that passes through? What land does the sun not reach to? How does the Torch Dragon light it? Why are the Jo flowers bright before Hsi-ho is stirring? What place is warm in winter? What place is cold in summer? Where is the stone forest? What beast can talk? Where are the hornless dragons which carry bears on their backs for sport? Where is the great serpent with nine heads and where is the Shu-Hu? Where is it that people do not age? Where do giants live? Where is the nine-branched weed? Where is the flower of the Great Hemp? How does the snake that can swallow an elephant devour its bones? Where are the Black Water that dyes the feet and the mountain of Three Perils? The folk there put off death for many years. What is the limit of their age? Where does the manfish live? Where is the Monster Bird?[63]

There are a number of other important mythological and ritual conceptions associated with the idea of Shu and Hu. One of these that I will only mention here is the relation between lightning and legends of serpentine arrows ritually shot at a leather sack called *hun-tun*. This is linked with a whole series of legends concerning the ritual importance of the owl at the time of an eclipse, the playing of a ritually "sacred" game, and ancient stories of dynastic change involving a ritual contest of shooting arrows into a blood-filled sack that is suspended from a tree.[64] The theme of a ritual shooting of an owl, gourd, or sack at important transitional times (seasonal and dynastic change, and also those religiously dangerous times of eclipse that represented a return to the primordial darkness of the chaos time) seems to be closely related to the mythological idea of the rupture, boring, or splitting of *hun-tun*. But more immediately relevant is the traditional Chinese symbolism associated with the source and nature of lightning. Lightning was said to issue forth from a gap or hollow space in the Heavens that was called Lieh-ch'üeh, and lightning itself is said to be but one form of *ch'i*[a].[65] This, for example, is indicated by the above-mentioned "Yüan Yu" poem from the *Ch'u Tz'u* where the culmination of the mystic's journey in the "Great Beginning" takes him "up to the lightning's fissure and down to the Great Abyss."[66] The journey to the two extremes of the sky's fissure and the earth's abyss is the way back to the central realm where all opposites become the shapeless "one," the kingdom of Emperor Hun-tun of the creation time. As in chapter 1 of the *Tao Te Ching*, the two extremes ultimately are the same (*t'ung*[a]). The unification of the two is the "gate" back to the "dark mystery" of the Tao.

Granet points to the possible connection of this with archaic metallurgical motifs and the significance of fire as the synthesizing element for refining metals. It is true that much of the *hun-tun* symbolism has such associations. Thus, the yellow, sacklike Hun-tun bird in the *Shan Hai Ching* is called "red as fire" and the term *hun-tun* is found in relation with the sacklike bellows of the forge (which is bipartite, hollow, and open at both ends; thus it is a "chaos form" basically similar to the double hemispherical calabash gourd or cocoon and the twin cones of Mt. K'un-lun). It is also linked with a whole series of symbols of what may be called the magic "empty" vessel motif (pot, bowl, drum, jar, sack, chaotic box, etc.) which, like heaven, possessed a central cavity that may vomit a magic fire of creative transmutation.[67] This kind of metallurgically oriented symbolism is finally found in the *Tao Te Ching* (chap. 5) where it is said that it is best "to keep to the center" since the sacred emptiness, form, and function of heaven and earth are like a bellows:

> Heaven and Earth and all that lies between is like
> a bellows [*t'o*[a]]

> In that it is empty [*hsü*[a]], but gives a supply that
> never fails.
> Work it, and more comes out.[68]

More noteworthy than the specific attachment to a hypothetical, archaic metallurgical tradition is that the symbolism of the bellows, sack, gourd, cocoon, or jar whose emptiness (*hsü*[a]) contains *ch'i*[a] (fire, water, breath, semen, blood, sap—i.e., all of the various manifestations of the life-force that are responsible for creation and rebirth) expresses the basic idea of the "chaos form" as the cosmogonic unity of the "three"—the harmonious meeting of two in the emptiness of the center. The flexibility of this symbolism has already been suggested by the fact that it is related to the symbolism of the *axis mundi* or "central thing" of fertile emptiness connecting heaven and earth. The "place" of creation as the gap or fissure in Heaven (the *lieh-ch'üeh*) that spits out the fire of transmutation and the abyss of earth (the *ta-ho* or *kuei-hsü*) can also be transposed into the mythically equivalent terms of cosmic mountain/tree (*k'un-lun* or *k'ung-t'ung*), spring or fountain life (*yüan*[c]), land of the dead (the "yellow springs," *huang-ch'üan*), primordial whirlpool (*wei-lu*), or labyrinth (*wei-lei shan*). Like the journey in "Yüan Yu" back through the chaos realm of Hsüan Ming and Chuan Hsü, through the twin gates of lightning's fissure and the Great Abyss, which lead back in time to the Great Beginning, the *Chuang Tzu* also speaks of a mythical journey of the sage to the land of the dead ("Yellow Springs") where all is harmonized: "To him [the sage] there is no north or south—in utter freedom he dissolves himself in the four directions and drowns himself in the unfathomable. To him there is no east or west—he begins in the *Hsüan ming* and returns to the *Ta-t'ung*" (chap. 17).[69] Analogously, in chapter 23 the Taoist sage Keng-sang Ch'u goes to the labyrinth or "Zig-zag" mountain of Wei-lei where he attained a "corpse-like" (*shih*[c]) condition.[70]

All of these "places" may be said to recapitulate the tripartite chaos condition of the beginning. In this sense, the idea of returning to the chaos time in Taoism frequently takes the form of the mystical journey to the "center" through a chaos region (labyrinth, dark cave, wilderness, desert, ocean, etc.).[71] This is the place of the creative "union," "meeting," or "Great Equalization" (*ta-t'ung*) of the two.

2. Reciprocity and Kindness

A second consideration concerns the decision on the part of Hu and Shu to pay back (*pao*[a]) the virtue (*te*[a]) of Hun-tun by "civilizing" him, by giving him the exterior openings that constitute the human condition of feudal culture and society (the various qualities of respectability such as *jen*, *i*[b], *hsiao*, etc.). As Hu and Shu say, Hun-tun is "alone" (*tu*; cf. the usage in the *Tao Te Ching*) and does not have the seven openings of the face that constitute ordinary human existence. They desire, therefore, to initiate him into the world of human culture. What we have in these lines is the motif of the "fall"—that moment of the creative rupture from the cosmogonic period of the sacred history of "three" to that of the human world of death and the Ten Thousand Things. This is often represented in mythologies as a break in the connection between heaven and earth, between the gods and men, a primal combat between chaos and the representatives of cosmos, or, in this case, the destruction of the paradise condition of "three" because of some "ritual fault."

In this case it would seem that the "fault" suggested is that Hu and Shu take it upon themselves to act according to *pao*[a] (the principle of ritual reciprocity) defined in terms of the prestige of having a human face.[72] A significant point here is that before Hun-tun had "face," before he was civilized, he was already virtuous and acted with kindness (*shan*[b]). Like the kindness or goodness (*shan*[b]) of the sage king in chapter 49 of the *Tao Te Ching* whose "mind was chaotically whole [*hun hsin*]," this story of Emperor Hun-tun suggests that true kindness and virtue is an internal quality not dependent on the openings of face or the discriminating faculties of sense knowledge. The kindness that flows spontaneously from man's inner virtue (*te*[a]) is the true basis of authentic social reciprocity. The values of face only artificially mask (as a persona) the real man within. What is implied is that a civilized condition does not necessarily bring about the fulfillment of human nature. Indeed, from the Taoist point of view it amounts to the fall of man from the godlike condition of the paradise time. As Kaltenmark has said:

> Chaos had the perfection of a sphere; it possessed the original simplicity (*p'u*[a]) of an undifferentiated being, the autonomy of the embryo, which is a concentration of life folded in upon itself. An untimely zeal [Hu and Shu] would wish to make it like everybody else, and initiate it into civilized life by giving it the sense organs that destroy its unity. The myth is a perfect symbol of the Founding Kings' original sin.[73]

The idea of the fall of man from a paradise condition constitutes an almost universal motif in world mythology. In Taoist tradition this theme would seem to be concerned not strictly with the creation of man but with the creation of the *fallen* human world. It is also interesting to see that this theme as presented in the Hun-tun story may be attached to another whole series of Chinese myths concerning a deluge or great flood. Maspero has analyzed many of these flood myths, and as I will show in Chapter 7 they can be said to correspond typologically to the general cosmogonic theme of *hun-tun*.[74] As already pointed out, the term *hun-tun* is related to the notion of a watery chaos condition; and generally the idea of the "flood" may be seen as one of those periods of return to the primordial watery condition of the absolute beginnings.[75]

The story of Emperor Hun-tun, therefore, emphasizes a creation mythology attempting to explain the fall from the paradise condition of the beginnings to a permanent civilized form of existence. This is the transition usually referred to as the passage from "chaos" to "cosmos"; but in the Taoist interpretation, the true meaning and "order" of cosmos already existed in the time of primitive totality. As I will show in the following chapter, early Taoism makes a distinction between the sacred condition of the *hun-tun* time and a secondary degeneration into the "chaos" (*luan*) of civilized "order." The Taoist accepts the fact of being born into a civilizational order but does not accept the possibility that civilizational values define what it means to be fully alive and human. The acceptance of phenomenal existence requires a more profound recognition of the fact that the fulfillment and renewal of human life depends on a periodic return to a chaotic or primitive condition.

3. *Bored for Seven Days*

The next significant element in the story is the seven days of the "drilling" or "boring" (*tso*) of the holes that would make Hun-tun human. As was disparagingly noted by a Western commentator in the nineteenth century, this "looks somewhat like a burlesque of the Scriptural account of Creation which the seventh day saw completed, Chaos being reduced to order."[76] Despite the disdain of this reference, there is certainly an interesting parallel here and one that does emphasize the cosmogonic nature of the *hun-tun* story. It should be stressed, however, that in this story the seven days or periods of creation refer to the secondary creation of human civilization from a preexisting paradise world.

As the sage king in the *Tao Te Ching* (chap. 28) is "one who does not carve up," so also is his condition one of being "uncarved." The fault or sin responsible for the fall from paradise is, therefore, the meddling with nature in the name of civilization and respectability—the values of *pao*[a] or social reciprocity—on the part of the Confucian culture heroes. The carving (*tso*) of Emperor Hun-tun is, then, only a more mythologically explicit elaboration on the philosophy of Tao seen in the *Tao Te Ching* (chap. 11):

> Doors and windows are cut out [*tso*] to make a room,
> But it is on its non-being that the utility of the room depends.
> Therefore while being the tangible or phenomenal has advantages,
> It is non-being that makes it useful.[77]

The method of accomplishing this creative act most probably recalls some sort
of mythically based initiation ceremony where, as in many tribal societies, the
initiate is inducted into the fully human world of culture (receiving the "face"
or mask of the ancestors of the tribal society) through such ritual practices and
bloody ordeals as incision, tooth extraction, circumcision, tatooing, beating, or
mutilation—simulating a sexual reversal, an identification with the dead ancestors, or a death to the ways of the child and a rebirth into the world of adult
human society.[78]

The numerical reference to seven, seven holes and seven days of drilling, is
especially significant in the Taoist initiatory symbolism of self-realization, but
it is also an issue that is extremely difficult to evaluate.[79] Interpretation of the
symbolism of seven is complicated by various cross-cultural ideas concerning
the sacredness of seven and also for the reason that in China the meaning of
seven is related to other numerical and ritual systems emphasizing three, five,
nine, and ten.[80] Despite these complicating factors, it would seem that throughout most of the early Taoist texts the numbers three, seven, and nine may be
taken as symbolically equivalent numbers indicating completion or hermaphroditic wholeness—in a sense, a return to the primordial condition of one. In
terms of the number symbolism of seven and the interrelated transitional phases
of social activity and quiescence (*yang* and *yin*, expansion and contraction,
creation and return, life and death, cosmos and chaos), Granet notes that in
traditional China:

> The separation of the sexes starts at 7 years; at 70 years it is terminated; at 70
> years old people are free from long periods of ritual mourning; up until 7
> years an infant who dies is lamented but extensive mourning rituals are not
> carried out for him. At 70 an old person retreats to prepare for death (at 7
> months, a fetus is formed and ready for birth); at 7 years a young man
> prepares to enter the common life of the schools. Before 7 years and after 70
> years—which is equivalent to the condition of death—there is no sexual
> differentiation.[81]

Cosmogonically, being at seven or nine is to be at a transitional period of
return to the condition of *hun-tun*, the condition of three that equals the
perfection of one. As the twenty-fourth hexagram of the *I Ching* states: "on the
seventh day comes return." This is also traditionally the time of the winter
solstice whose image is the thunder of creation and the New Year.[82] As all
creative acts are a replication of the cosmogonic process (in this case, the
sequence in the *Tao Te Ching* of one – two – three, where three or the third term
of cosmic synthesis might be taken as equivalent to seven or nine, the "union"
of two or three series of three) so is the act of creating the civilized human world
of face a process involving seven (three or nine) stages.

What the Taoist is concerned with is the reversal of this kind of process, which also involves seven (nine or three) stages of returning to the faceless condition of Hun-tun, an infant, a fetus, ambiguous sexuality or the dead. The symbolic significance of seven in Taoism, therefore, primarily finds meaning in terms of the cosmogonic theme of *hun-tun* and refers to the idea that any creative religious act (meditation, ritual, etc.) achieves fruition only in emulation of the cosmic process established at the beginning, the mythic sequence of events leading from the condition of the one through three, five, seven, or nine stages. Indeed, at all levels of microcosmic and macrocosmic life there is a reduplication of this basic process. Thus, the theme of the *hun-tun* time of wholeness before the birth of the profane world is suggested by the sexual ambiguity of an infant, an old person, or the dead, as well as by the idea of embryological development where the embryo came to fetal completion during the seventh month.[83] In this way, the frequent Taoist motif of *regressus ad uterum* (especially in later Taoist alchemy) fits precisely with the cosmogonic theme of *hun-tun*—the possibility of reattaining the primordial wholeness of the creation time. This may be imagined as a reidentification with the time before biological birth, going back to the period of the seventh month when the fetus has reached full development and is perfectly united with the mother through a closed internal circuit of life and sustenance.

4. *Death, Sacrifice, and Fall*

The last factor to be noted is the reference to the death of Hun-tun after the face-giving operation was completed on the seventh day. Here the implication is that at the cosmogonic level a destruction of the paradise condition was necessary to establish the world of human culture and, at the level of the individual, that rebirth or entry into any new mode of being requires a symbolic death and reenactment of the creation story. But where rebirth would ordinarily be the result of an initiatory death, the emphasis in the *Chuang Tzu* is placed on the fact that equating human values with the civilized values of face is but a loss of the true meaning of life. Whereas in the later, yet typologically analogous, P'an-ku accounts, the creation of the human world is accomplished through the voluntary sacrificial death (dismemberment) of the cosmogonic giant, in the Emperor Hun-tun story death is forcibly accomplished and nonsacrificial in nature.[84] The coercive death of Hun-tun accomplishes only a negative creation of something new and not something better than that which existed before.

The paradox and dilemma here, as in the *Tao Te Ching*, is that the "fall" at one level is necessary and essential—that is, the existential fall that gives rise to *something* rather than nothing, the creation of the actual world and man. Yet an acceptance of the reality of the phenomenal world and human nature need not require a secondary replacement of natural values with false cultural values. The dilemma for the Taoist is that the world has fallen a second time to the civilizing efforts of the culture heroes. For the Taoist this is a death to the true meaning of life, a "sin" against nature.

From the standpoint of the principle of *creatio continua*, the eternal "going out" and "coming back" of the Tao, the goal of the Taoist is not to return to the beginning as a final end, to dissolve himself in the timeless condition of nothingness before the creation of the world. It is rather that the Taoist in sympathy with the life of the Tao must reject the finality of either chaos or cosmos. In living a true life a Taoist must submit to the natural way of things, the constant cyclic interplay between chaos and the re-creation of the world. Chaos is the germ and ground of the world; but more important is that the fulfillment of human life only comes from embracing at the same time both chaos and cosmos, nothing and something, and living the perpetual round of beginning and return. The fault of the culture heroes Hu and Shu, like Yao and Shun, was to believe that chaos, nature, or primitive culture can be permanently replaced by civilization, or to believe that cosmos does not constantly depend on a periodic return to chaos. Another way to say this is that the sin of Confucianism from the Taoist standpoint is its replacement of a mythological vision of life as eternal return with a more historical conception of progressive cultural development.[85]

The *Chuang Tzu* admits the fact of the fall into civilization but not its desirability or finality, not as the permanent creation of a better "order." It would seem that the reason for the fall, the movement from a sacred to a profane condition, was exactly the self-deception of seeing the death of Hun-tun as a rebirth—the acceptance of the civilized values of life as ultimate and normative for human nature. The Taoist must also experience a death, but it is to be a death to the ordinary condition of the "civilized" world and a return to the primordial, primitive, or mythic life of Hun-tun. This is inculcated as a basic pattern of meaning in early Taoism that emphasizes the symbolism of the reversal of the death of Hun-tun through a mystic initiation involving seven stages of meditative closure and reunification of the bodily and psycho-mental processes. What is suggested in Taoism is that this is more than a theory, more than an allegorical or literary device, and that it is possible for a man to return to and reexperience the faceless condition of the Emperor Hun-tun.

THE "ARTS OF MR. HUN-TUN"

The plausibility of the above interpretation can only be judged in relation to an overall examination of the *hun-tun* theme in the early texts, and this must be an examination that would bear in mind the complicated multivalency of the symbolism involved. To indicate the relevancy of such an enterprise I would like to consider a few additional passages from the *Chuang-Tzu* where the *hun-tun* theme seems to underlie much of the symbolism of mystic self-realization. Most generally the way of "embracing the one" and "returning to the root" appears to be structured on a symbolic reversal of the cosmogonic process suggested in the story from chapter 7 and is variously referred to in the *Chuang Tzu*, and the *Tao Te Ching*, as the sage's ability to "hold fast to the source" or to "hold to the beginning" (chap. 5). Becoming one with the Tao is a matter of knowing and living the "mysterious workings of the Tao" (chap. 2) that were established in the creation time. The Tao as the "source" and "root" of life is that which in chapter 22 is said to be "chaotic, dark, or hidden (*hun jan*) and "without form" (*pu-hsing*). For a man who has returned to this condition:

> [his] body is like a withered corpse,
> mind like dead ashes,
>
> . . . .
> dim dim, dark dark [*mei-mei hui-hui*],
> [he is] mindless [*wu-hsin*].[86]

Throughout the *Chuang Tzu* there is a constant and generally consistent symbolic reference to specific techniques or "arts of the Tao" (*tao-shu*[a]) that allow the Taoist to repossess the faceless totality of the Emperor Hun-tun. In fact, such references to *tso-wang*, *hsin-yang*, *hsin-ning*, and *ch'i-hsin*[87] as "arts of the Tao," or methods of self-realization, might more aptly be referred to as the initiatory arts of becoming a Mr. Hun-tun.

This is asserted in a passage found in chapter 12 of the *Chuang Tzu* that discusses the attributes of a truly natural man of "complete virtue."[88] This man was a simple gardener who did things otherwise than the ordinary, artificial norms of conventional society. He avoided the use of "bored" (*tso*) contrivances that would have made his life superficially easier. Yet despite his uncivilized, humdrum, and bucolic ways he "held fast to the Tao and his virtue was complete": "Being complete in virtue, he is complete in body; being complete in body, he is complete in spirit; and to be complete in spirit is the Tao of the sage." In relation to the values of the ordinary world he was "chaotic, [*mang*[a]] yet his purity was complete." His was a method that involved the "breaking up of the bodily form."

The story relates that it is Tzu-kung, Confucius' disciple, who meets this simple gardener. Upon reporting on the encounter to Confucius, the Master identifies the gardener as a follower of the Taoist arts, a practitioner of the "arts of Mr. Hun-tun":

He is one of those who falsely practice the arts of Mr. Hun-tun [*hun-tun shih chih shu*]. . . . He is a person who understands returning to simplicity [*su*] and through effortless action [*wu-wei*] has returned to the uncarved state [*p'u*ᵃ]. He has embodied nature [*hsing*] and embraced spirit [*pao-shen*] wandering freely [*yu*ᵇ] in the midst of the world.[89]

Confucius concludes by agreeing that Tzu-kung was rightly perplexed by such strange matters: "As for the arts of Mr. Hun-tun, you and I need not bother to find out about them."[90] From the standpoint of the gardener and his uncarved condition, the failure of Confucius and Tzu-kung to understand the arts of Mr. Hun-tun is due to their acceptance of the values of face and "fame." This is the condition of the fall, which replaces natural values with false, civilized values. In the words of the simple gardener, Tzu-kung and his master Confucius have "machine hearts": "with a machine heart in your breast, you've spoiled what was pure and simple; and without the pure and simple, the life of the spirit knows no rest. Where the life of the spirit knows no rest, the Tao will cease to buoy you up."

Evident in this and other similar passages is the particular technical use of such terms as the "arts of *hun-tun*" to indicate a form of meditation and a unique experiential condition linked to some of the key ideas (*su, p'u*ᵃ, *wu-wei, yu*ᵇ, *pao-shen*, etc.) of Taoism. There is an important connection between what a Taoist does in meditation (in returning to an identification with the Tao) and the cosmogonic model suggested by chapter 7 of the *Chuang Tzu* and chapters 25 and 42 of the *Tao Te Ching*. Moreover, the various descriptions of a progressive return to the extraordinary *hun-tun* condition suggest a close similarity with the stages of meditation and trance described in many mystic traditions. There are certainly very probable allusions to such trance-inducing methods as breath manipulation, seclusion, purification, concentration, and posture; and, even more significant, the presence of symbolic references and a periodization (three, seven, or nine days, months, or years) relating to the *hun-tun* theme that suggest psychic "signs" of successful progress toward the unique experience of unification with the Tao.

1. *Stages of Return*
This is suggested by numerous passages, but let me only point to a few prominent examples. One of these is found in chapter 14.[91] This passage implies that there are various stages of trance that lead to a progressively more profound experience of enlightenment (*ming*ᵈ) or what might be described as a condition of "chaotification." Significantly, the Yellow Emperor (Huang Ti) is presented as a Taoist master who describes the path to the Tao by making an

analogy to different levels of performing music. For the Taoist in the practice of his art there are three stages of progressively more meaningful "harmony"—the third and final stage being reached when "your body melts into the empty void, and you are brought to an ideal freedom." This is the stage reached through a preliminary withdrawal (the Yellow Emperor performs his music "in the wilds") and period of meditation. It constitutes an initiatory regression to the chaos time:

> There seemed to be a chaos where things grew thickly together [*hun chu ts'ung sheng*], a maturity where nothing takes form, a universal plucking where nothing gets pulled, a dark chaotic obscurity [*yu hun*] where there is no sound. It moved in no direction and rested in mysterious shadows. Some called it death, some called it life, some called it fruit, some called it flower. . . . I end it all with confusion [*huo*] and because of the confusion there is stupidity [*yü*[b]].

This description of what can only be called an extraordinary trance experience concludes with the observation that because of the unique condition of sacred "stupidity," "there is the Tao, and this is the Tao that can be lifted up and carried around wherever you go."[92]

In this passage there is an explicit connection being made between mystic experience as a kind of "garden of unknowing" attained through the arts of the Tao and the mythological imagery of the *hun-tun* condition. In another passage from chapter 12 there is a description of a "man of spirit" (*shen-jen*) that similarly suggests the practice of the mystic arts of *hun-tun*:

> He [spirit man] lets his spirit ascend and mount upon the light; with his bodily form he dissolves and is gone. This is called the Illumination of Vastness [*chao-k'uang*]. He lives out his fate, follows to the end his true form, and rests in the joy of Heaven and Earth, while the ten thousand cares melt away. So all things return to their true form. This is called Chaotic Darkness [*hun-ming*].[93]

In a story from chapter 6 the true "method of a sage" (*sheng-jen chih tao*) is explained as encompassing a number of distinct stages or phases of trance gradually moving one back to an experience of absolute oneness.[94] It is said that: after three days—one is "able to put the world outside of oneself"; after seven days—one is able "to put things outside of oneself"; and after nine days—one is "able to put life outside of oneself." At this point one has reversed all that is ordinary in life and has achieved a mystic "completion." The sage has achieved that experience of complete identification with the Tao that is here called *ying-ning* or what has been translated by Chang Chung-yüan as "tranquilisation in chaos." Chang goes on to refer to this as the condition of the "purified" mind or the "enlightened" condition of *ming*[d].[95] As the Tao was in the beginning, the sage is alone (*tu*) and witness to the "dawn" of creation. This is seemingly the unique mystic condition where all distinctions of past and present, life and death, are collapsed into a total oneness of pure consciousness.

The passage is concluded by a recitation of the sources for the sage Ju Yu's method of returning to the Tao. This has been said to be but a simple literary "parody of the filiations of the other schools of philosophy";[96] but it can also be seen to be a listing of nine "sources" corresponding to the nine stages of initiatory return that lead progressively back to the condition of *hun-tun*. While it is not possible to determine the mythological basis for all of the terms used, the last three "sources" are generally linked to the cosmogonic themes under investigation. The seventh, eighth, and ninth sources of this "method of a sage" are called revelations from *Hsüan-ming* ("Dark Mystery"?) *Ts'an-liao* ("Participation in Mystery"?), and *I-shih* ("Congealed Beginning"?).

The terms *hsüan-ming* and *ts'an-liao* are frequently linked to a cosmogonic scenario, but more important is the problem concerning the meaning of the term *i-shih*. It has been noted, and I think correctly, that the graph *i* is probably a corruption since *i-shih* (to "doubt the beginning") seems to make no sense in the context of the passage. Watson amends this to read *ni-shih*, which he translates as "copy the source."[97] But even more probable and convincing, however, would be to see that *i* is likely to be a textual corruption of *ning*[a], which runs in the same word family as *ning*[b] used by Ju Yu to name the ninth stage of meditation achieved by the sage. That this is the most probable emendation is corroborated by the use of *ning*[a] elsewhere in the *Chuang Tzu* (and the *Lieh Tzu*) to refer to the condition of the "spirit man" (*shen-jen*) who has "congealed [or concentrated] his spirit [*shen ning*]."[98]

Ning[a] generally connotes the meaning of "to congeal, coagulate, to curdle." As a compound with *t'ai* it means "embryo," and the expression *ning ssu mo hsiang* suggests the idea of meditation. As with the ideas of returning to the one, the uncarved block, the root, or the source, the condition attained by the sage is a symbolic closure of the holes of face, an embryonic infolding, coagulation, concentration, or congealment of the spirit into a chaotic mass— the recovery of the condition of totality that is an identification with the mythic *hun-tun*.

Achieving this condition involves a process of "reduction" and "unification" or, more in keeping with the symbolic imagery, a process of returning to the faceless condition of the Emperor Hun-tun. In another similar passage from chapter 6 relating the techniques of *tso-wang*, it is stated that the sage must become shapeless by "smashing up his limbs and body, driving out hearing and seeing; and casting off form and doing away with knowledge." Finally, it is said that this is necessary in order to achieve a reunification (*t'ung*[a]) with the Great Unity (*ta-t'ung*[b]).[99]

Also reflective of specific meditation techniques is a passage found in chapter 21 that describes an encounter between Confucius and Lao Tan (Lao Tzu) during which Lao Tan is seen to be experiencing a trancelike state.[100] His body was deathlike and darkly mysterious—his "form and body seemed stiff as an old tree" as if he "had forgotten everything and had taken leave of men." Lao Tan was motionless as if "he were not even human [*fei jen*]" since, "standing in singular aloneness [*tu*]," he had attained an identification with the primordial condition of the Tao.

Lao Tan explained his condition to the amazed Confucius by saying that he was simply practicing the techniques whereby his "mind was wandering in the beginning of things [*yu hsin yü wu shih ch'u*]." Having attained the condition of the "perfect man" (*chih-jen*), he goes on to further explain his unique condition by appealing to a type of cosmogonic scenario:

> Perfect *yin* is stern and frigid; perfect *yang* is bright and glittering. The stern and frigid comes forth from Heaven; the bright and glittering emerge from the Earth. The two mingle, penetrate, come together, harmonize, and all things are born therefrom. Perhaps someone manipulates the cords that draw it all together, but no one has ever seen his form.[101]

Further amplification of this cosmogonic context of the "one," the "two," and the "three" (the mysterious chaotic unification of the two) is provided by Lao Tan in the following way:

> In this world, the ten thousand things come together in the One, and if you can get [*te*[b]] that One and become unified [*t'ung*[a]] with it, then your four limbs and one hundred joints will become dust and sweepings; life and death, beginning and end will be mere day and night, and nothing whatever can confound you, certainly not the trifles of gain and loss, good or bad fortune.

"Getting" the Tao, then, involves a "great return" (*ta-kuei*, from chap. 22), which is a kind of mythical journey to the K'un-lun mountains in the "central" realm of the Emperor Hun-tun.[102] In an analogous fashion chapter 11 relates a story of the Yellow Emperor who goes to the K'ung-t'ung mountains for instruction from the Taoist master Kuang Ch'eng.[103] Kuang Ch'eng reports that the "highest Tao" (*chih-tao*) is "profound and chaotic [*yao-yao ming-ming*] . . . chaotic and mysterious [*hun-hun mo-mo*]." To achieve the return to the Tao, the Yellow Emperor must be led through the "Gate of Yao-ming"; and, as is said elsewhere in this chapter, this method of returning to the beginning will lead to an extraordinary condition where one will "command a corpse-like stillness, dragon vision, the silence of the watery abyss, and the voice of thunder."[104]

2. *The Cosmogonic Context of Return*

What should be emphasized for all of these passages is the fact that the "arts of the Tao" are almost always linked to a cosmogonic model. This is brought out in a passage from chapter 12 that opens with a narration of the processes of creation during the "Great Beginning" (*t'ai-ch'u*) when things were in the chaos state: "In the Great Beginning, there was nonbeing; there was no being, no name. Out of it arose One; there was One, but it had no form. Things got [*te*[b]] it and came to life, and it was called virtue [*te*[a]]."[105]

This passage then goes on to link the operations of the creation time directly to the methods and goals of the Taoist. The Taoist is concerned above all with the methods of returning to a condition of inner wholeness by a training of his "inborn nature" (*hsing*):

> If the nature is trained, you may return to Virtue, and Virtue at its highest peak is identical with the Beginning [*t'ung yü ch'u*]. Being identical, you will be empty [*hsü*[a]]; being empty, you will be great. . . . You may join with Heaven and Earth. Your joining [*ho*] is chaotic [*hun-hun*[b]], as though you were stupid [*yü*[b]], as though you were confused [*hun*[a]]. This is called Dark Virtue [*hsüan-te*]. This is a unification with the Great Concordance [*ta-shun*].[106]

The cosmogonic context is also found in chapter 6 of the *Chuang Tzu* where it is stated, in a way reminiscent of chapters 21 and 14 of the *Tao Te Ching*, that the Tao "can be passed down yet cannot be received. Can be obtained yet cannot be seen. It is of itself the source and root."[107] This passage goes on to echo the mythological scenario seen in chapter 25 of the *Tao Te Ching* where it was said that the Tao was that mother of chaotic wholeness (*hun-ch'eng*) that gave birth to heaven and earth.[108]

What follows this passage is a further indication of the mythological context since there is a recounting of various mythological figures of the chaos time (Hsi-wei, Fu-hsi, P'ing-i, Huang Ti, Chuan-hsü, Hsi-wang-mu, etc.) who "got" (*te*[b]) the Tao. The idea of the passage seems to be similar to that of the Hun-tun story of chapter 7 in that it suggests that the present profane period of civilization is the time when the Tao is "hidden" (*yin*[a]) and extremely difficult to possess in its fullness. The time of the hidden Tao must be distinguished from the paradise time of *hun-tun* when there was direct access to the sources of cosmic life.

The mythological idea of "getting" the Tao can be equated with other terms (such as *pao*[b], *shou*, *fu*[a], etc.) symbolic of a return to the One and the establishment of a "connection" with the Tao through the harmonious balance of the two things, *yin* and *yang*. These same ideas are suggested in another passage found in chapter 12.[109] There it is stated that the "return to virtue [*fan te*]" comes from a training of human nature so that virtue is not the artificial trappings of face and morality but is that which is "unified with the beginning." The "return" called for in the concluding part of the passage is directly linked to the opening verses where a cosmogonic context of meaning similar to that seen in the *Tao Te Ching* is set forth: "In the Great Beginning [*t'ai-ch'u*], there was nonbeing; there was no being, no name. Out of it arose one."

Like chapters 42 and 25 in the *Tao Te Ching*, the "one" is identified as that chaotic thing "without form." As the various mythological figures in chapter 6 "got" the Tao, so here also in a more abstract cosmological sense "things got hold [*te*[b]] of it [the shapeless one], and came to life." The passage continues by linking these cosmic processes to individual human nature:

Things got hold of it and came to life, and it was called Virtue [*te*[a]]. Before things had forms, they had their allotments [*fen*]; these were of many kinds, but not cut off from one another, and they were called fates. Out of the flow and flux, things were born, and as they grew they developed distinctive shapes; these were called forms. The forms and bodies held within them spirits, each with its own characteristics and limitations, and this was called inborn nature [*hsing*].

In chapter 18 there is a similar evocation of these mythological themes. One passage states:

The inaction [*wu-wei*] of Heaven is its purity;
The inaction of Earth is its peace.
These two combine and all things are transformed [*hua*[a]].
Chaotically, Mysteriously [*mang . . . wu*]!
There is no place they come out of.
Chaotically, Mysteriously [*mang . . . mang*]!
They have no sign.[110]

The emphatic reduplicated use of *mang*[a] may be identified with the theme of *hun-tun* by its particular conjunction with *hun*[d] in chapter 26 for the idea of the paradise time. The term *mang*[a] is linked to the word-family of terms with meanings like "blind, deluded," "vast, vague," and "confused, abundant, mixed, blended." Moreover, mang[a] can be specifically connected with a mythical figure who was identified with Huang, one of the sixteen legendary Hsia kings. The mythic Mang was also called Ho (literally "union"), a deity that was frequently paired with Hsi and said to be a descendant of the primordial couple Chung-li.[111] Finally, in the syncretistic chapter 33, Chuang Tzu himself is described as being "chaotic [mang[a]] and arcane, he is one who has never been completely comprehended."[112]

Mang[a] is also used for the idea of the cosmogonic chaos time in the passage immediately following the above section—that is, the well-known passage recounting the parable of the death of Chuang Tzu's wife. In this story in order to explain his eccentric funeral behavior of "pounding on a tub and singing" to his more traditionally minded friend Hui Tzu, Chuang Tzu justifies his actions with a response that recalls the basic cosmogonic theme of hun-tun. Chuang Tzu states that he did grieve like anyone else when his wife first died; but he then

> Looked back to the beginning and the time before she was born. Not only the time before birth but to the time before form; not only the time before form but the time before the ch'i[a]. [This was the] time [when all] was in the midst of Chaos [mang wu]. It changes and produces ch'i[a] and ch'i[a] changes [pien[b]] producing form. Form changes and gives birth. Now [with regard to my wife] there has again been a change [pien[b]] and there is death. It's just like the natural change of the four seasons: spring, summer, fall, and winter.[113]

The emphasis here is upon the creative process of change established at the beginning. It is a mysterious pattern or order that can be described as a chaotic void that yet has an internal "life" potency giving rise to all creative transformations (hua[a] or pien[b]). As Chuang Tzu says at the conclusion of the famous butterfly parable from chapter 2, the chaotic order of the Tao is "the great transformation of things [wu hua]."

3. Forgetting Face in Chapter 6

Lest it appear that my focus hinges too much on the later chapters of the Chuang Tzu, let me go back to a consideration of some of these themes as developed in chapter 6.[114] I previously pointed out the significance of the cosmogonic passage found in this chapter and its general structural relation to the Hun-tun story of chapter 7 and the mythic patterns presented in the Tao Te Ching; but it is instructive to examine briefly some of the ways these mythic themes are symbolically embellished and applied to the methods and goals of being a "true man" (*chen-jen*) of Tao.

This chapter opens with a parable describing the condition of the Taoist holy man, the "true man" mentioned above, who is able to achieve the fullness of life and the state of a true "fullness of knowledge." [115] It is implied that he attains this state by emulating the practices of the ancients of the paradise time whose "breath came from deep inside." That is, a Taoist makes use of arts that seem to include meditation techniques of breath manipulation or, as it is put here, he learns to "breathe from his heels" in distinction to ordinary men who breathe from the bored openings of the mouth and nose. [116] By use of such a meditation technique the Taoist initiates the process of return wherein "His mind forgets, His appearance is calm [*chi*c], His brow unfurrowed." [117]

He is now on the path of achieving a reidentification with the cosmic life of the Tao where all the opposites (hot and cold, joy and anger, *yin* and *yang*, etc.) are blended and pass as naturally as the four seasons change. This is the condition where he has forgotten (*wang*a) the civilized values instilled by Yao and the other sage emperors. He has achieved the reverse transmutation back to the original wholeness of the Tao (*hua ch'i tao*)—the "Great Clod" or "Pupa" (*ta-k'uai*). [118] Achieving this experience, the Taoist then learns to "hide" (*ts'ang*) himself in the world and avoids any further life-destroying self-deception.

In this section, which has been paraphrased above, there are traces of specific forms of meditation such as breathing techniques and the yogalike reference to *tso-wang* (literally "sitting and forgetting"). It also would appear from subsequent sections in this chapter that the process of meditation as a symbolic return to the beginning is to be understood as encompassing a number of distinct stages or phases.

In another section of chapter 6 there is a story of Tzu-kung and Confucius where Confucius is ironically made into a spokesman for the Taoist position. [119] Here the symbolism of the condition attained by the sage resembles the condition of death, which is also equivalent to a return to the chaos time. In this case the reference is to the sage Sang Hu who in death had achieved the reversal of the creation process and had "returned [*fan*b] to his true [form]."

In this passage it is important to stress the general symbolic relation to a basic cosmogonic structure that is grounded in the theme of *hun-tun*. Therefore, after Tzu-kung had observed Sang Hu's friends singing at Sang Hu's funeral, he wondered what sort of men would ignore "proper behavior, disregard their personal appearance [the requirements of maintaining "face" or ritual respectability]" and "sing in the very presence of a corpse." In a similar way to the parable of the "death of Chuang Tzu's wife" from chapter 18, Confucius explains that they were men who were "joined with that which is the creation of things" and were "able to wander in the one *ch'i*[a] of Heaven and Earth." Like the condition of Emperor Hun-tun of the center, they had unified all "differences" into one unified mass (*t'ung-t'i*). Like Sang Hu in death, they had "forgotten" (*wang*[a]) their faces and had "cast aside their ears and eyes." In this condition their life was the sacred life of the beginnings. They experienced a condition of cosmic harmony that was a recovery of the central "realm" inhabited by the mythical Hun-tun. They had

> Cast aside ears and eyes . . . Reversed the beginning and end. Not knowing of starting and finishing and lost in a chaotic void [*mang jan*], they were outside the realm of dust and dirt, wandering free and easy [in the perfect freedom] of *wu-wei*.

They were practitioners of the "art of Tao"; singular or eccentric men (*chi-jen*) who, like fish forgetting themselves in perfect watery freedom of rivers and lakes, had mutually forgotten themselves in the art of the Tao.

The constant reference to methods of "forgetting" one's ordinary human face in order to return to the condition of *hun-tun* is found in a subsequent passage in chapter 6 that uses the technical term of *tso-wang*.[120] This term arises in the context of a story about Confucius who comes across a certain Taoist sage, Yen Hui, practicing this method. Here emphasis is given to the fact that Yen Hui, by making use of this technique, has been able to reverse the life-destroying aspects of having face by "forgetting" *jen* and *i*[b], rites and music. Yen Hui explains that *tso-wang* is a method whereby he has been able to "smash up his limbs and body, drive out hearing and seeing; and cast off form and do away with knowledge." The passage concludes with Confucius meekly remarking that he would like to become the follower of such a method.

There is one final passage from chapter 6 that I would like to examine here.[121] This passage, like the ones above, shows that there is an underlying structure giving symbolic coherence to the various terms and parables employed. In this instance the tale is told of the meeting of a certain I Erh-tzu and Hsü Yu.[122] I Erh-tzu has been following the ways of the Sage Emperor Yao and seeks guidance from the Taoist master, Hsü Yu. Hsü Yu responds by noting that I Erh-tzu has too willingly accepted drilling in Yao's ways of *jen* and *i*[b] (literally, the expression here is to being "tattooed" and having "the nose cut off," which were common punishments of the time but also may relate to the idea of initiatory mutilation seen in the Hun-tun story of chapter 7). Because of this, I Erh-tzu cannot expect to be able to achieve the condition of carefree "wandering" (*yu*[b]).

I Erh-tzu is unwilling to accept this verdict and begs to be given some training in the Taoist methods. He says that in the past other men such as the Yellow Emperor were able to forget the condition of discriminating knowledge (*wang ch'i chih*) and were transformed—"recast and remolded in the midst of a furnace [*lu*ᵃ]."[123] For some it was possible to follow the methods of Hsü Yu and return to the condition of identity with "that which created things." This was the *hun-tun*-like condition where one's "tattoo was filled in and one's nose was replaced"—the condition of wholeness (*ch'eng*).

Hsü Yu replies by reminding I Erh-tzu that his method is one that ultimately finds its source not among the ways of men but back at the creation time (literally, Hsü Yu's "teacher" was "older than the most ancient time"). His method was established by that thing that mythically "covered Heaven and bore up the Earth"[124]—that mysterious thing from which all shapes and forms were carved. Hsü Yu concludes that his method consists of the return to, and reexperience of, the condition that existed at the beginning. Hsü Yu has identified himself in this life with the mythical condition of the Emperor Hun-tun and experiences total freedom and the intense fullness of life at its very source. This is the sacred realm that he "wanders" in by employing the arts of the Tao.

These kinds of themes are also found in chapter 7 where there is a section that refers to the Taoist as one who has learned to wander in the "village of Not-Even-Anything" and live in the "Broad and Borderless Wasteland" beyond the six directions of the world.[125] This can be said to be the central realm of Hun-tun, the mystic "place" of the paradise time where one no longer has face or is *only* human (*fei jen*).[126] This is the condition of the "Nameless Man" (*wu-ming jen*) who has learned that to be a sage it is necessary to experience a mystic chaotification by

> Letting your mind wander in simplicity,
> reunifying your *ch'i*ᵃ with the Void,
> following the spontaneity of things [*tzu-jan*] and
> not relying on [personal] feelings [of face].
> These [principles] order the world!

4. *"Mind Nourishment": Hu Tzu (Gourd Master) and Hung-Meng (Big Concealment)*

Let me conclude this discussion of the *Chuang Tzu* by offering only a few other characteristic illustrations of the *hun-tun* theme. The initiation sequence suggested by the teachings of Ju Yu in chapter 6 is, for example, found in the previously mentioned parable from chapter 7 of the Taoist master Hu Tzu,[127] who instructs Lieh Tzu in a method of returning to the Tao that is different from the methods of a shaman (*shen-wu*). In this story Hu Tzu as a "Gourd Master" progressively reveals his "true form"; and the sequence that is presented recalls a reversal of the cosmogonic process. It is a method that involves a gradual return through nine forms of the primordial chaos condition. Ultimately, Hu Tzu reports to Lieh Tzu that he had gone back to an embryonic state: "I appeared as that which had not yet come forth from my source. I was empty [*hsü*ª] and wriggling like a snake [*wei she*]." After three years of putting these teachings into practice Lieh Tzu was also able to "return to the uncarved condition" (*fu p'u*). He was able to stand primordially "alone and clod- [or pupa-] like [*k'uai jan tu*]." [128]

To take another example that explicitly recapitulates the *hun-tun* theme, it is worthwhile examining the parable of Hung-meng found in chapter 11. [129] Hung-meng is a figure specifically connected with the *hun-tun* mythology and in this story is presented as a Taoist master who gives instruction in the art of returning to the beginning. [130] In this case the "art of the Tao" is called *hsin-yang* or "mind nourishment."

Hung-meng, like Hun-tun in the *Shan Hai Ching*, is said to be shamanically "slapping his thighs" and "hopping and dancing like a bird," which is a technique of "aimless wandering" (*fu-yu*) and "madness" (*ch'ang-k'uang*). [131] Hung-meng eventually explains that his method consists of the following:

> Rest in inaction [*wu-wei*] and things will transform themselves. Smash your form and body, spit out hearing and eyesight, forget you are a thing among other things. You may then achieve the great unity [*ta-t'ung*ª] of the deep and boundless [*hsing ming*]. Undo the mind, slough off spirit, be blank and soulless, and then ten thousand things one by one will return to the root. Return to the root and yet not know why.

Hung-meng concludes his instruction by saying that this is the faceless condition of "*hun-hun tun-tun*":

> Dark and undifferentiated chaos [*hun-hun tun-tun*]—to the end of life none will depart from it. Do not ask what its name is, and do not try to observe its form. Things will live naturally and of themselves [*tzu sheng*].

This unique condition is adumbrated by the passage immediately following the Hung-meng story. [132] In contrast to the "common man" who in valuing face "welcomes those who are like him and scorns those who differ from him," the Taoist "Great Man" (*ta-jen*) is one whose "face and form has blended with the Great Unity [*ta-t'ung*ª]." The Great Man is one who sees only "nothingness'' (wu^b) and, like Emperor Hun-tun, stands alone at the center—''he is the true friend of Heaven and Earth.''

With regard to the symbolism of an initiatory rebirth displayed throughout these passages, I want again to draw attention to the characteristic reduplicated use of the *hun-tun* terminology as seen in the *Tao Te Ching* and in the parable of Hung-meng. From the standpoint of comparative linguistics the function of reduplication is often linked to the development and use of ''secret languages'' that in a primitive religious context can have associations with initiation ritual in general, and more specifically, with the shaman's ability to speak the language of the ancestral spirits or divine animals.[133] Whether or not the reduplicated word of *hun-tun* and its associated terminology possess an auditory or mantra quality in the early texts is only speculation, but in later Taoism the invocation of special sounds clearly is an important part of meditation.

By returning to the creation time a Taoist has become a ''no-man'' (*fei jen*) or has achieved the shapeless and faceless condition of the great mythic ancestor of the beginning, Emperor Hun-tun. As suggested by chapter 11, this transformation involves the extraordinary trance condition of being ''corpse-like'' (cf. chaps. 2, 22). He is no longer simply human but commands a ''dragon vision and the silence of the watery abyss.''[134] Recalling the mythological imagery of thunder and lightning that pierces the central gap of the creation time, as well as possibly later esoteric meditation practices (''grinding the teeth'') that emulate the sounds of thunder and drumming, this passage concludes by saying that a Taoist possesses the ''voice of thunder.''[135]

Reviewing the discussion presented in this chapter, it can be said that in the *Chuang Tzu*, especially the inner chapters, the Taoist is seeking to achieve an individual reunification with the primordial Tao, that which infolds all things back into the harmonious whole of cosmic life. This is the ''Butterfly Way'' of *creatio continua*, a life that is ''blank, boundless, and without form; transforming, changing, never constant'' (chap. 33).[136] In chapter 5 the Taoist is said to ''store up the Ten Thousand Things. . . . make ornaments of his ears and eyes and unify the knowledge of what he knows.''[137] In chapter 2 the description of the Taoist sage is extended to include the theme of the sacred fool seen in chapter 20 of the *Tao Te Ching*: the man of Tao is ''stupid and blockish'' since he has returned to ''simplicity in oneness.'' For the Taoist, ''all the Ten Thousand Things are what they are, and thus they infold each other.''[138]

These are only selections from passages too numerous to quote extensively; but, along with the extended discussion throughout this chapter, they document the point that in the *Chuang Tzu* there are mystic techniques or ''arts of the

Tao'' (chap. 33) that allow one to repossess the cosmic totality of the Emperor Hun-tun. Most salient is that the various mystic techniques of a salvational ''return'' are all modeled on mythological symbolism related to the *hun-tun* theme. In short, there is a connection between what a Taoist does and experiences in meditation and an underlying cosmogonic theory or story.

My focus here has been on the ''arts of Mr. Hun-tun'' as suggesting a mysticism of individual renewal. As will be shown in the following chapter, this is also thematically intertwined in some chapters with a social doctrine of the paradise age—that time when the ''ancients'' lived ''in the midst of the Hun-mang'' (chap. 16). A Taoist seeks to withdraw from the ''great confusion'' (*ta-luan*) caused by the civilizing work of Yao and Shun who went around ''boring'' (*tso*) holes in things (chap. 23).

4

CHAOTIC ''ORDER'' AND BENEVOLENT ''DISORDER'' IN THE *CHUANG TZU*

> In this age of Perfect Virtue men live the same
> as birds and beasts. . . . In uncarved simplicity
> [*su p'u*] the people attain their true nature. Then
> along comes the sage, huffing and puffing after
> benevolence, reaching on tiptoe for righteous-
> ness . . . and the world for the first time is
> divided. . . . If the Way and its Virtue had not
> been cast aside, how would there be any call for
> benevolence and righteousness? If the true form
> of the inborn nature had not been abandoned,
> how would there be any use for rites and music?
> If the five colors had not confused [*luan*ᵃ] men,
> who would fashion patterns and hues? . . . That
> the Way and its Virtue were destroyed in order
> to create benevolence and righteousness—this
> was the fault of the sage.
>
> —*Chuang Tzu*, Chapter 9
> (trans. Burton Watson)

JOSEPH NEEDHAM HAS pointed out that in the early Taoist texts certain words like *p'u*ᵃ and *hun-tun* seem to be important technical terms associated with the elaboration of a Taoist ideology of ''primitivism.''[1] For Needham this implies most of all a kind of social ideal that on the one hand attacks the rise of the Confucian feudalistic hegemony and on the other hand recommends a return to what was remembered as the golden age of "primitive agrarian collectivism."[2] The key words of *p'u*[a] and *hun-tun* are interpreted as being primarily terms linked to political themes or to what Needham refers to as the Taoist desire to reestablish the paradise condition of "social homogeneity."[3]

I have already questioned Needham's exclusive linking of these terms, especially the theme of *hun-tun*, to an original social philosophy that allows for only the secondary development of a personal mystical ideal of the unique experiential condition of an "undifferentiated" union with the Tao.[4] There is little doubt, however, as to the legitimacy of Needham's general observation concerning the importance of these terms for a technical vocabulary evocative of the theme of "paradise lost" as seen in the *Tao Te Ching*, and even more prominently, in the *Chuang Tzu* and the *Huai Nan Tzu*.

My basic concern in this chapter is to extend Needham's observations by showing that in working with a text like the *Chuang Tzu* the important term of *hun-tun* is used in an ideologically significant way, especially as it is specifically distinguished from the term *luan*[a] (ordinarily meaning "disorder, confusion, etc."). The possible importance of this distinction is that it may have some bearing on the philosophical antagonism between the Taoist and Confucian understanding of the Tao as the foundation of natural, personal, and social "order" (*ch'ih/chih*[b]). More particularly, as I will try to demonstrate in a preliminary way by an examination of some of the other early Taoist and Confucian texts, the discussion of the usage of *hun-tun* and *luan*[a] may help to resolve a certain philological conundrum associated with the classical usage of *luan*[a].

The problem I am referring to is the peculiar contradictory usage of *luan*[a]— that is, its more common usage as "disorder" (and, in this sense, it can be potentially associated semantically with the ordinary meaning and usage of *hun-tun*);[5] and, surprisingly, its other classical usage as "order" (especially political and social "order" as related to the term *ch'ih*[b]). I do not want to anticipate my argument, but let me point out that this last usage of *luan*[a] as "order" is almost exclusively found in the Confucian classical canon (e.g., *Shu Ching, Tso Chuan*). In the *Lun Yü*, for example, the usage of *luan*[a] as order (*ch'ih*[b]) is linked to the civilizing activities of the legendary culture heroes so that as King Wu of the Chou dynasty was said to have "ten able ministers [*luan-ch'en*]," the great sage of antiquity, Shun, had "five able ministers [*luan-ch'en*] and the empire was well governed [*ch'ih*[b]]."[6]

HUN-TUN AND LUAN IN THE CHUANG TZU

To bring out the particular relationship between the terms *hun-tun* and *luan*[a] I would like to examine four characteristic golden age passages found in chapters 10, 16, and 11 of the *Chuang Tzu*. The first of these passages from chapter 10 presents the views of "Robber Chih" who condemns the deception and confusion brought about by the benevolent and righteous (*jen, i*[b]) ordering of human affairs by the Confucian sages—"when the sage is born, the great thief appears." The explanation for the false order present in the world is linked to a mythological theme of the original paradise time and a subsequent degeneration brought about by the labors of the Confucian culture heroes. The passage in question is as follows:

> Have you alone never heard of that age of Perfect Virtue [which in a previous passage is related to the condition of "Mysterious Leveling" or *hsüan-t'ung*[a] where benevolence and righteousness are wiped away]? Long ago, in the time of Yung Ch'eng, Ta T'ing, Po Huang, Chung Yang, Li Lu, Li Hsü, Hsien Yüan, Ho Hsü, Tsun Lu, Chu Jung, Fu Hsi, and Shen Nung,[7] the people knotted cords and used them. They relished their food, admired their clothing, enjoyed their customs, and were content with their houses. Though neighboring states were within sight of each other, and could hear the cries of each other's dogs and chickens, the people grew old and died without ever traveling beyond their own borders [cf. the famous paradise-age passage in the *Tao Te Ching*, chap. 80]. At a time such as this, there was nothing but the most perfect order [*chih ch'ih*].
>
> But now something has happened to make people crane their necks and stand on tiptoe . . . . [what follows is a description of the degenerate order brought about by the coming of feudalism].[8]

The reasons for this decay are attributed to the disease of "coveting knowledge [*hao chih*]," which is described as the condition of "great confusion [*ta-luan*]": "the world is dulled and darkened [*mei-mei*] by great confusion [*ta-luan*]. The blame lies in this coveting of knowledge [*hao chih*]." The confusion of the natural and social order is further depicted in the concluding section of this passage:

> In the world everyone knows enough to pursue what he does not know but no one knows enough to pursue what he already knows. Everyone knows enough to condemn what he takes to be no good, but no one knows enough to condemn what he has already taken to be good. This is how the great confusion [*ta-luan*] comes about, blotting out the brightness of sun and moon above, searing the vigor of hills and streams below, overturning the round of the four seasons in between. There is no insect that creeps and

crawls, no creature that flutters and flies that has not lost its inborn nature [*hsing*]. So great is the confusion of the world [*luan t'ien-hsia*] that comes from coveting knowledge [*hao chih*]! From the Three Dynasties [Hsia, Shang, Chou] on down, it has been this and nothing else—shoving aside the pure and artless people and delighting in busy, bustling flatterers; abandoning the limpidity and calm of inaction [*wu-wei*] and delighting in jumbled and jangling ideas. And this jumble and jangle has for long confused the world [*luan t'ien-hsia*].

In this passage, which is at the heart of one of the most homogeneous sections of the *Chuang Tzu*,[9] the term *luan*[a] seems to be used as a key descriptive term for the Taoist conception of the fall of man from the paradise condition. This conclusion is prompted by the sheer quantitative presence of *luan*[a] in this passage (nine occurrences in a passage of thirteen lines) and also by the three special uses of the intensive compound expression of *ta-luan* for the time and condition of the "great confusion."

Luan[a], therefore, appears to be consciously used in a technical sense to refer to the devolution of human society; and within a mythological context it is specifically placed in contrast with the true life-order of Tao that existed most fully during the creation time—the time of "perfect order [*chih ch'ih*]." In addition to the social-political implications, there is some indication in this passage that the paradise time should also be identified with the experiential condition of "undifferentiated" knowledge or *hsüan-t'ung*[a], which is an expression found here and in the *Tao Te Ching* and is most probably linked to the more mythologically relevant term of *hun-tun*.[10]

To bring out this connection it is necessary to consider the golden age passage found in chapter 16.[11] This short chapter (entitled "Mending Inborn Nature" [*shan hsing*]) starts out by suggesting that the Tao is the basis of "harmony and order [*ho li*]" but has been corrupted and lost through the pernicious prevalence of the artificial order of benevolence and righteousness. The loss of perfection and the corruption of one's "inborn nature [*hsing*]" suggest that the whole "world has fallen into disorder [*t'ien-hsia luan*]" due to the overemphasis that is "placed on the conduct of rites and music." Mending one's inborn nature can only be accomplished by a "return to the beginning [*fu ch'i ch'u*]" that is a kind of *regressus ad originem* in the mystical sense.[12]

As in chapter 10, the explanation for this fallen condition is understood in terms of a mythological scenario that immediately follows the introductory verses. It is here that the paradise time is identified as the time of *hun-mang*— the primordial time of "perfect unity [*chih-i*[a]]" and "spontaneity [*tzu-jan*]." Moreover, this paradise time when men "dwelt in the midst of crudity and chaos [*hun-mang chih chung*]" is set in contrast with the fall when "virtue began to dwindle and decline" through the misguided efforts of the legendary heroes Sui-jen, Fu-hsi, Shen-nung, Huang Ti, Yao, and Shun.[13]

Because of this, the true order of the beginning time was "pulled apart for the sake of goodness and virtue was imperiled for the sake of conduct." The great fault of these culture heroes was in their self-righteous "meddling" (see chap. 11, and below), whereby in setting out "to order and transform the world [*ch'ih hua chih liu*]" they only ended up by "defiling purity and shattering simplicity [*chiao ch'un san p'u*]." After this,

> inborn nature [*hsing*] was abandoned and minds were set free to roam, mind joining with mind in understanding; there was knowledge, but it could not bring stability to the world. After this, "culture" [*wen*] was added on, and "breadth" [*po*] was piled on top. "Culture" destroyed the substantial, "breadth" drowned the mind, and after this the people began to be confused and disordered [*huo luan*].

The world had lost the Tao and men "had no way to return to the true form of their inborn nature [*hsing*] or to return once more to the Beginning [*fu ch'i ch'u*]." From this time on, the Tao and its virtue were "hidden [*yin*[a]]" to the world.

Although the expression *ta-luan* is not used in this passage,[14] the same polarity between the naturalness of the paradise time and the confusion of the "civilized" order is present. Indeed, in two other Primitivist-type passages from chapter 11 the same pattern is repeated. The first of these is the paradise lost story of the Yellow Emperor who used "benevolence and righteousness to meddle [*ying*; cf. *hao chih* below and from chap. 10 above] with the minds of men."[15] After the Yellow Emperor,

> Yao and Shun . . . worked till there was no more down on their thighs, no more hair on their shins, trying to nourish the bodies of the men of the world. . . . But still some men would not submit to their rule, and so they had to exile Huan Tou to Mount Ch'ung, drive away the San-miao tribes to the region of San-wei, and banish Kung to the Dark City.

As will be seen in the Confucian texts to follow, this reference to the "legendary rebels" who "would not submit" to the benevolent rule of Yao and Shun is an important theme connected with the idea of *hun-tun*, a term that is used as the nickname of Huan-tou and also refers to one of the San-miao.[16] In general, these figures (the "four ominous ones" or "four punished ones") might be said to symbolize the forces of the precivilized "chaos" that still had to be overcome by the sage kings.[17]

The passage continues by saying that with the coming of the Three Dynasties and the rise of the Confucians and the Moists, the world was in "great consternation [*ta-hai*]," which is further identified as the time of the "great confusion [*ta-luan*]":

> There was no more unity to the Great Virtue [*ta-te pu t'ung*], and the inborn nature [*hsing*] and fate shattered and fell apart. The world coveted knowledge [*hao chih*] and the hundred clans were thrown into turmoil. Then there were axes and saws to shape things, ink and plumb lines to trim them, mallets and gouges [*tso*] to poke holes in them, and the world, muddled and deranged, was in great confusion [*ta-luan*]. The crime lay in this meddling [*ying*] with men's minds.

The solution to all of this is to return to the unsullied condition before the sages came "huffing and puffing after benevolence" (see chap. 9). Therefore, the passage concludes, "cut off sageness, cast away wisdom, and the world will be in perfect order [*ta-ch'ih*]." To further identify the contrast presented here, I would like to note that in a golden age passage from chapter 2 of the *Huai Nan Tzu* the time of "perfect or great order [*ta-ch'ih*]" is described as the time when "men lived in the midst of dark chaos [*hun-ming*]." The serenity of this period is set in opposition to the "confusion of spirit [*luan . . . shen*]" during the present age.[18]

The second of the passages from chapter 11 is the previously discussed *hun-tun* parable of Hung-meng, who spent his time "amusing himself by slapping his thighs and hopping around like a bird."[19] Interrupting his thigh-slapping and birdlike hopping, Hung-meng speaks of the "confusion [*luan*ᵃ] of Heaven's 'order' [*ching* or literally 'constant strands']" and the "violation of the true form of things" that destroys both the human and natural order of things: "Beasts will scatter from their herds, the birds will cry all night, disaster will come to the grass and trees, misfortune will reach even to the insects."

All of this, as in the other cited passages, is "the fault of men who 'govern' [*ch'ih-jen*]." The way to overcome this condition is to make use of what is called *hsin-yang*, or as Burton Watson translates, "mind-nourishment." Like the "return to the beginning" called for in chapter 16 and the condition of *hsüan-t'ung*ᵃ mentioned in chapter 10, this seemingly involves a mystic technique of returning the mind to its original inborn "paradise" condition. And, as noted in the previous chapter, this "return to the root" (*fu ch'i ken*) is named with emphatically reduplicated expression of *hun-hun tun-tun*.

These few textual illustrations are sufficient to suggest that there is an emergent pattern (involving a social and/or mystical ideal) that is associated generally with the paradise lost theme and more specifically with a particular contrast between the terms *hun-tun* and *luan*ᵃ. Even more convincing is the fact that it is possible to demonstrate this pattern in tabular form.

I have already discussed the paradigmatic significance of the *hun-tun* theme in the *Chuang Tzu* (especially in relation to the famous Emperor Hun-tun parable of chap. 7) and in the *Tao Te Ching*, so I would only like to point out summarily by means of table 1 that out of the sixty usages of *luan*[a] in the *Chuang Tzu*, all of them either refer generally to the Taoist analysis of the disorder and confusion of the present age or, within the context of the golden age passages, describe the specific reason for the fall of man. This is also a pattern that is reflected in varying degrees in the other early Taoist texts. Thus in chapter 38 of the *Tao Te Ching* (cf. chap. 18) it is said:

> When the Tao is lost, only then does the doctrine of virtue [*te*[a]] arise.
> When virtue is lost, only then does the doctrine of benevolence [*jen*] arise
> When benevolence is lost, only then does the doctrine of righteousness [*i*[b]] arise.
> When righteousness is lost, only then does the doctrine of propriety [*li*] arise.
> Now propriety is only the husk of loyalty and faithfulness [*chung hsin*];
> It is the beginning of all confusion and disorder [*luan*[a]].[20]

Conversely, all of the *hun-tun* passages are found within an opposite context of meaning (see table 2). Whereas *hun-tun* could theoretically be used as a synonymous term for *luan*[a], in every instance in the *Chuang Tzu* it connotes the true mysterious and original order of the Tao and man's inner nature (*hsing*) that was lost through the intervention of the Confucian sage heroes. Furthermore, as seen in the tables and as will be developed in the following section, the term *hun-tun* is almost exclusively found in the Taoist texts; and in those few instances of its use in Confucian texts, it is ordinarily a term of opprobrium and condemnation related to the suppression of the "barbarians" or the "legendary rebels."

HUN-TUN AND LUAN IN THE CONFUCIAN CANON

When some of the more important early Confucian texts are examined, the possible significance of the pattern detected in the *Chuang Tzu* becomes more apparent since it is only in the Confucian classics that *luan*[a], along with the common meaning of disorder, is found with the special meaning of "order" (=*ch'ih*[b]).[21] Thus, in the *Shu Ching*, *luan*[a] takes the meaning of "order," "aptness for government" (=*ch'ih ts'ai*, the quality of a good minister), and "ministers of government."[22] These passages are characteristically related to the establishment of a new political order so that, for example, in a passage

TABLE 1

USE OF *LUAN*

(4:71.4 = Vol. 4 of Legge: p. 71. line 4)

Texts	Total usage	"DISORDER"			"ORDER" =*CH'IH* =GOLDEN AGE
		Before Yao and Shun	After Yao and Shun Fall/Present Age	Other	
TAOIST TEXTS					
Tao Te Ching (before 300 B.C.)	4	—	× chaps. 18, 38	= × chaps. 3, 64	—
Chuang Tzu (*c.* 290 B.C. + later add.) chaps. 1–7	3	—	×?	= × chaps. 1, 4	—
Other Chaps.	57	—	× chaps. 10, 12, 16, etc.	= × passim	—
Huai Nan Tzu (*c.* 120 B.C.)	16+	—	× chap. 13, etc.	= × passim	—
CONFUCIAN TEXTS					
Shu Ching (*c.* tenth to fifth cent. B.C. + later add.)	10+	—	× passim (rebellion, confusion, etc.)	× passim (ferry) etc.	× 4:71.4; 240.4; 245.6
Shih Ching (*c.* ninth to fifth cent. B.C. + later add.)	17+	—	× passim (rebellion, confusion, etc.)	× passim (ferry) etc.	—
Lun Yü (*c.* 465 to 450 B.C. + later add.)	11+	—	× passim (insurrection, confound, etc.)	× passim (musical term)	× 1:214.8 (Cf. *Shu*)
Tso Chuan (*c.* 430 to 250 B.C. + later add.)	202+	—	× passim (rebels, rebellion, etc.)	× passim	× 5:539.8; 701.2 (Cf. *Shu*)
Meng Tzu (*c.* 290 B.C.)	18+	× = 2:279–284	× 2:279–284; passim	= × passim	—

TABLE 2

USE OF *HUN-TUN*

Texts	Total usage	PRIMORDIAL "ORDER"			DISORDER/CONFUSION		
		Primal Chaos	Golden Age	Undifferentiated Knowledge	Barbarians	Legendary Rebels	Other
TAOIST TEXTS							
Tao Te Ching	4	× ch. 25 ch. 14?	—	× ch. 15 ch. 20	—	—	—
Chuang Tzu Chaps. 1–7	5	×? = ch. 7	× = ch. 7	×? ch. 7	—	—	—
Other Chaps.	6	× ch. 11	× ch. 16	× chaps. 11, 12, 14	—	—	—
Huai Nan Tzu	10	×? =	× = chaps. 2, 8, 10	×?	—	—	—
Lieh Tzu (*c.* third cent. B.C. – A.D. 300)	2?	× ch. 1	—	—	—	—	—
CONFUCIAN TEXTS							
Shu Ching	0	—	—	—	—	—	—
Shih Ching	1+	—	—	—	× (=I^c) 4:441.3	—	—
Lun Yü	0	—	—	—	—	—	—
Tso Chuan	14	—	—	—	× (= Jung) 5:666. 6–8	× 5:280.9, 13	× 5:841.2, 13
Meng Tzu	1	—	—	—	—	—	× 2:324.8

describing the foundation of a new capital city of the Shang dynasty, the *Shu Ching* states:

> But God [Shang Ti] about to restore the virtue of my [P'an-keng, an emperor of the Shang] High Ancestor [*kau-tsu*] and secure the good government [*luan*[a]] of our empire, I with the sincere and respectful [*sic*] of my ministers felt a reverential care for the lives of the people, and have made a lasting settlement in this new city.[23]

Even more revealing is that the *Tso Chuan* quotes the *Shu Ching*'s "Great Declaration" of King Wu, one of the semilegendary founders of the Chou dynasty: " 'I have of ministers, capable of government [*luan-ch'en*], ten men, one in heart, and one in practice.' It was through this that Chow [*chou*] arose."[24] This usage of *luan*[a] in the *Shu Ching* and the *Tso Chuan* is therefore set in the context of the Confucian "paradise time" of the foundations of the Chou dynasty and is generally equated with the establishment of the "civilized" order by the sage heroes of the Three Dynasties. As noted in this chapter, the *Lun Yü* mentions this story of King Wu as a paradigmatic emulation of the *Shu Ching*'s mythical model of Shun, who was said to have had "five able ministers [*luan-ch'en*] and the empire was well governed."[25]

What is noteworthy with respect to the *hun-tun/luan* contrast found in the Taoist texts is that the pattern is reversed in the Confucian documents (see tables 1 and 2). While the term *hun-tun* is not found at all in the *Shu Ching, Lun Yü, I Ching, Chung Yung, Ta Hsüeh,* or *Meng Tzu*,[26] it is used in a particular and significant way in the *Shih Ching, Ch'un Ch'iu,* and *Tso Chuan*.

In the *Shih Ching* the term *hun*[d] is only found in reference to the northern barbarian tribe known as the *hun-i*[b].[27] In the *Tso Chuan*, however, a certain Confucian pattern of meaning related to the use of *hun-tun* and *luan*[a] is brought into relief. Whereas the *Tso Chuan* at times links *luan*[a] with the creation of a "civilized" order by the Confucian sage heroes, the term *hun*[d] is related to a certain tribe of Jung barbarians (mentioned in the *Ch'un Ch'iu*) and, as the figure of Hun-tun, is mentioned as one of the four "legendary rebels" who had to be subdued during the establishment of the feudal order.[28]

Thus in the *Tso Chuan*'s commentary on book 6 of the *Ch'un Ch'iu*, there is an important long passage that deals with the problems during the "Spring and Autumn" period of the Chou dynasty (722–481 B.C.).[29] The perspective, as with all of the Classics, is that the rectification of the present is to be found in the models of the past; and, in this spirit, the passage first of all invokes the example of the Duke of Chou who set down the principles of order for Chou civilization. "By means of the model of conduct you can see a man's virtue. His virtue is evidenced in his management of affairs. From that management his merit can be measured. . . . He who overthrows [the laws of conduct] is a villain."

It should be noted that in this passage the crucial issue concerning "good" or "true" order and conduct has to do with ability and merit as a minister, which is precisely the context of meaning associated with the special use of *luan*[a] as *ch'ih*[b] found in the *Shu Ching*. Furthermore, as *luan*[a] is associated with the benevolent and righteous order initiated by Shun and the other legendary founders, *hun-tun* appears in this passage as an untalented (*pu-ts'ai*) and villainous (*hsiung-te*) minister. He was one of the four wicked rebels (i.e., Chaos, Monster, Block, and Glutton) banished by Shun when he became Yao's good (*luan*?) minister.

This whole passage is introduced as a vindication of the conduct of a certain Chi-sun Hang-fu of the state of Lu who condemned and banished P'u of Chu[30] for his unfilial and disloyal actions in the murder of his father, the ruler of the state of Chu. The justification of Chi-sun's decree of banishment is asserted by the Grand Historian of Lu in terms that appeal to the exemplary conduct of the great sages of the past. Starting with the invocation of the Duke of Chou's "rules" mentioned above, it retrogressively appeals to the actions of the various legendary founders of Chinese civilization. Ultimately the story of Yao and Shun is recounted to affirm the correctness of Chi-sun's behavior:

> In the time of Yaou [*yao*[a]], he was not able to raise them [the legendary sixteen good ministers, the "eight harmonies" and the "eight worthies"] to office. When Shun, however, became Yaou's minister [*ch'en*], he raised the eight Harmonies to office, and employed them to superintend the department of the minister of the Land. All matters connected with it were thus regulated, and everything was arranged in its proper season:—the earth was reduced to order, and the influence of heaven operated with effect [*ti p'ing t'ien ch'eng*]. He also raised the eight worthies to office, and employed them to disseminate through the four quarters of knowledge of the duties belonging to the five relations of society. Fathers became just and mothers gentle; elder brothers kindly, and younger ones respectful; and some became filial:—in the empire there was order, and beyond it submission [*nai p'ing wai ch'eng*].

What follows this section is a discussion of the problems that plagued the period before Shun's ordering of society:

> The ancient emperor Hung [=Huang Ti?] has a descendant devoid of ability [and virtue]. He hid righteousness from himself, and was a villain at heart; he delighted in the practice of the worst vices; he was shameless and vile, obstinate, stupid, and unfriendly, cultivating only the intimacy of such as himself. All the people under heaven called him Chaos [*hun-tun*].[31]
> The emperor Shao-haou [*shao-hao*] had a descendant devoid of ability

[and virtue]. . . . All the people under heaven called him Monster [*ch'iung-ch'i*].

[The emperor] Chuen-Heuh [=Chuan-hsü?] had a descendant devoid of ability [and virtue]. . . . All the people under heaven called him Block [*t'ao-wu*].

During the time of Yao these three were "acknowledged for their wickedness" and seen as models of social and moral confusion;[32] but Yao "was not able to put them away." The passage then describes another evil minister during the time of Huang Ti known as Glutton (*t'ao-t'ieh*). Like Chaos, Monster, and Block, he also was "devoid of ability and virtue," thereby serving only to thwart the creation of a proper social order.

Finally, when "Shun became Yao's minister," the "four wicked ones" were banished:

> [Shun] cast them out into the four distant regions, to meet the spite of the sprites and evil things. The consequence of this was that, when Yao died, all under heaven, as if they had been one man, with common consent bore Shun to be emperor, because he had raised to office those sixteen helpers, and had put away the four wicked ones. Therefore, the Book of Yu [part of the *Shu Ching*],[33] in enumerating the services of Shun, says, "He carefully set forth the beauty of the five cardinal duties, and they came to be universally observed:"—none were disobedient to his instructions; "being appointed to be General Regulator [i.e., Shun], the affairs of each department were arranged according to their proper seasons:"—there was no neglect of any affair; "having to receive the princes from the four quarters of the empire, they all were docilely submissive:"—there were none wicked among them. Shun's services were shown in the case of those 20 men (i.e., the sixteen good ministers and the four rebels), and he became emperor.[34]

This passage is remarkable in a number of respects and, as Legge says, it is "worthy of careful study."[35] Thus, Chi-sun "in condemning Puh of Keu [P'u of Chu], and vindicating his own conduct in expelling him from Loo [*lu*], seems altogether unconscious of crimes in Loo nearly affecting himself, hardly less atrocious than those of which Puh had been guilty."[36] At a more fundamental level, however, it seems clear that the whole episode is more political than historical in nature; and in this respect the apparent inconsistency is not really so significant. More important is the overall frame of reference, which needs the justification and functional validation of a mythological paradigm of behavior. What seems important in this passage, as with many of the legendary stories found in the Classics, is not what really happened but how the past is interpreted or retold in terms of its meaning for the present. The assumption is always that there is a meaningful story to be found in archaic events, a story that must be moralistically linked with the present age. In fact, Legge seems to be aware of this since in a parenthetical comment he remarks that "the references to men and things in what we may call the prehistoric period were, no doubt, in accordance with traditions current at the time, though we cannot accept them as possessed of historical authority, more especially as there is an anticonfucian spirit in what is said of Yaou."[37]

Legge, as shown later by Maspero's discussion of the mythological under-pinning of the *Shu Ching*,[38] is certainly correct in this observation. And, as the distinction between *hun-tun* and *luan*[a] in the *Chuang Tzu* is found within the mythological context of the Taoist paradise lost theme, so also is the mytholog-ical and symbolic imagery of the Confucian golden age used here. As with most forms of myth, the past is used as the explanation, foundation, or charter for the present order of things. But whereas Taoist ideology harkens back to the mythical creation time of *hun-tun before* the coming of the culture heroes of the Three Dynasties, the Confucian mythos ignores and denigrates cosmogony and focuses entirely on the secondary creation of the civilized order.

As a final demonstration of the relevance of this pattern, I would like to consider the case of the *Meng Tzu* (Mencius), where we find another presenta-tion of the Confucian golden age theme and also the use of the expression *ta-luan* first pointed out in the *Chuang Tzu*. The *Meng Tzu* is particularly interesting in that while *luan*[a] is not used in the special sense of "order" or an "able minister," the expressions *luan*[a] and *ta-luan* are given a different interpretation than that found in the *Chuang Tzu*.

The two passages in question (from book 3) involve a variation on the golden age story, which in this instance incorporates the legends of a great deluge.[39] The first of these passages opens as follows:

> In the time of Yao, when the world had not yet been perfectly reduced to order [*wei p'ing*], the vast waters [*hung shui*], flowing out of their channels, made a universal inundation [*fan lan*]. Vegetation was luxuriant, and birds and beasts swarmed. The various kinds of grain could not be grown. The birds and beasts pressed upon men. The paths marked by the feet of beasts and prints of birds crossed one another throughout the Middle Kingdom [*chung-kuo*]. To Yao alone this caused anxious sorrow.

To establish order in the world, to create a civilized cosmos (*chung-kuo*) in the midst of the watery chaos, Yao called upon his ministers:

> He raised Shun to office, and measures to regulate [*ch'ih*[b]] the disorder were set forth. Shun committed to Yi [*I*[d]] the direction of the fire to be employed, and Yi set fire to, and consumed, the forests and vegetation on the mountains

and in the marshes, so that the birds and beasts fled away to hide themselves. Yü separated the nine streams. . . .

With the completion of these labors by Shun, I, and Yü, the world was organized and "centered" into the nine provinces of the middle kingdom. Out of the chaos was created an enclave made fit for an agriculturally based civilization—"it became possible for the people of the Middle Kingdom to cultivate the ground and get food for themselves." Shun then appointed other ministers in charge of agriculture (Hou-chi) and moral education (Hsieh). It was this last minister who was responsible for establishing the principles of *jen*, *i*[b], *hsiao*, and the five relationships.

I would also like to note that immediately after this golden age passage, Mencius paraphrases Confucius' extolling of the model virtue of Yao and Shun (cf. *Lun Yü*, bk. 8, chaps. 18, 19):[40]

> Confucius said, "Great indeed was Yao as a sovereign. It is only Heaven that is great, and only Yao corresponded to it. How vast was his virtue! The people could find no name for it. Princely indeed was Shun! How majestic was he, having possession of the kingdom, and yet seeming as if it were nothing to him!. . . ."[41]

Mencius, however, omits any reference to the very next chapter in the *Lun Yü* (bk. 8, chap. 20), which continues by praising the "able ministers [*luan-ch'en*]" of Shun and King Wu.[42] This is interesting because in Mencius' second golden age passage presented below the same term *luan-ch'en* is used but with the opposite meaning—that is, as "rebellious ministers."

In a later section (part 2) of book 3 the same story is told again, but this time there are a number of important embellishments.[43] One adumbration is that the history of man is now presented more equivocally as a kind of oscillation between periods of good and bad order—"a long time has elapsed since this world of men received its being, and there has been along its history now a period of good order, and now a period of confusion [*i ch'ih i luan*]."[44]

Mencius goes on to explain the meaning of this principle:

> In the time of Yao, the waters, flowing out of their channels, inundated the Middle Kingdom. Snakes and dragons occupied it, and the people had no place where they could settle themselves. In the low grounds they made nests for themselves on the trees or raised platforms, and in the high grounds they made caves. It is said in the Book of History [*Shu Ching*], "The waters in their wild course [*chiang shui*] warned me." Those "waters in their wild course" were the waters of the great inundation [*hung shui*].[45]

Order is finally established by Shun who "employed Yü to reduce the waters to order [*ch'ih*[b]]," and "after this men found the plains available for them, and occupied them.'' But after the death of Yao and Shun, "the principles that make sages fell into decay;" and by the time of King Chou of the Yin dynasty the world was again in a condition of "great confusion [*ta-luan*]" similar to the original watery chaos.

This period of confusion is finally overcome with the rise of the Chou dynasty and the efforts of King Wu and the Duke of Chou who destroyed the Yin dynasty and reestablished Shun's order in the world. This is, however, only a temporary interregnum, since "again the world fell into decay, and principles faded away. Perverse speakings and oppressive deeds waxed rife again. There were instances of ministers who murdered their sovereigns, and of sons who murdered their fathers."[46] It is for this reason that Confucius is said to have written the "Spring and Autumn Annals" (*Ch'un Ch'iu*), but he was unsuccessful in having the great principles of the past put into practice.

Mencius continues by saying that the present world was still in a state of confusion: "sage sovereigns cease to arise, and the princes of the states give the reins to their lusts. Unemployed scholars indulge in unreasonable discussions." As for the "unemployed scholars," Mencius singles out Yang Chu and Mo Tzu as acknowledging neither "king nor father" and thus reducing man to "the state of a beast."

This passage concludes with a recapitulation of Mencius' whole argument:

> In former times, Yü repressed the vast waters of the inundation, and the country was reduced to order. Chau-kung's [Chou-kung, the duke of Chou] achievements extended even to the barbarous tribes of the east and north [*i ti*], and he drove away all ferocious animals, and the people enjoyed repose. Confucius completed the "Spring and Autumn," and rebellious ministers [*luan-ch'en*] and villainous sons were struck with terror.
> It is said in the Book of Poetry [*Shih Ching*], "He smote the barbarians of the west and north [*jung ti*]; . . ." These father-deniers and king-deniers [i.e., Yang Chu and Mo Tzu] would have been smitten by Chau-kung. . . .
> Whoever is able to oppose Yang and Mo is a disciple of the sages.

While the school of Yang Chu cannot be wholly identified with the early Taoist traditions of Lao Tzu and Chuang Tzu, these schools were frequently seen to be compatible in spirit. This passage, therefore, can be read as a partial and muted attack on Taoism, or at least that kind of Taoism associated with the school of Yang as found in some chapters of the *Chuang Tzu*.[47]

In this sense it is interesting that the terms *ta-luan* and *luan*[a] are used in a way different from the usage in the *Chuang Tzu*. Both texts agree that the present age is one that suffers from a great confusion of values; but whereas in the *Chuang Tzu luan*[a] and *ta-luan* are equated with the activities of the Confucian sage heroes, here they are used for those periods of decay *after* the work of Yao and

Shun. While there is no evidence that Mencius was reacting to a Taoist argument, this usage is in some ways similar to the Taoist point of view since Mencius agrees that, despite the best efforts of the sage kings and of Confucius, the present world is still in a state of *luan*[a]. The crucial difference is that for the Taoists the *luan*[a] of the present world is a *result* of the misguided labors of Yao and Shun and is qualitatively inferior to the chaos-order *before* the coming of the sage gentlemen and their loyal ministers. Mencius, however, maintains that the present *luan*[a] is equivalent to the great watery confusion of the primordial precivilized period.

Finally, given the pattern set out with reference to the idea of *hun-tun* in the *Tso Chuan*, it seems significant that the creation of order is identified with the expulsion of rebellious ministers and sons, ferocious animals, and barbarian tribes (i.e., the *i*[c], *jung*, and *ti*[b]—all of which are variously associated with the term *hun*[d]). In the context of the various Confucian texts under discussion all of these categories seem to be equated politically with what is inimical to the maintenance of a "good" social order. Like the flood of the creation time, they are collectively symbolic of the cosmogonic chaos that had to be overcome in order to carve out a proper cosmos, a middle kingdom, in the midst of the wilderness.

This is expressive of the "combat motif" seen in many world mythologies and especially in relation to Hun-tun as a mythological figure of the chaos time. As Fontenrose remarks, the combat-myth is ultimately "a myth of beginnings, a tale of conflict between order and disorder, chaos and cosmos."[48] In the case of China a mythic figure (representing the forces either of chaos or cosmos) is considered a hero or villain depending on the particular interpretation of the mythic legacy asserted by either a Confucian or Taoist point of view. The early Taoist texts emphasize the more ambivalent mythological conception where chaos and cosmos, demon and hero, are necessarily interrelated. For example, despite the historicizing efforts of the Confucian school, the great civilizing hero and tamer of the flood, Yü, like Yao and Shun, is originally more of an ambiguous figure. In a mythological context he is the son of Kun who is related to the chaos monster Kung-kung. In this way, myth, in distinction to history, always implies that "order" is born out of, or is ultimately dependent on, the condition of chaos. Fontenrose, therefore, summarizes the intentionality of the mythological combat theme by saying:

> In general the hero-god champions the forces of creation, life, activity, and order. For creation is an active, life-asserting process that gives shape and form to unordered material. Life requires order, which means putting a limit upon action in certain directions. But an order that resists all change and

further creative activity denies life and turns into its opposite; it becomes a state of inactivity and death. The dragon enemy champions the forces of chaos, destruction, inaction, and death. For the kind of activity that turns solely to disorder and destruction destroys life along with order, and so returns to chaos and death. This is only to say that both life forces and death forces are necessary in a properly balanced individual and world.[49]

There is something of a counterpoint between a Taoist nostalgia for the time of the "noble savage" and a Confucian advocation of a doctrine of historical development—in other words, a fundamental opposition between "nature" and "culture," "raw and cooked," "uncarved and carved" or a distinction between an ideology that holds onto a mythical foundation of the creation and an ideology that equates the "Beginnings" only with the start of human history. For both it is the "creation" or the "beginning" that constitutes the true principles of order and meaning in the world; and for both the issue is one of the emulation of a paradigmatic model from the past. The decisive difference is in terms of where that past is located and how it is evaluated. It may even be legitimate to speculate that with the dominance of the Confucian point of view, we are close to one of the reasons why cosmogony, and mythology in general, seems so submerged and hidden in early Chinese tradition.

THE RAW AND THE COOKED

It is perhaps fitting that I conclude by referring to what Needham has proposed as a "hypothesis for further research."[50] Before doing so it will be best to summarize some of the findings presented here:

First, in the *Chuang Tzu* (and it would seem for the other early Taoist texts) the terms *hun-tun* and *luan*[a] are frequently paired in a contrasting way within the context of the paradise lost theme. For the Taoists *hun-tun* (and related vocabulary such as *p'u*[a], *hsüan-t'ung*[a,b], *k'un-lun*, *hung-tung*, etc.) seems, therefore, expressive of the Taoist ideal of social and personal harmony. It represents the true "order" of the Tao that was present during the paradise time. This ideal prompts various political and mystical prescriptions for "returning to the beginning" before the "great confusion [*ta-luan*]" caused by the coming of the culture heroes.

Second, in the Confucian texts something of a reverse pattern is revealed. The term *luan*[a] is found with the special meaning of the proper civilized "order" established by the legendary founders of Chinese civilization. The term *hun-tun*, however, is rarely encountered; but in those few instances of its use, it almost always receives a pejorative connotation related to the forces that were thwarting the creation of the middle kingdom (i.e., the "birds and beasts,'' barbarian tribes, banished ministers, and legendary rebels).

One general conclusion with reference to both of these points is that whereas a term like *hun-tun* may have been originally attached to a particular local culture in the context of a tribal creation myth or ancestral hero,[51] the term is ultimately used in a generalized ideological and symbolic sense by both the Taoists and the Confucians. For Taoism it seems to be appropriated as a key symbolic theme (along with others) representing the Taoist vision or story about the true nature of reality, the true mystery of the Tao as the hidden ''order'' inherent in nature and man. This was an order that once prevailed in the past but now needs to be reembodied in human society and rediscovered in individual human nature.

For Confucianism, the theme of *hun-tun* is avoided wherever possible in favor of a pseudohistorical story of the ''creation'' that coincides only with the beginnings of human civilization. When the term is used, there is again a suggestion that it was probably originally linked to an early local culture or cultures; but in the *Tso Chuan*, possibly through the pressure of the rival ideology of Taoism, it is used symbolically to represent ''barbarians'' in general or the legendary rebels subdued and banished by Shun. Somewhat like the symbolism found on the bronze TLV mirrors of ancient China, the theme of *hun-tun* in Confucianism might be said to represent the ''barbaric'' or ''chaotic'' order outside the centered ''square'' of the middle kingdom. *Hun-tun* becomes a term symbolic of anything ''non-Chinese,'' or more accurately, anything non-Confucian.[52] What we are confronted with is a binary opposition between the orders of the ''raw and the cooked,'' which as a matter of fact, involves the precise terminology of ''raw barbarians [*sheng-fan*]'' versus ''cooked or sinified barbarians [*shu-fan*].''[53]

The reverse of this ''barbaric'' order is sometimes represented in the Confucian texts by the term *luan*[a], which indicates the benevolent order or hierarchical civilization established as a part of the coming of early Chinese feudalism. But the use of *luan*[a] also reveals a certain ambiguity or indecision. Texts like *Tso Chuan* and *Lun Yü* use it in the special sense of order (*ch'ih*[b]) based on the paradigmatic authority invested in the legendary story of the origins of Chinese culture found in the *Shu Ching*; but, inasmuch as its more common meaning implies disorder and confusion similar to the idea of *hun-tun*, the special and rare usage of *luan*[a] seems to be avoided or forgotten in other texts like the *Meng Tzu*. It should, however, be recalled that all of the works under discussion are for the most part composite texts dating to different periods and representing different points of view. A perfect consistency should not therefore be required or expected. Nevertheless, it does seem safe to suggest that for early Taoism and Confucianism there were two antithetical patterns of meaning associated with the themes of *hun-tun* and *luan*[a].

Like the term *hun-tun*, *luan*[a] was probably also originally related to mythological figures and themes associated with different ancient local cults. Thus, the term *luan*[a] is perhaps linked to *luan*[b], the word for a fabulous multicolored solar bird. In some of the ancient texts, the Luan bird was said to be the helper of the mythological Feng-huang and identified with the masculine values of *yang* and the coming of spring.[54] The *Shan Hai Ching* says that "it is a bird resembling a pheasant striped in five colors, and renowned under the name of *luan*[b]. When it appears, it is a sign of peace."[55] In addition to this, the Luan bird is sometimes associated with courtly dress (i.e., a bird headdress); and, in the *Chou Li*, it is associated with funeral rites where it seemed to symbolize the deceased's soul, which came out of the coffin and flew up to heaven.[56]

It is impossible to sort out all of these fragmentary associations, but it seems clear that, like *hun-tun*, the term *luan*[a] had an important mythological heritage. Especially in the case of bird symbolism, which was frequently absorbed in a rationalized way into the ancient feudalistic and imperial court traditions, fabulous birds such as the Luan or Feng had positive symbolic value—that is, as a sign of the continuation of the social order or as "a sign of peace." While partaking of many of these same values, the Luan also had associations with the time of the return to the *yin* condition of chaos and death. Most of the solar bird symbolism stressed the associations with the *yang* principle of life in nature. The bird Luan, on the contrary, is somewhat different as a "solar symbol associated with the idea of death."[57]

Whether or not these observations offer any clues to the contradictory usage of the term *luan*[a] must, however, be left to further investigation. It is sufficient for my purposes to show that the significance of *luan*[a] and *hun-tun* must be approached in relation to their symbolic and mythological context of meaning.

To take up now some of the broader implications, it is worthwhile considering Needham's tentative hypothesis concerning the possible historical and cultural background. Briefly stated, Needham suggests that behind the symbolism of *hun-tun*, and especially the theme of the "legendary rebels," we can "see the leaders of that pre-feudal or proto-feudal class-differentiated society."[58] And as Needham points out in relation to the speculative work of Granet, the symbolism of *hun-tun* and the legendary rebels is almost always linked to archaic religio-cultural traditions of metallurgy and totemic shamanism.[59]

The possible importance of this observation is precisely that, if the reconstructions of Granet are at least accepted on heuristic grounds, the "beginning

of bronze-working was connected with the rise of Chinese proto-feudalism"
and references to such figures as Hun-tun, Huang Ti, the legendary rebels, the
Three Miao, and the Nine Li represent "metal-working confraternities" or
metallurgical initiatory brotherhoods.[60] In this sense the "leaders of pre-feudal
collectivist society would . . . have attempted to resist the earliest feudal lords,
and to prevent them from acquiring metal-working as the basis of their
power."[61]

Recognizing the tentative nature of Granet's reconstructions and putting
aside some of Needham's favored vocabulary (such as his constant refrain of an
early "collectivist" or "communistic" society), there is much to recommend
this theory. Thus the theme of *hun-tun* is especially associated in later Taoism
with the alchemical tradition, which tended to preserve much of the symbolism,
ritual, and religious spirit found in archaic traditions of the sacred task of
working with metals.[62] Moreover, there is a "vast mass of folklore . . .
available from Han and pre-Han texts" (embracing "such diverse subjects as
the origins of towns in Chinese proto-feudalism, the position of totemism and
ritual dances, the secret societies of the first bronze-founders, human and other
sacrifices, drums, potlatch, ordeals, rain-and-foam magic, etc.") supportive of
the main lines of this hypothesis.[63]

In addition to the above, and not developed by Needham, there is another
whole area of corroborating testimony coming from comparative considerations found in the history of religions, especially studies on the symbolism of
initiation associated with archaic metallurgical traditions.[64] This kind of perspective also tends to serve as a check on Needham's proclivity for neglecting
or downgrading the religious significance of a symbolic theme like *hun-tun* in
favor of a kind of sociological functionalism. It is more accurate to say that the
pattern of *hun-tun* and *luan*[a] detected in the *Chuang Tzu* seems to involve both a
social and a mystical ideal. Furthermore, it does not seem possible to separate
the two in terms of historical priority.[65] Indeed, this same ambiguity (or
simultaneity of ideals) is present in the *Tao Te Ching* and the *Huai Nan Tzu*.
Therefore, although Needham is correct in observing that the personal mystical
or occult interpretation of *hun-tun* is especially pronounced and one-sided in
later Taoism, this does not seem to be only the result of the failure or collapse of
the Taoist social-political ideal in the face of the dominance of the Confucian
imperium.

Both early Taoism and early Confucianism justify their vision of the world in
terms of different myths of the "creation," as is shown by the contrasting uses
of the themes of *hun-tun* and *luan*[a]. In this chapter I have tried to demonstrate

some of the significance of these competing stories; but further work is needed to clarify the complex historical and cultural dynamics associated with these themes. It would seem permissible, however, to suggest that such research might best follow the procedure recommended by the *Chuang Tzu*—that a determination of the symbolic interplay between Confucianism and Taoism can only be accomplished by "returning to the beginning."

5

COSMOGONY AND CONCEPTION IN THE *HUAI NAN TZU* AND *LIEH TZU*

Heaven and earth were perfectly joined [*tung-t'ung*], all was chaotically unformed [*hun-tun wei p'u*]; and things were complete [*ch'eng*] yet not created. This is called [the time or condition] of the Great One [*t'ai-i*[a]]. All came from this unity which gave to each thing its differences: the birds, fish, and beasts. This is called the lot [or division, *fen*] of things. . . . If we examine [*chi*[e]] the Great Beginning of Antiquity [*ku t'ai-ch'u*], we find that men were born from nonbeing and were formed from being. Having form, one is ruled by things. But one who is able to return [*fan*[b]] to that from which he was born and become formless again [*wei yu hsing*] is called a True Man [*chen-jen*]. The True Man is one who has not been separated [*fen*] from the Great One.

— *Huai Nan Tzu*, chap. 14

T HE *Huai Nan Tzu* (ca. second century B.C.) and the *Lieh Tzu* (ca. third to fourth century A.D. and some earlier material) may be considered the last works of the early classical tradition of Taoist philosophy.[1] Comparatively speaking, the *Huai Nan Tzu* and the *Lieh Tzu* are more eclectic and syncretistic in nature than the *Tao Te Ching* or the first seven chapters of the *Chuang Tzu*; and this is a situation that generally reflects a partial accommodation to a triumphant Confucianism and an adaptation to the universalistic philosophy of *yin-yang-wu-hsing* after the rise of the Han dynasty.[2] Given the complex syncretic cast of the thought, it is impossible here to offer any adequate or detailed characterizations of the overall nature of these works. Another debilitating factor is that both of these texts have received relatively less critical attention. Because of this, formidable problems of textual analysis, dating, and authorship still remain.

With this cautionary note it is perhaps not wholly imprudent to observe that both the *Huai Nan Tzu* and the *Lieh Tzu* constitute the richest compendiums of mythological, legendary, and forkloric material seen among the early Taoist texts. There is, in fact, a progressive intensification of such material leading from the *Tao Te Ching*'s cryptic and austere allusions down through the more overt parabolic passages found in the later chapters of the *Chuang Tzu*, the *Huai Nan Tzu*, and the *Lieh Tzu*. Such a state of affairs should not, however, be a reason to think that such materials are only later literary inventions or extraneous factors that seemingly "contradict" Taoist philosophy.[3] It is clear that most of the important mythic materials and allusions are prefigured in earlier periods and are basically consistent with the imagery and implicit mythic themes already seen in the *Tao Te Ching* and the *Chuang Tzu*. Most of all, the phenomenon of the inflated use of all sorts of diverse mythological imagery seems to reflect the general spirit of the age during the Han period as well as a progressive popularization of Taoist thought that reclaimed archaic images and themes kept alive at the folk levels of society. Part of this process is, for example, reflected in parallel, and partially contiguous, currents of thought related to the development of the so-called *hsien* cult of immortality.[4] These movements were surfacing for the first time during the former Han dynasty and drew upon many ancient religious themes. While it is probably wrong to see either the *Huai Nan Tzu* or the *Lieh Tzu* as being rampant with the theories of *hsien*-ship, it is nevertheless evident that much of the tonality and style of these documents was influenced by such movements.

"WHAT IS BELOW IS LIKE WHAT IS ABOVE"

There is, at times, much that is foreign, or even contradictory, to the classical fabric of thought seen in the *Tao Te Ching* and the *Chuang Tzu*; but there is also a common ground in the revelation of the message of "returning to the beginning." More specifically, the real basis for the delineation of a consistent religious trajectory in these works is that the soteriological doctrine of return continues to be couched in an imagery expressive of the *hun-tun* theme of creation and fall. The return called for in the *Huai Nan Tzu* and the *Lieh Tzu* is fundamentally a reworking of the paradigmatic story of Emperor Hun-tun seen in the *Chuang Tzu*.

The continuity of this vision is again demonstrated by the presence of the twin themes of an individual and social return to the paradise "order" of the cosmogonic chaos condition. In the *Huai Nan Tzu*, for example, the theme of paradise lost is most pronounced (see below and chaps. 2/13b−14b, 8/2a, 10/1b, 11/1a, and 13/4b) and is almost always developed within the mythological imagery of the *hun-tun* theme. The *Huai Nan Tzu* recounts the golden age and fall with respect to its essential relationship with cosmogony (see below and especially chaps. 2/1a−2a, 3/1a−3b, 7/1a−1b). As will be seen in this chapter, the *Lieh Tzu* basically follows the same model.

While the theme of the golden age is a constant refrain throughout these works, in the *Huai Nan Tzu*, and the *Lieh Tzu* (and also in the first seven chapters of the *Chuang Tzu*) the imagery of paradise lost is used mostly as an illustration of the condition to be achieved by an individual—especially the Emperor as the model for society (see chap. 8, *Huai Nan Tzu*). In this way there is something of a partial loss of faith in the real possibility of collectively renovating society as is suggested in the *Tao Te Ching* or the Primitivist document of the *Chuang Tzu*. Rather than desiring to reinstitute the paradise time as a realistic social goal, the *Huai Nan Tzu* "hoped only to utilize the knowledge of undifferentiated unity which characterized those earliest times."[5]

The focus on seeking paradise lost *within* the individual is characterized by another elaboration on the mystical philosophy of an initiatory return and transformation of man. Thus the thought in the *Huai Nan Tzu* is the most explicit development of the Taoist theory of the identification of man as a microcosm of the greater macrocosmos, a theory that is related to Han thought in general and constitutes the heart of much of the later alchemical and liturgical traditions.[6] The importance of this theory is that the cosmogonic and cosmological operations of Tao are immediately and intrinsically linked to the conception, birth, life, and bodily-psychic structure of the individual. Every man relives in miniature the creation, sacred history (=conception and period of gestation), and fall (=birth into the world).[7] The *Huai Nan Tzu* equates cosmogony and conception and, analogously, the human body reflects the cosmological structure of the world: "the head is round, the shape of heaven, and the feet are square, the shape of earth."[8] Like the cosmic "child" or chaotic "mass of flesh" that is the offspring of the incestuous union of its primordial parents, man is the unique product and agent of the Tao in the universe, the one who takes responsibility for continuing the creative transformation of the world.[9] Man in this sense is the third term of creation, the one who by virtue of his intrinsic, yet unfulfilled or lost, identification with the Tao, stands alone in the place of union, the central gap between what is above and what is below. Human nature (*hsing*) must, therefore, be understood in terms of its original, prefallen, condition of pure spontaneity and creativity associated with the myth of Emperor Hun-tun. "Returning" to one's original nature implies a personal reincarnation of the Tao, the creation of a "Taoist body" that is the cosmogonic body of Hun-tun, P'an-ku, or in later organized Taoism, the body of the savior god, Lao Chün.[10]

Part of this newly accentuated emphasis may be reflected in the substitution of "man" for the third term of union between heaven and earth in place of the more abstract cosmological notions seen in the *Tao Te Ching* and parts of the *Chuang Tzu*. What was previously implicit is now made the keystone of the mystic's path of salvation. Returning to the beginning in relation to the equation of microcosm and macrocosm involves a reverse recapitulation of the life history of the individual, a return to the womb, which is at the same time a reiteration of the creation of the world: embryology recapitulates cosmogony.

THE *HUAI NAN TZU*: REMEMBERING HISTORY AND MYTH

To initiate the analysis of the *Huai Nan Tzu* I want to emphasize that, more so than the other works under discussion, the mythological theme of creation and paradise lost literally reverberates throughout the whole work.[11] Because of this abundance of mythological material I will be able to examine only a few of the more important passages. But while my investigation will be delimited, the cosmogonic vision embodied in the text may be taken as an overall frame for the *Huai Nan Tzu*'s central concern for the reappropriation of an undifferentiated or comprehensive knowledge of the Tao, the One and the Many.

The quest for a comprehensive knowledge of the world and its underlying unity in the hidden order of Tao implies both an outer and inner cultivation of the mind. This new stress on a kind of historical knowledge (also exemplified by the roughly coterminous *Shih Chi*, ca. first century B.C.), as well as mystical knowledge and experience, seems different from the emphasis in the *Tao Te Ching* and the *Chuang Tzu* where the deprecation of discriminating or outward knowledge is paramount. On the other hand, if Needham's observations are given any credence, the seeming difference of the *Huai Nan Tzu* might only be a more explicit extension of what was already implicit in both the *Tao Te Ching* and the *Chuang Tzu*.[12]

Needham has been duly criticized for reading too much of an "empirical" or even "scientific" attitude into the earliest Taoist texts, but it is really not necessary to take sides on this issue. Despite what may be a certain difference of emphasis, the ultimate goal of these works is basically the same. It is the case, therefore, that the *Huai Nan Tzu*'s stress on the "investigation or examination [*chi*e] of things," the empirical knowledge of the real multiplicity of the phenomenal world, leads to a further level of mystic insight where multiplicity is blurred and all the Ten Thousand Things are experienced as the constant transformation of the primordial oneness of Tao. To achieve this understanding an investigation of the past is necessary because history as the manifestation and development of things in time is the clearest exemplar of the "Great Transformation" and its relation to an underlying first-principle of order. History demonstrates the need for man to follow the constant "way" of perpetual beginning and return, the cyclic interplay of chaos and cosmos.

An essential difference may be noted between the *Huai Nan Tzu* and the historical consciousness of the *Shih Chi*, which seeks to understand the present in terms of the legendary "Three Sovereigns" (Fu-hsi, Nü-kua, Shen-nung) who were said to be civilizing culture heroes even before the time of Yao, Shun, and Yü (and the other "Five Emperors").[13] Ssu-ma Ch'ien goes further back into legendary and mythic origins than earlier Confucians to account for historical development. While the ancient three sovereigns, like Yao, Shun, and Yü, were originally attached to cosmogonic themes, these figures are rationalized and euhemerized as the founders of the civilized order of the empire. Hun-tun, somewhat as in the *Tso Chuan*, is only mentioned as an euhemerized figure who followed the "three sovereigns" and the "five dragons" as a minor ruler in the empire. In distinction to the civilizing activities of the three sovereigns and five emperors, Hun-tun was notably *forgotten*: "since the written documents do not recall them [Hun-tun along with fifteen other figures], one does not know either the duration of the rule of their families or their genealogies, nor the place where they had their capitals."[14] There apparently was a need, therefore, to expunge the significance of a figure like Hun-tun from the official historical view of the past.

In the *Huai Nan Tzu* and *Lieh Tzu* the depth of the historical perspective is expressly pushed back to embrace the absolute beginnings of the world before either the three sovereigns or five emperors. From the Confucian perspective, history is self-contained and explains reality in terms of the beginnings of man and human culture. For the Taoist texts, on the other hand, a historical vision of reality is only a propaedeutic to a deeper mythic vision of the ultimate pre-human and precosmic origins. In the *Huai Nan Tzu*, history, or the investigation of the past, is fulfilled and completed by the myth of creation. Hun-tun, dramatically unlike the *Shih Chi*'s conception, is to be *remembered* as one of the most important symbols of the sacred time of the beginnings. In this way, *anamnesis*, or the remembering of the essential connection between the historical present and the mythic past, the beginning and continuing transformation of all things, is the real basis for Taoism's soteriological theme of return.

A fundamental difference between a Confucian and Taoist consciousness consequently hinges on their respective emphasis on either a "historical" or a "primordial" memory.[15] In Confucianism, knowledge starts with and depends on historical or civilizational origins. In Taoism, on the other hand, history is only the human continuation of a more ancient, more mythic, story of life. To remember the connection between myth and history in Taoism is to re-member or rearticulate the "original" human nature, to reassemble the parts of the body of the primordial giant (P'an-ku) who was dismembered in the creation of the world. Analogously, it is a closing of the holes of face bored into Emperor Hun-tun. Having a comprehensive and undifferentiated insight into the parts of his body and the world, a Taoist knows the Many and the One simultaneously. In this way, history (whether personal or social) is not an end in itself but only another path back to a time, condition, or knowledge that was not historically ordered. Taoism remembers history ultimately to forget it in the absolute freedom of the Tao.

1. *Remembrance and Mystical Return*

In the *Chuang Tzu* a man of Tao has to realize that his personal history or "face" is only given meaning because of its prior attachment to the universal history or "great transformation" of the Tao. So also here in the *Huai Nan Tzu*, a "true man" must forget himself to remember what is more precious and meaningful. Above all else, a Taoist must remember the true story of life, which is a story of the creation time before the fall. From the Taoist point of view, life fundamentally embodies a form that is more mythic than historical in nature.

The imagery that shapes and colors a remembrance of the beginnings is particularly attached to the theme of *hun-tun*. This has already been indicated in a cursory way by my analysis of the cosmogonic passage from chapter 7 of the *Huai Nan Tzu* in relation to chapter 42 of the *Tao Te Ching*. What I would like to bring out and stress here, as with the other chapters, is the important relation between this mythic remembrance and its application to mystic techniques of return. "Going back" as an effort of the mind in the *Huai Nan Tzu* involves the symbolism of reinacting the creation scenario.

To demonstrate and reinforce the significance of this for the *Huai Nan Tzu* I want to recall briefly the important cosmogonic passage from chapter 14 that is given in the epigram to this chapter.[16] In this passage there is a compact restatement of the overall theme of beginning and return that I have been tracing throughout this work. Furthermore, it is noteworthy that there is a consistent use of technical language invoking the ideas of the chaos time or condition. Aside from the term of *hun-tun* itself, attention should be drawn to the homophonically and semantically significant use of the reduplicated terminology of *tung-t'ung*; the reiteration of the idea of the "completeness" (*ch'eng*) of the chaos condition similar to the terminology of *hun-ch'eng* from the *Tao Te Ching*; the terminology and idea of the "one" or "great one" (*t'ai-i*[a]); the priority of the "great form" of the "formless" (*wu-hsing*); and finally, somewhat like the "boring" of Emperor Hun-tun, the creation of the ordinary world of things through "division" (*fen*). This passage goes on to emphasize that it is only through the "examination" (*chi*[e]) of the past, leading back to a knowledge of the "Great Beginning," that one is able to understand the true meaning and destiny of human nature. As in both the *Tao Te Ching* and the *Chuang Tzu*, only by means of the Taoist arts of knowing the "Great Beginning" is one able to return (*fan*[b]) to an experience of the undifferentiated condition.

This same movement from the creation paradigm to methods of personal return is also found in chapter 7 where the passages following the opening cosmogonic section with its microcosmic-macrocosmic equation invoke the symbolism of initiation and suggest the use of meditation methods.[17] These later passages reassert the *Tao Te Ching*'s symbolic refrain of "closing the eyes and ears" to experience, as it is called here, the condition of "mysterious fulfillment" (*hsüan-ta*).

The meaning of this is further reiterated in chapter 7 where it is said that the "true man's nature is unified with the Tao" when his "essence and spirit [*ching shen*] hold to the root, and life and death are without difference to him. This is therefore called the Highest Spirit[ual condition, *chih-shen*]."[18] He has achieved that condition of emptiness (*hsü*[a]) that was perfectly present only at the beginning of the universe and the beginning of human life in the womb. It is the condition of dwelling in the realm of the one (*ch'u ch'i i*) and is further described using terminology encompassing much of the important analogous symbolism of the *hun-tun* theme:

> [The true man] knows primordial simplicity [*t'ai-su*].
> He acts naturally [*wu-wei*] and has returned to the
> uncarved block [*fu p'u*].

> His body is at the source and infolds spirit [*pao shen*],
> and he is able to float [*yu*[b]] throughout
> the universe.[19]

The reference to *yu*[b] (or the common cognate term of *yu*[c]) for the condition of cosmic freedom or *wu-wei* is suggestive of the frequent mythological allusions to the watery nature of *hun-tun*—the time of the waters of creation, the time of the flood, or the condition of the fetus floating freely in the amniotic sac in perfect harmony with the mother.[20] In this vein Bauer has noted:

> The term *yu*, "to wander" is interesting for its ambiguity. For it refers both to aimless wandering, roaming about, vagabondage, and also to leisurely, recreative strolling, which has no aim other than itself. In contrast to the Taoists, the Confucians always felt negatively about both meanings. . . . "Leisure," "swimming," (especially in Taoist literature, it is not the radical for "walking" but that for "water" which is used. This is intentional. It gives the character the meaning of "swimming," "playing") was not really consonant with the Confucian concept of a life of duty.[21]

Another mythologically relevant consideration is that whereas "spiritual wandering" is frequently understood within the shamanic context of bird and flight symbolism,[22] the allusion to the "floating" condition may also suggest in a more direct fashion the cosmogonic symbolism of the magic gourd-egg-boat that is responsible for the salvation of a primordial couple. In south Chinese tradition there is an important legendary cycle connected to the *hun-tun* theme where, during the time of a great flood, a divine brother-sister pair is saved by floating across the flood waters in an ark made out of a gourd, drum, or cauldron. The creation of man was then accomplished through the incestuous union of this pair after the flood waters had subsided.[23]

I will develop some of the possible import of this mythic cycle in the next two chapters, but the ambivalence of the symbolism should be noted here. The medium of salvation (the gourd-drum-egg-cauldron-boat) can be identified both with the chaotic waters of the flood, and by extension, with the more cosmogonically relevant symbolism of the cosmic egg-gourd and primordial waters. It may even be suggested that the symbolism of the gourd-egg-boat-etc. as a magic vessel of salvation is given meaning because of its ultimate attachment to a cosmogonic cycle of mythology where sacrality and the powers of creation were embryonically contained within a hollow, chaotic mass (cosmic egg-gourd). The two are saved, or unified, by the third term of the hollow *hun-tun* egg-gourd, and this is the necessary precondition for the subsequent creation of man through *hieros gamos*. As in the *Chuang Tzu*, the two agents of the creation of the human world come together in the central realm of Hun-tun.

As a final observation pertinent to the mythological context of meaning just mentioned, the etymological connection between the terms yu^b (and yu^c) and fu/fou^c (meaning "to float," "to drift," or "giddy," "frivolous," "excessive") should be noted. Stein has shown that the significant use of these terms in the Taoist corpus is linked to "le thème du séjour paradisiaque."[24] One of the most famous parables recounting this theme is also a story that specifically suggests the mythic symbolism of the magic gourd-egg-boat of salvation. This is the story of the "useless" gourd found in chapter 1 of the *Chuang Tzu*.[25] In this story, which is directly related to a whole series of parables concerning the "use of the useless" found in the inner chapters, Chuang Tzu argues with the logician Hui Tzu about the possible uses of an extraordinarily large gourd (*ta-kua*). Hui Tzu remarks that because of its size and weight this gourd was useless for making even ordinary household objects like a water container or dipper. Even by carving or splitting it up, it was still too unwieldy. Hui Tzu's only solution to this dilemma was to smash the gourd to pieces. Chuang Tzu retorts that Hui Tzu was "certainly dense when it comes to using big things." For Chuang Tzu the whole secret of its use is to be found in its original uselessness or emptiness. As Chuang Tzu sarcastically concludes, "Why didn't you think of making it into a great tub so you could go floating [fu^c] around the rivers and lakes, instead of worrying because it was too big and unwieldy to dip into things! Obviously you still have a lot of underbrush in your head!" To be "buoyed up by the Tao" one has only to drop the pretensions of face and one's reliance on the logic and values of the civilized world. For both the *Huai Nan Tzu* and *Chuang Tzu* the secret arts of salvation are therefore absurdly simple and self-evident. The Taoist is one who learns how to pilot himself back to an appreciation and experience of the underlying undifferentiated order of the world: "The torch of chaos and doubt—this is what the sage steers by. So he does not use things but relegates all to the constant. This is what it means to use clarity."[26]

To return now to chapter 7 of the *Huai Nan Tzu*, the passage under consideration goes on to state that the Taoist's "freedom" (his "floating" condition) emulates the cosmic spontaneity of the Tao at the beginning, its *tzu-jan*. In this passage, however, this idea is significantly referred to as "*mang jan . . . hao-hao tang-tang*," terms that are related to the idea of the chaos time of the primordial waters or great flood. It is further said that the Taoist who has realized this condition has "equalized life and death"—that condition that might be interpreted as a mystic return to the paradise time wherein the Taoist lives as a mythological god-man in the central realm between heaven and earth, *yin* and *yang*, life and death.[27]

The Taoist has achieved that "inner concentration of the mind [*hsin chih chuan yü nei*]" that the *Chuang Tzu* spoke of as a mysterious unification, melting, congealing, or chaotification. It is the state of complete identification with the One, a state of consciousness different from the ordinary mode of knowing (it is *pu-chih*). The man of Tao knows and acts spontaneously, with the effortless freedom of *tzu-jan, wu-wei*, or as it is here called, *hun-jan*.[28] This is but another direct indication that such important technical terms as *tzu-jan* and *wu-wei* are to be understood within the mythological context of meaning associated with the theme of *hun-tun*.

The Taoist described here resembles the "nameless man" of the *Chuang Tzu* (chap. 5) because he has "forgotten the five viscera" and identified with the empty, faceless condition of primordial totality. He has "embraced the source of Great Purity [*pao ch'i t'ai-ch'ing chih pen*]" and his dualities of physical essence (*ching*) and spiritual essence (*shen*[a]) are harmonized. He has dedicated himself to the "uncarved purity of the *Ta-hun* [*ta-hun chih p'u*]." By achieving internally a condition that emulates the mythic condition of the Emperor Hun-tun, the Taoist has relived his own personal creation as well as the birth of the universe; he has "returned to the beginning and end" of all things.[29]

2. "Beginning and Return" in Chapters 1 and 3

Chapter 1 is another extremely important chapter containing passages explicitly related to the theme of *hun-tun*. This chapter opens with a somewhat disjointed cosmogonic section that is generally supportive of the scheme I have been explicating. Particularly significant is the use of additional mythological and symbolic allusions. The chapter starts by describing the cosmogonic origins of the Tao, and the image presented is basically that of the perfect "chaos form" of "three" seen in other texts. It is said that the Tao (of the creation time): "Filled heaven and supported earth, extended to the four quarters and touched the eight poles."[30] Like an egg or womb this primal Tao "infolded within itself heaven and earth [*pao kuo t'ien-ti*] and endowed that which was without form [*wu-hsing*]."[31] Again, the image here is one of the Tao in its cosmogonic condition before the creation of the fallen world, the condition of the sacred "oneness" of the "two" things called *hun-ch'eng* or *ta-hun*. And, as I will show, this symbolic motif must surely be connected with the later mythological accounts of P'an-ku, the primal giant who was born from the chaos egg of *hun-tun* and supported the two things of heaven and earth. P'an-ku gives the form of "three" to the paradise period of the cosmos. Chapter 8 of the

Huai Nan Tzu (see below), in fact, says that "heaven, earth, and the universe are the body of one man. This is why it is called the *ta-t'ung*[a]." This is a statement echoed by the *Lü Shih Ch'un Ch'iu*.[32]

The common image of water is presented in the following verses suggesting that the Tao's creative primordiality is like a "spring that chaotically wells up, bubbles and begins to overflow."[33] It is chaotically murky (*chuo*) and teeming with the germs of life.[34] This description of the watery, fertile condition of the Tao concludes with the characteristic reduplicated ejaculation: "*hun-hun ku-ku*."[35] It is interesting that like *hun* and *tun* (and their variants), *ku*[a] (read *hua* in modern usage) has a range of meanings that includes the ideas of "confused, cunning, humorous, slippery, polished." It is also related to *hua*[b] meaning "artful, treacherous, cunning" and seems to recall the legends of the "boneless king" (King Hsü). Folklore associated with the birth of a hero from an egg, gourd, or stone is related here; in particular, there are legends that tell of the birth of a shapeless lump of flesh (or toad) that are connected with the theme of *hun-tun*.[36] In this mythological sense, and recalling the primal solitude (*tu*) of the Tao, it is curious that the term *ku*[b], consisting of the elements of "son" and "gourd," means "orphan, alone." Boodberg points out the following series of etymological associations for the phoneme *ku* in archaic Chinese: "**GSo* < **GLoG* is connected with the etymon 'gourd' ~ 'neck of a bottle' ~ 'neck' ~ 'throat' ~ 'dewlap' ~ 'opening' ~ 'mouth' (of a vessel) . . . **GL-* is well attested in **g'uo*—'bottle-gourd.' " In relation to the theme of sacred madness associated with *hun-tun*, it is interesting that a "survival of **GS-* in **kuo*— 'coarse' . . . 'stupid' we see in colloquial *hu-t'u*—stupid.' " The terms *ku*[c] ("drum, to drum or to swell, bulge") and *ku*[d] ("to float, confusion, throw into disorder") can also be related to this sound series.[37]

Subsequent verses from chapter 1 offer a further description of how the primal chaotic matrix gave life and form to the cosmos yet paradoxically remains "one" at the heart of all the Ten Thousand Things. In the chaos time the Tao is that ordering "center" of the two things and everything. It is "the axis of the four seasons and contains the *yin* and *yang*. It binds together the universe and makes bright the three sources of light [moon, sun, and stars]."[38] Its creative power is the source of all life and is responsible for the harmonious functioning of all of the dualities of phenomenal existence. It is one thing yet "three" since it equalizes the dualities of the world.

In a later passage there is an additional rehearsal of the same scenario reflective of even more archaic mythological ideas. It is said that in the "great ancient time [*t'ai-ku*]" there were "two emperors [*erh huang*]" who had "gotten [*te*[b]] the authority of the Tao." These two deities lived in a "central" realm (*li yü chung yang*) like the Emperor Hun-tun. The creative power of their spirits (*shen*[a]) transformed itself and flowed outward giving form to the world. Their spirits were responsible for maintaining the constant harmonious life of the cosmos during the sacred period of the paradise time:

> Their spirit [force] transformingly flowed out [*hua yu*] in order to rule the four directions. Therefore, the heavens are able to move and earth is stable, turning and revolving without exhaustion.[39]

I might paraphrase this by saying that what was created was the "chaos-order" or "chaosmos" of the paradise time where all things revolve in an endless closed cycle of harmonious life and change. This could be said to be the true meaning of the "natural" order of the world where everything follows the spontaneous internal ordering principle (*tzu-jan* or *hun-jan*) of the primordial Tao. The order of life during the sacred history of the creation time is one of constant revolution, alternation, creative transformation, biological metamorphosis—wherein life is always a matter of the dialectical process of two things achieving synthesis, returning to the one and thus going out again giving rise to new life. Here the frequent mythological motif of creation resembling the action of a potter's wheel is invoked, indicating that both cosmic and human time are essentially cyclic and must always return to the beginning to initiate a new creation: "Like a potter's wheel [*chun*], revolving round and returning [*fu*[a]] to the starting point. Now carving, now polishing, it returns to the uncarved block [*p'u*[a]]."[40]

All of this is then applied to the principles of life the Taoist must personally adopt in order to emulate and return to an identification with the source, to learn to reexperience the sacredness of a truly "natural" life. This is said to be the meaning of *wu-wei*. By uniting with the Tao the Taoist symbolically becomes the mythic emperor of the center or the giant P'an-ku since, like the primordial condition of the "three," he "supports heaven and earth, harmonizes the *yin* and *yang*, divides the four seasons, and orders the five elements."[41]

In a later passage there appears the common emphatic declaration of the mysterious life-giving nature of the Tao. Much of this kind of terminology (such as the reduplicated use of *hu-huang*) has already been witnessed in the other texts, but attention should be paid to some of the other expressions (e.g., *yu-ming*[b] and *sui-tung*, that suggest the idea of a chaotic, murky condition teeming with life) symbolic of the "chaos" condition of the Tao as the cosmic principle of life and transformation:

> How chaotic and obscure [*hu . . . huang*]! Without form [*wei-hsiang*]! How chaotic [*huang . . . hu*]!

How exhaustionless! Dark and obscure [*yu . . . ming*]!
How fittingly without shape [*sui . . . tung*]! How complete and mysterious
[*sui . . . tung*]! Never emptied of movement![42]

Following these verses is a mytically significant story concerning the legendary charioteers Feng-i[b] and Ta-ping who were men of Tao:

> [They] had lost themselves in heaven's gate and floated [*yu*[b]] [in the "chaos" realm] above the boundless wasteland and below entered the gate of "formlessness" [*wu yin chih men*].[43]

Feng-i[b] and Ta-ping are mythological chaos figures like Emperor Hun-tun. In the story from chapter 6 of the *Chuang Tzu*, P'ing-i (or Feng-i[a]) "got the Tao and wandered [*yu*[c]] in the great river"; and here the *Huai Nan Tzu*, in distinction to the Confucian texts where such figures are either condemned or forgotten, presents them as an illustration of what it means to return to the Tao.[44] Furthermore, the *Ch'u Tz'u*'s first "Heavenly Question" links the term *feng-i*[b] to a cosmogonic context of meaning:

> What means are there to examine what it was like before heaven above and earth below had taken shape? How is it possible to probe into that age when the light and darkness were still undivided? And how do we know of the chaos [*feng-i*[b]] of insubstantial form?[45]

There is finally another section from chapter 1 that requires some discussion.[46] This is a passage that opens with the characteristic equation of Tao with water. Tao is metaphorically like water in its quality of acting as the universal solvent of all dualities, yielding and responding perfectly to any situation. As in the *Tao Te Ching*, these metaphors are linked to the mythic idea of the primordial watery condition of the Tao at the creation time. This is indicated by the fact that the metaphorical description leads directly into a reiteration of the basic cosmogonic themes associated with the Tao. Like water, the Tao's power resides in its "empty nothingness or formlessness [*hsü wu*]" and its constant flowing back and forth from the state of chaotic unity:

> [It] loses itself in the formless [*wu-hsing*], and that which is called the formless is called the One. What is called the One is that without equal in the world. It stands lofty and alone. It dwells clodlike and alone [*k'uai jan tu ch'u*].

This "clod-like" or "pupa-like" condition (*k'uai jan*) is the closed and shapeless "chaos-form of" the "three."[47] It unifies the above and below, heaven and earth, the "two" things: "Above it fills the nine heavens. Below it penetrates the nine wastes." The passage concludes by saying that the Tao is that which is "greatly chaotified [or the "Great Chaos," *ta-hun*], and constitutes the one." In chapter 6 there is a similar passage that says that the "chaos condition of heaven and earth is that which is the one [t'ien-hsia hun erh wei i]" and Kau Yu comments that the "one" is to be identified with the condition of hun-t'ung.[48]

Chapter 3 opens with much of the same technical cosmological terminology, but it is worth considering for some of the additional mythological imagery employed. The description basically concerns the creation time before heaven and earth became separate.[49] It says that the "heavens were shapeless" (wu hsing), which was a condition or time of feng-feng i-i, tung-tung shu-shu. These reduplicated terms are directly expressive of the chaos condition of hun-tun. The term feng-i[b] has already been examined; and tung, as throughout the Huai Nan Tzu (cf. chaps. 14 and 10), is an extremely important technical term that in later Taoism has the various symbolic associations of a tripartite cave, grotto, or paradise world of the immortals. There is unquestionably a connection here with the already encountered terms of t'ung[a,b] and hsüan-t'ung[a,b] for either the cosmogonic or experiential condition of "equality."[50] Moreover, as with the probable homophonic associations of hsüan-t'ung[a,b] and hun-tun, the reduplicated used of tung-tung or tung-t'ung may also betray something of a conscious punning on the sound quality of hun-tun.

The cosmogonic backdrop seen in the Huai Nan Tzu should be especially stressed since it may provide some explanation for tung becoming one of the most important technical terms in the later Taoist tradition. As Bauer points out, along with Stein and Soymié, the idea of tung as "cave," or tung-t'ien as "cave heaven," became the common expression for a certain kind of Taoist paradise. More generally, the term tung evoked the idea of a blissful condition and was "used in countless Taoist concepts, including book titles."[51] Here, as with the word family associated with hun-tun, the etymology of tung helps to tell some of the story of its significance and, at the same time, suggests many of the underlying symbolic and mythological themes. Bauer remarks:

> The term "cave" [tung] had something special about it . . . . The Chinese sign is written with the radical "water" on the left, and thus first suggests "flowing." Actually, the word often has the meaning "flowing rapidly" in early texts. When it is read tung (from *d'ung > d'ung), the sound permits us to assign it to a word family which includes concepts such as t'ung (from *t'ung > t'ung), "to pass through," "to connect," "to have a connection with," or t'ung (from *d'ung > d'ung), "pipe," which has the same sound; indeed probably even the word for "equal," t'ung (from *d'ung > d'ung), . . . as in the ideal of the Great Equality.[52]

Bauer goes on to note that "the concept 'equal' . . . did not so much bring to mind the idea of a static identity, but that of a reciprocal adaptation based on an exchange." The term *tung* or "cave" therefore did not just "evoke the association of 'grotto,' i.e. a closed vault in a rock or the ground, which might serve as a temporary hiding place," but also that "of a 'passage,' a 'transition.' It was not the darkness of the cave that attracted attention, but rather the light of day shimmering far away at its end, and which promised a new world."[53]

Bauer also suggests, and my analysis supports his contention, that these associations especially connote the Taoist motif of initiation or the "archtype of a 'rebirth' in a non-Buddhist sense."[54] He consequently concludes by saying that the Taoists always understood salvation

> [in a sense] which ran altogether counter to the Buddhist view (and therefore could not be appropriated by Buddhism), a liberating rebirth into a life wholly of this world. Entry into this earthly paradise did not call for the "superman" who leaves earth on luminous wings, but the "new man," who dug his way back through the womb of mother earth and thus actually returned to the condition of the old, the original "true man" (*chen-jen*), as the Taoists called him.[55]

The *chen-jen*, of course, is the figure from chapter 14 of the *Huai Nan Tzu* who had returned to the condition of *hun-tun wei p'u*, the uncarved chaos condition of "great antiquity."[56]

After the descriptive refrain of *feng-feng i-i tung-tung shu-shu*, chapter 3 goes on to call this condition the great origin of brightness or the *t'ai-chao*; and, as in chapter 42 of the *Tao Te Ching*, the Tao is that which gives rise to the one "empty" (*hsü-k'uo*) thing. The image of the *hsü-k'uo* is of a vast, mist-laden hollow at the center of the Tao, a fertile "emptiness" that subsequently gives birth to the "cosmos" (*hsü-k'uo sheng yü-chou*). Within the hollow of the primordial cosmos (*yü-chou* = that which is stretched out or swollen), *ch'i*[a] is engendered.

Ch'i[a], as the visible and invisible "stuff," "connective tissue," or "circulating fluid" of creation, organizes itself through an alternate separation and fusion into the paradise condition:

> *Ch'i*[a] has branches and roots. The pure *yang* [*ch'i*[a]] drifted up and became heaven and the heavy and turbid congealed [*ning*[a]] downwards and became earth. . . . heaven and earth unified [*hsi*[b]] their essence [*ching*] making *yin* and *yang*. *Yin* and *yang* blended and circulated their essence [*ching*] and produced the four seasons. And the four seasons in scattering their *ch'i*[a] produced the Ten Thousand Things.[57]

It is clear that while the overall sequence of events is somewhat confused and distorted, this passage represents a more elaborate and mythologically evocative gloss on the cosmogony seen in chapter 42 of the *Tao Te Ching*. This stage or condition of the creation time is further ordered through the manifestation of the creative life-force of *ch'i*[a], eventually giving birth to the "two" offspring of heaven and earth. There is also a suggestion that heaven and earth may be imagined as male and female twin deities since the birth of *yin* and *yang* is said to proceed from a kind of marriage union (*hsi ching*). All of this, then, can be read as a richly embellished reworking of a mythological account of the creation time.

In the remaining verses of the opening section of chapter 3 the rupture from the sacred time is recounted in terms of the combat myth of Kung-kung, the rebellious deity who broke the central axis uniting heaven and earth and is responsible for the "broken" or profane condition of the world:

> Long ago Kung-kung and Chuan-hsü fought over who was to be king, and in their rage they dashed against Pu-chou mountain. The heavenly pillar was broken and the earthly cord was cut. The heavens listed to the northwest and so the sun, moon, and stars move in that direction. Earth was lowered in the southeast and thus water and soil flows in that direction.[58]

In the combat between Kung-kung and Chuan-hsü, the tripartite paradise form of the harmonious connection (the third term, umbilical, "pillar," or "cord"; cf. the later myths of P'an-ku whose body supported heaven and earth) between the two things of heaven and earth was broken. The battle between Kung-kung and Chuan-hsü, therefore, functions mythically like the decision on the part of Hu and Shu to carve up the primal unity of Hun-tun. Again the ambiguity of this symbolism should be noted since both Kung-kung and Chuan-hsü are divine beings of the chaos time and can be symbolically identified with the nature and function of Hun-tun as a mythological being.[59] The Kung-kung legends are, for example, especially related to flood stories; and, as Boodberg notes:

> The "Flood Story" of the archaic texts is, as is well known, nothing but a euhemerized Creation legend. It must have passed through a stage where it was interpreted as a myth of the primeval struggle between the powers on high . . . and the monster of Chaos. The latter was undoubtedly designated as **Glung* ~ **Glun*, an etymon which is reflected in [*lung*] *Glung— "dragon," [*kung*] *Glung—"flood" (as in *kung-shui* and *kung-kung*).[60]

It is noteworthy that rhyming binomials like *kung-kung* and *hun-tun* appear to be phonetically and semantically related, since as Boodberg says, "it would be comparatively easy to demonstrate how most of the names of the mythological characters in the Flood Story are but variations (dialectical or graphic) of only two or three original etymons which composed the primeval mythological theme of the Creation Legend, and how many motifs in it were developed through the semantization of graphs or specialization of complex semantemes."[61]

The flawed or profane "order" (*luan*[a]) is thus established, and man must seek a return to the paradise age of *hun-tun* (here referred to as *tun chih nieh*). This movement from an initial recounting of the sacred history of the beginnings to the fall from the primordial condition, along with a description of the necessary methods of reversal and return to the paradise condition, exemplifies the basic ideological pattern running throughout the *Huai Nan Tzu* (cf. especially chap. 8 of the *Huai Nan Tzu*).

3. *"Moist Mystery": The Seven Stages of Cosmogony, Gestation, and Return*

Even more reflective of the pattern outlined above is the narrative of the beginnings found at the start of chapter 2.[62] Again, there is a certain amount of syncretic supererogation, but the basic mythological structure is intact and can be extracted. The time of the beginning is spoken of in terms of seven stages of creative development, seven periods that recall the seven days of boring in the *Chuang Tzu*'s Hun-tun story, the seven cosmogonic phases referred to in chapter 2 of the *Chuang Tzu*, or the seven stages leading to the murky condition of *hun*[d] seen in chapter 15 of the *Tao Te Ching*. The *Chuang Tzu* passage from chapter 2, which is closest in structure to the *Huai Nan Tzu*, states:

> There is a beginning [1]. There is not yet beginning to be a beginning [2]. There is a not yet beginning to be a not yet beginning to be a beginning [3]. There is being [4]. There is nonbeing [5]. There is a not yet beginning to be nonbeing [6]. There is a not yet beginning to be a not yet beginning to be nonbeing [7].[63]

In a less whimsical way the seven stages of creation found in chapter 2 of the *Huai Nan Tzu* can be taken as being equivalent to the movement from one to two to three found in the *Tao Te Ching*. All seven of these stages are analogous to the mythological condition of the *hun-tun* time and are generally descriptive of the wholeness and internal life process of the cosmic Tao. The description of each of these stages is important in revealing more of the mythological foundation for the idea of the "chaos" time and the mystery of its "order." These stages parallel the Chinese ideas of embryological development and biological metamorphosis and again bring to the fore the mythic image of the cosmic egg.

It is reported that in the first stage of creation nothing yet had issued forth or had taken shape. It is "*wu-wu juan-juan,*" an expression that is interesting for the somewhat unusual use of the rare character *juan*, which is basically suggestive of something that manifests movements like an insect or snake.[64] In a subsequent verse from this chapter the term *juan tung* is used, which again recalls the peculiar wriggling movement of a snake or insect.[65] There is an intimation that this refers to the idea of the internal embryonic life within an egg, seed, womb, or the larval contractions within a pupa or cocoon. This reechoes Gourd Master's return to the beginning from chapter 7 of the *Chuang Tzu* (cf. *Lieh Tzu*):

> Hu Tzu said, "Just now I appeared to him as Not Yet Emerged from My Source. I came at him empty, wriggling and turning [*wei she*], not knowing anything about 'who' or 'what,' now dipping and bending, now flowing in waves."[66]

Or, to cite another passage from the *Chuang Tzu* (chap. 12), it is said that in the time of Perfect Virtue men "wriggle around like insects [*chung tung*], performing services for one another, but do not know that they are being kind."[67] The passage from the *Huai Nan Tzu* goes on to say that this first, shapeless thing (*wei yu hsing*) of creation already possessed a latent potency to give birth to things. But the creation process was not yet completed.

At the second stage, an internal ordering (splitting, separation, rising and falling, evacuation, etc.) has started to take place within the primordial undifferentiated mass:

> Heaven's *ch'i*[a] started to descend and earth's *ch'i* started to rise. *Yin* and *yang* alternately merged, mutually flowing among the elements of the *yü-chou*. There was only the fluid watery movement of blending and interpenetration, and there was no complete appearance of form yet.

With the third stage of cosmic development, the image is one of the establishment of an internal hollow (similar to the *hsü-k'uo* of chap. 3) filled with the life-force of the *ch'i*[a] and connecting the preformal shapes of heaven and earth. Heaven and earth, the "two," were still blended (*ho-ho, huai*) into the unity of the *ch'i*[a] and had not yet completely separated (ascended and descended, *chiang yang*). It was a condition that was "an empty void, still and solitary [lonely and desolate, cf. the term *tu*]. A vapory, moist, drizzling, humid state in which there was now a glimmer of form." The *ch'i*[a] floating in this space has achieved the "order" of the chaos condition called here *ta-t'ung ming-ming*. Kau Yu comments that, at this stage, the "Tao was that which was in the midst of the *hun-ming ta-ming*."[68]

The fourth stage involves the development of definite forms: "Germs and embryos, roots, stems, tissues, twigs, leaves of variegated hues appeared."

Form and shape was not manifest to the extent that it could be "felt, grasped, and seen."

The fifth stage implies that the forms of the preceding stage were all internal manifestations and that outwardly the Tao still had "no form . . . no sound . . . no tangibility," which is reminiscent of the *i-hsi-wei* refrain from chapters 14 and 21 of the *Tao Te Ching*. It was still a chaotic closed unity, great watery mass, or moist embryonic mystery called *hao-hao han-han*. The term *hao* has already been seen in the context of the cosmogonic chaos condition of *hao-hao tang-tang* from chapter 7. *Hao* evokes the idea of flood waters and in this way is related to the term *han*, which is an archaic word that generally means "ocean," especially the northern ocean or wasteland. Used in the compound *hun-han*, it means a "vast expanse of water" or a "flood."[69]

In the sixth stage there was still the egglike or embryonic internal unity of all forms. Heaven and earth were "wrapped up [*pao-kuo*]" (cf. chap. 1 of the *Huai Nan Tzu*, see above) into a single chaotic mass that was constantly shaping and forging all things. *Pao*[b] generally means "to wrap" and is linked to the word family of "womb" (*pao*[c]), "embrace" (*pao*[d], cf. *pao-i*[a] in the *Tao Te Ching*), and "placenta" (*pao-i*[b]). *Kuo* means to "wrap or bind" but is associated with the ideas of "wrapping up a corpse" (*kuo-shih*) or wrapping a body in a skin, which suggests the scapegoat motif of the *hun-tun* sack or bag that was made out of skins.[70] This stage, then, can be called a continuation of the "shut up" chaos "order" or "shape." It is characteristically called the *ta-t'ung hun-ming*[b], which is also used as a golden-age expression at the end of chapter 6. There was "nothing," yet all things were complete and preformed internally. The "world" was already perfectly present.

Finally, in the seventh stage the cosmogonic process is complete and there is no rupture or separation (*wei p'ou, wei p'an*) between the "two" things of heaven and earth or *yin* and *yang*. Kau Yu comments here that this means things were *hun fen* or "chaotically separate (chaotically fused yet distinct)."[71] It was a quiescent state of harmonious form that can be equated with the centered condition of "three" seen in the *Tao Te Ching*. In a concluding verse recalling the association with the condition of the primordial waters, this stage is said to be "peaceful and quite like a vast watery expanse [*wang jan*], still like [*chi jan*] clear water."

As a final point concerning the passage from chapter 2 of the *Huai Nan Tzu*, the term *wang*[b] should be singled out for attention. *Wang*[b], therefore, can be taken as a chaos term connoting a watery condition (such as the compound *wang-mang* meaning a "vast expanse of water") and is also connected with terms suggesting the motif of sacred madness—that is, *k'uang*[b] ("mad"), *wang*[c] ("crooked" or "depraved"), and *wang*[d] ("emaciated or crippled").

What follows throughout the rest of this chapter are various descriptions of the sacred history of the paradise time—a time, as it is said, when men lived "in the midst of *hun-ming*." Like the state of sacred madness or the unique experience of unification with the Tao sought by the Taoist, the ancient men of the paradise time lived as "wild men" (*ch'ang-k'uang*).[72] This was a golden age where nothing was "ordered" according to the principles of "discriminating" knowledge (*chih*):

> [These ancient men] did not know directions. They ate and wandered [*yu*[c]] about in complete freedom, drumming their bellies [*ku fu*] and rejoicing.

The curious reference to the men of the paradise time "drumming their bellies" in carefree joy recalls the *Tao Te Ching*'s "belly knowledge" and the *Chuang Tzu*'s Hung-meng who went around dancing and "slapping his thighs" and is similar to the description of the golden age found in chapter 9 of the *Chuang Tzu*. There are no doubt shamanic implications here, but it is perhaps more revealing to recognize mythological connections with drumming and thunder symbolism. Granet, for example, notices that the "fools in the *Huai Nan Tzu* appear to be possessed by the Spirit of Thunder."[73] The same motif is seen in the *Shan Hai Ching* (chap. 13) having the totemic associations of the spirits of thunder and lightning, and signaling a moment of creative union or the folly of divine possession.[74] Here the thunder and lightning associations of Hu and Shu from the story of Emperor Hun-tun should be recalled.

The age of carefree abandonment and joy is further described in chapter 2 as the sacred time of the "Great Order" (*ta-ch'ih*) or the time of *mang-mang ch'en-ch'en*—terms that connote the idea of the *hun-tun* time. *Ch'en* in its reduplicated use with *mang* refers to a watery chaos condition and usually means "to sink or perish"—such as the compound *ch'en-lun* meaning "to perish." Furthermore, *lun* (and its cognate *lun* without the "water" radical) can have the meaning of "to drown" or "to engulf" and may be seen as related to the expression *hun-lun* found in the cosmogonic section of the *Lieh Tzu* (see below).

The "wild men" of this period are subsequently depicted as the "true men" of the ancient time whose condition the Taoist hopes to reattain. That is, he hopes to return individually to an "enlightened" condition (*ta-ming*) and reestablish for himself the "time of the Great Peace [*t'ai-p'ing*]." This was the time when, like the mythical Emperor Hun-tun, men were "established at the center of heaven and earth; wandered freely [*yu*[c]] in the midst [of this central realm] and embraced the *te* in a fused [*yang*] harmony [*ho*]."[75] During this period the Tao was like a web (*ching chi*) that bound all things into a closed cosmic unity. To return to this condition the sage must revert to the uncarved condition of Emperor Hun-tun: "[the sage] forgets [*wang*ᵃ] his viscera, abandons his eyes and ears, and floats alone [*tu fu yu*] in the realm of nothingness. United [*ho*] with heaven and earth, he has embraced the Primordial Simplicity [*t'ai-su*]." This passage goes on to introduce metallurgically relevant imagery (cf. the term *yang* above) by suggesting that the condition of having returned to the center may be related to the purity of jade found on the mythical cosmic mountain of K'un-lun, jade that has been refined and transformed for "three days and three nights."

The Taoist has now "obtained" (*te*ᵇ) the "one source" (*i yüan*) of life and has returned to the beginning of the Ten Thousand Things (*kuei yü wan wu chih ch'u*). His spirit (*shen*ᵃ) is stored in the *ling-fu* and again shares in the primordial condition of the creation time: "He is in the midst of the 'chaos' condition [*ming-ming chih chung*]." To achieve this condition he must, as in the *Tao Te Ching* and *Chuang Tzu*, remove his "face"—close up the openings bored into his original condition of wholeness:

> Close up the nine openings [*pi chiu ch'iao*] . . . and return to the condition of "non-distinguishing" [*wu-shih*] which is "chaos-like" [*mang-jan*].

Subsequent sections of this chapter elaborate on the idea of a past golden age that is called the time of *hun-tun ts'ang-ts'ang*. This was the age when "primordial unity had not been destroyed [*shun p'u wei san*]" and when all the "Ten Thousand Things enjoyed a great abundance."[76]

4. *Paradise Lost, One Body, and the Closure of the Senses*

To conclude my discussion of the *Huai Nan Tzu* I want to comment briefly on chapter 8 where the motif of paradise lost is especially pronounced and represents a more embellished variation on the description of the golden age (*hun-hun ts'ang-ts'ang*) just seen in chapter 2. In chapter 8, which like much of the *Huai Nan Tzu* is garbled and highly repetitious, the basic Taoist salvation theme is presented in the context of the fall from the paradise condition or what is initially called the *T'ai-ch'ing* or Most Pure Age.[77] This was a time of the natural harmony of cosmos, society, and man. In such a mythic age, "men's minds were contented and without artificiality [*pu wei*]."

Then came the "decadent age" (*shuai-shih*) when men gave into their inclinations "to bore" (*tso*) into the one body of earth and man in order to regulate and control the world by artificial human standards: "there was a rupture of the connection between *yin* and *yang* and the succession of the four seasons failed. Thunder brought destruction."

After this description of the fall into the bored order of the civilized condition, or what was called *luan*ᵃ in the *Chuang Tzu* and in other sections of the *Huai Nan Tzu*, the lessons of life that can be learned from the model of the ancient golden age are developed. The key issue is for man to learn how to rediscover the principle of balance and natural order. In the fallen condition, the third term of reunion is man or, more specifically, the "*ch'i*ᵃ of man." As the principle of the cosmic *ch'i*ᵃ was the third term of cosmogonic union and the principle of the perpetual return to and reunion of the one (*tao*) and the two (*yin* and *yang*, heaven and earth) in the *Tao Te Ching*, here it is asserted that man's *ch'i*ᵃ, or more properly the *ch'i*ᵃ of the emperor as the agent and model for all men, is responsible for the "harmony [*ho-ho*] of heaven and earth and the [continued] creative transformation [*tsao hua*] of the Ten Thousand Things through the principles of *yin* and *yang*."

This is a lesson that directly expresses the formula of microcosm-macrocosm since human knowledge and action must be "timely" to insure the return to, and maintenance of, the creative order and great transformation of all life. Learning the saving need for a constant periodic return to the beginning, the time of cosmic equilibrium and rebirth, is, therefore, equated with the transitional or chaos time of the "forty-six day period before the time of the winter solstice [*tung-chih*]."[78] This is the crucial ritual time of cosmic return or "closure," which is the precondition for either future growth or decay, creation or destruction:

> Heaven retains harmony [*han ho*] and does not descend; and the earth embosoms [*huai*] *ch'i*ᵃ and does not ascend [i.e., representing a return to the cosmogonically quiescent state of *tu*]. *Yin* and *yang* are stored up and waiting. [Their] breath is like a vast watery deep [*chin yen*] containing what is yet to be refined.

This passage ends with the refrain that "heaven, earth, and the universe are the body of one man," which is a phrase that reaffirms the textual basis for relating the early chaos cosmogony of *hun-tun* with the later cosmic body mythology of P'an-ku and Lao Tzu (Lao Chün).

In a subsequent passage, a second description of the golden age and its relevance for fallen man is presented. This was the "ancient time when men were unified [*t'ung*ᵃ] in their *ch'i*ᵃ with heaven and earth."[79] At this point the specific terminology of *hun-tun* is introduced since this time when man's *ch'i*ᵃ was in union with the cosmic body of heaven and earth, the condition of "three" as in the *Tao Te Ching*, is further identified as the period when men lived naturally in the "midst of the chaos condition [*hun-ming chih ch'ung*]." This primal condition of *hun-ming* is equated with Tao in Kau Yu's commentary.[80]

As with the other texts, a return to the chaos condition of primordial unity involves for the individual a "closure" (pi) of the sense openings (ears, eyes, heart, and mouth) or the protection of one's "essence" (ching).[81] By accomplishing this inward retreat one will be "submerged (or drowned) in Tao [tao lun]" (cf. the Lieh Tzu's technical use of the cosmogonic term of hun-lun). This closure, similar to the "wrapped up" or inchoate state of yin and yang during the winter solstice period, the pupa condition of an insect, or the closed, faceless condition of the Emperor Hun-tun, is the source of "the spirit light [shen-ming] which is hidden [tsang] in shapelessness [wu-hsing]." It constitutes the "return of spirit and essence to the 'perfect body' chih-chen]."[82]

Having returned to such a condition,

> The eye will be bright but not concerned with seeing; the ear will be acute but not concerned with hearing; the heart (mind) will be intelligent yet not anxious or thinking. . . .
> Essence [ching] fills the eye and so one sees clearly. It is present in the ear and so one hears acutely. It is in the mouth and so one speaks correctly. And it gathers in the heart (mind), so one is penetrating in thought.

"Therefore," as the passage goes on to say:

> The closure [pi] of the four senses means that the body is without trouble and that all of its individual parts are without sickness. There is no death, no life, no gaps or excess. This is called [the condition or "body" of] the True Man [chen-jen].

The passage concludes by contrasting the "perfect or true body" of the Taoist sage who has returned to the beginning with the ordinary fallen or disordered condition (luan[a]) of man.[83] Luan[a] in this context is understood as the abuse of the senses or what is said to be the excessive, ornamental, or extravagant use of the five elements (wu-hsing). As it explains further on in the description of the improper use of the five elements, the loss of, and failure to return to, the natural "chaos-order" of the Tao is a matter of tso—the destructive or excessive carving up, or boring into, the primal integrity of the world and man.[84] These passages represent a summation of almost all of the terminology and motifs related to the hun-tun theme. In this way chapter 8 is one of the best demonstrations of the continuity and coherence of the mythic intentionality and meaning in early Taoist thought from the pre-Ch'in works of the Tao Te Ching and Chuang Tzu down to the Han dynasty.

THE LIEH TZU: GOURD MASTER'S RETURN

My analysis of the Lieh Tzu will be necessarily truncated and directed only toward the selection of several passages that most clearly demonstrate the ubiquity of the chaos theme.[85] Most helpful is to examine the opening sections of chapter 1 where there are a series of parables directly concerned with creation themes. The first of these passages is attributed to Lieh Tzu's legendary master, the already encountered Hu Tzu or "Gourd Master," whose teaching reasserts the familiar mythic scenario seen in the other texts.[86] As with the other Hu Tzu passages in the *Chuang Tzu* and in chapter 2 of the *Lieh Tzu*, Hu Tzu's teaching harkens back to the mythic wisdom of the cosmic egg-gourd. It is the philosophy of a "dead man" who was able to return to the condition that existed "before we first came out of our Ancestor."[87] In chapter 1 the enigmatic meaning of this is explained in terms of its connection to the cosmogonic theme of the constant "return" of the "unborn" (*pu-sheng*) and "unchanging" (*pu-hua*):

> There are the born and the Unborn, the changing and the Unchanging. The Unborn can give birth to the born, the Unchanging can change the changing. The born cannot escape birth, the changing cannot escape change; therefore birth and change are the norm. Things for which birth and change are the norm are at all times being born and changing. They simply follow the alternations of the *yin* and *yang* and the four seasons.

The significance of this cosmogonic refrain is that it expressly links the terminology of *sheng*[a] and *hua*[a] (change or transformation), which were separate in the *Tao Te Ching* and *Chuang Tzu*, as well as expanding on the *Tao Te Ching*'s themes of the primordial Tao as the "nameless" (*wu-ming*) and "shapeless" (*wu-hsing*) "nothingness" (*wu*[b]) of "chaotic wholeness" (*hun-ch'eng*) before heaven and earth (*Tao Te Ching*, chaps. 1 and 25). The verses that immediately follow this in the *Lieh Tzu* imply that the law of the Tao's constant "return" and perpetual creative activity is something that microcosmically applies to man as well as to the universe:

> The Unborn is by our side yet alone [*tu*].
> The Unchanging goes forth and returns [*fu*[a]].
> Going forth and returning, its successions
>   are endless;
> By our side and alone [*tu*], the Tao is bound-
>   less.

As a further development of the meaning of Hu Tzu's teaching, chapter 6 of the *Tao Te Ching*, attributed to the lost "Book of the Yellow Emperor," is invoked:[88]

> The Valley Spirit never dies:
> It is called the dark female.
> Is called the root of Heaven and Earth.
> It goes on and on, something which almost exists;
> Use it, it never runs out.

The section that follows these opening verses offers a further expansion on the creation theme in terms of Lieh Tzu's own teaching.[89] Lieh Tzu says that in the past the sage kings had civilized the world and had "reduced Heaven and Earth to a system by means of *yin* and *yang*." But the crucial question remains as to what took place *before* the civilizing activities of the culture heroes—since "if all that has shape was born from the shapeless [*wu-hsing*], from what were Heaven and Earth born?"

The answer that is provided is a restatement of the sacred history of the chaos time and is similar to that offered by the *Huai Nan Tzu*. Before the two things of heaven and earth (or *yin* and *yang*) were born as separate shaped "things," there were four developmental states or conditions: *t'ai-i*[b] ("primal change or transformation"), *t'ai-ch'u* ("primal commencement"), *t'ai-shih* ("primal beginnings"), and *t'ai-su* ("primal simplicity"). All of these terms may be taken as names for that "One" primordial Tao that, as in chapter 3 of the *Huai Nan Tzu*, manifests an internal life or metamorphosis resembling embryological development. A sequence of creative development is presented that is roughly analogous to the stages of three, seven, or nine seen previously— although in this case there are actually five stages, which probably reflects the influence of the *yin-yang-wu-hsing* philosophy.[90] Thus:

> Primal Change is before there is any visible appearance of *ch'i*[a]. Primal Commencement was the beginning of *ch'i*[a] and Primal Beginning was the start of the shaping of *ch'i*[a]. Primal Simplicity was the beginning of substance. [But these three things of] *ch'i*[a], shape [*hsing*] and substance [*ch'i*[b]] were not yet separated from each other.

This would appear to correspond to the stage of *hun-ch'eng* or the mysterious condition of "three" seen in chapter 42 of the *Tao Te Ching*, a condition that was also a perfect blending of *ch'i*[a]. Yang Pai-leng's commentary, therefore, specifically identified it with the *Tao Te Ching*'s *hun-ch'eng* and the *Chuang Tzu*'s Emperor Hun-tun. It is the condition of the "Great Abyss" (*t'ai-hsü*) that is "congealed and still" (*ning chi*).[91]

Indeed, in the *Lieh Tzu* there is a fifth stage that completes the previous four stages and blends the "three": *ch'i*[a], form, and substance. This is the stage called *hun-lun*; the character *lun* is a homophonic analogue to *hun*[d] *or tun*[a] and is in a word-family having the "chaos-order" connotations of "complete," "whole," "constant or regular," "revolving or turning," and, in reference to the flood or primordial-waters imagery, the idea of "eddying water," "ruined, engulfed, lost." The condition of *hun-lun* is explained in terms that recall the ideas of *hun-ch'eng* and the "third term" from the *Tao Te Ching*: "*Hun-lun* means that the Ten Thousand Things were chaotically [*hun-lun*] whole yet not separate from each other.''

Another cosmogonic passage immediately follows the above.[92] It essentially repeats the ideas dealt with in the preceding verses but equates the five-stage scenario with the symbolism of one, seven, and nine. The passage opens by paraphrasing the *Tao Te Ching* (chaps. 14 and 21) concerning the mysterious nature of the Tao: "In looking at it, it cannot be seen; in listening to it, it cannot be heard; and in grasping for it, it cannot be touched."

This is the Tao of "Change" or "Simplicity," without shape (*wu-hsing*) or bounds. It experienced an inner transformation and became one (*pien erh wei i*). Then, "the One transformed [*pien*[b]] seven times and the seven transformed nine times. [This] brought the process to completion." Upon reaching the stage of completion (three, five, seven, or nine; or that condition which is also called the *hun-ch'eng, hun-tun,* or *hun-lun*), the process cyclically reverses itself and reverts to unity: "then the transformations reverse and become one [*fu pien erh wei i*]."

This "one" is the source for a new creation or a new process of metamorphosis wherein heaven and earth assume the form of "higher" and "lower." This new creation culminates in the creation of man. The "third term" of the "chaotically blended" *ch'i*[a] (*chung ho ch'i*, cf. chap. 42 of *Tao Te Ching*) between the two things of heaven and earth "makes man" (*wei jen*).

This whole passage presents different numerological systematizations of a single cosmogonic idea. The third, fifth, seventh, or ninth stage is a time or condition of completion and reversal perfectly reflecting the condition of primordial unity. *Hun-lun, hun-tun, hun-ch'eng,* and so on are the names for this sacred creation condition, a condition that may be reappropriated by the Taoist in his emulation of the Tao's constant return to the beginning.

1. *Infancy, Death, and Rebirth: Man's "True Home"*

Throughout the rest of chapter 1 the saving message of life reappears in various ways, but it is always something that finds its source in the mystery of the Tao's *creatio continua*. In this way the initiatory symbolism of returning to the condition of either infancy or death is homologous with the cosmic return to the chaos condition. This is demonstrated by several passages from chapter 1. One of these states that the life of a man passes through four great changes or transformations (*hua*[a])—infancy, youth, old age, and death.[93] But in this scheme, infancy and death are symbolically equivalent. Death from the perspective of the cosmic life of the Tao is, therefore, but a return to the condition of infancy where "one's energies are concentrated [*ch'i chuan*] and one's inclinations are unified [*chih i*ᵇ]—the ultimate of harmony [*ho chih chih*]." When a man dies it is a return to the beginning, which recalls Chuang Tzu's eulogy to his dead wife.[94] Here it is said that when a man dies, "he goes to his rest, rises again to his zenith."

As noted by another passage in chapter 1, one ancient term for "the dead," *kuei*ᵃ, means " 'one who has gone home [*kuei*ᵇ],' they have gone back to their true home."[95] The method of Hu Tzu as a Gourd Master consequently involves a return to the Tao as the primordial gourd-egg. By accomplishing this kind of initiatory return, it can therefore be said that he resembled a "dead-man"—one who had reexperienced the faceless and shapeless condition of the beginning.[96] Returning to the beginning as the fundamental art of the Tao (meditation and trance) is experientially both to die and to be reborn. It is the "Great Transformation" of Chuang Tzu's "Butterfly Way."

Suggesting at times the additional influence of the *hsien*ᵃ cult or the school of Yang Chu with its emphasis on "tending life,"[97] the theme of death as return runs throughout chapter 1 and other sections of the *Lieh Tzu*. Death is constantly said to be "a return to where we set out from when we were born,"[98] or in another passage:

> Dying is the virtue in us going to its destination. The men of old called a dead man "a man who has gone back" [*kuei*ᵇ]. Saying that the dead have gone back they implied that the living are travellers. The traveller who forgets to go back is a man who mistakes his home.[99]

Above all, the Taoist here, as in the *Huai Nan Tzu*, is one who must remember how to "go back" to his true home while still living.

As with the other early Taoist texts, the remembrance of the myth of chaos implies specific methods of returning to the primordial condition and requires a symbolic recapitulation of the stages of creation. One example that is found in both chapters 2 and 4 of the *Lieh Tzu* is the method called *hsin-ning* or the "concentration-congealing of the mind." It is said that after a certain period of time (three, five, seven, and nine years) the Taoist is able to go back and reexperience, in a sense, the primordial condition of Emperor Hun-tun. At the culmination of the meditation process of "congealing the mind," the sage's "bones and flesh were fused" and "his eyes were like his ears, his ears like his nose, and his nose like his mouth." The sage is like a dead man; and in contrast to normal men, he is faceless: "my eyes became like my ears, my ears like my nose, my nose like my mouth; everything was the same."[100]

2. Paradise Lost and Recovered: The "Journey of the Spirit"

It is pointless to multiply any more examples of these fundamental themes; but inasmuch as my emphasis has been on the individual Taoist's "arts of Mr. Hun-tun," it is worthwhile to mention at least briefly some of the symbolism of paradise lost also found in the *Lieh Tzu*. In general, the symbolism of the paradise time is congruent with the imagery already seen in the other texts; and, like the *Huai Nan Tzu*, the *Lieh Tzu* is particularly rich in golden age passages that preserve remnants of ancient mythologies (see especially chaps. 2, 3, and 5).

One interesting aspect of these new descriptive passages is that the symbolism of K'un-lun and K'ung-t'ung as paradise places connecting heaven and earth are presented in terms of images suggesting the idea of the cosmic egg-gourd, which is constantly related to the overall theme of chaos. In this sense, "paradise" is found both at the beginning of time and, contemporaneously, at the ends of the earth—that is, beyond the borders of the civilized world. As noted before, the spatial and temporal dimensions of paradise are collapsed in Taoism. As it says in chapter 2, the paradisical "place" that one returns to is a "place that cannot be reached by boat or carriage or on foot, only by a journey of the spirit [*shen-yu*]."[101] One's "true home" is within the "mind" and "belly" of man.

In the *Lieh Tzu* there are several descriptions of paradise lands that speak of a mythic "calabash mountain" (Fang-hu or Hu-ling shan in chap. 5). Hu-ling mountain (Calabash or Urn Peak) is, for example, "shaped like a pot with a small mouth" and is located in the "utmost north," the traditional region of the Yellow Springs or land of the dead.[102] It lies outside the region civilized by Yü after the great flood. Hu-ling mountain, furthermore, stands in the center of a paradise land, irrigating the country and rejuvenating the people with water issuing from the "divine spring" on its summit. As for the fabled country itself, it is a place of perfect equilibrium, both cosmically and socially:

> The climate is mild, and there are no epidemics. The people are gentle and compliant by nature, do not quarrel or contend, have soft hearts and weak bones, are never proud or envious. Old and young live as equals and no one is ruler or subject; men and women mingle freely, without go-betweens and betrothal presents. Living close to the waters, they have no need to plough and sow, nor to weave and clothe themselves, since the climate is so warm. They live out their span of a hundred years, without sickness and early deaths, and the people proliferate in countless numbers, knowing pleasure and happiness, ignorant of decay, old age, sorrow and anguish. By custom they are lovers of music; they hold hands and take turns to sing ballads, and

never stop singing all day. Hungry and tiring they drink the Divine Spring, and are soothed and refreshed body and mind, and so drunk, if they take too much, that they do not wake for ten days. When they bathe and wash their hair in the Divine Spring, their complexions grow sleek and moist, and the fragrant smell does not leave them for ten days.

A detailed analysis of such golden age passages in the *Lieh Tzu* would be most revealing; but perhaps it is sufficient here to comment, along with Bauer, on one other similar passage. This is the passage from chapter 3 that describes the land of Ku-mang, which is distinguished from the civilized central realm (*chung-kuo*) of China proper.[103] As representative of a "chaos" realm outside of the civilized order of the central kingdom, Ku-mang (literally the "Ancient Chaos Land") is a place where all the opposites are perfectly equalized:

> The *yin* and *yang* breaths do not meet there, so there is no distinction between cold and heat. The light of the sun and moon does not shine there, so there is no distinction between day and night. Its people do not eat or wear clothes and sleep most of the time waking once in fifty days. They think that what they do in dreams is real, and what they see waking is unreal.

Bauer remarks that the *Lieh Tzu*'s sympathy for the Ku-mang land is "demonstrably characteristic of Taoism from the very beginning" since it always stresses "preexistence rather than excessive existence."[104] In Bauer's masterful study of Chinese conceptions of paradise, it is almost always the case that "the genuinely paradisiacal lands are . . . like the Ku-mang land."[105] Although not entirely absent from Confucianism, it is especially Taoism that stresses the cosmogonic condition of "preexistence" in relation to the idea of paradise. For Bauer, and in essential agreement with my analysis of the chaos theme, this special emphasis on the ideal of "preexistence" is because "this phase *prior* to the polarization of the fundamental forces can hardly be distinguished from the stage of balance *between* those same forces."[106] This is but another way of saying that in the mythological logic of Taoism, three equals one.

3. *The Paradise Within: Remembering to Forget*

Like the *Huai Nan Tzu* and the *Chuang Tzu*, these descriptions of paradise are primarily illustrative of the individual's mystic journey back to an experience of the primordial void of the creation time. In fact, the idea of the primal void or abyss (the *kuei-hsü*) is found in the *Lieh Tzu* as a kind of bottomless whirlpool that contains five floating paradise islands or mountains (one of which is Fang-hu or the calabash mountain).[107] Moreover, the idea of the paradise condition that is to be sought within the mind of man is clearly indicated in both chapters 3 and 5 where the story of King Mu's dreamlike "spirit journey" (*shen-yu*) to K'un-lun is the underlying context for the various golden age passages.[108]

In the spirit of the "butterfly parable" from the *Chuang Tzu* where dream and reality are constantly blurred in the great transformation of things, these passages from the *Lieh Tzu* suggest that, as "dreaming" was the normal state of mind in the Ku-mang land, a Taoist practicing the art of Tao is able to forget the deceptive surface reality of everyday consciousness and, by submitting to a dreamlike or undifferentiated consciousness attained in meditation, remember the primal state of man, the condition of man before the fall.

It is finally suggested that the mind of the sage who has fully returned to the realm of Calabash mountain, K'un-lun, or the Ku-mang land is beyond even the conscious and unconscious distinctions of the awakened and dreaming mind. He enters a land of perfect equilibrium and harmony where all dualities are blurred into oneness. This unique state when "the spirit is concentrated" (*shen ning*) is said in chapter 3 to be the condition where

> Imagination and dreaming diminish of themselves. What those who trust the time when they are awake do not explain, and those who trust in dreams do not fathom, is the arrival and passing of the transformations of things.[109]

This passage concludes by remarking that "it is no empty saying that the True Men of old forgot themselves when awake and did not dream when they slept!"

The secret of returning to the undifferentiated knowledge and action of paradise is to forget to remember one's fallen condition, one's reliance on the bored openings of face; or as it says in another parable from chapter 3:

> "Formerly when I forgot," said Hua-tzu [a figure who had lost his "memory" and was beyond the "understanding" of someone like Confucius who sought to waken Hua-tzu to the everyday world], "I was boundless [*tang-tang*]; I did not notice whether heaven and earth existed or not. Now suddenly I remember; and all the disasters and recoveries, gains and losses, joys and sorrows, loves and hates of twenty or thirty years past rise up in a thousand tangled threads. I fear that all the disasters and recoveries, gains and losses, joys and sorrows, loves and hates still to come will confound [*luan*[a]] my heart just as much. Shall I never again be able to return to and attain the [*fu te*] moment of forgetfulness?"[110]

Hua-tzu's problem was one of a natural amnesia that serves as a general illustration of the Taoist point of view in contrast to the Confucian perspective. Most important is that the Taoists had a specific solution to Hua-tzu's lament of

never being able to find again a "moment of forgetfulness"—that is, the arts of
return that made it possible to recover the bliss of the paradise or *hun-tun*
condition hidden in the depths of the human mind.

As it says in chapter 2 these arts involve a "journey of the spirit."[111] Having
accomplished such a mystic journey backward in time and space, the Highest
Man (*chih-jen*) "walks under-water and does not suffocate, treads fire and does
not burn, walks above the myriad things and does not tremble." Such a man has
learned "to hold fast to his purest *ch'i*[a] [*ch'un ch'i chih shou*]" and "to grasp
and fathom the Unshaped [*pu-hsing*] from which things are created, the
Changeless [*wu suo hua*] by which they are brought to a stop."[112] In this
country of the mind;

> There are no teachers and leaders; all things follow their natural course
> [*tzu-jan*]. The people have no cravings and lusts; all men follow their natural
> course. They are incapable of delighting in life or hating death, and therefore
> none of them dies before his time. They do not know how to prefer
> themselves to others, and so they neither love nor hate. They do not know
> how to turn their faces to things or turn their backs, go with the stream or
> push against it, so nothing benefits or harms them. There is nothing at all
> which they grudge or regret, nothing which they dread or envy. They go into
> water without drowning, into fire without burning; hack them, flog them,
> there is no wound nor pain; poke them, scratch them, there is no ache or itch.
> They ride space as though walking the solid earth, sleep on the void as
> though on their beds; clouds and mist do not hinder their sight, thunder does
> not confuse their hearing, beauty and ugliness do not disturb their hearts,
> mountains and valleys do not trip their feet—for they make only journeys of
> the spirit [*shen-yu*].[113]

The symbolism of paradise as a metaphor of undifferentiated knowledge, or
the condition of preexistence as the primordial balance of all opposites, is
something that colors the imagery of the Taoist holy man in the *Lieh Tzu* as well
as in the other texts. In chapter 2 of the *Lieh Tzu*, and in similar passages found
in the *Huai Nan Tzu* and the *Chuang Tzu*, the condition of the "Spirit Man"
(*shen-jen*) is described in terms basically analogous to the Ku-mang land or
country of the Calabash peak. By returning to the beginning, the Spirit man has
reentered paradise:

> His mind is like a bottomless spring, his body like a virgin's [*ch'u-nü*]. He
> knows neither intimacy nor love, yet immortals and sages serve him as
> ministers. He inspires no awe, he is never hungry, yet the eager and diligent
> act as his messengers. He is without kindness and bounty, but others have
> enough by themselves; he does not store and save, but he himself never
> lacks.[114]

The passage ends by describing the new uncarved territory of his mind and mode of being in a way that echoes the harmony of Ku-mang land:

> The *yin* and *yang* are always in tune, the sun and moon always shine, the four seasons are always regular, wind and rain are always temperate, breeding is always timely, the harvest is always rich, and there are no plagues to ravage the land, no early deaths to afflict men, animals have no diseases, and ghosts have no uncanny echoes.

4. *In the "Country of Women"*

As a final point, and something that leads directly into a consideration of the mythic context of this symbolism as well as the symbolism of the faceless Emperor Hun-tun, the Spirit Man in the paradise condition is described as someone "who inhales the wind and drinks the dew, and does not eat the five grains."[115] This reference is clearly related to the development of specific Taoist dietary techniques of "nourishing the *ch'i*" (*yang-ch'i* or *yang-hsing*);[116] but such descriptive details can also be shown to be rooted in the mythic themes of the "people without anuses" and "the country of women" where people lacked the normal alimentary apertures and were nourished by the wind and the steam or vapor of food.[117]

The importance of such comparative considerations will be developed in the next two chapters. Let me only remark here that an analysis of the mythic repertory associated with Taoist symbolism may help to link the ideas of the cosmic egg-gourd, paradise land, and especially the paradigmatic tale of Emperor Hun-tun into a coherent pattern of thought. As a forecast of the significance of this, it should be noted that in the *Lieh Tzu*'s description of the Spirit Man who had returned to the beginning, his "body was like a virgin's." He had taken on the characteristics of a hermaphrodite (the equilibrium of male and female); and he was, in a sense, "faceless," or at least mouthless, in his inability to eat and drink normally.

The continuity of this kind of symbolism is suggested by Schipper's observation that in later Taoism the adept is said to urinate in a squatting position like a woman![118] As it says in chapter 41 of the *Tao Te Ching*, when an ordinary man confronts the Tao, or the "Taoist body" as the case may be, he can only, somewhat embarrassingly, laugh.[119] Gourd Master's teachings are surely peculiar and even frightening (recall the shaman who fled in terror when Hu Tzu's primordial body was revealed). This is only to say that a true transformation of man, both body and spirit, is no easy or "normal" matter. The return to the chaos condition, which is the basis for the saving transformation in Taoism, mythically reveals man as more than conventionally human. Myth, not history, tells the true story of human identity.

PART THREE

AND ALL THE KING'S HORSES AND ALL THE KING'S MEN

COMPARATIVE ANALYSIS

It all gathers,
humming *[hun-hun tun-tun]*
in the egg.
> —*Gary Synder,*
> *"The Egg," in*
> *Turtle Island*

Somewhere there must be primordial figures the bodies of which are only images. If one could see them one would know the link between matter and thought; what being consists of.
> —Flaubert, *The Temptation*
> *of St. Anthony*, in
> Stanley Diamond, *In Search*
> *of the Primitive*

6

EGG, GOURD, AND DELUGE: TOWARD A TYPOLOGY OF THE CHAOS THEME

The heavens are like a hen's egg and as round as
a crossbow bullet; the earth is like the yolk of
the egg, and lies alone in the center. Heaven is
large and earth small. Inside the lower part of
the heavens there is water. The heavens are
supported by *ch'i*, the earth floats on the waters.

—*Hun I Chu*
(trans. Joseph Needham)

I N THE PREVIOUS chapters I have shown that the early Taoist texts reveal a
pattern of religious meaning structured on the underlying cosmogonic
theme of chaos. As was evident throughout my analysis of the complex
constellation of symbols associated with the creation scenario of chaos, the
thematic paradigm of *hun-tun* does not represent a single mythic narrative.
Rather, as the texts themselves are in great measure composite in nature and
extend over a time span from pre-Ch'in to Han, the mythic structure is a
combination of a number of different mythological traditions and has gone
through various religious, philosophical, and literary transformations. The
problem is simply that while the early Taoist tradition roots its message of
salvation in the image of the primordial chaos time, order, or condition, the

thematic structure is clearly made up of different typological units that originally derive from diverse cultural and religious situations.

As a further step in my analysis it is imperative to try to establish some of the particular mythological heritage of the *hun-tun* theme. The relevance and importance of this task is that even a preliminary elucidation of some of the basic types of myth associated with the *hun-tun* theme, in the first instance, will help to clarify some of the archaic cultural and religious matrices of thought related to the origins of Taoism and, secondly, will provide a basis for a comparative consideration and refinement of the meaning and significance of the early Taoist vision of reality. The study of early Chinese mythology is still in its infancy, but it will nevertheless be possible to show that the chief typological units of creation myth linked to the chaos theme ultimately support and amplify a single ontological and religious intentionality.

THE PROBLEM OF CULTURAL ORIGINS

An examination of the cultural and mythological origins of Taoist tradition is crucial for a fuller understanding of the chaos theme; but I want to emphasize that no final solution is possible. The issue of tracing the cultural and historical origins of a civilizational tradition as complex as Taoism is always fraught with intractable problems relating to the paucity of historical evidence and the presuppositions of methodology. There is, however, sufficient evidence to say that most of the mythic units associated with the exposition of the *hun-tun* theme generally suggests a "southern" focus of cultural origin.

For some scholars such as Izutsu and Fung a belief in the southern origin of Taoism is prompted by what is seen to be a special connection with the ancient tradition of Ch'u, especially Ch'u shamanism, which was an important cultural component in the development of Chinese civilization during the Chou period.[1] There is, no doubt, a good deal of truth in this observation but it is, at the same time, too much of an oversimplification. A more expansive and balanced perspective on the "southern" origins of the mythology associated with the chaos theme is indicated by the work of several scholars who point to the general linguistic and cultural significance of the so-called Austroasiatic and Austronesian (=Mayalo-Polynesian) traditions or, more particularly, to the role of various local tribal traditions in the ancient cultural areas of south China, Indo-China, and insular southeast Asia.[2] Moreover, while the ultimate origins of Ch'u probably go back to "northern" cultural sources (northeastern, northwestern, or "Hunnish"), even to the extent of having possible connections with the ancient Shang tradition and showing some traces of Altaic and Indo-European influence, the traditional (i.e., post-Chou) significance of the

Ch'u culture is at least to some degree related to this same complex of "southern" local cultures.[3]

Maspero and Erkes were the first to emphasize the importance of primitive tribal culture and mythology for the study of Chinese myth and, as Inez de Beauclair notes for the tribal folklore of the Miao, "the motives of their myths, which they share with a number of peoples of southeast Asia and certain islands of the Pacific, may preserve the clue to the ancient Chinese cosmogony."[4] The implications of this for a reconstruction of ancient Chinese mythology have been especially developed by Eberhard, who traces "chains" of mythology and ritual back to specific archaic local cultures that were formative factors in the shaping of Chinese civilization. In this way he finds that the chain linked with the *hun-tun* theme is primarily reflective of an extremely ancient southern Liao[b] (=Lao) culture, along with traits coming from the Yao[b] and Thai cultures. For Eberhard this cultural matrix most probably can be traced back to an Austroasiatic cultural sphere. Eberhard concludes that "it is a chain that was important for the high culture during the earliest times."[5]

Eberhard's theory of "local cultures" and identifiable "chains" is controversial in theory and not wholly demonstrable in terms of evidence; but the work of Porée-Maspero, Kaltenmark, and Ho Ting-jui helps to substantiate and develop many of his findings, especially with regard to the cultural underpinnings of the *hun-tun* theme. Thus, Porée-Maspero's study of the Cambodian cycle of calendric rites is primarily addressed to an analysis of the myth-ritual pattern that she calls the ancient Man cultural complex. For Porée-Maspero, the Man Complex represents a religio-cultural pattern that is to some degree connected with Central Asiatic (especially the Shaka, Yue-Tche, Hun, and Parthians), Austroasiatic, and Austronesian language families and underlies many aspects of "barbarian" Chinese (i.e., such traditional Chinese ethnic groups as the Jung, Ti, I, Miao, Man, Yao[b], Liao[b], etc.),[6] Indo-Chinese, and southeast Asian traditions. Ho's work is similarly directed toward a comparative analysis of the folklore and mythology associated with insular, south Chinese, and Indo-Chinese cultures that can be traced back to Asiatic and Austronesian origins.[7]

Finally, Kaltenmark's monograph on the legends and symbolism associated with the honorary Chinese military title of *Fu-po chiang chün* ("general tamer of the flood") builds on the earlier work of Maspero and is directly pertinent to these considerations.[8] The legends of the Fu-po go back to the later Han period, or earlier, and are attributed to the historical figure of Ma Yüan who suppressed the revolt of the ancient Annamite tribes of Indo-China in A.D. 42. As Kaltenmark points out, the title of Fu-po, while applied to a historical figure and incident, harbors complex mythological motifs and refers to the heroic taming of the southern barbarians who had not been fully incorporated into the Chinese empire. From the Chinese point of view, the barbarians were usually understood in mythical terms so that the "flood" referred to in this official title suggests the mythic equation of "barbarian" with the *ssu-hai* or "four seas" outside the boundaries of the central kingdom.[9]

A parallel instance of a foundational "history" of a hero rooted in mythic themes is provided by Porée-Maspero, who analyzes the Chinese accounts of Hun-hui (or Hun-t'ien[b]), a barbarian hero from the south, and the origins of the kingdom of Fu-nan in Indo-China. It is significant, as Porée-Maspero remarks, that the name of the hero, Hun-hui, most probably represents a mythic theme transformed into a historical account since "*hun*, or *kun*, designates 'troubled waters,' a chaos, and *hui* has the sense of a 'river which has overflowed its banks' or 'disorder, confusion,' "[10] Moreover, it might also be noted that the alternate term for *hui* is *t'ien* (or *tien, chen*), which connotes the "settlement" of a kingdom or, more mythically, the rumbling and crashing sounds of drums and thunder. Porée-Maspero concludes, therefore, that the "name of the hero was 'deluge.' Can it be simply by chance that the accounts of the origins of Fu-nan reveal a story of the hero-saviour of the deluge?"[11]

Kaltenmark demonstrates that, in the process of civilizing the barbarians, the mythology and legends of the southern tribes were adopted or sinicized into an official Chinese ideology of cosmological and historical order. The symbolism related to the figure of the Fu-po was originally derived from various southern barbarian myths dealing with a demiurge hero (especially in the form of a dog, horse, or serpent) who orders the chaotic waters of the creation time. In this way, for example, the dog god P'an-hu of the Man culture is similar to the demiurge P'an-ku—"both are related with the deluge and chaos."[12] More generally, the figure of the Fu-po assimilates the mythological symbolism of the barbarian myths "where a demiurge puts an end to the deluge" and subsequently gives rise to a new creation.[13] The ambivalent hero of the creation time is at least partially identified with the vanquished chaos condition since in the creative act of establishing the ordered or human world, the demiurge always "risks reconstituting a new chaos by reuniting the assailed Heaven and submerged Earth into a single unformed mass."[14] As in the Emperor Hun-tun story from the *Chuang Tzu* where "lightning [Hu and Shu] put an end to Chaos by giving his sack-like form a human figure, Fu-po, as a great military figure, puts an end to anarchy by subduing the barbarians with the thunder of his drums and the virtue of his arrows [these are also details in the Hun-hui accounts]. . . . The Chinese tried to 'sinicize' the barbarian divinities: their military becomes the thunder which represents celestial justice; the vanquished divinities, chained to a column, become the guardians of the Chinese order."[15]

As indicated by this quotation, many of the mythic motifs uncovered by Kaltenmark are identical with the theme of chaos found in the Taoist texts. Kaltenmark's findings, therefore, support the contention that there is a special southern or "barbarian" focus for the mythological symbolism associated with *hun-tun*. Kaltenmark's analysis also helps to clarify the process of "siniciza-tion" or the "Chinese" reinterpretation of elements from various local cul-tures—that is, the process whereby mythic themes from local religious cults are reworked into an official sacred history that validates the imperial order. The imperial or Confucianized "sinicization" of the barbarian myths associated with the figure of Fu-po represents an obverse parallel to the Taoist assimilation of many of the same materials. Whereas in the official version the emphasis is on the heroic triumph over a destructive chaos condition (deluge, barbarian revolt, etc.) and the reestablishment and preservation of the civilized order, the Taoist reinterpretation of similar mythic themes stresses the artificiality of the human order and the need to reidentify with the condition or creature of chaos. Furthermore, it is important to realize that in the Confucian and Taoist sinicized versions of tribal mythology the original demiurgic figure (animal ancestor) is fundamentally ambiguous with respect to the chaos condition and can be either the heroic "tamer of the flood" or the agent responsible for, and identified with, the return of chaos.

Both Ho and Porée-Maspero's findings, along with Kaltenmark's corrobo-rating work, will prove to be valuable in the next chapter when I set out the salvation pattern of egg-gourd-deluge; but at this point I would like only to stress the relevance of Porée-Maspero's thesis for suggesting a general linguis-tic, historical, and cultural foundation for the "foreign" or "barbarian" connotations associated with the *hun-tun* theme in Taoism. Porée-Maspero, in fact, describes the overall religio-cultural pattern of the southern Man tradition as the "*k'un-lun* complex" or what could also be called the *hun-tun* com-plex.[16] Functionally, as I will develop below, the K'un-lun mythology (themes of deluge, animal ancestor, and the salvation of a primal couple in a gourd-drum boat) is closely related to many of the primary symbolic motifs found in the Taoist use of the chaos theme. *K'un-lun* is a term (as well as the term *hun-tun*) initially related to the ancient Jung tribes in Chinese texts and "the name of K'un-lun was equally used to designate the populations of Indo-China: Chams, Khmers, inhabitants of the Prome region."[17] Porée-Maspero goes on to say:

K'un-lun* was primitively the name of one of the Jung tribes, and it is in relation to the Jung that we find the first historical mention of bronze drums. Certain Jung were also said to be born from a dog and they are also associated with the downfall of the Yin [Shang] . . . M. Rolf Stein has shown that the theme of the calabash-gourd as a perfect closed world, grotto or ancestral cavern, and the *cornucopia* motifs, are all equivalent to the idea of *k'un-lun* which is also related to the theme of chaos as the vast watery condition of the flood.[18]

In this sense the myth-ritual pattern reconstructed by Porée-Maspero depicts K'un-lun as a veritable Mt. Ararat, which appeared in the midst of the chaotic waters of the deluge and served as the landing place for the gourd-drum-boat of the primordial couple. This was also the place for the subsequent creation of man and the regeneration of the world.[19]

Porée-Maspero notes that the use of coupled words where only the initial sound is differentiated, such as *hun-tun* and *k'un-lun* (as well as many archaic Sanskrit words like *Pulinda-Kulinda, Anga-Vanga, Kosala-Tosala*, etc.), may betray the influence of the ancient Man cultural complex and, linguistically speaking, reveal a linkage with that "vast family of Austroasiatic languages which in India is related to the Munda, or Kolarian, languages."[20] There is, however, no monolithic solution to the problem of linguistic origins since the word *hun*[d] shows a complex affinity with various central and western Asiatic nomadic cultures (i.e., the Huns and the Hsuing-nu), which have perhaps some ultimate connection with Indo-European languages and traditions.[21]

From the standpoint of the imperial Chinese tradition, inculcated with the chauvinistic values of Confucianism, words like *hun-tun* and *k'un-lun*, which were originally associated with mythologies of the deluge and chaos, became general derogatory expressions for uncouth, uncivil, or "barbarian" peoples. Maenchen-Helfen points out, for example, that the term *hun*[d] was used by the Chinese as a "transcription of **aryun* 'half-breed,' the offspring of a mixed marriage"; and Link has noted that the famous Buddho-Taoist Tao-an was called "Little K'un-lun"—an epithet that was "used as a vulgar term of opprobrium in a somewhat similar way that 'little Darky' has been used in our own language."[22]

Despite the general "barbarian," "asiatic," or "southern" (used broadly to refer to a mixture of cultural factors some of which originally had a central or northwestern cultural origin) locus of this terminology, it is important to reiterate that this does not make the *hun-tun* theme in Taoism essentially non-Chinese. Different local cultures go back to the very beginnings of the Chinese civilization in the neolithic and Shang periods and were integral factors in the shaping of the high tradition throughout the Chou and Han periods.[23] The real issue of the foreignness of the *hun-tun* terminology is more a matter of the evaluation and interpretation of Chinese civilization from the standpoint of what became the official or orthodox ideology of Confucianism. It must be remembered that Confucianism itself also harbors important traits that may be labeled as ''barbarian'' in origin.[24] It is therefore not so much the case that *kun-lun* or *hun-tun* were really foreign words or concepts but that they were terms applied to those elements outside the norms of the self-defined Great Tradition of Confucianism.

Pertinent to this whole discussion is the need to avoid theories that tend to resolve the contrast between Confucianism and Taoism into a simple north-south cultural polarity—the view that the more ancient and more properly ''Chinese'' northern cultural matrix engendered Confucianism as its basic ideological and symbolic mode of expression and that later extrinsic additions from southern ''barbarian'' cultures nurtured Taoism as a basic mode of expression.[25] The problem is that such theories grow out of the attempt to validate the traditional self-image of Confucianism as the purest manifestation of Chinese culture. From a more neutral historical perspective that respects the complexity of Chinese cultural origins, it is almost possible to stand this type of xenophobic theory on its head. Thus the so-called ''southern'' cultures, or what more properly involves a complex blend of Austroasiatic, Austronesian, and central, or originally ''northern'' and ''western'' Asiatic (Altaic as well as Indo-European) elements are crucial in the development of Chinese civilization. Furthermore, such ''foreign'' cultural elements may also have played a role in the evolution of the earliest Chinese neolithic and Shang traditions.[26] It is sufficient to emphasize that if the *hun-tun* theme possesses ''le caractère méridional,'' this does not necessarily mean that it is foreign or peripheral to the mainstream of Chinese tradition.[27]

As a final point on the issue of cultural origins, it would be disingenuous if I did not stress that, while there is much merit in the theory of a special connection between the *hun-tun* theme in Taoism and a ''southern'' cultural sphere, such an identification has only a very general applicability and relevance. It is helpful comparatively since it provides some clues as to a specific context of culture and myth, but it cannot be taken as a controlling factor in my analysis. Even more so than with the unresolved problems associated with the Indo-European hypothesis, there is still a great deal of controversy concerning the origin, nature, coherence, and interrelationship of those languages and cultures called ''Austroasiatic'' and ''Austronesian.''[28] Despite the wealth of detailed evidence and suggestive argument provided by Porée-Maspero, these problems are only compounded when one postulates the existence of an ancient Indo-Chinese cultural tradition known as the Man or K'un-lun complex.[29]

For my purposes it is enough to mention the likelihood of this kind of linguistic and cultural backdrop to the *hun-tun* theme as found in Taoism. Since it is only possible to outline some very broad vectors of cultural influence, the rest of my discussion will adopt the more prudent strategy of sidestepping the problems of historical-cultural origins in favor of a more functional and typological treatment of the main mythological and symbolic patterns.

TYPOLOGIES ASSOCIATED WITH THE HUN-TUN THEME

In this section I want to present a preliminary classification of some of the more obvious and important variations of the *hun-tun* theme. It is my contention that there is a common symbolic intentionality connecting the various units described here, especially as they cluster around and elaborate on the basic cosmogonic idea of "creation out of chaos"; but it is premature to suggest that a complete formulation of functional and typological relationships is possible. More properly, this chapter constitutes only a general survey of the different mythic themes and images associated with the idea of returning to the *hun-tun* condition. Such a comparative gathering of analogous mythic units, and especially an analysis of the various and diverse symbolic motifs incorporated into the Taoist texts, will primarily serve to give more depth and meaning to the religious and philosophical implications of the *hun-tun* theme.

To arrive at a manageable number of mythic units or typologies, it is helpful first of all to examine Chang Kwang-chih's delineation and classification of what can be called the traditional sequence of events constituting a mytholgical "sacred history" for China. Chang finds that at least six major mythological periods may be set out in terms of a movement from the time of the primordial creation to the time of the creation of the human world of civilization. These six periods are:[30]

1. The precosmic condition of chaos (*hun-tun*), which is most frequently symbolized by the image of the cosmic egg (or gourd).

2. The splitting of the egg and the birth of a cosmic giant (P'an-ku) who gives form to the prehuman cosmos by separating heaven and earth. P'an-ku's body acts as a kind of living axis or column connecting heaven and earth. The subsequent creation through the creative activities of a goddess (usually Nü-kua) or primal couple (usually Fu-hsi and Nü-kua).

3. After the creation of man there were at least two great cataclysmic disasters representing the reappearance of a primordial chaos condition: a) the simultaneous appearance of ten suns threatening the destruction of all life, a problem that is rectified by the archer I[d] shooting down nine of the suns; and b) the collision and breaking of the cosmic mountain Pu-chou by the wrathful god Kung-kung, which causes a great flood and disrupts the harmonious

balance of heaven and earth. The goddess Nü-kua eventually repairs and props up the heavens by making four poles out of the legs of a giant tortoise and stops the flooding (in other accounts the god Yü may be responsible for controlling the flood).

4. Cosmic order is reestablished, but the human world is still partially "chaotic"—that is, there are no proper class distinctions, no "civilization," and men "know their mothers rather than their fathers." The men of this chaos time have no clothes or tools and they live in caves and nests like animals. This stage therefore represents the condition of life maintained by barbarian or tribal cultures.

5. The first period of the culture heroes (especially Fu-hsi and Shen-nung) who taught the people the arts of agriculture and civilization.

6. Further civilizing activity by other culture heroes (especially the Yellow Emperor and Yao, Shun, and Yü) who initiate the political institutions of feudalism.

What is represented here is a product of later periods of traditional Chinese historical reflection when it was necessary to give an arbitrary rational order and systematic unity to various individual mythic units. In another article also concerned with the classification of Chinese myth, Chang develops the notion that the artificial movement from the cosmic activities of the gods down to the civilizing actions of the semihuman culture heroes betrays a fundamental shift in the Chinese religious ethos.[31] From the Shang to the Chou there is a progressive separation between the World of the Gods and the World of Man to the extent that man ultimately challenges the very authority and significance of the sacred realm. Such an anthropocentric shift is revealed, for example, by the changing conceptions of god, animal, and ancestor in the archaic artistic tradition and was probably motivated by changes in the kinship system as it relates to religious and political authority.[32] On the whole it is a movement raised to the level of a conscious philosophy of life by the Confucian school.

It is clear that each mythological "period" in the above sequence is a combination and reworking of different and originally separate myths. Chang therefore finds it possible to distinguish at least ten basic mythic units or constituent typological motifs. The *hun-tun* or cosmic egg mythology is clearly one of the primary typologies and is particularly associated with a limited number of other mythologies of cosmic and human creation—especially the mythic units of the cosmic giant, animal ancestor-hero, and primordial couple. To this must also be added a third interrelated category of deluge mythology since the destruction and regeneration of the world represents a recapitulation of the cosmic processes of creation and, specifically in the case of the Chinese themes of deluge and combat between monster and hero, involves the reworking of the cosmogonic symbolism of *hun-tun* as cosmic egg or gourd, the primordial couple theme, and the cosmic giant or animal ancestor themes. As noted in an earlier chapter, Chang more synthetically classifies the various creation mythologies under the two basic rubrics of "Separation" (i.e., especially the cosmic egg, heaven and earth separation, and primordial couple myths) and "Transformation" (i.e., especially cosmic giant and ancestral-animal hero myths).[33] These categories represent originally separate cultural and mythological traditions, but in the texts of the Chou and Han they were creatively rearticulated into a common mythological pattern of meaning.[34]

In the scheme presented by Chang there are really three creations or reduplicated phases of creation leading to the establishment of the complete cosmic, social, and political order of Chinese civilization: 1) the period of the original chaos and the creation of the paradise world (and man in some cases) by a demiurgic giant, animal ancestor, female deity, or primordial couple; 2) the second period of chaos caused by the disorder of the sun or waters, a condition that is overcome by the heroic labors of I[d], Yü[a], or Nü-kua; and 3) a third "chaos" condition or lack of a fully civilized cosmic order finally transformed by the actions of the sage kings of antiquity. Although this sequence makes use of different mythic units and arbitrarily links all of them into an artificial historical narrative, it should be noted that each stage is really only a recapitulation of the cosmogonic process established during the original creation time. Thus in a transformed and pseudohistoricized way, the mythic intentionality concerning the basic nature and processes of life and creation is primarily related to the cosmic egg idea associated with the absolute beginnings. In this manner a cosmogonic intentionality is carried throughout each of the other stages and is to be found, no matter how disguised, at the heart of the understanding of almost any new creation or transition in Chinese tradition. In the sequence set out above, therefore, the following interrelated functional and symbolic analogies can be delineated:

> *Precosmic "Order"*: chaos: cosmic egg: body of P'an-ku: ten suns: flood: barbarian condition: etc. (As a condition of "chaotic wholeness" or embryonic unity, this stage already contains or presupposes the other categories of manifest creation.)
>
> *Agent of Transformation—Creation*: P'an-ku: Nü-kua: Primordial Couple: I[d]: Kung-kung: Yü[a]: Fu-hsi: Shen-nung: Sage Kings: etc. (All of these are to some degree related to the first category.)
>
> *Cosmic "Order"*: duality (heaven and earth, etc.) plus axis (pillar, column, mountain, etc.—order of three): one sun: controlled waters: four

pillars plus center (order of five): civilization (agriculture and feudalism—the order of nine): etc. (All of these are "contained" by the first category.)

Based on the above considerations and especially Chang's careful determination of some of the fundamental mythic units, an analysis of the mythological heritage of the *hun-tun* theme in Taoism is made possible in relation to five basic interrelated typologies. First, most general, and in some ways serving as a controlling focus of intentionality for the other units, is that species of creation mythology designated as the cosmic egg type (including also heaven and earth separation myths), which involves primarily the "separation" thesis of a primal egg-shaped substance (or analogues such as the important variant of cosmic gourd) splitting into dual principles that are constitutive of the primal or paradisical cosmic form (the order of three). Associated with this kind of typology would be the three other interrelated typologies (and their variant forms) of cosmic giant, animal ancestor, and primordial couple. These units can involve both the idea of the primal "transformation" of a cosmic ancestor and the idea of "separation." Finally, the mythologies of deluge as a return to the creation time of chaos and its associated themes (the creation or recreation of the profane human world) must be examined in relation to all of the other units. For all of these categories there will necessarily be a certain amount of arbitrary classification and selection since the Chinese texts, as well as the relevant comparative considerations introduced into the discussion, constitute an extremely entangled and overlapping mass of material.

CHAOS AND THE TYPOLOGY OF THE COSMIC EGG-GOURD

The typology most frequently suggested by the *hun-tun* theme of chaos is that general species of creation mythology emphasizing the image of a cosmic egg or gourd (as well as other analogous symbolic images of a closed embryonic state)—that "one" thing of the creation time that contained within its watery interior the perfect germlike totality of the phenomenal world. Aside from the texts already examined, a characteristic expression of the relationship between the images of egg and chaos that stresses the technical vocabulary of *hun-tun* states that "before the two powers separated in the ancient time there was something whose name was *hung yüan ming hsiang meng hung*. It was like a chicken's egg and is properly called *hun-tun*."[35]

The special philosophical and religious relevance of the cosmic egg mythology for the *hun-tun* theme in Taoism is also suggested by the fact that in Sproul's survey of world mythologies there is commonly a close association of the primordial egg mythologies with the mythologies of a watery chaos or nothingness, the myths of a primordial giant or ancestor, and the myths of a primordial couple. In general, the mythologies of "egg," "chaos," "nothing," hermaphroditic giant, and incestuous primordial couple can be understood to represent wholeness and the fullness of being "rather than the absence of any being" and emphasize a "primordial unity of the sexes, thought immensely fertile."[36]

It is precisely these kinds of linkages that are revealed by the synthesis of myths found in the Taoist texts. Of course, the simple recognition of a special relationship between the *hun-tun* theme and a cosmic egg typology is not really so helpful since the category of "Creation Egg" mythology can be broken down into at least four different units as to general content and intentionality.[37] These may be enumerated as the following:

1. "Cosmic Egg or World Egg" myths proper that describe the creation of the universe.

2. "Man or Mankind Egg" myths that depict the birth of mankind or the first human ancestor out of an egg.

3. "God or Hero Egg" myths wherein prominent tribal deities, fabulous animal ancestors, or culture heroes are born from an egg.

4. "Magic Egg" stories in which marvelous and/or demonic things come forth from an egg or egg-shaped vessel such as a sack, vase, gourd (especially the *hu-lu* or calabash gourd-vase), seed, drum, bell, cauldron, cocoon, or stone.

The complicating factor is that in the Taoist use of the *hun-tun* theme, all four of these categories are represented, sometimes simultaneously. An example of this would be the P'an-ku mythology where the First Ancestor is born from the world egg of *hun-tun* and is subsequently both the creator of the cosmos and mankind. For Taoism it seems clear that the various types of egg myths are functionally interrelated and are ultimately linked to the primary category of the cosmogonic myth of the cosmic or world egg. As Eberhard says, "the concept that single persons or groups or people may be born out of an egg or an egg-like lump of flesh seems to be connected with the myths in which the whole world is born from an egg or a lump of flesh."[38]

Along with the connection with the P'an-ku or cosmic giant mythology is the relation of the cosmic egg typology to myths concerning the idea of a primordial couple. As Charles Long points out, primordial couple myths need not be necessarily linked with cosmic-egg creation myths and, in fact, may convey different religious ideas about creation. Thus, in the symbolism of the cosmic egg:

The beginning of things is spoken of as a totality which includes the opposite modes of sexuality in relation. This is a *coincidentia oppositorum*, a form of symbolism which is different from that of the Primordial World Parents. Sexuality is not represented here by World Parents but by the precise creative power of each sex, who, though related, are capable of independence and separate determination. In other words, the actual *power of creativity* is already present in the beginning. . . . In the cosmic egg the concrete forms of the two sexual principles are united. This unity is a symbol of perfection. Again we must emphasize that this unity is not the same as the unity of the primordial World Parents; rather it is the unity of sexuality which has expressed its potentiality and power as separate from the other sexual principle.[39]

Despite these differences, in Taoism both the primordial couple and cosmic giant mythologies are specifically linked to the cosmic egg mythology of *hun-tun*. The reason for their coalescence may, in the first instance, be related to the symbolic multivocality and adaptability of the image of the cosmic egg as witnessed in many world mythologies. More particularly, however, it must be accounted for by the Taoists' interpretation of the myths' symbolic compatibility in potentially expressing and amplifying a single idea about the ultimate nature of reality. In this way for primordial couple myths, the implications of sexual reunion and creation—especially the motif of an *incestuous* relation between the primordial couple (or their offspring)—may afford the "connecting link" with the strict world egg and cosmic giant mythologies.[40] The functional identification here is in terms of what the Taoist texts interpreted as basically analogous ways of expressing a single idea of primordiality—that is, the idea of the primal unity of the egg, the sexual wholeness of the hermaphrodite, and the return to an original unity through an incestuous sexual union.[41]

There is an additional association with *hun-tun* as cosmic egg that displays another functional overlapping of various categories of myth. This is the relation the theme of *hun-tun* has to what Eberhard calls "thunder-egg" stories, mythic tales that are most closely related to the category of "God or Hero Egg" myths.[42] In fact, it is clear that Eberhard's category of "thunder-egg" stories and Hellbom's related category of "God or Hero Egg" myths primarily reflect an instance of the combination of the typologies of cosmic egg, cosmic giant, and animal ancestor—as well as the deluge and primordial couple themes, which are frequently linked to the myths of the cosmic giant-animal ancestor.[43]

The primary factor in the "thunder-egg" stories is that lightning and thunder are the creative forces or obstetrical agents responsible for the miraculous birth of an ancestral god, or more particularly a thunder god such as Lei-kung, from an egglike container.[44] The symbolism in these tales, which are associated with the various legends of the thunder god, various local-myth cycles such as those of P'an-hu, and stories of fabulous animals like the one-legged *lei*[c] (depicted as an amorphous lump that produces thunder noises at midnight), is homologous with the symbolism of *hun-tun* as a cosmic egg, sack, drum, gourd, or shapeless "mass of flesh."[45] Needless to say there is an obvious and special connection with the story of Emperor Hun-tun from the *Chuang Tzu*. Another factor may be the seeming importance attributed to the very sounds associated with the theme of *hun-tun* in the Taoist texts in that there appears to be a linkage with religious ideas rooted in an archaic ritual cycle emphasizing certain seasonal periods of transition, or a periodic return to chaos, signaled by thunder and lightning and the coming of fertilizing rain.[46]

With respect to the whole emergent series of symbolic analogies linking the themes of *hun-tun*, thunder god, animal ancestor, primordial couple, and deluge, Kaltenmark notes:

> The god of thunder [is] born from an egg miraculously revealed by a dog. It is not without interest to note that Thunder is the god of justice, or order and fecundity. He is therefore a god importantly related, if not with the origins of the world, with the cycle of universal life and with the renovation of the universe when order is destroyed. In the myths of the deluge or flood which have been gathered from aboriginal populations from the south-west provinces of China and North Vietnam, the deluge or great flood is often started by the god of thunder; and in several versions the primordial brother-sister couple, father and mother of mankind, escape the disaster by entering into a drum which takes them to a safe place. In other variants it is a gourd.[47]

For my purposes it is enough to recognize this series of homologous themes and avoid getting lost in a labyrinth of interconnected symbolism. The final outcome of all of these variant typologies associated with the category of the cosmic egg seems to be that there is always the preservation of a common cosmogonic idea concerning the ultimate nature of the first principle of creation. Namely, the emphasis is always on the periodic salvific return to a condition of absolute totality exemplified most fully by the symbolism of the cosmic egg or gourd. In this respect it might also be said that it is especially the symbolism of thunder and lightning that emphasizes the eternal periodic return of the time of chaos and creation.

The "idea" behind most cosmic egg symbolism is the need to see the ultimate nature of reality and life in terms of the mystery of *coincidentia oppositorum* whereby the beginning and end of all things is a perfect embryonic equilibrium of dualities. As in the *hun-tun* theme in Taoism, cosmic egg symbolism in general displays a world view where a "cosmological dualism comes to the fore. The myths of this type posit the dualism, but they show at the same time the necessary relation between the two active principles."[48] In the most general sense, then, the significance of *hun-tun* in the primary category of the cosmic egg is found in the basic embryological analogy to the mysterious nature of a seed or egg—that which possesses an internal life-force completely prefiguring the finished form.

In many instances in Taoist texts the theme of *hun-tun* as egg, watery substratum, or original formless mass would seem to imply the priority of a feminine principle as mother and womb of creation. And it is true that egg symbolism frequently refers to primordiality in a feminine context: "the egg is the potential source of all life. It is the incubator and therefore the homologue of the womb. This symbolism can be extended to cover shells, caverns, dark places, the earth, etc."[49] Especially in the *Tao Te Ching* there would seem to be an emphasis given to the maternal quality or primordial femaleness of the Tao.

More accurately, however, the Taoist idea of *hun-tun* as a primordial egglike substrate and source of all life goes deeper than a mother-earth type of symbolism. The primary emphasis conveyed by the use of the *hun-tun* theme seems, therefore, to concern an idea of an absolute wholeness that necessarily includes both male and female dimensions. In a way that is related to the Taoist use of the cosmic egg idea,

> "Femininity" does not seem to have been thought of as a primordial mode of being. "Femininity," like "masculinity" also, is already a particular mode of being, and, for mythical thinking, this particular mode is necessarily preceded by a *whole* mode of being. . . . One might call this primordial state a neuter and creative wholeness.[50]

In relating this to the particular case of China, Eliade goes on to note Granet's contention that the most primitive idea of sacrality was essentially neuter or bisexual in nature—so that, for example, a " 'holy place' was perceived as an undifferentiated religious power, as a primordial *Grund* which preceded and supports all subsequent manifestations."[51]

This emphasis on a complementary dualism represents a general Chinese conviction and tends to show why the Taoists would find the category of cosmic egg mythology so amenable to their views. In cosmic egg myths the "essential complementary relationship of the sexual modes of being is emphasized" and it would seem that this kind of intentionality serves as a cardinal element distinguishing cosmic egg mythology from other types of world mythology.[52] Long consequently notes that in Baumann's discussion of primitive traditions, cosmic egg mythologies can be seen as a philosophical and religious attempt to deal with the problem of duality posited by primordial couple or heaven-earth separation myths:

> The cosmic egg symbolism, insofar as it includes bisexuality, represents the attempt to come to terms with the religious meaning of the powerful antithetical symbols of sexuality. In the egg symbolism the union of the sexual principles in twins as in a bisexual deity is an attempt to overcome the dualism involved in the revelation of the sacred in one or the other sexes. This is not the old primordial union of earth mother and sky father. In this symbolism the emphasis is on the passive togetherness of the sexes. Though myths always state that the World Parents have offspring, the full meaning of sexuality as unique and separable principles is not emphasized.[53]

It may be said, then, that the chaos theme of *hun-tun* in its mythic form as cosmic egg sets a basic pattern of mythological intentionality and constitutes an underlying frame upon which other mythic types were added. In theory, the emphasis always tends to stress a complementary dualism or an equilibrium of opposites as the basic mode of creation, both cosmic and human. The periodic reappropriation of a primordial wholeness, the mysterious union of the two things, the return to the *hun-tun* condition—this is the way of the Tao and man and can be symbolized by a homologous series of mythic themes: the cosmological and embryological perfection of the world egg, the miraculous birth of the animal ancestor from the primal egg, the hermaphroditic totality of the cosmic giant, or the incestuous sexual union and "chaotic" offspring of a primordial couple. Man is an articulation of the "two," but there is a loss of equilibrium that demands an initiatory reenactment of the cosmogonic process, a reversal of the outward movement of the Tao into manifest duality and a return to that original paradise condition when the "two" found harmony in the central realm of the Emperor Hun-tun.

From these considerations would follow the significance of "transitional moments" in Taoism since all of those sacred "times" that were part of an archaic ritual cycle of cosmic renewal signaled by thunder and lightning need only to be reactualized at the microcosmic level of man himself. While Taoism is broken from any particular primitive agrarian ritual cycle of periodic social regeneration, there is still a symbolic remembrance and personal initiatory reenactment of a return to the chaos time. The return to, and identification with, the life of the Tao that is sought by the Taoist consequently makes use of the symbolism and mythic themes associated with seasonal "transitional moments"—those ritual periods that recover the cosmogonic condition of the unity of "three."

The archaic ritual context of this is almost impossible to reconstruct with any degree of confidence, but in a very general way it might be said that the ideas of "return" and "transitional moments" in Taoism are especially connected with those traditional Chinese periods of seasonal and temporal renewal, such as spring and autumn festivals, solstice and equinox periods, changes in lunar phases, and diurnal cycles. Particularly important would seem to be those ancient festivals associated with fertility during the fifth day of the fifth month (summer solstice), the seventh day of the seventh month (fall full moon festival), and the winter solstice-new year festivals.[54] In later esoteric Taoism these macrocosmic periods of ritual renewal are microcosmically reenacted during the practice of meditation. The hours of the day represent a microcosmic year, one cycle of birth-chaos-rebirth; and the periods of meditation must be adjusted to certain hours related to the union of *yin* and *yang*.[55] In this regard it is significant that in the traditional system of the Twelve Branch cycle of the year, the twelve characters correspond to the months and to the hours of the day doubled. Moreover, the first and sixth stages of the cycle (*tzu* and *ssu*) are the most important transitional periods in the alternation of *yin* and *yang* and represent the nodal periods of the "return" or "union" of the *yin* and *yang*, the time of "three" that is the threshold time of a new creation.[56] As Granet has noted:

> The initial point [of the Twelve Branch system] is placed in relation to the north, the winter solstice, midnight: it is symbolized by the character *tzu* which signifies "the infant," "an egg," "a seed," "semen". . . . The sixth cyclic period in the normal order . . . is marked by the character *ssu* which can be taken as the figure of an embryo. The Time of Origins, the initial point, the winter solstice, midnight, north (*tzu*, "the infant, the seed") is the place where the two cosmogonic sexual principles, whose inverse and antithetical action constitute the continuity of time, coexist without separation.[57]

RELATED MYTHOLOGICAL THEMES: ANIMAL ANCESTOR, COSMIC GIANT, AND PRIMORDIAL COUPLE MYTHS

I have already suggested that along with the primary typology of the cosmic egg, there are, at least, the four other related mythological themes of the animal ancestor, cosmic giant, primordial couple, and deluge. As with the cosmic egg theme, the problem is that only transformed and intermixed remnants of originally coherent, mythic cycles remain in the Chinese texts. Thus the preserved fragments of a demiurgic cosmic giant (especially the figure of P'an-ku) are commonly merged with what may be considered its more primitive or folkloric prototype of the animal ancestor (such as P'an-hu). Similarly, as I will show in the next chapter, the best guess as to an overall "primitive" ("southern" or "barbarian") mythic typology that links the various images of egg, gourd, ancestor, and primordial couple with the salvational theme of returning to chaos is a reconstructed mythology of the deluge.

1. Animal Ancestor and Cosmic Giant Symbolism

With regard to traces of cosmic giant or primordial ancestor myths, it is necessary to examine the figures of P'an-hu, P'an-ku, and Huang Ti. In Taoist tradition all of these figures can be shown to lend elements to the symbolic embellishment of the *hun-tun* theme and all are specifically linked to an underlying cosmogonic intentionality of the cosmic egg or gourd. It can perhaps also be said that the few traces of Hun-tun as an actual mythological figure (*Chuang Tzu, Shan Hai Ching, Tso Chuan, Shih Chi*) most immediately suggest the primitive theme of the thunder egg, deluge, and animal ancestor mythologies. Because of this, the figure of P'an-hu is particularly important as a possible analogue for an original mythology involving a Hun-tun deity. In a similar fashion the figures of P'an-ku as cosmic giant and Huang Ti as semi-divine king, prominent Taoist figures related to the *hun-tun* theme, are also composed of various symbolic traits revealing a general mythic prototype of the animal ancestor who is identified with the primal chaos condition of creation and cyclic transformation.

P'an-hu and the Theme of the Animal Ancestor

From the ancient Chinese historical sources, as well as from comparative materials gathered by Ho, it appears that the figure of P'an-hu was originally a totemic ancestral dog deity of the Man tribes of south China ("Man" in this context having reference to about a dozen tribal groups—especially the Miao, Yao[b], Lolo, Liao[b], Li, and Shaka).[58] Most important, however, is to recognize the fact that the legends of a dog ancestor represent an assimilation of the various anthropogonic myths of the deluge, cosmic egg-gourd, and incestuous primordial couple.[59]

This congruence is shown by a whole series of symbolic details and functional associations, particularly those involving the symbolism of the "magic egg" and calabash gourd (*hu-lu*). The figure of P'an-hu is therefore connected with that cycle of myths wherein a divine brother and sister survive a great deluge by floating over the turbulent waters on a gourd, drum, or some other boatlike object. Indeed, the very name of P'an-hu, literally "platter-gourd," suggests the creation theme and cosmology of *hun-tun*. In at least one account that links P'an-ku with P'an-hu, P'an-hu is saved from the chaotic deluge by mounting a plateau supported by a huge gourd. After this he becomes the ancestor of a newly created mankind.[60] As with the accounts where P'an-ku's body is the column supporting heaven and earth, thus representing the condition of three that is the precondition for his sacrificial dismemberment and creation of the phenomenal world, the P'an-hu account of the deluge and regeneration of man emphasizes the return to a chaos condition, the reestablishment of the world and man through the salvific agency of a kind of cosmic gourd-pillar (mountain) identified with the name and substance of the ancestor god.[61] A similar conclusion is reached in consideration of another derivation for the name P'an-hu offered by a commentator on the *Hou Han Shu*. In this version the dog god was said to be born from a silkworm cocoon that was put in a gourd (*hu*) covered with a bowl (*p'an*). Aside from the symbolism of the cocoon and gourd, which can be homologized with the image and cosmogonic function of the cosmic egg, the most noteworthy detail in this commentary is that the cocoon is specifically called *hun-tun*.[62]

There is no need to go into the numerous associations of the cocoon, gourd, and calabash in Taoist tradition. This, along with the symbolic and etymological connections of the calabash vessel *hu-lu* with the theme of *hun-tun*, has already been treated by Lo, Stein, and Eberhard.[63] But it should be made clear that the P'an-hu, cocoon, gourd, and *hu-lu* symbolism has magical, transformative, or healing significance primarily because of the attachment to the creation themes of *hun-tun* as cosmic egg and as the salvation vessel (gourd, drum, cauldron, boat, etc.) or creative "mass of flesh" of the great deluge. In fact, the cosmological significance of the gourd is clearly suggested in early Chinese works like the *Li Chi* where it is said that "to offer sacrifices in the countryside use pottery containers of a gourd shape in order to symbolize the nature of Heaven and Earth."[64]

Aside from the magic vessel connotations, the connection with the cosmogonic theme of *hun-tun* in the Taoist texts is shown by a number of additional details found in the P'an-hu tales. One of these factors is the symbolism linking the tradition of the dog ancestor with the "thunder-egg" cycle of myths.[65] Another factor is that some of the P'an-hu legends are suggestive of the initiatory ordeal of "boring," death, and transformation into a human form found in the Emperor Hun-tun story from the *Chuang Tzu*. The Man tribes of Wu Ning, for example, are reported to " 'stab heaven' because P'an-hu, after his death, had been put on a tree and pricked with needles."[66] As with the initiatory implications of becoming profanely human and having face after the death of a primordial ancestor in the Emperor Hun-tun story, the tribal remembrance of the death of P'an-hu, which is associated with the "pricking of needles," is suggestive of southern aboriginal rites of initiatory tatooing and the primitive theme of becoming the tribal ancestor, taking his animal face (cf. the reference to the "multicolored garments" of P'an-hu's children in the *Hou Han Shu* account below).[67]

A final association here concerns the detail of the hanging of P'an-hu from a tree and the "stabbing of heaven." This recalls several references in early Chinese literature that report a ritual ordeal of shooting arrows at a *hun-tun* or leather, blood-filled sack that is hung from a tree. In these accounts it is said that this constitutes "shooting at heaven."[68] As in other uses of the *hun-tun* theme in Confucian inspired texts, these stories appear to be particularly related to the significance of "transitional moments," or the periodic return to chaos, that is symbolically associated with a change in a ruling house, a change of dynasties, or the suppression of rebel and barbarian challenges to the established political order. While presented as "history" in the Confucian texts, it is clear that such accounts represent disguised adaptations of origin myths. Most important is that a mythological connecting link for all of these details of cutting, boring, pricking, stabbing, or tatooing is the deluge theme of *hun-tun* as a deformed "mass of flesh" or gourd that is chopped up in order to create the human world.[69]

The conclusion that is emerging from all of these considerations is that Hun-tun and P'an-hu (as well as Yao, Shun, Yü, Huang Ti, etc.) were most probably the names of originally different local deities or tribal ancestors. Whatever specific myths were originally a part of a Hun-tun cycle is impossible to know with any detail, but they were certainly related in terms of general typology and symbolism with the animal ancestor tales associated with the figure of P'an-hu. It is even the case that in the *Shen I Ching*, Hun-tun is specifically described as a bearlike dog god with long hair who lived on Mt. K'un-lun. Echoing the account of the amorphous Emperor Hun-tun, this creature is described in the following way:

> It has eyes but can't see, walks without moving; and has two ears but can't hear. It has the knowledge of a man yet its belly is without the five internal organs and, although having a rectum, it doesn't evacuate food. It punches virtuous men and stays with the non-virtuous. It is called Hun-tun.

The passage concludes by quoting the *Ch'un Ch'iu*: "Hun-tun was Meng-shih's untalented son. He always gnaws his tail, going round and round. Everyone ridiculed him."[70]

Despite some differences in detail between the various Hun-tun and P'an-hu stories, it is clear that their basic features are homologous and refer primarily to a similar cosmogonic intentionality. In this regard it is instructive to examine the earliest Chinese record of the P'an-hu legend. This account is found in the "Biography of the Southern Barbarians" chapter of the *Hou Han Shu* (Annals of the Later Han), which, as with other *hun-tun*-type stories and the theme of Fu-po and Hun-hui in Confucian influenced texts, characteristically relates what is essentially a mythic or folkloric theme to the "history" of the political subjugation of barbarian tribes within the Chinese empire. The story, however, preserves much of the idea that the creative acts of P'an-hu as the ancestor of the Man tribes were but a reenactment of the processes of the creation time. The account is as follows:

> In ancient times, Emperor Kao-hsin was troubled by the banditry of the Ch'uan-jung [a barbarian tribe of the west]. Concerned over their depredations he attacked but did not subdue them. Then seeking the enlistment of anyone within the empire who could take the head of General Wu, General of the Ch'uan-jung, he offered the gift of a thousand *i* of gold, a fief of ten thousand families, and, in addition, the hand of a younger daughter. At that time, the Emperor had a tame dog whose hair was of various colors named P'an-hu. After the promulgation of the order, P'an-hu then arrived at the gate of the imperial palace holding in his mouth a human head. When the officials, marvelling, examined it, it was the head of General Wu. The Emperor was greatly delighted but considering that P'an-hu should not be granted his daughter in marriage and could not be enfeoffed, he deliberated, wishing to make a reward but not knowing what was fitting. The Emperor's daughter, hearing of it, and considering that the Emperor's order should not be repudiated, accordingly asked his permission to carry out the promise. The Emperor could do nothing but espouse his daughter to P'an-hu. Having gained the daughter, P'an-hu, taking her on his back, went to the southern mountains, and stopped in a stone chamber situated over a precipice inaccessible to the footsteps of man. Thereupon, the daughter took off her clothes, tied her hair into a "P'u-chien" and donned "Tu-li" garments. The Emperor, grieving for her, sent messengers to seek her. Constantly encountering wind, rain, thunder, and darkness, the messengers could not proceed. Three years passed, and she bore twelve children—six sons and six daughters. After the death of P'an-hu, the children then married each other. They wove and twisted bark and hides and dyed them with grass juices. They liked varicolored garments which were cut out in the form of a (?) tail. Afterwards, their mother returned and reported their condition to the Emperor who, thereupon, sent messengers to welcome them all. Their clothing was varicolored and striped. Their speech was unintelligible. They preferred to go to the mountains and valleys and disliked level land. The Emperor according to their wishes endowed them with renowned mountains and wide

marshes. Afterwards, expanding and spreading, they were called the Man-i. Outwardly they appeared like simple folk, but inwardly they were clever.[71]

This story fits with the previously related Confucianized accounts of Hun-tun as a barbarian rebel or monster that must be tamed and brought into the established political order. Even more important than the overt political implications of this passage is that the tale still retains a structure recalling a creation scenario. While the legend is presented primarily as a kind of etiological account of the tribal origins of the Man culture, there is also an allusion to the fact that the creation of man, in this case the Man-i tribe, is but a recapitulation of the creation of the world. All creation is a matter of a return to the sacred marriage union of the "two" during the chaos or deluge time.

In this sense P'an-hu may not only be understood as a great tribal ancestor but also as equivalent to the demiurgic chaos giant who is born from the primal substance and is responsible for the creation of the world and man. In the analogous deluge cycle of the recreation of the world, these identifications are even more explicit in that the primordial animal ancestor or thunder god is simultaneously responsible for the return to chaos and symbolically linked with the agent of salvation (gourd-drum-boat), the facilitator of the marriage union of the primordial couple, and the offspring ("mass of flesh," gourd) of the marriage that gives rise to the human world.[72]

Creation necessarily involves a retreat to the chaos condition or a chaos realm—the stone chamber that is "inaccessible to the footsteps of man."[73] The daughter of the king also returns to a condition of absolute primordiality and identification with her husband P'an-hu. This is indicated by her nudity and rejection of the ordinary human world. Moreover, she has attained a new mode of barbarian or chaotic being symbolized by her *P'u-chien* and *Tu-li* garments—terms that are evocative of her status as a goddess of the creation time.[74] It should also be noted that the detail of the marriage of the King's "younger" daughter is a fundamental aspect of the overall dog-ancestor cycle and, like the references to the marriage of Hun-tun (as a "warty toad") among the Ch'uan Miao, represents the beauty and the beast motif of the "animal spouse," a motif that has numerous worldwide folkloric parallels.[75] As Porée-Maspero has also shown, the preference given to the younger daughter specifically suggests the kinship tradition of ultimogeniture that was practiced by many southern local cultures.[76]

The creation itself is a process that is signaled by "wind, rain, thunder, and darkness" and extends over a period of three years. The product of the primordial couple's sacred marriage union during this period is the appearance of twelve children, six sons and six daughters. Through the incestuous union of the children, a kind of uncivilized paradise world was created. This was a *hun-tun*, chaotic, or barbarian condition where men lived in primal simplicity—their speech was unintelligible and they wore motley garments (an identification with their animal progenitor?).

Other variants of the dog-ancestor legend make use of a similar narrative structure but add such motifs as the floating over the ocean in a special boat that recalls the deluge theme of returning to chaos.[77] Composite assessment of the various stories reveals the interrelated presence of the themes of the animal spouse, the origin of tatooing, incest, and the transformation of animals into men.[78] This last-mentioned theme of transformation is especially important in relation to the Hun-tun story in Taoism in that it stresses the identification of man with an animal ancestor. Some of the tales therefore indicate that transformation is due to the magical powers of a bell, cauldron, or drum; and these are details that can all be taken as analogous to the creative power of the primordial egg, cocoon, or gourd.[79]

Ho has assembled many accounts of the dog-ancestor tale and has shown that, comparatively speaking, they are all related to the idea of creation. Ho's overall conclusion, therefore, indicates that the dog-ancestor cycle is basically linked to the Austronesian mythologies, which characteristically focus on the creation of mankind and involve the three basic subthemes of 1) the origin of man from an egg, gourd, rock, bamboo joint, etc.; 2) the animal ancestor origin tales; and 3) the stories of the creation of a new race from the incestuous relations of a divine couple after the deluge.[80] I need only remark that these same three subthemes are fundamental to the Taoist elaboration of the *Hun-tun* theme. The most important difference is that in the Taoist accounts the origin and nature of man is explicitly understood as the recapitulation of the creation of the world. For the Taoists who were incorporating various mythologies into their grand cosmogonic vision, there was clearly a philosophical and religious realization that any form of creation necessarily depends on the processes established at the absolute beginnings of the world. Every significant macrocosmic or microcosmic transformation or change in life is ultimately cosmogonic in structure and meaning.

P'an-ku and the Theme of the Cosmic Giant

Concerning the P'an-ku mythology, it is impossible to present here a full analysis of all its ramifications in later Chinese tradition. What is of interest is that a probable reason for its importance in later Taoism is its relation to the earlier creation theme of *hun-tun* as cosmic egg-gourd, as well as to the southern deluge and animal ancestor cycle of myths. Ferguson described the traditional aspects of the P'an-ku myth in this way:

> The scholarly interpretations of cosmogony . . . are entirely eclipsed by the vulgar theories of Taoism which have captivated the minds of the majority of the Chinese people and which may be accepted as the teachings of present day Taoism. According to these the Great Creator was P'an Ku. He came from the great chaos, and his body was four times the size of that of an ordinary man. Two horns projected from his head, and two tusks from his upper jaw. His body was thickly covered with hair. Knowing the principles of Heaven and Earth and the inherent changes of the dual fires of nature, he was able to excavate the deep valleys and pile up high mountains. He taught men to build boats and bridges; he understood the qualities of the rocks and was able to select those that were of value to mankind. With his hammer and chisel he brought the universe into shape. From his high throne he issued his instructions to the people, whom he divided into the two classes of nobles and commoners. Above are the sun, moon, and stars, he said, and below are the four seas. Listening to his discourse on the manner in which chaos was reduced to order, the people forgot their fatigue. After he had exhausted his instructions to them, one morning he disappeared and was never again heard of.[81]

This account draws upon late popular versions of the myth where there is an emphasis on P'an-ku's role as a kind of culture hero or Thor-like god wielding a thunder ax. In other popular accounts, P'an-ku was considered as one of the gods of medicine and the father and lord of all living creatures.[82] Chinese Buddhism also adopted versions of the P'an-ku mythology in the elaboration of its cosmological vision; but most commonly in Taoist popular mythology, P'an-ku was combined with the *yin-yang* theory—"certain tales relate that P'an-ku is born from *yin* and *yang* with the mission of creating Heaven and Earth out of the primal chaos. . . . A poem describes P'an-ku as springing forth from chaos which appeared with the division of the *yin* and *yang*. It is through the agency of the two principles that he creates the Heaven, Earth and man."[83] These are all late traditional depictions of P'an-ku, but they serve to show that the ancient *hun-tun* cosmogonic formulation of the "two" and the "three" (*yin-yang* and *axis*: Hun-tun, K'un-lun, P'an-ku) persisted as a basic underlying cosmological model.

In the earliest versions of the myth there is a clear connection with a cosmic egg cosmogony. Therefore, despite the fact that the P'an-ku myth does not really appear in name before the third century A.D. in China and is probably influenced by an Indo-European prototype, it is related in general form and function with the earlier *hun-tun* creation themes involving the notions of the cosmic egg-gourd, animal ancestor, primordial couple, and deluge.[84]

The earliest extant version of the myth from the third century A.D. tells the story of P'an-ku in the following way:

> Heaven and Earth were in the chaos condition [*hun-tun*] like a chicken's egg, within which was born P'an-ku. After 18,000 years, when Heaven and Earth were separated, the pure *yang* formed the Heaven and the murky *yin* formed the Earth. P'an-ku stood between them. His body transformed nine times daily while his head supported the Heaven and his feet stabilized the Earth. Each day Heaven increased ten feet in height and Earth daily increased ten feet in thickness. P'an-ku who was between them daily increased ten feet in size. After another 18,000 years this is how Heaven and Earth came to be separated by their present distance of 90,000 *li*.[85]

Here P'an-ku is identified with the cosmic egg of *hun-tun* and, in this sense, is related to the primal condition of chaos. Aside from the obvious similarity with P'an-hu in name and symbolism (especially the thunder-egg theme), there is no consensus as to the derivation of the name P'an-ku. One suggestion in keeping with the mythic overtones is that it means something like "coiled up (like a snake or embryo) antiquity."[86] In a literal sense *p'an* signifies a "bowl, dish, or tub," which relates to the idea of the curved eggshell or gourd that embraces the universe in the Hun-t'ien[a] system or, also, "to examine," "to coil up, wriggle"; and *ku* means "old, ancient" or "firm, solid."[87] Perhaps the most intriguing of these philological speculations, and one supportive of the interlocking network of mythological images, is that offered by Wen I-to. He shows "that the name of P'an Ku may have been originally rendered with the characters *p'an-hu*" signifying the gourd symbolism of the dog ancestor of the Man.[88]

A fundamental functional aspect of the myth quoted above is that P'an-ku plays the role of an *axis mundi* or central pivot of equilibrium between the two things of heaven and earth. As with the primordial wholeness of P'an-ku within the *hun-tun* egg, so also is the second period of the creation process after the formation of the basic cosmic form of duality still a perfect reflection of unity. P'an-ku represents the cosmic condition of the "three," the time of cosmic incubation. As a final point of verification, Kaltenmark notes that the themes of P'an-ku are linked to the imagery of Mt. K'un-lun, which serves as a cosmic pillar (in the shape of a column of bronze or calabash gourd) and landing place for the primordial couple during the deluge.[89]

As in the Emperor Hun-tun tale in the *Chuang Tzu*, other versions of the P'an-ku myth stress the idea of the sacrificial death, dismemberment, and transformation of the primal giant into the "body" of the universe and man:

After the death of P'an-ku, his breath became the wind and clouds, his voice the thunder, his left and right eyes the sun and moon, his four limbs and five "bodies" (fingers) the four quarters of the earth and five great mountains, his blood the rivers, his muscles and veins the strata of earth, his flesh the soil, his hair and beard the constellations, his skin and body-hair the plants and trees, his teeth and bone the metals and stones, his marrow gold and precious stones, and his sweat the rain. The parasites on his body, impregnated by the wind, became human beings.[90]

This form of the myth is especially close to, even possibly influenced by, Indian texts telling of the cosmic man Purusa-Prajapati coming forth from the cosmic egg (*brahmanda* or the "golden germ," *hiranyagarbha*) and creating the world through self-sacrifice; but even allowing for Indo-European influence there is no doubt, as Chang shows, that this kind of transformation thesis basically resonates with earlier Chinese cosmological thought.[91] This myth cannot, therefore, be considered simply a foreign importation.[92]

Stein has shown that this type of transformation myth has as much to do with the cosmological classification of the world in correlation with the human body as it does with creation per se.[93] In later Taoism this mythology was especially significant for its emphasis on the macrocosmic-microcosmic identification of the primordial giant-ancestor, the world, and man. All constitute the one "body" of the Tao and are directly related to Taoist meditation theory and liturgical practice.[94]

It also should be noted that the connecting element between this version and the previous myth is the idea of P'an-ku's creative "transformation" (*pien*[b] or *hua*[a], he "transformed himself nine times during the course of one day"). The reference to the "nine" transformations is a formulaic expression for completion, wholeness, unity, or continuity in Taoism and is functionally analogous to the sevenfold transformation and death of the Emperor Hun-tun. A whole series of related mythological themes of transformation can consequently be set out for the later Taoist theory of Lao Tzu as the cosmic man.[95]

    a. Huang Ti (Nü-kua) creates by transformation—the Tao (Lao Tzu, Lao Chün) is the one who fashions all beings.
    b. P'an-ku is born before the creation of the world—the Tao (Lao Tzu) exists before the separation of the heaven and the earth.
    c. The body of P'an-ku (Lao Tzu) is the universe—the created universe is the visible aspect of the Tao.
    d. Lao Tzu (P'an-ku) is transformed nine times (forever). Lao Tzu swells and contracts with the seasons—the Tao is nothing other than the alternation of *yin* and *yang*, the seasonal rhythm.

Seidel has demonstrated these correlations in a most convincing fashion for later religious Taoism, but I would like to reiterate the significance of this mythic model for even the earliest Taoist texts. Man's original sacredness is affirmed by virtue of the fact that his being is but a disarticulated part of the cosmic body of the Tao. Throughout Taoist tradition, therefore, there is general agreement on the need for man to find a way of remembering and reexperiencing the primal unity of the paradise time, a way of rearticulating the primordial body of P'an-ku or plugging the holes bored into the faceless Hun-tun. The method of doing this symbolically involves a sevenfold or ninefold initiatory transformation of man (a "sacrificial death") back to the prehuman condition of chaotic totality.

Many elements, especially popular iconographical and folkloric details, that were taken into the overall mythology of P'an-ku in China betray not only a similarity with the Indian themes of Purusa-Prajapati but also with the deluge themes of southern local cultures. Indeed, the areas in the south of China where P'an-hu was venerated as a tribal god are the same areas where the majority of temples dedicated to P'an-ku are located.[96] As will become evident in chapter 7, the connecting symbolic link between the southern mythologies of the deluge, the P'an-ku mythology, and the Taoist themes of Emperor Hun-tun, as well as the later accounts of the cosmic transformation of Lao Chün, appears to be the deluge motif of the "mass of flesh" that is cut up into many pieces in order to create the human world.[97] The presence of this Demalike motif in various Man and Miao myths of the deluge resonates closely with the ideas of the death of Emperor Hun-tun and the dismemberment and transformation of P'an-ku's corpse. As the offspring or "third term" of the primordial couple, the faceless "mass of flesh" represents the positive, creative side of the chaotic forces unleashed during the deluge. It is possible that this motif is especially important in the Taoist assimilation of the various mythic themes of the animal ancestor, the gourd-egg-drum of salvation, the cosmic mountain, the primordial couple, and the primordial giant into a metaphysics of Hun-tun and Tao.

The safest assessment of these factors is that, while representing different mythic cycles, the deluge and cosmic giant mythologies were incorporated by the Taoists into the general philosophical and religious theme of *hun-tun* as cosmic egg-gourd. As already indicated, the hagiographies of the divine Lao Tzu-Lao Chün are modeled on the idea of the Tao's cosmogonic transformation: "Lao Tzu is one with the primordial chaos of *hun-tun*."[98] In this sense, when the P'an-ku type of myths entered the Chinese milieu, they could easily be assimilated as alternate versions of the earlier southern deluge cycle and as but another instance of the *Tao Te Ching*'s basic creation formula of the one-two-three. Most of all, it is clear that the mythological complex underlying later Taoist theories of the cosmic body of Lao Tzu were "not newly introduced into China by the myth of P'an-ku."[99]

In a comparative vein it is worthwhile to point out that the significance of the cosmic giant mythology in Taoism is paralleled by its use in Indian religion and philosophy. In the Vedic conception, for example, there is a close connection between the Purusa-Prajapati theme and the idea of the cosmic egg. This kind of mythology commonly involves the idea of the heating (*tapas*), incubation, and transformation of the cosmic man:

> The cosmic egg, formed and incubated in the primal waters, gives birth to the first man called Prajapati. After this, Prajapati speaks, an act lasting one year. His first words, which manifest themselves in the creation, are *Bhur* (Earth), *Bhuvar* (atmosphere), and *Svar* (Heaven). These words constitute the Earth, the intermediary region, and the Heaven.[100]

In the beginning was the tripartite word of Prajapati, who was newly hatched from the cosmic egg. Also prominent are the ideas of *tapas* as the mysterious energy of incubation and the atmospheric breath (*bhuvar*), which, like Prajapati's body in other versions, links heaven and earth; and these are notions that are analogous to the Taoist theme of the primordial *ch'i*[a] and *hun-tun* (as well as the Tao as that which is "spoken"?). These themes, along with other variants emphasizing the dismemberment and transformation of the cosmic giant, are crucial to the theoretical development of ancient Brahmanic ritual and the use of magical spells. Even more significant is that the evolution of Indian philosophical and religious thought can be traced in relation to the progressively interiorized reinterpretation of the Purusa-Prajapati cosmogony (especially in Samkhya-yoga and Vedanta[101]).

In the light of my findings here with respect to early Taoism and in relation to the recent work on religious Taoism, it is evident that a similar paradigmatic correspondence between an archaic mythological pattern and religio-philosophical thought and practice exists in Taoist tradition. At the same time it should be stressed that the surprising relationship between a particular creation mythology and religious thought in both India and China does not constitute an argument for the influence of Indian tradition on Taoism. There are hints of some slight early exchange, and certainly with the arrival of Buddhism there are specific cases of mutual influence with respect to the P'an-ku mythology; but, as maintained in this chapter, the primary sources of Taoist cosmogony cannot be ascribed to Indian origins.[102] As Porée-Maspero suggests, it is rather the case that the "southern" or Man cultural complex may represent a common source for both Chinese and Indian tradition—especially Taoism and Buddhism.[103]

The Yellow Emperor: Animal Ancestor and Culture Hero

The enigmatic figure of the Yellow Emperor (Huang Ti) is traditionally the ancestor of man, the emperor of the golden age, the patron of magic, sexual mysticism, medicine, and alchemy. Only a thin historical veneer, applied liberally in the classical texts, separates this figure from the more blatantly mythological personages of P'an-hu and P'an-ku. Especially in the Taoist adoption of the Yellow Emperor as a kind of foundational patriarch alongside Lao Tzu (the Huang-Lao movement of the Han dynasty), he is revealed as a kind of demiurgic cosmic giant or animal ancestor. In this way his legendary history is intimately connected with the overall development of the *hun-tun* theme in Taoism.[104]

A significant factor in the assessment of the Yellow Emperor is the problem of his curious ambivalence in the *Chuang Tzu* where he is subject to either praise or condemnation. At times the Yellow Emperor is presented as an example of the perfect Taoist sage and emperor of the golden age, while at other times he is said to be the one responsible for bringing about the "great disorder" (*ta-luan*) of Confucian civilization into the world.[105]

Part of the reason for this ambivalence is surely to be understood in relation to Huang Ti's original nature as a tribal god or demiurgic ancestor who was both born from chaos and, at the same time, responsible for the creation of the cosmos and world of man. As with the sinicization of the Fu-po and Hun-hui materials, this kind of symbolic ambivalence can be decided in dialectically contrasting ways. From a Confucian perspective, emphasis is placed on his heroic triumph over chaos as a culture hero; but from a Taoist point of view, the Yellow Emperor's essential identification with the true source of all creativity in the prehuman chaos condition is stressed. The presence of these two kinds of evaluations of the Yellow Emperor in the single Taoist text of the *Chuang Tzu* demonstrates the composite nature of the text and suggests the complexity of trying to assess the early Taoist use of mythological figures and themes.

Part of the difficulty of evaluating the role of the Yellow Emperor may be indicated by the fact that by the time of Ssu-ma Ch'ien, the legends of the Yellow Emperor, which originally had only the status of local myths (perhaps having to do with metallurgical guilds and secret societies), were subsumed into a universal history making the Yellow Emperor the first of the great culture heroes and the one who initiated the main patterns of Confucian civilization.[106]

It would seem that the Confucian historicization of the Yellow Emperor myths would be an obvious problem for the composition of the *Chuang Tzu*. While certain early sections of this work were written when the Yellow Emperor could be exclusively claimed by Taoism and identified with the general cosmogonic theme of *hun-tun*, other parts were being composed during that period when the Yellow Emperor was being made part of an official sacred history giving sanction to a Confucian religio-political ideology of the Chinese empire. The early Taoist ambivalence toward the Yellow Emperor might be said, then, to reflect the rivalry concerning a Taoist or Confucian interpretation of the Yellow Emperor's status as either a mythic ancestor of the cosmogonic/ deluge time or a culture hero of feudal civilization. Seidel, in fact, feels that the Taoist adoption of the Yellow Emperor and the development of the Huang-Lao cult during the Han represent an attempt to synthesize more fully the early mystical ideal of the sage with the later political ideal of the emperor. This issue should be clarified as the Ma-wang-tui "Yellow Emperor" texts are studied. [107]

In the official Confucian context during the Han, the Yellow Emperor assumes the paramount role as the first of the legendary five sage emperors and is said to be one of the great civilizing heroes who banished the "legendary rebels" from China and solidified the cultural and political unity of the empire. [108] It is recounted that the Yellow Emperor banished Huan-tou, a "rebel" or mythological deity who may be identified with Hun-tun. [109] However, in the more archaic understanding of the Yellow Emperor preserved by Taoism, the Yellow Emperor was but another local deity mythologically equivalent to the "rebels" of Huan-tou and Hun-tun. In the *Shan Hai Ching*, for example, the Yellow Emperor is said to be the ancestor of the barbarian tribes of the Jung, Ti, Miao, and Mao—tribes that were also identified with Hun-tun. [110]

As with the almost impossible task of reconstructing the archaic cultural and mythological legacy of Hun-tun as a tribal ancestor, the Chinese sources only provide various ambiguous traces of the Yellow Emperor as a mythological personage. There is, however, a pattern evident amid the mythological residue that suggests a special connection with what Granet postulates as ancient metallurgical bronze-working guilds. Granet was the first to notice the important identification of the Yellow Emperor with the symbolism of the forge, owl, bellows, and the "legendary rebels" (Huan-tou, Hun-tun, etc.). Because of this, Granet feels that the Yellow Emperor was originally a patron god or totemic ancestor of certain prefeudal traditions of metal working. [111]

The possible relevance of this to the Yellow Emperor's later significance for Taoist alchemy is obvious; and, given the religious implications, it should be noted that an archaic technology like bronze working must be considered a shamanistic art of the transformation of matter wherein man emulated the cosmogonic activities of the gods.[112] Furthermore, in Porée-Maspero's delineation of a "southern" Man complex of culture and religion associated with the *hun-tun* theme in Taoism, the creation themes of the deluge, incestuous primal couple, and animal ancestor were interrelated with the ritual and mythology of bronze working.[113] This, for example, is shown by the special ritual role of bronze drums in these "barbarian" local cultures and, in a mythological context, by the role of the drum as an important analogue for the gourd-boat of salvation during the deluge. The magic and ritual power of these drums was associated with its power to reproduce the thunder of the creation time, and the "hourglass" form of the drums seems to have been based on the cosmological prototype of the sacred calabash gourd.[114]

How all of these details relate to the development of early Chinese tradition is only speculation; but Needham, in sympathy with Granet, remarks that the various metallurgical guilds' secret of religio-political power (coming from the godlike ability to work with metals) would have made them the leaders of prefeudal local cultures. They would "have attempted to resist the earliest feudal lords, and to prevent them from acquiring metal-working as the basis of their power."[115] Because of the eventual triumph of feudalism and the need to coalesce authority and legitimize the usurpation of power originally held by various local metallurgical guilds and local cultures, it is reasonable to surmise that it would have been particularly helpful to adopt one of the chief archaic metallurgical gods as a defender of the new unified social order of feudalism and set him in opposition to other gods representing the older tribal orders. It was in this sense necessary to erect a theology of history, the T'ien-ming theory, justifying the authority of the new feudal order while maintaining a religious continuity with the chief symbols of power in earlier periods.[116]

From this kind of perspective, Granet notes that the tension between Confucianism and Taoism is especially reflected by the varying attitudes adopted toward the Yellow Emperor. Even by the end of the Former Han dynasty when the Yellow Emperor was consciously being fitted into the universalist Confucian scheme of imperial history, Ssu-ma Ch'ien's work was criticized by some more orthodox scholars for starting ancient history with the Yellow Emperor and not Yao, Shun, or Yü.[117] Thus, the *Shih Chi* at one point mentions the Yellow Emperor in relation to a passage "in which the states of the Jung and the I are idealized and said to be much better governed than the Chinese states because they are not burdened with the institutions of civilization," and Ssu-ma Kuang's commentary notes that this passage was "written under Taoist influence."[118] In the *Chuang Tzu*, then, the Yellow Emperor theme would be subject to two conflicting tensions: on the one hand, the symbolic identification of the Yellow Emperor with the *hun-tun* theme at the heart of the Taoist vision and, on the other hand, the problem of setting this more archaic understanding apart from the absorption of the Yellow Emperor into official Confucian history.

Of course, one way to deal with this problem is to identify partially with the Confucian idea of kingship. Thus, during the Han period, the prestige given to the Yellow Emperor was related to the Taoist elaboration of the *wu-wei* theory of the sage king. Seidel consequently notes that for the Huang-Lao movement during the Han, which acted as a kind of intermediary stage between the early Taoism of the *Tao Te Ching* and *Chuang Tzu* and the later Taoism of the Six Dynasties, the "Huang-Lao masters attached their teachings to Huang Ti in order to make them acceptable to the princes as an art of government."[119] Elements of this kind of syncretistic compromise with imperial ideology are apparent in sections of the *Chuang Tzu* and *Huai Nan Tzu*; but alongside this later development persisted the more archaic mythological conceptions of the Yellow Emperor as creator and ancestor, which originally allowed for his incorporation into the cosmogonic theme of *hun-tun*.[120]

An example of this synthetic assimilation is found in a cryptic passage from chapter 17 of the *Huai Nan Tzu* that states that "Huang Ti gave birth to *yin* and *yang*. Shang P'ien and Sang Lin [two other deities] created ears, eyes, hands and feet; and that is why Nü-kua performed the seventy [=72 or a multiple of 9] transformations [*hua*[a]]."[121] Plaks remarks that the passage represents the "skeleton of a cooperative 'creation' myth."[122] This is certainly the case, but because the passage is so truncated only a few general comments are possible. First of all, it is important to see the figure of the Yellow Emperor presented as a mythological demiurge of the creation time linked to the P'an-ku notion of "transformation." Secondly, there is at least a suggestion of the Emperor Hun-tun motif of the creation of the human form (eyes, ears, hands, and feet) through the activities of two deities (Hu and Shu). In a very abbreviated and confused sense, therefore, there is at least a glimmer of the fundamental cosmogonic scenario of the one (Yellow Emperor), the two (*yin* and *yang*, Shang P'ien and Sang Lin), and the three (Nü-kua as the creatress or third term who accomplishes the final transformation of the human world). As with the animal ancestor, cosmic giant, and primordial couple and deluge associations broadly hinted at here, the Yellow Emperor is one who is identified with the processes of creation during the chaos time.

Like the yellow, birdlike Hun-tun of the *Shan Hai Ching* and Hun-tun as the Emperor of the Center in the *Chuang Tzu*, Huang Ti was traditionally associated with the color yellow, linked with theriomorphic bird symbolism (the owl, crane, swan, crow, pelican, etc.), and related with the symbolism of the "center" or *axis mundi*—that which balances and harmonizes heaven and earth, *yin* and *yang*, and the four seasons. [123] The *Chuang Tzu* reports that the Yellow Emperor made a pilgrimage to Mt. K'ung-t'ung, "rested" on K'un-lun, and "got" the Tao like "Hsi-wei who held up Heaven and Earth." [124] It should be recalled that K'un-lun is the central place of creation after the deluge in some of the P'an-hu stories. Moreover, in the *Chuang Tzu* and *Lieh Tzu*, K'un-lun is especially depicted as the place of the Yellow Emperor's "death" to the human world and his transformation (=ascension, flight as a bird-man) into an immortal in heaven. [125]

As Major points out, the idea of a "central axis is intimately connected with one of the most potent of the ancient gods, Huang Ti, the Yellow Emperor, who corresponds to Saturn in Western versions of the myth [of creation]. He was a smith and teacher of metallurgy, hence one of his claims later, as a euhemerized Confucian sage, to being a founder of civilization. Most important, he is the god of the center; not only of earth, but of the universe itself." [126] In sum it can be said that throughout Taoist tradition, the Yellow Emperor is associated with medical, alchemical, sexual, and mystic arts of returning to the center, a return to the saturnalian chaos time, in order to achieve the condition of the immortals. [127]

The cosmogonic and cosmological significance of the Yellow Emperor is further indicated by his prominent role in the *yin-yang-wu-hsing* theory of Tsou Yen; and this may, in turn, be related to his special ancestral role in the ancient state of Ch'i. [128] The connection with the northeastern coastal state of Ch'i may also be suggestive of the role of the northern and southeastern barbarian cultures known as the I[c]. Like *hun* and *k'un-lun*, *i*[c] is a general term for "barbarian" or "non-Chinese" and in the form Hun-i is equated with the Kun-i and Chüan-jung barbarians. [129] The people of these cultures were traditionally known as the "bird men" and seemed to have had a central myth of the birth of their tribal ancestor from a primal egg similar to the ancient Shang oviparous ancestor myth. [130] There are many traces of the thunder-egg type of mythology here that directly suggest the deluge and cosmic egg cycles of mythology linked with the *hun-tun* theme in Taoism. Furthermore, Kaltenmark has shown the influence of these factors in the development of the Taoist ideas of the "feathered" immortal (*hsien*[b]) and the metallurgical techniques of transformation practiced by the *fang-shih* magicians of Ch'i. [131]

Whether or not the Yellow Emperor can be exclusively identified as a primordial bird ancestor of these tribes is impossible to substantiate, especially since Chinese accounts of the Yellow Emperor, like those of Emperor Hun-tun, already represent an amalgamation of different mythologies from various local cultures. Despite these problems there is enough evidence to demonstrate the Yellow Emperor's origin in an animal ancestor and thunder-egg type of mythology. The core of symbolism surrounding the Yellow Emperor points finally to a thematic structure basically amenable to the constellation of mythological themes associated with *hun-tun*.

2. *Primordial Couple Myths*

Myths concerning a primordial divine couple, especially an incestuous brother and sister pair, appear to be one of the earliest typologies incorporated into the *hun-tun* theme of creation.[132] There are hidden and degraded references to such a primal couple in many of the early Chinese texts. In ancient works like the *I Ching, Lun Heng, Li Chi*, and *Han Shu* the concept of father Heaven and mother Earth is common, and "it is also an old idea that the various beings come into existence through the union of heaven and earth."[133] A characteristic Taoist expression of this mythic motif as related to the chaos theme is found in chapter 7 of the *Huai Nan Tzu*, which speaks of two deities (*shen*[a]), identified with *yin* and *yang*, who were "chaotically" (*hun*[d]) born. They were responsible for establishing the cosmic form of heaven and earth. As previously noted, this chapter of the *Huai Nan Tzu* specifically invokes the *Tao Te Ching*'s creation scheme of one-two-three. In relation to the mythology of the primordial couple, the two deities found in this passage are particularly reminiscent of the figures of Fu-hsi and Nü-kua.

Fu-hsi and Nü-kua, along with the figure of Chung-li, are the clearest early examples of a primordial couple in early Chinese tradition; but as with many of the other euhemerized mythological figures in Chinese sources, they are often presented as separate, unrelated ancient heroes associated with the ideas of the cosmic egg-gourd, the deluge, the creation of man, and the bringing of a civilized order to the world.[134] This image of the figures is but another instance of the artificial historicization of mythology. This kind of tension between myth and history is, for example, represented in the *Chuang Tzu* where, like the Yellow Emperor, Fu-hsi appears either as an exemplar of the precivilized paradise time or as a culture hero who established feudal civilization.[135]

In general terms, the traditional view of Fu-hsi and Nü-kua "completely falsifies their character, making both of them male rather than emperor and wife, brother and sister"; but there are still certain details preserved in these euhemerized accounts that point to Fu-hsi and Nü-kua's nature as a divine couple of the creation and deluge times.[136] One of these factors is that both

Fu-hsi and Nü-kua were linked with the institution of marriage, a theme that is important in the animal ancestor, animal spouse, and deluge cycle of myths. Fu-hsi was, therefore, "recognized as an originator of the rules of matrimony, specifically inventing the archaic custom known as *li-p' i*, in which animal skins are exchanged as some sort of wedding present, dowry, or mutual guarantee."[137] This detail recalls the motif of wedding garments found in the legend of P'an-hu recounted above and, also, in a way similar to the theme of ultimogeniture in the animal ancestor tales, may point to specific southern tribal kinship rituals.

With regard to Nü-kua, Wen I-to and Granet have shown that this mythic figure was related to the ancient practice of marriage rituals performed at the time of equinoxes.[138] Other evidence leads to the conclusion that these deities were originally consanguineous, animallike gods (especially of serpent form) associated with water and thunder. Like the dragon-snake associations for Fu-hsi, Nü-kua is revealed as a serpent or snail goddess, her name having the cognate meanings of "snail, frog, water hole, pond, etc."[139] It is tantalizing to recall here the *Tao Te Ching*'s evocation of the "profound female" who was the "valley spirit who never dies."[140] More explicitly, the *Lieh Tzu* reports that "Fu-hsi, Nü-kua, Shen-neng, and the Emperors of the Hsia dynasty had snake bodies, human faces, heads of oxen and tigers' snouts."[141] Such hints as to the true animal ancestor nature of Fu-hsi and Nü-kua are further corroborated by the Han iconographical depictions of them as half-human creatures with intertwined, caduceuslike, serpent tails.[142]

The uniped and serpent qualities of these figures, especially Nü-kua, are significant in that suggestions of a dragon nature are frequently linked with the mythic figures in the chaos theme and are central to the southern tribal mythology.[143] As I have already shown, there is much linguistic evidence that indicates an affinity with terms like *hun-tun* (chaos, primal egg-gourd-sphere), *k'ung-tung* (sacred grotto-cave), and *k'un-lun* (cosmic mountain); and this etymological constellation of related words and mythic themes can be extended to include the word *lung* (dragon) whose archaic root **klung* embraces the meanings of "arched," "vault," "cavern," "canopy," "dome," "chamber," "rainbow," "hollow," "hillock-mound," "rain serpent," etc.[144]

The idea of creation I have been tracing throughout this study is clearly brought out in a compilation of texts where the following traits can be noted for Nü-kua as a primal creatress:[145]

1. In the *Huai Nan Tzu* she is linked with the Yellow Emperor as the great "transformer," and in another passage she is presented as the repairer of heaven and earth with multicolored stones after a great catastrophe and

flood (yin^b—a term also having the meanings of lewd, immoral, or incestuous behavior).

2. In the *Shan Hai Ching* one of her divine colleagues, who is "dragon-bodied and human-headed," makes "the thunder by drumming on his (her) belly." In the same text her "intestines are transformed [hua^a] into deities" in a manner "reminiscent of P'an-ku's generative dissolution."

3. In the Han period *Feng Su T'ung I* she creates mankind by patting yellow earth together and dragging a string through mud.

Because of these and other passages, Plaks concludes that Nü-kua's creative activity most ordinarily comes after the origin of heaven and earth, the time of the secondary creation of the human world after a deluge or some other catastrophe that ends the paradise condition. Like P'an-ku, she is primarily associated with the idea of transformation or the continuous creation and regeneration of the world.[146] This kind of creative function is furthermore especially related to the motif of an incestuous marriage union with a sibling male god. This is brought out in a T'ang story of Nü-kua and Fu-hsi, which is a folkloric variant of the southern deluge cycle of myths:

> Long ago, when the universe had first come into being, there were no people in the world, only Nü-kua and her brother on Mount K'un-lun. They considered becoming man and wife, but were stricken with shame. And so (Fu-hsi) and his sister went up on K'un-lun and (performed a sacrifice), vowing: "If it is Heaven's wish that my sister and I become man and wife, let this smoke be intertwined. If not, let the smoke scatter," whereupon the smoke was intertwined, and his sister did cleave unto him.[147]

The necessary linkage between marriage union and creation is prominent in Taoist texts that stress the *hun-tun* theme of a complementary union between two different, yet equal dimensions of the one undifferentiated reality, the Tao. For Taoism, the divine couple mythology expresses the idea of the "third term," or union, of the "two" things of the creation time. This represents a reunion of the primordial one and a return to the chaos state as the necessary prelude to any creative transformation. In this way, the linkage with the overall *hun-tun* theme is precisely that the primordial couple symbolism can convey a conception of primordiality congruent with the cosmic egg-gourd or cosmic giant type of mythology. What is important for the Taoists is that the marriage of Fu-hsi and Nü-kua harbors a metaphysical idea upon which the creation and endurance of the world depends, as well as the salvation of society and man. As Plaks remarks more generally for Chinese tradition, "The marriage of Nü-kua and Fu-hsi emerges as a metaphysical one, not only providing for a contract of cooperation and a promise of continued creation, but in effect embodying the very structural and functional principles of an orderly universe."[148]

Like all of the various motifs of "returning to the beginning" found in early Taoism, the reappropriation of the sacrality of the beginnings involves the notion of "union" or the perfect chaotic blending of the dualities. In fact, the theme of an incestuous sexual union or marriage is a constant factor in Taoist tradition and gives rise to the "suspicion that 'long life' essentially stands for 'sexual love.' "[149] Recall also that the word family of *hun* includes the meaning of "marriage," and compounds such as *tun-lun* refer to "sexual intercourse."

The ritual use of the halves of a gourd as a sacred wedding cup in antiquity together with the consideration that the seventh day of the seventh month was traditionally the most fortuitous time for conjugal union—both fit together with the various elements outlined above to show that in ancient China marriage was seen as a significant "transformation" of life necessarily involving a recapitulation of a cosmic egg-gourd type of cosmogony. In regard to the symbolism of the gourd, primordial couple, and cosmic marriage, it is striking that along with the gourd associations in the names of P'an-ku and P'an-hu, Wen I-to has traced "the characters *p'ao*[a] and *hsi*[f] used in variants of the names of Nü-kua and Fu-hsi . . . back to the ideographs *p'ao*[b] and *hu*[i], also signifying the *hulu* gourd." Similar to the ritual use of drums based on the prototype of the calabash in the southern cultural tradition, Wen notes that "the musical instruments credited to Nü-kua [*sheng*[b] and *huang*[c]] were originally constructed from gourd shells."[150] These linguistic connections and the "motival similarity" of the cosmic egg, primordial couple, and cosmic giant typologies take on a "particular significance if we recognize the *hulu* gourd as a specific Chinese variant of [the] image of autochthonous generation."[151]

A final assessment of the evidence leads to the conclusion that the closest analogue to the Chinese primordial couple lore is seen in the deluge cycle of legends related to the local folklore of south China.[152] It should be made clear that these folkloric materials derive from traditional Chinese records and from modern ethnographic accounts very distant in time and context from the ancient texts under consideration. Plaks therefore remarks that "in the case of myths recorded by anthropological field workers . . . we should not overlook the centuries and millennia of oral redaction that have gone by in the interest of cultural demands external to 'original' myth."[153] Despite the necessary caution called for in handling these materials, and recognizing the fact that the original or "pristine form" of archaic mythology will never be adequately recovered, it is nevertheless possible to view them as preserving some of the essential traits of ancient mythologies lost within the elite tradition. In this sense a pattern of symbol and myth referring to a specific typology of deluge mythology reveals a structural symmetry with the ancient *hun-tun* theme and its interrelated motifs of the cosmic egg-gourd, animal ancestor, cosmic giant, and primordial couple. In composite form this cycle of deluge mythology tells of a great flood caused by an enraged thunder god, a brother and sister pair who are saved by a magic gourd-boat, the incestuous marriage of the couple, and the re-creation of man and the world. In addition, to these details, an important variant of this pattern describes the offspring of the marriage union as a formless mass of flesh, gourd, or bloody lump which, when cut into pieces, produces the human race.[154] A representative version of this kind of story is the following legend of the Ch'uan Miao that reveals a linkage between the mass of flesh and people without anuses motifs:

> (After a great flood that destroyed the world): the people of the earth were all drowned by the water, and there were left only Mi Long . . . and T'u Nyi . ., a brother and a sister. [After a series of tests on a mountain preserved from the flood], the brother and sister reported to heaven and earth and became husband and wife. The next morning they gave birth to a son. This son was a queer thing (called *hun-tun*). It was like a piece of wood. There was no head on top of it, and below there was no means of urinating or relieving the bowels. The two talked the matter over and took the son and cut it into many pieces and threw one piece onto a peach tree and another piece onto a willow tree, and some onto every kind of tree and onto other objects. On the third morning the two arose and saw that there was smoke (from fires made by the people) everywhere. Then people arose everywhere and called on them to be mother and father, and they named all things.[155]

Another version of the Man tribes identifies the pair as Fu-hsi and Nü-kua:

> Heaven decided to punish mankind. Fu-hsi and his sister [Nü-kua], to whom Heaven sent a messenger, sought refuge in an enormous gourd which floated on the waters of the flood. As the sole survivors, they were stranded on the mountain K'un-lun. The bamboo and the black tortoise told them to marry one another. The man cut the tortoise and bamboo into bits which soon reformed themselves; and, since that time, the bamboo has nodes and the black tortoise still bears the marks of the event. The couple joined together. The woman gave birth to a mass of flesh (bloody lump or gourd). The father cut the lump into pieces which became men.[156]

There are many other variants of this tale (see the Appendix). In fact, the Japanese creation myth in the *Kojiki*, which tells of the primordial couple Izanaki and Izanami's deformed firstborn called Hiruko or "leech child," is a direct parallel and has probable connections with southern Austronesian cultural sources.[157] In world mythology the primordial couple myth is widely spread so that there are, for example, many versions in American Indian tradition that involve the failure of the firstborn and show a strong affinity with a Ymir typology where the world is created from the corpse of the cosmic giant.[158]

The important mass of flesh motif as related to the primordial couple deluge mythology just recounted demonstrates a close similarity with some of the details found in the *Chuang Tzu*'s Emperor Hun-Tun story. Recall, for example, the presence of the two deities of Hu and Shu who have water, lightning, thunder, and serpent connotations and who have a special relation (*pao*[a]— having to do with archaic marriage rights and duties?) with the faceless Hun-Tun. Like the father and mother of the lump of flesh, Hu and Shu are the ones who cut up Hun-Tun in order to create the world. It is from the sacrificial dead corpse (like the transformational sacrifice of P'an-ku) that the chaos time of the beginnings or deluge is ended and the profane human world is established. These associations are too pronounced and consistent to be mere coincidence in the Taoist texts and collectively point to a particular mythological pattern coming primarily from "southern" cultural sources.

The identification of the primordial couple and the formless mass of flesh with the *hun-tun* theme in Taoism and the clear analogy with "P'an-ku's dissolution into the infinite phenomena of creation, reminds us of the 'universal egg' motif appearing in mythical tales the world over." [159] The compatibility of the symbolic intentionality of *creatio continua* in the primordial couple, animal ancestor-cosmic giant, and cosmic egg-gourd typologies is certainly a factor in the Taoist amplification of a cosmological metaphysics of *hun-tun*. The Taoist religio-philosophical orchestration of these mythic themes in relation to a particular vision of creation is therefore a good illustration of the methodological principle that all myths and rituals reflect, to some degree, the prestige of cosmogonic myth: "The creation of the World being *the* pre-eminent instance of creation, the cosmogony becomes the exemplary model for 'creation' of every kind."[160]

7

EGG, GOURD, AND DELUGE: THE MYTHOLOGICAL PROTOTYPE OF THE CHAOS THEME

> We are in the presence of one of the marvels of the vegetable world: the plant that gives bottles.
> —Villaneuva (quoted by Heiser, *Gourd Book*)

> Planted is this seed. It grows; it leafs;
>   it flowers; lo! it fruits—this gourd vine.
> The gourd is placed in position; a shapely
>   gourd it is.
> Plucked is the gourd, it is cut open.
> The core within is cut up and emptied out.
> The gourd is this great world, its cover the
>   heavens. . . .
> —Hawaiian "Prayer of the Gourd"
>   (*Pule Ipu*),
>   from Heiser, *Gourd Book*

THE PATH I have been following is overgrown with many layers of cultural and historical foliage, but it has been possible to reach a point in the analysis that allows for some synthetic conclusions as to the cultural, mythological, and symbolic heritage of the chaos theme in Taoism.

First let me quickly review the main points of the inquiry thus far:

1. The *hun-tun* theme in early Taoism represents an ensemble of mythic elements coming from different cultural and religious situations.
2. The symbolic coherence of the *hun-tun* theme in the Taoist texts basically reflects a creative reworking of a limited set of interrelated mythological typologies: especially the cosmic egg-gourd, the animal ancestor-cosmic giant, and primordial couple mythologies. The last two of these typologies are especially, although not exclusively, linked to what may be called the deluge cycle of mythology·found primarily in southern local cultures.
3. While there may also be a cultural connection between the southern deluge cycle and the cosmogonic scenario of the cosmic egg (i.e., via the "thunder-egg," "origin of ancestors [culture hero] from egg or gourd," and "origin of agriculture and mankind from gourd" myths), the fundamental linkage for all of these typologies is the early Taoist, innovative perception of a shared symbolic intention that accounts for, and supports, a particular cosmogonic, metaphysical, and mystical vision of creation and life.

In harmony with the analysis of mythic fragments in the previous chapter, I would like to extend the implications mentioned in the second and third points above—namely, to clarify the specific "southern" mythological paradigm that appears to be foundational for the Taoist development of the *hun-tun* theme; and then to set out more precisely the nature of the early Taoist metaphysics as related to its mythological and symbolic lineage.

THE MYTHOLOGICAL PROTOTYPE OF THE CHAOS THEME

I have maintained throughout this study that the chaos theme in Taoism is most directly expressive of the strict cosmogonic intentionality of a cosmic egg typology. On the other hand, it is clear that the theme, as creatively amplified and structured throughout the early texts, basically draws upon the mythologies of southern local cultures that collectively refer to the theme of the deluge, the regeneration of mankind, and the development of agricultural tradition. In the southern deluge cycle traced by Porée-Maspero and Ho, the creation of the world is taken for granted or hardly mentioned, and the focus in terms of "creation" is almost entirely on the secondary creation of man and human culture. This fact, however, does not invalidate my main thesis since, even for the deluge cycle, the emphasis is always on the implicit cosmogonic idea of "returning to chaos" as the necessary precondition for any new creation or transition. The anthropogonic deluge mythology in a symbolic and philosophical sense depends on, and presupposes, the cosmogonic idea of a watery chaos condition or agent as the mysterious unity of the "one" and the "two"—the creative source and foundation for all natural and cultural life.[1] In the animal ancestor and primordial couple typologies that make up the deluge cycle, the motif of an incestuous marriage, which is analogous to the cosmic egg idea of a moist embryonic *coniunctio*, is emphasized along with the idea of the special product of that union (gourd, mass of flesh, etc.) that preserves both unity and duality. The Taoist synthesis and transformation of these key images represents a philosophical and mystical interpretation of the idea of chaos as ultimately symbolic of the Tao as cosmogonic *arche*, or perhaps most properly, the Tao as Cosmic Gourd.

The Taoist interpretation of the deluge mythology in terms of the philosophical and mystical ideal of the cosmic egg is most probably affected by the crucial function of cucurbitic symbolism in the flood accounts and in the associated typologies of the animal ancestor and primordial couple. The prominent role of the gourd as salvation vessel, place of refuge, and offspring of the primordial couple strongly hints that cucurbits represent a paramount symbolic factor that allows for an explicit cosmogonic understanding of the deluge cycle. My reasoning behind this inference has to do with the botanical, cultural, and linguistic significance of cucurbits in Asia (and elsewhere)[2], their ubiquity in "southern" or Austronesian mythology and religious symbolism, and their special relation with the myths of the origin of agriculture.[3]

The deluge symbolism of the gourd (=mass of flesh, egg, deformed child, leather sack, etc.), which when cut up (=sacrificial death) gave rise to men and plants, suggests, in fact, the Austronesian Dema mythological complex of agricultural origins so richly developed by the ethnologist Adolph Jensen.[4] In a composite and abbreviated form, Dema mythology tells of the ancient time when, during or after a marriage ceremony, a mysterious child (=the Dema deity, who is usually female and identified with certain animals—boar, pig, bird, fish—and food plants—coconut, taro, yam, gourd, etc.) is murdered, cut into pieces, and buried.[5] The sacrificial dismemberment of the Dema deity is a "creative death" since it establishes the ordinary human world of sexuality and mortality.

The murder of the Dema child "is not only a 'creative' death, it is also a way of being continually present in the life of men and even in their death. For by feeding on the plants and animals that sprang from her body, men actually feed on the very substance of the Dema-divinity."[6] It is furthermore the case that in the primitive world of the tropical paleocultivators, this kind of mythology has a foundational connection with traditions of ritual sacrifice (and head hunting), systems of dual classification, sexual antagonism, and masculine initiation rites whereby a man can attain a higher worldly and spiritual status by his symbolic usurpation of the feminine powers of the Dema goddess.[7] A man, in distinction to a woman, can gain the special social prestige of "face" through his participation in ritual ceremonies that reenact the primal murder of the Dema. It is tempting to conjecture that in the cultural areas imbued with the Dema ethos, the common usage of a ritually significant penis sheath made out of a gourd shell implies the masculine appropriation of one of the most religiously potent and mythically validated signs of creative power and fertility.[8]

Besides the surprising resonance of some of these details with the symbolism seen in the Emperor Hun-tun story, it is also interesting to observe that a similar pattern is found within the synthetic national mythology recorded in the Japanese *Kojiki*. Obayashi Taro, for example, notes that in the *Kojiki* there is a linkage between the cosmogonic phase of creation ("origin of the land" involving a primordial couple and their incestuous union that produces a deformed child—a "leech child" identified with an earlier state of undifferentiated chaos before the appearance of duality and with the Chinese *hun-tun*) and the later origin of the human world and agriculture.[9] Obayashi concludes that the "form of agricultural crop-origin myth that appears . . . in Japanese mythology is the one in which the agricultural crop is believed to have emerged from a corpse, and this falls under the category that Jensen called the Hainuwele [or Dema]-mythologem."[10]

Jensen's Dema thesis concerning the primitive origins of vegeculture (=root crop agriculture) is admittedly controversial because of his diffusionist leanings and his use of contemporary ethnological evidence to argue for the historical development of culture.[11] But it is not necessary to adopt all of Jensen's theoretical edifice to see the value of his general descriptive discussion of a Dema-type mythology. For my purposes the point remains that within the civilizational and literate tradition of the *Kojiki* there is a cosmogonic and synthetic reinterpretation of myths very similar in cultural background and typological structure to those found in the Taoist use of the *hun-tun* theme. Obayashi feels that Japanese mythology relates especially to south Chinese tradition where it seems that two mythological cycles, one a Dema corn-deity type relating to the origin of agriculture (e.g., the Chinese accounts of Hou-chi, Lord Millet, from whose grave the five cereals grew spontaneously) and the other the P'an-ku cosmogonic myth of world creation, coexisted and shared the same structure. Obayashi's final speculative assessment is that "this form of agriculture crop origin myth belongs to the millet cultivation type of the swidden culture in the southern part of China."[12] With respect to the possible origins of the Taoist *hun-tun* theme, I need only add that this type of agriculture (swidden or "slash and burn") was particularly characteristic of the southern local culture of the Yao[b].[13] The Liao[b] culture, which Eberhard thinks is most closely related to the *hun-tun* theme in the Chinese literate tradition, seems to have adopted swidden agriculture from the Yao[b] and, later, wet-field agriculture from the Thai.[14]

In view of the relation between a Dema-type mythology and the origins and nature of root crop and swidden forms of agriculture, the prominence of cucurbitic symbolism in these and other related myths may have some particular significance. There is seemingly something about the natural botanical existence and consequent cultural role of gourds that has determined their status as a kind of common denominator for most of the myths under consideration. It, first of all, should be reemphasized that gourds (especially the bottle gourd, calabash, or *Lagenaria siceraria*, meaning "bottle-like drinking vessel")[15] in east, southeast, and insular Asia are traditionally a commodity of utmost value, being honored for their extreme cultural utility (especially as containers/ utensils, musical and gaming devices [*t'ou-hu*], insect and bird cages, fishing floats, an artistic medium, etc.), their medicinal and religious significance, and also, though of less importance, their nutritive value as a food source. In reference to East Asian tradition, Ho remarks:

> [The] *Lun-Yü* . . . of the fifth century says "*i tan shih, i piao yin*" (one "*tan*" [a basket] container of food and one "*piao*" [the *p'iao* gourd] container of drink). In Taoist tradition the shape of the constricted gourd is said to be analogous to that of the isles of the Immortals, as well as being the symbol of the world. The gourd is also an emblem of one of the eight immortals and is believed to have contained the elixir of life; hence Chinese apothecaries selected the constricted gourd as their sign-board. Among the Puyuma of Formosa, a gourd in the altar is identified as the dwelling place of departed souls, and among the boat-people of Canton, gourds are tied to the backs of children to assist them in floating in case they fall into the water.[16]

From the broader perspective of worldwide cultural history, the botanist Charles Heiser writes that the bottle gourd was clearly "one of man's most important plants before the invention of pottery."[17] *Lagenaria*, in particular, gave rise to a truly amazing inventory of different uses: as containers, as food, in medicine and surgery, as floats and rafts, pipes and snuffboxes, cricket cages and bird houses, masks, games, charms, offerings, penis sheaths, carved decorations, musical instruments (especially rattles, drums, and cordophones), and as a pervasive subject of myth and ritual.[18] The bottle gourd was, perhaps, the "world's most widely distributed plant" in ancient times.[19]

The cultural antiquity and pantropical universality of the bottle gourd is shown by the fact that, despite the existence of two primary subspecies (*Lagenaria siceraria siceraria=afrikana* and *L. s. asiatica*) and several varieties, "no wild ancestor has been determined with certainty."[20] The absence of a wild ancestral bottle gourd, in other words, suggests that *Lagenaria* was domesticated at an extremely early period in human cultural development, one scholar putting the "earliest cultivation of bottle gourds in tropical Africa by 40,000 B.P."[21] With regard to the antiquity of the Asian subspecies of *Lagenaria*, which may have had its distant prehistoric origins in Africa, there is the recent, albeit controversial, evidence of the Spirit Cave findings in Thailand that points to the very early cultural selection of the gourd (ca. 9,000 B.P.?).[22] Bottle gourds may have "occured naturally in southeastern Asia prior to the time of the human occupation of Spirit Cave, on the basis of the fact that the history of *Lagenaria* is so little known at present that we cannot state anything definite about its natural distribution at the end of the Pleistocene."[23]

Along with the growing ethnobotanical and archaeological attention that is being paid to the cultural legacy of the gourd, there is also the rich corroborating evidence of comparative data in the history of religions. In Ho's comparative analysis of an extensive gathering of Asian mythological materials, as well as in Porée-Maspero's similarily focused study, the evidence testifies to an almost archetypal presence of gourd symbolism in the deluge cycle of tales that are concerned with the origin of man and plants: "the gourd, besides magically yielding grain, appears in many ways. Mankind emerges from a gourd; men escape from the deluge by drifting in a gourd; the gourd's vine serves as a sky-rope for ascending to heaven," and so on.[24] Ho finds that the "popularity and versatility of the gourd is far greater than that of any other kind of fruit."[25] It seems reasonable to conclude, therefore, that in the earliest versions of the deluge mythology, the primary magic fruit of salvation and creation is "the gourd and that the other kinds of fruit appear later."[26]

The persistent emergence of gourd symbolism in relation to the *hun-tun* theme in the early Taoist texts is additional confirmation of the singular significance of cucurbitic imagery in the mythological context under consideration. Yet another powerful indication of these linkages is brought out by the semiotic matrix that unfolds when the various Chinese words for "gourd," and their word-family associations, are comparatively examined. In the preliminary survey condensed in table 3, it is telling that there is a special abundance of Chinese terms for *Lagenaria siceraria asiatica*. While the semantic range for phonetically related words is by no means a closed system, it becomes obvious that most of the seemingly diverse meanings fall into a definite pattern that essentially reproduces the mythological typologies and related motifs that I have collectively labeled the *hun-tun* theme. The full thematic range and interconnected mythological significance of the multi-form motifs and sub-motifs recorded in table 3 will be pursued throughout the rest of this chapter; but when table 3 is placed alongside tables 4 and 5, which summarily map the mythological structure of the Taoist *hun-tun* theme, it already becomes evident that the almost exact morphological congruence goes beyond mere coincidence.

"Map is not territory," but maps can have some real reference to the objective world of space, time, and gourds if they help to show how "this" is connected with "that." They help to show how and why one has gotten to a certain destination, and they indicate something about the propinquity of a future course of action. Tables 3 and 4 in this sense may be said to chart out a truly homologous relationship between gourds and their symbolic meaning in China since what is depicted clearly depends on a complex historical and linguistic network that has some common natural and cultural origin.

1. *Culture, Agriculture, and "Mother Gourd"*

One of the common cultural factors may have to do with the overall issue of the early neolithic origins of agriculture in south China and Southeast Asia, the relative priority of types of plant cultivation (i.e., the cultural primitivity of root cropping versus cereal agriculture as well as affiliated cultivation technologies: digging stick, house gardening, and swidden practices in relation to the more complex techniques of cereal cultivation, especially those involving water management), and finally the economic sequence of certain grains, particularly millet and rice, within the context of the development of Asian seed farming. With respect to the human exploitation of plants, the role of the animal ancestor and the primordial couple's marriage-union themes in the same southern deluge cycle of mythology raises an additional consideration concerning the cultural history of animal domestication (most archaically, it seems, the pig, dog, and buffalo) and the evolution of social and religious ideas pertaining to kinship and sexual stratification (or, perhaps, the "domestication" of women from the men's point of view?).[27]

These are all complicated and hotly debated questions and it does not behoove me to claim that any overarching or definitive solution is forthcoming. I will therefore not pretend to proffer answers to all of the cultural and historical issues mentioned; but, the focus on the single problem of agricultural origins highlights some intriguing clues embedded in the mythological material and affiliated gourd symbolism that indicate, at least, a plausible hypothesis. With

TABLE 3

SEMIOTIC MATRIX OF CHINESE CUCURBITIC TERMINOLOGY

phonetic/word family associations — gourd terminology	CHAOS/NATURE/ PRIMITIVE/BARBARIAN — semantic traits							Passage/Fall Primal Sacrifice Cutting/Carving	COSMOS/CIVILIZATIONAL/ HIERARCHICAL — semantic traits								
	1	2	3	4	5	6	7		8	9	10	11	12	13	14	15	16
KUA, R. 97 瓜 爪 — Cucurbitaceae gourd, melon, cucumber, etc. espec. C.m., C.s.	1a	2a,2c 2d,2e	3c,3d		5a			X					12		14a		
HU 瓠 葫 壺 espec. L.s. Cf. HUN, HUNG, HOU	1e,1g 1d	2b,2d 2c	3,3d 3b,3e 3c		5b		7	X		9	10 10a				14b	15b 15c	16c
JANG 瓤 — gourd pulp, pith	1e,1g 1d		3				7								14a,	15a	16a
KOU 瓤 — gourd	1g	2b	3a,3e				7									15a 15b 15c	16c 16b
K'UA 瓣 — C.s.						6	7									15b	
LEI 蓏 (Cf. LUAN, LUN) premature ripe C.s., gourd	1e,1d	2b	3b	4a					8a		10a				14d 14b 14c 14a	15b, 15	16c

TABLE 3 (continued)

SEMIOTIC MATRIX OF CHINESE CUCURBITIC TERMINOLOGY

phonetic/word family associations — gourd terminology	CHAOS/NATURE/PRIMITIVE/BARBARIAN — semantic traits							Passage/Fall Primal Sacrifice Cutting/Carving		COSMOS/CIVILIZATIONAL/HIERARCHICAL — semantic traits							
	1	2	3	4	5	6	7	X	8	9	10	11	12	13	14	15	16
LIEN (pulp, pith)	1d				5	6	7					11	12		14c, 14b	15	16c
LOU (C.s., gourd, etc.)	1g	2c	3d,3e	4	5a	6a	7	X		9					14d		
LU (L.s.)	1g,1f, 1e	2b,2a	3e,3c, 3d,3b		5b	6,6b, 6a	7	X	8a	9	10, 10a	11	12		14d	15a, 15b	16b, 16a, 16c
PAN (P'AN) (pit, pith, gourd)	1d	2e,2a, 2c	3,3e	4a			7	X			10a		12			15a	16a, 16c
P'AO (PAO, PO) (L.s., C.m.)	1d,1e, 1b	2a,2b	3	4a	5,5b, 5a	6	7	X		9	10		12			15, 15c	16c, 16a
PENG (P'ENG) (gourds of same vine)	1d,1e	2d,2a, 2c	3,3e	4b			7				10a, 10		12			15	
P'IAO (PIAO) (L.s., ladle, etc.)	1b,1c, 1d	2c,2b, 2e,2d, 3a	3a,3c	4a,4b			7	X							14d	15c	16b, 16c
P'IEN (PIEN) (pit, pith)	1b,1f	2c,2a	3	4a			7	X	8a				12		14c, 14b	15, 15b	16c
T'ANG (TANG) (large C.m., L.s.)	1d,1e	2e,2c	3a	4,4b	5		7	X	8,8a		10a, 10				14c, 14b	15, 15b	16a, 16c

Character / Description	1	2	3	4	5	6	7	8	9	10	11	12	13	14	15	16
T'IEH (TIEH) large/small L.s., C.m. immature gourds	1g,1d	2c	3c,3d / 3e	4a			7	8a		10a	11	12		14c	15a	
T'UN (TUN) name of gourd, melon		2b,2a	3c,3b / 3d.3		5a		7	8a	9	10				14d / 14c		
YAO C.s., C.M., gourd	1d,1b / 1c	2b,2a	3.3d / 3e.3a	4	5.5a	6		8		10a						16a / 16c
YUNG (YING) gourd, melon	1d.1g / 1e	2c.2a	3.3e / 3d	4a	5		7	8a		10 / 10a	11			14a / 14c	15 / 15a	16c
YÜ fruit of same vine	1f,1g	2a,2b / 2c	3b,3d / 3a	4	5.5a		7	8.8a	9	10a / 10		12	13	14b / 14c	15b	16c / 16a

LEGEND FOR TABLE 3

Sources: *Tz'u Hai*; Karlgren, *Analytical Dictionary*; Couvreur, *Dictionnaire Classique*; Mathew, *Dictionary*.

Abbreviations: C.m. = *Cucumis melo*, C.s. = *Cucumis sativus*, L.s. = *Lagenaria siceraria*

SEMANTIC TRAITS/NARREMES

A) CHAOS/NATURE

1. Deluge Theme
   1a. primordial couple
   1b. water/air, wet/dry, etc. contrasts
   1c. drifting, floating, etc.
   1d. revolving, swirling, flowing motion
   1e. thunder (noise, drumming, etc.)
   1f. boat/ark/drum
   1g. mound, pillar

2. Animal Ancestor Theme
   2a. bird/fish
   2b. mammal
   2c. insect/amphibian
   2d. hairiness
   2e. striped, varicolored, tattoo, etc.

3. Confusion, Obscurity, Mixed
   3a. sexual license

LEGEND FOR TABLE 3 (continued)

3b. stupidity, clumsiness, foolishness, (stupidity-intelligence contrast)
3c. blind, lost, dizzy, darkness, (dark-clear contrast)
3d. unclear noise, sound
3e. barbarian, rebel, primitive, shame, vulgar

4. Disease, Deformity
4a. leprosy, lame, tumors, etc.
4b. swollen, bloated

5. Shut-Up/Empty/Hollow Condition
5a. alone, solitary, protected
5b. cave, womb, cocoon, shelter, etc.

6. Bodily Parts
6a. head, skull
6b. belly

7. Growth/Change/Abundance/Uncontrolled
   Vitality/Progeny-Descendants/Harmony

B) COSMOS/CIVILIZATIONAL

8. Culture-Civilizational Hero
8a. flood control, dikes, boundaries, controlled order

9. Agricultural Arts

10. Culinary Arts
10a. utensils, containers, etc.

11. Metallurgical Arts

12. Clothing/Sericulture

13. Musical/Gaming Arts

14. Religious/Priestly Arts
14a. sacrifice, divination, etc.
14b. ritual vessels
14c. burial, funerary ritual
14d. tower, ceremonial center, central mound, mountain

15. Military Arts
15a. ritual combat
15b. boasting
15c. weapons, etc.

16. Political Arts
16a. ritual reciprocity
16b. marriage alliance/political alliance
16c. prestige/authority—ranked order, measure

this in mind it is noteworthy that in relation to the origins of cereal cropping in East Asia, if not Southeast Asia, millet (*Setaria italica* and *Panicum miliaceum*) was apparently cultivated before rice (*Oryza sativa*)[28]; and, in the earliest legends collected by Ho, there is a clear preference given to millet over rice.[29] Rice eventually became the dominant food staple for these cultures, and a mythology of rice is substituted for the tales involving millet. Among the five grains in ancient China, only the spirit of millet (Hou-chi) was worshipped as a deity at the first harvest; and it seems that millet was the cereal that was symbolically dominant in the first mythologies of the origins of seed plants and human culture.

It is fascinating that Hou-chi as Lord Millet, the ancient Minister of Agriculture under Shun in the Chinese Classics, is depicted in relation to mythological fragments suggestive of an archaic gourd mythology. In the *Shih Ching* it is said that after his fabulous birth as the culture-hero of the Chou and still as a child:

> [Hou-chi] looked majestic and intelligent.
> When he was able to feed himself,
> He fell to planting large beans.
> The beans grew luxuriantly;
> His rows of paddy shot up beautifully;
> His hemp and wheat grew strong and close;
> His gourds yielded abundantly.[30]

Gourds also appear as sacrificial vessels (cf. *hu*[g]) used ritually to validate the political foundations (after a period of wandering) of a feudal prince and his newly created state during the early Chou period. The *Shih* reports that Duke Liu, a descendant of Hou-chi:

> Went up to the dais and leant upon a stool.
> Then to make the pig-sacrifice
> They [the people] took a swine from the sty:
> He [Duke Liu] poured out libation from a gourd,
> Gave them food, gave them drink;
> And they acknowledged him as their prince and founder.[31]

As it says elsewhere in the *Shih* concerning the culture hero Tan-fu (a rival to Hou-chi): "The young gourds spread and spread. / The people after they were first brought into being / From the River Tu went to the Ch'i."[32] Waley comments in passing that "it is most likely that imbedded in this line is an allusion to a forgotten belief that 'the people when they were first brought into being' were gourd seeds or young gourds."[33] More tentative is the possibility that Hou-chi may have originally been part of a mythological primordial couple since the word *hou* has the dual meaning of "empress" and "king," which is allusively insinuating of a gender alteration similar to the one performed on Nü-kua in the official historicized annals. There is, moreover, some further etymological likelihood that *hou* has a word-family linkage with the basic hu^{b-i} series of terms for the bottle gourd.

Coming to essentially the same conclusions from the standpoint of his own independent comparative analysis of mythology, Ho states that "the earliest version of [the grain origin theme] must be a *Magic Gourd that Yields Millet*."[34] The implications of this in the mythological record are that "the other fruits which produce rice are later modifications that conform to a changing social reality, since millet is replaced by rice, and the pumpkin or squash become more frequently spoken of than the gourd in certain communities."[35]

In line with these observations, the unexpectedly fertile matter of the comparative significance of gourd mythology and symbolism also offers a basis from which to address the larger question of the antecedents and mechanism of the origins and development of agriculture. I have already noted in company with the findings of several other scholars that the Dema and deluge mythologies, which involve the symbolism of the gourd, often have special reference to archaic tropical and semitropical forms of root cropping and swidden practices. When this information is aligned with the archaeological and botanical evidence, there is good reason to presume that the gourd (*Lagenaria*, as well as bamboo, fruit trees, and root crop plants like the yam and taro) was one of the most ancient, if not the most ancient, of all cultigens in Asia and elsewhere.[36] When this is all put together, there is the very real possibility of arguing for the central agency of the gourd in the agricultural transformation of the human world.

Since this point of view tends to favor the priority of root cropping over cereal agriculture, it not only suffers from an overindulgence in gourd infatuation but runs counter to prevailing archaeological opinion, which asserts the greater antiquity of seed crop cultivation.[37] This is not to say that there have not been serious challenges to the orthodox position. Carl Sauer's hypothetical case (following Vavilov and Haudricourt) for the archaic tropical root cropping of southwestern and eastern Asia as the cradle of world agriculture is one prominent and respected early example of maverick opinion and one that fits well with the cultural characteristics of the Dema mythology set out by Jensen.[38] There is also the later and largely supporting work of D. G. Coursey on the passage from yam "ceremonialism" to yam cultivation in Africa and Asia and the more theoretical publications of David Harris on swidden systems and tropical agriculture.[39] Most recent and most directly related to the topic at hand is the enticing and bold work of the anthropologist, Donald Lathrap, who proposes an elaborate speculative model for the origins and development of agriculture.[40] Lathrap, it should be made clear, is primarily basing his argument on evidence related to an African genesis and later diffusionist developments in South America; but given the role of *Lagenaria* as the keystone in his understanding of the inception and development of plant domestication, much of his discussion, as he recognizes, is relevant to the Asian situation. Writing before Lathrap's views were published, Chang Kwang-chih cautiously embraced a similar theoretical model for agricultural development in Southeast Asia and southern China.[41]

Briefly stated, Lathrap emphasizes the importance of the bottle gourd for the development of garden horticulture among paleolithic fishing (hunting)/ gathering communities living along tropical river banks. The need of primitive fishermen for containers, dippers, net floats, fish poisons (from bitter gourd pulp or seeds?), and other culturally useful paraphernalia would have led them to exploit that kind of tropical plant which naturally exists as a buoyant bottle. The maintenance of a steady supply of these plants, then, gave rise to the relatively unstable protocultivation of gourds in weeded clearings or house gardens. Through gradual experimentation in the raising of other tropical plants (like yam, taro, manioc, etc.) more directly related to the improvement of the available food supply, there was a shift from a fishing economy to a more extensive swidden root cropping in areas separate from the original house gardens and closer to the jungle's edge.[42] These changes are in turn reflected in the religious symbol systems of these cultures since the house garden and its gourd crop were considered a safely controlled spiritual domain (having feminine associations) as distinguished from the more remote swidden clearings carved out of the tropical forest, which were charged with a more ambiguous ''aura of spiritual disorder'' and ''potent sexuality'' (the associations here are primarily masculine).[43]

This rough sketch does not do justice to the wealth of detail marshalled by Lathrap or the imaginatively synthetic tenor of his thesis. Of course, as specialists like Heiser and Charles Reed have been careful to point out, neither the weight of sporadic archaeological detail nor the appeal of Lathrap's theoretical imagination constitutes proof with regard to such complex issues.[44] There is no need for me to enter into the fray concerning the final validity of Lathrap's hypothesis of agricultural origins and development. I would, however, like to embrace and highlight Lathrap's impressive cucurbitic evidence as testifying at least to a particular kind of cognitive significance attributed to gourds. The unassailable fact is that the gourd, more so than many other objects of the natural world, has existed in human cultural history as a prototypical botanical symbol for the idea of creation. The gourd lived in human consciousness as the "mother" of both natural and cultural life, the uncarved and carved orders of existence. Regarding the "peculiar set" of religious beliefs and rituals associated with the gourd (especially concerning sexual dualism and antagonism) that he collected from South American, Melanesian, and African sources, Lathrap says that "we may conclude that metaphorically the gourd is a womb, that it is the whole universe, or, stated more simply, the universal womb."[45]

2. Gourd as "Botanical Egg": The Power of Natural Emptiness

Remembering the Old English derivation of "true" from a word meaning "firmly planted like a tree (*treowe, trywe*)," I would like to propose that the metaphorical truth of the gourd, its prolific linguistic and cultural fruitfulness, must be something that is deeply rooted in nature. Regardless of any symbolic connotations, the fruit of the gourd plant is botanically a womb. The "semiotic role of the cucurbits," as Ralf Norrman and Jon Haarberg put it, "is mainly to be sought in the physiology of the plant."[46] Moreover, it is necessary not only to study the morphological and physiological distinctiveness of individual cucurbitaceous traits in the world of flora but also to explore the "naturalness" or meetness of the connection that gourds have with certain kinds of mythological stories. One must, in other words, seek out the narrative element in the growth process or life cycle of gourds. Symbols give rise to thought by first giving birth to stories.

In their gloriously erudite and monomaniacal analysis of cucurbits in world literature, Norrman and Haarberg have done the initial spadework in this direction.[47] Since much of the paradigmatic system of cucurbitic symbolism uncovered in their survey has already been encountered in this study, there is no need to reproduce their results. But because they indiscriminately approach the whole family of *Cucurbitaceae* as literary critics primarily acquainted with Western tradition, it is possible to extend, refine, and cross-fertilize their work by bringing forward the Asian material presented here and by stressing the special significance of the genus *Lagenaria* amid the garden of all other gourds. Finally, in relation to my focus as historian of religions, it will be helpful to examine more closely the "cosmogonic" narrativity of the life and growth of the gourd as a paradigm for the mythological symbolism found within the Chinese context.

In the morphological spirit of Goethe's *Urpflanze*, or better in this case, the *Urkürbis*, the most effective way to demonstrate the connection between the cosmogonic theme of *hun-tun* seen in the Taoist texts and the natural analogue of the gourd will be to consider some botanical details relevant to the existence of *Lagenaria* in both space and time. Most remarkable in this regard is that the "narrative element" in the life and death of *Lagenaria* naturally tells the creation and fall story of "one-two-three" in the *Tao Te Ching* and of Emperor Hun-tun's primal sacrifice in the *Chuang Tzu*.

One way to begin is simply to list some of the basic botanical facts that serve to classify the family of *Cucurbitaceae* and genus of *Lagenaria*.[48] Most generally *Cucurbitaceae* (composed of 100 genera and almost 1000 species, mostly tropical in origin) can be characterized as a tendril-bearing vine plant with three or five lobed, alternately arranged leaves, producing unisexual flowers born on the same plant, and developing a fruit or gourd (technically a *pepo* or form of berry) with a hardened outer dermis containing many seeds ordinarily attached in three places on the outer wall. *Lagenaria* shares these family traits but is more specifically distinguished as a mesophytic annual plant producing creeping and climbing vines up to fifty feet in length and showy white, pubescent flowers and bearing a durable hard fruit that is extraordinarily variable in size and shape (the bipartite "hourglass" or "dumbbell" shape being particularly noteworthy in Asian accounts; other popular names give some indication of their morphological and symbolic multivalence: ball-egg, club, dipper, drum, snake, swan, ridged fish, warty toad, and kettle/retort). The large tangled leaves have a distinctive musky odor (related to the ento-mophilous character of the plant?); and the nocturnally blooming flowers are usually pollinated by beetles, bees, moths, birds, butterflies(?), and bats(?).[49] It may also be said *Lagenaria* is monoecious (hermaphroditic) and auto-incestuous since pollen from a male flower (staminate) will fertilize a female flower (pistillate) on the same plant and, curiously, inbreeding seems to result in little loss of vigor.[50]

It might be said interpretively that incest is functional in the natural order of the gourd while, within the cultural order, incest is held to be cognitively (and to a lesser degree, biologically) disfunctional and taboo. The human offspring or "gourd-kin" of the mother gourd, like the cereal grains that also mythologi-cally come from the primal gourd of the deluge, must practice the hybridization of cross-fertilization (exogamy) to maintain cultural vigor.

The most revelatory aspect of the growth of *Lagenaria* is finally the explo-sive swelling, shaping, and coloring (white/green) of its fruit (the actual gourd), which, upon maturity, contains a watery, undifferentiated, and pulpy mass embedded with the seeds of future life. As it naturally ages, this "first chaos" stage of the gourd is transformed from its youthful soft, downy-hairy condition into a hard, dry, smooth (sometimes warty or ridged), and hollow container colored a dark reddish or yellow brown. In the jostle of independence that comes from their separation from the fleshy pulp as it dries, the germs of life within the central cavity of the gourd signal their presence through sound: they rattle and roll. Hollow, light, and sonant with the stirrings of new life, the gourd has become the vegetable bottle that floats. It is, in fact, the gourd's ability to float that constitutes the basic mechanism for the propagation and distribution of its phenomenal bounty—its "ten thousand" seeds—which are dispensed when the shell is broken.[51]

This is not meant to be an exercise in armchair botany; but, from the few details and brief interpretive commentary presented so far, it becomes evident that the bottle gourd exists in nature as a remarkable cypher for the story and mystery of creation told of in the Taoist *hun-tun* theme: the "one" truly gives birth to the "two," the "two" to the "three," and, thrice "three" to the "Ten Thousand Things." The gourd's shapeless omnipotence is truly a gift from the divine ancestors. By being bored, cut, or carved, it freely yields (*jang*[a,b]) its ambivalent natural life to man so that the human world may be created. *Lagenaria*'s unique creative aptitude is rooted in the power of its emptiness, a *wu-wei* that accomplishes all things. Both its natural fertility and cultural utility are dependent on the nothingness of its fruit; and the bipartite form of the constricted type of bottle gourd emulates the balanced cosmic form of heaven and earth, *yin* and *yang*, linked by the empty yet pregnant force of *ch'i*[a]. These naturally symbolic factors, as well as the more precise analysis presented in figure 3, recommended *Lagenaria* as the Chinese and Southeast Asian botanical equivalent, or prototype, of the mythological cosmic egg. The gourd exists as a kind of "earth egg" in form, growth, and function. Even more meaningful than egg symbolism, which naturally tends to require some version of a divine Mother Goose, the bottle gourd in its emptiness and self-yielding, its *wu*[b] and *tz'u-jang* (cf. *tzu-jan*?), emphasizes the *creatio ex nihilo* mystery of spontaneous self-generation out of "nothing."

Birds are, of course, related both to the *hun-tun* theme (e.g., the *hun-tun* "bird" in the *Shan Hai Ching*; reference to types of geese and swans [*hung*[a]], other water or predatory birds like the kingfisher, owl, etc.; "feathered" Taoists [=*hsien*[b]]; and the *hun*[j] soul that "ascends" to heaven) and to the natural growth of gourds (as pollinators and as feeders on insects found on the plants).[52] But, in distinction to the naturally symbolic implications of the egg that require a biological progenator as a necessary cause (e.g., the theistic

Biblical imagery of a creator God "hovering over the waters"), birds as a part of the Way of the gourd are only peripheral agents in a larger organismic process of creation and life that originally depends on the chaos of empty nothingness. In fact, bird imagery, stressing the important role of an avian actor, or "holy spirit," in the drama that furthers the sexual reunion and continuation of the eternal life-cycle, is more correctly subsumed into a dualistic system which accentuates the contrasting, yet ecologically interrelated, symbolism of BIRD (:air:drought:sky:dry:male:kite flying ritual: etc.) versus FISH (:water reptiles:dragon:water:flood:earth:wet:female:dragon boat ritual: etc.).[53]

Insects and other anomalous creatures (like the bat, some nocturnal mammals, and some amphibians), it may be added, seem to be symbolically significant because they can be identified with either pole or, even more ambiguously, as "third term" creatures; they exist in the twilight region between the more distinct divisions in the zoological and cultural worlds. For Chuang Tzu in the opening story in the "inner chapters," it is exactly this mythologically and ecologically grounded contrast between the fish ($k'un^c$) and bird ($p'eng$) that serves as a basic Taoist lesson in the primacy of the relativistic and empty order of the chaos-gourd in life, that order which is responsible for the ultimate transformation of fish into bird, $k'un^c$ into $p'eng$—as well as the blurred interrelationship of cicada and dove, north and south, big and little, dark and light, earth and heaven, man and butterfly, *hun* and *tun*, and vice versa.[54] There is an empty and dynamic power of nothingness, hidden in the interstices of all life, that blends, unites, and overcomes all ordinary distinctions. The gourd as the shapeless "great form" of creation is the plant that has the ability to take the animal shape of both a bird and a fish.

The growth of *Lagenaria* (i.e., in the temperate and semitemperate climate of north and south China) from implanted seed in the springtime after the last frost, to axial stem, to luxuriantly meshed leaves and spiralling tendrils, to flowered sexuality, and to fruited maturity ordinarily takes about seven lunar months of growth.[55] Maturity is botanically indicated by a color change in the stem and fruit, the stem turning hard and brown and the gourd-fruit taking on a mottled (or striped) lunar hue of a milky white/light green color.[56] In China the time of a gourd's ripe fruition was traditionally known as the "gourd month" (*kua-yüeh*), the seventh (or eighth) lunar month. In the seasonal round of south China and Southeast Asia, this marks the crucial transitional or chaos time of passage from the heat and rains of summer to the cool, dry darkness of winter. As in many other ancient traditions, this was an ambivalent negative/positive Halloween time (in China, the ritual time of the seventh or fifteen day of the seventh month) when the unquiet and hungry dead return to haunt the living and threaten an eternal winter. It was a time when lanterns were lit and gourds hung from rafters.[57] More positively, the gourd month is also the time that celebrates the foundations of the social order of the living and dead and the civilizational arts associated with women.[58] As suggested by the legends told of the swan maiden or Cinderella-like weaver girl, it is the "pumpkin coach" and gourd-eating time of propitious marriage union that insures the continuation of the cultural order of man.[59] The ancient text of the *Tso Chuan* records that the "gourd time" (*kua-shih*) is auspicious for any significant change whether for well or ill.[60]

The malevolent potential for perpetual winter, cold dryness, and death (or eternal summer, heat, rain, and uncontrolled life) is overcome by a gourd's ability to protect its inner fertility (its seeds, which possess the power of *creatio continua*) by hardening and emptying itself in preparation for a future rebirth. The universality and symbolic significance of this is suggested in Western tradition by the ninth century Christian monk, Walahfrid Strabo, who writes that the splendor of a gourd is that "they are all belly, all paunch./ Inside that cavernous prison are nourished, each in its place, the many/ Seeds that promise another harvest as good as this one."[61]

Suspended from its umbilical stalk and coming to ripeness in the sun, the gourd must be prematurely separated from the vine, before the fruit has had a chance to harden and hollow itself, to allow rot to consume its flesh and seeds. After it has developed a brittle protecting shell and its withered epidermis has taken on a scaly, leprous appearance, it is only when its "cavernous belly" is punctured, cut, carved, bored, or broken that the ten thousand embyronic offspring are subject to premature disease, corruption, and death.[62] Granting the kind of poetic and religious license that was so meaningful and dear to the Taoist saints who carried a suspended bottle gourd from a staff as an emblem of their holiness, it may be said that the gourd, because of its emptiness, harbors the sacred powers of hibernation and longevity.[63] *Lagenaria* seeds, in fact, have been shown experimentally to retain germination viability after six years of floating in salt water within the gourd container.[64] The bottle gourd overcomes a permanent uncontrolled or undifferentiated chaos in the world by returning temporarily to the original "ordered chaos" of buoyant emptiness that existed at the beginnings of all life. A gourd, in this sense, is the botanical equivalent of the Chinese sacred tortoise whose hard shell mimics the cosmological structure of the universe and whose life is protected and extended by its yearly retreat into the formless mud of the earth.

Within the cultural sphere it is the cut and carved ornamental emptiness of the gourd that is the basis for the creation of the utensils of the civilizational order. Suspended, uncarved, and whole, the gourd is the Taoist model for mystical unity and naturalness; when carved, its utility is the model for the foundational arts of human civilization. The point of civilization, it may be said, is to be "out of its gourd"; the concern of Taoism, to be within the empty paradise of the uncarved gourd.

Since I have previously discussed the role the gourd may play in the development of the agricultural origins of civilization, I need only remark here that the carved-gourd paradigm certainly has some involvement in the development of a whole range of civilizational arts and crafts. The creation and evolution of container technologies associated with the craft of potting are related to a natural gourd prototype, one instance of this being the traditional Chinese spoon/ladle/dipper that is modeled on the form of a split gourd.[65] Other craft traditions—such as, perhaps, culinary, food preservation (drying), measurement (hu^a meaning ancient measure or goblet), metallurgical, marine, medicinal, dying and cloth-making technologies, as well as the ritual arts of kinship, marriage, sacrifice, divination, and statecraft—also show suspicious affinities with the cultural potential released by boring the *hun-tun* gourd. Gourds are finally linked with the making of musical instruments (rattles, flutes, lutes, zithers, and especially drums) in ancient Chinese tradition. The primordial couple of Fu-hsi and Nü-kua, after their salvation within an uncarved gourd-boat, are related to the invention of musical devices made out of gourd shells.[66] As it is the chaos gap or central cavity of the gourd that manifests the creative and culturally meaningful power of sound in music, so also can it be said that all of the useful gourd-arts of civilization are connected with the controlling and taming of the gourd's originally unsullied power of emptiness. A Taoist dwells within the floating uncarved gourd as an ark of salvation (cf. *Chuang Tzu*, chap. 1); the civilizational order forgets this naturally useless use by remembering only the primal sacrificial act of carving and death that gives it its cultural utility and creativity. The Taoist teeters with Humpty Dumpty and Mr. Hun-tun on the wall, while "all the king's horses and all the king's men" are left with only the aftermath of the fall, when Humpty Dumpty is smashed into ten thousand useful, but unrepairable, pieces.

The irony here, and the difficulty modern man has in taking the symbolic truth of the gourd seriously, is that in the course of civilizational history, gourd symbolism (like myth and religion even more generally) suffers a progressive and inevitable infantilization of meaning to the point where today in the West its ritual significance is reduced to the eating of frozen pumpkin pies and the carving of a jack-o'-lantern at Halloween. Semantically depleted and vaguely ridiculous, the gourd lingers in modern memories, whether Chinese or Western, as only an ornamental plant, not as the foundational ornament in the creation of the cosmos. While the gourd was originally associated with human sacrifice as the most profoundly serious of mythico-religious acts, in time, in the historical time of a social order that seeks to deny the validity of the mythological time of the beginnings, a gourd, along with plastic melons, phallic cucumbers, and delirious pumpkins, is fated to satiric lampooning or morbid silence among the polite circles of society and scholarship.

This process is not only a modern phenomenon, since suffering deadly bores like Confucius, who as an agent of civil man would make the whole world polite, was always the bane of the early Taoists. In fact, this same kind of clash over the profound or ridiculous meaning of gourds and cosmogony is curiously shown by Saint Irenaeus' mock satire on the "absurd" cosmic egg creation schemes of the Gnostic opponents of orthodox Christianity. From Irenaeus' point of view, Gnostic accounts like Valentinus' aeons and emanations could be nothing more than empty words and "could just as well be replaced" by cucurbits:[67]

> There is a kind of first beginning, royal, before and above comprehension, a power before and above substance, rolling itself ever onward. Now with this exists a power, which I call a gourd: and with this gourd is a power, which also I call perfect emptiness. This gourd, and perfect emptiness, being one thing, emitted, without emitting it, a fruit, in all respects visible, eatable and sweet, which fruit their speech calls a Cucumber. But with this fruit is a power of the same tendency with it, which also I call a Pompion. These powers, the gourd, and the perfect emptiness, and the cucumber, and the pompion, emitted the rest of the multitude of Valentinus' delirious pompions.[68]

Church fathers, like Confucian bureaucrats, always had trouble with the empty words, and the "perfect emptiness," of heretics and Taoists who challenged the official order of things. Chuang Tzu's words, after all, were "goblet words" (*chih-yen*) that upset themselves when full and righted themselves when empty.[69] They were words "that adapt to and follow along with the fluctuating nature of the world and thus achieve a state of harmony."[70] Irenaeus upon hearing this would surely agree with Confucius that "as for the arts of Mr. Hun-tun, you and I need not bother to find out about them."

It is pointless to continue this cucurbitic litany as related to the symbolic roots of early Taoism and the cultural foundations of ancient Chinese civilization. I will consequently leave any further comparison of the nature-culture significance of the gourd to what has been more conveniently condensed in figure 3. This table shows quite dramatically, I think, the resonance the life

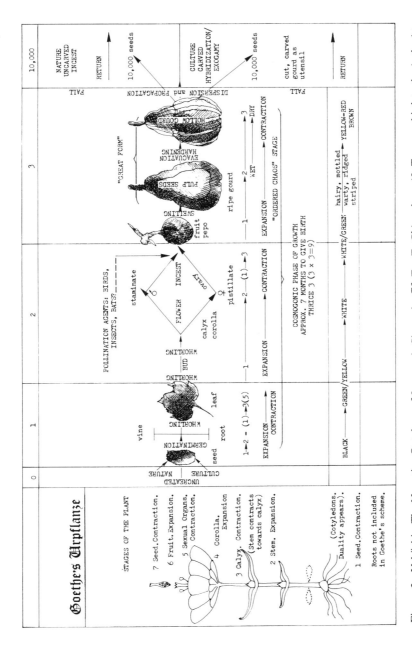

Figure 3. Urkürbis: The Narrative Ontology of *Lagenaria Siceraria*. Cf. *Tao Te Ching* chap. 42: Tao gave birth to the 1, the 1 to the 2, the 2 to the 3, and the 3 to the 10,000 things.

cycle of *Lagenaria* has with both the symbolic content and the narrative form of the *hun-tun* theme examined throughout this work. It is the natural way, or Tao, of the gourd that is most expressive of the inner Tao of all life and the mystical path of early Taoism. The panoply of botanical and symbolic gourd lore presented here suggests, finally, some of the context for the Taoist meditation on the metaphysical meaning of the one and the two of existence.

The gourd lives in human culture as a symbol. For man the gourd is both a model "of" and a model "for" reality in the sense that it creates meaning by telling the true story of natural and cultural life—that is, it gives objective, cognitive form to the world by shaping itself to the psycho-social reality of the human world and by shaping that world to itself.[71] As a part of its very being and becomingness it tells the mythic story of the cyclic, inexhaustible creativity of the world and man, a creativity that ultimately depends on emptiness. Lao Tzu (chap. 4), of course, never tires of remarking that the Tao, as the "ancestor of all things," is "empty (like a bowl, bottle, container, cocoon, gourd?). It may be used but its capacity is never exhausted."[72] The existential mystery of this is that utility depends on "nonbeing or nothingness" (*wu*[b], chap. 11). The Taoist sage knows how to "turn being into advantage" by resting in nothingness, emptiness, or "non-action" (*wu-wei*).[73] The Taoist (*Tao Te Ching*, chap. 12) is concerned with the belly ("they are all belly, all paunch"), not with the bored openings of the eyes.[74]

As seen in the early Taoist texts, the power of a symbolic image "rests on its comprehensiveness, on its fruitfulness in ordering experience."[75] In this way, also, the gourd is "a natural form with a moral import."[76] In early Taoism its fabled content acts as a source of moral ethos (i. e., *jang*[a], *tz'u*, *tzu-jan*, *shan*[b], *wu-wei*, etc.) because of the "fidelity with which it expresses the fundamental nature of reality".[77] *Lagenaria* is a rebus (and *rebis*?) of the meaning and moral purpose of life.

By his assimilation of a mode of being that is uncarved and gourdlike, a Taoist sage, pot-bellied and gourd-headed, learns the salvational and medicinal secrets of natural life. Classically in the early texts, he is a Hu Tzu or Gourd Master; traditionally in later Taoist saintly legend and folklore, a true Taoist is the "Old Man of the Gourd" who knows the magical art of overcoming the weariness of ordinary time by retreating into the belly of a suspended gourd:[78]

Once in an ancient city there was an old man who was a popular street vendor of medicines and herbs. No one knew his name, so he was called the Old Man of the Gourd, because of a gourd that he hung by the wall as a symbol of his trade. A man named Fei lived on the same street, and one day, having nothing better to do, he watched the old man from his window and wondered about him. Finally after dark he saw that old man pack up his wares and, looking around to see that no one was watching, clap his hands and jump into the gourd. Fei could scarcely believe what he saw; he realized that the old man was not a mere mortal but one skilled in magic ways.

The story continues by saying that after the old man was invited to Fei's house for tea, the old man, in the reverse sense of Hu and Shu's reciprocation of Hun-tun's kindness, decided to pay back Fei by showing him the secrets of his gourd. The old man clapped his hands and Fei suddenly

found himself inside the gourd with the old man. What a surprise, for it was a beautiful mansion, elaborately decorated with priceless objects. "Make yourself at home," the old man said, "we have food and wine on yonder table."

But after "the sumptuous feast with much wine, Fei remembered nothing more, and when he awoke, he was in his own bed." Fei, as a good and decent citizen, was simply unprepared to accept the fantastic truth of the old man's gourd. A good man prefers a warm bed to religious truth. But this was, after all, a fairy tale and "the Old Man of the Gourd was never to be seen again."

The reduplicated word *Cucurbita* comes from the Latin term for "gourd," which also carried the meanings of "fool," "idiot," and "adulteress."[79] The tale of the gourd, like the parable of Emperor Hun-tun, is simultaneously wise and silly, profound and pathetic in its linguistic, mythological, and religious implications. The interpretation of the gourd's meaning as a symbol will always be as paradoxical as the cosmogonic antipodes of chaos. A gourd's emptiness is both, and at the same time, a positive cypher of salvation, sanity, growth, and health (it produces and contains the medicine of longevity) and, more negatively for conventional society, the sign of an "empty" *Kürbiskopf*.[80] From the Taoist point of view both of these potentially antagonistic values of sanity and stupidity are conjoined in the uncarved wholeness of the gourd or in the paradoxical personality of the sage as a Gourd Master. The sage (cf. *Chuang Tzu*, chap. 1) knows how to use emptiness and freely float through life.

GOURDKIN: THE DELUGE AND ANIMAL ANCESTOR NARRATIVE SCHEME

The natural ontology of the gourd has undergone numerous cultural permutations in Southeast Asian and Chinese traditions, not the least of which has been its literary, philosophical, and religious transformation in the early Taoist texts. Throughout this long history of creative reinterpretation and cognitive *bricolage*, the "narrative element" has perdured as a constant, if disguised, structural factor. In the interests of clarifying this mythological structure, its related themes, and its general religious intentionality, it will be helpful to consider the kind of narrative scheme that can be reconstructed from the various literary and folkloric materials coming from the "southern," or to use Porée-Maspero's expression, the K'un-lun cultural complex. Some of the myths and legends that have gone into the construction of a prototypical narrative structure can be found in the appendixes, but the following Yao[b] myth can be taken as a specific and characteristic instance of the kind of mythological material involved:

> Formerly there was a great flood which submerged all the world. All mankind drowned except for the Fu-i brother and sister, who escaped the flood by hiding in a gourd. After the water subsided, the two discussed whether or not they should marry. They agreed that if they burned incense and planted bamboo trees in two different places and the smoke and tree-tops came together, they would marry; otherwise, they would not. They prayed to the heaven and burned incense and planted bamboo trees on two separate mountains. Eventually the smoke and the tree-tops came together and they married. From them was born a leather bag [mass of flesh, egg, gourd, deformed child, etc.] from which ten boys and ten girls, emerged. They became the ancestors of mankind.[81]

The pattern that emerges from this and the other mythological accounts is a temporally and geographically composite configuration, but it does represent an "ideal" typology in the Weberian sense and has been convincingly established in the work of Porée-Maspero. In summary form, as developed in table 4, the symbolic kith and kin of the mother gourd trace out an ancestral line that displays a "mythic combat" or "Noah's ark" type of narrative sequence.[82]

It is evident that the hypothetical scheme presented in table 4 is constitutive of the *hun-tun* theme in form and content as found in early Taoism. Indeed, a very similar narrative pattern, and many of the "associated themes," have already appeared throughout my analysis of the Taoist texts and in the semantic matrix related to Chinese gourd terminology (table 3). And it would be possible to document specific examples for all of the other themes in Chinese sources, as in fact much of Granet's earlier work tends to confirm. Apropos of the animal ancestor myths of P'an-hu and P'an-ku discussed in the previous chapter, I should mention in keeping with Porée-Maspero that the "animal-spouse" theme has special prominence in the deluge cycle (see Appendix 3). Moreover, vestiges of social and ritual practices (kinship and marriage alliance symbolism, initiatory tattooing, tooth laquering, masked ritual, and ritual ball games or other ritual contests such as alternate chanting, ceremonial boasting, kite flying, and dragon/bird boat races) are discernible in these tales.[83]

TABLE 4

I. Narrative Scheme

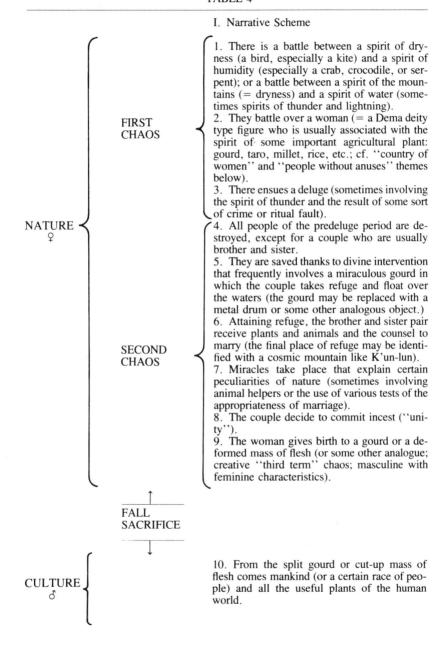

NATURE ♀

FIRST CHAOS

1. There is a battle between a spirit of dryness (a bird, especially a kite) and a spirit of humidity (especially a crab, crocodile, or serpent); or a battle between a spirit of the mountains (= dryness) and a spirit of water (sometimes spirits of thunder and lightning).
2. They battle over a woman (= a Dema deity type figure who is usually associated with the spirit of· some important agricultural plant: gourd, taro, millet, rice, etc.; cf. "country of women" and "people without anuses" themes below).
3. There ensues a deluge (sometimes involving the spirit of thunder and the result of some sort of crime or ritual fault).

SECOND CHAOS

4. All people of the predeluge period are destroyed, except for a couple who are usually brother and sister.
5. They are saved thanks to divine intervention that frequently involves a miraculous gourd in which the couple takes refuge and float over the waters (the gourd may be replaced with a metal drum or some other analogous object.)
6. Attaining refuge, the brother and sister pair receive plants and animals and the counsel to marry (the final place of refuge may be identified with a cosmic mountain like K'un-lun).
7. Miracles take place that explain certain peculiarities of nature (sometimes involving animal helpers or the use of various tests of the appropriateness of marriage).
8. The couple decide to commit incest ("unity").
9. The woman gives birth to a gourd or a deformed mass of flesh (or some other analogue; creative "third term" chaos; masculine with feminine characteristics).

FALL SACRIFICE

CULTURE ♂

10. From the split gourd or cut-up mass of flesh comes mankind (or a certain race of people) and all the useful plants of the human world.

TABLE 4 (continued)

II. Associated Themes

1. The metal smith
2. The cave from which emerges mankind
3. The animal guide
   3a. Hairiness
   3b. Spotted, striped, varicolored, etc.
4. The animal spouse
5. The tower and/or star of morning
6. The vine that connects heaven and earth
7. The lame man, leper, or man covered with tumors (or some other deformity/abnormality)
8. The split tree that is reunited
9. The marvelous sword
10. The bronze drum or gong (bell)
11. The conquest of cultivated grains (especially rice and millet) and the lessons given by the gods

To assess this scheme as the most probable mythological backdrop for the *hun-tun* theme, it must be reiterated that the early Taoists have transferred the tribal myth-ritual scenario and symbolism onto a mystical and philosophical plane of meaning. The primitive elements of an initial battle between the divine forces of dryness and wetness (mountain and water, bird and fish, etc.) are suppressed, or more accurately, transposed into the cosmogonic and philosophical context of a metaphysical dualism. The basis for finding a common intentionality in the gourd's natural emptiness, in the noncivilizational emphasis on deluge (reflecting a tropical or semitropical monsoon cultural origin but transformable into the dangers of seasonal flooding found in an ancient hydraulically based agricultural civilization like China), and in the early Taoist concern with a mystical cosmogony is grounded in the shared conviction that the re-creation and continuation of life requires a periodic return to the condition of chaos. In early Taoism the basic narrative form and symbolic content of myth are largely preserved but are understood as a model for a man's personal healing intunement with the Great Tao.

Such a reinterpretation of older mythologies in relation to an altered cultural and religious situation is a common occurence in the general history of religions. To take but one ready example from Western tradition, it is well known that the Israelite Bible in many ways incorporates and religiously transforms Ugaritic (and other ancient Near Eastern) myths of a primordial battle between the forces of chaos and cosmos. Extending Herman Gunkel's pioneer work in this matter, Mary Wakeman has shown that the muted echoes of the cosmic battle between God and the Leviathan-Chaos-Monster in the apocalyptic sections of the Hebrew scriptures represent a reinterpretation of a mythological scenario typologically akin to the Asian pattern outlined here.[84] This is especially so since the Near Eastern materials often manifest a pattern involving the ritual implications of a contrast and tension between the natural forces of dryness and wetness (drought and flood, earth and water, desert and river, etc.) and the cultural forces of nomadism and agriculture (tribalism and kingship, monotheism and polytheism, patrilineal and marilineal kinship, etc.) Although Wakeman perceives that the Chaos figure in many of the Israelite and other Near Eastern accounts is not permanently overcome, she fails to "appreciate fully the deep ambiguity of such figures."[85] Within all of these ancient Near Eastern materials, as in the Asian materials under investigation in this study, the deeper ambiguity is that while the chaos figures in mythology "represent a threat to, or a repression of, creativity, they are also frequently depicted as the very source of creative power."[86]

I need only add that this kind of recognition is the crux of the Taoist reinterpretation of the southern deluge and combat myths. It is the Taoist mystical intuition into these kinds of myths that leads to their understanding that the real meaning of "chaos" is not simply resolved by siding with either camp in the dualistic division of life. More exactly from the Taoist standpoint, chaos is that which stands as a third term betwixt and between all extremities. In the life of the gourd, in the common narrative plot of the Asian deluge myths, or in the Taoist mystical sensibility, chaos creates meaning in the world by the fact of creation—through a creative self-transformation that leads from a first stage of utter chaotic undifferentiation to the later fruition of an empty "ordered chaos." It is impossible to understand chaos as only chaos, but it is possible to know and love its wondrous *hun-tun* child, no matter how strange and fantastic it may be.

GOURDKIN'S PECULIAR PROGENY: THE "COUNTRY OF WOMEN,"
"PEOPLE WITHOUT ANUSES," AND THE "MASS OF FLESH"

There are a few other important themes that fit with the narrative scheme just developed and directly relate to some of the symbolic details found in the *hun-tun* theme in Taoism. The most notable of these additions to the ancestral heritage of the gourd are the tales of the "country of women" and the "people without anuses." These interconnected story cycles, also found within the same general "southern" Asiatic cultural sphere, seem to represent more detailed commentaries on the predeluge phase of the narrative scheme (i.e., point 2 in table 4) or, also, a more specialized description of the deluge period itself (points 3 through 9 in the narrative scheme) before the birth of the differentiated order of agricultural life. Stressing either the cultural importance of sexual or bodily distinctions, both of these tales refer to what I have called the cosmogonic "first" stage of an undifferentiated or unproductive chaos condition. Finally, both the "country of women" and "people without anuses" show a particular relationship with the peculiar progeny of the incestuous union in the deluge scheme. This is the "second" or creatively potent chaos stage symbolized by the "mass of flesh" (empty yet fertile, warty gourd; deformed wonder child; lame culture hero; sacrificial cosmic giant; hairy animal ancestor; faceless Emperor Hun-tun; etc.).[87]

Ho finds that these mythical tales, along with other related "vagina dentata" or the familiar "Peach Boy" stories, possess a common narrative form and cognitive intention.[88] The basic mythological issue concerns the transition from a prehuman or preagricultural "chaos" time to the dualistically ordered world of human culture. The relation between the "mass of flesh" theme and the "people without anuses" is clear since the two are often linked within a single narrative—for example, the primal couple gave birth to a deformed son called Hun-tun who had no head or "means of urinating."[89] The same kind of connection is indicated for the "country of women" tales since they sometimes involve the submotif of a "deformed birth" and, even more commonly, describe the apertureless condition of the women by saying that they, like the people without anuses, could only eat by absorbing the wind and the vapor of cooked food (see appendixes). The mythological logic seems to be that while the "mass of flesh" is a certain creative advance over the earlier condition, it, at the same time, represents a specialized or "ordered" reappearance of the previous chaos state. It partakes of both the absolute unity or first chaos condition of "one" (variously having predominant feminine characteristics or being without the holes of face, sexuality, or evacuation) and the dualistic, more masculine, order of "two." Superficially chaotic in outward appearance, the repulsive and apparently irrelevant "mass of flesh" hides the powers of creation and life. It is a "third sex" or male "thing" that has the female ability to give birth by means of a sacrificial act. What women accomplish naturally, men achieve heroically and ritually.

An example that characteristically combines the three themes is the following tale from the Garawan culture of Formosa:

> Formerly there was a village of women called Saipahahan. The people of Saipahahan were without anuses and lived by smelling the vapor of cooked food. Once a man called Lubugots went there and played with the women so

that they conceived male children. However he became homesick, and he told them that he would like to make an anus for each of them. He put a hot iron rod into several women and ran for his home. The people of Saipahahan knew they were fooled and started to pursue him. En route they found a hole of anteaters and suspected that Lubugots had hidden inside the hole. When they struck inside with bamboo lances, they found that the lances were stained red. So they started to dig a hole with their lances, but it was only a dye-yam which Lubugots had put in. Lubugots returned safely to his home.[90]

This tale is typical in that a composite scenario for both the "country of women" and "people without anuses" legends often tells of a tricksterlike culture hero who puts an end to the unordered and unhuman condition by boring holes into the anusless people with a pointed stick or iron rod.[91] The references to a planting stick (used in the swidden root-cropping of the Garawan), as well as the "iron rod" and the related themes of the "origin of grains by stealing" recorded by Ho, bring to the fore again the special affinity these stories have with myths concerned with the rise of agriculture and other cultural arts like metallurgy and cloth dying.[92] A certain masculine bias is obvious here in the sense that it is the male culture hero who takes credit for the creation of human culture while implicitly conceding the original feminine control of the secrets of fertility and new life.

It may also be said that the culture hero figure is but a particular transformation of the "mass of flesh" symbolism since, when sacrificially bored, cut, or broken, it is the heroic container of plants and men. This kind of permutation is suggested by the motif of Lubugots's salvation through his deceptive use of dye-yams (dye-yams can be used to make a red dye, suggesting that the men have an artificial cultural control over blood that surpasses the natural feminine powers of blood-menstruation). By tricking the women, Lubugots is symbolically equated with the yams; their substitutionary bloody "death" and his continued life make his subsequent return home and the creation of the ordered human world possible. Through his male yamkin that proceeded from his union with the anusless women, Lubugots is the creator of a cosmos ornamented in terms of the "right" ritual standards of male prestige, privilege, and "face." It was from this point on that mankind knew their fathers and not their mothers.

Like the deluge scenario and the *hun-tun* theme in Taoism, these stories tell of the passage from a chaos time to the world of human culture—the transition from nature to culture, the raw to the cooked, the female to the male, the faceless to faced, anusless to excremental orders. From the point of view of tribal culture the condition represented by the country of women or people without anuses is equivalent to the dangerous deluge conditions of chaotic

disorder. This is a condition that has to be overcome through divine intervention in order to establish the "normal" cultural order—that is, to establish
the superiority of the phallic masculine order over the bloody feminine order by
the giving of a proper human face and alimentary openings to what is spawned
by a union with a woman. To give "face" in this sense is intimately connected
with the ritually accomplished ways of kinship and eating in a tribal culture.
The "purity and danger" of the interrelated cultural concern for proper sexual/
kin relations and dietary/hygiene regulations are central to "totemistic" traditions such as these and, as seen here, are validated by the remembrance of a
mythic model.[93]

The cognitive significance of food and eating, eating and ethos (especially
the consumption of "cooked food" and the eating of special foods at ritually
important times), is shown by the tabooed sacrality of particular "ancestral"
plants and animals (depending on the local tradition) and the practice seen in
some of these "southern" Asian traditions where a periodic ritual reenactment
of the foundation myth involves a communal banquet of the "pulpy" or
"fleshy" mass of the ancestor.[94] Symbolically this kind of practice ritually
dramatizes the story of the raw mass of flesh, animal ancestor, primal man, or
mediating offspring of the primordial couple which, when cut up, sacrificed,
made into food, cooked, and eaten (sometimes prepared as a stew, soup, broth,
vegetable and meat curry, minced pie; a substitution for human sacrifice or
ritual anthropophagy?), reinvigorates the normal cultural order.[95]

The continuation and replenishment of human culture is dependent on a
ritual return to, identification with, and eventual killing and eating of the
mediating chaos agent, which is made into a mincemeat pie, soup, sausage, or
stew (cf. cucurbitic concoctions like baked pumpkin pie)—a pattern apparent
in the ritual dragon boat festivals of south China, in the southern cultural
complex studied by Porée-Maspero, and in Jensen's Dema mythologem.[96]
From my discussion of "soup, symbol, and salvation" from chapter 1, it is
perhaps warranted to propose that this represents a probable primitive prototype
for the ritual eating, during the Chinese new year festival period, of a soup
made of wonton skins filled with the mixed and minced flesh of plants and
animals.

In his study of the Na-khi peoples of southwest China, Anthony Jackson
shows that "floods, fertility, and feasting" are mutually expressive of the same
myth/ritual structure of meaning.[97] To generalize from Jackson's work and the
material presented in this study, it may be said that sacrificial food and feasting
function as the most basic mediating agents between nature and culture, the
ancestors and men. Cooking and eating in this sense are always religiously and

ethically significant acts. The rituals of sharing food—table manners—are finally the basis of all forms of cultural morality and social reciprocity. And in terms of the development of culture in history, when one sex, group, or class eats better or differently than some other group, when "sharing" and "kin(d)-ness" are qualified in some way, there will be a corresponding shift in the understanding of ethical prerogatives.

As Lévi-Strauss remarks, food, sacrifice, and cooking are "*absolute* or *extreme*" operations that cognitively relate to an "*intermediary* object."[98] In a civilizational context where feudal lords eat the best foods, sacrificial ritual (and the sacrificial cooking of special humble foods—for example, a *keng* soup, see above, chap. 1) "resembles, though it is at the same time opposed to them," the rites and values termed sacrilegious, barbarian, or primitive (such as incest, beastiality, boorish and unseasoned foods, etc.) "which are *intermediary* operations relating to *extreme* objects."[99] Sacrifice, as a ritual expression of mythological logic, "seeks to establish a desired connection between two initially separate domains": nature and culture, primitive and civilized, folk and elite.[100]

Early Taoism, while drawing upon these same kinds of themes, reverses the ordinary civilizational evaluation and views the passage from chaos to cosmos as fundamentally a fall from a previous, more perfect cultural/natural condition. The Taoist sage seen in the earlier chapters is, therefore, very often described with the composite characteristics of a woman, hermaphrodite, animal ancestor, bumpkin, gourdkin, or as a Mr. Hun-tun with the faceless features and strange ritual habits of the "people without anuses" and the "mass of flesh." As the classic and self-styled "outsiders" to their own elite civilizational culture, Taoists define the issue not as the acceptance of the mythic validation of the normal order but as the mystical possibility of returning to a special "chaos" condition that combines the best of both the worlds of nature and of culture. Taoist mysticism, in keeping with its underlying mythological logic, "seeks to establish a desired connection between two initially separate domains." It seeks to heal the breach between body and spirit, individual and nature, the individual and other individuals. A Taoist goes back in time to the ultimate undifferentiated beginnings of the world in order to return home and live in the intermediary paradise condition that exists within the shell of an empty *hu-lu* gourd.

It is true that the Taoist imagination embraced the "people without anuses" theme of Han Shan's poem, which fondly recited the verses of "how pleasant were our bodies in the days of Hun-tun./ Needing neither to eat or piss!"[101] But an important qualification is required here since, while frequently prone to

excremental exaggeration in the face of machine-hearted and puritanical Confucians, the Taoists were not nihilistically concerned with a completely nonhuman realm where one never eats or pisses. Chuang Tzu, it must be remembered, finds the Tao within the piss and shit (chap. 22)![102] The point is to accept
the relative equality of all things as mediated by the central kingdom of the Tao.
Men and women, like barbarians and civilized men, may eat and piss differently, but such real differences do not mean that one or the other way is
necessarily better than the other.

"PUTTING HUN-TUN BACK TOGETHER AGAIN":

STRUCTURE AND MEANING OF THE CHAOS THEME

In consideration of all the various factors examined in this chapter and throughout my textual analysis, it is possible to outline a hypothetical structure for the
hun-tun theme in Taoism where the cosmogonic and mystical implications are
linked with the narrative form of the deluge cycle and its more important
associated themes. What follows in table 5 is only an incomplete mapping of
the creative orchestration of different symbolic elements in harmony with the
inner mythic logic of the chaos theme found in the early Taoist texts:[103]

TABLE 5

HYPOTHETICAL SALVATIONAL SCHEME FOR THE HUN-TUN THEME

Cutting the Gourd is the Beginning
of Dismemberment (*kua fen chih tuan*).
Chinese Proverb

The myriad things returning [10,000]
lead to the Three [3],
The Three to the Two [2],
The Two to the One [1],
The One to the Tao of Transcendence [0].
Yellow Court Canon

(trans. M. Saso)

I. FIRST UNDIFFERENTIATED CHAOS AND NATURAL SEASONAL RETURN:
   ANTEDILUVIAN PERIOD AND THE CREATION OF THE WORLD

"0" = UNCREATED TAO (uncreated "nothingness" or "emptiness" + hidden
      "great form")

"1" = CREATED TAO = HUN-CH'ENG

yinyang = created undifferentiated unity; cosmic egg-gourd; primordial waters;
           asexual; unconsciousness; young pulpy gourd; etc.

TABLE 5 (continued)
HYPOTHETICAL SALVATIONAL SCHEME FOR THE
HUN-TUN THEME

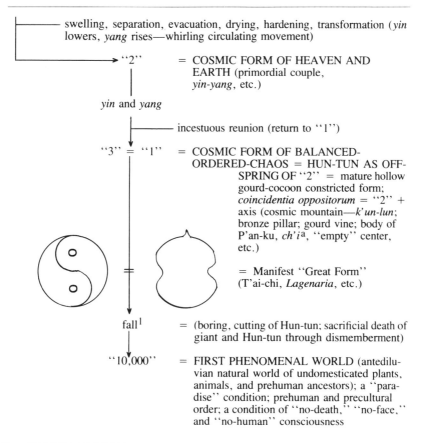

swelling, separation, evacuation, drying, hardening, transformation (*yin* lowers, *yang* rises—whirling circulating movement)

"2" = COSMIC FORM OF HEAVEN AND EARTH (primordial couple, *yin-yang*, etc.)

yin and *yang*

incestuous reunion (return to "1")

"3" = "1" = COSMIC FORM OF BALANCED-ORDERED-CHAOS = HUN-TUN AS OFF-SPRING OF "2" = mature hollow gourd-cocoon constricted form; *coincidentia oppositorum* = "2" + axis (cosmic mountain—*k'un-lun*; bronze pillar; gourd vine; body of P'an-ku, *ch'i*[a], "empty" center, etc.)

= Manifest "Great Form" (T'ai-chi, *Lagenaria*, etc.)

fall[1] = (boring, cutting of Hun-tun; sacrificial death of giant and Hun-tun through dismemberment)

"10,000" = FIRST PHENOMENAL WORLD (antediluvian natural world of undomesticated plants, animals, and prehuman ancestors); a "paradise" condition; prehuman and precultural order; a condition of "no-death," "no-face," and "no-human" consciousness

II. SECOND ORDERED CHAOS AND RITUAL RETURN: DILUVIAN PERIOD AND THE CREATION OF PRIMITIVE HUMAN CULTURE

UNITY OF DILUVIAN PARADISE WORLD (nonagricultural paleolithic situation; prehuman ancestors and gods; imagery of "country of women" and "people without anuses")

TRANSITION FROM NATURE TO CULTURE: IMBALANCE, SEPARATION, AND RETURN TO FIRST COSMOGONIC CHAOS (COSMIC BATTLE, RITUAL FAULT, ETC.)

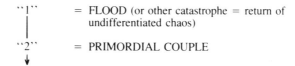

"1" = FLOOD (or other catastrophe = return of undifferentiated chaos)

"2" = PRIMORDIAL COUPLE

TABLE 5 (continued)
HYPOTHETICAL SALVATIONAL SCHEME FOR THE
HUN-TUN THEME

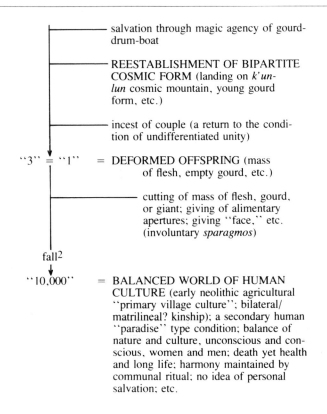

salvation through magic agency of gourd-drum-boat

REESTABLISHMENT OF BIPARTITE COSMIC FORM (landing on *k'un-lun* cosmic mountain, young gourd form, etc.)

incest of couple (a return to the condition of undifferentiated unity)

"3" = "1" = DEFORMED OFFSPRING (mass of flesh, empty gourd, etc.)

cutting of mass of flesh, gourd, or giant; giving of alimentary apertures; giving "face," etc. (involuntary *sparagmos*)

fall^2

"10,000" = BALANCED WORLD OF HUMAN CULTURE (early neolithic agricultural "primary village culture"; bilateral/matrilineal? kinship); a secondary human "paradise" type condition; balance of nature and culture, unconscious and conscious, women and men; death yet health and long life; harmony maintained by communal ritual; no idea of personal salvation; etc.

III. THIRD FALLEN CHAOS AND POLITICAL/MYSTICAL RETURN: POST DILUVIAN PERIOD AND THE CREATION OF URBAN CIVILIZATION

PARADISE IDEAL OF PRIMITIVE, VILLAGE, FOLK, OR BARBARIAN CONDITION (cf. chap. 80 of *Tao Te Ching*, symbolically equivalent to above "second" paradise stage)

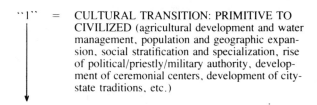

"1" = CULTURAL TRANSITION: PRIMITIVE TO CIVILIZED (agricultural development and water management, population and geographic expansion, social stratification and specialization, rise of political/priestly/military authority, development of ceremonial centers, development of city-state traditions, etc.)

TABLE 5 (continued)
HYPOTHETICAL SALVATIONAL SCHEME FOR THE
HUN-TUN THEME

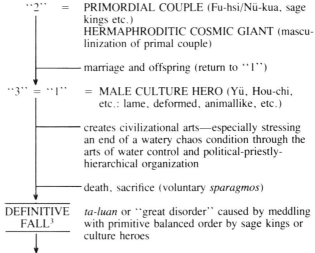

``2`` = PRIMORDIAL COUPLE (Fu-hsi/Nü-kua, sage kings etc.)
HERMAPHRODITIC COSMIC GIANT (masculinization of primal couple)

—— marriage and offspring (return to ``1``)

``3`` = ``1`` = MALE CULTURE HERO (Yü, Hou-chi, etc.: lame, deformed, animallike, etc.)

—— creates civilizational arts—especially stressing an end of a watery chaos condition through the arts of water control and political-priestly-hierarchical organization

—— death, sacrifice (voluntary *sparagmos*)

DEFINITIVE FALL[3]   *ta-luan* or ``great disorder`` caused by meddling with primitive balanced order by sage kings or culture heroes

``10,000`` = UNBALANCED WORLD OF FEUDAL CIVILIZATION (hierarchical ritual order: male over female, *yang* over *yin*, elite over folk, urban over rural; social reciprocity based on values of social prestige or ``face``; *li* over *jang*[a]; dis-ease, desire, private property, premature death, etc.)

``RETURN`` within this situation of definitive fall involves three considerations:

a) NATURAL RETURN: In nature, the sacred chaos-order continues as the process of *creatio continua*.

b) POLITICAL RETURN: Within the hierarchical civilizational order, there is a need to deny, exorcise, or control permanently the natural powers of chaos through political/military/ritual means.

This, however, involves a recapitulation of the cosmogonic process:

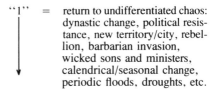

``1`` = return to undifferentiated chaos: dynastic change, political resistance, new territory/city, rebellion, barbarian invasion, wicked sons and ministers, calendrical/seasonal change, periodic floods, droughts, etc.

TABLE 5 (continued)

HYPOTHETICAL SALVATIONAL SCHEME FOR THE

HUN-TUN THEME

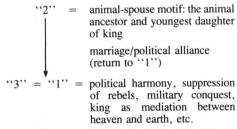

"2" = animal-spouse motif: the animal ancestor and youngest daughter of king

marriage/political alliance (return to "1")

"3" = "1" = political harmony, suppression of rebels, military conquest, king as mediation between heaven and earth, etc.

c) MYSTICAL RETURN: Born into the fallen order of civilization, a Taoist can reidentify himself with the balanced life of nature and "primitive" social values by a personal recovery of the ordered third-term *hun-tun* condition of chaos.

This scheme portrays the early Taoist interpretation of the meaning and development of human life. It is an understanding that is premised on the idea of a series of progressively radical breaks with the natural processes established during the cosmogonic time. Existence in the most general sense requires the first creative chaos and fall in order to have the natural life of the world and, also, the second chaos and fall to have human nature and culture. Both of these increasingly profound falls into matter, time, and history can be evaluated *positively* from the Taoist perspective since each represents a "paradise" type condition.

In distinction to the first two stages, the third fall into the civilizational condition is seen as unnatural, unnecessary, and ultimately destructive of authentic human nature and the organismic balance between social and cosmic life. Because the political and rational order of civilization attempts to suppress and deny the natural values of chaos or the relativity of existence, there is a definitive break with the sacred order of the beginnings. Once Humpty Dumpty is smashed into ten thousand pieces, all the loyal agents of feudal civilization, "all the king's horses and all the king's men," cannot put Humpty Dumpty back together again. The problem of a shattered Humpty Dumpty or a bored Mr. Hun-tun is the fundamental salvational issue posed by Taoism in its rejection of the ethical valorization of the feudal order espoused by Confucian tradition. Like the Humpty Dumpty nursery rhyme, the theme of Mr. Hun-tun betrays remnants of a political protest based on the imagery and form of a mythic paradigm.[104]

The early Taoists were not anticulture, antisociety, or, for that matter, antiritual. It is really a question of the kind of culture, society, and ethos ("primitive," pre-urban, or folk "communitas" versus feudal class society), as well as the kind of ritual (ritual of the "gift" shared by gods, ancestors, and men versus the ritual legitimation of the ruling power of an elite class), that is seen to be most meaningful for the fulfillment of human nature.[105] The "fall" was indeed the result of a "ritual fault," not in the literal sense of some form of divine disobedience but in the symbolic sense that the fall represents the passage from a "primitive" condition (where ritual was a cathartic and creative means of "yielding" to the ambivalent life-power of the gods and ancestors) to a civilizational situation of the "ceremonial center" (where priestly cultus becomes the basis for political aggrandizement and social stratification).[106]

Primitive ritual that expressed a fundamental "ambivalence to all authority" changes with the onset of urban genesis to the compulsive and schizophrenically dualistic ritualism, and domesticated thought, of those who have fixed authority and "face," those who rule religiously or politically over others.[107] Civilizational ritual, like the Confucian elevation of the feudal codes of *li* to ethics, strives "toward repression of ambivalence rather than its recognition and cultural use."[108] Adopting a civil point of view, the problem for Confucianism is always "whether the difference between the *appearance* of morality in ritual and the *reality* of morality in ritual and humanity can be made sufficiently prominent to forestall arrogant pride."[109] The fatal temptation for Confucianism is "to confuse the order of a society that makes human value possible with a mere order of social domination."[110] From the Taoist perspective, the ritual sin of feudal civilization and Confucianism is their need to seek a permanent end to the barbarian reign of Emperor Hun-tun who ruled by not ruling, by giving up everything he had.

Unlike the diluvian or "primitive" phase of culture, civilizational man in the name of historical, religious, political, and moral betterment no longer remembers the ambivalent natural and social roots of his well-being. From the historical perspective of civilization the human story is told by and about men, back to the first sage kings, and has no place for a Tao that is chaotic and nonhuman. The value and meaning of the Great Tao is reduced to the artificial and static codes of human conduct that assert the superiority of one class or standard over another. Taoism, however, remembers the story of man as being essentially mythological in nature. It leaves room for the sacred madness, freedom, imagination, and creativity of man's primitive nature. Knowing the true story of man provides a way of personally reliving that story. And to retell the story of life one must always start with "once upon a time." In contrast with "all the king's horses and all the king's men," Taoism knows the Way to put Humpty Dumpty back together again.

A CUCURBITIC ONTOLOGY: THE PROBLEM OF DUALISM AND THE TAOIST METAPHYSICS OF HUN-TUN

Along with a clarification of the prototypical botanical, mythic, and cultural structure underlying the chaos theme, there is a need to elucidate some of its metaphysical implications. It is important to appreciate that the mystical and philosophical intentionality of the theme cannot be divorced from its mythic structure. Myths are most adequately interpreted mythically, comparatively, and imaginatively; and this has been an operant principle throughout this study. By their very nature, as Eliade and Lévi-Strauss have shown from contrasting theoretical perspectives, there is always a tedious redundancy in mythic form and content. To make use of a method where myths constantly give rise to other myths consequently has the frustration of a spiral-like circularity, the telling of stories about stories not all of which may be equally spellbinding. For these reasons it is helpful to try to extract somewhat more analytically what could be called the "archetypal pattern of conceptualization" suggested by the *hun-tun* theme.[111]

1. *The Two and the Three*

The meaning of the Tao in Chinese tradition raises the perennial problem of the one and the many. Otherwise stated, this is the problem of the Chinese analysis of reality in terms of the dual principles of *yin* and *yang*: "*yin* and *yang* are the elementary terms used to express a fundamental premise of Chinese thought: they convey the idea of the polar quality of all effects."[112] This is a philosophical issue that early Taoism, while not originally using the technical, abstract nomenclature of *yin* and *yang*, solves by its appeal to a mythological understanding of reality where the image of the cosmic egg-gourd suggests the metaphysical principle of the "chaos-order" of the "third term" that is simultaneously identified with primordial unity and the multiplicity of phenomenal existence. The "two" came forth from "one"; yet also cosmogonically, the "two" produce a third "empty" state that centers all polar phenomena.

The meaning of life from this perspective is that life is not a binary manipulation of two different kinds of "things," not movement between two separate and static antipodes, but the pure process or constant creative transition that can only be artificially or culturally cut into discrete bits, categories, ideas, words, utensils, and containers. Life as process properly requires the propriety of carving and cutting to be used culturally as, in fact, the creation of the world involved an original passage from what was not (wu^b) to what is (yu^a). What was not, however, was not not, just as what is, is not without not. Chuang Tzu (e.g., chap. 2 of the "inner chapters") would mischievously add several further negations to confuse the issue, but the point remains that it is finally confusion itself, an imaginative confusion, that is responsible for the creation of all order and meaning. It is the *fact* of creation (that there is not just not or not not) as the event, act, passage, or "great transformation" from one to two that is the muddled ground of the existence of, as well as the real similarity and real difference between, all dualities.[113]

Duality in the "southern" cultural context is primarily a problem mythically related to the cosmic battle between the forces of dryness and wetness. The story of the diluvian return to chaos is reenacted yearly in the alternation of the seasonal rains, the agricultural cycle, and the round of ritual and social life. It is also the case that, like China, these cultures are basically characterized by a dualistic social structure expressed in the kinship structures and overall life of the people.[114] There is, in fact, a demonstrable similarity between this kind of cognitive world view and Granet's reconstruction of archaic Chinese culture and its seasonal rituals of sexual interaction.[115]

For both Porée-Maspero and Granet (following Durkheim and Mauss), cosmological duality is primarily an abstract formulation of a cultural reality related to a fundamental tension, rivalry, and interaction of the sexes in society.[116] Socially and psychologically, this tension is validated, or periodically resolved, in the ritual reenactment of the mythological scenario. Thus, the primordial couple-deluge mythology tends to reflect the underlying sexuality of all creative processes and the psychosexual orientation of social conflicts. Despite this mythological affirmation of an existential sexual dualism, these myths almost always evoke the idea of an original sexual unity. Even when these myths emphasize the domination of a male over a female deity, as with the elevation of Fu-hsi and the masculinization of Nü-kua, an underlying idea of the complementary relationship and primordial unity (or reunion) of the sexes still commonly persists.[117]

There is no need to adopt Granet's sociological principles of causality in order to see that ancient traditions of myth and ritual influenced the development of the basic Chinese ontological dualism, or "complementary bipolarity," of the *yin-yang* theory.[118] *Yin-yang*, and the related theory of *yin-yang-wu-hsing*, are the principles that guide traditional Chinese thought and religion, whether Taoist or Confucian. In traditional Chinese cosmology, the cosmos is but a more complicated permutation of the *Tao Te Ching*'s principle of the "great transformation" of one, two, and three: the world evolves out of "a series of progressions from the one Great Ultimate, the T'ai Chi, to the two principles, *yin* and *yang*, the three sources, heaven, earth, and man, the four seasons, five elements [*wu-hsing*], eight trigrams, and so forth. From the combination of *yin* and *yang* the myriad creatures are produced."[119]

In an exemplary analysis Plaks has set out a number of formal characteristics of the *yin-yang* theory: 1) "bipolarity," which means that "the apprehension of experience is realized in terms of the relative presence or absence of opposites rather than absolute states"; 2) "ceaseless alternation" wherein "phenomenological change is conceived of in terms of regular and ceaseless alternation towards and away from the hypothetical poles of each duality"; 3) "presence within absence" or that "the ascendance of one term immediately implies its own subsequent diminution"; and 4) "infinite overlapping" or that the endless overlapping of the polar axes of change "manifests what is on the surface a random chaos, but what eventually adds up to a convincing illusion of plenitude, and hence the perception of reality."[120]

The perceptiveness of Plaks's discussion of these abstract assumptions underlying the *yin-yang* theory is that he recognizes that they are all ultimately rooted in a mythic context of meaning. The *yin-yang* theory shows its "derivational nature" by virtue of the fact that the polar principles are usually cited in Chinese texts as an "intermediate step from nothingness to totality," or from one to two to three to the ten thousand things of the *Tao Te Ching*.[121] I would also add that there may be a covert mythological explanation here for the standard pairing of *yin* before *yang* since, in view of my earlier discussion of chapter 42 from the *Tao Te Ching*, the act or process of "giving birth" and the condition of one as the initial cosmogonic manifestation of the embryonic womb of undifferentiated nothingness both have maternal, *yin*, or feminine associations even though these are finally *not just* feminine characteristics.[122]

I am generally in agreement with Plaks's discussion of an archetypal mythological pattern of meaning, but I must finally take issue with his conclusion that, even though "the dualism in Chinese thought carries an implication of unity, it is generally not talking about unity."[123] For Plaks, "even when we are told that 'the myriad things revert to unity' . . . , it is the sheer infinitude of existence—its all-ness—that brings us around full circle to the idea of one-ness."[124] Plaks argues that it is the "logic of myth" that "leads us from the unity of the universal egg-gourd, the common womb of brother and sister, to a marriage that while essentially a union is quintessentially dual. It is the separateness between male and female rather than their merging into one that makes the union fruitful and results in the harmonious continuity of creation."[125] From this point of view the "paired concepts of the Chinese system by very definition can never reach an ultimate synthesis. . . . Instead, the polarities of Chinese thought remain forever distinct, producing and destroying each other in a ceaseless process of mutual displacement."[126]

It is true that traditional Chinese thought never asserts a monistic solution to the problem of dualism, never denies the reality of the two. But as I have extensively shown, the early Taoist texts proffer a unique, if perplexing, solution to the problem of the relation between the one and the two in the cosmogonic and mystical idea of a third term, the special triadic condition of *hun-tun*. It is the *tertium quid*, the fact of dialectical *relation* in life, that accounts for the reality of one and two.

Being lost in the broken world of the Ten Thousand Things, man, according to the Taoists, has the real possibility of returning to a state of union and meaningful relation with the Tao that does not involve a complete or permanent dissolution of personality. Man returns to the first chaos stage of absolute undifferentiated nothingness in order to give birth to the second state of ordered-chaos that represents the perfect harmony of the two. In this way it must be said that both forms of chaos, along with the one and the two, are indispensable for the Taoist. The journey back to the first stage is the necessary transitional prelude for the creation of the second, but the experience of the first undifferentiated chaos is a mystical "high" that is before man or before even the creation of the world. The nature of the mystic experience of total union is something that as a "high" is momentary. One must "come down" from a "high" and reenter the world to be human. It is this second phase of rebirth back into the world, consciousness, and society that is the destination that is not an end for the Taoist.

Plaks misreads his mythological documents when he claims that it is the separateness of the primordial couple and not their union that is responsible for the continuity of creation. The meaning of creation and the constant regeneration of life more accurately depends, both mythically and philosophically in the Taoist texts, on the real existence of the two but also on their return to unity as symbolized by their incestuous marriage. Moreover, the continued real presence of unity in the world is a result of the hidden "great form" of the third term that is the fruit of the orgasmic reunion of the two. The third term, or ordered-chaos condition, is mythically equivalent to the deformed offspring of the couple's incestuous union (gourd, mass of flesh, *hun-tun*). This important detail is overlooked by Plaks as he also neglects the significance of the "three" in the *Tao Te Ching*'s creation scenario. In a primordial couple mythology, the emphasis may be placed on the separateness of the sexes, but it is especially in the Taoist assimilation of this theme into a cosmogony of the cosmic egg-gourd that the special metaphysical formula of *coincidentia oppositorum* comes to the fore.

2. *Struggle and Conflict in Chinese Dualism*

A further complication is that the complementary dualism of *yin* and *yang* tends at times to be seen in terms of the superiority of the *yang* principle (male, active, fiery, etc. = life, health, sacrality) over the *yin* (female, passive, watery, etc. = death, disease, profanity). Despite the ancient philosophical formulations of complementarity, popular Chinese tradition manifests a movement toward the interpretation of dualism in antagonistic terms.[127] As De Groot has said for the popular tradition:

> All *shen* or gods, being parts of the *yang*, are the natural enemies of the *kwei*, because these are the constituents of the *yin*; indeed the *yang* and *yin* are engaged in an eternal struggle. . . . The worship and propitiation of the gods, which is the main part of China's religion, has no higher purpose than that of inducing the gods to protect man against the world of evil, or, by descending among men, to drive spectres away by their intimidating presence. . . .[128]

Even in Taoist tradition where the complementary aspects of dualism, and the fact of complementarity as the third term of life, are particularly important in both a philosophical and religious sense, there is eventually in later sectarian Taoism a popular preference given to the "life-giving" force of *yang* that verges on an identification of the primordial Tao with the *yang* power—"if one could imitate nature and hold in his grasp the principle of life and *yang*, then the process from life to death could be reversed."[129] The *T'ai P'ing Ching*, a Han dynasty classic of sectarian Taoism preserved in the *Tao Tsang*, is a specific example of this tendency since, on the one hand, it tends to affirm the early Taoist theme that salvation comes from a return to the original unity of *yin* and *yang*, yet, on the other hand, it displays a kind of ethical dualism that places *yang* ahead of *yin*.[130]

Aside from Granet's pioneering work, the relationship between a complementary and antagonistic interpretation of dualism has never been adequately treated for China. It is an issue, however, that has potentially revealing consequences for an analysis of the Chinese understanding of the problem of evil since, from a comparative perspective, "it will be interesting to determine precisely in what cultures, and at what epochs, the negative aspects of life, until then accepted as constitutive and unexceptionable moments of the cosmic totality, lost their initial function and began to be interpreted as manifestations of *evil*.''[131] In religions ''dominated by a system of polarities, the *idea of evil* arises slowly and with some difficulty. . . .''[132]

In many religions there tends to be a resolution of the problem of dualism in terms of a root tension between two separate sexual modalities or the ''irreducibility of the two modes of being in the world, those of man and woman.''[133] But while this is also an important factor for China and later Taoism, the essential thrust of the early Taoist mystical theme of ''returning to the origin'' is directed toward another type of solution, a solution that overcomes the separateness and priority of polarities in terms of a third condition of duality-in-unity most fully and naturally symbolized by the empty *hun-tun* gourd.

3. *Comparative Considerations: The Dayak* Tertium Quid

It is instructive to compare early Taoist thought to some primitive mythological conceptions of dualism.[134] In the Kogi Indian culture of the Sierra Nevada region, for example, mythology is rooted in a cosmic egg cosmogony where it is not the fact of dualism that is important, but the attainment of a perfect equilibrium of the polarities. For the Kogi ''the central problem of the human condition is precisely how to bring [the] two contraries to equilibrium and yet maintain them as complementary forces.''[135] In a way surprisingly similar to the Taoist idea of *hun-tun*, the ''fundamental concept'' in the Kogi cosmic egg mythology is ''*yuluka*, a term that can be translated 'being in agreement,' 'being equal,' 'being identified.' Knowing how to balance the creative and destructive energies, 'being in agreement,' is the guiding principle of human behavior.''[136]

In a more controlled comparative context, an interesting parallel to the early Taoist metaphysics of *hun-tun* is provided by the cosmological conceptions of the Indonesian tribal culture of the Ngaju Dayak. The Dayak system of mythological and religious thought has been carefully studied by Hans Schärer and, as shown by Porée-Maspero and Matsumoto, can be related to the Austronesian southern cultural complex.[137] Allowing for the obvious differences in cultural and historical complexity, it can be said that, to some degree, the Taoist and Dayak traditions share the same mythological roots.

For the Dayak the phenomenal cosmos is equated with polarity, but tribal life involves a periodic ritual recovery of a cosmogonic totality. Dayak tradition primarily expresses the mythological idea that ''by its own mode of being, the polar antagonism aims to annul itself in a paradoxical union of contraries.''[138] This conception implies that the ''polarities, by clashing together, produce what could be called a 'third term,' which can be either a new synthesis or a regression to a previous situation.''[139] In Dayak tradition, ''individual and collective life has a cosmological structure: every life constitutes a cycle, whose model is the sempiternal creation, destruction, and recreation of the world."[140] Given the common elements in their respective mythological foundations, it seems possible to say that for the Ngaju Dayak and for early Taoism, "the synthesis of the polarities, the 'third term,' though representing a new creation in regard to the immediately preceding stage, that of polar-antagonism, is at the same time a regression, a return to the primordial situation when the contraries coexisted in a non-differentiated totality."[141]

The whole symbolic and ritual structure of Austronesian culture commonly involves a mythologically sanctioned confrontation of dualities that is resolved by a "higher unity"—a "third, intangible element . . . which harmonizes the two antithetical elements and keeps them in balance."[142] In light of the development of Chinese cosmology in terms of the imperial order of "five" (*yin-yang-wu-hsing*), it is furthermore interesting to observe that in Justus Van Der Kroef's study of Javanese and other Indonesian societies, a system of five is a frequent, and symbolically equivalent, substitution for an order of three. In the ancient fivefold-clan ordering of Javanese society, "the fifth element, that of kingship, represents . . . a 'third' element, harmonizing the two social antitheses into a 'higher unit,' relating them also to the immutable cosmos."[143]

Like the natural world of cucurbits, human culture in time produces three- or five-lobed foliage. Saying this does not mean, however, that social organization and classification in China somehow depends on the morphology of the Cucurbitacea. It would seem rather that these two forms of existence, natural and cultural, are seen by men to share some ideal "likeness" or third term that is present, yet hidden, in the heart of all living things. Despite this interpretive qualification, the bottle gourd in Asia may be said to be a historically prior, symbolic prism for discovering the inner process of "centering" in life.

I would like finally to remark that the idea of the Tao as the "third term" or quintessence of existence is directly related to the basically optimistic evaluation of the world and nature seen in Taoist thought. While this is also true for Chinese tradition in general, Confucian thought, at least classically, tends to shift its interest away from the mystery and meaning of creation and nature to the problem of maintaining the civilizational order of human life. In this way the dualistic implications of the creation process start to be evaluated in a more moralistic, rational, and historical manner that avoids the mythological ethos of life where the "chaos-order duality" of the creation time cannot be interpreted negatively.[144]

A certain kind of negative evaluation of chaos is also seen in the tribal mythologies of the flood that stress the combat motif of triumph over chaos in order to establish and perpetuate the normal cultural order. But in contrast with the finality sought by the civilizational formulation of the same combat theme in terms of the suppression of the "barbarians," tribal cultures reveal a fundamental ambivalence toward the chaos order—that is, the rectification of cultural entropy ultimately depends on the constant periodic return to the time of the flood. This crucial ambivalence in the southern flood mythologies is exactly the factor accentuated cosmogonically and mystically by Taoism and is something that legitimates the notion of the "primitiveness" of the early Taoist vision.

In the context of the ontology associated with Cosmic Gourds and Emperor Hun-tun, all of the phenomenal polarities of life find their meaning in the ceaseless process of going out and coming back to the condition of trinitary union established during the creation time. Both the world and man are at once part of the grand synthetic totality of the Tao and both organically participate in the constant temporal recapitulation of the cosmogony. Man in his fallen civilizational condition, however, needs to rediscover that his personal time is still intrinsically linked with the Time of the "Great Transformation." Darkly mirrored in the cosmic processes of nature, man's true face, mottled like a wizened and warty gourd, shines back as the faceless ancestor of all men.

PART FOUR

COULDN'T PUT
HUMPTY DUMPTY BACK
TOGETHER AGAIN

CONCLUDING SPIRALS

When you use the word "chaos," it means there is no chaos, because everything is equally related—there is an extremely complex interpenetration of an unknowable number of centers.

—John Cage

It is the size of a chicken egg, its color yellow like a sweet orange. Expired it is half; inspired it is entire. If you can keep it, the Ten Thousand Things are complete.

—*Ling Pao Wu Fu Hsü*
(trans. J. Lagerwey)

8

THE ORDER OF CHAOS: SYMBOLIC ASPECTS OF TAOIST MYSTICISM

> Dwelling alone, peaceful and placid, in spiritual brightness—there were those in ancient times who believed that the ''art of the Tao'' lay in these things. The Barrier Keeper Yin and Lao Tan heard of their views and delighted in them. They expounded them in terms of constant nonbeing and being, and headed their doctrine with the concept of the Great Unity.
>
> —*Chuang Tzu*, chapter 33
> (trans. Burton Watson)

T HE ANALYSIS of the mythological heritage and metaphysical implications of the *hun-tun* theme lends itself to a fuller appreciation of the ''maximal appropriateness'' of some of the more outstanding symbolic expressions of early Taoist mysticism.[1] Many examples of the ''tendency of symbols to cluster'' in a paradigmatic way have already come to light in the chapters devoted to textual exegesis,[2] but I would like to summarize and extend these findings by presenting a brief interpretive catalogue of a few of the primary symbolic motifs associated with the ''art of the Tao.''

The motivations for such an enterprise are both to amplify the inner coherence of Taoist symbolism as it creatively incorporates and transforms various aspects of ancient Chinese religious tradition and also to indicate some of

Taoism's comparative resonance with patterns of symbol, myth, and ritual coming from other cultures. Along with emphasizing the related motifs of mystical effacement and a knowledge that is centered in the paunch of a gourd or abdomen, I will selectively focus this discussion on the early Taoist infatuation with the redemptive significance of chaos as a sacred "rule of folly." The Taoist advocacy of the hidden order of chaos is that which finally breaches all ordinary boundaries between sense and nonsense. This kind of symbolism in early Taoism, like the imagery of the fool in the most general sense, rejects the assumption that the conventional distinction between order and chaos was "where we thought it was and that it had the character we thought it had: that of affirming whatever we have taken for granted and in that way protecting us from the dark unknown."[3] Accepting the order of chaos "allows us to maintain a playful contact with undeveloped possibilities."[4] In sympathy with the spirit of chaos, I need only add that what is attempted in this chapter remains largely within the realm of "undeveloped possibilities."

IMAGO DEI: FACE AND NO-FACE

> All men have seven openings in order to see, hear, eat, and breathe, Hun-tun alone doesn't have any. Let's try boring him some. Each day they bored one hole and on the seventh day Hun-tun died.
>
> —*Chuang Tzu*, chapter 7
> (trans. Burton Watson, p. 97)

The idea of returning to the beginning fundamentally refers to the use of "arts" or practices of meditation and trance so as to "fast the heart," "still the mind," or "close up" the sense organs that give a man a particular self-understanding, "face," or mode of being defined by ordinary social, moral, and intellectual standards. A Taoist goes against the grain of normal life by forgetting his personal history in the world. By forgetting "his" history, the Taoist is able to remember a more meaningful and therapeutic identification with the "great image" of the Tao.

From the Taoist perspective, "face" and "name" are the fatally deceptive characteristics of a fallen human nature that accepts the values of human culture as ontologically definitive and normative. Taoism therefore seeks to recapture a sense of the cosmic context of human life—that man's well-being is primarily related to and defined by nature even while he lives within the cultural order. The symbolism of Emperor Hun-tun who gains a human face only to lose his real self is in this way a controlling image in the Taoist concern for an "undifferentiated knowledge" of the world and man: "The elimination of all personal characteristics, the complete identification with a nature whose namelessness was no accident, the 'forgetting' which they never tired of preaching (a concept both linguistically and graphically related to 'losing' and 'dying' in Chinese), was for [the Taoists] only a loss of what was superficial, a reduction of the personality to the truly inalienable."[5] To be reidentified ecstatically with the faceless Hun-tun, with the protean visage of the Tao, is for the early Taoists the very source of a more authentic human existence.

The Chinese tradition of the idea of "having face" (indicated by the terms *mien-tzu* and *lien*) is connected with the desire for social prestige and the means of attaining it. "Face," to borrow from Erving Goffman's study of the rituals of social interaction, "may be defined as the positive social value a person effectively claims for himself by the line others assume he has taken during a particular contact. Face is an image of self delineated in terms of approved social attributes."[6] *Mien*, the more archaic term, suggests "a reputation achieved by getting on in life, through success and ostentation . . . prestige accumulated by means of personal effort or clever maneuvering."[7] The word *lien* has more of the connotation of moral character or the "respect of the group for a man with a good moral reputation. . . . it represents the confidence of society in the integrity of ego's moral character."[8] Despite certain differences in the moral criteria associated with the two terms, the general idea of "face" in Chinese tradition is basically influenced by a Confucian context of meaning.

"Confucian" is taken here as a generic label for the traditional Chinese ethical system that affirmed the importance of becoming fully human through social interaction. It was built on the idea of having face or a self-definition that involved the cultivation of hierarchical values derived from the ritual ethos of early feudal civilization. This is the kind of "face" or "face work" rejected by the Taoist concern for the original no-face condition of Emperor Hun-tun.[9] Value for the early Taoists is not a matter of social ranking or a code of ethical-moral precepts located in social history. First and foremost, it is a question of rediscovering a natural treasure or inner power (te^a) that cannot be qualified by ordinary social standards. It is not something accumulated in time but rediscovered as always having been present; not something dependent on clever manipulation or reputation but a matter of "not acting" with a concern for honor or shame. Within the natural order of creation established by the Tao, all men are truly equal as long as they do not totally surrender to the carved order of human culture, as long as they do not sacrifice their inner integrity to a superficial and destructive quest for social privilege.

Of course the whole issue of "face" and "prestige" is quite complicated in Chinese tradition, and it is an oversimplification to make an overly neat distinction between Confucian "face" and Taoist "no-face." In both early Confucianism and early Taoism there is a shared concern for an original and pure human nature; but for the former, self-definition is normatively grounded in the beginning-time of human history and civilization, while for the latter, true human nature is ultimately to be found in the time before human history. The mythic values of the Taoist sage in this way reflect the "nonbenevolent" (*pu-jen*) order of the Tao at the creation time (see, for example, the *Tao Te Ching*, chap. 5). The paradox of myth, and the difficulty of appreciating the Taoist's mystical reentry into mythical time, is that both myth and Taoism are cultural creations that exist to say that the cultural order can never fully circumscribe the meaning of creation in human life.

The different understandings of the creative source of creation and self-definition in early Confucianism and Taoism also relate to the question of the nature and face of the "ancestors": were the "ancestors" originally gods or men, mothers or fathers, animal ancestors or semihuman culture heroes? Using Christian and Islamic theological nomenclature, it is the question of man being made in the image and likeness of God. [10] For the Taoists the face of the primal ancestor was no-human-face; it was the fetal face of all men in the symbolic sense of ontogeny recapitulating phylogeny. As the Ch'an Buddhists would put it later on, the goal of meditation was to "see one's face before one was born." [11]

Some of the contrast between the early Confucian and Taoist points of view may be seen in the changing symbolism of the gods and ancestors who originally and mythologically had animal "faces" and communicated with the human world through animal spirits. Standing face to face with the gods required the shamanistic donning of an animal mask. By emphasizing the identification of human and animal nature, Taoism preserved more of an archaic religious consciousness where "the mythological animal served as a link between the world of man and the world of the ancestors and the gods." [12] In the Eastern Chou period a humanistic movement that can most closely be associated with the development of Confucian thought "euhemerized deities into ancestral heroes and transformed mythical and potent animals into human subjects." [13] These are the historicized legends of the culture heroes who established human civilization by permanently triumphing over the forces of chaos—the old bestial gods and ancestors. This development represents a new humanistic dispensation in Chinese thought that decisively challenges the authority and significance of the older mythological understanding of man. As

Confucius says in the *Analects*, he is not the type of man who "herds together with the birds and the beasts" (XXVIII.6).[14]

The issue raised here is related to the overall evolution of ideas about the ancestors and the condition of the dead in ancient China and cannot be easily simplified or summarized. However tentatively, this kind of inquiry is worth pursuing since the concepts of the ancestors and the dead, along with the associated symbolism of ancestral masks and tablets, are helpful in suggesting a broader perspective from which to understand the archaic religious foundations of early Taoist thought concerning the no-human-face or animal ancestor condition of Emperor Hun-tun.

1. *Face and Mask*

Comparatively speaking, primitive rites involving the use of masks often relate to the technique of status reversal during the liminal period of initiation. Within collective "rites of passage," masking serves to insure the regeneration of the normal cultural order; but masks may also have reference to more dramatic, secret, and personal cults (secret societies and shamanism) that imply the transcendence of the ordinary social world.[15] When members of a secret society put on an animal face, "they act out a myth of beginnings: how in days primordial the Ancestor met his death—changed his state and became 'other'—and afterward revealed to the people the mysteries of death and resurrection through the dramatic ceremonies of initiation."[16]

The relation of this with the symbolism of a mystic's discovery of a nonhuman or ancestral identity is seen by the primary religious function of the ritual mask as a "primordial implement" for returning man to the sacred condition of the mythological time.[17] The visage of "natural man" as originally the offspring of an animal ancestor is made visible both in the symbolism of the archaic mask and the symbolism of mystical ecstasy: "hence the creative, participating ecstasy which the mask calls forth and disseminates. It is a magic implement, which enables man at any moment to apprehend that situation and find the road into a broader, more spiritual world, without departing from the world of natural existence."[18]

Only secondarily, and in terms of the overevaluation of the civilized social order, is the mask exclusively equated with the ideas of monster, demon, concealment, and terror;[19] and it is especially in this more negative context that the ritual and exorcistic use of masks is seen in orthodox Chinese literature after the Eastern Chou period.[20] Taoist literature of the same period, however, reveals a certain continuity with a more "primitive" point of view that preserves the positive ambivalence of the mask and animal ancestor symbolism.

As the *Lieh Tzu* (chap. 2) says, the primordial couple of Fu-hsi and Nü-kua "did not look like men, but they had the virtue of great sages."[21] The human ancestors, the Confucianized emperors or sage kings of the Hsia, Shang, and Chou dynasties, "all shared with other men the same looks, and the same seven holes in their heads, but they had the minds of beasts." Because of this, "ordinary men," who evaluate things on the basis of the superficial standards of "face," are sure to be deceived.[22] The disturbing fact for Taoism, it may be said, is that man "has lost sight of the distinction between [his] true self and the veil of personality that is its present costume, its current shroud, but which will be laid aside when the play is over."[23] The Taoist sage, therefore, discards his false face or *persona* in order to rediscover the "true form" of man, which bears the embryonic visage of all men, the animal shape of the cosmogonic ancestors, or the amorphous condition of the dead.

2. *Face and Ancestral Tablets*

Related to the religious symbolism of the mask is the Chinese lore of the ancestral tablet (*shen-chu*). Granet has pointed out that in the ancient period there was a ritual need to "fix" (*ts'un*) the ancestral image or "face" of the deceased, to insure his "human" identity, since immediately after physical death the deceased has in a sense "returned" [*kuei*[b]] to the prehuman or precultural condition of chaos: "that is why ghosts are called *kuei*[a]" (*Lieh Tzu*, chap. 1).[24] This is an extremely dangerous situation for society since the dead soul is uncontrollable and antisocial. It is evidently important to insure ancestral continuity with the society of the living by the creation of a new face or ancestral identity represented by the tablet or mask. An annotation to the *Shuo Wen* consequently states: "the *hun*[j] soul of the dead wanders [*yu*[b]]; that is why one fixes it by making a mask [*ch'i-tou*]."[25]

The idea of controlling the dead by the giving of a permanent ancestral "face" is connected with later traditional practices concerning the use of ancestral tablets at the time of death. Ancestral tablets probably evolved from phallic statues and anthropomorphic figurines, finally becoming simple wooden plaques marked with the holes of "face" (especially important were the markings to indicate the eyes). At a later stage of development the writing of the name of the deceased on the tablet became equivalent to the idea of giving a proper ancestral status to the tablet.[26]

What is exemplified in the ritual consecration of the ancestral tablet is the theme of the struggle between the Taoist advocacy of the chaos-order of the "unfixed" and "wandering" (*yu*[b]) dead who have returned to the liminal condition of the beginnings and the traditional concern for insuring the continuation of the civilized order of society even after death. Civilization in the orthodox sense is a cosmic "order" that embraces both the worlds of the living and the dead. Like Emperor Hun-tun, the dead represented by the uncarved wooden tablets must be civilized by a face-giving operation that recapitulates the original creation of the human world. The afterworld must be made to submit ritually to the civilized order as does the world of the living.

It seems, in fact, that the traditional ritual ceremony of punctuating or marking the ancestral tablets is modeled on a creation scenario since the conventionalized northern ritual of adding a final dot to a written character (purposely left incomplete on the tablet) is most probably an abridgement of the more archaic southern ceremonies that involve the creation and initiatory symbolism of the giving of a human form to the unshaped wood:

> There the tablet, wrapped up with red cloth, is carried in the funeral procession in an open palanquin preceding the bier. . . . A member of the family who is highest in rank, or an official who is on friendly terms with the family, now removes the red cover from the tablet and touches it six times with dots in vermillion, two pairs of dots in the middle denoting eyes and ears, one above and another below representing head and feet and interpreted from the thoughts of nature philosophy as symbolizing heaven and earth, man being considered the product of the union of the two. This explanation is recited in a verse by the officiating writer during the ceremony, and this verse, doubtless, is very old:
>
> > I am painting heaven, may heaven always be bright over his grave.
> > I am painting earth, may the site of the grave be of powerful effect.
> > I am painting the ears, may the ears well listen (i.e. to the prayers of the descendants).
> > I am painting the eyes, may his eyes penetrate through all (i.e. be open to the needs of the descendants).[27]

Here there is a remembrance of the cosmogonic basis of the ritual in terms of the ancient idea of the "union of the two." As with the operation of Hu and Shu on Hun-tun, the creation of a human face is implicitly justified in terms of the principle of reciprocity (*pao*[a] in the Hun-tun story) since it insures a permanent civil relationship between the societies of the living and the dead. The wood of the tablet having been transformed from the uncarved to carved, natural to cultural, chaotic to cosmic, orders of life, Laufer concludes that "in this punctuation rite, accordingly, a mystic and magic shorthand figure of a man is drawn, and it is this very act which renders the tablet alive and useful, capable of serving as the domicile of a soul."[28]

The deceased, who potentially has a place in the interrelated social hierarchy of the living and dead symbolized by the tablet, is dangerously potent until it is fixed with a "face" or the ancestral mode of being. It may also be significant, therefore, that the tablet is only made and marked with "face" at a moment that is somewhat comparable to the practice of "second burial" seen in some archaic cultures.[29] After the initial physical death and entry into the nonhuman condition of chaos, the human community tries to insure the deceased's reentry into the ancestral community of the living and the dead by a funerary rite of passage—that is, by giving face, by accomplishing a definitive rebirth into "the life beyond the grave: when one fully becomes an Ancestor."[30]

3. Death and "Pumpkinification"

There are other factors that allude to the same set of ideas, but let me only point out with relation to burial customs that it was an early Taoist theme to reject a coffin burial and the ordinary rites of mourning. Inasmuch as the symbolism of the coffin and tomb represents the continuation of human society into the afterlife, the early Taoists seemed to prefer more primitive and less "civilized" practices resembling "ritual exposure."[31] In light of this, the legends of the tree burial of P'an-hu should be recalled as well as, perhaps, the theme of "hanging" or "suspending" the *hun-tun* sack (or *hu-lu* calabash) upside down and the later legends of the Taoist sage who enters a suspended gourd or sack.[32]

It is tantalizing to speculate that these factors may also account for some of the context of meaning underlying Chuang Tzu's famous satirical recommendation for his own funeral:

When Chuang Tzu was about to die, his disciples expressed a desire to give him a sumptuous burial. Chuang Tzu said, "I will have heaven and earth for my coffin and coffin shell, the sun and moon for my jade discs, the stars and constellations for my pearls and beads, and the ten thousand things for my parting gifts. The furnishings for my funeral are already prepared—what is there to add?" "But we're afraid the crows and kites will eat you, Master," said his disciples. Chuang Tzu said, "Above ground I'll be eaten by crows and kites, below ground I'll be eaten by mole crickets and ants. Wouldn't it be rather bigoted to deprive one group in order to supply the other?"[33]

In this passage Chuang Tzu mockingly espouses a kind of cosmic reciprocity that transcends the propriety required by the social code. In distinction to the ordinary emphasis on an ancestral, communal, or moral definition of human nature in both the worlds of the living and dead, the early Taoists sought to define human nature in terms of a more profound experience that could be symbolized by the cosmic reunion attained by the "unfixed" dead. This was an experience and a mode of being that could not be achieved by having "face" or by accepting standards whose primary function was to maintain the civilized order.

Taoism in this sense expresses a soteriological need "for a personal religious experience engaging man's entire existence."[34] The rise of Taoism to some degree resembles the rise of mystery religions in Greece by suggesting that "a personal religious experience could not flourish in the framework of public cults whose principal function was to ensure the sanctification of communal life and continuance of the state."[35] Somewhat like the mystery tradition of Eleusis, early Taoism represents a creative reinterpretation of archaic religious and mythological traditions. Even though Taoism and Eleusis incorporated the mythological structure of primitive agricultural rites, the religious "secret" no longer "referred to fertility of the soil and prosperity of the community but the spiritual destiny of each individual initiate."[36] The "secret" of life for Taoism was the mystical art or internalized ritual of returning personally to a condition that was more than being simply human, a mode of being that was the reversal of all ordinary social and cultural values.

The condition of the dead, the cosmogonic condition of chaos, and consequently the symbolism of the *hun-tun* experience are the basic images of what it means to be a "true man"—to have no-human-face. The secret harbored by Taoism is the secret of returning to chaos while still living or, to echo the famous Zen poem, to learn to be a dead man in this life: "While living be a dead man, / Be thoroughly dead— / And behave as you like, / And all's well."[37] Shen Tao in the *Chuang Tzu* "discarded knowledge, did away with self," and chaotically "revolved like a whirlwind."[38] He followed the "ideals of a dead man."[39] Similarly, as the *Lieh Tzu* says, the old man of the gourd, the Taoist Gourd Master Hu Tzu, in his meditation resembles a "dead man" (there was "damp ash in him").[40] He has returned to that condition "before we first came out of our Ancestor."[41]

The Taoist forgets the artificial self of face and name given to him as a member of society but remembers his original more-than-human self as a Mr. Hun-tun. He remembers his face before he came out of the womb. As a "Gourd Master," one who has mastered the principles of creation, he achieves the deathlike condition of "pumpkinification." This last reference is taken from Seneca's famous contrast between *apocolocyntosis* ("pumpkinification") as the rotting degradation of the dead and *apotheosis* as the ancestral deification of the dead in heaven.[42] Confucius, like Seneca, stands on the side of civilization and can only mock the pumpkin-headed madness of the Taoist's desire for a mystical pumpkinification.

In contrast to the Confucian value system that defined human nature in terms of the "face work" of ritualized social interaction, a Taoist stands alone (*tu*), away from the crowd, and embraces the chaotic values of the "dead," "barbarian," "bumpkin," or "pumpkin-headed fool"—someone who is either dangerously or laughably outside the bounds of all ordinary standards. The true Taoist must accept the opprobrium of being a *hun-jen*—someone who has "lost face," "humbled," or "shamed" (*hun*[f]) himself in the eyes of society.[43] A fatheaded and potbellied numskull, the Taoist sage is someone who goes his own peculiar way, someone who "dwells alone, peaceful and placid, in spiritual brightness" (*Chuang Tzu*, chap. 33).

SIGHT AND INSIGHT: EYE AND BELLY KNOWLEDGE

> The sage is concerned with the belly and not the
> eye. He accepts the former and rejects the latter.
> —*Tao Te Ching*, chapter 12 (trans.
> W. T. Chan)

Another way to view the contrast between face and no-face, ritual "face work" and mystical effacement, would be to stress an epistemological distinction between Confucian and Taoist modes of knowledge. "Knowing" in the Confucian sense implies a doctrine of the rational and hierarchical ordering of reality. It is a knowing of reality that is dependent upon the external sense openings of face or, more properly, the linguistic objectification or "naming" of nature.[44] It is especially the openings of the eyes that allow for "acquired knowledge"—that is, the discrimination and understanding of the world in terms of a spatialized hierarchical perspective: bigger-smaller, higher-lower, brighter-darker, and so on. For Confucianism this is a process that ultimately reflects the cosmic and human order of moral discrimination: superior-inferior, good-bad, beautiful-ugly, face-no-face, civilized-barbarian, human-animal.

Sight, perhaps, can be said to be the most civilized, discriminating, or rational of the senses because it has less of the chaotic ambiguity and variability of the other senses. As Foucault says of the situation in the West after the eighteenth century, the cosmizing of the world in terms of the visible order, "seeing is believing," leaves "sight with an almost exclusive privilege, being the sense by which we perceive extent and establish proof, and, in consequence, the means to an analysis *partes extra partes* acceptable to everyone."[45]

From the Taoist point of view all such distinctions are artificial and strictly "human"—affirming a false connection with sight, language, and reality. For

Taoism, seeing and knowing must be turned inward through the reactivation of the more primordial, preverbal, intuitive, or tacit modes of knowledge. The need to return to the "blind" condition of *hun-tun*, to close up the openings of face, is therefore to refer to a latent power of insightful knowledge activated through various meditational techniques. By making use of the belly instead of the eye, the Taoist can overcome the ordinary reliance on the ultimacy of "seen" reality—the reality structured by language and exteriorized forms of knowing. True knowledge of reality, the right method of "caring for life" (*yang-sheng*), is an instinctual knack communicated by the inner spirit (*shen*[a]) in harmony with the Tao, not through the bored holes of the eyes. Chapter 3 of the *Chuang Tzu*, it will be remembered, tells the story of Cook Ting who worked his knife without looking—"in perfect rhythm as though he were performing the dance of the Mulberry Grove." In explaining his method, Ting said:

> What I care about is the Tao, which goes beyond skill. When I first began cutting up oxen, all I could see was the ox itself. After three years I no longer saw the whole ox. And now—now I go at it by spirit [*shen*[a]] and don't look with my eyes. Perception and understanding have come to a stop and spirit moves where it wants. I go along with the natural makeup, strike in the big hollows, guide the knife through the big openings, and follow things as they are. So I never touch the smallest ligament or tendon, much less a main joint.[46]

For the Taoists there is an inner mode of "empty" knowing and doing. It is a wisdom that comes from the instinctual center of the belly, an image that is expressive of the hollow, womblike condition of *hun-tun*. It is a way of knowing that allows the mind to resonate directly with the cosmic pulse of life and nature. The Confucian, through the exercise of his "evaluating mind," seeks a "path to privilege" within an "aristocracy of merit."[47] The Taoist, however, seeks a "path to the mirror" wherein his mind naturally reflects the larger nonhuman or "chaotic" order of primordial life:

> Be empty, that is all. The Perfect Man uses his mind like a mirror—going after nothing, welcoming nothing, responding but not storing.[48]

In distinction to the "normal" man who accepts the fallen condition of being carved, drilled, or molded into a particular closed system of perceiving reality, the Taoist seeks to return to an inward vision (*nei-kuan*) of his faceless self, the possibility of "seeing" his original state as an "uncarved block" possessing all of the inborn latent powers of creative growth, spontaneity, and life in seedlike wholeness.[49] Through such techniques as *hsin-yang, hsin-chai, tso-wang,* and *nei-kuan* the Taoist seeks to attain that mode of being symbolized by Hun-tun's condition of totality: Lao Tan said, "I was letting my mind wander in the Beginning of Things."[50]

Because of the apparent reference to meditation techniques and mystic experience in early Taoist texts, there is a strong suggestion that the "belly" as the true center of human action and wisdom is more than a simple literary metaphor. This is explicitly the case in later Taoist mysticism where the mysterious *huang-t'ing* or "Yellow Court" as a focal point of meditation is most ordinarily associated with "a spot in the belly . . . situated somewhere 'under' the navel."[51] The mystical return to the Yellow Court in the belly (or sometimes the "alchemical field" in the head—i.e., there is a symbolic equivalence between the head and belly in Taoist mysticism) is, in a sense, a return to the hermaphroditic condition of the chaos time or the country of women. Thus the adept's Yellow Court is symbolically the womblike matrix for the gestation of the *ch'ih-tzu* or immortal embryo of sainthood. As Schipper remarks, the Yellow Court of the belly, the residence of Lao Chün and the *ch'ih-tzu*, can "be identified semantically with *hun-tun*."[52]

For Taoism, knowing the true order of life is like listening to a parable told by the beasts, a parable that is communicated to man through his gut—his inner self as a Mr. Hun-tun. The *Shan Hai Ching* stated that Hun-tun was a creature that was without "face and eyes"; and as I have shown throughout this study, the motif of being faceless or blind is closely connected with the mystic theme of returning to the beginnings. The *Huai Nan Tzu* (chap. 2) says that the ancient men of the *hun-tun* time "did not know directions. They ate and wandered about in complete freedom, drumming their bellies and rejoicing."[53]

The imagery of the ancients of the paradise time who "drummed their bellies and rejoiced" (cf. *Huai Nan Tzu*, chaps. 2, 4; *Chuang Tzu*, chap. 9; and *Shan Hai Ching*, chap. 13) evokes the mythological prototype of the great flood signaled by the drumming rumble of thunder and lightning. In the *Huai Nan Tzu* the god of thunder is described as a semihuman animal ancestor who "drums his belly in amusement," and the condition of sacred folly (*ch'ang-k'uang*) is specifically related to the masked identification of shamanic revelers with the god of thunder at festival times.[54]

There is an evident connection here between archaic shamanic ecstasy (or the frenzy of masked possession) and the mystic experience sought by the Taoist. Both are expressive of a common mythological model of meaning. "Knowing with the belly" identifies the Taoist with the sacred madness of the ancestral gods of the creation time.

SACRED MADNESS: THE TAOIST SAGE AS FOOL

> Hung-meng said, "Aimless wandering [*fu yu*]
> does not know what it seeks; demented drifting
> [*ch'ang k'uang*] does not know where it goes. A
> wanderer, idle, unbound, I view the sights of
> deception. What more do I know?"
>   —*Chuang Tzu,* chapter 11 (trans.
>   Burton Watson)

Another image I would like to develop briefly is that of the Taoist as the "wise fool." The reversal of conventional human standards is characteristically described in images suggesting a sacred madness, stupidity, foolishness, or deformity so that the "true Taoist must, in his perfect simplicity, give the appearance of a fool."[55] Chapter 20 from the *Tao Te Ching* says that the sage is a "fool" (*yü-jen*) because his mind is "muddled and chaotic" (*hun-hun*[a]).[56]

Taoist images of madness are related to the mystical experience of the chaos condition and to the unique effortless freedom of *wu-wei,* the sage's playful freedom beyond human, or even humane, bounds. The Taoist as a "demented drifter" is aloof and indifferent to the normal order of the world. From the perspective of his belly knowledge, the Taoist is a wayfarer who knows that "the way things appear to be—permanent, predictable, manageable—is not the way things really are in an ultimate vision of the real."[57]

In the early Taoist texts, terms such as *yü*[b] ("stupid, fool"), *ch'ih*[a] ("idiot"), *ju-su* ("unsophisticated"), *san-jen* ("loafer"), *yeh-jen* ("rustic, bumpkin, simpleton"), and *k'uang*[b] ("demented, mad") are all expressive of the mythological paradigm of *hun-tun* and suggest the unique experiental condition and mode of behavior attained by the Taoist. The "man of Tao" is often pictured as a simple and uncivilized farmer, rustic, gardener, wood cutter, fisherman, or as someone who is physically deformed (especially as a hunchback or as one-legged). In the *Chuang Tzu* the Taoist seeks to make himself stupid and giddy or as humdrum and useless as a "withered tree" (*san mu* or *kao mu*).[58] Throughout the use of many of these terms there is the implied contrast between "rural" and "urban" or, as previously discussed, between "barbarian" (or "criminal, ugly, deformed, etc.") and "civilized."

Symbols tend to cluster and "connotations flock together" so that there is sometimes a surprising linkage of words and meanings related to the symbolism of *hun-tun.*[59] Even in modern vernacular Chinese, expressions such as *hu-li-hu-t'u* for madness, deformity, confusion, stupidity, foolishness, boorishness, idiocy, and so on are related to the word families of hu^{b-i} (gourd, calabash, confusion, muddled, foolish) and hun^d.[60] Moreover a term like ya^a for "humpback, ugly, or deformed" can be associated with other characters such as ya^b meaning "dumb or speechless," o meaning "wicked or bad," and hu^h, the calabash vase or gourd.[61]

This kind of symbolic pattern can also be found in the later iconography and symbolism of the *hsien*, especially that type of *hsien* called the "banished immortal" (*che-hsien*).[62] There is apparently a connection with the general theme of a tricksterlike figure, holy man, or religious eccentric found in popular Chinese literature (such figures as No Cha, Lu Ya, Tung-fang Shuo, and Sun Wu-k'ung).[63] Schipper refers to such figures as representing the Taoist typology of the "bouffon-mediateur divin."[64] This figure often has traces of an ambivalent sexuality and, as the primordial clown-immortal-exile, inhabits the chaos region between heaven and earth. He is the autonomous mediator or "third term" that incorporates into himself the dual principles of *yin* and *yang*, heaven and earth, sacred and profane. In later Taoism he transmits sacrality to man by acting as the agent of revelation.[65]

The particular grounding of this in the theme of *hun-tun* may be indicated by recalling those passages from the *Tso Chuan* where Hun-tun, along with the other "legendary rebel" monsters, is put in the context of ancient spectacles involving ritual buffoon figures who were licensed to act outside the bounds of the normal values of the society. The very identification of Hun-tun as a "rebel" or "barbarian" in the Confucian-inspired literature may derive from the archaic ritual importance of seasonal periods of nonconformity and antisocial behavior, transitional periods of returning to the life-order of chaos. Granet consequently maintains that the description of Hun-tun and the other "rebels" strongly suggests that their characters were modeled on ancient dramatic rituals involving a buffoon or scapegoat figure.[66] Becoming a Mr. Hun-tun in the form of a ritual buffoon or clown symbolized all that was opposed to the ordinary civilized order.

The same relation to ancient traditions involving the role of buffoon figures or "demon impersonators" during festival periods and times of ritual exorcism is suggested by the term $k'uang^b$. It appears that in the archaic period $k'uang^b$ was a name for comedic clowns, buffoons, or fools (the *k'uang-fu*, or the shamanically "possessed") who participated in masked ceremonies during spring and autumn periods of the ritual renewal of the agrarian cycle—especially the No festival at the time of the New Year.[67] It is also said that these *k'uang-fu* wore a characteristic motley dress (*p'ien-i*) indicating their lack of "political" or "civilized" wisdom.[68] Yet, at the same time, a *k'uang-fu* was "a kind of sage whose words were worth being taken into consideration."[69]

FOOLISH COMPARISONS

[Fools] have a magical affinity with chaos that might allow them to serve as scapegoats on behalf of order; yet they elude the sacrifice or the banishment that would affirm order at their expense. . . . They wrest life from the "destructive element" while ridiculing the ancient dream that victory over it is possible—and while ridiculing even more the idea that victory over it may be achieved through the observance of rules of conduct. Fools induce chaos by violating those rules. They may look on passively, innocently, even benignly, while the sympathetic magic that binds them to it works. Though they may seem innocently detached from it, it may be an active form of their folly. It may be overtly demonic, but it may also take a playful form, and it may emerge as the fool's guiding spirit in a transvaluation of values with him as its center.

—William Willeford, The Fool
and His Scepter

The kind of symbolism roughly sketched out above is reflective of worldwide traditions involving the idea of a sacred fool or scapegoat figure, traditions that are especially linked to primitive ideas of fertility magic and seasonal renewal. The typology of the sacred fool both in China and in other cultures is in this way connected with the mythological theme of transitional periods in the round of cosmic and social life, those times in the life passage when there is a return to the chaos condition as a prerequisite for the re-creation of the ordered world. These were the "carnival" times usually associated with the coming of the new year and marked by frenzied, chaotic, or orgiastic behavior; periods when folly reigned in the figure of a mock king, scapegoat, trickster, jester, buffoon, or "wylde" man. In medieval Europe these festival periods were known as *ludus de homine salvatico*.[70]

To consider only some of the more obvious parallels it should be noted that in European tradition the theme of the wild man commonly recalled a cosmic giant type of mythological figure variously modeled on Biblical imagery, pagan deities, or the primal man Enkidu in the Gilgamesh epic. Resembling the Chinese P'an-ku, Enkidu's "wylde" or chaotic condition is indicated by his speechless, hairy, and horned appearance.[71] There is also an important connection with initiation rituals since in some cases the reward for taking on the role of the wild man was reception into a secret society.[72]

In addition to these observations, there is a striking similarity between what may be called the comparative typology of the fool in Western tradition and the idea of sacred madness in Taoism. The basic symbolic features are congruent (physical deformity, dress, and psychic aberration); and even the derivations of the English terms of "fool" and "buffoon" (and other expressions) are reminiscent of some of the etymological details found in relation to the theme of *hun-tun*. Both "fool" and "buffoon" go back to Latin and Italian words for "puffing, blowing, filled with wind" or, as in the associations for *hun-tun*, allude to the image of a bellows, an empty windbag, drum, sack, gourd, and so on.[73] Moreover a series of erotic and sexual connotations in both the Chinese and Western symbolism of the fool suggest archaic mythological and ritual traditions that were concerned with creation and fertility.[74]

More significant than these random factors is that thematically, the times of licensed folly in Western tradition were dramatically expressive of the tension and ambiguous relationship between the civilized and wild orders. Within the social context the most important part of the festival period was the hunting, capture, and death of the wild man, which represented his reintroduction back into the human world.[75] The wild man or fool, like Hun-tun, the animal ancestors, or the wandering dead, is thus an ambivalent figure in relation to society. He is both a creator and a destroyer, a harbinger of fertility yet at the same time a demon who is identified with the return of the dead spirits in the late winter carnival periods.[76] In the manner of Emperor Hun-tun or P'an-ku, the wild man must die in order to insure the continuation of a stable human cosmos, the normal order of the world.

From the standpoint of society, the periods of the irresponsible and contrary behavior of the fool must be made to serve the values and standards of the existing social order. The very idea of "civilization" and "civilized values" as the "right/rite order" of human life may be seen to some degree in relation to a progressive denial of the mythic need to celebrate periodically the forces of chaotic folly. This is but another way of saying that demythologization coincides with the development of an all-encompassing civilizational order of life built on the increasingly intense conviction that chaos, the gods, or the sacred are essentially extraneous and meaningless.[77]

But in early Taoist thought, and in reference to the overall comparative meaning of the fool, there is always a necessary and vital relation between order and chaos. Chaos in the figure of the ritual fool or foolish mystic affirms the presence of a higher and more authentic "order" that stands in judgment on the legitimacy and meaning of the social order. It is only with reference to the experience of chaos that a "transvaluation of values" is accomplished, that change, a new creation or revolution, is effected in either social or individual life.[78]

In this way the symbolism of a ritual or mystic return to chaos may not be just a prelude to the re-creation of the existing human order but an experience that attacks the whole meaning of order as the simple antithesis of chaos. The mythic basis for this, as it has surfaced in this study, is that order, or existence itself, originally and continually depends upon the cosmogonic priority of chaos. Mythologically, chaos is the secret source and rule of creation just as the symbolism of the fool both validates and transcends all conventional standards.

Like the multiple and sometimes contradictory meanings associated with the *hun-tun* theme in China, and especially the contrast between the early Taoist and Confucian understandings of chaos and order, the traditional European figures of the wild man and fool had complex sociological, psychological, and metaphysical connotations that challenged many of the presuppositions of established Christian society. In medieval European literature the wild man's condition was finally felt to be somehow superior to that of the civilized order:

> Wildness meant more in the Middle Ages than the shrunken significance of the term would indicate today. The word implied everything that eluded Christian norms and the established framework of Christian society, referring to what was uncanny, unruly, raw, unpredictable, foreign, uncultured, and uncultivated. It included the unfamiliar as well as the unintelligible. Just as the wilderness is the background against which medieval society is delineated, so wildness in the widest sense is the background of God's lucid order of creation. Man in his reconstructed state, faraway nations, and savage creatures at home thus came to share the same essential quality. This quality was one which held considerable fascination for many men in the Middle Ages, as a counterpoise against traditional imitations of thought and behavior. It is true that to venture into the woods and there to prove one's mettle by slaying the dragon, the giant, or the Saracen meant to combat the ever present threat of natural and moral anarchy, and thus to strengthen the beneficent rule of Christianity. But wildness embodied not only a task but a temptation, to which one exposed oneself by plunging into the great wild unknown. No wonder that, before the Middle Ages were out, it became fashionable to identify oneself with savage things, to slip into the wild man's garb, and thus to repudiate that very principle of hieratic order upon which medieval society was founded.[79]

By substituting "Confucian" for "Christian" and "Taoist sensibility" for "wildness" in this quotation it is possible to see that the *hun-tun* theme found in China touches on issues universally rooted in human history and consciousness. The whole meaning of the conventional, cosmetic, ornamental, rational, or civilized idea of order and life is being questioned by Taoism and its foolish concern for becoming a Mr. Hun-tun. The Taoist sage follows out his inner urge to "slip into the wild man's garb, and thus to repudiate that very principle of hieratic order" upon which early Chinese feudal society was founded.

Lastly, I would like to remark that the Taoist understanding of man as a "sacred fool," or *homo ludens*, may offer a way of viewing the significance of *wu-wei* as "natural," or wildly spontaneous and free, behavior contrary to the accepted order. The return to the condition of *hun-tun* implies the possibility of a certain kind of conduct that emulates the unique life-order, continual self-createdness, and freedom of the primoridal Tao—its *tzu-jan*. *Wu-wei* is not so much a principle of utter passivity or "non-action" but the idea of a "natural," "purposeless," "playful," or "disinterested" mode of action set in distinction to the willful and socially structured "face work" emphasized within Confucian tradition.[80] But this kind of simple contrast would seem to be reflective of the deeper mythological and metaphysical issues that have been discussed in this study. Schipper, for example, has noted that inasmuch as *wu-wei* must be seen as a mode of conduct modeled on the cosmic life of the Tao, the "alternative between the Confucian ideology and the Taoist attitude could just as well turn out to be the difference between two different cosmologies."[81] In other words, the difference comes from the differing conceptions of the ultimate meaning of life, order, and behavior seen in Taoism and Confucianism—that is, their respective interpretations of "creation." Taoism and its theme of *hun-tun* prompt the conviction that "folly is one of the supreme facts about human nature, perhaps even about the world."[82]

9

CONCLUSION
THE CONUNDRUM OF
HUN-TUN

> How can I live with men whose hearts are
>   strangers to me?
> I am going a far journey to be away from them.
> I took the way that led towards the K'un-lun
>   mountain: A long, long road with many
>   turnings in it.
> —"Li Sao" (trans. D. Hawkes, *Ch'u Tz'u*)

THE LONG JOURNEY that has led this study to the vicinity of Emperor
Hun-tun's "neighborhood of the Great Beginning" has followed a
sinuous path with "many turnings in it." This is in keeping with the
mythological logic of my subject since Hun-tun as the animal ancestor, the
Shen I Ching tells us, "always gnaws his tail, going round and round."[1] The
end of this inquiry, in other words, is only the beginning of an understanding of
the significance of the chaos theme in Taoism. The final conundrum of *hun-tun*
is that in the early Taoist texts, in some aspects of later Taoist meditative ritual,
and more broadly in the general history of religions, the religious and philosophical truth of "chaos" as a mythological and metaphysical principle maintains its integrity by revealing itself chaotically: "there is an extremely complex
interpenetration of an unknowable number of centers."[2]

CHAOS AND CONTINUITY IN TAOIST TRADITION

> The great saints of old taught a profound medi-
> tation in which one had to shut the nine aper-
> tures, relax one's body, and become similar to
> chaos, inside which the circulation of the
> breaths makes a closed circuit as with the
> embryo in the womb.
>
> —*T'ai P'ing Ching* (paraphrased by
> M. Kaltenmark, *Facets of Taoism*)

Building on the pioneering studies of the Paris school of sinology and the important contributions of modern Japanese scholarship, a remarkable group of young scholars is for the first time gradually unveiling the hidden riches of liturgical and esoteric Taoism.[3] These studies are crucial for a more precise understanding of the history of Chinese religions and, also, from a hermeneutical perspective, allow the historian of religions to start to make some interpretive judgments concerning the relation between classical and later Taoism. Taoism, especially the sectarian or liturgical tradition, has been the most neglected of major religions, but the advances in recent scholarship are now making it possible to fit the overall Taoist tradition more meaningfully into the comparative history of world religions. These are immense tasks that can only be adequately accomplished after further scholarship and comparative reflection has taken place.[4]

Granting the provisional nature of any interpretive ventures at this time, it can nevertheless be said that, if the mythological theme of chaos constitutes one of the central religious insights of early Taoist thought and practice, then it will be of extreme interest to see whether or not, or in what specific ways, a similar pattern of meaning is manifest in later forms of orthodox Taoism. To perceive some underlying structural continuity between the early classical texts and the later, fantastically varied, aspects of institutionalized Taoism is not to argue for the identity of all forms of Taoism. It is to suggest, however, that when post-Han Taoism became conscious of itself as an organized religious movement it creatively drew upon a preexisting history of religious ideas most closely associated with the early classical texts.

Part of the problem here is the tendency to set up a predetermined dichotomy between the early and later texts in terms of either a "philosophical" or "religious" intention. "Religious" is this sense is usually used to define a system of thought directed toward a supernaturalistic goal of immortality. Unfortunately for the cogency of this position, the one thing that is relatively clear in the study of Taoism is that there is never simply a goal of transcendent or otherworldly immortality.[5] By the same token, the early Taoist texts cannot just be called "philosophical" if this is intended to disallow any sort of religious intent or action.

From a comparative point of view the "most powerful innovative constructs" of a tradition "will be those that achieve their force against . . . the inevitability of personal death"; but this kind of innovation does not necessarily represent a completely different religious foundation.[6] In distinction to Creel's attempt to distinguish classical and *hsien* Taoism on the basis of their "logical" incompatibility, it is more correct anthropologically to recognize that a religious tradition "can never be adequately summed up as a logical ordering or closed system of internally consistent propositions."[7]

The unity and coherence of the Taoist religious vision is fundamentally a matter of a "logic" that is symbolic and mythological in character. As a "system of symbols" involving mythological formulations of a "general order of existence," religion can be more broadly defined as thought and action directed toward salvation.[8] The meaning of "salvation" from this definitional perspective is determined by the particular mythological formulations and refers to the permanent or temporary rectification of some significant ill in human life.[9] In this way, the early Taoist texts show a concern that is as fully religious as that found in the *Tao Tsang*.

Despite inevitable differences relative to a changing sociological situation, or what Ninian Smart calls a "milieu transformation," the fact is that the later Taoists themselves saw reason to embrace a "core of religious striving" first made explicit in the early texts.[10] To say that orthodox Taoism is built largely on beliefs and practices adopted from popular religion is really to say that the later tradition continues, intensifies, and institutionalizes a process of creative transformation initiated by the early texts. The appropriation and reinterpretation of the primitive, folk, or popular legacy of Chinese religion has always been the unique genius of Taoism, whether of the early texts or of the lineage of Chang Tao-ling.[11]

To dismiss assertions of religious unity on the part of later Taoist spokesmen as due primarily to a self-serving hindsight that sought the confirmation of ancient authority is to beg the question that stands behind the meaning of the idea of a "tradition." The idea of a historical tradition is not that there is a "fixed intellectual content independent of time and space"[12] but that there is always a constantly changing series of interpretations and forms relative to a nuclear set of a few basic, and open-ended, religious convictions. Referring to the Taoist "tradition" as including both the sociologically disparate early texts and the later, more coherent and definable, Taoist sectarian movement is to say nothing more than certain items in a chronological sequence have been *interpreted*, by Taoists or by historians, as having *something* in common with respect to the general meaning and method of salvation. Such an interpretation of tradition as a *process* of constant reinterpretation is surely bound to respect the realities of Chinese social history but, at the same time, rests on the identification of some flexible core of salvational intent concerning symbolic formulations of a general order of existence and a way to cope with the fragility of the human predicament.

To say that this romantically reduces the unity of Taoism to a loose symbolic patchwork of ''congenital sentiment'' is only accurate to the extent that the common pattern of religious symbolism remains undefined or tritely universal. [13] One result of this study has been to show that the central religious sentiments in early Taoism need not remain vaguely sentimental. The early texts reveal a specific and definable structure of religious symbolism. Religious sentiment, in other words, is embodied in a particular system of symbols; and the ''core of religious striving'' in the early texts has a discernable symbolic shape as well as more amorphous moods and motivations. Both are subject to transformation, but the underlying symbolic form changes more recalcitrantly than its associated feelings.

Here it is well to invoke Clifford Geertz's advice that the anthropological study of religion is a ''two stage operation: first, an analysis of the system of meanings embodied in the symbols which make up the religion proper, and second, the relating of these systems to social structural and psychological processes.''[14] Geertz admonishes his anthropological colleagues by remarking that too much of contemporary work on religion is devoted to the second stage, to the neglect and exclusion of the first. [15] The problem with some contemporary recommendations concerning the study of Taoism is exactly comparable to the situation criticized by Geertz. The issue is not that sinological scholars are properly concerned with the social history of Taoism but that they have tended to neglect, or reject, the importance of paying primary attention to the *religious* history of Taoism as a system of meanings embodied in symbols.

Finding a kind of structural continuity in early and later Taoism that legitimates the use of the term ''tradition,'' therefore, is not just to discover some curious ''parallels'' of language but to see how, amid all of the obvious differences of interpretation and application, there may be some coherent symbolic trajectory of salvational intent regarding the meaning and method of ''returning to the beginning.'' The meaning of tradition as a ''longue durée'' of some fundamental cultural systems of religious symbolism is finally like the meaning of the Tao: it stays the same by constantly changing. [16]

1. *Unity and Diversity in Taoist Tradition*

In order to trace some of the unity and diversity of Taoist tradition in the manner indicated, I would first like to stress how certain core ideas are subject to significant reinterpretation. One clear instance of this pertains to the popular amelioration of the old utopian and revolutionary social implication of the *hun-tun* theme. Sivin points out that "far from being politically revolutionary, orthodox Taoist sects after the Han period played no active role in rebellions, messianic or otherwise, and never represented rebellion as desirable."[17] Rejecting the radical social and mystical implications of the "faceless" Emperor Hun-tun, orthodox Taoism as a mass religious movement "consistently sought the favor of the temporal powers, provided support for the government, and modeled relations with the gods on the usages of the imperial bureaucracy."[18]

Even more generally it can be said that the vast liturgical apparatus of sectarian Taoism was primarily directed toward the maintenance and regeneration of ordinary society (the *chiao*[b] rites), the protection of the normal social order through exorcistic ritual, and the procurement of heavenly blessings for the dead (the *chai* rites).[19] For the layman the attainment of these goals was the result of good works and grace mediated by the liturgical performances and magical rites of the priests (*Tao-shih*) on behalf of the divine Lao Tzu (Lao Chün) and the celestial hierarchy of gods.

The gods of the Taoist church are associated with two realms—the visible or profane gods of the "Posterior Heavens" worshipped by the ordinary believers and the hidden cosmogonic gods (especially in the form of a trinity) of the "Prior Heavens" associated with the private meditational ritual of the priests.[20] As Seidel and Schipper have shown, the sacred biography of Lao Tzu as a savior god in sectarian Taoism is generally modeled on the scenario of the primal chaos and the related cosmic giant mythology of P'an-ku.[21] The relation between the cosmogonic birth of Lao Tzu, who was coterminous with the primordial *hun-tun*, and his historical incarnations is the revelatory and salvational link between the cosmogonic condition of the "Prior Heavens" and the "fallen" divine world of the "Posterior Heavens." Revelation implies a "fall" of the gods into human time.

The priest is the one responsible for maintaining a balanced connection between the different divine and human worlds by virtue of his liturgical manipulation of the divinities of the "posterior" realm, by his ritual dealings with "prior" gods, and finally through his meditational identification with the cosmogonic or "mystical body" of Lao Tzu, triune and hermaphroditic in nature. The efficacy of communal liturgy to some degree depends on rubrical perfection, *ex opere operato*; but in the sense of *ex opere operantis*, ritual is "vastly enhanced and elevated" by the interior spiritual life of the Taoist priest who is privately concerned with the mystical truth of returning to the *hun-tun* condition.[22] The esoteric practices of ritual meditation performed by the Taoist priest in this way continue much of the original pre-Han religious significance of the chaos theme even though the personal attainments (or "merit," *kung/kung-fu*) of the priest are concerned with the benefit of the whole community.

Some of the change in the direction of an "inner" mystical and "outer" liturgical understanding of the religious goal of Taoism is seen in the popular view of the cosmic giant mythology, which tends to depict P'an-ku, as well the divine Lao Chün, as a Confucian type of culture hero who carves a civilized order out of a prior chaotic situation.[23] Rather than being identified with the saving power of chaos, the popular ideal of a mythological demiurge is presented as a theological savior-hero who triumphs over what was originally dark and shapeless. In the communal liturgy of temple Taoism, there is a shift away from the mystery of "chaos" to an emphasis on the suppression of the demonic forces that constantly threaten the traditional social fabric.

The danger of the early Taoist mystical solicitude for *hun-tun* was always that, in lieu of any actual political or social reform, the image of chaos could only be popularly understood as an obstacle to human life. This is a conclusion that is amply demonstrated by the developing stress on an antagonistic *yin-yang* dualism and the importance of magical rites of exorcism. The old formulaic contrast between the sacrality of a "chaos-order" and the profanity of "benevolent disorder" gave way in Han and post-Han Taoism to a Mencian *Heilsgeschichte*-type idea of *i-chih-i-luan* where the cyclic interplay of social decline and redress is primarily focused on maintaining the hierarchical order.[24] Sectarian Taoism of the Six Dynasties period thus fit itself into the mainstream institutional structures of civil respectability and ancestral piety.

Part of the reason for the popular reinterpretation of the old salvational ideal may be suggested by Peter Berger's general theoretical observation that "to deny reality as it has been socially defined is to risk falling into irreality."[25] A mystic counterdefinition of the world is impossible to maintain without the support of general society, and the popular success of sectarian Taoism can be said therefore to reflect a kind of sociological routinization of the more charismatic and anarchistic religious strivings of the early texts. The wistful impracticality of the early Taoist political ideal of primitivism as seen in the *Tao Te Ching* and parts of the *Chuang Tzu*, the elitish exclusivity of a wholly mystical understanding of the meaning of salvation, the syncretistic popularization of

Taoism during the Han, the influence of Mahayana theory and ecclesiology, and the abortion of the Taoist theocratic rebellions at the end of the Han prompt the speculative conclusion that there were only two interrelated options. Esoterically, as it applied to the priestly elite or individual adepts, the mystical ideal of returning to chaos continued to harbor revolutionary metaphysical and imaginative implications; but as an institutionalized mass movement, Taoism was forced to adapt itself to the conventional definitions of social reality.

From the anthropological perspective of Victor Turner, a mystical vision and its sociological corollary of a nonhierarchical social order of "communitas" flounder because of the impossibility of making the antistructure of liminality a permanent condition of human life.[26] By its very nature a chaos condition can only be a temporary counterpoint to the structured social world or rational mind. It is *yin* in constant dialectical relation to *yang*; it is *homo ludens* in mirror relation to *homo hierarchicus* and vice versa. As Turner has observed, and this is a point with some bearing on the development of sectarian Taoism during and after the Han dynasty (especially concerning the Way of Great Peace and Way of the Heavenly Masters),[27] one solution to the problem of society returning to the kingdom of god on earth is the development of messianic/eschatological/apocalyptic doctrines that assert a final, even imminent, return to the paradise condition of "great equality" at the end of historical time.[28] As an end that would be the permanent reappearance of the beginning, this event symbolically represents the eternal crystallization of the original cosmogonic condition of egalitarian unity. While waiting for this future event, however, it is best to make the most of the face-work of ordinary social life and the grace-work offered by the gods and church.[29] The problem is that the pristine future event never quite arrives and one is left only with waiting. Even though mystics, fools, and children will continue to be impatient and bored with such a tactic, it can perhaps be said that making the most of "waiting for Godot" is finally the destiny of any religion when it becomes ecclesiastically orthodox.

2. *Solve et Coagula* in Esoteric Taoist Meditative Ritual

The orthodox tradition can be distinguished in terms of the public practices of communal liturgy and the private ritual meditation of the priest or adept. Notwithstanding the changes relative to the mass appeal and functionality of Taoism, it is finally the case that the individual priest understands ritual as necessarily related to an internal meditation that is homologous, both in form and in experience, with the cosmogonic model of the early texts. Indeed, the doctrinal unity and very meaning of "orthodox" ritual is basically founded on the mystical philosophy of returning to the *hun-tun* condition:

> If the purpose of orthodox ritual can be stated in a single sentence, it is perhaps this: the Taoist, by his or her ritual, attempts to progress from the myriad creatures, back through the process of gestation, to an audience with the eternal, transcendent Tao. In a series of ritual meditations, the Taoist adept empties out the myriad spirits, until he or she stands in the state of *hun-tun*, or primordial emptiness. At that moment, the Tao of transcendence, *wu-wei chih Tao*, comes of itself to dwell in the emptied center of man. This process is called *hsin-chai*, or fasting (voiding) the heart. Orthodox ritual is thus defined by ritual purpose. Taoists who perform their liturgies for the purpose of union are called orthodox.[30]

Saso speaks of this as implying a cosmological metaphysics of "transcendent dualism" where the transcendent uncreated Tao is to some extent distinct from the created manifestation of Tao in the cosmogonic process of one, two and three.[31] In this sense there is a certain shift in emphasis from the original theories of Taoism but no real contradiction; and this is a shift that may basically reflect a compromise in the tension between the adept's mystical point of view and the demands for a popular theology of liturgical salvation. In terms of the priestly perspective, the basic paradox of the classical idea of *coincidentia oppositorium*, the relation between the created and uncreated as the third term of *creatio continua*, remains as the basic underlying formula for the mystery of creation, life, and salvation.

The priest's ritual meditation, therefore, exemplifies and continues the classic cosmogonic structure. Through the priest's efforts in meditation he reaches the time before time, the threshold of creation itself, which is identified with the condition of *hun-tun*, *t'ai-chi*, or *t'ai-i*[a]. This is but a preparation for a final stage of sainthood that gratuitously comes as a kind of beatific vision of the "transcendent" Tao. At the moment of undifferentiated union in the last ritual meditation of the priest, the "final document for blessings for all laymen and women is sent off to the heavens . . . and the potency for standing before the Tao of Transcendence is made available."[32] As Saso remarks, "in the basic meaning of esoteric religion, it is the master (the Taoist [priest]) who attains immortality for himself, and he passes on the inwardly won blessings to the community by ritual."[33]

Regardless of the various theological elaborations, it is evident that the inner meaning and form of later Taoist ritual meditation is essentially similar to the mythological logic and structure of early Taoist mysticism. The ancient formula of returning to the beginning endures as the basic goal of the ritual meditation performed by the Taoist priest.[34] The secret of return via liturgy and meditation is revealed in the canonical texts and involves both mind and body through the interrelated work of thought, word, and action (interior psycho-mental meditation, mystic prayer, and ritual). From the standpoint of the esoteric understanding of Taoist liturgical doctrine, this involves a kind of alchemical process of refinement, or the microcosmic "great work" of *solve et coagula*, where the initial separation and purification of the three life principles of spirit, breath, and vital essence (*shen*[a], *ch'i*[a], and *ching*) leads to the final stage of chaotic fusion.[35]

In esoteric Taoist theory the formulation of man's fallen condition also builds on the cosmogonic analysis found in the early texts. Man, as born into the world, mistakenly defines reality in terms of the grasping discriminations of his sense organs and the societal definitions of "face." This is an illusory conviction since objects presented to the senses, though really existing, have no value in themselves. Individual things are not permanent or final causes in themselves but only the constantly changing manifestations of the *creatio continua* of the Tao, the "Great Transformation" of things. The fundamental delusion of man is that the external world, as presented by the senses, is deemed worthy of pursuit by the will and capable of satisfying one's desires. Running pell-mell after the things of the world only results in selfish despair, conflict, and a dissipation of the psychosomatic life energies of breath, spirit, and vital essence. This existential hubbub leads to bodily/psychic anxiety and premature death.[36]

The priest or adept is concerned with another way of knowing and being in the world: a realization of the authentic inner self of no-human-face that comes about through a mystical closure of the holes of sense discrimination and desire normally responsible for exhausting the generative energies (especially *yang* forces) of the Tao within man. In later Taoist tradition, man cannot accomplish this by himself and needs the downcoming of the Transcendent Tao in the sacred scriptures, ritual spirit registers (*lu*[b]), talismans (*fu*[b]), the gods of the posterior heavens, and the incarnate Lao Chün of the Prior World. The "Tao opened a path" that is contained in the scriptures, liturgy, and rules of Taoist morality.[37] Because of revelation:

> The bodily state could be transcended
> By a higher state of union with the Tao,
> By preserving the life essences,
> Through performing the rituals,
> And promising to fulfill the moral commandments,
> The Heart is quiet and contemplates darkness (*yin*);
> The will is fixed on undivided brightness (*yang*);
> All thought is reduced to the one (*hun-tun*).[38]

In fact, the scriptures themselves, as the primary medium of revelation, are said to originate in the mythological *hun-tun* condition. In the Ling-pao tradition, the scriptures have a kind of preexistence as the radiant "jade characters" or "red script of the chaos cavern" (*hun-tung hung-wen*). These sacred words were the "very first coagulation of the *yüan-ch'i* accessible only to the highest deity Yüan-shih t'ien-ts'un (the first emanation of *yüan-ch'i* and, in a way, a personification of the Tao) who preaches them to the lesser gods until they reach humanity."[39] In this way the scriptures are a self-revelation of the primordial Tao before the separation of heaven and earth. "In the beginning was the Word," is for the Taoist tradition "the best authentication any scripture can get."[40]

The above can be taken only as a very general sketch of some of the form and content of esoteric Taoist doctrine. While recognizing the almost impossibly arcane nature of much of the later tradition, it is most significant that even a cursory perusal of this material, based on current scholarly information, points to a remarkable coherence with the mythological structure and symbolic intent of the earlier *hun-tun* theme. To further substantiate this, and to suggest some avenues for future research, I would like to devote the rest of this section to a closer, yet again only preliminary, examination of the mythological underpinnings of the savior god doctrine of Lao Tzu (Lao Chün) and the process of ritual meditation prescribed by the *Yellow Court Canon* (*Huang T'ing Ching, nei* and *wai*).

I have already noted that the sacred biography of the divine Lao Chün is modeled on the chaos cosmogony. In esoteric theory as distinct from popular belief and iconography, Lao Chün is identified with P'an-ku as the cosmic giant whose corpse was transformed into the world and represents the hermaphroditic "mystical body," "mass of flesh," or *hun-tun* form of the transcendent Tao. Moreover, the mystery of the divine Lao Chün as the created "body" of the Tao is understood by means of the trinitarian formula of the "three in one," hypostatized as the divinities known as the "Three Pure Ones" (San-ch'ing or some other analogous term).[41] I need only remark that this theological scheme clearly partakes of the cosmogonic enigma of the uncreated Tao and its relation to the created "chaos" principles of "one" and "three" seen in chapter 42 of the *Tao Te Ching*.

In the cosmogonic prehistory of the Tao, recorded in the canonical *Tao Tsang* corpus, Lao Chün as the divine offspring of the Tao is said to undergo nine transformations that represent three recapitulations of the primary process of one-two-three seen in the *Tao Te Ching*. In one of the texts recounting Lao Chün's divine biography there are three distinct stages of creation involving various multiple transformations: the first creation leads to the appearance of the trinitarian gods of the prior heavens; the second creation, proceeding out of the "empty," swollen, or pregnant condition of *k'ung-t'ung*, gives rise to the pantheon of the posterior heavens and the mysterious identification of Lao Tzu with his own mother; finally, the third creation involves the historical revelation of Lao Tzu to the Heavenly Masters (*t'ien-shih*) on earth.[42] In another text known as the *Hun Yüan Huang Ti Shen Chi* (Hagiography of the Ruler of the Origin of Chaos), the technical identification of Lao Tzu (= Lao Chün), *k'ung-t'ung*, *k'un-lun*, and *hun-tun* is clearly asserted. In this text the Tao is transformed into *k'ung-t'ung* (or the hollow mountain of *k'un-lun*), which is consubstantial with the embryonic "real one" (*chen-i* = *ch'ih-tzu*) or unborn chaos-body of Lao Tzu.[43]

This same type of narrative structure is revealed microcosmically by the Taoist priest in the practice of ritual meditation. Saso, Schipper, and Robinet have provided the clearest and most accessible descriptions of this internal process based on studies of the important meditation scriptures known as the *Yellow Court Canon* (along with its commentaries, its related texts, and its living embodiment in contemporary religious Taoism on Taiwan).[44] In the history of Taoism, the *Yellow Court Canon* is associated with the important south Chinese Mao Shan revelations of the fourth century A.D. that gave rise to the meditation sect of Shang-ch'ing (Highest Purity) and had a great impact on all of subsequent Taoist history (especially in relation to medicinal and alchemical theory).[45]

In the *Yellow Court Canon*, meditation is primarily a process of internal alchemical refinement where the three life principles (personified as three spirits: Primordial Heavenly Worthy [= *ch'i*[a]], Tao [-*te*[a]?] Heavenly Worthy [= *ching*], and Ling-pao Heavenly Worthy [= *shen*[a]]; these microcosmic spirits are equivalent to the macrocosmic San-ch'ing) return to the "original state of *hun-tun* or primordial chaos."[46] This process recalls the intention and structure of the *Chuang Tzu*'s *tso-wang* and *hsin-chai* practices but even more directly rehearses the *Chuang Tzu*'s Emperor Hun-tun story and the creation scenario from chapter 42 of the *Tao Te Ching*. In the most general sense the practice of meditation found in the *Yellow Court Canon* involves a reversal of the microcosmic process of gestation and the macrocosmic process of creation:

> The myriad things [= Ten Thousand Things]
>   returning lead to the Three,
> The Three to the Two,
> The Two to the One,
> The One to the Tao of Transcendence.[47]

This represents a "strictly religious interpretation" of the classic texts;[48] but as I have tried to show throughout this study, it is most probable that these religious, if not theological, implications were present from the very beginning.

To further demonstrate how the practice of meditation is specifically linked to the creation scenario, figure 4 should be consulted and compared with the scheme developed in chapter 7 (cf., also, the Sung philosopher Chou Tun-i's "Diagram of the Great Ultimate" [*t'ai-chi t'u*]).[49] Briefly stated, the alchemical stage of *solve* is concerned with the inner imaginative visualization of the myriad spirits of the body and mind. This is a process initially involving the use of "spirit registers" (*lu*[b]) in order to visualize, control, and reduce the multiple spirits of the microcosm (associated with the viscera of the body) down to five spirits and then down to the three "Heavenly Worthies" or life principles.[50] These three primary spirits of life and creation are organized around three internal foci (the *ni-wan* in the head, the *ch'iang-kung* in the heart, and the *tan-t'ien* in the belly) that correspond to the tripartite cosmological structure of the heaven, earth, and the central axis (or watery underworld).[51]

By way of analogy it can be said that the myriad psychomental and bodily parts of fallen man—the cut-up parts of the mass of flesh, dismembered body of P'an-ku, or bored openings of the mortified Emperor Hun-tun—are rearticulated back into the perfect triune "paradise" form of the hollow K'un-lun mountain, bottle gourd, or cocoon. As in the tales of the *hsien* immortals who return to paradise by magically leaping inside a hollow gourd, the Taoist as a mystic "gourd master," "pumpkin head," or "egghead" reassembles the primordial body of man. Indeed, it is tempting to speculate that the exaggerated head and belly iconography of the typical Taoist saint is to some extent a remembrance, or a "re-membering," of this kind of archaic symbolism.

Using the imagery of Emperor Hun-tun, the bored holes of face are closed. A commentary to the *Yellow Court Canon* consequently states:

> The seven sense apertures [eyes, nostrils, ears, mouth]
> Must be jointed in an inward union,
> All filled with a brilliant light;
> The light of holy Yin and holy Yang.
> The light penetrates and fills the
>   Yellow Court.[52]

Once the myriad spirits have been refined to the three life principles, a "spiritual fire" (an internal brooding "heat" of incubation similar to the *ignis innaturalis* or *ignis gehernnalis* of Western alchemy or the *tapas* of India) is

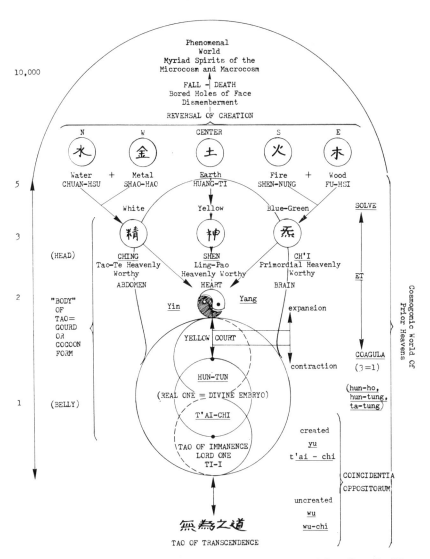

Figure 4. Taoist Meditative Alchemy. "Solve et Coagula" in the Yellow Court Tradition

said to incubate, congeal, and unify the three into the mysterious primordial state of three-in-one, *ta-t'ung*[a], *ta-tung, t'ai-i*[a], *t'ai-chi*, or *hun-tun*:

> The three components are one in
>   principle.
> A wondrous mystery that cannot be told![53]

This last stage occurs in the crucible of the Yellow Court, the empty (*hsü*[a]) center of man esoterically located somewhere below the navel or between the kidneys (the spleen?) recalling the central place of belly-knowledge seen in the *Tao Te Ching*.[54] The location of the Yellow Court is, however, ambiguous and variable in the texts, suggesting an esoteric symbolic equivalence among the three "centers" of belly, heart, and head. Moreover, there is a special correspondence between the "belly" and "head" as the place of chaotic fusion in the symbolism of Yellow Court that resembles the Western alchemical idea of the "rotundum"—the "round" vessel in the skull that is the place of the final alchemical transmutation of *unus mundus*, the creation of the cosmic, whole, or "round" Man.[55]

In other texts such as the *T'ai P'ing Ching* and *Ta Tung Ching* (= *Shang Ch'ing Ching*), this crucial stage of *coagula*, or mystic union, in the overall process of return is referred to as the method of chaotic reunification or "unitive fusion"—*hun-ho* (or variously: *hun-tung, ta-hun, hun-i*[d], etc.).[56] The condition of chaotic reunification is the basic point of departure for the initiatory rebirth and transformation (*hun-sheng* = "birth by fusion" and *hun-hua* = "transformation by fusion") sought in meditation.[57] Furthermore, the relation of this to the creation scenario and principle of *creatio continua* seen in the earlier texts is suggested by the interrelated and contrasted twin process of *hun-ho*, the return of the Tao or reversal of creation back to the condition of one, and *fen-hua*, which like the boring of Hun-tun is the process of separation, multiplication, and division of the one into the Ten Thousand Things of the microcosm and macrocosm.[58] The overall process is sometimes called *li-ho* or "separation and reunion" wherein the "two movements, division and union, correspond to the expiration and inspiration [of breath], to the *solve et coagula*, to the expanding movement of *yang* which makes the world and the contracting movement of *yin* which reabsorbs the world."[59]

Maspero in his studies of the Taoist internal alchemical techniques of breath manipulation (or "embryonic breathing"—*t'ai-hsi*) had long ago brought forth evidence of a central ideological foundation in the archaic mythological idea of the cosmic egg. Maspero constantly draws attention to the fact that the breathing method is validated by its microcosmic duplication of a cosmogonic model.[60] The goal behind all of these alchemical methods was the personal identification of the adept with the cosmic Tao, and they may be collectively referred to as arts for the "centering of the *ch'i*[a]," "reverse circulation of the *ch'i*[a]," or the "return to the original *ch'i*[a]" (*yüan-ch'i*, identified with *hun-tun*). In the more popular currents of late Taoist tradition these methods were referred to as arts for reunifying the *yin* and the *yang*—methods, like *hun-ho*, commonly called *ho-ch'i, ho-ho,* or *hun-ch'i.*[61]

It is also said that the famous eleventh-century alchemist Chang Po-tuan was taught "the Tao of *hun yüan.*"[62] In explaining this the commentator Hsieh Tao-kuang remarked that *tao hun yüan* means: "There was something formed by mixing before the heaven and the earth. This thing has been put into words contrainedly and is known as the Tao of *hun yüan.*"[63] More recently a contemporary handbook of Taoist internal alchemy states that the process of meditation reverses the cosmogony: *hun-tun* is the "time of the refining of the 'pill of immortality' when the *shen*[a] and *ch'i*[a] are conjoined. It is a condition wherein one gives the appearance of idiocy and stupidity. An ancient immortal has said that before the birth of Hun-tun, Hun-tun was round and whole but its meaning is difficult to make known."[64]

The constant round of creation and return, expansion and contraction (*fen* and *hun*[d]), seen in the cosmos is thus duplicated microcosmically in the body and mind of the Taoist. Having accomplished the return to the beginning, the adept is at the "Gate of Destiny" (*ming-men*) and is open to the indwelling of the Tao and the creation of an immortal esoteric body (= "pill of immortality," "infant," "divine embryo," "real self," etc.).[65] Most of all it should be stressed that the religious meaning of the overall process is fundamentally rooted in the metaphysics and mythic logic of chaos: "Three is One and One is Three."[66] In this sense it may be that Saso's "Transcendent Tao" more properly reflects a theological elaboration of the greater mythological mystery of *coniunctio.*

In summary fashion, a rapid review of some of the late Taoist meditation and liturgical texts of the Mao Shan or Shang Ch'ing tradition demonstrates the following pattern of salvational intentionality:[67]

1. Meditation primarily consists of the technique of "inner vision" (*nei-kuan*), which involves a psychomental and physical synesthesia of the sense experiences of light, sound, and smell. This requires the simultaneous work of thought (inner vision or concentration), word (recitation and incantation), and deed (ritual). In Taoist meditation, cosmology and psychology are inseparable and complementary. Therefore, the adept's inner sight or "creative imagination" is first cultivated in order to imagine, visualize, assemble, and control the microcosmic gods of the body; this, at the same time, effects a response and descent of the myriad gods of the greater cosmos (especially astral deities). These complex exercises may be called the *solve* stage of the overall process.

2. Once the gods are properly assembled (imagined or "seen") in the five

viscera and three "cinnabar fields" of the body and marshalled to guard (or close) the bored orifices of the body, the second stage of return ("reversing the inner circulation of *ch'i*ᵃ"), or *coagula*, is initiated. The ten thousand gods are reduced and refined through a series of seven or nine stages (or multiples of these numbers) to five ("quintessence"), to three ("trinity"), and finally to the beatific vision of the "Three-in-One" or hermaphroditic supreme god, Lord One (TiI). This is the unique experience of undifferentiated or chaotic unity that is called "chaotic fusion" (*hun-ho*).

3. Aside from the therapeutic experience of "chaotic fusion" itself (the first chaos stage), the basic point of this operation is not to rest in the undifferentiated chaos state but to accomplish the eventual birth, through repeated refining "returns," of a third term or "ordered-chaos": the "immortal embryo-divine child-real self-etc." Esoteric meditation recapitulates cosmogony and, after a long process of multiple regressions to the beginning, results in the initiatory or "astroalchemical" preparation of a glorified, astral, cosmic, or spirit body for the adept that is impervious to death.[68] A kind of "physical immortality" is accomplished via an *imitatio dei* of Lord Lao or Emperor Hun-tun.

This theory of "physical immortality," along with other details in the process just outlined, certainly represents salvational innovations in the old idea of return; but, at the same time, these innovations can also be seen to be interpretive developments that organically grew out of the more ancient theme of *hun-tun* found in the early texts. In a way surprisingly similar to Paracelsian medicinal alchemy and Renaissance Neoplatonism, the immortal "Taoist Body" is metaphysically and cosmologically related to the mystic experience of returning to the *tertium quid* or primordial "great form" (*ta-hsiang*) of the Tao. A "light" body (in both weight and radiance) of refined *ch'i*ᵃ is produced, which implies the alchemical formula of *coincidentia oppositorum*.[69] Like the implications of early Taoist thought, later Taoist meditational theory ultimately affirms duality without sacrificing the idea of cosmic continuity and unity.

"CARESSING CROCODILES AND WHALES": CHAOS AND CHINESE ALCHEMY

(The Tao is like) Chaos [*hun*ᵈ], or like an ocean, or like wandering in the Great Beginning [*t'ai-ch'u*]. Sometimes it (is to be studied in) metals, sometimes in jade, sometimes in manure, sometimes in earth or mud, sometimes in flying birds, sometimes in running animals, sometimes in the mountains and sometimes in the abyss. (The sage studies) every point, and evaluates (every change). So he seems (to the ignorant) to be like a madman or a fool. . . .

If you know that the *chhi* [*ch'i*ᵃ] emanates
from the mind you will be able to attain spiritual
respiration and will succeed with the alchemical
transmutations of the stove. . . .

If you know that the Tao, which is formless
can change the things that have form, you can
change the bodies of birds and animals. If you
can attain the purity of the Tao, you can never
be implicated in things; your body will feel
light, and you will be able to ride on the phoenix
and the crane. If you can attain to the homogeneity (*hun*ᵈ) of the Tao, nothing will be dark,
and you will be able to caress crocodiles and
whales.

—Kuan Yin Tzu
(trans. Joseph Needham)

The esoteric meaning of "return" and "rebirth" seen in the Mao Shan tradition
of ritual meditation indicates that the chaos theme in later Taoism is closely
related to the symbolism of initiatory refinement found in the theory and
practice of Chinese alchemy. Alchemical theory involves the reduplication and
manipulation of the processes of creation in order to glorify what is fallen,
leaden, or base.[70] Chinese alchemical tradition in this way draws upon the
cosmological metaphysics and religious strivings associated with the Taoist
understanding of *hun-tun*. Remembering that the spagyric symbolism of *solve
et coagula* was already suggested by aspects of the early mythological heritage
of chaos, as well as by its possible relation to ancient metallurgical tradition, I
think it may be appropriate to say that the theme of *hun-tun* in the history of
Taoism has a special affinity for expressing itself as a kind of alchemical
science of salvation.

Like the connection alchemy has with certain forms of esoteric religious
theory in other cultural traditions (i.e., Indian, Hellenistic, Islamic, and post-
Renaissance European traditions), the phenomenon of alchemy in Chinese
cultural history reveals a particular coincidence with the religious concerns of
Taoism. There is, in fact, some reason for thinking of Taoism as the alchemical
tradition par excellence since the salvational idea of an "elixir" or medicinal
drug of life, which from Needham's perspective serves to define what is truely
"alchemical" in intent, is uniquely related to Taoist tradition both in terms
of alchemy's priority in world history and in reference to its religious
implications.[71]

The complex history of Chinese alchemy, akin to the development of the interrelated exoteric liturgical and esoteric mystic dimensions found in later Taoism, is commonly distinguished in relation to two typological constructs: an "inner art" (nei-tan), which was primarily concerned with the adept's personal mystical refinement of body and spirit, and an "outer art" (wai-tan) which was associated with an actual laboratory craft and directed toward more mundane goals. As the work of Jung and Eliade has shown for the general history of alchemy, and that of Needham and Sivin more specifically for China, the distinction between an inner and outer alchemy is finally moot.[72] Both types of alchemical pursuit are constantly and ambiguously intermingled in the history of Taoism to an extent that suggests that the complete soteriological "work" of alchemy necessarily implies the synthesis of the inner and outer, microcosmic and macrocosmic, spiritual and organic dimensions of life. As it says in the Kuan Yin Tzu, "if you know that the ch'i[a] emanates from the mind you will be able to attain spiritual respiration and will succeed with the alchemical transmutations of the stove."[73] Although the sociological context, religious application, and stated goals may differ, both the inner and the outer art ideally merge by virtue of their shared roots in a symbolic system of thought that presupposes the creation theme of returning to the beginning of time.

An example of the interrelationship between the inner and the outer art is seen in the Ts'an T'ung Ch'i, which is reputedly a text of the second century A.D. and represents the earliest complete alchemical treatise in the world history of alchemy.[74] In this work the basic theoretical outline of thought involving an elaborate system of correspondence (yin-yang, five elements, colors, numbers, symbolic animals, internal organs, etc.) is couched within the hun-tun theme and is "unambiguously cosmogonic" in nature.[75] This text seemingly has reference to external laboratory operations; but, inasmuch as the Yellow Court Canon constitutes a kind of commentary on its esoteric significance for meditation,[76] it is clear that it is impossible to make a neat separation between the internal and external dimensions of the Taoist alchemical opus.

Because of these interconnections it may be expected that the hun-tun symbolism in the early Taoist texts and in later Taoist ritual meditation will be carried over into the laboratory art. This, indeed, is the case and much of the very shape and terminology of Chinese alchemical equipment is based on "chaos forms" and language associated with the cosmogonic symbolism of the embryo, egg, or gourd (especially the lu series of characters: lu[c], gourd, and lu[a,c,d], stove). Ho and Needham, for example, have shown that the alchemical reaction vessel is often named in a way that directly recalls the chaos theme: hun-tun ting (chaos vessel), hun-tun chi-tzu shen-shih (magical chaos egg-shaped reaction chamber).[77] It should be pointed out that there is a parallel here with the symbolism of Western alchemical apparatus (e.g., furnace and retort symbolism such as the *cucurbit* flask that was a gourd, egg, or womb vessel), as well as a similar theoretical formulation in terms of the metaphysics of the cosmic egg, cosmic giant, or primordial couple mythology.[78] In Jung's words, "the cosmogonic brother-sister incest, like creation itself, had been from ancient times the prototype of the alchemists' great work."[79]

In short, the mythological theme of chaos is a unifying thread running throughout many specialized and diverse aspects of later Taoist theory and practice. The basic unity of Taoism that structurally links the mysticism of the early texts and the later forms of liturgy, ritual meditation, and alchemy might, therefore, be found in the concept of the "hierogamy of *yin* and *yang*, heaven and earth, which gave birth to the immortal embryo."[80] This is but another way of saying that the inner religious unity of Taoist tradition is revealed by the cosmogonic theme of returning to chaos, which, along with other mythological typologies, incorporated the primordial couple mythology. More accurately and technically than the idea of the incestuous hierogamy of *yin* and *yang*, the overall Taoist vision is concerned with the offspring of that marriage union—the *mysterium coniunctionis* condition of *hun-tun*, not as absolute One (transcendence) or Two (immanence) but as the two-in-one third term, divine child, mass of flesh, or glorified cosmic body of the Tao.

COMPARATIVE ALCHEMICAL GIBBERISH

First we must assume that we have obtained the hidden, unrevealed, chaotic *Materia Prima*, 'our chaos.' This is always likened to the state of the world at the beginning of Genesis, before the constitution and separation of all things into distinct elements. It will thus be clear that the alchemical process is a microcosmic reconstitution of the process of creation, in other words a re-creation. It is affected by the interplay of forces symbolized by two dragons, one black and one white, locked in an eternal circular combat. The white one is winged, or volatile, the black one wingless, or fixed; they are accompanied by the universal alchemical formula *solve et coagula*. This formula and this emblem symbolize the alternating role of the two indispensable halves that compose the Whole.

—S. de Rola, *Alchemy*

If it is meaningful to describe the unity of Taoist tradition in terms of the theme of attaining the alchemically refined "cosmic body" of Hun-tun, then it may also be possible to perceive some convergence of form and purpose among other, non-Chinese, alchemical traditions. This is especially so in the sense that post-Renaissance Western alchemy is fundamentally a medicinal art of the "elixir" or "stone" that is commonly described in images of "its permanence (prolongation of life, immortality, incorruptibility), its androgyny, its spirituality and corporeality, its human qualities and resemblance to man (homunculus), and its divinity."[81] Western alchemy, like Taoism, is religiously concerned with the methods of returning to the condition of the glorified cosmic man, Adam, before the fall. The preparation of the Philosopher's Stone through a repetition of the creation is "at the same time a fabrication of the glorified body."[82]

Titus Burckhardt has seen the need to distinguish between the transcendental aims of Christian mysticism and the more cosmological intent of Western alchemy:

> The essence and aim of mysticism is union with God. Alchemy does not speak of this. What is related to the mystical way, however, is the alchemical aim to regain the original "nobility" of human nature and its symbolism; for union with God is possible only by virtue of that which, in spite of the incommensurable gulf between the creature and god, unites the former to the latter—and this is the "theomorphism" of Adam, which was "displaced" or rendered ineffective by the Fall.[83]

Burckhardt goes on to state that "alchemy is based on a purely cosmological vision and therefore can only be transposed indirectly to the metacosmic or divine realm";[84] and this might be extended to include not only Taoist alchemy but also the general thrust of Taoist thought given the Taoists' unconcern for the relevance of a wholly transcendent principle and their passion for the cosmological totality of *hun-tun*, the Adam-like P'an-ku or Lao Chün. Even the theological notion of the "transcendent Tao" suggested by Saso's discussion of liturgical Taoism seems more properly subsumed into the cosmogonical/ cosmological category of the coincidence of opposites. Both the alchemical secret of the Stone in the West and the mythological secret of *hun-tun* in Taoism paradoxically refer to a "prime matter" that is *trinus et unus*. Both depend on a cosmological metaphysics of the *principium* of creation as a *creatio continua* or *natura perpetua et infinita*. Tao, to borrow appropriately enough from Western alchemical metaphor, is that which is cosmogonically a *radix ipsius*, the "root of itself" that is autonomous and dependent on nothing. "Returning to the root'' in order to become a "round" or "whole" man again, to become a *corpus rotundum, unus mundus,* or *hun-tun,* is the summation of the work.[85]

1. *Hun-tun* and *Unus Mundus*

Because the possibilities for comparison are manifold, I can only offer here a few additional comments. One of these has to do with the type of cosmogonic model emphasized within the Western alchemical tradition, inasmuch as it frequently involves the idea of the *tertium quid* or mediating third term unifying the opposites. Jung, for example, relates this to the notion of the *unus mundus* of Western alchemy, which in the sixteenth-century scheme of Dorneus (or Dorn), a follower of Paracelsus, is linked to the idea of the alchemical quest for *coniunctio* as a cosmogonic process involving the mediation of the "third term":

> In the beginning God created one world; He divided this into two parts, Heaven and Earth. But in these two parts is hidden a third part which has the quality of a mediator, it is the original whole which exists also in both the other parts. These cannot exist without the other two. The third part is the original totality of the world but the division into two parts was necessary in order to transfer the "one" world from a condition of potentiality into the state of reality.[86]

In Dorneus' scheme, like the procedure in the *Yellow Court Canon,* alchemy involves the *"subjective reproduction of creation in meditation"* through an inner reversal of the original cosmogonic process.[87] The three principles of body, psyche, and spirit (= salt, sulphur, and mercury; remotely equivalent to the three Taoist life principles) are first made separate (*solve*) as a prelude to the work of reunification (*coagula*) involving the stages of *unio mentalis, unio corporalis,* and *unus mundus. Unio corporalis* is the "producing of the immortal body within the mortal body, the production of a *corpus glorificationis.*" In distinction to many earlier medieval mystical texts, a kind of Taoist sensibility is revealed here since, as Von Franz notes, the idea of *unio corporalis* uniquely affirms the importance of the body as a factor in the redemptive process of inner reunification.[88]

As seen from figure 5 (cf. figure 4), *unio corporalis* leads to the final stage of cosmic unity that reproduced in man the primordial condition of *unus mundus*—the "third term" linking the uncreated and created.[89] Jung says that for Dorneus, therefore, the "third and highest degree of conjunction was the union of the whole man with the *unus mundus.* . . . [this] meant the possibility of effecting a union with the world—not with the world of multiplicity as we see it

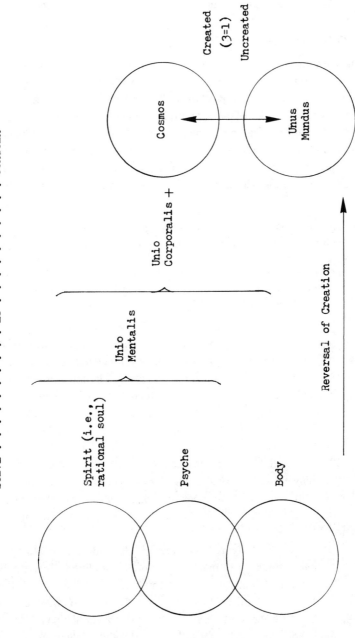

Figure 5. Dorneus's *Unus Mundus*

but with a potential world, the eternal ground of all empirical being, just as the self is the ground and origin of the individual personality past, present, and future."[90]

In alchemy, and in earlier medieval theology, the concept of *unus mundus* is not the actual material cosmos but the "model" or "great form" of creation eternally existing in the mind of God as His Wisdom (*Sapientia Dei*, a feminine principle) or logos (Christ before his birth on earth or the divine hermaphroditic body of Adam as the cosmic man).[91] The *unus mundus* or the *mundus archetypus* of the Scholastics was the "potential world of the first day of creation when nothing was yet 'in actu,' i.e., divided into two and many, but was still one."[92] This idea above all stresses the identity of the "inner" and "outer" aspect of the art or, more generally, affirms the mystery of the necessary relation between spirit and body, God and world, unity and multiplicity. With this formula also, as Jung points out, the Paracelsian alchemists went beyond the traditional medieval creation doctrine of *creatio ex nihilo*:

> Paracelsus and his school assumed that matter was an "increatum," and hence coexistent and coeternal with God. Whether they considered this view monistic or dualistic I am unable to discover. The only certain thing is that for all the alchemists matter had a divine aspect, whether on the ground that God was imprisoned in it in the form of the *anima mundi* or *anima media natura*, or that matter represented God's "reality." In no case was matter dedeified, and certainly not the potential matter [= Chaos] of the first day of creation.[93]

What is so provocative here is that the relation between the actual created cosmos (the realm of "two": heaven and earth, male and female, etc.) and the uncreated "one" of the *unus mundus* exactly parallels the mystery of the relationship between the uncreated and created Tao, nonbeing and being, *wu* and *yu*, chaos and cosmos, seen in the Taoist metaphysics of *hun-tun* as the "great form" (*ta-hsiang*) of Tao.

Striking and worthy of further investigation is the similarity between the Paracelsian and Taoist understanding of "chaos" as both the undifferentiated "one" and as the "third term" that united the one and two, uncreated and created (perhaps, also, it is possible to distinguish between a kind of inferior, dark, or leaden chaos state, *plumbum*, and the superior/glorified/refined/golden chaos of *hun-tun*).[94] While not dealing with this particular point, Needham has gone so far as to say that alchemy in the West represents in some ways a kind of Taoist spirit in Occidental tradition.[95] From the standpoint of his magisterial global reconnaissance of alchemy, Needham, along with Mahdi-hassan on somewhat less compelling grounds, would even go further to suggest that post-Renaissance alchemy manifests the influence, via Islamic culture, of the earlier Taoist tradition of alchemy.[96] While it is impossible to demonstrate an actual historical connection between Chinese and Western tradition, it does seem that both traditions are rooted in a similar mythological understanding of the nature and significance of creation.

These comparative considerations, whether archetypally or historically grounded, suggest an important connection with what might be called the constant medicinal understanding of "salvation" found in both Taoism and Western alchemy. "Salvation" in both the Taoist and alchemical context (especially the tradition of the "elixir") is more a matter of the healing of man to the fullness of cosmic life than it is a saving from the world.[97] The implication seems to be that if a man can truly learn to reexperience *his* time as the primordial rhythm of Cosmic Time there will be a therapeutic effect bringing health, longevity, freedom, and wisdom. The result of the return to the beginnings is a physical and spiritual wholeness but not an escape into a condition of absolute transcendental perfection. I think it may be said, therefore, that the cosmogonic theme of chaos in both Taoism and Western alchemy seems never to "have the complete (spiritual) 'extinction' of the individual in view, as have such concepts as the Hindu *moksha*, Buddhist *nirvana*, Sufi *fand'u'l-fand'l* and likewise the Christian *unio mystica* or *deificatio*."[98] The sympathy between Taoism and Western alchemical soteriology may in fact explain to some degree Jung's special fascination with Western alchemy and Taoist internal alchemy since "for Jung, the ideal that man should pursue was totality, not perfection. Perfection was abstract and inhuman. Totality meant the union of opposites—the integration of the angelic and demonic in man."[99]

2. *Hun-tun, Tumtum,* and *Zimzum*

Another interesting topic related to these themes is the Kabbalistic tradition of Jewish mysticism and alchemy. G. Scholem points out that the Kabbalistic tradition is unique within Judaism for its restoration of a mythic dimension to Jewish theology, particularly since it replaces the orthodox theologies of creation with the mystical idea of a mythological "chaos." Whereas in the rationalist tradition of Rabbinic theology the "substitution of nothingness for chaos seemed to provide a guarantee of the Creator God's freedom as opposed to all mythical determination by fate," in the Kabbalistic tradition of mysticism "the chaos that had been eliminated in the theology of the 'creation out of nothing' reappeared in a new form. This nothing had always been present in God, it was not outside Him, and not called forth by Him."[100]

Resembling the Taoist mythology of *hun-tun* and the Adamic P'an-ku, the Kabbalistic God (in the *Zohar*) known as the Sefiroth is identified with Adam Kadmon, the "tailed Adam" or androgynous Primordial Man, and is fit into a cosmogonic model of the cosmic egg involving seven periods of creative activity.[101] Adam Kadmon, in this sense and somewhat like the relation of P'an-ku and *hun-tun*, can be identified with the figure of the *tumtum* (reduplication of the Hebrew root $\sqrt{tmm}$, "to be covered"), which in ancient Jewish lore was a hermaphroditic "third sex" outside the bounds of the ordinary covenental Law.[102] There is also the important connection here with the symbolism of a shapeless lump, "mass of flesh," homunculus, or, more particularly within the Kabbalistic tradition, the legends of the making of the Golem that are related to the cosmogonic theme of Adam Kadmon as the embryonic man, or cosmic giant, of the chaos time.[103]

The closest parallel to the Taoist cosmogony of *hun-tun* is found in the tradition of the Lurianic Kabbala of the sixteenth century. The Lurianic interpretation of Kabbala "introduced far-reaching changes in the structure of Kabbalistic thought" primarily because of its doctrine of *zimzum* (= *tsimtsum*), which basically refers to the idea of the "contraction," "evacuation," or "withdrawal" of God (= Ein-Sof) that initiates the creation process.[104] *Zimzum* is therefore the primordial empty "place" (*tehiru*), "body," or "form" of creation that mysteriously contains a hylic mixture of light emanations from the Ein-Sof. Out of this chaotic hyle and within the embryonic sack of *zimzum*, the primordial man or Adam Kadmon is formed. Recalling the idea of *hun-tun* as the womblike "gap" or "third term" of creation embryonically filled with the invisible *ch'i*[a] and giving birth to the cosmic giant of P'an-ku, we can see the amazingly close approximation of the Taoist theory. Based on the discussion and analysis of Scholem and Jürgen von Kempski, it can even be said that the Lurianic doctrine of *zimzum* reads almost like a commentary on the Taoist theory of creation.[105] A historical explanation for this curious semantic and phonetic similarity is, no doubt, improbable. But given the strong congruence in mythological structure as well as a convergence in religious-mystical intentionality, the peculiar sympathy between the Taoist *hun-tun* and Kabbalistic *zimzum* is an issue that merits further comparative consideration.

CHAOS AND THE MODERN MYSTIQUE OF SUPERMAN

> Je finis par trouver sacre le desordré de mon
> propre esprit.
> > —Rimbaud (quoted by Carrouges, *La*
> > *Mystique du Surhomme*)

> It is hard to adapt to chaos, but it can be
> done. . . .
> > —K. Vonnegut, *Breakfast of*
> > *Champions*

> I would like to have wings, a carapace, a bark,
> to bellow smoke, to possess a trunk, to divide
> myself into everything, to be in everything, to
> be in the emanation of perfumes, to grow like
> plants, flow like water, vibrate like sound, to
> shine like light, to crouch in all forms, to pene-
> trate each atom, to descend to the depth of
> matter—to be matter.
> > —Flaubert, *The Temptation of*
> > *St. Anthony* (quoted by Stanley Diamond,
> > *Search of the Primitive*)

> Do not fear disorder.
> > —Mao Tse-tung

The dream of the human possibility of a godlike freedom through a transformative participation in the very processes of creation is witnessed in Western
alchemy, Kabbala, and Taoism. In all of these traditions a kind of a Faustian or
Nietzchian "mystique du surhomme," associated with a revalorization of
chaos, comes to the fore; and it may be appropriate to suggest that modern
movments preaching the primacy of confusion, such as Dada and Surrealism,
are to some extent thematically and metaphysically analogous. In Dada, especially, the archaic mythic wisdom of the fool, the saint as child ("da-da"),
again asserts its importance for a more balanced understanding of reality.

Civilized society, Western or Chinese, maintains itself by disciplining the
chaotic forces of life.[106] For the Taoist as well as for the Surrealist or Dostoevski's idiot, however, this is a destructive rejection of what is finally generative
and creative for both the individual and society.[107] Writing during the interwar
years at the start of this century, Hermann Hesse sees Dostoevski's Myshkin
(along with other Dostoevskian "forerunners of Chaos": Rogozhin, Nastasya,
the four Karamazoffs—all epileptics, criminals, hysterics, etc.) as a prophetic
commentary on the cultural and spiritual confusions of the modern world:

> Highest Reality in the sense of human culture is the division of the World
> into Light and Dark, Good and Evil, Allowed and Forbidden. Highest
> Reality for Myshkin is the magical experience of the reversibility of all
> institutional forms, of the existence of a negative equivalent to all moral
> values. The Idiot finally considered, introduces the Mother-claim of the

Unconscious, he is the blaster of Civilization. He does not break the Tables of the Law, he simply turns them round and shows that the contrary to them is written on the other side.[108]

In a manner somewhat similar to the Taoist portrayal of the "hidden sage" as a humble yet more-than-human chaos figure, a bumbling Clark Kent superman rather than a rampaging General Zod, the key to the secret identity of Dostoevski's idiot antihero is that "this enemy of Order, this fearful destroyer, does not appear as a malefactor but as a charming, shy creature full of childlike grace, full of warm-hearted unselfish goodness."[109] The Taoists always understood that the sacred humility of the saint is terrifying.

Victor Turner suggests that once traditional societies are broken from a myth-ritual pattern that allows for a periodic regenerative return to chaos, rebellions of irrationality and antistructure ("liminoid phenomena") haphazardly resurface to challenge the validity of a permanently structured order of human life.[110] Dada, Hippies, Mao's cultural revolution, Lévi-Straussian structuralism, Primal Scream therapy, Kurt Vonnegut, Richard Brautigan, Thomas Pynchon, and Tom Robbins's literary inanities, Jim Jones' People's Temple, Aleister Crawley's magik, and the Incredible Hulk, among many other possible examples, are cultural expressions of the need for the periodic regression to chaos; and at the same time they reveal to different degrees the dangers of trying to institutionalize chaos as a permanent condition. As the Taoists and David Banner knew so well, the secret of life is not just the nihilistic return to chaos as an end, but the embodiment of the cosmic process of diastole and systole, the continued self-creation of all things. This necessarily involves the dialectical phases of chaos and cosmos, return and recreation, *yin* and *yang*, antistructure and structure, spontaneity and discipline, individual and society, *solve et coagula*.

In a remarkable analysis of some modern artistic and literary themes, M. Carrouges notes that, in relation to the rise of modern bourgeois society and culture in the West, the major significance of Dada and Surrealism was to have reemphasized the "necessity of contradiction and chaos."[111] In the Taoist spirit of *hun-tun* as the generative source of fresh life, the principle of chaos must be seen as innocently immoral as an infant or as spontaneously impartial as a thunderstorm. The *Tao Te Ching* (chap. 5), after all, tells us that Heaven and the sage treat all things as if they were straw dogs. A storm destroys yet finally invigorates the old and gives rise to what is new. Most of all, the meaning and significance of chaos is related to the idea of creation:

Creation presupposes nothingness and chaos. All creation postulates a positive force of affirmation which causes new being to shoot forth, but it also, at the same time, requires the negative force of a prior totality. In that which preexists it is necessary that an empty fault (or cavity) be opened without which that which is going to be born will never be able to surge forth from its vital source. This is the Kabbala's idea of signs wherein the creation of the world by God is accompanied by a mysterious contraction [or withdrawal = *zimzum*] of the Creator without which his thundering plenitude would not allow any creature to exist.[112]

To translate this into a Taoist context, the principle of chaos in life is especially to be imagined as the empty center or "third term" of mediating union that allows for the very possibility and fulfillment of any new creative development. Life as the flow of the Tao requires a hollow space in order to move, change, grow, swell, or create. Moreover, the image of the "empty" chaos can be simultaneously linked to the symbolism of the paradise condition at the beginning and end of time, the sacrificial "death of God" seen in the myth of P'an-ku, and the creation of the "glorified man" in Taoist ritual meditation that recalls the birth of the wonder-child or "mass of flesh" from the primordial parents. As Carrouges says, "it is in the womb of chaos that the 'death of God' and the birth of the superman is accomplished. . . ."[113] The images of the "death of God," chaos, and paradise must not be seen as separate but rather as "simultaneous or at least closely interrelated" aspects of creation and the ongoing process of life.[114]

Having roots in Romanticism and protean figures like Goethe and Blake, the eccentric prodigies of occult artists like Yeats, Rimbaud, Brancusi, and the surrealists in recent Western history directly acknowledged the intrinsic "coexistence and symbiosis of chaos and the world."[115] For Carrouges this was only to rediscover what was already known by primitive man; and, I may add, what was known by the Taoists and alchemists. Carrouges in fact, perspicaciously recognizes that in China the soteriological goal of Taoism and Ch'an Buddhism "was always the glorified man who reigns within the womb of the glorified cosmos-chaos."[116] Recalling the impact of Oriental religions on Hesse's literary and philosophical vision, Carrouges implies that this is a lesson from the East that needs to be relearned by more than the alchemists, surrealists, and visionary artists of Western tradition.[117]

A discussion such as this could obviously be extended to include a whole gamut of fascinating comparative reflections on the cultural, religious, and philosophical meaning of chaos in both the West and China. I will, however, mercifully avoid a lengthy dissertation on the subject of the popular iconography of Godzilla and the Incredible Hulk and only draw attention to the possible intimation of these ancient Taoist conceptions in Mao's understanding of the dialectical life and "revolutionary immortality" of the Chinese "New

Man.''[118] Some of Mao's key ideas on "contradiction," the "unity of cognition and reality," the "masses," the people as "poor and blank," and the interrelationship of "transformation," "disorder," and "matter," while consciously indebted to the dialectical philosophy of Hegel and Engels, may also betray a resonance with the traditional metaphysics associated with the creation theme of *hun-tun* seen in early Taoism and the *I Ching*.[119] In Mao's curiously celebrated swims in the Yangtze, which Bauer sees as "a kind of cultic act performed . . . with almost ritual necessity on the eve of the Great Leap Forward and again on the eve of the Cultural Revolution," it is tempting to suggest that Mao, as the incarnate archetype of the "New Man" or "New Adam," was unconsciously appealing to the age-old Chinese religious symbolism of swimming (a return to the watery chaos condition of infinite potential) as the necessary prelude for the creation of a communistic society of "great equality."[120]

But it is beyond the scope of this study to extend the unwieldy implications of the chaos theme any further. Suffice it to say that early Taoism and its mythological vision of chaos not only show a continuity with later Taoist thought and practice but also are reflective of a number of archetypal patterns of religious, philosophical, and artistic thought. Despite the obvious and rather extreme speculative fancy of this phase of my discussion, it can be affirmed that modern man still has something to learn from the foolish wisdom of Emperor Hun-tun—even if it is only a matter of "getting" the gist of a rather perverse shaggy dog (P'an-hu?) story. That my ruminations have not been entirely due to the undifferentiated delirium that comes from chaos and cosmic gourds is fortunately indicated by some other more sober analytical studies in the general intellectual history of Western cultural tradition. To take one specific example, I would like to note the work of the Whiteheadian philosopher David Hall, who discusses cogently and at length the proposition that an appreciation of the mythic meaning of chaos in both Western and Eastern tradition may be important for a philosophical and spiritual revisioning of modern culture.[121]

Hermann Hesse comes to a similar conclusion in his study of Dostoevski's idiots and madmen:

> The future is uncertain but the road which [Dostoevski] shows can have but one meaning. It means a new spiritual dispensation. This takes us beyond Myshkin, it points toward magical thinking, to the acceptance of Chaos, to return to anarchy, back into the unconscious, into formlessness, into the beast, back far beyond the beast, back to the beginnings of everything.[122]

As in the Taoist vision, the final point is not to slumber in the night of chaos: "Not to stay there, not to become beast or primeval matter but to start in a fresh direction, to discover new springs of development and action deep down in the roots øf our being in order to reach to a higher and nobler creation and valuation and division of the world.''[123] But "no programme can teach us to find this road, no revolution will cast down the walls that we may enter into it.''[124] The Way that beckons the Taoist and Dostoevski, therefore, implies that "each one must approach it alone, each one for himself.''[125] "Each one of us," Hesse continues, "must in one hour of his life stand on the threshold of the border-land," that empty center where Myshkin and the idiot Hun-tun stood, "where truths cease and new ones begin.''[126]

THE CHAOS OF CHAOS

"It's very provoking," Humpty Dumpty said, . . .
"to be called an egg—very!"
—Lewis Carroll, *Through the Looking Glass*

When we make an effort to understand, we destroy the object of our attachment, substitut-ing another whose nature is quite different. That other object requires of us another effort, which in its turn destroys the second object and substi-tutes a third—and so on until we reach the only enduring Presence, which is that in which all distinction between meaning and the absence of meaning disappears: and it is from that Presence that we started in the first place.
—Lévi-Strauss, *A World on the Wane*

Writer: Diabetes, what you're suggesting is chaos!
Actor: Is freedom chaos?
Writer: Is freedom chaos? Hmm. . . . That's a toughie. (To the audience) Is freedom chaos? Did anybody out there major in philosophy?
—Woody Allen, *Without Feathers*

I have now come full circle in this study and it appears that as the alchemical Ouroboros devours itself, chaos devours meaning. But that is one of the lessons taught by the arts of Mr. Hun-tun. At the end the beginning reappears and there is only order in relation to chaos. It will be recalled that Chuang Tzu had "something" to say about this:

There is a beginning. There is not yet beginning to be a beginning. There is a not yet beginning to be a not yet beginning to be a beginning. There is being. There is nonbeing. There is a not yet beginning to be nonbeing. There is a not yet beginning to be a not yet beginning to be nonbeing. Suddenly there is nonbeing. But I do not know, when it comes to nonbeing, which is really being and which is nonbeing.[127]

Or, as Chuang Tzu says elsewhere, there is a real condition of life where "this" and "that" no longer are opposed. This is called the "pivot of the Tao" (*tao-shu*[b], chap. 2) or "Heavenly Equality" (*t'ien-chün*, chap. 27): "The Ten Thousand Things all come from the same seed, and with their different forms they give place to one another. Beginning and end are part of a single ring and no one can comprehend its principle."[128]

Possibly the lesson here, the lesson of an "ordered" or "sensitive" chaos, is to make us respect the refusal of Erasmus' Mother of Fools "to expound myself by definition, much less divide myself. For it is equally unlucky to circumscribe with a limit her whose nature extends so universally or to dissect her in whose worship every order of being is at one."[129] The real life-order of chaos is too much a part of the texture of our own lives, too much of the warp and woof of reality to be captured in a description. The *Tao Te Ching* (chap. 41) reminds us that if we did not laugh at this proposition it would not be worth the name of the Tao.

The problem in pursuing the meaning of the *hun-tun* theme is that, as with other symbolic themes of a mythic dimension, the "links of analogy are so adhesive that they spread all over the universe."[130] Thus my analysis of the theme of chaos in Taoism demonstrates the fact that the "pursuit of one mythic complex tends to absorb all other myths into it."[131] This is exactly the point at which the theme of *hun-tun* becomes "curiouser and curiouser" in relation to myriad cross-cultural comparisons.

As suggested by the semantic and phonetic humble-jumble of themes already noted, there is the very perplexing conundrum that the reduplicated sound quality of *hun-tun* has a number of surprising phonosemic correlations in other traditions unrelated in history, language, and culture. As an exercise in the mummery of *hun-tun* or the sense of nonsense let me only enumerate a few of these tantalizing items culled somewhat indiscriminately from different traditions:

1. The first and most noteworthy of these curiosities is the "striking linguistic parallel" of Humpty Dumpty that, at least in popular English folklore, alludes to the same type of cosmic egg scenario seen in the *hun-tun* theme.[132] It is probable that the original rhyme was basically an allegory of political protest

without any egg associations; but the fact remains that in English folk tradition there is a seemingly natural linkage made between the reduplicated words of hump-dump or Humpty-Dumpty (having the primary meanings of a mixed drink of ale and brandy; drunkenness; and a hump or hunch-backed man) and egg symbolism.[133]

2. Another phonetically and semantically related parallel is found in the Kurnai tribal culture of southeast Australia where the secret rites of initiation (the Jeraeil ritual) were founded by the god Tundum who is associated with the sacred thundering creation sounds of the ritual bullroarers.[134] Aside from the fact that Tundum is said to be the son of the high god, Munganngaua, and marries a primordial goddess in order to create human culture, I have not been able to document any extensive mythology for Tundum. It should be recalled, however, that many of the Australian creation and initiation myths are similar to the ''southern'' prototypical myths of a ''shapeless,'' ''faceless,'' or ''anus-less'' primordial chaos divinity. Without being aware of this special typo-logical relationship, Waley perceived the mythic character of the *Chuang Tzu*'s Emperor Hun-tun by recounting such an Australian ''tundum'' myth: '' 'In the beginning Anjir was lying in the shadow of a thickly-leaved tree. He was a black-fellow with very large buttocks, but peculiar in that there was no sign of any orifice. Yalpan happened to be passing by at the time and noticing this anomaly made a cut in the usual place by means of a piece of quartz-crystal.' ''[135]

3. In the Mayan *Popol Vuh* there is an interesting mythic analogue to the deluge-animal ancestor typology that tells of Hun-Hunahpu who was the principle deity of the Quiche Mayan culture and the twin son of the primordial couple, Zpivacoc and Xmacane. Hun-Hunahpu, who figures in the ''third'' creation period, must be sacrificed and his skull changed into a calabash (a tree gourd, *Crescentia cujete*) in order for the human world to be created.[136]

4. Finally there is what R. Guénon calls the ''mysteries'' of the Arabic letter *nun*. Guénon points out that this letter is the central letter of the Arabic alphabet (the fourteenth of twenty-eight symbols) and pertains to an esoteric interpreta-tion of the Arabic alphabet as being revelatory of the process and structure of creation. Moreover, in Islamic tradition *nun* is said to represent El-Hut, the chaos whale or fish of the primordial waters of the creation time or flood: ''it is by reason of this meaning that *Seyidna Yunus* (the prophet Jonah) is called *Dhun-Nun*. This naturally refers to the traditional symbolism of the fish and more especially to certain aspects of this symbolism. . . , notably that of the 'Fish-Saviour,' represented by the *Matsya-Avatara* of the Hindu tradition and the *Ichthus* of the early Christians.''[137] In a way similar to Hun-tun as the gourd

(cf. Jonah's gourd in the Bible),[138] ark, or watery serpent-dragon of salvation in the Chinese context, Guénon states that in Semitic tradition:

> The whale, instead of simply playing the part of the fish which conducts the Ark, is in reality identified with the Ark itself; thus Jonah remains enclosed in the body of the whale, like . . . Noah in the Ark, during a period which is for him also, if not for the exterior world, a period of "obscuration," corresponding to the interval between two states or two modalities of existence; here again the difference is only secondary, as the same symbolic figures are always susceptible of a double application, macrocosmic and microcosmic. Moreover, the emergence of Jonah from the belly of the whale has always been regarded as a symbol of resurrection, and thus of the passage of the being to a new state; and this in turn may be related to the idea of "birth" attaching to the letter *nun*, particularly in the Hebrew Kabbalah, to be understood spiritually as a "new Birth," that is to say as a regeneration of the being, individual or cosmic.[139]

Fascinating, also, is that the very form or shape of the Arabic letter *nun* (ن) points to the cosmogonic conception of the cosmic egg-gourd:

> The lower half of a circumference is . . . . a figure of the Ark floating on the waters, and the point at its centre represents the germ enclosed within the Ark; the central position of this point shows in addition that this germ is the "germ of immortality," the indestructible "core" which escapes all exterior dissolutions. It may also be remarked that the half-circumference in question is a schematic equivalent of the cup; thus, like the latter, it has in some respects the signification of a "matrix" in which the as yet undeveloped germ is contained, and which, . . . is identical with the inferior or terrestrial half of the "World Egg."[140]

Guénon continues by relating this to a series of images that especially recall some of the initiatory and alchemical symbolism seen in the Chinese chaos theme:

> As the "passive" element of spiritual transmutation, *El-Hut* also represents in a certain sense every individuality in so far as it contains the "germ of immortality" as its centre, represented symbolically as the heart; and in this connection we will recall the strict relationship which exists between the symbolism of the heart and that of the cup and the "World Egg." The development of the spiritual germ implies that the being emerges from his individual state and from the cosmic environment to which it belongs, just as Jonah's restoration to life coincides with his emergence from the belly of the whale; and we may mention in passing that this emergence is equivalent to the issuing forth of the being from the initiatic cavern, the concavity of which is similarly represented by the half-circumference of the letter *nun*.[141]

Aside from an apoplexy of parallelomania, what does all of this mean?

Probably nothing at all. These bizarre similarities of sound, form, and meaning raise problems susceptible to no easy solution and, furthermore, conjure up the spectre of the "ding-dong" or "bow-wow" theories of echoic symbolism and language origin.[142] Nevertheless in a discussion of a principle of meaningful chaos the mantric invocation of some authentic mumbo-jumbo may not be entirely improper. In view of the absurdity of pursuing such a tenuous line of comparison, it is best to conclude by again quoting Lewis Carroll's Humpty Dumpty, who said "with a good short laugh" that "*my* name means the shape I am—and a good handsome shape it is, too."[143]

At this point it can most likely be said that after yielding itself to comparative analysis, the mythic theme of chaos only enriches its meaning by becoming progressively more impenetrable to abstract dissection. Analytically speaking, and in view of the fact that scholars are always agents of "all the king's horses and all the king's men," it is impossible for me to put all the broken pieces of Humpty Dumpty or Hun-tun back together again. The implication behind any true myth of creation is that the final dissection would come only when there is nothing left to dissect. To operate further on the carcass of myth would require the use of Cook Ting's cleaver, which with a "zip and a zoop" gets to the empty heart of the matter. This method goes beyond analytical skill since "perception and understanding have come to a stop and spirit moves where it wants."[144]

The "meaning" of *hun-tun* as the mythological and metaphysical principle of chaos embraces, therefore, the fundamental question of the meaning of meaning. Chaos from the Taoist perspective is not ultimately a negative concept but rather a vision concerning the true order of cosmic and human life. It is a condition that is not the complete absence of order in the sense of *privatio boni* but rather the experience and insight that reality is a fluid fusion of chaos and cosmos. As the true meaning of the inner life-order of nature and man, *hun-tun* is a condition that is not outside the Great Time, transforming round, or "Butterfly Way" of the universe. The Chinese word and symbol for "butterfly" (*hu*[j]), after all, connotes, etymologically and entomologically, the mythological story of that gloriously free creature of air, pollen, and nectar, "flitting and fluttering around," that issues forth from the great "transformation of things" and is responsible for the incestuous reunion of duality. *Hu*[j] is a character showing the hidden traces of the *hun-tun* theme since it is composed of the root for "insect" (*ch'ung*[b], radical 142) coupled with the phonetic particle, *hu*[k (f,g,h)], meaning variously "stupid," "foolish," "muddled and blind," "calabash gourd," "pot or vase," "sacrificial vessel used to contain grain," and "long life." Chuang Tzu's gnomic "dream" as a Taoist master of cosmic gourds and cocoons was that "he was a butterfly, a butterfly flitting and fluttering around, happy with himself and doing as he pleased" (chap. 2).[145]

Early Taoism is fundamentally concerned with the humbling and healing arts of Mr. Hun-tun, the difficult arts of relearning childlike ease, of returning to the natural condition of faceless selfhood, spontaneity, creativity, health, and wisdom. This is especially the case in the sense that creativity, change, transformation, or freedom is the activity or "play" (*wan*) of the Tao. To be really and authentically free for man implies a return to the mythic Time of the Tao. This is not the "ordinary" time of the human world but the greater "chaotic" rhythm or larval wriggling of universal life—the *tzu-jan* of the Tao. There is no implication that the return to the beginnings is but a step toward a final escape of the world or time, a turning "in" that is ultimately denied in the absolute perfection of being "out." As Izutsu has noted, this may be called a form of transcendence, but it is a "very peculiar kind of 'transcendence' because it is—again by the principle of *coincidentia oppositorum*—at the same time 'immanence.' "[146]

Quoting Whitehead, Hall has felicitously referred to this Taoist view of life as a "clutch at vivid immediacy":

> If we view life as the "clutch at vivid immediacy," we may believe that the art of life is promoted best either through the functioning of reason as a means of realizing the balanced complexity of the aesthetic intensities inherent in the selection of a single order from out of Chaos, or through the functioning of creativity as the realization, in a single intuitive insight, of Chaos as the sum of all orders. The Taoist chooses the latter path.[147]

A Taoist turns inward to rediscover the vital rhythms of organic life; and by achieving this reintegration with the cosmic Time of the Tao, he is able to fulfill his destiny, to live out his "time." In other words, a Taoist is a Gourd Master who has learned the secrets of creation and stores the elixir of life within an empty calabash. Sacrificially cut in two, a calabash usefully serves as a ladle or dipper to feed the desires of ordinary social life; whole and empty, it is the container of wine and medicine, ecstasy and salvation. Chuang Tzu would have it that the best use of a gourd is to respect its original uselessness by "making it into a tub so you can go floating around the rivers and lakes."[148]

While the presence of the *hun-tun* theme may be recognized throughout Taoist thought and practice, the paradoxical idea that the Tao is somehow an "ordered chaos" is certainly, as the sinologist and missionary James Legge remarked, "fantastic and unreasonable."[149] Taoism tends to suggest that, like the trickster monkey Sun Wu-k'ung born from the primal rock of *hun-tun*, the Primal Man as the Animal-Ancestor (Hun-tun, P'an-hu, P'an-ku, Lao Chün, or

Adam Kadmon) had a tail; and "if Adam had a tail, and Adam was created in the image of God and is God's likeness, what does this tell us of the *Imago Dei*?"[150] Like the faceless Chaos-Trismegistus in China, the Egyptian baboon god Thoth was mute, but from his numb dumbness "comes the Word."[151] In the central hollow place at the Beginning, the Sound and Light of creation thunders forth: *hun-hun-tun-tun*. The universality of the sacred monkey business of the chaos principle is suggested by the fact that the "language of nature is ineffable; it has only signs. That mute monkey, forming his glyphic signs, his phallic token always on display, is the reformer, re-orderer, and re-generator."[152] In Thoth, Hun-tun and the monkey king, Sun Wu-k'ung, "gibberish and instruction, sexuality and logos, aged wisdom and Hermes are one."[153]

How, finally, do I say what the Tao means, other than it is laughably nonsensical? As Chuang Tzu said (chap. 2), "Now I have just said something, but I don't know whether what I have said has really said something or whether it hasn't said something." Taoists never say things clearly; they mumble.

APPENDIX 1

THE DELUGE AND ANIMAL ANCESTOR TALES

References: AM Hugo Adolf Bernatzik, *Akha and Miao*, trans. A. Nagler (New Haven: Human Relations Area Files, 1970), pp. 300–309.

ICM Scott, "Indo-Chinese Mythology," in *The Mythology of All Races*, ed. J. MacCulloch (Boston: Marshall Jones Co., 1928), vol. 12, pp. 253–321.

ML Ho, *Myths and Legends*, pp. 267–280.

RA Porée-Maspero, *Rites agraires*, pp. 821–844.

Man Coc (RA)

Chang Lo Cuo made a house of banana leaves. Lord Thunder knocked down the house, then changed himself into a cock. He was put in a cage by Lo Cuo. Lord Thunder bartered for a little water, giving one of his teeth to Lu Cuo. As soon as he drank, he resumed his original form, broke the cage and ascended to heaven.

When the tooth was sown it yielded a plant which bore an enormous gourd. Advised by a bird from the sky, Pu Hay and his younger sister entered the gourd.

Chang Lo Cuo caused the waters to swell unto heaven in order to reach his enemy. Carried by them, he knocked vehemently on the doors of heaven. Lo Cuo opened the water-gates (of heaven); the waves gushed forth carrying Lo Cuo, who smashed his head on the mountain Quan Lon (K'un-lun).

All men were drowned except Pu Hay and his sister, who, stranded on the Quan Lon, received from the tortoise and the bamboo the counsel to marry each other. The brother cut (the tortoise and the bamboo) into bits, which miraculously came back together, but one still sees the scars on them. In the light of the miracles, the brother and sister decided to marry each other.

The young woman delivered a gourd (or lump of flesh) of which she sowed the seeds, but instead of sowing those which would yield some Man on the plain, and those which would give some Tho in the mountains (as her husband told her to do), she switched (them) so that the numerous Man ought to be content with the mountains, while the less numerous Tho possess the fertile plains.

Miao (RA)

Thunder, in order to punish a man, wished to destroy his house; but he fell by the fireplace, and the man put him in an iron cage. Then there was a great drought.

The brother and the sister came to look at him; with his fingers moistened with saliva, he rubbed the bars of his cage and sparks shot up. He asked the children for water; when he had it, refreshed, he caused the bars of his cage to melt and reascended to heaven. He gave to the children some gourd seeds, telling them of the flood.

The brother and sister sailed in the gourd. They beached on a rock, where they lived on chicken which an eagle brought each day to her brood. The eagle, in order to rid herself of them, carried them onto the plain.

The brother and sister, in order to know if they were able to unite themselves seeing that they were alone, hurled down two millstones from the top of an incline. The millstones came together again; they married one another. The woman bore a lump of flesh, from which would spring forth three human couples. They were mutes, but when their father dug up fire (which he had buried in the ground before the flood), they fled letting out different yells, which are the names of fire among the people of which they are the ancestors.

Miao (AM)

In the beginning the earth was flooded by the ocean. When the water had gradually created its own pathways and earth became visible, a pair of siblings was living there. The brother impregnated the sister, and she gave birth to a gourd, which instead of seeds contained germ cells from which, in the course of time, human beings developed.

Miao (AM, RA)

Each morning two brothers saw their furrow was filled in. They hid themselves and saw an old man intent at undoing their work. The elder (brother) wished to kill the old man, the younger wished first to question him. The old man foretold the approaching flood. He told the elder to put himself in a iron drum, and the younger brother to accompany his sister in a barrel of very heavy wood, with a pair of each kind of animal and one seed of each kind of plant.

The Lord of the Sky questioned the brother and the sister when they climbed to heaven. They responded that it was because of the flood; and the Lord, leaning toward the earth, saw it was covered with water.

He sent the rainbow dragon to dry up the earth. An immense eagle came to light upon the barrel and took the brother and sister under his wing in order to place them on a high and dry place. In gratitude, as the eagle did not find anything to eat on earth, the brother and sister gave him pieces of their own flesh, taken from the head, under their arms and behind their knees, whence are derived the cavities men have in their occiput, the armpits and the back of the knee.

Wishing to marry, the brother and sister decided to consult the Master of the Sky on the matter. Two millstones rolled from the top of a mountain did not join themselves together again. Two needles thrown together fell reunited, as did two coins.

The child who was born was round as an egg. They cut him and the pieces which fell to earth became children. They also took care to cut the remainder in as many pieces as possible. And so the earth was repopulated.

Having become numerous the men tried to climb to heaven by constructing a tower. The Lord of the Sky struck those who climbed with lightning and dispersed the others by causing them to speak in different languages.

LoLo (RA)

During a war between the Man-zi and the M'ti (Thai), the former people burned the houses of the latter, who asked the Sky to avenge them. A brother and a sister had not taken part in the crime and took refuge in a temple. The Sky advised them to enter a gourd, which was as large as a house, where they amassed provisions. They floated on the waters, and when they receded, they found themselves beached on the peak Piaya, the only escapees.

Leaving the gourd, they scoured the mountain in order to find wedding-partners. A tortoise advised them to marry for all humanity had been destroyed; they killed her, burning her shell in hopes of some signs. The signs indicated to them to marry. They hesitated for a while, but the bamboo told them to join together and they obeyed him. From their union came three sons and three daughters, who copulated and gave birth to Man-zi, Mung and M'ti.

Li-su and Shui-t'ien (RA)

All humanity was destroyed by a flood, save for a brother and a sister placed in a gourd which floated on the water.

The brother wished to marry the sister, and, since she continually refused, the brother suggested that each of them roll one millstone from the top of a mountain onto the plain, he himself taking the upper stone and she the lower; they would marry if the two stones came together. And that is what came to pass.

The woman gave birth to two balls of flesh, which she threw. The one fell at the foot of a sweet-smelling catalpa tree, the other at the foot of a Jujube-tree. Some men sprang forth from these trees. These are the ancestors of the two Li-su groups.

The Wa (ICM)

In the beginning of time, they say, three pappada ("hills") were inhabited by two beings, who were neither spirits nor human, and who, though they seem to have been of differing sex, had no earthly passions. They existed spontaneously from the union of earth and water. These the Wa call Yatawm and Yatai, while the Shans name them Ta-hsek-khi and Ya-hsek-khi. The Creator Spirit, who is styled Hkun Hsang Long, saw them, and reflecting that they were well suited to become the father and mother of all sentient beings, he named them Ta-hsang Ka-hsi ("Great All-Powerful") and Ya-hsang Ka-hsi ("Grandmother All-Powerful"); and from his dwelling-place in the empyrean, which is called Mong Hsang, he dropped two hwe-sampi, or gourds, down to them.

Picking up the gourds, Yatawm and Yatai ate them and sowed the seeds near a rock. At the end of three months and seven days the seeds germinated and grew into large creepers; and in the course of three years and seven months the creepers blossomed, each producing a gourd, which, by the end of the full period, had swollen to the size of a hill. At the same time Yatawm and Yatai and the twelve kinds of creatures (concerning whom no details whatever are given) came to know the sexual passion. . . . When the gourds had reached their full size, the noise of human beings was heard inside one, and the noise of all kinds of animals inside the other.

Ya-hsang Ka-hsi at the same time grew great with child and gave birth to a girl who had the ears and the legs of a tiger, whence her parents called her Nang Pyek-kha Yek-khi ("Miss Queen Phenomenon") and made over to her all the expanse of earth and water and the two gourds. Apparently the eating of the first two gourds had brought death into the world as well as passion, for the two first beings, we are told, were now well stricken in years, so that they called aloud and addressed the Nats and Thagyas, the spirits and archangels, vowing that whosoever was able to split the gourds should have their daughter to wife.

At this time there was one Hkun Hsang L'rong, who had come down from Mong Hsang in the skies and, by eating the ashes of the old earth, had become so gross and heavy that he lost the power to reascend to his own country. This suggests the *thalesan*, or flavored rice, of Burmese legend, which brought about the debasement and fall of the original celestial Brahmas. Hkun Hsang L'rong was, therefore, constrained to remain upon earth and be associated with the spirits of the hills and dales, the trolls and pixies and kelpies, and he wandered far and wide. He passed through the three thousand forests of Himawunta (the Himalayas), he wandered to the foot of Loi Hsao Mong, which seems to be a Wa equivalent for Mount Meru, and he crossed mighty rivers and falls to the sources of the Nam Kiu (the Irrawaddy), and thence over to the Nam Kong (the Salween), which borders the Wa country on the west. Finally he came to the place where Yatawm and Yatai lived, and when he saw their young daughter Nang Pyek-kha Yek-khi, he fell in love with her, in spite of her tiger's ears and legs, and asked for her hand in marriage. The old people were not unwilling, but they told him of the vow which they had made to the spirits of the air, and insisted that only the man who had the power to split two gourds should wed their daughter.

Then Hkun Hsang L'rong recalled the pilgrimages which he had made and the merit that he had thereby gained for himself, and he called aloud and said: "If indeed I be a Bodhisattva who, in the fullness of time, am destined to become a Buddha and to save all rational beings, then may the Hkun Sak-ya (Indra) and the Madali Wi-hsa-kyung Nat, that powerful spirit, descend and give me the two-handed Sak-ya sword, the celestial weapon!" Thereupon the two eternal beings came down from the Elysian Fields and gave him the magic falchion, two-edged and wonderful. With this he cut open the two gourds; first that which enclosed all the animals of the earth, and then that in which the human beings were contained. Before he struck, however, he called to warn those inside. The hare and the crab were very anxious to get out. The hare curled himself up in a ball with his head between his legs and watched for the stroke of the sword; but the crab crept beside him and took no precautions. When the blade fell, the hare leaped out of the way, but the crab was cut in half. Such was the glory of the sword that there was no stain of blood upon it, and ever since crabs have remained bloodless creatures. Then Hkun Hsang L'rong took up the shell of the crab and said: "If in truth this world is to be the abode of rational beings and the birthplace of the five Buddhas, then let this be for a sign, that where the shell of this crab falls, there shall a lake be found.'' With these words he flung the crab's shell down on the mountaintop, and thus the lake Nawng Hkeo was formed, and on its shores Hkun Hsang L'rong built a city called Mong Mai. This Nawng Hkeo Lake is the sacred mere of the Wa and covers a large area on the crest of a whale-back ridge not far from the Chinese frontier. Since this place was the motherland, and its inhabitants were the parents of all the generations of men, it was afterward named Sampula Teng, and the people were termed Sampula, the first of the children of men on this world, called Badda (Palibhadda, ''good''). Hkun Hsang L'rong, however, named it Mong Wa (''the Country of the Wa'') and said: ''Whoso attacks or injures Mong Wa and harms its children, the La Wa Hpilu Yek-kha, may he be utterly destroyed by the Sak-ya weapons!'' He declared the land to be independent forever of all the countries surrounding it, so that it has remained a purely La Wa Hpilu Yek-kha region from the beginning till now; and he made the country rich with the seven kinds of metals—gold, silver, iron, copper, lead, tin, and the soil of the earth, the latter being a metal according to Burmese notions.

The races of men that came out of the great gourd were sixty in number, and they were divided into four classes; those who lived on rice; those who lived on maize; those who lived on flesh; and those who lived on roots. Each had its own language and raiment and manner of living. From these are descended the five clans of Yang (Karens), two clans of Pawng (who they were does not appear), five clans of Tai (Shans), six clans of Hke (Chinamen), ten clans of Hpai (also undetermined), two clans who were neither Hke nor Tai, and thirteen clans of Hpilu Yek-kha. . . .

APPENDIX 2

ORIGIN OF ANCESTORS FROM GOURDS AND EGGS

Reference: Ho, *Myths and Legends*, pp. 246–256.

1. *Origin from a Gourd*

Ivaho, The Burun, Formosa

If we were to tell you the story of how we human beings were born long ago, we would say that a gourd fell down from heaven, broke open, and two persons came out of it.

The man and the woman from the gourd became husband and wife, and their children multiplied. Among the children were girls as well as boys; the girls and boys intermarried, and from them many children were born and human beings became plentiful.

The Illocanos, Luzon

There was a couple who had prayed for a child for many years. One year they grew in their yard a white squash which produced a beautiful white fruit. Because they had no vegetables at the time, they decided to eat it. When they started to open it, a voice came from within which said, "Please be careful that you do not hurt me." They carefully opened the fruit, and there inside was a fine baby boy who could already talk and stand alone. The man and his wife were overjoyed.

The Dondo, Middle India

A raja had a son and a daughter and the two used to play together. One day the girl got a gourd seed and threw it away on the rubbish heap. It grew and a great flower came from it and then a mighty gourd. The boy made a hole in the gourd and hollowed it out inside. He said, "If ever it rains too much we can hide in this gourd." One day the rain fell and the brother and sister went to play inside this gourd. As they were playing several days passed, but the rain never stopped and the whole world was flooded with water. The gourd floated on the surface and the children grew hungry and began to cry. Mahaprabhu heard them and came to see what was the matter. "Who are you?" he asked. "We are brother and sister and we are very hungry." Mahaprabhu went to the wild boar and told it what had happened. The boar went to the Underworld to Kermo Deota and stole earth from him. With the earth he stole seven kinds of trees—the mango, tamarind, mahua, sago palm, dumar and pipal figs, and banyan.

The boar smeared the mud on its body and bathed. When it came out of the water, it shook itself and the earth flew over the ocean and the world was made. Some of the boar's bristles came out and turned into grass. The seeds of the seven trees were also scattered across the world; from them has come the jungle.

Then Mahaprabhu took the brother and sister out of the gourd and changed their appearance by smallpox so that they did not know each other. They married and mankind has come from their union.

The Bugun, Northeastern Frontier of India

. . . He ran far far away and, as he went, he found two gourds growing. He picked them and took them home where he put them away carefully in one corner. Now he was all alone in his house and he had to cook for himself and fetch his own water as well as go hunting. And then one day when he came home from the forest, he found the house had been cleaned and that there was food cooking on the hearth. This happened for several days and at last Phoiphua said to himself, "This is a very extraordinary thing, for there is nobody else in the forest, so who can be getting me water and cooking me food?"

The next day Phoiphua hid behind the house, and, after a little while, he saw the girl come out of one of the gourds and clean the house, fetch water and cook the food. When she had finished and was about to return into the gourd, Phoiphua came out from his hiding-place and caught her by the hair. She struggled to escape but he held on tight and at last he broke the gourd and persuaded the girl to live with him as his wife.

The children of this couple were the ancestors of the Buguns (Khowas), and the Buguns even today tie their hair in a knot at the top of their heads, for this resembles the shape of the groud from which they came.

2. *Origin from an Egg*

Makazayazaya, The Paiwan, Formosa

In ancient days the sun came down to the top of the Chokaborogan Mountain and laid two eggs, one white and one red. The Vorun snake came to hatch them, and two deities, a male and a female, came out. The male deity was called Boraboran; the female deity, Giarumjuru. They became ancestors of the chief family of the village. The common men originated from the eggs of the green snake.

Kolo, The Sedeq, Formosa

In ancient days a fly came out of nowhere and laid eggs. The eggs hatched, and two persons, a man and a woman, came out of them. They are ancestors of mankind.

The Miao, Southwest China

It is said that at the very beginning there were nine eggs in a certain mountain cave. (It was not known whence the eggs came.) After having been hatched by "Mother Sun," eight sons were born; the eldest was Thunder, the other seven being Dragon, Snake, Tiger, Nine-headed Monster, Python, Wolf, and Monkey. The last one who came out said that the ninth refused to follow him. The mother thought it was a spoiled egg and she was about to crush it when she heard a voice inside saying, "Mother, do not crush me. I am coming out in three days. My name is Lao Yen. When I come out I should be the eldest brother." The mother complied and hugged the egg for three more days when at last a boy was born. This son was the cleverest of all and immediately was able to talk. It is said that he is closely related to mankind.

The Miao, Southwest China

A tame pigeon laid an egg and gave it to a wild dove to hatch. She sat upon the egg until Lan Lang's wing grew out. She hatched out Man Yoh Men, who was very strong. She sat upon the egg twelve days at one time and thirty days at another time. The pigeon egg was fine on top and was also fine-grained inside. When the egg was hatched it changed into a man named Pao Ch'eng Kiang ("one who protects a high official"). When the egg on top opened it changed into a person named Mi Wang Sen. Mi Wang Sen got up and was able at once to write. He then went to the heavenly land of Ntzi. Pao Ch'eng Kiang also went to the land of the King of Heaven (Lo Fa Dail) to study. . . .

APPENDIX 3

THE ANIMAL-SPOUSE TALES

References: ML Ho, *Myths and Legends*, pp. 256–266.
RA Porée-Maspero, *Rites agraires*, pp. 846–847, 849.

The Story of P'an-Hu (Yao version) (RA)

Some thiefs carried off the son of a king. The latter promised the hand of his daughter to his dog, if he found him again. When the son was freed, he regretted his promise, but a spirit advised him to put the dog under a bell, leaving it there for seven days at the end of which the dog would be transformed into a man. Impatient, the king lifted up the bell after the sixth day, the metamorphosis stopped, and the princess had to marry a man with the head of a dog.

Origin of the Man Tien (RA)

Born of a union of the Emperor Jade and the Earth, a princess, in order to amuse herself, organized some games during which a large dog mated with her. Pregnant, she was chased by her father into the mountains and bore a son and a daughter with the bodies of dogs and the heads of men. They mated and their descendants little by little lost the animal form.

Moken (RA)

A daughter of the king of China had intercourse with her dog and became pregnant. The king made her embark with provisions on a raft, which ended up running aground on an island. A son was born who, two days later, became a man. She told her son to take himself to the other end of the island, where he would find a young girl whom he would marry. She transformed herself and went to mate with her son; from them came the Moken.

Na-Khi Legend About the Origin of the LoLo (RA)

The wife of a king suffered from an eye disease and the king promised his daughter to whomever would cure the queen. A jackal came and licked her diseased eyes. The jackal led the princess into the forest. From the couple, considered as ancestor of the Lolo, was born a son and a daughter.

Taroko, The Sedeq, Formosa (ML)

Formerly there was a chief who was ashamed to keep a malformed daughter. He gave much treasure to her and put her and a dog in a boat and set them adrift on the sea. The boat arrived at the beach of Taroko after several days adrift. They landed there and found a place to settle. The dog hunted animals and caught fish to feed the daughter. Thus several years passed. One day the dog said to the daughter, "I have sought food to serve you several years but have never received any special favor so I am thinking of leaving you." The chief's daughter said, "Since I have received your sincere care, how could I forget your reward? Fortunately, I know a girl who has a tattooed face so I will go and bring her to you for your wife." A few days later, after tattooing herself, the chief's daughter came back. She married the dog and from them the Taroko people descended.

The Ketangalan, Formosa (ML)

In olden days when our ancestors still lived in Shan-Shi (unidentified place name), there was a minister whose daughter was hopelessly afflicted with leprosy. The minister prayed to heaven saying, "If anyone could cure my daughter, I would award my daughter to him."

One day a dog came and started to lick his daughter's decomposed skin. This was repeated for several days, and, strangely enough, her disease was completely cured. The minister thought it was a pity to give his daughter in marriage to the dog, but he could not break his promise. He then put her and the dog in a boat and set them adrift on the sea. The boat arrived on Formosa. Through ages the descendants from the minister's daughter and the dog multiplied and they established Kimpaoli village.

The Shaka, South China (ML)

Once upon a time there lived a king named Bukoo, who fought a great battle against another king. Because he had not many soldiers, Bukoo could not defeat his foe. So he issued an order that if anyone could bring him his enemy's head, that person might marry the princess, his daughter.

On hearing this, the King's dog went to the enemy's army quarters. Having entered the enemy's chambers, he suddenly bit off his head and carried it back to his master. When Bukoo saw his enemy's head he was intoxicated with joy and ordered at once that the dog should be awarded, given a high rank, better food and accommodations, for it was a meritorious dog. But the dog was not happy at all. The dog ran into the princess's room with the bloody head and would not come out.

Remembering his promise, Bukoo then told the dog that it was not fitting that he should marry the princess. "For," said the King, "you are a dog." As soon as the dog heard this, he put the head down on the floor and said to the King, "Put me under a bell for forty-nine days and do not allow anyone to peep in during that time." This was done, but on the forty-eighth day they thought the dog must be dead of hunger and took away the bell. Then they saw a man where the dog had been, but he had not yet had quite enough time to change himself entirely and still had the head of a dog. Bukoo then felt bound to keep his word and married the princess to this dog-headed husband. People called her the dog-headed princess. The princess was ashamed of her dog-headed husband, so they went far away and lived in the forest. The princess was afraid to look at her husband's face, so she dressed her hair up on the top of her head and tied a piece of red cloth to it. When her husband came near, she pulled the red cloth down over her face so as not to see him. The princess had three sons, to whom Bukoo gave the names Lui, Pan and Lan respectively.

The Yao, North Vietnam (ML)

Pen Hung, who was at that time ruler of the Chinese province of Su, promised his daughter's hand and half of his kingdom to the hero who should rid him of the conquering marauder Cu-Hung, who was menacing his security. The invader's reputation for valour had preceded him and was such that no man dared match swords with him. When all seemed lost, a dog named Phan-Hu undertook the task of destroying the enemy, and, having succeeded in slaying Cu-Hung in mortal combat, he returned to claim from the king the fulfillment of his promise. The king gave his daughter to the victor, but in order to keep himself the more fertile portion of his kingdom, he assigned only the uncultivated mountain-tops as the dog's share. This unfairness was resented by the Dog-King, and, to remedy it special concessions were granted to his descendants.

APPENDIX 4

THE "COUNTRY OF WOMEN" AND "PEOPLE WITHOUT ANUSES" TALES

Reference: Ho, *Myths and Legends*, pp. 350–381.

1. *The Country of Women*

Takonan, The Atayal, Formosa

In a certain place there were women living, and moreover there was no one there but women. When their sexual desire was aroused, they climbed up a cliff and, when they let the wind into their private parts, they became pregnant. All the children that they bore were girls. This was the situation in former times. Though there were only women, it was not as if they had no chief. An old woman was the chief.

These women had never seen a man. One day a dog belonging to one of our ancestors became lost, and so he went out to look for it. And he came to the place where the women lived. The man said to the woman, "Is my dog around here? He went chasing after a wild boar." The women said, "No, he isn't here. No dog ever comes to our place." The man said "Hmm, is that so? That's all right. Then, I'll go and look somewhere else." The woman said, "What is that thing hanging between your thighs? We've never seen anything like it. Why is that thing dangling so between your thighs?" Whereupon the man said, "We have people like you (women) living where I come from but, say, don't you have any mates?" Then the women said, "If you don't mind, let us have a little try." The man said, "Well, then, let's go to your sleeping quarters and sleep together." The women said, "Let all of us try a little." And they went into the

323

sleeping quarters and took turns having intercourse with the man. However much they worked, they were not satisfied. This was because there were too many women, and however much he worked his private parts, he could not have intercourse with all of them. After they had finished, they called the old woman who was the chief and said, "Old woman, old woman, come here a minute and try it. It feels good." The old woman came smiling and said, "What is this thing that you say feels so good?" The old woman arrived and went to the sleeping quarters, but the man had had so much intercourse that, try as he could, he could not have more. Then the old woman said, "Why didn't you let me have intercourse first? Am I not your chief?" She became provoked and, taking a hatchet, cut off the private parts of the man who had come looking for his dog. Whereupon the man died.

We Atayal waited and waited, but the man did not come back. When we inquired, we heard the rumor that the women who lived in the good region had killed him. Our ancestors said, "They've killed him, so we'll go and kill them."

Our ancestors started out and surrounded the women they were going to kill. This was because the women had been the first to start the fight. The men shot at the house with their guns, but no one came out, and there was no noise in the houses. Only bees came out, and our ancestors were chased by hornets, but the women they came to kill did not come out. Our ancestors returned home, but their clothes were full of red ants, wasps, bees, hornets, etc. These came to build hives in the trees where we live. When the bees make hives we burn them and eat them, and they taste very good. And we hadn't had any red ants and black ants before, but they came back with the men who went to lay seige to the women, and now they are all over the place.

The women said, "They came to kill us, but didn't succeed. The reason they stopped their attack then and there was because they were afraid of the bees." But our ancestors said, "That was only to throw them off their guard." They again went and beseiged them, and without warning burned the thatch grass which surrounded their houses. And the bees and the ants and the women were all burnt up. The houses, too, were all burnt black.

When they went to see the burnt remains of the houses, they found a pigpen with a small girl child trembling in it. A man said, "We're fortunate to have a child." They carried the child on their backs and took her home. The people who brought the child back and cared for her were people from Tahajakan village. They raised the child, and when she grew up they found a husband for her. Then a child was born to them. Afterwards, whenever he wanted anything, he used magic and could get it. He also taught his son to use magic. Now, the people of Tahajakan village are descended from a line of sorcerers, but at present there are no longer any sorcerers left in Tahajakan village. This is because they killed them. All right, even if they have their sorcerers there, what can they do?

Rarukruk, The Paiwan, Formosa

The people of Caovaivai village were all women, and there were no men. So one day they said, "We would like to bear children." And they went to a mountain, and bent down, and thrust out their buttocks to the wind. Then they became pregnant and bore children. But the children they bore were only girls; moreover, they were all cripples, and in addition, they were not strong.

So they again went to the mountain and bent down. Just at that moment, a man from Caozajazaja village came hunting. He climbed a tree, and when he looked around, he saw the women bending down. The man looked and said, "I wonder why the women are doing that." And he visited the women. Whereupon the women got to like the man and seized him and had intercourse. And they had male children. So the people in the village increased, so tradition says.

The Wancho, Northeastern Frontier of India

There was a village of Konyaks where only women lived; there was no man there. Whenever there was a big storm the women conceived by the wind. If a girl was born they rejoiced, but at the birth of a boy they wept. They let the boy grow until he was ten or twelve years old and then killed and ate him.

The Chinese

They say, in the Ocean there was a country of women which was inhabited solely by women. In that country there was a holy spring which caused women to conceive.

Still further to the southeast there is a country of women. Here the water constantly flows east. . . .

In olden days, whenever a ship was wrecked by a tempest on these shores, the women would take the men home with them, but they were all dead within a few days. At last a cunning fellow who stole a boat at night managed to get away at the risk of his life and told the story.

The women of this country conceive by exposing themselves naked to the full force of the south wind, and so give birth to female children.

2. *The People Without Anuses*

Bangatseq, The Atayal, Formosa

Now in the days of our ancestors there was a tribe of Singuts which was said to have led, by their own choice, an unusual life. This tribe of Singuts was said to have eaten only the steam from cooked rice and boiled vegetables.

There was a man called Sijuma who went there and saw that while they cooked the rice and boiled the vegetables, they did not eat the food but only swallowed the steam from the cooking. Now Sijuma ate up the rice and the vegetables just as they were. Thereupon, the Singuts, seeing this, were astonished and wondered from where the food was going to come out. Then Sijuma explained to them, saying, "We're not like you people without any hole in the buttocks. We gradually eliminate what we eat." Saying this, he showed them by relieving himself right there and then, it is said.

Then one of the Singuts said, "We would certainly like to learn from you who don't eat the steam from cooked food. Isn't there some way of making a hole in the buttocks?" So Sijuma replied, "Well then, I'll make a hole in the buttocks for you. Then you can eat rice and vegetables and gradually eliminate them just as I do." It is reported that the Singut was very happy and said, "Please make a hole in my buttocks right away." Sijuma then heated some iron and, when it had become red-hot, had the Singut turn his back toward him and suddenly, with a hissing sound, thrust the iron into his buttocks. The Singut died instantly and so Sijuma fled stealthily.

Now these Singuts were very light and fleet of foot. This was because they ate nothing but steam. When the other Singuts woke up the next morning, they found the Singut who had been abandoned by Sijuma after having been pierced in the buttocks lying dead. Sijuma had fled and was not there, so they knew that he had killed the Singut. Thereupon they started out in pursuit of him. Sijuma saw that the Singuts were after him and had almost caught up with him, so he quickly climbed a tree and hid there. Before long the Singuts, making a rustling noise like the wind, came in pursuit, but they failed to find Sijuma's footprints and so turned back.

After the Singuts had left, Sijuma came down, but he was afraid that they would come back in search of him. So he took dye-yam leaves and thrust them into the hole of the anteater and smeared them around the rim of the hole. Then he cleverly eluded the Singuts and returned home, it is said. After Sijuma had left, the Singuts came back in search of him, as was expected, and discovered the hole of the anteater. They saw blood stains and, thinking that he had surely gone into the hole, thrust their spears into it. When they withdrew them, they saw that the spearheads were covered with blood. Thereupon they were convinced that Sijuma was dead, and they returned home, it is said.

The Pazeh, Formosa

There were two brothers; the elder was called Damurirarus, the younger Upairarus. One day they went to the beach and they found a tortoise had laid its eggs there. When the elder brother tried to pick up the eggs, his hand was bitten by the tortoise, who dragged him into the water. After long drifting, the tortoise left him on an unknown island. When he was wandering he found cultivated fields, and much food was abandoned on them. Finally he found a village. The people of this village called Tanuhenuhe lived by only smelling the vapor of cooked food and threw the food away after the meal.

During a meal they just smelled the vapor of cooked food, but Damurirarus was so hungry that he ate a great amount of food. People around him were so surprised, and they told him since he ate so much food, the food would stick in his stomach. He felt strange about this word "stick," but when he observed carefully, he found these people were without anuses.

During the stay he saved many deerskins and used the skins to make a leather boat in which he finally returned home.

The Apayao, Luzon

In the early days when life was at its beginning, it came about that a man from Madatag met and wooed a woman named Pakiyan, who came from another place. They were married and went to live in the husband's house in Madatag.

Pakiyan noticed a strange custom which the people there had. They ate only the vapor which comes off of cooked rice. She became consumed with curiosity as to why they followed this custom. Finally she thought that maybe their bodies were different. So one night, full of curiosity, she went over the body of her husband and examined it. To her surprise, she found that there was no hole where the anus should be.

Pakiyan was very sorry for her husband and wanted to help him. So she took her sharp stick and made an anus for him. In the morning they found that he could now eat just as Pakiyan herself. The other people saw the husband eating rice and asked Pakiyan how it was done. She told them and showed them how to make an anus.

So now the people of Madatag are just the same as other people.

The Isneg, Luzon

The people of Madatag in former days were all stupid: they did not know how to eat. There was no hole in their breech: that was why they did not know how to eat. When they cooked rice, they ate it very quickly, as there was no hole in their breeches: that was why they merely ate the steam of the cooked rice; that is why they could not defecate. And, they say, their breeches were perforated when their relatives perforated their breeches. That is why the Madatag people are still stupid.

NOTES

Introduction

1. Michel Foucault, *The Order of Things, An Archaeology of the Human Sciences* (New York: Vintage Books, 1970), p. xv. In a more desultory manner, see also Paul G. Kuntz, ed., *The Concept of Order* (Seattle: University of Washington Press, 1968).

2. Foucault, *Order of Things*, p. xv.

3. Ibid.

4. Ibid., p. xxi.

5. Ibid., p. xx.

6. Ibid.

7. Octavio Paz, *Claude Lévi-Strauss: An Introduction* (London: Jonathan Cape, 1971), p. 94.

8. See, for example, Max Kaltenmark, *Lao Tzu and Taoism* (Stanford: Stanford University Press, 1969), pp. 24−37.

9. *CCT*, 5/2/47; and Watson, p. 42. It can be noted that the term for "confusion" (ku^a) is related to hua^b (ku), which recalls the mythological chaos theme of the "mass of flesh" or "boneless ancestor." See, for example, Eberhard, *LC*, p. 45.

10. See the discussion by David L. Hall, "Process and Anarchy—A Taoist Vision of Creativity," *Philosophy East and West* 28 (1978): 271−285.

11. Ibid., pp. 278−279.

12. Ibid., pp. 271−272; and also David Hall's *The Uncertain Phoenix: Adventures Toward a Post-Cultural Sensibility* (New York: Fordham University Press, 1979).

13. See, for example, Ernst Siecke, *Drachenkämpfe* (Leipzig: J. C. Henricks' sche, 1970); Hermann Gunkel, *Schöpfung und Chaos in Urzeit und Endzeit* (Gottingen: Vandenhoeck und Ruprecht, 1895); Mary K. Wakeman, *God's Battle With the Monster* (Leiden: E. J. Brill, 1973); Joseph Fontenrose, *Python: A Study of Delphic Myth and Its Origins* (Berkeley and Los Angeles: University of California Press, 1959); and Bernhard W. Anderson, *Creation Versus Chaos* (New York: Association Press, 1967).

14. See Jonathan Z. Smith, "The Wobbling Pivot," in his *Map is Not Territory* (Leiden: E. J. Brill, 1978), pp. 97−98.

15. See especially Barbara Sproul, *Primal Myths, Creating the World* (San Francisco: Harper and Row, 1979), pp. 5−14.

16. Smith, *Map*, p. 97.

17. See Jonathan Z. Smith's review of Wakeman's *God's Battle With the Monster*, in *Journal of Biblical Literature* 94 (1975): 442.

18. Smith, *Map*, p. 98; and Mircea Eliade, *Myth and Reality* (New York: Harper Torchbook, 1963), pp. 41−53.

19. Sproul, *Primal Myths*, p. 9.

20. Ibid., p. 10.

21. See Paul Wheatley, *The Pivot of the Four Quarters* (Chicago: Aldine Publishing Co., 1971), pp. 316–330.

22. See Paz, *Lévi-Strauss*, p. 74; Claude Lévi-Strauss, *The Savage Mind* (Chicago: University of Chicago Press, 1966); and Wheatley, *Pivot*, pp. 311–317.

23. Paz, *Lévi-Strauss*, p. 76.

24. See, for example, Werner Jaeger, *The Theology of the Early Greek Thinkers* (New York: Oxford University Press, 1967), pp. 13–14.

25. See F. M. Cornford, *Principium Sapientiae, The Origins of Greek Philosophical Thought* (Cambridge: Cambridge University Press, 1952), pp. 194–195, 202–238 (on cosmogony and the New Year ritual).

26. See Hall, *Uncertain Phoenix*, chapter 2; and Arnold Ehrhardt, *The Beginning* (New York: Barnes and Noble Inc., 1968).

27. Cornford, *Principium*, p. 197.

28. See Henry George Liddell and Robert Scott, *A Greek-English Lexicon*, New Ed. (Oxford: The Clarendon Press, 1940), p. 985. Liddell and Scott list the following semantic range: shamefully; good, natural, or governmental order; discipline; fashion; epithets; praise; honor/credit; ruler/regulator; world-order; firmament; inhabited world; sinful world.

29. See the discussion in Angus Fletcher, *Allegory, The Theory of a Symbolic Mode* (Ithaca: Cornell University Press, 1964), pp. 108–135.

30. On the New Testament idea of cosmos as the fallen, sinful, or estranged world see Liddell and Scott, *Lexicon*, p. 985.

31. Scc, for cxamplc, Mary Douglas, *Purity and Danger: An Analysis of Concepts of Pollution and Taboo* (New York: Frederick A. Praeger, 1966).

32. Presupposed here is Clifford Geertz's understanding of "religion as a cultural system." See his discussion in *Reader in Comparative Religion*, ed. William A. Lessa and Evan Z. Vogt (New York: Harper and Row, 1965), pp. 204–215. See also the complementary discussion by Patrick Burke, *The Fragile Universe, An Essay in The Philosophy of Religions* (New York: Barnes and Noble, 1979), p. 17. On "salvation" as a comparative category see Willard Oxtoby, "Reflections on the Idea of Salvation," in *Man and His Salvation; Studies In Memory of S. G. F. Brandon*, ed. Eric J. Sharpe and John R. Hinnells (Manchester: Manchester University Press, 1973).

33. Burke, *Fragile Universe*, pp. 17–18.

34. For a comparative discussion see Needham, *SCC*, 5:2, pp. 77–84.

35. See Geertz, "Religion as a Cultural System," pp. 209–212.

36. Ibid., pp. 212–214.

37. Victor Turner, "Myth and Symbol," in *International Encyclopedia of Social Sciences*, ed. David L. Sills (New York: Macmillan Co. and The Free Press, 1968), vol. 10, p. 526.

38. See Burke, *Fragile Universe*, pp. 17–18.

39. Walter Burkert, *Structure and History In Greek Mythology and Ritual* (Berkeley, Los Angeles, London: University of California Press, 1980), p. 3. See also the excellent discussion of Burkert's methodology by Larry J. Alderink, "Greek Ritual and Mythology: The Work of Walter Burkert," *Religious Studies Review* 6 (1980): 1–13. While

Mircea Eliade's methodology is less explicit than Burkert's, I think that it can be said that because of their non-Lévi-Straussian concern for the universal form and historical/thematic context of myth, Eliade and Burkert are finally complementary. See my "Imagining Eliade: A Fondness for Squirrels," in *Imagination and Meaning: The Scholarly and Literary Worlds of Mircea Eliade*, ed. N. J. Girardot and M. L. Ricketts (New York: Seabury Press, 1982); and also Seymour Cain, "Mircea Eliade: Attitudes Toward History," *Religious Studies Review* 6 (1980): 13–16.

40. See Eliade, *Myth and Reality*, pp. 1–20; Ian G. Barbour, *Myths, Models, and Paradigms* (New York: Harper and Row, 1974), pp. 19–28; and also Georges Gusdorf, *Mythe et metaphysique* (Paris: Flammarion, 1953), pp. 28–36.

41. Gusdorf, *Mythe*, p. 28 (his emphasis).

42. Burkert, *Structure and History*, p. 23.

43. See Eliade, *Myth and Reality*, pp. 21–38; Barbour, *Myths*, pp. 20–21; and also K. Bolle, *The Freedom of Man in Myth* (Nashville: Vanderbilt University Press, 1968), pp. 17–21.

44. Burkert, *Structure and History*, p. 3.

45. Ibid.

46. Ibid.

47. Ibid., pp. 5–18.

48. Ibid., p. 13.

49. See Eliade, *Myth and Reality*, pp. 162–193.

50. Andrew H. Plaks, *Archetype and Allegory in the Dream of the Red Chamber* (Princeton: Princeton University Press, 1976), p. 4. On the meaning of "paradigm" see also Barbour, *Myths*, pp. 8–11, 119–146; and Northrop Frye, "The Archetypes of Literature," in *Myth and Literature* (Lincoln, Nebraska: University of Nebraska, 1966), pp. 87–89.

51. See Nathan Sivin, "On the Word 'Taoist' as a Source of Perplexity," *History of Religions* 17 (1978): 303–330; and Michel Strickmann, "On the Alchemy of T'ao Hung-ching," in *Facets of Taoism*, ed. Holmes Welch and Anna Seidel (New Haven: Yale University Press, 1979), pp. 164–167.

52. See, for example, the discussions by Holmes Welch, "The Bellagio Conference on Taoist Studies," pp. 107–136; Arthur F. Wright, "An Historian's Reflections on the Taoist Tradition," pp. 248–255, in *History of Religions* 11 (1972); and T. Izutsu, *Key Philosophical Concepts In Sufism and Taoism* (Tokyo: Keio Institute, 1967), 2:1–27.

53. On the idea of "trajectory" and "tradition" see H. Koester and J. M. Robinson, *Trajectories Through Early Christianity* (Philadelphia: Fortress Press, 1971), pp. 13–15; and Smith, *Map*, pp. x–xi. See also Peter Slater, *The Dynamics of Religion* (San Francisco: Harper & Row, 1978), pp. 28–63.

54. See below, chapter 9.

55. See Burkert, *Structure and History*, p. 6.

56. See Victor Turner's discussion, "Myth and Symbol," pp. 526 ff; and my "Initiation and Meaning in the Tale of Snow White and the Seven Dwarfs," *Journal of American Folklore* 90 (1977): 298–300.

57. See Lewis Carroll, *The Annotated Alice*, Intro. and Notes by Martin Gardner (New York: Clarkson N. Potter, 1960), pp. 270–272.

58. Ibid., p. 263.

59. Ibid., p. 276, n. 10.

60. Ibid., p. 271, n. 7; and also James Joyce, *Finnegans Wake* (New York: Penguin Books, 1976), p. 3.

61. For this Sherlockian reference I am indebted to Jonathan Smith's heuristic perspicacity, *Map*, pp. 300–301.

62. See, for example, Frederick Mote, "The Cosmological Gulf Between China and the West," in *Transition and Permanence: Chinese History and Culture*, ed. David C. Buxbaum and Frederick W. Mote (Hong Kong: Cathay Press, 1972), pp. 3–21.

63. "Cosmogony and Religion," *China Review* 4 (1875): 12.

64. Ibid.

65. For discussion and relevant bibliography see my "Problem of Creation Mythology in the Study of Chinese Religion," *History of Religion* 15 (1976): 289–318. The emphasis on a spontaneous creation out of a chaos-nothingness is also honored in the *via negativa* tradition in the West—see, for example, Robert Neville, "From Nothing to Being: The Notion of Creation in Chinese and Western Thought," *Philosophy East and West* 30 (1980): 21–34.

66. Chang Kwang-chih, "Chinese Creation Myths: A Study in Method" (in Chinese with English summary), *Bulletin of the Institute of Ethnology*, Academica Sinica, no. 8 (1959), pp. 47–79. See also Sarah Allan, "Sons of Suns: Myth and Totemism in Early China," *Bulletin of the School of Oriental and African Studies* 44 (1981): 290–326.

67. Chang Kwang-chih, "A Classification of Shang and Chou Myths," in his *Early Chinese Civilization: Anthropological Perspectives* (Cambridge: Harvard University Press, 1976), pp. 157–158.

68. Ibid.

69. Ibid., pp. 157–159.

70. Ibid.

71. Ibid.

72. Ibid.

73. See below, chapter 3.

74. See Chang, "Classification," pp. 155–173; and his "Changing Relationships of Man and Animal in Shang and Chou Myths and Art," in *Early Chinese Civilization*, pp. 174–196. Especially important is the reciprocal relation between changes in myth and changes in the meaning of ritual kinship.

75. See the discussion in Plaks, *Archetype and Allegory*, pp. 3–26.

76. Gusdorf, *Mythe*, p. 244.

77. See Plaks, *Archetype and Allegory*, pp. 11–26.

78. See, for example, Lévi-Strauss' comments on the work of Karl Hentze, *Structural Anthropology* (New York: Basic Books, 1963), p. 246.

79. See Fred Eggan, "Social Anthropology and The Method of Controlled Comparison," *American Anthropologist* 56 (1954): 743–763; and E. A. Hammel, "The Comparative Method in Anthropological Perspective," *Comparative Studies In Society and History*, 22 (1980): 145–155.

80. Quoted by Guilford Dudley III, *Religion on Trial, Mircea Eliade and His Critics* (Philadelphia: Temple University Press, 1977), p. 154. See also Jean Rudhart, "Coherence and Incoherence of Mythic Structure: Its Symbolic Function," *Diogenes* 77 (1972): 14–42.

81. See Arthur F. Wright, "The Study of Chinese Civilization," *Journal of the History of Ideas*, 21 (1960): 232–255; and Maurice Freedman, "Marcel Granet, 1884–1940, Sociologist," in Marcel Granet, *The Religion of the Chinese People*, trans. Maurice Freedman (New York: Harper Torchbooks, 1975), pp. 1–32. On Maspero see Paul Demiéville, "Henri Maspero et l'avenir des études chinoises," *T'oung Pao* 38 (1947): 16–42; D. C. Twitchett's "Introduction" in H. Maspero, trans. F. A. Kierman, Jr., *China in Antiquity* (Amherst: University of Massachusetts Press, 1978), pp. ix–xxx; and T. H. Barrett, "Introduction," in H. Maspero, trans. F. A. Kierman, Jr., *Taoism and Chinese Religion* (Amherst: University of Massachusetts Press, 1981), pp. vii–xxiii.

82. See Marcel Granet's introductory comments in *DL*, pp. 1–59.

83. See George Dumézil's preface to the latest edition of Granet's *La religion des chinois* (Paris: Editions Imago, 1980), pp. v–viii; and the discussion of Granet's formative impact on Lévi-Strauss' first major work, *The Elementary Structures of Kinship*, trans. J. H. Bell, J. R. Von Sturmer, and Rodney Needham (Boston: Beacon Press, 1969), pp. 311–404. Granet's work is referred to throughout many of Eliade's scholarly publications.

84. See the discussion by Wright, "Chinese Civilization," pp. 232–255. Though not influenced by Granet, the fruitfulness of a comparative/structuralist/interpretive approach for Chinese studies is brillantly illustrated by the work, among others, of Chang Kwang-chih, Wolfgang Bauer, and Paul Wheatley.

85. Edmund Leach, "Lévi-Strauss in the Garden of Eden: An Examination of Some Recent Developments in the Analysis of Myth," in *Reader in Comparative Religion*, ed. William A. Lessa and Evon Z. Vogt (New York: Harper and Row, 1965), p. 581.

1. Soup, Symbol, and Salvation

1. Burton Watson, trans., *Cold Mountain, 100 Poems by the T'ang Poet Han-shan* (Taipei: Wen Feng Publishing Co., n.d.), p. 96. For the *Chuang Tzu* parable of Emperor Hun-tun see below, chapter 3. Chuang Tzu's "seven" holes and Han Shan's "nine" holes are symbolically equivalent.

2. See Anthony C. Yu, trans., *The Journey to the West* (Chicago: University of Chicago Press, 1977), vol. 1, p. 65; and Wilhelm Grube, trans., *Die Metamorphosen der Goetter*, 2 vols. (Leiden: E. J. Brill, 1912).

3. See Lin Yutang, *Chinese Theory of Art* (New York: G. P. Putnams, 1967), pp. 137–142; and Pierre Ryckman's "Les Propos sur la peiture de Shitao," *Mélanges chinois et bouddhiques* 15 (1968–1969): 1–242.

4. See below, chapters 2–4. More generally on utopian themes see Wolfgang Bauer, *China and the Search for Happiness* (New York: The Seabury Press, 1976).

5. See Granet, *DL*, pp. 540–545; and Eberhard, *LC*, pp. 441–442.

6. See Daniel Overmyer, "Folk-Buddhist Religion: Creation and Eschatology in Medieval China," *History of Religions* 12 (1972): 42–70.

7. Lo Meng-ts'e, "Shuo hun-tun yü chu-tzu ching-ch'uan chi yen ta-hsiang" (The Primeval State and Ideas of Creation in Early Chinese Philosophy and Classics), *Journal of Oriental Studies* (Hong Kong) 9 (January 1971–July 1971): 15–57, 230–305 (with short English synopsis). See also David C. Yu's discussion and translation of one brief

section, "On the 'Great Pupa,' " in *Myth and Symbol In Chinese Tradition*, ed. N. J. Girardot and J. S. Major, forthcoming.

8. Lo, "Primeval State," *passim*; and Yu, "Great Pupa."

9. Alfred Forke, *The World Conception of the Chinese* (reprint ed., New York: Arno Press, 1975), p. 21 (quoting Ko Hung from the *Chin Shu*). On the Hun-t'ien[a] system see also Needham, *SCC*, 3:216—219. Ko Hung's description basically follows Chang Heng's earlier account in the *Hun I Chu*—see Needham, *SCC*, 3:217.

10. Forke, *World Conception*, p. 18.

11. See Eberhard, *LC*, p. 440; and Edward Schafer, "The Development of Bathing Customs in Ancient and Medieval China and the History of the Floriate Clear Palace," *Journal of the American Oriental Society* 76 (1956): 69—98.

12. See Rolf Stein, "Architecture et pensée religieuse en extreme-orient," *Arts Asiatiques* 4 (1957): 163—186 (expanded in his "L'Habitat, le monde et le corps humain en extreme-orient et en haute Asie," *Journal Asiatique* 245 [1967]: 37—74). One specific ancient analogue is the so-called Ming-t'ang or Hall of Light—on this see the work by W. E. Soothill, *The Hall of Light: A Study of Early Chinese Kingship* (London: Lutterworth Press, 1951); and, more reliably, Henri Maspero's "Le Ming-t'ang et la crise religieuse chinoise avant les Han," *Mélanges chinois et bouddhiques* (1948—1951): 1—71.

13. See Rolf Stein, "Jardins en miniature d'extreme-orient," *Bulletin de l'ecole francaise de l'extreme-orient* 42 (1942): 53—54. On the notion of "word family" associations see B. Karlgren, "Word Families in Chinese," *Bulletin of the Museum of Far Eastern Antiquities* 5 (1933): 9—120. See also Karlgren's *Grammata Serica* (Gotenburg: Elauders Boktryckeri, 1940) and his *Analytical Dictionary of Chinese* (Paris: Paul Geuthner, 1923).

14. See Lo, "Primeval State," pp. 50—55. See also Yu's discussion, "Great Pupa," and James J. Y. Liu, *The Art of Chinese Poetry* (Chicago: University of Chicago Press, 1962), pp. 34—36.

15. On the complexities of the ancient Chinese calendrical system (a unique lunar/solar combination), see Derk Bodde, *Festivals in Classical China* (Princeton: Princeton University Press, 1975), pp. 26—34. See also Bodde's discussion of the relation between cosmology and apotropaism/exorcism, pp. 80—81, 112—117, 304—391.

16. Ibid., pp. 289—339. On gourd charms see Juliet Bredon and Igor Mitrophanow, *The Moon Year, A Record of Chinese Customs and Festivals* (New York: Paragon Book Reprint Corp., 1966, originally printed 1927), p. 318; and Eberhard, *LC*, pp. 279—280.

17. Personal observation while in Taiwan, 1970—1971.

18. Wolfram Eberhard, *Chinese Festivals* (New York: Henry Schuman, 1952), p. 90; and Bodde, *Festivals*, p. 317.

19. Eberhard, *Festivals*, p. 91.

20. See Liu Ts'un-yun, *Buddhist and Taoist Influences on Chinese Novels* (Wiesbaden: Otto Harrassowitz, 1962), vol. 1, pp. 261—76; and H. Doré, *Researches into Chinese Superstitions* (reprint ed., Taipei: Ch'eng-wen, 1967), vol. 9, pp. 111f.

21. See W. L. Hildburgh, "Note on the Gourd as an Amulet in Japan," *Man* 19 (1919): 25—29.

22. See C. Ouwehand, *Namazu-e and Their Themes* (Leiden: E. J. Brill, 1964), pp. 182 ff.

23. See, for example, the depictions in Charles Derry, *Dark Dreams, a Psycho-*

logical History of the Modern Horror Film (New York: A. S. Barnes and Co., 1977), p. 72.

24. Doré, *Researches*, 3:xx.

25. See F. Steiner's discussion of Frazerian comparison, *Taboo* (London: Cohen and West, 1956), p. 92; and Jonathan Z. Smith, "*Adde Parvum Parvo Magnus Acervus Erit,*" *History of Religions* 11 (1971): 76–80.

26. See J. J. M. de Groot, *Les fêtes annuellement célèbrees à emoui (amoy)* (Paris: Ernest Leroux, 1886), pp. 220–229; Eberhard, *LC*, pp. 419–422; and for the Han period spring observances, Bodde, *Festivals*, p. 277. See also Eberhard, *LC*, pp. 420–422.

27. See below, chapter 9. See especially Daniel Overmyer's "Dualism and Conflict In Chinese Popular Religion," in *Transitions and Transformations in the History of Religions*, ed. Frank E. Reynolds and Theodore M. Ludwig (Leiden: E. J. Brill, 1980), pp. 153–184.

28. See below, chapter 9.

29. See Eberhard, *LC*, p. 440.

30. Tjan Tjoe Som, trans., *Po Hu T'ung—The Comprehensive Discussions in the White Tiger Hall* (Westport, Conn.: Hyperion Press, 1949), vol. 1, p. 262.

31. Ibid.

32. See Eberhard, *LC*, p. 278; and Granet, *DL*, p. 220.

33. V. R. Burkhardt, *Chinese Creeds and Customs* (reprint ed., Hong Kong: South China Morning Post, 1953, 1955, 1958) 3 vols., 1:65.

34. Legge, *Chinese Classics* 5:679, 684; and K. C. Chang, "Ancient China," in *Food in Chinese Culture*, ed. K. C. Chang (New Haven: Yale University Press, 1977), p. 51, n. 2.

35. See Eberhard, *LC*, p. 440.

36. I am indebted to Edward Schafer for this felicitous expression—see his *Pacing the Void, T'ang Approaches to the Stars* (Berkeley, Los Angeles, London: University of California Press, 1977), p. 30.

37. I am, of course, alluding to Clifford Geertz's formulations of these methodological issues—see his "Religion As a Cultural System," and "Deep Play: Notes on the Balinese Cockfight," in his *The Interpretation of Cultures* (New York: Basic Books, 1973), pp. 412–454.

38. See Derk Bodde, *Annual Customs and Festivals in Peking as Recorded in the Yen-ching Sui-shih-chi by Tun Li-ch'en* (Peiping: Henri Vetch, 1936), p. 87. Unfortunately, Bodde fails to develop the significance of this proverb and only remarks in a note (pp. 87–88, n. 4) that the text refers to the *Han Shu* and continues with "a short and rather far-fetched explanation of the origin of the term *hun-t'un.*" See also Doré's reference to the eating of "glutinous rice dumplings called Hvan-t'wan [=*wan-t'uan*]" at the first New Year's meal—*Researches* 4:631. Doré connects this with *wan-hsi* meaning "great joy," but more probable is its rhyming and ritual associations with *hun-tun* or wonton. Other traditional ritual and cosmological foods like *man-t'ou* (=*manju* in Japan) cakes may also be thematically connected—see Edward Schafer, *The Vermilion Bird, T'ang Images of the South* (Berkeley, Los Angeles: University of California Press, 1967), pp. 249–250; and Eberhard, *LC*, p. 196 (sacrifical implications of *man-t'ou*). In Japan as U. A. Casal remarks, the New Year's *kagami mochi* rice cakes, which were traditionally molded with a flat bottom and arched top, probably embody the

Chinese "idea of a vaulted heaven over a level earth"—see his *The Five Sacred Festivals of Ancient Japan* (Rutland: Charles E. Tuttle, 1967), p. 13, n. 13.

39. On the ancient winter solstice and related ritual practices see Bodde, *Festivals*, pp. 165—188, 75—163. See also Bodde's discussion of the ancient system of multiple renewals of the year (correlated with the five elements theory), pp. 45—47. The Han system represents a composite rationalization of earlier systems.

40. See, for example, the theory of ritual developed in Evan Zeuss, *Ritual Cosmos, The Sanctification of Life in African Religions* (Athens, Ohio: Ohio University Press, 1979), pp. 238—243.

41. See Claude Lévi-Strauss, *The Raw and the Cooked* (London: Cape, 1970); and his *The Origin of Table Manners* (New York: Harper and Row, 1968), pp. 496—508. For the relation of food and ritual in China see Jordan Paper, "The Ritual Core of Chinese Religion," unpublished article.

42. See below, chapters 6 and 7.

43. See especially the various articles in Chang, *Food in Chinese Culture*.

44. See Bodde, *Festivals*, pp. 26—41; and Needham, *SCC*, 3:390—408.

45. See Eberhard, *LC*, p. 440. Eberhard feels that before the T'ang, wonton was known "only under the names of 'tun' and 'kun' . . . which at least traces the name and the thing to the Han time." Kun is the mythological father of the culture hero Yü and analogous to the mythological Hun-tun.

46. Chang, "Ancient China," pp. 39—52. Figure 1 is based loosely on Chang's diagram on p. 40 but has been adumbrated in line with my interpretations of the material (Chang, therefore, does not speak of "triads").

47. Yü Ying-shih, "Han," in *Food in Chinese Culture*, p. 57.

48. Chang, "Ancient China," p. 44.

49. Ibid.

50. See Yü, "Han," pp. 57—58. *Keng* stews eaten during normal, non-nodal, social time were "seasoned." For the "barbarian" quality of *keng* see Chang, "Ancient China," pp. 41—42.

51. Yü, "Han," p. 58.

52. Chang, "Ancient China," pp. 47—49; and Yü, "Han," p. 57.

53. Chang, "Ancient China," p. 48.

54. See below, chapter 3; and Granet's interpretation, *DL*, pp. 537—545.

55. Chang, "Ancient China," p. 46.

56. Ibid. One should, of course, remark that Granet was developing a similar speculative thesis more than fifty years ago (allowing for Bodde's cautious criticism, *Festivals*).

57. See Granet, *DL*, pp. 515—537; Eberhard, *LC*, pp. 153—162. See also Bodde's discussion of "peach soup" consumed on "New Year's Day as an effective agent against noxious vapors and demons"—*Festivals*, pp. 133—138; and Ling Shun-sheng, "Turtle Sacrifice In Ancient China," *Bulletin of the Institute of Ethnology, Academia Sinica* 31 (1971): 41—46.

58. Eberhard, *LC*, pp. 155.

59. See Eberhard, *Festivals*, pp. 69—96; Bodde, *Festivals*, pp. 314—316; and in a more detailed fashion, Goran Aijmer, *The Dragon Boat Festival on the Hupeh-Hunan Plain, Central China. A Study in the Ceremonialism of the Transplantation of Rice* (Stockholm: The Ethnographic Museum of Sweden, 1964).

60. See Bodde, *Festivals*, pp. 100–101 (during the New Year), pp. 290–291 (during the fifth month); and Eberhard, *LC*, pp. 149–153 (fifth month).

61. Eberhard, *LC*, p. 156.

62. Granet, *DL*, pp. 515–537.

63. On the combat theme see especially Joseph Fontenrose, *Python, A Study of Delphic Myth and Its Origins* (Berkeley and Los Angeles: University of California Press, 1959).

64. Needham, *SCC*, 2:120, n. b.

65. Ibid.

66. On the work of Yoshioka Yoshitoyo see Whalen W. Lai, "Towards a Periodization of the Taoist Religion," *History of Religions* 16 (1976): 75–85. The other scholars' views will be discussed throughout this book. See also David C. Yu, "The Creation Myth and Its Symbolism in Classical Taoism," *Philosophy East and West* 31 (1981): 479–500.

67. See my "Part of the Way: Four Studies on Taoism," *History of Religions* 11 (1972): 319–37.

68. See, for example, the general discussion of some of these points in Paz, *Lévi-Strauss*, pp. 58–76.

69. Mircea Eliade, *Myth and Reality* (New York: Harper Torchbook, 1963), p. 112.

70. Ibid.

71. Bauer, *Search for Happiness*, p. 32.

72. Ibid.

73. See Paz, *Lévi-Strauss*, pp. 73–74.

74. Ibid., p. 73.

75. See Jan Yün-hua, "Problems of Tao and Tao Te Ching," *Numen* 22 (1975): 208–234.

76. See Gerald J. Gruman, *A History of Ideas About the Prolongation of Life, Transactions of the American Philosophical Society*, New Series; vol. 56, part 9 (Philadelphia: American Philosophical Society, 1966), pp. 5–19, 28–48; and Needham, *SCC*, 5:2, pp. xvii–xxxii, 71–187.

77. See especially Mircea Eliade, *The Forge and the Crucible* (New York: Harper Torchbook, 1971); Stephen Toulmin and June Goodfield, *The Architecture of Matter* (New York: Harper and Row, 1962), pp. 109–138; and, for China, N. Sivin, "Chinese Alchemy and the Manipulation of Time," *Isis* 67 (1976): 513–526.

78. See R. C. Zaehner, *Concordant Discord* (Oxford: The Clarendon Press, 1970), p. 413. Zaehner, it should be noted, is one of the few Western commentators to discuss the religious implications of paradise and fall in the early Taoist texts (pp. 214–236). For the passage from the *Tao Te Ching* see *LTCK*, p. 278 and Chan, p. 176.

79. *LTCK*, p. 149; and Chan, p. 137.

2. *"Beginning and Return" in the Tao Te Ching*

1. While the *Lao Tzu* is the more traditional reference for this text, I have used the alternate title of *Tao Te Ching* because of its popularity in Western scholarship.

2. "On the Essentials of The Six Schools," *Shih Chi*, chap. 130. See Fung, *History*, 1:21.

3. See Ariane Rump, trans. (in collaboration with W. T. Chan), *Commentary of the*

Lao Tzu by Wang Pi (Honolulu: University Press of Hawaii, 1979); Paul J. Lin, *A Translation of Lao Tzu's Tao Te Ching and Wang Pi's Commentary* (Ann Arbor: Center for Chinese Studies, University of Michigan, 1977); Isabelle Robinet, *Les commentaires du Tao To King jusqu'un VII siècle* (Paris: College de France, 1977); and Ch'en Ku-ying, *Lao Tzu, Text, Notes, and Comments* (San Francisco: Chinese Materials Center, 1977). Collected Chinese commentary is also found throughout *LTCK*. For a discussion of the Ma-wang-tui *Lao Tzu* texts see Robert G. Hendricks, "The Philosophy of Lao-tzu Based on the Ma-wang-tui Texts: Some Preliminary Observations," *Bulletin of the Society For the Study of Chinese Religions* 9 (1981): 59–78.

4. For an interesting discussion of Fung's recent views, see Jan Yün-hua, "Problems of Tao and Tao Te Ching," *Numen* 22 (1975): 208–234. Chang Chung-yuan's views are found in his *Tao: A New Way of Thinking* (New York: Harper Colophon Book, 1975), pp. vii–xxviii.

5. Chang, ibid., p. ix. For additional comments from a Heideggerian perspective, see Charles Wei-hsun Fu's "Creative Hermeneutics: Taoist Metaphysics and Heidegger," *Journal of Chinese Philosophy* 3 (1976): 115–143.

6. E. M. Chen, "The Meaning of *te* in the *Tao Te Ching:* An Examination of the Concept of Nature in Chinese Taoism," *Philosophy East and West* 23 (1973): 463.

7. Ibid.

8. Charles Wei-hsun Fu, "Lao-Tzu's Conception of Tao," *Inquiry* 16 (1973): 377. See also Gelbert Beky's discussion in *Die Welt des Tao* (Freiburg/München: Verlag Karl Alber, 1972), p. 133.

9. See, for example, Nai-Tung Ting's discussion of "organic" imagery in his "Lao Tzu: Semanticist and Poet," *Literature: East and West* 14 (1970): 212–244; and also, Needham's discussion of the "organismic" nature of Taoist thought, *SCC*, 2:33–86.

10. Tom Stoppard, *Jumpers* (New York: Grove Press, 1972), p. 27. As Lévi-Strauss and Eliade have shown throughout their many works, the unique logic of mythic thought collapses the ordinary distinction between synchronic and diachronic, *sub specie aeternitatis* and *sub specie temporis.*

11. *LTCK*, pp. 166–170; and Chan, pp. 144–145. I have basically followed Chan's translations except where it has been necessary to alter them in view of my interpretations. For the last three verses of this passage I am following E. M. Chen's translation as found in her "Origin and Development of Being from Non-Being in The *Tao Te Ching,*" *International Philosophical Quarterly* 13 (1973): 404–405.

12. *CCT*, 16/6/29–30; and Watson, p. 81. For my translations, I have followed Burton Watson's excellent renderings except for modifications relative to my analysis.

13. D. Munro, *Concept of Man in Early China* (Stanford: Stanford University Press, 1967), p. 120, feels that in the *Tao Te Ching* the cosmogonic idea of the Tao as a "mother" or "ancestor" who gives "birth" (*sheng*) to the world is replaced in the *Chuang Tzu* with the more philosophical idea of the Tao acting as the principle behind the endless changing of things. See also below, chapter 3.

14. Quoted by Forke, *The World Conception of the Chinese* (reprint ed., New York: Arno Press, 1975), p. 109, n. q.

15. C. de Harlez, *Textes taoistes* (Paris: Annales du Musée Guimet, 1891), p. 21.

16. Ibid., and also Lin on Wang Pi's commentary, pp. 45–47.

17. E. Erkes, "Spüren einer kosmogonischen Mythe bei Lao-Tse," *Artibus Asiae* 8

(1940): 16–35; and also Needham, *SCC*, 2:78.

18. *LTCK*, p. 166.

19. See *LTCK*, pp. 133, 306–308. On the connection with *wu-chih* see also Lo, "Primeval State," pp. 20 ff.

20. See, for example, E. M. Chen, "Nothingness and the Mother Principle in Early Chinese Taoism," *International Philosophical Quarterly* 9 (1969): 391–405. Chapter 52 explicitly refers to the idea of the Mother in a cosmogonic context and then goes on to apply this understanding to the methods of returning to the Tao used by the individual Taoist. The Taoist "blocks the passages and shuts the doors" and reduplicates the cosmic processes established at the beginning. Man is instructed to "return and hold to the Mother," which is a way of "returning to the light." This is called *hsi-ch'ang*. It is significant that *hsi*[a] may also be read as *hsi*[b]. Chapter 27 uses the technical expression of *hsi-ming*, "following" or "unifying" the light—see *LTCK*, p. 184. These terms are connected with the idea of primordial unity. For example, the *Huai Nan Tzu* says that "the unification [*hsi*[b]] of the essence of heaven and earth gave rise to *yin* and *yang*," which links the idea of *hsi*[b] to a cosmogonic context of meaning— see *LTCK*, p. 325. Chapter 59 also relates the idea of the Mother to specific techniques of returning to the Tao.

21. Erkes on rather meager comparative grounds was the first Western commentator to suggest these parallels—see "Spüren," pp. 16–35. As will be discussed below in chapter 3, the *Shan Hai Ching* identifies Hun-tun as a faceless "divine bird" who is really the god Chiang (Ti Chiang). Erkes feels that Ti Chiang is related to Ti Hung. See Erkes, "Spüren," p. 30. On the mythological connection between Ti Chiang (Ti Hung) and Hun-tun, see Karlgren, "Legends and Cults," pp. 247, 253. See also n. 63.

22. *LTCK*, pp. 2–31; and Chan, pp. 97–100. On the problems of the punctuation and translation of these lines, see J. J. L. Duyvendak, *Tao Te Ching, The Book of Way and Its Virtue* (London: John Murray, 1954), p. 21; and Chan, pp. 97–100. They could also be read as "non-being is named the origin of heaven and earth. Being is named the mother of the Ten Thousand Things."

23. See Chan's discussion of this, pp. 97–98; and especially Chen's comments, "Origin and Development of Being from Non-Being," p. 411.

24. *LTCK*, p. 10; and Chan, p. 97. Cf. chap. 2: "Being and non-being produce (*sheng*[a]) each other," *LTCK*, p. 12 and Chan, p. 101.

25. See M. Eliade, "Le symbolisme des ténèbres dans les religions archaïques," in *Polarité du Symbole Études Carmélitaines* (St. Augustine: Desclée de Brouwer, 1960), pp. 15–28.

26. *LTCK*, pp. 38–40; and Chan, pp. 110–111. For the range of meanings associated with *hsüan*, see Peter A. Boodberg, "Philological Notes on Chapter One of the Lao Tzu, "*Harvard Journal of Asiatic Studies* 20 (1957): 600 f.; and Chen's discussion in "Origin and Development of Being from Non-Being," pp. 407–408. On "Lao Tzu's goddess" see Edward Schafer, *The Divine Woman* (San Francisco: North Point Press, 1980), pp. 41–43.

27. *CCT*, 30/12/39–40; and Watson, p. 132. This verse ("Cheeping and Chirping"), which is suggestive of the sounds of a hatching egg, is reminiscent of Ho-shang kung's commentary on chapter 1 of the Tao: The "eternal name" of the Tao is "like a chicken that has not yet broken through (the eggshell)"—see E. Erkes, *Ho-Shang-*

Kung's Commentary on the Lao-tse (Ascona: Artibus Asiae, 1958), p. 13.

28. *CCT*, 30/12/37–38; and Watson, p. 131.

29. *CCT*, 30/12/40–41; and Watson, p. 132 (reading *hun-hun*[b] for *ming-ming*). For the expression of *ta-shun* see also the *Tao Te Ching*, chap. 65.

30. *LTCK*, pp. 85–87; and Chan, pp. 126–127. For further discussion of chapter 15, see below.

31. *LTCK*, pp. 345–346; and Chan, pp. 199–200.

32. See below, chapter 3.

33. Ch'en Meng-chia, *Lao Tzu Fen Shih* (Chungking: n.p., 1945), p. 6. See *LTCK*, p. 346 and Chan, p. 200.

34. See below, chapter 4 (*CCT*, 24/10/27; and Watson, pp. 111–112).

35. *HNTCS*, pp. 153 (chap. 10), 235 (chap. 14). In chapter 6 of the *Huai Nan Tzu* there is a similar passage and Kau Yu (ca. 168–212) comments that the "one" is to be identified with *hun-t'ung*. Chapter 6 concludes with a characteristic golden age passage that is called the time of *ta-t'ung hun ming*[b]—see *HNTCS*, pp. 97–98; and below, chapter 5.

36. The Chinese text is found in *Wen Wu* 10 (1974): 42. For a translation and discussion of this text, see Jan Yün-hua, "The Silk Manuscripts on Taoism," *T'oung Pao* 63 (1978): 65–84. With some emendation, I have followed Jan's translation.

37. See especially Chen's discussion of the four stages of the Tao's going out and return—"Origin and Development of Being from Non-Being," pp. 404–416. The "Huan Tao" (the round Tao) chapter of the *Lü Shih Ch'un Ch'iu* is pertinent to this discussion—see Jan Yün-hua, "Problems of Tao," p. 221.

38. *Lü Shih Ch'un Ch'iu*, chap. 5. Paraphrase and Chinese text given by Forke, *World Conception*, p. 36.

39. *LTCK*, p. 265; and Chan, p. 173. In chapter 16 the term *fu-kuei* is used and chapter 28 uses the expression *fu-kuei yü p'u* (returning to the uncarved block). In the *Chuang Tzu* a constant refrain is *fu ch'i ch'u* or "return to the beginning."

40. *LTCK*, p. 173; and Chan, p. 144 (Chan translates: "And Tao models itself after Nature").

41. For a discussion of some of the problems associated with the important technical term of *tzu-jan* see "Rapporteur's Notes on the Bellagio Conference," Xerox copy (American Council of Learned Societies, 1968), pp. 27 ff. Also see A. Link, "Taoist Antecedents of Tao-an's Prajna Ontology," *History of Religions*, 9 (1969–1970): 196–197, 215.

42. *LTCK*, pp. 278–280 (including relevant Chinese commentaries); and Chan, pp. 176–177.

43. In the *Tao Te Ching* the terms *hun* and *tun* are used six times (see chaps. 14, 15, 20, 25, and 49).

44. Max Kaltenmark, "La naissance du monde en Chine," in *La Naissance du monde* (Paris: Éditions du seuil, 1959), p. 464; see also Erkes, "Spüren," pp. 16–35; and Needham, *SCC*, 2:78.

45. For a discussion of Tao in relation to the idea of "one" see Chen, "Origin and Development of Being from Non-Being," pp. 409–410; and Robinet, *Commentaires*, passim. See also *LTCK*, p. 252, where Chiang Hsi-ch'ang specifically identifies the "one" of chapter 39 with the cosmogonic idea of the Tao and one found in chapter 42.

46. *HNTCS*, p. 99 (line 13b); and below.

47. See *LTCK*, pp. 278-280 and Erkes's discussion of relevant commentary, "*Spüren*," pp. 16-28.

48. Chan, p. 176.

49. Erkes, "Spüren," p. 28; and below, chap. 9.

50. *LTCK*, p. 279. See also Fu's discussion, "Lao Tzu's Conception of Tao," pp. 376-379; and W. T. Chan, "Chu Hsi's Appraisal of Lao Tzu," *Philosophy East and West* 25 (1975): 132-141.

51. *LTCK*, pp. 76-78; and Chan, pp. 124-125. See below.

52. *LTCK*, p. 78; and Lo, "Primeval State," pp. 20 ff.

53. *LTCK*, p. 277; and Chan, p. 174.

54. For a discussion of some of the significance of these terms see M. Kaltenmark, "Ling-Pao: Note sur un term du Taoisme religieux," *Mélanges publiés par l'institute des hautes études chinoises* (Paris: University of France, 1960), pp. 581-582, 585-586.

55. Fung originally identified the one with *Chuang Tzu's ta-t'ung*[a,b], the two with heaven and earth, and the three with *yin* and *yang* and their harmonious interaction (*History* 1:178-179—originally written in the 1930s); but more recently he has put forth a more Marxian "dialectical" interpretation. See also Fu's discussion, "Lao Tzu's Conception of Tao," p. 376.

56. Within the context of imperial ideology Tung Chung-shu writes in his *Ch'un Ch'iu Fan Lu*: "Those who in ancient times invented writing drew three lines and connected them through the middle, calling the character 'king' [*wang*]. The three lines are heaven, earth, and man, and that which passes through the middle joins the principles of all three. Occupying the center of heaven, earth, and man, passing through and joining all three—if he is not a king, who can do this?"—Quoted from W. T. de Bary, ed., *Sources of Chinese Tradition* (New York: Columbia University Press, 1960), vol. 1, p. 163. See also H. Wilhelm, "The Interaction of Heaven, Earth, and Man," in *Heaven, Earth and Man in the Book of Changes* (Seattle: University of Washington Press, 1977), pp. 126-163.

57. See, for example, Munro, *Concept of Man*, pp. 121 ff. By the time of the *Huai Nan Tzu*, however, the idea of "man" for "three" is a factor in the Taoist interpretation—see below.

58. See Jan Yün-hua's discussion in his "Problems of Tao," pp. 213-216. On the general concept of *ch'i*[a] see M. Yosida, "The Chinese Concept of Nature," in *Chinese Science*, ed. Shigeru Nakayama and Nathan Sivin (Cambridge: Massachusetts Institute of Technology Press, 1973), pp. 71-89.

59. See the *Tz'u Hai* on these terms, pp. 1741-1742, 1756-1757; and below, chapter 8.

60. The etymology of the Greek term for "chaos" is related to the idea of a "yawning gulf or gap," a "hollow," or "space." See above, "Introduction."

61. On the Taoist idea of the "original" or primordial *ch'i*[a], the *yüan-ch'i*, see H. Maspero, "Les Procedes de 'nourir de principe vital' dans la religion taoiste ancienne," *Journal Asiatique* 228 (1937): 206 ff. Maspero states that in later Taoism "this interior breath, personal to each man, is the Original Breath (*yüan-ch'i*). In man this Original Breath corresponds to the primordial breaths which before the creation formed the Heaven and Earth" (pp. 206-207).

62. *HNTCS*, pp. 99-100; and see below, chapter 5.

63. Mythologically, Hung-meng is related to Ti Hung (or Ti Chiang) who was said to be the father of Hun-tun (see the *Tso Chuan* in Legge, *Chinese Classics* 5: 279–283). The terms *hung*[b,c,d] mean "flood waters," "cinnabar" (the metallurgical theme is frequently a factor with all of these terms) or, as in the compound *tung-hung*, suggest the idea of "communication"—see F. S. Couvreur, *Dictionnaire classique* (reprint ed., Taipei: Kuangchi Press, 1966), p. 537.

64. See below, chapter 3.

65. As Kaltenmark suggests, this may be a reference to a cosmogony involving a primordial couple—see "Naissance du monde," p. 466. Cf. *Tao Te Ching*, chapter 14; and see below.

66. Duyvendak, p. 99.

67. Chen, "Development of Being from Non-Being," p. 409, n. 12.

68. See the following: Granet, *DL*, pp. 537–548 (sack, drum, owl, and bellows symbolism associated with *hun-tun*); Stein, "Jardins en miniature," pp. 42–80 (calabash gourd); Eberhard, *LC*, pp. 438–446 (egg, sack, thunder); and Lo, "Primeval State," pp. 287 ff. (gourd and cocoon). See also David Yu, "Creation Myth and Symbolism in Classical Taoism," pp. 492–495 (discussion of Lo's views).

69. Erkes, "Spüren," p. 35.

70. See below, chapter 6; and Long, *Alpha: The Myths of Creation* (New York: George Braziller, 1963), pp. 109 ff.

71. On the possible, although improbable, Indian influence on the terms *i-hsi-wei* see Walter Liebenthal, "Lord Atman in the *Lao Tzu*," *Monumenta Serica* 27 (1968): 375. At one point in early Western scholarship it was even felt that these terms were a coded reference to Jehovah (i.e., *i-hsi-wei*=*Jud-hev-vav*). See, for example, Paul Carus, trans., *The Canon of Reason and Virtue* (1913; reprint ed, Chicago: Open Court, 1945).

72. *LTCK*, p. 76; and Chan, pp. 124–125.

73. *Hu*[b] is related to the following terms: *Hu*[c] meaning "round or whole" and *hu*[d,e] suggesting the idea of "obscurity" or "blurred vision." Word-family associations with the mythically relevant calabash gourd (*hu*[f,g,h]) are also noteworthy here. In a similiar way, the "huang" family of words is significant. Thus, *huang*[a] can mean "wild or mad" (*huang-k'uang* meaning "delirious" or "raving") and *huang*[b] means a "watery waste," a "wild uncultivated land." *Huang-hu* suggests "obscurity, confusion, and blurred vision."

74. See K. Schipper, "The Taoist Body," *History of Religions* 18 (1978): 361.

75. *LTCK*, pp. 142–146; and Chan, pp. 137–138. See also *LTCK* for the numerous variant readings of these lines.

76. On *miao-ming* (or *yao-ming*) and its relation to *hun-tun*, see below, chap. 4. *Ming*[a] can mean "dark, obscure, deep, profound, stupid, confused." It is also related to *ming*[b] ("vast, boundless, deep") and *ming*[c] ("blinded, to close the eyes").

77. On the significance of thunder and lightning in ancient China see Eberhard, *LC*, pp. 439 ff; and Granet, *DL*, pp. 520 ff.

78. *LTCK*, pp. 33–37; and Chan, pp. 105–106.

79. See Izutsu, *Key Concepts*, 2: 129. *Ch'ung*[a] may also be read as *chung* meaning "vessel or bowl"—see *LTCK*, p. 27.

80. See *LTCK*, pp. 33–37; and Lin on Wang Pi's commentary, p. 9.

81. Waley, *Way and Its Power*, p. 146.

82. Duyvendak, p. 27.

83. Chiang in *LTCK* (p. 33) specifically links the identity of ti^a to the cosmogonic passages in chapters 25 and 42.

84. *LTCK*, p. 30.

85. See Duyvendak's reference, p. 27.

86. "Bond"—*chi*. As Chan points out (p. 125, n. 5), chi^a literally means "a thread" but "denotes tradition, discipline, principle, order, essence, etc. Generally it means the system, principle, or continuity that binds things together." It could be that there is also a less abstract and more mythically symbolic meaning of the "cosmic web" as seen in other traditions. See Mircea Eliade's "Ropes and Puppets" found in *Mephistopheles and the Androgyne: Studies in Religious Myth and Symbol* (New York: Sheed and Ward, 1965), pp. 160–188; and his study "The 'God who binds' and the Symbolism of Knots" in *Images and Symbols* (New York: Harper Torch, 1958), pp. 92–124.

87. *LTCK*, pp. 148–419; and Chan, p. 137.

88. See Creel, *What is Taoism*, pp. 3–5.

89. See Munro, *Concept of Man*, passim.

90. Bauer, *Search for Happiness*, pp. 69–204.

91. *LTCK*, pp. 459–465; and Chan, pp. 238–239.

92. Needham, *SCC*, 2:100 ff.

93. See below, chapters 4 and 5.

94. See Bodde's discussion, "Myths," pp. 389–394.

95. See below, chapters 3 and 4. For a fascinating anthropological discussion of the Rousseauian contrast between the "primitive" and "civilizational" modes of culture, see Stanley Diamond, "The Search for the Primitive," in his *In Search of the Primitive* (New Brunswick, New Jersey: Transaction Books, 1974), pp. 116–175. See also below, chapter 7.

96. *LTCK*, pp. 114–117; and Chan, p. 131. On the contradictions concerning $tz'u$ in the *Tao Te Ching* (cf. chaps. 19 and 67), see Chan, pp. 219–220, n. 3.

97. *LTCK*, pp. 305–308; and Chan, pp. 186–187. Te^b (to get, attain) is interchangeable with te^a (virtue).

98. *LTCK*, pp. 306–308. Chiang specifically connects this passage with the *hun-tun* passage of chapter 20—particularly significant is the relation between *hsi-hsi*, *tun-tun*, and the idea of the Taoist sage achieving the condition of *wu-chih* or *hun-tun* (*LTCK*, p. 308).

99. *LTCK*, pp. 355–356; and Chan, pp. 203–204. In *LTCK* see also the variant readings for *ch'un-ch'un*.

100. *LTCK*, pp. 85–87; and Chan, pp. 126–127. See especially Chan's notes to this chapter, p. 127; and the variant readings given in *LTCK*.

101. *LTCK*, pp. 88–92; and Chan, pp. 126–127.

102. *Tun* ($t'un^{a,b,c,d}$) is related to a word family having meanings very similar to *hun*: honest, sincere, to conceal, to store, dull-witted, confused, chaotic, etc. $K'uang^a$ is related to $k'uang^b$ meaning "wild, mad."

103. Chan, p. 127, n. 4.

104. Maspero, *Le Taoisme* (reprint ed. Paris: University of France, 1967), pp. 227–242.

105. See below, chapter 4 (*CCT*, 20–21/7/28–29; and Watson, pp. 96–97). See

also the *Lieh Tzu*, chap. 2, where the same story is presented.

106. *LTCK*, pp. 122–141; and Chan, pp. 134–136. Variant readings and various textual problems should be noted in *LTCK* and Chan. Chiang notes that all of the special terms given here indicate the special condition of the Taoist's "no-knowledge" (*wu-chih*)—*LTCK*, p. 133.

107. See *LTCK*, p. 129.

108. Quoted in *LTCK*, p. 133.

3. Bored to Death: The "Arts of Mr. Hun-Tun" in the Chuang Tzu

1. This traditional division is based on Kuo Hsiang's (third century A.D.) edition of the text. See Watson, pp. 13–18.

2. See Watson, pp. 13–15.

3. A. C. Graham, "Notes on the Composition of Chuang-tzu," unpublished paper given at the Workshop on Classical Chinese Thought, Harvard University, August, 1976. A revised version of this article was published as "How Much of *Chuang Tzu* Did Chuang Tzu Write?" *Journal of the American Academy of Religion Thematic Issue*, ed. Henry Rosemont, Jr. and Benjamin I. Schwartz, 47 (1979): 459–502.

4. *CCT*, 5/2/53–55; and Watson, p. 43.

5. Graham, "Notes," p. 36.

6. See Chan's discussion of this point in relation to Neo-Confucianism, "Chu Hsi and Lao Tzu," pp. 132–135.

7. Munro, p. 120

8. *CCT*, 7/2/94–96; and Watson, p. 49.

9. See Needham, *SCC*, 2:78–83. As Needham points out, there is always a strong biological undercurrent in the idea of "transformation." See also Lo's discussion of transformation and cocoon symbolism, pp. 289–299.

10. See Schipper, "Taoist Body," pp. 361–374; and Seidel, *Divinisation*, pp. 58 ff.

11. See above, chapter 2.

12. See, for example, Creel's distinction between "purposive" and "contemplative" Taoism, *What is Taoism*, pp. 1–27; Munro's excellent discussion, pp. 118–121; and John Major, "The Efficacy of Uselessness: A Chuang Tzu Motif," *Philosophy East and West* 25 (1975): 275.

13. Waley, for example, says that this story is "no doubt an adaptation of a very ancient myth"—see *Three Ways of Thought*, p. 67. See also Chang's discussion of this story in relation to Chinese creation mythology in his "Chinese Creation Myths," pp. 55 ff., 61 ff; and Lo, "Primeval State," pp. 20 ff.

14. *CCT*, 21/7/33–35; and Watson, p. 92.

15. Needham, *SCC*, 2: 107–115.

16. Ibid., 2:112.

17. Ibid., 2:107, 112. There would seem to be a technical relation between the terms *fen*, *san*, and *tso* (also related are the terms *p'ou* and *p'an*) in Taoism that is linked to the cosmogonic idea of the rupture of the primordial deity.

18. See Waley, *Three Ways of Thought*, pp. 66–70.

19. Needham, *SCC*, 2:113.

20. Izutsu, *Key Concepts*, 2:18–19.

21. Ibid., 2:19.

22. See, for example, Eberhard, *LC*, pp. 75–79, 308–309; M. Eliade, *Shamanism: Archaic Techniques of Ecstacy* (New York: Pantheon Books, 1964), pp. 447–461; P. J. Thiel, "Shamanismus im alten China," *Sinologica* 10 (1968–1969): 149–204; and Needham, *SCC*, 2:132 ff.

23. Hawkes, *Ch'u Tz'u*, p. 81.

24. Ibid., pp. 86–87. The connection between space and time has been noted by J. Shih, "The Ancient Chinese Cosmogony," *Studia Missionalia* 18 (1969): 118–119; and Bauer, pp. 89 ff.

25. See especially Eberhard, *LC*, pp. 75–79, 308–309.

26. Izutsu, *Key Concepts*, 2:21.

27. Eliade, *Shamanism*, p. 460.

28. See, for example, Eliade, *Rites and Symbols*, pp. 1–40.

29. See below, chapters 6 and 7.

30. Granet, *Pensée*, pp. 320–321.

31. Ibid., p. 321.

32. See, for example, B. Malinowski's discussion of primitive burial rites in his *Magic, Science, and Religion* (Garden City, New York: Doubleday Anchor Books, 1954), pp. 149–215. See the discussion in the *Po Hu Tung*, trans. Tjan Tjoe Som, pp. 642–643.

33. *Hun-tun* symbolism in Taoism is generally congruent with the idea of death—a closed, bottled up, contained, or "returned" (*kuei*[b]) condition.

34. See Creel, *What is Taoism*, pp. 1–24.

35. See, for example, Graham, *Lieh Tzu*, pp. 46, 54.

36. *CCT*, 74–75/21/37–40; and Watson, pp. 300–301.

37. Granet, *DL*, p. 544.

38. Some diluted remnants of puberty initiation can, for example, be seen in the ancient Chinese "cap ceremony" wherein a boy at the age of twenty (or variously at the age of eighteen, sixteen, or twelve) was accepted into the community of adults. Generally the significance of the ceremony was in terms of the right to marriage and the ability to carry on the ancestral line—see Eberhard, *LC*, pp. 72–73.

39. For the classic discussion of initiation see Arnold van Gennep, *The Rites of Passage*, trans. Monika B. Vizedom and Gabrielle L. Caffee (Chicago: University of Chicago Press, 1960). See also V. Turner's more recent discussion in *The Ritual Process* pp. 94–130, 131–165.

40. See Eliade, *Rites and Symbols*, pp. 2–3, 61 ff, 81 ff, and G. Weckman, "Understanding Initiation," *History of Religions* 10 (1970): 62 ff.

41. E. M. Mendelson, "Initiation and the Paradox of Power: A Sociological Approach," in *Initiation*, ed. C. J. Bleeker (Leiden: E. J. Brill, 1965), p. 215. For Granet working within the French sociological tradition, the emphasis is always on the primacy of social reciprocity as a way of understanding Chinese religion.

42. Mendelson, "Initiation," p. 215.

43. See Granet, *DL*, p. 543, n. 2.

44. Ibid., pp. 515 ff.

45. Ibid., pp. 534 ff., 543–547.

46. Ibid., p. 544.

47. Waley, *Three Ways of Thought*, p. 67. Waley recounts the following myth: "In the beginning Anjir was lying in the shadow of a thickly-leaved tree. He was a black-fellow with very large buttocks, but peculiar in that there was no sign of any orifice. Yalpan happened to be passing by at the time and noticing this anomaly made a cut in the usual place by means of a piece of quartz-crystal." This is an obvious instance of the "people without anuses" type of legend that is discussed below, chapters 6 and 7.

48. Ibid., p. 68.

49. Ibid., pp. 66–67.

50. Izutsu, *Key Concepts*, 2:20.

51. For a discussion of the presence of totemism in ancient China see Huang Wen-shan, "The Origins of Chinese Culture. A Study of Totemism," *Sixth International Congress of Anthropological and Ethnological Sciences* (Paris: Musée de l'homme, 1962–1964), vol. 2, pp. 139–143; and Hwei-lin Wei, "Categories of Totemism in Ancient China," in *Folk Religion and the Worldview in the Southwestern Pacific*, ed. N. Matsumoto and T. Mabuchi (Tokyo: Keio Institute of Cultural and Linguistic Studies, 1968), pp. 73–83. On potlatch see Nobuhiro Matsumoto, "Religious Thoughts of the Bronze Age Peoples of Indochina," in *Folk Religion*, pp. 145 ff.

52. See Eliade, *Rites and Symbols*, pp. ix-xv.

53. Turner, "Myth," p. 526.

54. See Turner, *Ritual Process*, passim; and his "Betwixt and Between: The Liminal Period in *Rites de Passage*," in *Reader in Comparative Religion*, 3d ed., ed. William A. Lessa and Evon Z. Vogt (New York: Harper and Row, 1972), pp. 338–347.

55. Granet, *DL*, pp. 544–545, n. 5. On arrow symbolism in relation to the idea of a thunder god see Mircea Eliade, "Notes on the Symbolism of the Arrow," in *Religions in Antiquity*, ed. J. Neusner (Leiden: E. J. Brill, 1968), pp. 463 ff.

56. Quoting the *Ta Tai Li Chi* (second century B.C.?), see Needham, *SCC*, 2:269.

57. See Eberhard, *LC*, pp. 438–445; and below, chapter 6.

58. See Stein, "Jardins en miniature," pp. 50–54. See also M. Soymié on the "paradise form" of the sacred mountain in China—"Le Lo-feou Chan, étude de géographie réligieuse," *Bulletin de l'école francaise d'extrême-orient* 48 (1956): 68 ff.

59. See M. W. de Visser, *The Dragon in China and Japan* (reprint ed., Wiesbaden: Martin Sandig, 1969).

60. See Fontenrose, *Python*, pp. 491–499.

61. See Eberhard, *LC*, p. 70; and below, chapter 5.

62. See Granet, *DL*, p. 544, n. 5.

63. Hawkes, *Ch'u Tz'u*, p. 49.

64. Granet, *DL* pp. 540 ff. On the mythic significance of the game motif in other cultures see J. G. van Hamel, "The Game of the Gods," *Arkiv for Nordisk Fillologi* 50 (1934): 218-242. For the theme of the "sacred game" in China see Yang Lien-sheng, "A Note on the So-called TLV Mirrors and The Game of Liu-po," *Excursions in Sinology*, Harvard-Yenching Institute Studies No. 24 (Cambridge: Harvard University Press, 1969), pp. 138–165.

65. See Granet, *DL*, pp. 544–545, n. 5.

66. Hawkes, *Ch'u Tz'u*, pp. 86–87. See Maspero, "Légendes mythologiques," pp. 36–37, for the cosmological relation between *lieh-ch'üeh* and *ta-ho* (great abyss). *Ta-ho*

is related to the term *kuei-hsü* seen in the *Huai Nan Tzu*.

67. See Stein, "Jardins en miniature," pp. 58 ff.; and on the significance of *t'o*[a], Granet, *DL*, pp. 516 ff.

68. *LTCK*, pp. 34–36; and Chan p. 107.

69. *CCT*, 45/17/77; and Watson, p. 187. On the archaic significance of the "Yellow Springs" as the land of the dead see Granet, *Études sociologiques sur la Chine* (Paris: University of France, 1953), 216 ff.

70. *CCT*, 61/23/1; and Watson 248–254. The reference to *wei-lu* is found in chapter 17 of the *Chuang Tzu* (*CCT*, 42/17/8; and Watson, p. 176) and appears to be related to the mythological reference to the *kuei-hsü* whirlpool spoken of in the *Lieh Tzu* (chap. 5). *Kuei-hsü* has the vernacular meaning of "going to the grave—to die," and *hsü* (*hsü*[b]) generally means a "burial ground, wild waste, fair or market." There would appear to be an important relation here to the archaic significance of seasonal fertility rites held at the market place outside the city and the religious significance of the terms *hsü*[a], *hsü*[b], and *ch'iu*—see Eberhard, *LC*, pp. 224–227.

71. See Bauer's discussion, *Search for Happiness*, pp. 89–128; 177–202.

72. On the concept of *pao*[a] see Yang Lien-sheng, "The Concept of 'Pao' as a Basis for Social Relations in China," in *Chinese Thought and Institutions*, ed. John K. Fairbank (Chicago: University of Chicago Press, 1957), pp. 291–309. For a general anthropological discussion of "reciprocity" see Lévi-Strauss, *Elementary Structures of Kinship*, pp. 52–68, 311–324 (Chinese system based on Granet).

73. Kaltenmark, *Lao Tzu*, p. 101.

74. Maspero, "Légendes mythologiques," pp. 59 ff.

75. See below, chapters 6 and 7.

76. Anonymous, "Tauism," *The China Review* 1 (1873): 215.

77. *LTCK*, pp. 63–64; and Chan, p. 119. The term for "drilling," *tso*, seems to act as an important Taoist technical expression for the destructive acts of the sage kings who established class distinctions and the hierarchical "order" of civilization. See, for example, its use in the *Chuang Tzu*, chapters 23 and 26. In chapter 23 *tso* is particularly connected with the idea of the "great confusion" (*ta-luan*) caused by Yao and Shun. *Tso* is also a term that is used extensively throughout the *Huai Nan Tzu* as one of the "civilized" activities that brought an end to the golden age.

78. See Eliade, *Rites and Symbols*, pp. 21–40. It is most probable that the detail of "boring" (*tso*) alludes to primitive practices of filing or knocking out the front incisors (cf. *tso-ch'ih*). A mythological context is suggested by the *Huai Nan Tzu*'s reference to an evil monster or tribe known as Tso-ch'ih—see Eberhard, *LC*, p. 82. Erkes suggests the ritual idea of "whipping" or "beating"—"Spüren einer kosmogonischen Mythe," pp. 32–33, n. 2. Erkes would connect this motif with the ideas of beating (*chi*[d]), pregnancy (*t'ai*), and beginning (*shih*[d])—all of which relate to primitive ideas of fertility magic and appear to be mythically linked to the idea of *hun-tun* as an egg or sack. The *Lun Heng* significantly states that "some narrate of the emperor Ti Yi, the father of Chou, that he was in the habit of shooting at Heaven, and flogging the Earth. On an excursion between the Ching and the Wei (two rivers), he was struck by lightning and killed. Thus Heaven destroys depraved characters by a thunderbolt."—see Forke, *Lun Heng*, 2:29. See also A. Jensen's discussion of ritual scourgings as having their origin in mythic sources among primitive peoples—i.e., he sees a symbolic parallel between ritual

scourging and the myth of the killing of a primordial deity. See his *Myth and Cult Among Primitive Peoples*, pp. 249–252, 254.

79. In the *Chuang Tzu* see chapters 19, 20, 23, and 27. On the religious significance of seven in later Taoist tradition see K. Schipper, *L'emperour Wou des Han dans la légende taoiste. Han Wou-ti Nei-tchouan* (Paris: École francaise d'extrême-orient, 1965), pp. 51 ff. See also J. Ware, "The *Wei Shu* and the *Sui Shu* on Taoism," *Journal of the American Oriental Society* 53 (1933): 226, 227, 228, 242, 245. Despite the fact that by the time of the *Chuang Tzu* seven and nine are frequently equated, there would still seem to be a certain preference given to the "order" of seven. In this sense, it may be significant that in the early Chou period the system of nine was apparently connected with the establishment of the feudal order (see Granet, *DL*, pp. 236 ff.) and the banishment of *hun-tun* and the other "rebel monsters" (representing an earlier socio-religious order of seven?). For comparative aspects of the sacredness of seven see Heiler, *Erscheinungs-formen und Wesen der Religion* (Stuttgart: Kohlhammer, 1961): 161 ff.

80. On the significance of seven and nine see Granet, *Pensée*, pp. 234 ff. On Chinese numerology and the sacredness and "perfection" of certain numbers (especially five and the *yin-yang-wu-hsing* system) see S. Cammann, "The Magic Square of Three in Old Chinese Philosophy and Religion," *History of Religions* 1 (1960): 37 ff. It should also be noted that the *hun-tun* cosmogonic passage in the *Lieh Tzu* (chap. 1, where the particular term is the homophonic variant *hun-lun*) is related to a number system of seven and nine, which are equated with the "reversion" to unity. See below, chapter 5.

81. Granet, *Études sociologiques*, p. 212. On the relation between the numbers three, seven and ten see p. 212, n. 1.

82. See Richard Wilhelm, trans., rendered into English by Cary F. Baynes, *The I Ching or Book of Changes* (Princeton: Princeton University Press, 1967).

83. See above, chapter 2.

84. See below, chapter 6.

85. This, of course, is an oversimplification for Confucianism as, for example, is seen in the cyclic historical schemes of Mencius and Tung Chung-shu. On Mencius's conception see below, chapter 4.

86. *CCT*, 58/22/20–24; and Watson, p. 237. Cf. *LTCK*, pp. 133–140.

87. See, for example, chapter 6 (*tso-wang*), chapter 4 (*ch'i-hsin*), and chapter 11 (*hsin-yang*) of the *Chuang Tzu*. For the term *hsin-ning* see the *Lieh Tzu*, chapters 2 and 4.

88. *CCT*, 21/12/52–69; and Watson, pp. 134–46.

89. My translation and interpretation of these verses differ considerably from Watson's—i.e., Watson distinguishes between the one who follows the arts of Mr. Hun-tun *and* the "person who understands returning to simplicity. . . . "

90. The reference to the "arts of Mr. Hun-tun" may help to clarify the context of meaning surrounding one of the most cryptic of all mythic allusions in the *Chuang Tzu*. That is, in chapter 26 (*CCT*, 74/26/36) there is a reference to the "fashion of Hsi Wei" (*hsi wei shih chih liu*) that Watson (p. 300, n. 11) believes to be a reference to the "advocates of ancient simplicity within the Taoist school." While in all of ancient Chinese literature there is only the additional reference in chapter 6 of the *Chuang Tzu* (*CCT*, 16/6/31) to Hsi Wei as a mythical deity who "got" (*te*[b]) the Tao and "held up heaven and earth" there are a number of clues that suggest basically the *hun-tun* theme. Thus, *hsi*[e] generally means "pig" and *wei*[b] means "leather hide or skin." As Granet has shown (*DL*, p. 543), *hun-tun* would also seem to refer to a leather sack or bag. Related to

this would seem to be the general Taoist idea of the "closure" of the sense openings and the numerous archaic religious associations with the scapegoat idea of the "putting on of the skin" of the god (a magical or ritual personification of the deity) and returning to the paradise time. *Hun-tun's* association with the Thunder God is also important here since the traditional idea of the Chinese thunder deity is a composite figure made up of a number of different ancient, local-cult, ancestral animal gods—especially the owl, dog, monkey, bat, and pig. On the archaic religious significance of the pig in the southern local cultures of China see Eberhard, *LC*, pp. 242−260, 253−254.

91. *CCT*, 37/14/13−30; and Watson, pp. 156−158.

92. Cf. *Tao Te Ching*, chapter 20—*LTCK*, p. 133. See also chapter 2 of the *Chuang Tzu—CCT*, 6/2/78; and Watson, p. 47.

93. *CCT*, 32/12/75−77; and Watson, pp. 136−137. This parable involves the chaos figure of Chun-mang and is basically similar to the *hun-tun* story of Hung-meng in chapter 11—see below.

94. *CCT*, 16−17/6/36−45; and Watson, pp. 82−83.

95. Chang Chung-yuan, "Purification and Taoism," in *Proceedings of the XIth International Congress of the International Association for the History of Religions*, vol. 2 (Leiden: E. J. Brill, 1968), p. 140.

96. Watson, p. 83, n. 16.

97. Ibid.

98. *CCT*, 2/1/30; and Watson, p. 33. For its use in the *Lieh Tzu* see below, chapter 5. For its use in later Taoist texts see W. C. Doub, *A Taoist Adept's Quest for Immortality: A Preliminary Study of the Chou-shih Ming-T'ung Chi by T'ao Hung-Ching* (A.D. 456−536), (Ph.D. diss., University of Washington, 1971), p. 34; and the *Hsien Hsüeh Tz'u Tien*, p. 39, 162.

99. *CCT*, 19/6/89−93; and Watson, p. 90. See below, this chapter.

100. *CCT*, 55/21/24−39; and Watson, pp. 224−226.

101. Since the usual order of *yin* and *yang* is reversed here, it is possible that there is a textual error—see Watson, p. 225, n. 8.

102. *CCT*, 29/12/18−20; and Watson, pp. 128−129.

103. *CCT*, 26−27/11/28−44; and Watson, pp. 118−120.

104. *CCT*, 26/11/15; and Watson, p. 116. Cf. chapter 14.

105. *CCT*, 30/12/37−41; and Watson, pp. 131−132.

106. Reading *hun*[b] ("chaotic") for *min*.

107. *CCT*, 16/6/29−35; and Watson, pp. 81−82.

108. See above, chapter 2.

109. *CCT*, 30/12/39−40; and Watson, p. 132.

110. *CCT*, 46/18/12−13; and Watson, p. 191.

111. See Karlgren, "Legends and Cults," pp. 314, 232.

112. *CCT*, 93/33/69; and Watson, p. 374.

113. *CCT*, 46/18/15−18; and Watson, p. 192.

114. It should be noted, however, that there are passages in the chapter that appear to be later interpolations—see Watson, p. 79, n. 6.

115. *CCT*, 15−16/6/1−29; and Watson, pp. 77−81.

116. On the mystic significance of "heel breathing" see Waley, *Way and its Power*, pp. 116−120.

117. The cosmogonic significance of the term *chi*[c] is brought out in chapter 25 of the

Tao Te Ching where it would seem to be related in meaning to *tu* and *liao*[a], which suggest the "still, silent, calm, empty" nature of the primordial Tao.

118. On the "great clod" see Creel, *What is Taoism*, pp. 25 ff. In the *Huai Nan Tzu*, the idea of Tao as shapeless clod or lump is directly related to the theme of *hun-tun*—see below, chapter 5. Based on philological principles, Lo feels that *k'uai* refers to *k'uei* or "pupa" (as well as *kuei*[a,b]: "ghost" or "return"), pp. 293–299.

119. *CCT*, 17–18/6/60–74; and Watson, pp. 86–87.

120. *CCT*, 19/6/89–93; and Watson pp. 90–91.

121. *CCT*, 18–19/6/82–89; and Watson, pp. 89–90.

122. Hsü Yu is a mythical figure that is identified with the golden age period in *Chuang Tzu*.

123. Later alchemical symbolism is important here, especially the symbolism of the *lu*[a] as a "paradise form" similar to the *hu-lu* gourd—see Stein, "Jardins en miniature," pp. 35 ff., 53, 58, n. 2.

124. This is a common cosmological expression seen throughout the *Chuang Tzu* and *Huai Nan Tzu*. It suggests an image close to the symbolism of the cosmic egg surrounding heaven and supporting earth seen in the Hun-t'ien[a] cosmology—see above, chapter 2.

125. *CCT*, 20/7/7–11; and Watson, pp. 93–94.

126. *CCT*, 20/7/2; and Watson, p. 92.

127. It can be said that Hu Tzu (Gourd Master) is a Mr. Hun-tun figure. On the symbolism of the *hu-lu* and the legends of the "old man of the gourd" see Stein, "Jardins en miniature," pp. 55 ff. Hu Tzu or Hu Kung is one who is able to periodically return to the paradise condition through the agency of his magic calabash. He is also mentioned in the *Lieh Tzu*, chapter 1. See the reference to the legends of "Little Monk Leathersack" (*P'i-pu-tai*) found in the erotic novel *Jou P'u T'uan*—see F. Kuhn, *Jou Pu Tuan* (New York: Grove Press, 1963), pp. 9, 322 ff., 370. It should be noted that *pu-tai* refers to a varicolored or calico sack—that which is symbolic of the motley dress of the fool.

128. See above, chapter 2; *CCT*, 20–21/7/15–31; and Watson, pp. 94–97.

129. *CCT*, 27–28/11/44–57; and Watson, pp. 120–122.

130. Watson is mistaken when he states that Hung-meng is only a literary "invention of the writer"—Watson, p. 120, n. 10. Cf. *Huai Nan Tzu*, chapter 6 for the cosmogonic term *hung-meng hung-tung*. Mythologically, Hung-meng is related to Ti Hung (or Ti Chiang) who was said to be the father of Hun-tun—see Karlgren, "Legends and Cults," p. 225.

131. Cf. also chapters 4 and 7 of the *Chuang Tzu* for the use of the term *k'uang*[b] to indicate the sacred condition attained by the Taoist. There are obvious shamanic overtones here that may be connected with the so-called "step of Yü"—see Granet, *DL*, pp. 549 ff. The *Tz'u Hai* (pp. 1756–1757) reports that *hun-t'o*[a] was an ancient dance music that involved the wearing of a felt hat. *Hun-t'o*[a] was said to be a Tartar expression and in the T'ang dynasty it became a sign of evil and misfortune. *Hun-t'o*[a] can also mean a kind of ferry boat made of sheep skin. All of these details are important within the mythic context of the *hun-tun* theme. Thus, *hun-tun* as a gourd, boat, or leather sack floats across the primordial waters and saves man from the flood—see M. Kaltenmark, *Le Lie-sien Tchouen, biographies légendaires des immortels taoistes de l'antiquite* (Peking: Centre d'études Sinologiques Franco-Chinois, 1953), p. 164. The shamanic element is also suggested by the term *t'o*[b], which suggests the idea of a ritual nakedness

associated with the dance—on this see E. Schafer, "Ritual Exposure in Ancient China," *Harvard Journal of Asiatic Studies* 14 (1951): 130–184. The context of meaning surrounding the term *k'uang*[b] is also discussed by Schafer, "Ritual Exposure," pp. 160–161.

132. *CCT*, 28/11/57–66; and Watson, pp. 123–124.

133. See H. Key, "Some Semantic Functions of Reduplication in Various Languages," *Anthropological Linguistics* 7 (March, 1965): 93; and Eliade, *Shamanism*, pp. 93 ff. The reduplicated and rhyming words (*tieh-tzu*) that are so characteristic of the *hun-tun* theme in the Taoist texts are an important linguistic factor that may attest to the archaic nature of these etymologies—see P. Boodberg, "Some Proleptical Remarks on the Evolution of Archaic Chinese," *Harvard Journal of Asiatic Studies* 2 (1937): 329–372; James J. Y. Liu, *The Art of Chinese Poetry* (Chicago: University of Chicago Press, 1962), pp. 34–36; and especially Lo, part 4.

134. See above in this chapter.

135. See Maspero, "Nourrir le principe vital," p. 223.

136. *CCT*, 93/33/62; and Watson, p. 373.

137. *CCT*, 13/5/12; and Watson, p. 69. The mystic significance of "closure" or "storing up" is suggested by the use of the term *ling-fu* in another place in Chapter 5 of the *Chuang Tzu*. (*CCT*, 14/5/45). On the religious meaning of *ling* in Taoism see Kaltenmark, "Note sur un terme du Taoisme," pp. 567 ff. See also *Tao Hsüeh Tz'u Tien* and *Hsien Hsüeh Tz'u Tien* on the terms *ling* and *fu*.

138. *CCT*, 6/2/77–78; and Watson, p. 47.

4. Chaotic "Order" and Benevolent "Disorder" in the Chuang Tzu

1. See Joseph Needham, *SCC*, 2:99, 115. *P'u*[a] literally means "sincere, simple, raw," but in the Taoist tradition it is an important philosophical term with a rich semantic resonance (such as, for example, A. Waley's felicitous translation of mystical import—"the uncarved block").

2. Ibid., 2:100.

3. Ibid., 2:107.

4. It is certainly the case that *p'u*[a] and *hun-tun* are related in context and meaning in the Taoist texts. Thus, they are generally synonymous; but the theme of *hun-tun* seems more clearly connected to a particular mythological legacy and, in this sense, might be said to be supportive of the theme of *p'u*[a].

5. An example of this usage is found in the opening lines of the *Hsi Yu Chi*, which states in the context of the cosmogonic myth: "Chaos [*hun-tun*] had not separated and the world was in a state of confusion [*luan*[a]]." See Wu Ch'eng-en, *Hsi Yu Chi* (Records of the Journey to the West), (Taipei: Li Ming, n.d.): 1.

6. See James Legge, *The Chinese Classics* (reprint ed., Hong Kong: Hong Kong University Press, 1960), 5 vol., 1:214. It should be noted that the *Lun Yü* is quoting the *Shu Ching*—see below.

7. As Watson notes, these men "appear to be mythical rulers of antiquity, some mentioned in other early texts, some appearing only here"—*Complete Works*, p. 112, n. 11.

8. *CCT*, 25/10/29–41; and Watson, pp. 111–113.

9. Graham identifies chapter 10 (along with chaps. 8, 9, and 11/1–28, 12/95–102, 11/57–63; and possibly chapter 16) as part of the "primitivist" document. Graham dates these writings around 205 B.C. (during the breakdown of the Ch'in dynasty) and agrees with Needham that "the Primitivist's concerns are exclusively social and political." In this way, the Primitivist document has affinities with the utopian philosophy found in the *Tao Te Ching*. See Graham, "Notes."

10. See above, chapter 2. The expression *hsüan-t'ung*[a] is found in *CCT*, 24/10/27; and Watson, p. 111.

11. *CCT*, 41/16/1–11; and Watson, pp. 171–173.

12. For a discussion of the concept of *hsing* see Munro, *Concept of Man*, pp. 136–138, 145–151.

13. It should be noted that there is a certain amount of confusion in the *Chuang Tzu* concerning the status of the Yellow Emperor. In some places he is a Taoist hero, whereas here and in other passages he is condemned along with Yao and Shun. For a discussion of some of the textual tradition associated with Huang Ti see Karlgren, "Legends and Cults," pp. 206–207, 212–227, 230–233, 242–247, 260–278, 283–285. On the contradictory nature of the Yellow Emperor see below, chapter 6.

14. Besides the three instances of the use of *ta-luan* in chapter 10, this expression is also found in chapters 11, 23, and 33 of the *Chuang Tzu* (*CCT*, 26/11/24, and Watson, p. 117; *CCT*, 61/23/15, and Watson, p. 250; *CCT*, 91/33/11, and Watson p. 364); and in every instance it is specifically linked to the mythological theme of paradise lost. Thus, the passage from chapter 23 recounting the parable of Keng-sang may be taken as generally characteristic of the context of meaning constantly associated with the use of *ta-luan*: "I tell you, the source of all the great confusion [*ta-luan*] will invariably be found to lie right there with Yao and Shun."

15. *CCT*, 26/11/19–28; and Watson, pp. 116–118.

16. See Karlgren, "Legends and Cults," p. 255 (connection of Ti Hung, Hun-tun and Huan-tou); and Eberhard, *LC*, 438–439.

17. See below. For a discussion of the different legendary strains associated with the idea of the "four" rebels see Karlgren, "Legends and Cults," pp. 247–255.

18. *HNTCS*, pp. 21–22, 26.

19. *CCT* 27–28/11/44–57; and Watson pp. 120–123.

20. *LTCK*, pp. 243–251; and Chan, p. 131. At times, the term *hun*[a] (chap. 18) is equated with *hun-tun*, but in no instance in the *Tao Te Ching* or the *Chuang Tzu* are the specific terms *luan*[a] and *hun-tun* used synonymously—even though this might be expected in terms of their "ordinary" usage.

21. The reference to the "Confucian" Classics is meant to include those works traditionally taken to be expressive of the general philosophical outlook of Confucianism. Certain of these works, especially sections of the *Shu* and *Shih*, were written before the time of Confucius or before there was any Confucian school of thought; but the particular philosophy of history developed, and in this instance the usage of *luan*[a] and *hun-tun*, do seem to be factors in why they were eventually taken over (and edited) as exemplary models for a later Confucian ideology. For a discussion of some of these general textual and dating problems see Burton Watson, *Early Chinese Literature* (New York: Columbia University Press, 1962); B. Karlgren, "The Authenticity of Ancient Chinese Texts," *Bulletin of the Museum of Far Eastern Antiquities* (1929): 165–183;

and W.A.C.H. Dobson, "Authenticating and Dating Archaic Chinese Texts," *T'oung Pao* 53 (1967): 233–242.

22. Legge, *Chinese Classics*, 3:71, 240.

23. Legge, *Chinese Classics*, 3:245. In the *Shu Ching* the two contradictory uses of *luan*[a] as both order and disorder are about evenly divided—see *Chinese Classics*, 3:648 (concordance).

24. Legge, *Chinese Classics*, 5:702. For the passage in the *Shu Ching* see *Chinese Classics*, 3:292.

25. The *Lun Yü* cryptically notes that one of Wu's able ministers was a woman, so that in a literal sense "the able ministers were no more than nine men."

26. See Legge's concordances (not complete) at the end of each volume of the *Chinese Classics*. I have also consulted the Harvard-Yenching concordance for *Chou I* (*I Ching*) and *Meng Tzu*; and the Centre Franco-chinois d'études sinologiques indexes for the *Lu Shih Ch'un Ch'iu* and *Ch'un Ch'iu*. On the *Tso Chuan* see also E. D. H. Fraser's *Index to the Tso Chuan* (reprint ed., Taipei: Ch'eng-wen, 1966). It should be noted that there is one instance of the use of *hun*[d] in the *Meng Tzu*—as an onomatopoetic term for running water (see Legge, *Chinese Classics*, 2:324).

27. Legge, *Chinese Classics*, 4:441. For an interesting discussion of the I[c] culture in relation to Taoism, bird symbolism, and shamanic practice, see Kaltenmark, *Lie-sien Tchouen*, pp. 13 f.

28. Legge, *Chinese Classics*, 5:181, 293, 665–668, 691.

29. Legge, *Chinese Classics*, 5:279–283. For similar passages see Legge *Chinese Classics*, 2:349 (*Meng Tzu*) and 3:23 f., 39–40 (*Shu Ching*). As Karlgren notes, these last references (involving the personages of Kung-kung, Huan-tou, San Miao, and Kun) probably originally represented a separate legendary tradition; but by the time of the Han they are identified as a collective symbolic reference for what was considered outside of the accepted civilized order—see above, n. 17. The so-called barbarians were, of course, only various local cultures, or less advanced groups of Chinese, before the definitive solidification of the Chinese Empire in 221 B.C. For a general historical discussion of the idea of the "barbarians [*sheng-fan*]" in the ancient sources see Lien-sheng Yang, "Historical Notes on the Chinese World Order," in *Chinese World Order*, ed. J. K. Fairbank (Cambridge: Harvard University Press, 1968), pp. 20–33. See also below, chapter 6.

30. It may not be unwarranted to speculate that P'u[b] (like Hun-tun) may represent a disguised account of an original mythological personage and, in this sense, provides more of a symbolic context for the later philosophical meaning of *p'u*[a] similar to the context associated with *hun-tun*. See, for example, the account of P'u-niu found in the *Shan Hai Ching*—Karlgren, "Legends and Cults," p. 325.

31. See Karlgren, "Legends and Cults," p. 253, who notes that in the *Shan Hai Ching* Hun-tun is identified with Ti Chiang (=Ti Hung).

32. At this point in the text *luan*[a] is used once with its ordinary meaning to refer to Block who was "seeking to confound [*luan*[a]] the heavenly rules of society"—*Chinese Classics*, 5:283.

33. Cf. Legge, *Chinese Classics*, 3:31 ff.

34. Cf. Legge, *Chinese Classics*, 3:71 (*Shu Ching*), where in an echo of Shun's regulations (i.e., 3:31 ff) quoted here, Shun's minister of crime, Kau Yu, lists "aptness

for government [*luan*[a]]'' as one of the "nine virtues" of conduct.

35. Legge, *Chinese Classics*, p. 283.

36. Ibid.

37. Ibid. With reference to the inconsistent reference to Yao noted by Legge, it should be remembered that these are all composite texts drawing upon different fragments of a more ancient legendary tradition. Despite the honor attributed to Yao it is still the case that, here and in the *Meng Tzu*, Yao is personally impotent and otiose and must rely on his agents, Shun and Yü, to banish the rebels and overcome the great flood.

38. See H. Maspero, "Légendes mythologiques," pp. 1–100.

39. Legge, *Chinese Classics*, 2:250–254.

40. Legge, *Chinese Classics*, 1:213–214 (*Lun Yü*).

41. Legge, *Chinese Classics*, 2:253 (*Meng Tzu*).

42. See above, n. 6 and 24.

43. Legge, *Chinese Classics*, 2:279–284. See Maspero's discussion of this passage, "Légendes mythologiques," pp. 68–70. Maspero correctly notes that this passage is not simply a deluge legend but a type of creation story: "It is clear that Mencius considers that the world begins when Yü puts the earth and waters in order: this is for him the legend of the origin of man, it is not that which goes back to the absolute beginnings."

44. It should be noted that the philosophy of history articulated here, the inevitable cyclic interplay between order and disorder, is basically similar to the more elaborate orthodox Han cosmology systematized by Tung Chung-shu. For an interesting discussion of this as a paradigmatic principle in Chinese politics see Peter R. Moody, Jr., "The Romance of the Three Kingdoms and Popular Chinese Political Thought," *Review of Politics* 37 (1975):175–199.

45. Cf. Legge, *Chinese Classics*, 3:60 (*Shu Ching*).

46. Cf. the condemnation of P'u[b] who murdered his father and gives occasion for the legendary rebels story in the *Tso Chuan*; see above.

47. A. C. Graham feels that chapters 28, 29, 31 (and possibly chapter 30) of the *Chuang Tzu* represent the philosophy of the Yang Chu school—"Notes," pp. 33–44. Parts of the *Lieh Tzu* can, of course, also be attributed to the Yang school. Fung Yu-lan has recently argued for the close relationship between the philosophy of Yang Chu (especially the idea of self-preservation) and Taoism—see Jan Yün-hua, "Problems of Tao," pp. 211–216. For an interesting discussion of the significance of this passage for orthodox Confucian tradition, especially in terms of the denigration of Moism, see William A. Lyell, Jr., "The Birth and Death of the Yang-Mo symbol," M. A. diss. (University of Chicago, 1962); pp. 1–20.

48. Fontenrose, p. 465.

49. Fontenrose, p. 473.

50. Needham, *SCC* 2:119.

51. See Eberhard, *LC*, pp. 438–446 and Chang ("Chinese creation myths"), pp. 61 f. In general, there is a "southern" or "southwestern" focus for the theme of *hun-tun*. On some of the overall problems associated with the relationship of the term *hun*[d] with barbarian traditions (i.e., such traditional linkages as Ti, Jung, Hsiung-nu, Hsien-yün, Hsün-yü, and Hun) see J. Prusek, *Chinese Statelets and the Northern Barbarians in the Period 1400–300* B.C., (New York: Humanities Press, 1971), pp. 9–20. Eberhard argues for an Austroasiatic origin, and Prusek's conclusions tend to suggest

that there is more of an Indo-European linguistic and cultural connection than there are Turkic or Altaic connections. The possibility of some relation to archaic Indo-European tradition may be significant, given variants of the *hun-tun* theme as a "Cosmic egg" or "cosmic giant" type of creation myth (especially the later P'an-ku myths). On the mythic pattern of the Cosmic Giant in Indo-European tradition see Bruce Lincoln "The Indo-European Myth of Creation," *History of Religions* 15 (1975): 121–145. See below, chapter 6.

52. On the symbolism of the TLV mirrors see S. Cammann, "Types of Symbols in Chinese Art," in *Studies in Chinese Thought*, ed. A Wright (Chicago: University of Chicago Press, 1958), pp. 201–202. Another possible parallel is the later Taoist symbolism of the *hsien*[a] or, in this case, the "banished immortal [*che-hsien*]" who must remain outside the conventional human order like the banished Hun-tun of the *Tso Chuan*—see below chapter 8.

53. See Laurence G. Thompson, "Formosan Aborigines in the Early Eighteenth Century: Huang Shu-Ching's *Fan-su Liu-k'ao*," *Monumenta Serica* 28 (1969): 42.

54. See K. Hentze, *Chinese Tomb Figures* (London: Edward Goldston, 1928), pp. 41 ff. The *Erh Ya* dictionary (p. 17 of book I, Ssu-pu pei-ya ed.), for example, says that *luan*[a] means *ch'ih*[b] (order) and also *shen*[a] (gods or spirits). Moreover, the term *luan*[a] is related to the themes of *tsung*[a] (letting go, expansion) and *shu*[b] (drawing back, contraction), which are reminiscent of the creation scenario of the expansion and contraction of the primordial chaos (book I, p. 19 of the *Erh Ya*). I am indebted to Sun Lung-kee for this reference.

55. Quoted by Hentze, p. 42, n. 1.

56. Ibid. p. 43.

57. Ibid. p. 45.

58. Needham, *SCC*, 2:119.

59. See above, chapter 4; and Granet, *DL*, 2:503–548. Despite Karlgren's objections ("Legends and Cults"), the association of animals (especially birds) is surely significant here (although the term "totemism" must be used with caution).

60. Needham, *SCC*, 2:119.

61. Ibid. Needham notes that Granet "did not notice the connection between these legendary rebels and their subsequent favourable mention in Taoist texts."

62. See, for example, Mircea Eliade, *The Forge and the Crucible* (New York: Harper Torchbook, 1971), pp. 109–126; and Lu Gwei-djen, "The Inner Elixir (Nei Tan); Chinese Physiological Alchemy," in *Changing Perspectives in the History of Science*, ed. M. Teich and R. Young (London: Heinemann, 1973), pp. 76–79. One example of some of these connections is suggested on linguistic grounds. Thus, the word family of *hung*[a] (=Ti Hung Meng, the legendary emperor associated with Hun-tun) and *hung*[b] (=the primordial flood or chaos waters) is also related to *hung*[c] (mercury), *hung*[d] (red or cinnabar), *hung*[e] (discord, revolution, to make mischief), and *hung*[f] (to bake, roast, dry at a fire).

63. Needham, *SCC*, 2:119.

64. See Eliade, *Forge and Crucible* (especially the "Postscript," pp. 179–199); and Stanley J. O'Connor, "Iron Working as Spiritual Inquiry in the Indonesian Archipelago," *History of Religions* 14 (1975): 173–190. The fact that the earliest origins of bronze technology in Asia have been traced to Thailand (see O'Connor) and that the

mythology associated with *hun-tun* is especially linked to a southern "Man" or "K'un-lun" cultural complex in ancient China (see Eberhard and Porée-Maspero) may be a clue toward the further localization of the cultural origins of the *hun-tun* theme. See below, chapter 6. On the other hand, Cheng Te-k'un has recently restated his argument for the independent invention of bronze metallurgy in the Shang—see his "Metallurgy in Shang China," *T'oung Pao* 60 (1974): 14–229. See also Ho Ping-ti, *The Cradle of the East* (Chicago: University of Chicago Press, 1975), pp. 179–222. This, however, does not obviate the possible influence of other "western" or "southern" cultures.

65. Initiatory and shamanistic symbolism associated with secret societies or metallurgical brotherhoods involves both a socio-political and personal-religious significance for the initiate—see Eliade, *Rites and Symbols*, pp: 61–80. Eliade would maintain that in shamanic initiation we see the archaic roots of later traditions of mysticism—*Rites and Symbols*, pp. 81–102. Eliade, therefore, says that "initiation imposed upon entrance to a secret society, and initiation requisite for obtaining a higher religious status have a good deal in common. They might even be regarded as two varieties of a single class. What principally tends to distinguish them is the element of [personal] ecstasy, which is of great[er] importance in shamanic initiations"—p. 3.

5. *Cosmogony and Conception in the Huai Nan Tzu and Lieh Tzu*

1. See Graham, *Lieh-tzu*, p. 1. Graham refers to these texts as connecting the earliest writings with the later syncretistic thought of "Neo-Taoism." The notion of a philosophical movement known as "Neo-Taoism" is, however, very ambiguous and should be used with caution—see E. Zürcher, *The Buddhist Conquest of China* (Leiden: E. J. Brill, 1959), p. 87.

2. For a discussion of some of the general background related to these texts see Benjamin Wallacker's introduction to his *The Huai-Nan-Tzu Book Eleven: Behavior, Culture and the Cosmos*, American Oriental Series, no. 48 (New Haven: American Oriental Society, 1962); John Major, *Topography and Cosmology in Early Han Thought: Chapter Four of the Huai-nan-tzu*, Ph.D. diss., Harvard University, 1973; Cheng Te-k'un, "*Yin-yang wu-hsing* in Han Art," *Harvard Journal of Asiatic Studies* 20 (1957): 162–186; and H. H. Dubs, "The Victory of Han Confucianism," *Journal of the American Oriental Society* 58 (1938): 435–449. Traditional Chinese discussion of the *Huai Nan Tzu* is found in Liu Wen-tien, ed., *Huai Nan Hung Lieh Chi Chieh* (Collected Commentaries on the *Huai Nan Tzu*), (Shanghai: Commercial Press, 1923).

3. See Graham, *Lieh-tzu*, p. 16.

4. See Kaltenmark, *Lie-sien Tchouan*, pp. 1–25; Yü Ying-shih, "Life and Immortality in Han China," *Harvard Journal of Asiatic Studies* 25 (1964–1965): 80–122; and Creel, *What is Taoism*, p. 19.

5. See Jeffrey Howard, "Concepts of Comprehensiveness and Historical Change in the *Huai-Nan-Tzu*," paper delivered to the Harvard Conference on Classical Chinese Philosophy, 1976. See also Roger T. Ames, "*Wu-wei* in 'The Art of Rulership' Chapter of *Huai Nan Tzu*: Its Sources and Philosophical Orientation," *Philosophy East and West* 31 (1981): 193–213. Ames notes that chapter 19 ("Hsiu Wu") of the *Huai Nan Tzu* attacks the early Taoist extreme idealization of primitivism—p. 213, n. 16.

6. See Needham, *SCC*, 2:294 ff; Ho Ping-yu and J. Needham, "Theories of

Categories in Early Medieval Chinese Alchemy," *Journal of the Warburg and Courtauld Institutes* 22 (1959): 173–210; and Tenny L. Davis, "The Dualistic Cosmogony of *Huai-nan-tzu* and its Relations to the Background of Chinese and of European Alchemy," *Isis* 25 (1936): 327–340. From a comparative standpoint, see George Perrigo Conger, *Theories of Macrocosmos and Microcosmos in the History of Philosophy* (New York: Russell and Russell, 1967).

7. From a comparative point of view see F. B. J. Kuiper, "Cosmogony and Conception: A Query," *History of Religions* 19 (1971): 91 ff.

8. See above, chapter 2 (the quotation is from chapter 7 of the *Huai Nan Tzu*).

9. See below, chapters 6 and 7.

10. See Schipper, "Taoist Body," pp. 358–365.

11. The text used throughout is *HNTCI*. The complete work has never been translated; but for partial translations see the works by Major and Wallacker (chapters 4 and 11); and less reliably E. Morgan, *Tao, the Great Luminant* (Shanghai: Kelly and Walsh, n.d.; reprint ed., Taipei: Ch'eng-Wen Publishing Co., 1966), (chaps. 1, 2, 7, 8, 12, 13, 15, 19), and de Harlez, *Textes Taoistes* pp. 171–212 (chaps. 1–8; 12, 14, 20). Wherever possible I have generally followed Morgan's translations.

12. See Needham, *SCC*, 2: 71–99 (on Taoist empiricism).

13. On the *Shih Chi* see Watson, *Chinese Literature* pp. 92–103; and E. Chavannes, *Les mémoires historiques de Se-ma Ts'ien* (reprint ed., Leiden: E. J. Brill, 1967), vol. 1.

14. Chavannes, ibid., pp. 19–20.

15. For a discussion of the mythic and mystic significance of *anamnesis* see Eliade, *Myth and Reality*, pp. 114–138.

16. *HNTCI*, p. 235.

17. *HNTCI*, p. 101, 1. 7a; and Morgan, pp. 61–62.

18. *HNTCI*, p. 103, 1. 10a; and Morgan, p. 64. Cf. the description of the "true man" (*chen-jen*) in chapter 15 of the *Chuang Tzu*.

19. *HNTCI*, p. 103, 1. 12a; and Morgan, pp. 64–65.

20. See Soymié, "Le Lo-feou chan," pp. 68 ff.

21. Bauer, *Search for Happiness*, p. 181.

22. See, for example, Eliade, *Shamanism*, pp. 447–461.

23. See Kaltenmark, *Lie-sien Tchouan*, pp. 19–20; and his "Naissance du monde." p. 458. See also below, chapter 6.

24. Stein, "Jardins en miniature," pp. 52–53.

25. *CCT*, 2–3/1/35–42; and Watson pp. 34–35.

26. *CCT*, 5/2/47; and Watson, p. 42.

27. *HNTCI*, p. 103; and Morgan, p. 65.

28. *HNTCI*, pp. 103–104, 1. 15b, 1a–b; and Morgan, pp. 65–66.

29. *HNTCI*, p. 104, 1. 10b–13a; and Morgan, p. 66.

30. *HNTCI*, p. 1, 1. 1; and Morgan, p. 2. On the ancient Chinese cosmological ideas of four quarters and eight poles, see Maspero, "Légendes mythologiques," pp. 29 ff; and Major, "Topography and Cosmology," pp. 19–35.

31. *HNTCI*, p. 1, 1. 2; and Morgan, p. 2.

32. *HNTCI*, p. 115, 1. 8 (see below); and *Lü Shih Ch'un Ch'iu*, chapter 13. See Sun's discussion, "Mythical World-View," pp. 30–34; and below, chapter 6.

33. The term *ch'ung*[a] is used here. Cf. above, chapter 2. For the later Taoist use of

this term see *Hsien Hsüeh Tz'u Tien*, p. 82.

34. *Chuo* is the term that is related to *hun* in chapter 15 of the *Tao Te Ching* (see above, chapter 2). *Chuo* generally means "muddy, turbid, or corrupt"; and, as with the ambivalent meanings attributed to *hun-tun*, it can have the meaning of "evil age" (such as the compound *chuo-shih*) or "foolish" (*chuo-ts'ai* meaning "fool" or *chuo-wu* meaning "stupid or lout").

35. For this and the above lines, *HNTCI*, p. 1, 1. 3; and Morgan, p. 2.

36. See Eberhard, *LC*, pp. 410 ff; and D. Crockett Graham, *Songs and Stories of the Ch'uan Miao*, Smithsonian Miscellaneous Collections, vol. 123 (Washington, D.C.: Smithsonian Institution, 1954), pp. 179–181.

37. Boodberg, "Evolution of Archaic Chinese," p. 367, n. 80.

38. *HNTCI*, p. 1, 1. 7; and Morgan, p. 2.

39. *HNTCI*, p. 1, 1. 11–13; and Morgan, p. 3. See Kaltenmark's comment on this passage in relation to the primordial couple mythology, "Naissance du monde," p. 466.

40. *HNTCI*, p. 2, 1. 1; and Morgan, p. 3. The idea of the cosmic process of the Tao being identified with the image of potting is a common mythological theme and in later Taoism gives rise to the technical expression *t'ao-hua*—see Link, "Taoist Antecedents of Tao-an," p. 196. As the reduplicated sounds associated with *hun-tun* seem to have the mythological significance of thunder so also do terms like *hun-yüan*, *hun-lun*, and *hun-lun* suggest the revolving motion of flowing water (especially in the sense of a whirlpool) or the turning of a wheel (cf. *yun*)—see the *Tz'u Hai* on these terms. In later Taoism the technical expression of *hui feng hun ho* suggests the idea of the microcosmic internal circulation and blending of the *ch'i*[a] during esoteric meditation—see *Hsien Hsüeh Tz'u Tien*, p. 113.

41. *HNTCI*, p. 2, 1. 2–5; and Morgan, p. 3.

42. *HNTCI*, p. 2, 1. 14; and Morgan, p. 3.

43. Feng-i[b] in chapter 3 of the *Huai Nan Tzu* is another mythic name for the chaos time. Feng-i (also called Wu-i and P'ing-i) is frequently depicted as a water god who dwells in the deep—see Werner, *Dictionary of Chinese Mythology*, p. 126.

44. See above, chapter 3.

45. Hawkes, *Ch'u Tz'u*, p. 46. Hawkes also notes with reference to the "Li Sao" that the "Ch'u poets show an unusual tenderness" for other unpopular chaos figures like Kun (p. 26, n. 2). On the mythology associated with Kun see Eberhard, *LC*, pp. 349–362.

46. *HNTCI*, p. 11, 1. 2–8; and Morgan, pp. 17–18.

47. On *k'uai* see above, chapter 3. Couvreur points out the significant phrase *k'uai-jan wu-chih* meaning "lumpish and stupid"—*Dictionnaire Classique*, p. 177.

48. *HNTCI*, p. 97, 1. 14. Chapter 6 concludes with a characteristic golden age passage that is called the time of *ta-t'ung hun-ming*[b], (*HNTCI*, p. 98, 1. 1).

49. Ibid., p. 35, 1. 1.

50. See Chapter 10 (Ibid., p. 153, 1. 6) for *hsüan-t'ung*[a,b].

51. Bauer, *Search for Happiness*, p. 192. See also Stein, "Jardins en miniature," pp. 42 ff; and Soymié, "Lo-feou chan," pp. 88 ff.

52. Bauer, ibid., pp. 191–192. Cf. also the associations of "water" or "rapidly flowing" and *hun-tun*.

53. Ibid.

54. Ibid.

55. Ibid.

56. See the epigraph at the head of this chapter.

57. *HNTCI*, p. 35, 1. 1–5.

58. Ibid., p. 35, 1. 7–9. On the myths of Kung-kung see Maspero, "Légendes mythologiques," pp. 47 ff; and Karlgren, "Legends and Cults," pp. 218–255.

59. It should be recalled that in the *Tso Chuan*, Chuan-hsü was the father of one of the four "monsters" of antiquity before Yao and Shun. See above, chapter 4.

60. Boodberg, "Evolution of Archaic Chinese," p. 370, n. 90.

61. Ibid.

62. *HNTCI*, pp. 19–20; and Morgan, pp. 31–33.

63. *CCT*, 5/2/49–51; and Watson, p. 43.

64. See *Tz'u Hai* under *juan*.

65. *HNTCI*, p. 19, 1. 8–9; and Morgan, p. 31.

66. See above, chapter 3.

67. *CCT*, 32/12/80–84; and Watson, p. 138.

68. *HNTCI*, p. 20, 1. 1.

69. See *Dictionnaire Classique*, p. 544.

70. See Granet, *DL*, pp. 337 ff.

71. *HNTCI*, p. 20, 1. 2.

72. *K'uang*[b] has already been encountered in the *Chuang Tzu*; see above, chapter 3. *Ch'ang* generally indicates a "mad or frenzied condition" or "raving, wild singing." See Schafer, "Ritual Exposure," pp. 160–161.

73. Granet, *DL*, p. 326, n. 3.

74. Ibid.

75. The reference to *yang* again brings out the metallurgical context of thought. The idea of a metallurgical "fusion" of metals seems to be equated with the idea of the sacred "union" sought by the Taoist. *Ho* is also an extremely important technical term in Taoism that is associated with the idea of the sacred union or closed condition of chaos. For the cosmogonic association with *ho* see the discussion of *t'ai-ho* in *Hsien Hsüeh Tz'u Tien*, p. 64; and below, chapter 9.

76. *HNTCI*, p. 28; and Morgan, pp. 43–44.

77. *HNTCI*, pp. 113–115; and Morgan, pp. 80–84.

78. See above, chapter 2.

79. *HNTCI*, p. 115, 1. 10 ff; and Morgan, p. 84.

80. *HNTCI*, p. 115, 1. 12 b.

81. *HNTCI*, pp. 120–121, 1. 12 ff; and Morgan, pp. 93–94.

82. Kau Yu comments that *chen* should be taken as *shen*[b] or "body"—*HNTCI*, p. 120, 1. 16.

83. *HNTCI*, p. 121, 1. 4 ff; and Morgan, pp. 84 ff.

84. See, for example, the use of *tso* in *HNTCI*, p. 121, 1. 9.b.

85. For this section on the *Lieh Tzu* I used the *Lieh Tzu Chi Shih* compiled by Yang Pai-Chün (Taipei: Ming Lun Publishing Company, 1971). Cited as *LTCS*. I have also consulted A. C. Graham's excellent English translation, *The Book of Lieh-tzu*. Generally, I have made use of Graham's rendering of the text except where it has been necessary to draw out particular points. See also K. Schipper's review of Graham's

translation in *T'oung Pao*, 51 (1964): 288–292. For a discussion of the textual problems associated with the *Lieh Tzu* see A. C. Graham, "The Date and Composition of Liehtzu," *Asia Major*, 8 (1961): 139–198.

86. *LTCS*, pp. 1–3; and Graham, pp. 17–18.

87. *LTCS*, pp. 43–44; and Graham, pp. 47–48.

88. For a discussion of the Yellow Emperor tradition see Kaltenmark, *Lao Tzu*, pp. 14–15; and below, chap. 6.

89. *LTCS*, pp. 3–4; and Graham, pp. 18–19.

90. On the complex number symbolism from the time of the Han on, see especially the discussion in chapter 4 of the *Huai Nan Tzu*. In this system 2, 3, 5, 7, 8, 9, 10, 12, 60, and 64 (and their multiples) are particularly significant as meaningful cosmological numbers. See Major's discussion "Topography and Cosmology," pp. 19–35. On this passage from the *Lieh Tzu* compare the *Po Hu Tung*, trans. Tjan Tjoe Som, p. 591.

91. *LTCS*, p. 4.

92. *LTCS*, pp. 4–5; and Graham, p. 19.

93. *LTCS*, pp. 12–13; and Graham, p. 23.

94. See above, chapter 3.

95. *LTCS*, p. 12; and Graham, p. 23.

96. *LTCS*, pp. 43–44; and Graham, pp. 47–48.

97. See *LTCS*, chapter 6.

98. *LTCS*, p. 15; and Graham, p. 25.

99. *LTCS*, pp. 16–17; and Graham, p. 26.

100. *LTCS*, p. 29; and Graham, pp. 36–37. *Ning*[a] is also used in a cosmogonic context in chapter 3 of the *Huai Nan Tzu* (*HNTCI*, p. 35) and in the *Chuang Tzu*, see above chapter 3.

101. *LTCS*, p. 25; and Graham, p. 34 (see below).

102. *LTCS*, pp. 102–103; and Graham, pp. 102–103. See also Maspero, "Légendes mythologiques," pp. 34–38.

103. *LTCS*, pp. 64–65; and Graham, pp. 67–68. The commentary explains that *mang*[b] means *mo lang ch'ieh*—"where everything is unclear."

104. Bauer, *Search for Happiness*, p. 93.

105. Ibid.

106. Ibid.

107. *LTCS*, pp. 94–95; and Graham, p. 97.

108. *LTCS*, pp. 57–59; and Graham, pp. 63–64.

109. *LTCS*, p. 64; and Graham, p. 67.

110. *LTCS*, pp. 67–69; and Graham, pp. 70–71.

111. *LTCS*, p. 25; and Graham, p. 34.

112. *LTCS*, p. 30; and Graham, p. 37.

113. *LTCS*, p. 25; and Graham, p. 34.

114. *LTCS*, pp. 27–28; and Graham, p. 35.

115. *LTCS*, p. 27, 1. 7–8; and Graham, p. 35. See also the passages in the *Chuang Tzu*, *CCT*, 2/1/28–30; and Watson, p. 33 (reference to *shen-ning* and *ch'u-tzu*, which refer to a young woman or recluse).

116. See, for example, Needham *SCC*, 2:143; Maspero, "Nourrir principe vital," passim.

117. See Ho Ting-jui, *A Comparative Study of Myths and Legends of Formosan Aborigines* (Taipei: The Orient Cultural Service, 1971); and below, chapters 6 and 7.

118. See Schipper, "Taoist Body," p. 365.

119. *LTCK*, p. 278; and Chan, p. 171.

6. *Egg, Gourd, and Deluge: Toward a Typology of the Chaos Theme*

1. See above, chapter 3, for Izutsu's views; and Fung Yu-lan, *A History of Chinese Philosophy*, trans. Derk Bodde (Princeton: Princeton University Press, 1952) 1:175–176.

2. Besides the works of Eberhard, Kaltenmark, Porée-Maspero, and Ho cited below, see Obayashi Taro, "The Origins of Japanese Mythology," *Acta Asiatica* 31 (1977): 1–23; Franz Numazawa, "Background of Myths on the Separation of Sky and Earth from the Point of View of Cultural History," *Scientia* (Milan), 88 (1953): 28–35; Leopold Walk, "Das Flut-Geschwisterpaar als Ur-und Stammelternpaar der Menschheit. Ein Beitrag zur Mythengeschichte Süd-und Südostasiens," *Mitteilungen der Anthropologischen Gesellschaft in Wien* 78–79 (1949): 60–115; Toichi Mabuchi, *The Ethnology of the Southwestern Pacific* (Taipei: Orient Cultural Service, 1974), pp. 65–160, 221–242; and Chang Kwang-chih, "Prehistoric and Early Historic Culture Horizons and Transitions in South China," *Current Anthropology* 5 (1964): 359–406.

3. See Major, "Research Priorities," pp. 227–230; and Eberhard, *LC*, pp. 70–71 (especially in relation to the Yao[b]).

4. Inez de Beauclair, *Tribal Cultures of Southwest China* (Taipei: Orient Cultural Service, 1974), p. 99. Maspero's "Légendes mythologiques" points to the comparative significance of the White and Black Thai myths in Indochina; and Erkes in his "Chinesisch-Amerikanische Mythenparallelen," *T'oung Pao* 24 (1941), provides an even broader base of comparison (i.e., myths of the Battak of Sumatra, the Semang of Malacca, and the Goldi of the Amur). On "southern" local cultures see H. J. Wiens, *Han Chinese Expansion in South China* (n.p.: Shoe String Press, 1967); and F. M. Lebar, G. C. Hickey, and J. K. Musgrave, *Ethnic Groups of Mainland Southeast Asia* (New Haven: Human Relations Area Files, 1964).

5. Eberhard, *LC*, p. 446.

6. E. Porée-Maspero, *Étude sur les rites agraires des Cambodgiens* (Paris: Mouton and Co., 1962, 1964, 1969), 3 vols. pp. 567–569, 703 ff., 771 ff.

7. Ho, *Myths and Legends*, pp. 165 ff.

8. M. Kaltenmark, "Le Dompteur des flots," *Han-hiue* (Peking), 3 (1948), pp. 1–112.

9. Ibid., p. 1.

10. Porée-Maspero, *Rites agraires*, p. 795.

11. Ibid., p. 796. See also pp. 532–533.

12. Kaltenmark, "Dompteur des flots," p. 76.

13. Ibid., p. 78.

14. Ibid.

15. Ibid., pp. 79–80.

16. Porée-Maspero, *Rites agraires*, pp. 703 ff., 783 ff. See also Kachorn Sukhabanij, "Two Thai MSS on the K'unLun Kingdom," in *Symposium On Historical,*

Archaeological, and Linguistic Studies on Southern China, South-East Asia, and the Hong Kong Region, ed. F. S. Drake (Hong Kong: Hong Kong University Press, 1967), pp. 70–74.

17. Porée-Maspero, *Rites agraires*, p. 786.

18. Ibid., p. 787. See also L. de Saussure, "L'etymologie du nom des monts K'ouen-louen," *T'oung Pao* 20 (1921): 370–371.

19. Porée-Maspero, *Rites agraires*, pp. 832–833; and Kaltenmark, "Dompteur des flots," p. 56.

20. Porée-Maspero, *Rites agraires*, p. 780.

21. O. Maenchen-Helfen, "The Ethnic Name Hun," in *Studia Serica Bernhard Karlgren Dedicata*, ed. Sören Egerod (Copenhagen: E. Munksgaard, 1959), pp. 223–238. See also B. Laufer, *Sino-Iranica* (1919; reprint ed., Taipei: Ch'eng-Wen, 1967), pp. 248–249. On the linguistic relation between Malayo-Polynesian and Sino-Tibetan see especially Chang Kwang-Chih, "A Working Hypothesis for the Early Cultural History of South China," *Bulletin of the Institute of Ethnology, Academia Sinica* 7 (1959): 95–97.

22. Maenchen-Helfen, "Ethnic Name," p. 224; and A. Link, "The Biography of Shih Tao-an," *T'oung Pao* 46 (1958): 10.

23. See especially Eberhard, *LC*, on this, pp. 1–31; and also Judith Triestman, *The Prehistory of China* (New York: Doubleday and Co., 1970), pp. 103–143.

24. As, for example, found in the official cosmological-historical theories of Tsou-yen and Tung Chung-shu—see John S. Major, "Myth, Cosmology, and the Origins of Chinese Science," *Journal of Chinese Philosophy* 5 (1978), pp. 1–20.

25. See P. Pelliot, *T'oung Pao* 28 (1931): 468; and Granet, *Pensée*, p. 412.

26. See, for example, Major, "Research Priorities," pp. 231–233; and his review of K. C. Chang and Ping-ti Ho's works on Chinese cultural origins—in *Isis* 68 (1977): 639–640. See also David Keightley's review, "Ping-ti Ho and the Origins of Chinese Civilization," *Harvard Journal of Asiatic Studies* 37 (1977): 381–411. For possible Indo-European influence see E. G. Pulleyblank, "Chinese and Indo-Europeans," *Journal of the Royal Asiatic Society* (1966): 304; Tor Ulving, "Indo-European Elements in Chinese," *Anthropos* 63/64 (1968/1969): 944–951; Major, "Myth and Origins," passim; and Prusek, *Chinese Statelets*, pp. 9–20. For a discussion that essentially supports the view adopted here see Chang Kwang-chih, "A Working Hypothesis for the Early Cultural History of South China," pp. 75–103. Chang considers the ancient cultural complex of south China to be a "Lungshanoid" extension of the north China neolithic, a perspective that recognizes that "various local phases came into being in the South as the result of adaptations to various kinds of environment and of different historical experiences" (p. 94).

27. See Pelliot, *T'oung Pao*, 28 (1931): 428.

28. See, for example, Nancy Kleiber, "The Controversy About the Austronesian Homeland," *Anthropologica* 11 (1969): 151–163; Isidore Dyen, "The Austronesian Languages and Proto-Austronesian," in *Current Trends in Linguistics*, ed. Thomas A. Sebeok (The Hague: Mouton, 1963) 8:5–12; Paul K. Benedict, *Austro-Thai Language and Culture* (New Haven: Human Relations Area Files, 1975), pp. 464–490 ("Austro-Thai and Austroasiatic"); B. J. Terwiel, "The Origin of the T'ai Peoples Reconsidered," *Oriens Extremus* 25 (1978): 239–258; and, most recently, Donn Bayard,

"The Roots of Indochinese Civilisation: Recent Developments in the Prehistory of Southeast Asia," *Pacific Affairs* 53 (1980): 89—114.

29. See Frank Reynolds, "Buddhism and the Anthropologists: Some Comments Concerning Recent Works on Southeast Asia," *History of Religions* 11 (1972): 303—313; and A. de Hauteclocque, "Agriculture et religion: rites et légendes des cambodgiens," *Annales Economies-Sociétés-Civilisations* 18 (1963): 1002—1006. Some note should be taken of the panbabylonian theories of Ling Shun-shen who argues for a linguistic and cultural origin of K'un-lun symbolism in the tradition of Mesopotamian ziggurats—see his "K'un-lun chiu yü Hsi Wang Mu," *Bulletin of the Institute of Ethnology, Academia Sinica* 22 (1966): 253—255 (English summary). Occam's razor suggests that this kind of hypothesis is least probable as a satisfactory explanation of the material.

30. Chang, "Chinese Creation Myths," pp. 48—50. See also his "Classification," pp. 149—173; and Major, "Myth and Origins," pp. 3—18.

31. Chang, "Classification," pp. 170—173.

32. Chang, "Relationships of Man and Animal," pp. 174—198. See also Michael Loewe, "Man and Beast, The Hybrid in Early Chinese Art and Literature," *Numen* 25 (1978): 97—117.

33. See above, Introduction.

34. Chang, "Classification," p. 153.

35. Quoting the *T'ai Shih Ching*—see *Tz'u Hai*, p. 1741.

36. Sproul, "Prolegomena," p. 212. See also Ho, *Myths and Legends*, pp. 68—74.

37. Hellbom, "Creation Egg," pp. 64—65.

38. Eberhard, *LC*, p. 438.

39. Long, *Alpha*, pp. 116—117.

40. See Eberhard, *LC*, p. 438.

41. On the problem of the functional relationship among cosmic egg, cosmic giant, and primordial couple myths see H. Baumann, *Das Doppelte Geschlecht* (Berlin: D. Reimer, 1955).

42. Eberhard, *LC*, pp. 253 ff.

43. On the linkage of deluge-primordial couple-animal ancestor see Porée-Maspero, *Rites agraires*, pp. 821—851; and Ho, *Myths and Legends*, pp. 56—86.

44. See Eberhard, *LC*, pp. 253 ff.

45. Ibid., pp. 440, 57—60.

46. See, for example, Eberhard's discussion of "Thunder and Spring" rites within Thai culture—Ibid., pp. 257—258; and Porée-Maspero, *Rites agraires*, passim.

47. Kaltenmark, "Naissance du monde," pp. 457—458.

48. Long, *Alpha*, p. 121.

49. Ibid., p. 113.

50. Eliade, *Myths, Dreams, and Mysteries* (New York: Harper Torchbooks, 1967), p. 178.

51. Ibid. (quoting Granet).

52. Long, *Alpha*, p. 119.

53. Ibid., p. 115 (referring to Baumann's work—see above, n. 41). See also Eliade's review of Baumann in *Revue de l'histoire des religions* 153 (1958): 89—92.

54. See Eberhard, *LC*, pp. 118 ff., 280 ff., 154 ff.

55. See Maspero, "Nourrir le principe vital," pp. 354 ff; and Schipper, "Taoist Body," pp. 365 ff.

56. Granet, *Études sociologiques*, p. 206.

57. Ibid.

58. See Ho, *Myths and Legends*, pp. 74–81. See also C. H. Liu, "The Dog-ancestor Story of the Aboriginal Tribes of Southern China," *Journal of the Royal Anthropological Institute* 62 (1932): 361–368; and de Groot, *Religious System*, 4: 263–271; and Ruey Yih-fu, "A Study of the Miao People," in *Symposium On Historical, Archaeological, and Linguistic Studies on Southern China*, pp. 49–58.

59. See Porée-Maspero, *Rites Agraires*, pp. 845 ff.

60. Ibid., p. 518, n. 1; and Kaltenmark, "Dompteur des flots," pp. 67–68, 71–77.

61. For another discussion of the relation between P'an-hu and P'an-ku see E. Mestre, *Annuaires 1945–1946 et 1946–1947 de l'école pratique des hautes études*, pp. 28–31, 108–116.

62. Seidel, *Divinisation*, p. 95, n. 2; and Porée-Maspero, *Rites agraires*, p. 518, n. 1. On *hun-tun* and cocoon symbolism see especially Lo, "Primeval State," pp. 285 ff.

63. Stein, "Jardins en miniature," passim; and Eberhard, *LC*, pp. 279, 281, 429. The symbolism with regard to this category is particularly rich for China and Japan—especially the *hu-lu* (calabash) motif. For Japan see Ouwehand's *Namazu-e* (pp. 114–131). The most complete discussion of the Chinese and Japanese sources for gourd symbolism is found in Shime Suigan's *Hyotan monogatari* (n.p., 1922). For the Chinese context of meaning see the interesting essay by Lao Han [pseud.], "Hua Hu-lu (Talking about the Bottle Gourd)," *Culture World* (Taipei), 1 (1971): 26–28. See also below, chapter 7.

64. Lo, "Primeval State," pp. 287 f. See also his discussion of the cosmological implications of cocoon symbolism in relation to the calabash bipartite form, the theme of "slender waist transforms," and the *T'ai-chi* symbol—pp. 287 f.

65. See Eberhard, *LC*, pp. 44–46.

66. Ibid., p. 54.

67. See Ho, *Myths and Legends*, pp. 76–79; and Eberhard, *LC*, pp. 288–390.

68. Eberhard, *LC*, pp. 441–442; and Granet, *DL*, pp. 540 ff.

69. See below in this chapter.

70. See Eberhard, *LC*, p. 439. The *Shen I Ching* is a work of the fourth to fifth centuries A.D.

71. Lin Yueh-hwa, "Miao-Man Peoples of Kweichou," *Harvard Journal of Asiatic Studies* 5 (1941): 261–345. See de Groot's somewhat different version in *Religious System* 4: 263–264.

72. See below in this chapter.

73. The symbolism of the stone chamber relates to the theme of the sacred tripartite cave or grotto (*tung*) as a place that duplicates the condition of the creation time. In a T'ang dynasty commentary it says that P'an-hu's "stone chamber" had "three compartments"—see DeGroot, *Religious System* 4: 264, n. 1.

74. Both *p'u*[b] and *tu* are terms having specific cosmogonic connotations in the *hun-tun* theme developed in the early Taoist texts. Berthold Laufer notes that these terms mean that "she adopted the hair-dressing and costume of the indigenous Man tribes."

See his "Totemic Traces Among the Indo-Chinese," *Journal of American Folklore* 30 (1917): 420.

75. Such as the "swan maiden" type of tale—see Eberhard, *LC*, pp. 167, 282—284. This might also be referred to as a "beauty and the beast" story. Thus, there are numerous stories concerning the marriage of a woman to a dog-, snake-, or toad-shaped husband (*LC*, pp. 382 ff.). For the connection with the idea of *hun-tun* see Graham's *Songs and Stories of the Ch'uan Miao*, pp. 180—188 (marriage of the "warty toad"); and below in this chapter. See also Eberhard, *Folktales of China* (Chicago: University of Chicago Press, 1965), pp. 41—72.

76. See Porée-Maspero, *Rites agraires*, pp. 852—861.

77. Ibid., pp. 821—851.

78. Ho, *Myths and Legends*, pp. 74 ff.

79. Ibid.

80. Ibid.

81. J. C. Ferguson, "Chinese Mythology," in *The Mythology of All Races*, ed. J. McCulloch (Boston: Marshall Jones Co., 1928), pp. 57—58. See also J. Dyer Ball, "Scraps from Chinese Mythology," *The China Review* 11 (1882): 76—86.

82. Hoahn-son Hoang-sy-Quy, "Le Mythe indien de l'Homme cosmique dans son contexte cultural et dans son evolution," *Revue de l'histoire des religions* 175 (1969): 137.

83. Ibid.

84. On the relation to Indo-European cosmogony see ibid., pp. 134—139; and Lincoln, "Indo-European Myth of Creation," pp. 121—145. With reference to the relation with the southern deluge cycle see Eberhard, *LC*, pp. 442—443, 445—446.

85. See Chang, "Chinese Creation Myths," p. 48; Bodde, "Myths of Ancient China," pp. 3S2—383; and Seidel, *Divinisation*, pp. 93—96. The text quoted is from the *San Wu Li Chi* (third century), which is cited in the *T'ai P'ing Yu Lan*.

86. Bodde, "Myths of Ancient China," p. 382.

87. See Hoanh-son, "Le mythe indien," pp. 136—137. See Lo, "Primeval State," pp. 287 ff. for the relation between *p'an-ku*, *p'ao-hu* (gourd), and *hun-tun*.

88. See Plaks, *Archetype and Allegory*, p. 37. For a more negative evaluation of these apparent etymological connections and the identification of P'an-ku and P'an-hu see Paul Pelliot's review of W. Köpper's *Der Hund in der Mythologie der zirkumpazifischen Völker*, in *T'oung Pao* 28 (1931): 467—468.

89. Kaltenmark, "Dompteur des flots," pp. 56, 67—68, n. 233.

90. Chang, "Chinese Creation Myths," p. 48 (Chinese text given); and Bodde, "Myths of Ancient China," p. 383. This text is from the sixth century *Shu I Chi*.

91. Hoanh-son, "Le mythe indien," pp. 143 ff; and Chang, "Classification," pp. 155—159.

92. See especially Seidel, *Divinisation*, pp. 93—96.

93. Ibid., p. 95, n. 1.

94. Ibid., pp. 95—96.

95. Ibid. See also Schipper, "Taoist Body," pp. 361—365.

96. See Kaltenmark, "Dompteur des flots," pp. 67—68; and Eberhard, *LC*, pp. 442—443.

97. See below in this chapter.

98. Seidel, *Divinisation*, p. 56.

99. Ibid., p. 94.

100. Hoanh-son, "Le mythe indien," p. 148; and Sproul, "Prolegomena," pp. 183–185, 218.

101. Hoanh-son, "Le mythe indien," pp. 148 ff.

102. For Chinese Buddhist versions see ibid., pp. 138–139; and Porée-Maspero, *Rites agraires*, p. 843 (see also n. 2).

103. Porée-Maspero, *Rites agraires*, pp. 731 ff., passim.

104. For the best general discussion of the Yellow Emperor see Seidel, *Divinisation*, pp. 34–58; and Charles Le Blanc, "A Re-examination of the Myth of Huang Ti," in *Myth and Symbol in Chinese Tradition*, ed. N. J. Girardot and John S. Major, forthcoming. See also Kaltenmark, "Naissance," p. 466; Joseph Edkins, "Place of Hwang Ti in Early Tauism," *The China Review* 15 (1886–1887): 233–239; and Major, "Myth and Origins of Chinese Science," pp. 1–20.

105. See above, chapter 3; and Seidel, *Divinisation*, pp. 22–23. Chapter 11 of the *Chuang Tzu* is a good example of this conflict. In one parable the Yellow Emperor is said to be the "meddler" (*ying*, cf. *Tao Te Ching*, chap. 13) who initiated the great confusion (*ta-luan*) in the world and in a subsequent story the Yellow Emperor is presented as an example of a true Taoist seeking the "perfect Tao." The *Chuang Tzu* is also ambivalent and, at times, contradictory with regard to the figure of the ancient "sages" or *sheng-jen*. See also the significance of the Huang-Lao tradition in relation to the ideas of emperor and sage discussed in Seidel, "Image of the Perfect Ruler," pp. 228 ff., 228 n. 37; and *Divinisation*, p. 52.

106. See Granet, *DL*, pp. 45, 534 ff.; and Seidel, *Divinisation*, pp. 21–22.

107. Seidel, *Divinisation*, pp. 50–58. See also Tu Wei-ming, "The 'Thought of Huang-Lao': A Reflection on the Lao Tzu and Huang Ti Texts in the Silk Manuscripts of Ma-wang-tui," *Journal of Asian Studies* 39 (1979): 95–110; and Jan Yün-hua, "The Silk Manuscripts on Taoism," *T'oung Pao* 63 (1978): 65–84.

108. See Kaltenmark, "Religion and Politics in the China of the Ts'in (Ch'in) and the Han," *Diogenes* No. 34 (Summer, 1961): 16 ff.

109. See above, chapter 6; Needham, *SCC*, 2: 117; and Karlgren, "Legends and Cults," pp. 249, 254.

110. Seidel, *Divinisation*, p. 22.

111. Granet, *DL*, vol. 2, passim; and Needham, *SCC*, 2: 115 ff.

112. See Eliade, *Forge and Crucible*, passim.

113. Porée-Maspero, *Rites agraires*, vol. 2, passim.

114. Ibid., pp. 672 ff; Eberhard, *LC*, pp. 363–374; and Nobuhiro Matsumota, "Religious Thoughts of the Bronze Age Peoples of Indochina," in *Folk Religion and the Worldview in the Southwestern Pacific*, ed. N. Matsumota and T. Mabuchi (Tokyo: Keio Institute, 1968): 141–157.

115. Needham, *SCC*, 2: 119.

116. On the "Mandate of Heaven" theory in the Early Chou period see especially H. G. Creel, *The Origins of Statecraft in China*, vol. 1 (Chicago: University of Chicago Press, 1970), pp. 81–100. See also Dubs, "Archaic Royal Jou Religion," pp. 275 ff.

117. Granet, *DL*, pp. 45, 535, n. 2.

118. See Creel, *Statecraft*, 1: 227, n. 130.

119. Seidel, *Divinisation*, p. 52.

120. Ibid.

121. *HNTCI*, p. 292; and see Plaks, *Archetype and Allegory*, pp. 30–31.

122. Plaks, *Archetype and Allegory*, p. 30.

123. See Granet, *DL*, pp. 442 ff; 510 ff; Kaltenmark, "Naissance," p. 466; and Erkes, "Spüren," pp. 30 ff.

124. See above, chapter 3; and Watson, *Complete Works*, pp. 118, 192, 81–82.

125. See above, chapter 3; Watson, *Complete Works*, p. 82; and Yü, "Life and Immortality," pp. 103–108 (on the ascent motif).

126. Major, "Myth and Origins," p. 5. On the "chaos" figure of Saturn in Western tradition see J. E. Cirlot, *Dictionary of Symbols* (New York: Philosophical Library, 1962), pp. 265–267. On Saturn and chaos in Western alchemy see C. G. Jung, *Mysterium Coniunctiones* (New York: Pantheon Books, 1963), p. 335.

127. See, for example, H. Levy and A. Ishihara's *The Tao of Sex* (Yokohoma: Shibundo, 1968); and I. Veith's *The Yellow Emperor's Classic of Internal Medicine* (Berkeley and Los Angeles: University of California Press, 1966).

128. See Seidel, *Divinisation*, pp. 21–58. On the relation between Ch'i and the southern culture of Ch'u, see Major, "Research Priorities," pp. 239–241.

129. See Porée-Maspero, *Rites agraires*, p. 532.

130. See Kaltenmark, *Lie-sien Tchouan*, pp. 1–26. On Tsou-yen see Kaltenmark's "Les Tch'an-wei," *Mélanges de l'Institute de hautes études chinoises*, 1 (1957): pp. 366–370.

131. See Seidel, *Divinisation*, pp. 21–58 and Kaltenmark, *Lie-sien Tchouan*, pp. 1–26.

132. See, for example, Kaltenmark, "Naissance," pp. 458 f; and Eberhard, *LC*, pp. 443–445.

133. Eberhard, *LC*, p. 443.

134. See Ibid., pp. 443–445 (on Chung-li as a primordial couple and as associated with the southern Ch'u culture).

135. See chapters 4, 6, 10, 16, and 21 of the *Chuang Tzu*; and Plaks, *Archetype and Allegory*, pp. 39–40.

136. Kaltenmark, "Naissance," p. 458.

137. Plaks, *Archetype and Allegory*, p. 37.

138. See ibid., pp. 31–32. In general, see Wen I-to, "Fu-hsi k'ou" (Examination of Fu-hsi) and "Ts'ung jen-shu she-shen hsiang t'ou tao lung yu t'u-t'ung" (Beings with Human Heads and Serpent Bodies Considered as Dragon Totems) in *Wen I-to Ch'uan Chi* (Collected Works of Wen I-to), vol. 1 (n.p.: K'ai Ming Bookstore, 1948); pp. 3–12, 13–46.

139. See E. Schafer, *The Divine Woman: Dragon Ladies and Rain Maidens in T'ang Literature* (Berkeley, Los Angeles, London: University of California Press, 1973), pp. 29–32; and Plaks, *Archetype and Allegory*, pp. 27–42.

140. *LTCK*, pp. 38–39 (chap. 6); and Chan, pp. 6–7.

141. See Graham, *Lieh-tzu*, p. 54.

142. For a depiction of the iconography see Needham, *SCC*, 1: 164; and Plaks, *Archetype and Allegory*, pp. 238–239.

143. See Porée-Maspero, *Rites agraires*, pp. 361–478.

144. See Schafer, *Divine Woman*, pp. 13–14; and his, *Pacing the Void*, pp. 251–252.

145. See Plaks, *Archetype and Allegory*, pp. 29–33.

146. Ibid., pp. 34–35.

147. Ibid., pp. 35–36.

148. Ibid., p. 38. See also Plaks's discussion of "Complementary Bipolarity and Multiple Periodicity," pp. 43–53; see also below, chapter 7.

149. Eberhard, *LC*, p. 128.

150. Plaks, *Archetype and Allegory*, p. 37.

151. Ibid.

152. Ibid., p. 36; and see Porée-Maspero, *Rites agraires*, pp. 821 ff; Ho, *Myths and Legends*, pp. 56–86; and below, chapter 7.

153. Plaks, *Archetype and Allegory*, p. 19.

154. Ibid., pp. 36–37; Porée-Maspero, *Rites agraires*, pp. 831–836; Inez de Beauclair, "A Miao Tribe of Southeast Kweichow and Its Cultural Configurations," *Bulletin of the Institute of Ethnology*, Academia Sinica, No. 10 (1960): 154–156; and Hugo Adolf Bernatzik, *Akha and Miao*, trans. A. Nagler (New Haven: Human Relations Area Files, 1970), pp. 300–309.

155. Graham, *Stories of Ch'uan Miao*, pp. 179–180; and on the "people without anuses" legends, see Ho, *Myths and Legends*, pp. 134–137.

156. Porée-Maspero, *Rites agraires*, pp. 832–833.

157. See Obayashi Taryo, "Origins of Japanese Mythology," pp. 3–7.

158. See Anna B. Rooth, "The Creation Myths of the North American Indians," *Anthropos* 52 (1957): 500–502.

159. Plaks, *Archetype and Allegory*, p. 37.

160. Eliade, *Myth and Reality*, p. 21.

7. *Egg, Gourd, and Deluge: The Mythological Prototype of the Chaos Theme*

1. See Matthieu Casalis, "The Dry and the Wet: A Semiological Analysis of Creation and Flood Myths," *Semiotica* 17 (1976): 35–67. For an analysis of the structural relation between cosmogonic, anthropogonic, and flood myths in the "south" China context under investigation here see Anthony Jackson, "Floods, Fertility, and Feasting" *Ethnos* 40 (1975): 212–243.

2. On the worldwide botanical, cultural, and symbolic significance of cucurbits see Charles B. Heiser, *The Gourd Book* (Norman: University of Oklahoma Press, 1979); and Ralf Norrman and Jon Haarberg, *Nature and Language, a Semiotic Study of Cucurbits in Literature* (London: Routledge & Kegan Paul, 1980).

3. See Porée-Maspero, *Rites agraires*, pp. 672–680; Ho, *Myths and Legends*, pp. 153–158; Ouwehand, *Namazu-e*, pp. 182–202; and Eberhard, *LC*, pp. 279–285.

4. Jensen, *Myth and Cult*, pp. 83–134. See also Mabuchi, "Tales Concerning the Origin of Grains in the Insular area of Eastern and South-eastern Asia," in *Ethnology*, pp. 65–160; Atsuhiko Yoshida, "Les excrétions de la Déesse et l'origine de l'agriculture," *Annales Économies-sociétés-civilisations* 21 (1966): 707–728; and Mircea Eliade, *Myth and Reality* (New York: Harper Torch Books, 1963), pp. 103–107.

5. A. Jensen, "Das Weltbild einer frühen Kultur," *Paideuma* 3 (1944): 34–38—English translation in J. Campbell, *The Masks of God: Primitive Mythology* (New

York: The Viking Press, 1959), pp. 173–176.

6. Eliade, *Myth and Reality*, p. 106.

7. Jensen, *Myth and Cult*, pp. 147–190.

8. Ibid., pp. 162–208; and Campbell, *Masks of God*, pp. 170–215. On the gourd's ritual use as a penis sheath see Heiser, *Gourd Book*, pp. 145–160.

9. Obayashi, "Japanese Mythology," pp. 3–12.

10. Ibid., p. 8.

11. For criticism of Jensen see J. Z. Smith, "A Pearl of Great Price and a Cargo of Yams: A Study in Situational Incongruity," *History of Religions* 16 (1976): 1–19.

12. Obayashi, "Japanese Mythology," p. 11.

13. See Eberhard, *LC*, pp. 92–98.

14. Ibid., p. 451.

15. See Heiser, *Gourd Book*, p. 72. The term *Lagenaria vulgaris* is often seen but is currently out of date. The name "calabash" is commonly taken to mean a bottle gourd (especially of the constricted "dumbell" shape in East Asia) but is ambiguous as a reference to a particular member of the family Cucurbitacae. The term calabash in this book will always refer to the bottle gourd (*Lagenaria siceraria asiatica*).

16. Ho, *Myths and Legends*, p. 156. For Chinese and Japanese textual sources concerning gourds see Shime Suigan, *Hyotan monogatari*, passim. The significance and role of gourds in ancient China is shown by the fifth to sixth century A.D. *Ch'i Min Yao Shu* (Essential Arts of the People)—see Li Hui-lin, "The Vegetables of Ancient China," *Economic Botany* 23 (1969): 253–260.

17. Heiser, *Gourd Book*, p. 71.

18. Ibid., pp. 71–228. See also Angelo de Gubernatis, *La mythologie des plantes* (1878–1882; reprint ed., New York: Arno Press, 1978), pp. 97–191; Gertrude Jobes, *Dictionary of Mythology, Folklore and Symbols* (New York: Scarecrow Press, 1961), p. 680; and Charles Pickering, *Chronological History of Plants* (Boston: Little, Brown, and Co., 1879), pp. 137–138.

19. Heiser, *Gourd Book*, p. 71. See also Don and Patricia Brothwell, *Food In Antiquity* (New York: Frederick A. Praeger, 1969), pp. 124–129.

20. Charles A. Reed, "Origins of Agriculture: Discussion and Some Conclusions," in *The Origins of Agriculture*, ed. Charles A. Reed (The Hague: Mouton Publishers, 1977), p. 932. See Heiser's technical discussion, "Variation in the Bottle Gourd," in *Tropical Forest Ecosystems in Africa and South America: A Comparative Review*, ed. Betty J. Meggers, Edward S. Ayensu, and W. Donald Duckworth (Washington: Smithsonian Institution Press, 1973), pp. 121–128.

21. See Reed's discussion of Donald Lathrap's work, "Origins of Agriculture," p. 930 (on Lathrap see below).

22. Ibid., pp. 905–917; and Heiser, *Gourd Book*, pp. 81–85 (based on his personal examination of fragments of the "bottle gourd" specimen from Spirit Cave, Heiser is now of the opinion that this material is most probably not from an archaic gourd— pp. 82–83). If the archaeological material for the gourd at Spirit Cave does not hold up under specialized scrutiny, this means that presently the oldest records of the gourd in Asia are to be found in the semimythical accounts in the Chinese classic known as the *Shih Ching* (ninth to fifth cent. B.C., plus later additions). On this literary evidence see Hsuan Keng, "Economic Plants of Ancient China as Mentioned in *Shih Ching* (Book of

Poetry)," *Economic Botany* 28 (1974): 391–410.

23. Reed (referring to a personal communication from Heiser), "Origins of Agriculture," p. 908, n. 5.

24. Ho, *Myths and Legends*, p. 156. See also Heiser's random collection of "myth, legend, and fable" materials, *Gourd Book*, pp. 202–228.

25. Ho, *Myths and Legends*, p. 156.

26. Ibid.

27. See generally Ho, *Myths and Legends*; Eberhard, *LC*; Porée-Maspero, *Rites agraires*; Granet, *DL*; Jensen, *Myth and Cult*; A. Haudricourt, "Domestication des animaux, cultures des plantes, et civilisation d'autri," *L'Homme* 2 (1962): 40–50; and his "Nature et culture dans la civilisation de l'igname, origine des clones et des clans," *L'Homme* 4 (1964): 93–104.

28. See P. T. Ho, *Cradle of the East*, pp. 18, 57; and Reed's discussion of Ho (who claims a date of ca. 7000 B.P. for the first cultivation of millet), "Origins of Agriculture," pp. 902–904, 905–917 (on Southeast Asia). See also Chang Kwang-chih's corroborating archaeological discussion in "The Beginnings of Agriculture in the Far East," *Antiquity* 44 (1970): 175–185. Based on P. T. Ho's work, Chang states that "the dominating importance of millets (*Setaria italica* and *Panicum miliaceum*) above all other crops is plain" (p. 182). See also Hsuan Keng, "Economic Plants," pp. 395–399.

29. Ho, *Myths and Legends*, p. 157. Like the substitution of rice for millet, it is clear that gourds are replaced by other more economically significant vegetables in Chinese cultural history—see Li, "Vegetables of Ancient China," pp. 253–254 (table 1).

30. Legge, *Chinese Classics*, 4:468–469; for other gourd allusions in the *Shih* see 4:53, 231, 375; and Hsuan Keng, "Economic Plants," pp. 391–410. Legge (4:53) remarks in a note that empty gourd shells were commonly used as flotation bladders for children in China. The "gourds" in the *Shih* are variously *Lagenaria siceraria, Lagenaria leucantha,* and *Cucumis melo*—see Li, "Vegetables of Ancient China," p. 254; and K. C. Chang, "Ancient China," in *Food in Ancient China*, p. 28.

31. Waley, *Book of Songs*, p. 245.

32. Ibid., p. 248. See also Legge, *Chinese Classics*, 4:437.

33. Waley, *Book of Songs*, p. 248.

34. Ho, *Myths and Legends*, p. 157.

35. Ibid. The cucurbits, pumpkin and squash (*Cucurbita pepo*), are "American plants and probably did not reach China and southeastern Asia until the sixteenth century or later"—Heiser, personal communication and his *Gourd Book* pp. 30–33.

36. See Chang's conclusion, "Beginnings of Agriculture," pp. 179–181 (although it should be noted that in this article Chang accepts the identification of *Lagenaria* from Spirit Cave).

37. For a statement of the dominant position among archaeologists see Kent V. Flannery, "The Origins of Agriculture," *Annual Review of Anthropology* 2 (1973): 271–310.

38. See Carl O. Sauer, *Agricultural Origins and Dispersals, The Domestication of Animals and Foodstuffs* (1952; reprint ed., Cambridge: The Massachusetts Institute of Technology Press, 1969). For criticism and discussion see Paul C. Mangelsdorf's review of *Agricultural Origins* in *American Antiquity* 19 (1953): 87–90; and the more balanced discussion by Reed, "Origins of Agriculture," pp. 910–912; Li Hui-lin, "The Origin of

Cultivated Plants in Southeast Asia,'' *Economic Botany* 24 (1970): 3—19; and G. A. Wright, ''Origin of Food Production in South Western Asia: A Survey of Ideas,'' *Current Anthropology* 12 (1971): 447—477. See also the earlier work of N. I. Vavilov, ''The Origin, Variation, Immunity, and Breeding of Cultivated Plants,'' trans. K. S. Chester, *Chronica Botanica* 13 (1949/1951): 1—364; and A. Haudricourt and L. Hedin, *L'Homme et les plantes cultivées* (Paris: Gallimard, 1943).

39. See D. G. Coursey, ''The Civilization of the Yam: Interrelationships of Man and Yams in Africa and The Indo-Pacific Region,'' *Archaeology and Physical Anthropology In Oceania* 7 (1972): 215—233; and his ''The New Yam Festivals of West Africa,'' *Anthropos* 66 (1971): 444—484. For David R. Harris' work see his ''Swidden Systems and Settlement,'' in *Man, Settlement, and Urbanism*, ed. Peter J. Ucko, et al. (London: Duckworth, 1972), pp. 245—261; and ''Agricultural Systems, Ecosystems and the Origins of Agriculture,'' in *The Domestication and Exploitation of Plants and Animals*, ed. Peter J. Ucko and G. W. Dimbleby (Chicago: Aldine Publishing Co., 1969), pp. 3—15.

40. See Donald W. Lathrap, ''Our Father the Cayman, Our Mother the Gourd: Spinden Revisited, Or a Unitary Model for the Emergence of Agriculture in the New World,'' in *Origin of Agriculture*, ed. Charles A. Reed, pp. 713—751.

41. See Chang, ''Beginnings of Agriculture,'' pp. 179—181. See also W. Watson, ''Neolithic Settlement in East Asia,'' in *Man, Settlement, and Urbanism*, p. 338; and Li, ''Origin of Cultivated Plants,'' pp. 3—19.

42. For Lathrap's argument, see ''Our Mother the Gourd,'' pp. 729—735.

43. Ibid., pp. 734—735. For the Asian/Pacific context of this kind of spatial, agricultural, and sexual dualism see Jacques Barrau, ''L'Humide et le Sec: An Essay on Ethnobiological Adaptation to Contrastive Environments in the Indo-Pacific Area,'' *Journal of the Polynesian Society* 74 (1965): 329—344 (wet, triangular ''female'' taro as distinct from dry, phallic ''male'' yams). See also Paul Sillitoe, ''The Gender of Crops in the Papua New Guinea Highlands,'' *Ethnology* 20 (1981): 1—14.

44. Heiser, *Gourd Book*, pp. 105—118; and Reed, ''Origins of Agriculture,'' pp. 930—935.

45. Lathrap, ''Our Mother the Gourd,'' p. 719. African gourd mythology and symbolism is especially rich, and in many instances, parallels the Asian accounts—see Geoffrey Parrinder, *African Mythology* (London: Paul Hamlyn, 1967), pp. 21—22, 32, 42; and Marcel Griaule, *Conversations with Ogotemmeli* (London: Oxford University Press, 1965), pp. 106—107, 110.

46. Norrman and Haarberg, *Nature and Language*, p. 8.

47. For the ''semiotic matrix of cucurbits,'' see ibid., pp. 13—79 (see also the visual imagery recorded on the plates between pp. 80—81).

48. For most of my botanical information I have relied heavily on Heiser, *Gourd Book*, passim; Thomas W. Whitaker and Glen N. Davis, *Cucurbits* (New York: Interscience Publishers, 1962); and Carolyn Mordecai, *Gourd Craft* (New York: Crown Publishers, 1978), pp. 45—60. See also Thomas W. Whitaker and G. W. Bohn, ''The Taxonomy, Genetics, Production and Uses of the Cultivated Species of Cucurbita,'' *Economic Botany* 4 (1950): 52—81; and J. A. Kobiakova, ''The Bottle Gourd,'' *Bulletin of Applied Botany, Genetics and Plant Breeding* 23 (1930): 475—520 (in Russian with English summary). Within the Chinese context see J. C. Liu, *Flowering Families in*

North China (Peking: Henri Vetch, 1931), pp. 132–135; N. M. Porterfield, Jr., "The Principle Chinese Vegetable Food Plants of Chinatown Markets," *Economic Botany* 5 (1951): 32–37; Li, "Vegetables of Ancient China," pp. 253–256; Hsuan Keng, "Economic Plants," pp. 391–401; and Berthold Laufer, *Insect Musicians and Cricket Champions of China* (Chicago: Field Museum of Natural History, 1927), pp. 6–14 (and plates).

49. Information on the pollination of *Lagenaria* is scanty—see Heiser, *Gourd Book*, pp. 72–74 (who documents the agency of moths, bees, birds, and beetles). My tentative addition of butterflies and bats (not unknown in the pollination of some cucurbits) to the list of pollinators is based on inference coming from the mythological, symbolic, and linguistic evidence analyzed here. On the bat associations with gourds and *hun-tun* see Eberhard, *LC*, p. 280; and for bat pollination of *Crescentia cujete* (calabash tree) see Anthony Huxley, ed., *The Encyclopedia of the Plant Kingdom* (New York: Chartwell Books, 1977), p. 36. Also, Lo Meng-ts'e shows that the life cycle of the silk worm/ cocoon/moth (=butterfly?) is an important metaphor for the idea of "great transformation"/metamorphosis related to the *hun-tun* theme—pp. 293–299. It should be noted that there is apparently some relation between the symbolic significance of gourds, cocoons, and rituals associated with sericulture in China—see Eberhard, *LC*, pp. 34–35, 197, 246, 302 (especially with reference to the symbolism of sacrifice during the Dragon Boat festival time); and also Bodde, *Festivals*, on the ritual of the "First Sericulturalist"—pp. 263–272 (a third month festival in the Han). The gourd and the cocoon (as well as the mulberry tree) appear to have been especially important symbols that calendrically marked nodal times of renewal in the ancient festival cycle.

50. The relative lack of vigor and heterosis following inbreeding, while not documented for *Lagenaria*, is reported for other cultivated species of cucurbits—see Whitaker and Bohn, "Taxonomy of *Cucurbita*," pp. 73–74.

51. On floating as the basic dispersion mechanism for *Lagenaria* and its far-reaching implications for the transoceanic diffusion or propagation of ancient mother cultures see Heiser, *Gourd Book*, pp. 99–117; and Lathrap, "Our Mother the Gourd," pp. 720–729.

52. See Eberhard, *LC*, pp. 282–287.

53. See Porée-Maspero, *Rites agraires*, passim; and Lorenz G. Loffler, "Beast, Bird, and Fish, An Essay in South-East Asian Symbolism," in *Folk Religion and the Worldview in the Southwestern Pacific*, ed. N. Matsumoto and T. Mabuchi (Tokyo: Keio Institute of Cultural and Linguistic Studies, 1968), pp. 21–36.

54. *CCT*, 1/1/1–17; and Watson, pp. 29–31.

55. Heiser reports an average of six to eight months for African *Lagenaria* and four to six months for the Asian species by modern calendrical dating—a range that fits well into the seventh/eighth lunar month frame (August/September) indicated by the evidence from traditional China. See Heiser, "Variation in the Bottle Gourd," p. 122.

56. Lunar symbolism is especially important in relation to the ripe gourd in China— see Eberhard, *LC*, pp. 279–280.

57. See Ibid., pp. 279–282, 198–199 (cf. practices on the fifth day of the fifth month). Eberhard also notes that P'an-hu's birthday was originally celebrated during the seventh or eighth month—p. 46.

58. Ibid., pp. 281–283. On the ancient Han festivals of the seventh and eighth

months (''Autumn's Beginning'') see Bodde, *Festivals*, pp. 327—359.

59. Eberhard, *LC*, pp. 283—286. On the associations with Taoist lore see Schipper, *L'emperour Wou des Han*, p. 51. It is clear that the folkloric weaver girl story is typologically structured on the narrative scheme developed in this chapter—see below and compare Eberhard, *Festivals*, pp. 143—145.

60. Reference found in *Mathew's Dictionary*, entry number 3508. I have been unable to locate this in Legge. The *Shih Ching* records that the eighth month was the time to cut down bottle gourds—Legge, *Chinese Classics*, 4:231.

61. *Hortulus, Walahfrid Strabo*, trans. Raef Payne (Pittsburgh: The Hunt Botanical Library, 1966), p. 37.

62. For the ''disease'' (leprosy, tumors, scales, etc.) associations see table 3 and below. Like the alchemical elixir, the gourd was related to both sickness and health (poison/medicine). Medicinally, gourd infusions ''were found useful in treating beriberi, the vitamin B^1 deficiency disease in the predominantly rice-eating south''—see Edward H. Schafer, ''T'ang,'' in *Food in Chinese Culture*, p. 138, n. 5.

63. See, for example, the accounts given by Stein in ''Jardins en miniature,'' passim; and the legends of the ''Eight Immortals,'' in Doré, *Researches*, 9:35—63.

64. Heiser, *Gourd Book*, p. 101; and T. W. Whitaker and George F. Carter, ''A Note on the Longevity of Seed of *Lagenaria siceraria* (Mol.) Standl. after Floating in Sea Water,'' *Bulletin of the Torrey Botanical Club* 88 (1961):104—106.

65. See, for example, Berthold Laufer, *Chinese Pottery of the Han Dynasty* (Leiden: E. J. Brill, 1909), pp. 106—112 (and pl. 22). Laufer quotes a Han text that says that the *p'ao-tou* ''are ladles resembling a bottle-gourd after it has been cut into halves. . . . Among the materials for the eight musical instruments, the gourd takes the first place, and embodies in its form the nature of heaven and earth. Nowadays the shape of the ladle is derived from the gourd, an idea inherited by the ancients'' (pp. 107—108). See also Ouwehand, *Namazu-e*, pp. 182—202.

66. See Plaks, *Archetype and Allegory*, pp. 34—37; and Porée-Maspero, *Rites agraires*, pp. 672—680.

67. Norrman and Haarberg, *Nature and Language*, p. 53.

68. Ibid. (Latin text) and pp. 221—222 (English translation).

69. *CCT*, 75/27/1, 93/33/65; and Watson, pp. 303, 373.

70. Watson, p. 303, n. 1.

71. I am paraphrasing Geertz's discussion of symbol here—see ''Religion as a Cultural System,'' in *Reader*, p. 207.

72. *LTCK*, pp. 27—30; and Chan, p. 105.

73. *LTCK*, pp. 63—65; and Chan, p. 119.

74. *LTCK*, pp. 63—67; and Chan, p. 121.

75. See Clifford Geertz ''Ethos, World View, and the Analysis of Sacred Symbols,'' in *Interpretation of Cultures*, p. 128.

76. Ibid.

77. Ibid.

78. See Heiser, *Gourd Book*, p. 222.

79. Ibid., p. 30.

80. See Norrman and Haarberg, *Nature and Language*, pp. 38—39 (cf. *Kürbiskopf* [gourd head] : Croation, *Tvrda tikva* : Italian, *cocomero, zucca, zuccone, peponella*,

mellone, citrullo : French, *melon, citrouille, gourde, cornichon* : Spanish, *calabaza, sandio* : etc.). On these foolish associations see below, chapter 8.

81. Ho, *Myths and Legends*, p. 275.

82. See Porée-Maspero, *Rites agraires*, pp. 821–851. The scheme presented here has been amended in relation to my analysis. See also Jackson, "Floods, Fertility, and Feasting," pp. 212–243. Eliade sees a connection with an "Earth Diver" type of mythology—see his *Zalmoxis* (Chicago: University of Chicago Press, 1972); pp. 115–130 (useful also for his bibliography).

83. Porée-Maspero, *Rites agraires*, passim. For a corroborating discussion of basic cultural traits associated with this "southern" complex see K. C. Chang, "Working Hypothesis For the Cultural History of South China," pp. 90–98. See also E. N. Anderson, *Mountains and Water* (Taipei: Chinese Association for Folklore, 1973), pp. 33–40, 147–166, for a discussion of the south Chinese ecological context for religion.

84. See Mary K. Wakeman, *God's Battle with the Monster* (Leiden: E. J. Brill, 1973); H. Gunkel, *Schöpfung und Chaos in Urzeit und Endzeit* (Göttingen: Vandenhoeck und Ruprecht, 1895); and Bernhard W. Anderson, *Creation Versus Chaos* (New York: Association Press, 1967).

85. Jonathan Z. Smith, review of Wakeman in *Journal of Biblical Literature* 94 (1975): 422.

86. Ibid.

87. Ho, *Myths and Legends*, pp. 127–137.

88. Ibid., p. 127.

89. See above, chapter 6.

90. Ho, *Myths and Legends*, p. 356.

91. Ibid., pp. 128–129, 135–137.

92. Ibid., p. 135; and see Eberhard, *LC*, on the significance of the agricultural digging stick among the Yao[b], pp. 94–97.

93. See Porée-Maspero, *Rites agraires*, pp. 361–478. In general, see Mary Douglas, *Purity and Danger: An Analysis of Pollution and Taboo* (New York: Frederick A. Praeger, 1966). For the Chinese context see Wei Hwei-lin, "Categories of Totemism in Ancient China," in *Folk Religion and the Worldview*, pp. 73–83. The concept of "totemism" is too ambiguously broad to be used as a specific cultural or religious denominator. In fact, as Lévi-Strauss shows, "totemism" defines a universal structure of human existence, not a particular primitive culture or stage in cultural history—see his *Totemism*, trans. R. Needham (Boston: Beacon Press, 1963).

94. See Porée-Maspero, *Rites agraires*, pp. 361–478; Eberhard, *LC*, pp. 52, 100–102 (on cooking pots: bamboo, gourds?), 202, 379; and Jensen on "sacrifice," *Myth and Cult*, pp. 166–190.

95. For associations with the *hun-tun* theme in China see Eberhard, *LC*, pp. 446–450 (headhunting, skull cult, and cannibalism). See also Jensen's comments on the sacrificial cutting up, or sacred murder, of the Dema diety, *Myth and Cult*, pp. 160–190. In the Burmese Kachin mythology of the flood the deformed offspring is made into a curry—see *Standard Dictionary of Folklore*. Compare also the *Shih Ching*'s allusion to gourd symbolism, sacrifice, and food—see above in this chapter.

96. See, for example, Porée-Maspero, *Rites agraires*, pp. 361–478. Comparatively

see the discussion of Scandinavian "savior sausages" by Nils-Arvid Bringeus, "Food and Folk Beliefs: On Boiling Blood Sausage," in *Gastronomy, The Anthropology of Food and Food Habits*, ed. Margaret L. Arnott (The Hague: Mouton Publishers, 1975), pp. 251—274.

97. Jackson, "Floods, Fertility, and Feasts," pp. 212—243. Also important in Jackson's study is his discussion of the transformations of the mythic structure in relation to different periods and groups in ·Na-khi cultural history. On cooking and eating symbolism see also Anderson's discussion of Cantonese "ethnohoptology"— *Mountains and Waters*, pp. 109—120.

98. Lévi-Strauss, *Savage Mind*, p. 225.

99. Ibid.

100. Ibid.

101. See above, chapter 1.

102. *CCT*, 59/22/43—44; and Watson, pp. 240—241.

103. The development of this scheme was influenced by Wheatley's understanding of Chinese civilizational development—see *Pivot of The Four Quarters*, pp. 316—330.

104. On Humpty Dumpty see Albert Muson Stevens, *The Nursery Rhyme* (Lawrence, Kansas: Coronado Press, 1968), pp. 67—82.

105. For a discussion of the basic contrast between pre-urban and urban culture see Wheatley, *Pivot of Four Quarters*, p. 317.

106. Ibid., pp. 316—330.

107. See Diamond's discussion, *In Search of the Primitive*, pp. 150—159.

108. Ibid., p. 153.

109. See Robert Neville, "From Nothing to Being: The Notion of Creation in Chinese and Western Thought," *Philosophy East and West* 30 (1980):32.

110. Ibid.

111. I borrow the phrase "archetypal pattern of conceptualization," as related to a mythic structure, from Plaks, *Archetype and Allegory*, pp. 43—53.

112. M. Porkert, *The Theoretical Foundations of Chinese Medicine*, (Cambridge, Mass. MIT Press, 1974), p. 9.

113. See Neville's discussion of the Taoist *creatio ex nihilo*, "Nothing to Being," pp. 25—28.

114. See Porée-Maspero, *Rites agraires*, pp. 361—478; Jensen, *Myth and Cult*, pp. 147—161; Lévi-Strauss, *Structural Anthropology*, pp. 132—163; and Barrau, "L'humide et le Sec," pp. 329—346.

115. See Granet, *Pensée*, pp. 101—126; and his *Fêtes et chansons*, pp. 244 ff. See also Aijmer's discussion, *Dragon Boat Festival*, passim.

116. See E. Durkheim and M. Mauss, *Primitive Classification*, trans. R. Needham (Chicago: University of Chicago Press, 1963). For discussion of this approach see R. Needham's comments, pp. xvii—xviii, xxvi—xxvii; Lévi-Strauss, *Elementary Structures of Kinship*, pp. 311—392; and Eliade, *Quest*, pp. 127—133.

117. See Sproul, *Prolegomena*, pp. 204—207.

118. See Plaks, *Archetype and Allegory*, pp. 43—53.

119. Saso, *Cosmic Renewal*, p. 9.

120. Plaks, *Archetype and Allegory*, pp. 44—47. See also Porkert's discussion, *Theoretical Foundations*, pp. 9—43.

121. Plaks, *Archetype and Allegory*, p. 47.

122. See Porkert, *Theoretical Foundations*, pp. 19–22, for the "chaos" qualities of *yin*.

123. Plaks, *Archetype and Allegory*, p. 48.

124. Ibid.

125. Ibid.

126. Ibid., p. 49.

127. See D. Bodde's discussion, "Harmony and Conflict in Chinese Philosophy," in A. Wright, ed. *Studies in Chinese Thought* (Chicago: University of Chicago Press, 1953), pp. 54, 61–62. Some of the ideas in this section profited from a reading of Daniel Overmyer's "Dualism and Conflict in Chinese Popular Religion."

128. De Groot, *Religious System*, 6: 930–931.

129. Saso, *Cosmic Renewal*, p. 10.

130. See Max Kaltenmark, "The Ideology of the T'ai-P'ing Ching," in *Facets of Taoism*, pp. 19–52.

131. Eliade, *Quest*, pp. 174–175. See also Hsu Sung-peng, "Lao Tzu's Concept of Evil," *Philosophy East and West* 26 (1976): 301–316.

132. Eliade, *Quest*, pp. 174–175.

133. Ibid., p. 134.

134. Without treating the particular significance of *hun-tun*, Eliade has insightfully noted that "the comparison of the notion of *tao* with the different primitive formulas of the 'third term' as a solution of polarities, constitutes a fascinating theme for the historian of ideas" (*Quest*, p. 173).

135. Ibid., p. 139.

136. Ibid.

137. Hans Schärer, *Ngaju Religion* (The Hague: Martinus Nijhoff, 1963); Porée-Maspero, *Rites agraires*, pp. 432–434, passim; and Nobuhiro Matsumoto, "Religious Thoughts of the Bronze Age Peoples of Indochina," in *Folk Religion and the Worldview*, pp. 148–149.

138. Eliade, *Quest*, p. 163.

139. Ibid.

140. Ibid., p. 80.

141. Ibid., p. 163.

142. Justus Van Der Kroef, "Dualism and Symbolic Antithesis in Indonesian Society," *American Anthropologist* 56 (1954): 852.

143. Ibid., p. 855; and his "The Roots of Javanese Drama," *Journal of Aesthetics and Art Criticism* 12 (1954): 318–327. In China the order of "five" seems especially related to the priestly/kingly order that balances the four quarters of the "middle kingdom." For this comment I am indebted to Sun Lung-kee's unpublished paper "The Mythical World-View and Cosmogonic Myths of the Ancient Chinese." Sun cites the work (which I have not been able to obtain) of Hu Hou-hsüan, "Lun wu-fang kuan-nien chi 'chung-kuo' ch'eng-wei chih ch'i-yüan" (On the concepts of the five positions and the origin of the title 'middle kingdom'), in *Chia Ku Hsüeh Shang Shih Lun Ts'ung Ch'u Chi* (First Collection of Essays on the Studies of Oracle Bones and Shang History). vol. 2 (Shantung: Ch'i Lu University, 1944). See also Granet, who points out that "five" represents a centered elaboration on the prior order of "three"—see *DL*, pp. 616–617.

144. See Sproul, *Prolegomena*, pp. 193–200.

8. *The Order of Chaos: Symbolic Aspects of Taoist Mysticism*

1. See Norrman and Haarberg, *Nature and Language*, pp. 112–115.

2. Ibid., p. 114.

3. William Willeford, *The Fool and His Scepter* (Evanston: Northwestern University Press, 1969), p. 108.

4. Ibid.

5. Bauer, *Search for Happiness*, p. 38.

6. Erving Goffman, *Interaction Ritual, Essays on Face-to-Face Behavior* (Garden City: Anchor Books, 1967), p. 5. On Chinese usage see Hsien-chin Hu, "The Chinese Concepts of 'Face,' " *American Anthropologist* 46 (1944): 45–64; W. Eberhard, *Guilt and Sin in Traditional China* (Berkeley and Los Angeles: University of California Press, 1967); pp. 12–13, 100–108, 119–124; and Leon E. Stover and Takeko Kawai Stover, *China: An Anthropological Perspective* (Pacific Palisades, Ca.: Goodyear Publishing Co., 1976), pp. 202–212.

7. Hu, "Concepts of Face," p. 45.

8. Ibid.

9. I borrow the term "face work" from Goffman, *Interaction Ritual*, pp. 5–45.

10. From a comparative standpoint see H. Corbin, "Face de dieu et face de l'homme," *Eranos Jahrbuch* (Zürich: Rhein-Verlag, 1968), pp. 166–228; and James Hillman, "Senex and Puer," *Eranos Jahrbuch* (Zürich: Rhein-Verlag, 1968), pp. 349–355.

11. See D. T. Suzuki, *Essays in Zen Buddhism, First Series* (New York: Rider, 1949), p. 208.

12. See Chang, "Man and Animal," p. 195; and Loewe, "Man and Beast," pp. 97–117.

13. Chang, "Man and Animal," p. 196.

14. Legge, *Chinese Classics*, 1: 334.

15. See Turner, *Ritual Process*, on the "masking function," pp. 172–177.

16. M. Eliade, "Masks, Mythical and Ritual Origins," in *Encyclopedia of World Art* (New York: McGraw Hill, 1964), 9:521.

17. C. Kerenyi, "Man and Mask," in *Spiritual Disciplines*, ed. J. Campbell (New York: Pantheon Books, Inc., 1960), p. 152.

18. Ibid., p. 167. See also Walter Sorell, *The Other Face: The Mask in the Arts* (Indianapolis: Bobbs-Merrill Co., 1973), pp. 7–16. It is interesting to note that the English word *mask* comes from the Arabic *maskharah* meaning "buffoon" or from the verbal root *maskh* referring to the "transformation of men into animals"—see *Encyclopedia of World Art*, p. 521.

19. See Kerenyi, "Man and Mask," p. 152.

20. For the Chinese tradition of masks, see L. Lanciotti, "Chinese Masks," *Encyclopedia of World Art*; Granet, *DL*, pp. 335 ff; and Bodde, *Festivals*, pp. 78–82.

21. *LTCS*, p. 51; and Graham, p. 54.

22. Ibid.

23. Huston Smith, *The Religions of Man* (New York: Harper and Row, 1958), p. 37.

24. See Granet, *DL*, pp. 335–336, n.1. The term *ts'un* generally means "to keep, retain, preserve, or to be in existence." For the *Lieh Tzu* quote see *LTCS*, p. 12; and Graham, p. 26.

25. Granet, *DL*, p. 335. Although it is relevant to this discussion, I am avoiding here the complicating factor of the ancient Chinese belief in a bipartite soul principle (i.e., the *hun*[j] and *p'o*[b] souls and their multiple manifestations)—see, for example, Needham, *SCC*, vol. 5, pt. 2, pp. 85–93. See also Lo's discussion of "funerary images" (*hsiang-jen* and *yung-jen*) in his "Primeval State," pp. 293–299. Lo sees a connection with the images of the chrysalis and cocoon.

26. Granet, *DL*, pp. 335–336, n. 1. For the problems associated with the archaic origin and meaning of the ancestral tablet see B. Karlgren, "Some Fecundity Symbols in Ancient China," *Bulletin of the Museum of Far Eastern Antiquities* (Stockholm) 2 (1930): 1 ff; E. Erkes, "Some Remarks on Karlgren's 'Fecundity Symbols,'" *Bulletin of the Museum of Far Eastern Antiquities* (Stockholm) 3 (1931): 63–68; B. Laufer, "The Development of Ancestral Images in China," in *Reader in Comparative Religion* ed. William Lessa and Evon Vogt (1913, in *The Journal of Religious Psychology*; reprint ed., New York: Harper and Row, 1965), pp. 445–450; and Ling Shun-sheng, "Ancestral Tablet and Genital Symbolism in Ancient China," *Bulletin of the Institute of Ethnology, Academia Sinica* 6 (1958): 39–46.

27. Laufer, "Ancestral Images," p. 447. See also de Groot, *Religious System*, I: 214–216.

28. Laufer, ibid. Laufer also recounts a similar ritual of the consecration of deity images by Taoist priests (p. 447). Compare also the ritual consecration of puppets—see K. Schipper, "The Divine Jester," *Bulletin of the Institute of Ethnology, Academia Sinica*, 21–22 (1966): 81–96.

29. Granet, *DL*, p. 336. On the practice of second burial in primitive cultures see R. Hertz, *Death and the Right Hand*, trans. Rodney and Claudia Needham (Glencoe, Ill.: Free Press, 1960), pp. 53 ff.; and Eberhard, *LC*, pp. 104–106.

30. Granet, *DL*, p. 336.

31. See Eberhard, *LC*, pp. 103 ff; and also de Groot, *Religious System*, I: 316–324.

32. Eberhard, *LC*. See also Stein, "Jardins en miniature," pp. 56 ff; Soymié, "Le Lo-feou chan," pp. 57 ff; and Granet, *DL*, pp. 532, 542.

33. *CCT*, 90/32/47–52; and Watson, p. 361. See de Groot's discussion of this passage, *Religious System*, 1: 305–306. On the primitive Dayak funeral practices involving the symbolism of the drum and bird-boat see Matsumoto, "Religious Thoughts of the Bronze Age Peoples of Indochina," pp. 148–155.

34. Eliade, *Rites and Symbols*, p. 113.

35. Ibid.

36. Ibid., p. 114. See also Maspero, *Taoisme*, pp. 13–16.

37. Shido Bunan, a Japanese Zen master of the early Tokugawa era.

38. *CCT*, 92/33/45–52; and Watson, pp. 370–371. It should be noted that in later Taoist mysticism the image of the "revolving whirlwind," like the swirling flood waters of the creation time, is expressly related to the chaos condition of mystic union—see Isabelle Robinet, *Méditation taoiste* (Paris: Dervy Livres, 1979), p. 160.

39. *CCT*, 92/33/45–52; and Watson, pp. 370–371.

40. *LTCK*, pp. 43–44; and Graham, pp. 47–48. Like Shen Tao's "whirlwind" imagery, this passage emphasizes the symbolism of swirling, floodlike waters, a whirlpool. Cf. *Chuang Tzu*, chapter 7; and see above, chapters 3 and 5.

41. Ibid.

42. See Richard B. Onians, *The Origins of European Thought* (Cambridge: Cambridge University Press, 1954), pp. 507–508; and Norrman and Haarberg, *Nature and Language*, pp. 54–62. More correctly, this is "gourdification" since there were no real pumpkins in ancient Rome—see Heiser, *Gourd Book*, p. 30.

43. The term *hun*[f] means "to dishonor, disgrace, shame" and is related to *hun*[g] meaning a "privy, confused, dirty, turbid" and *hun*[h], "pig sty, privy."

44. See E. M. Chen, "The *Tao Te Ching*'s Approach to Language," *Chinese Culture*, pp. 38–48; and in a comparative context see P. Fingesten, "Sight and Insight: a Contribution Toward an Iconography of the Eye," *Criticism* 1 (1959): 19–31.

45. Foucault, *Order of Things*, p. 133.

46. *CCT*, 7/3/2–7; and Watson, p. 50. On the significance of the "knack passages" see Needham, *SCC*, 2: 121 ff.

47. See Munro, *Concept of Man*, pp. 55 ff.

48. Ibid., pp. 140 ff. *CCT*, 21/4/31–33; and Watson, p. 97.

49. For a discussion of *nei-kuan* see Schipper's review of Graham's *Book of Lieh tzu* in *T'oung Pao* 51 (1964): 288–292. See also *Hsien Hsüeh Tz'u Tien*, p. 58.

50. *CCT*, 55/21/26; and Watson, p. 225.

51. Schipper, "Taoist Body," p. 369. See also M. Saso, *The Teachings of Taoist Master Chuang* (New Haven: Yale University Press, 1978), p. 228, n. 15.

52. Schipper, "Taoist Body," p. 370. It is interesting to observe that the Taoist symbolism of the belly extends into Japanese tradition in terms of the idea of the *hara* (belly) or the true center of man—see J. Evola, "The Japanese Hara-Theory and Its Relations to East and West," *East and West* 9 (1958): 76 ff; and Karlfried Dürckheim's *Hara, The Vital Centre of Man*, trans. Sylvia-Monica von Kospoth in collaboration with Estelle R. Healy (London: Unwin Paperbacks, 1962).

53. See above, chapter 5; and Granet, *DL*, p. 326, n. 3.

54. Granet, ibid.

55. Kaltenmark, *Lao Tzu*, p. 69.

56. See chapter 2.

57. Quoting from David Kinsley's discussion of sacred madness in Indian tradition, " 'Through the Looking Glass': Divine Madness in the Hindu Religious Tradition," *History of Religions* 13 (1974): 281.

58. *Chuang Tzu*, chapters 1, 2, 4, 21; see above, chapter 3.

59. On the matter of the "flocking" of connotations within this kind of semantic matrix see Norrman and Haarberg, *Nature and Language*, p. 114.

60. See Stein, "Jardins en miniature," p. 54, n. 1. Stein sees a special connection between the symbolic meaning of the *hu-lu* gourd, calabash, or vase and the idea of sacred madness/mystical experience; and it is curious to see a similar connection in Western languages—such as the idea of "pumpkin head," "bumpkin," or in French, *gourde*, meaning an "idiot, fathead, stupid person." In Italian *zucca* and *zuccone citrullo* are used as terms "injurieux contra les gros imbeciles"—see Gubernatis, *Mythologie des plantes*, pp. 99–100. On this see especially the discussion on "delirious pumpkins" in Norrman and Haarberg, *Nature and Language*, pp. 36–40.

61. See Karlgren, *Analytic Dictionary*, p. 87.

62. See Schipper, *L'empereur Wou des Han*, pp. 60–61; and Kaltenmark, *Lie-sien Tchouan*, p. 136.

63. On No Cha see Werner, *Dictionary of Chinese Mythology*, p. 247; and Doré, *Researches into Chinese Superstitions*, vol. 9, pp. 111 ff. On the figure Lu Ya as a *san-jen* in the Ming novel *Feng Shen Yen I* see Liu Ts'un-yan, *Buddhist and Taoist Influences on Chinese Novels* (Wiesbaden: Otto Harrassowitz, 1962), vol. 1, pp. 261–276. Tung-fang Shuo is discussed by Schipper, *L'empereur Wou des Han*, pp. 31 ff., 60 ff.

64. Schipper, *L'empereur Wou des Han*, p. 61.

65. Ibid., pp. 60 ff. On the symbolism of the immortal see Isabelle Robinet, "The Taoist Immortal: Fantasies of Light and Shadow, Heaven and Earth," in *Myth and Symbol In Chinese Tradition*, ed. N. J. Girardot and John S. Major, forthcoming.

66. See Granet, *DL*, p. 267, n. 1.

67. See Eberhard, *LC*, pp. 328 ff. On the ancient No festival see Bodde, *Festivals*, pp. 75–138.

68. Granet, *DL*, p. 324. On the symbolism of motley see Willeford, *Fool and His Scepter*, pp. 16 ff.

69. Eberhard, *LC*, p. 330.

70. See R. Bernheimer, *Wild Men in the Middle Ages* (Cambridge: Harvard University Press, 1952), pp. 56 ff. See also Enid Welsford, *The Fool* (London: Faber and Faber, 1935), pp. 55 ff.; Willeford, *Fool and His Scepter*, pp. 73 ff.; and the articles in E. Dudley and M. Novak, ed., *The Wild Man Within* (Pittsburgh: University of Pittsburgh Press, 1972).

71. Bernheimer, *Wild Men*, pp. 1–20.

72. Ibid., pp. 56 ff.

73. Willeford, *Fool and His Scepter*, pp. 91 f.

74. Ibid., pp. 11 ff.; and Bernheimer, *Wild Men*, pp. 121 ff. Like "fool" (Latin *follis*), which has the sense of scrotum or testicles, the Chinese term *hun-t'o*[b] can also mean the "sack" of the male genitals, the testicles. *T'o*[a] also means "bellows, drum, sack" and is specifically related to the *hun-tun* theme of the owl as an animal ancestor or demon—see Granet, *DL*, pp. 516 ff. The term *hun*[i] generally meaning "obscene jests or jokes" (or *hun-yen*) also appears in the compound *hun-i*[c] meaning "harlequin garments in black and white [motley] with obscene inscriptions."

75. Bernheimer, *Wild Men*, p. 52.

76. Ibid., p. 56.

77. See Willeford, *Fool and His Scepter*, pp. 100 ff.

78. Ibid., p. 101.

79. Bernheimer, *Wild Men*, pp. 19–20.

80. See Munro, *Concept of Man*, pp. 142, 144. For a comparative discussion of the religious significance of the idea of "play" see David Kinsley, *The Divine Player* (Delhi: Motilal Banarsidass, 1979). Like *luan*[a], the Chinese word *wan* has the contradictory meanings of "to play around" or "to examine, test."

81. Schipper, quoting from "Rapporteurs' Notes of the Bellagio Conference," pp. 21–22.

82. Willeford, *Fool and His Scepter*, p. xv.

9. *Conclusion: The Conundrum of Hun-Tun*

1. See above, chapter 6.

2. John Cage, *New York Times* 23 (May 25, 1969): 3.

3. I am particularly thinking of A. Seidel, K. Schipper, M. Saso, I. Robinet, M. Strickmann, and N. Sivin (building on the earlier work of Maspero, Stein, Soymié, and Kaltenmark). Some of these scholars have had, for the first time, access to the living esoteric lore of the initiated Taoist priesthood. On Japanese scholarship see Tadao Sakai and Tetsuro Noguchi, "Taoist Studies in Japan," in *Facets of Taoism*, pp. 269–288; and the articles in *Acta Asiatica* 27 (1974). See also Whalen Lai, "Toward a Periodization of the Taoist Religion," *History of Religions* 17 (1976): 75–85 (on Yoshioka Yoshitoyo's work); David C. Yu, "Present Day Taoist Studies," *Religious Studies Review* 3 (1977): 220–239; T. H. Barrett, "Introduction" in H. Maspero, *Taoism and Chinese Religion*, trans. F. A. Kierman, Jr., (Amherst: University of Massachusetts Press, 1981); pp. vii–xxiii; and the various articles on "Taoism" (by Seidel and Strickmann) in the 1974 "macropedia" edition of the *Encyclopedia Britannica*. Papers from the first and second international conferences on Taoism have been published respectively in *History of Religions* 9 (1969–1970) and *Facets of Taoism* (1979). A third international conference took place in Switzerland on September 3–9, 1979. It should be noted that the increased participation of mainland Chinese scholars at the third conference indicates a revived interest in Taoist studies in contemporary Chinese scholarship. For a bibliography of Western studies on Taoism see M. Soymié's compilation in *Dokyo kenkyu* 3 (1968): 1–72 and 4 (1971): 1–66. On more recent French publications see Seidel's bibliography in *Facets of Taoism*, pp. 17–18. Also helpful, though sketchy, is Li Shu-huan's encyclopedic dictionary of Taoism, *Tao Chiao Ta Tz'u Tien* (Taipei, 1979). This work is more balanced than the earlier *Hsien Hsüeh Tz'u Tien*.

4. See, for example, the introductory articles by Welch in *History of Religions* 9 (1969–1970): pp. 107–136; and in *Facets of Taoism*, pp. 1–18.

5. See especially Needham, *SCC*, vol. 5, pt. 2, pp. 71–114.

6. Quoting Roy Wagner, *Habu* (Chicago: University of Chicago Press, 1972), p. 9.

7. Ibid., p. 10. For Creel's position see his *What Is Taoism*, pp. 1–24; and my "Part of the Way," pp. 319–337.

8. I am borrowing and adapting here Clifford Geertz's definition of religion, "Religion as a Cultural System," pp. 204–215.

9. In addition to Geertz, see Burke, *Fragile Universe*, pp. 16–27. See also above, Introduction.

10. See Ninian Smart, *The Phenomenon of Religion* (London, 1978), pp. 114 ff. I am referring here to Sivin's discussion, "On the Word 'Taoist,' " p. 314, n. 21.

11. See the comments by Wright, "Historian's Reflections," pp. 248–255; Max Kaltenmark, "Le Taoisme religieux," in *Histoire des Religions*, vol. 1., pp. 1216–1248; and Rolf Stein, "Religious Taoism and Popular Religion from the Second to Seventh Centuries," in *Facets of Taoism*, pp. 53–82.

12. Quoting Sivin in "On the Word 'Taoist,' " p. 305.

13. See Sivin's counter position, ibid., p. 314.

14. Geertz, "Religion as a Cultural System," p. 216.

15. Ibid.

16. See the discussion of Fernand Braudel's idea of "la longue durée" in the cultural history of religions—*Bulletin of the American Academy of Religion* 10 (1979): 101–105.

17. Sivin, "On the Word 'Taoist,' " p. 323.

18. Ibid.

19. See Michael Saso, *The Teachings of Taoist Master Chuang* (New Haven: Yale University Press, 1979), pp. 193−233. For a critical appraisal of this work see Harvey Molé, *Journal of Asian Studies* 39 (1980): 580−581; and M. Strickmann, "History, Anthropology, and Chinese Religion," *Harvard Journal of Asiatic Studies* 40 (1980): 201−248.

20. See Saso, *Master Chuang*, pp. 193−233; and also his "Buddhist and Taoist Ideas of Transcendence: A Study in Philosophical Contrast," in *Buddhist and Taoist Studies I*, ed. Michael Saso and David Chappell (Honolulu: University of Hawaii Press, 1977), pp. 3−22.

21. See Seidel, *Divinisation*, pp. 93−96; and Schipper, "Taoist Body," pp. 355−386.

22. Saso, *Master Chuang*, p. 213.

23. See above, chapter 6. On the popular understanding of P'an-ku see Doré, *Researches* 10:34−36. In Taoist theology, P'an-ku (and the deity Hung-kung Tao-jen) is commonly identified with The Primordial Heavenly Worthy (Yüan-shih T'ien-tsun)—Doré, *Researches* 9:4−5.

24. See Saso, *Master Chuang*, pp. 127−192, 234−266; and Stein, "Religious Taoism and Popular Religion," pp. 53−82. The *Heilsgeschichte* implications of these developments were first suggested to me by Anna Seidel in a personal communication.

25. Peter Berger, *The Sacred Canopy* (Garden City: Doubleday Anchor Book, 1969), pp. 26−27.

26. See Turner, *Ritual Process*, pp. 94−130.

27. See especially Seidel, "Image of Perfect Ruler," pp. 216−247; and also Max Kaltenmark, "The Ideology of the T'ai-p'ing ching," in *Facets of Taoism*, pp. 19−52.

28. Turner, *Ritual Process*, pp. 139−158. For an interesting comparative discussion of millenary movements as a kind of "frozen new year's festival" see Zuess, *Ritual Cosmos*, pp. 163−176.

29. On the sociological dynamics of this kind of process in the history of religions see John G. Gager, *Kingdom and Community* (Englewood Cliffs: Prentice-Hall, 1975).

30. Saso, *Master Chuang*, p. 197.

31. Saso, "Buddhist and Taoist Ideas of Transcendence," pp. 5 ff.

32. Ibid., pp. 11, 17.

33. Ibid., p. 13.

34. This is not to say that there are not certain changes and embellishments in the esoteric theory of *hun-tun*, especially with reference to the influence of Buddhist thought—see, for example, David Yu, "The Creation Theme of Chaos in Dauist Religion," forthcoming in *Journal of Chinese Philosophy*. Prof. Yu was kind enough to provide me with a prepublication copy of this paper.

35. Saso, "Buddhist and Taoist Ideas of Transcendence," pp. 10 ff; and Saso, *Master Chuang*, pp. 193−233.

36. See Saso, "Buddhist and Taoist Ideas of Transcendence," p. 5.

37. *Wu Shang Pi Yao* (sixth century)—quoted by Saso, *Master Chuang*, p. 207.

38. Ibid. In a personal communication Robinet points out that Saso is sometimes guilty of poetic license in his translations—i.e., although the meaning is the same, *yin* and *yang* really read *mo* (obscure) and *ming*^{c} (clear). Saso's reference to *hun-tun* in the last line appears to be his interpretive interpolation for the esoteric meaning of returning to "one."

39. Anna Seidel, personal communication. In general see her *Divinisation*, passim; and Robinet, *Méditation*, pp. 32—48.

40. Seidel, personal communication; and see Saso, *Master Chuang*, p. 202.

41. See Seidel, *Divinisation*; and especially, Schipper, "Taoist Body," pp. 358—365.

42. Schipper, "Taoist Body," pp. 361—363. See also Robinet, *Commentaires*, pp. 168—173, 191—203.

43. Schipper, "Taoist Body," pp. 365—366.

44. See ibid.; Saso, "Buddhist and Taoist Ideas of Transcendence"; Saso, *Master Chuang*; and Robinet, *Méditation*, pp. 85—151.

45. See Robinet, *Méditation*, pp. 85—86; Saso, "Buddhist and Taoist Ideas of Transcendence," pp. 8—20; M. Strickmann, "The Mao Shan Revelations, Taoism and the Aristocracy," *T'oung Pao* 63 (1977): 1—64; and, more generally, Edward H. Schafer, *Mao Shan In T'ang Times* (Boulder: Society for the Study of Chinese Religions, 1980).

46. Saso, "Buddhist and Taoist Ideas of Transcendence," p. 16. Robinet comments that it is anachronistic to connect the Three Worthies mentioned by Saso to the *Yellow Court Canon* since these divinities do not "appear in the history of Taoism until several centuries later." Moreover, while the three principles of *ching-ch'i-shen* appear in the *T'ai P'ing Ching*, they are not found as a triad in the earliest *Yellow Court* texts— personal communication; and see her *Commentaires*, pp. 149—151, 174—185. In fairness to Saso it should be pointed out that his discussion is based on the contemporary priestly understanding of these texts.

47. Quoted by Saso, ibid., p. 16.

48. Saso, *Master Chuang*, p. 195.

49. Figure 4 is adapted from Saso, "Buddhist and Taoist Ideas of Transcendence," p. 12. On the *T'ai-chi t'u* see Julia Ching, "The Symbolism of the Great Ultimate (*T'ai-chi*): Myth, Religion, and Philosophy," (unpublished paper). Ching concludes that the diagram fundamentally expresses the metaphysical formula of *coincidentia oppositorum*. See also Robinet, *Méditation*, p. 164.

50. See Saso, *Master Chuang*, pp. 218—233; Saso, "Buddhist and Taoist Ideas of Transcendence," pp. 14—16; and Robinet, *Méditation*, pp. 93—129.

51. Saso, "Buddhist and Taoist Ideas of Transcendence," p. 14.

52. *Seal of the Heart Canon (Kao Shang Yu Huang Hsin Yin Ching)*. T'ang or early Sung—quoted by Saso, ibid., p. 20. While not crucial to the import of the text, Robinet mentions that "holy *yin*," "holy *yang*," and "Yellow Court" more accurately read holy sun, holy moon, and Golden Court—personal communication.

53. Ibid., p. 20 (*Seal of the Heart Canon*); on the "spiritual fire" see ibid., p. 15; and for Western tradition see C. G. Jung, *Mysterium Coniunctionis* (New York: Pantheon Books, 1963), pp. 441 f.

54. See Schipper, "Taoist Body," p. 369; and Robinet, *Méditation*, pp. 92—93.

55. See Jung, *Mysterium*, p. 514. On the *unus mundus* see below.

56. See Robinet, *Méditation*, pp. 163—169. In the system of esoteric correspondences found in Taoist meditation, *hun-tun* macrocosmically is equated with the North, the winter solstice, and the sign of the tortoise (Robinet, *Méditation*, pp. 120, 186).

57. Ibid., p. 165.

58. Ibid.

59. Ibid.

60. Maspero, "Nourrir le principe vital," p. 297. Cf. his quotation from the *Yüan Ch'i Lun*, p. 207, n. 1.

61. Ibid., p. 401. Maspero is of the belief that these ideas may derive from ancient religious rites involving orgiastic seasonal festivals wherein "hommes et femmes se mêlaient exactement comme des bêtes"—p. 402.

62. See T. L. Davis and Chao Yun-Ts'ung, "Chang Po-tuan of T'ien-t'ai, His *Wu Chen P'ien*, Essay on the Understanding of the Truth," *American Academy of Arts and Sciences* (Proceedings) 70 (1935–1936): 99.

63. Ibid.

64. See the *Hsien Hsüeh Tz'u Tien*, p. 147.

65. See Schipper, "Taoist Body," pp. 365–374. On the "Gate of Destiny" see Robinet, *Méditation*, pp. 123–125.

66. See, for example, Robinet, *Méditation*, p. 187; and her *Commentaires*, pp. 149–203.

67. Based primarily on Robinet's study, *Méditation*, passim.

68. See I. Robinet, "Randonnées extatiques des Taoistes dans les Astres," *Monumenta Serica* 32 (1976): 159–273; and M. Strickmann, "On the Alchemy of T'ao Hung-ching," in *Facets of Taoism*, pp. 123–192.

69. In a comparative context see H. Crobin, *The Man of Light in Iranian Sufism* (Boulder: Shambala, 1979).

70. See Eliade, *Forge and Crucible*, passim; and Sivin, "Chinese Alchemy and The Manipulation of Time," *Isis* 67 (1976): 513–526.

71. See Needham, *SCC*, vol. 5, pt. 2, pp. 71–126.

72. See Jung, *Psychology and Alchemy*; Eliade, *Forge and Crucible*; Needham, *SCC*, vol. 5, pt. 2; and N. Sivin, *Chinese Alchemy: Preliminary Studies* (Cambridge: Harvard University Press, 1968).

73. Quoted by Needham, *SCC*, 2:449.

74. On the *Ts'an T'ung Ch'i* see Needham, *SCC*, vol. 5, pt. 3. See also Lu-ch'iang Wu and Tenny L. Davis, "An Ancient Chinese Treatise on Alchemy entitled 'Ts'an T'ung Ch'i,' " *Isis* 18 (1932): 210–285; and Fukui Kojun, "A Study of *Chou-i Ts'an-t'ung-ch'i*," *Acta Asiatica* 27 (1974): 19 ff. The dating of this text is controversial—i.e., the extant text is probably of the T'ang period.

75. Quoting from N. Sivin's draft manuscript, "The Theoretical Background of Chinese Alchemy," final version to be published in vol. 5, pt. 4, of Needham's *SCC*. I am indebted to Prof. Sivin for giving me access to this work. On the Chinese correspondence theory in alchemy see Ho Ping-yu and J. Needham, "Theories of Categories in Early Medieval Chinese Alchemy," *Journal of the Warburg and Courtauld Institute* 22 (1959): 173–210.

76. See Saso, "Buddhist and Taoist Ideas of Transcendence," p. 8.

77. Ho Ping-yu and J. Needham, "Laboratory Equipment of the Early Medieval Chinese Alchemist," *Ambix* 7 (1959): 62–77.

78. See, for example M. J. Sheppard, "Egg Symbolism in Alchemy," *Ambix* 6 (1958): 140–148; S. Mahdihassan, "Creation, Its Nature and Imitation in Alchemy," *Iqbal Review* (1968), pp. 80 ff; and on gourd associations, J. E. Cirlot *A Dictionary of Symbols*, trans. Jack Sage (London: Routledge & Kegan Paul, 1971), pp. 266–267.

79. Jung, *Mysterium*, p. 516.

80. Quoting Welch's summation of Schipper in "Bellagio Conference," p. 128.

81. Jung, *Mysterium*, p. xiv.

82. Marie-Louis Von Franz, *Creation Myths* (Zurich: Spring Publications, 1972), p. 222. See also her discussion of the *hun-tun* myth, pp. 92–95.

83. Titus Burckhardt, *Alchemy* (Baltimore: Penguin Books, 1967), pp. 25–26.

84. Ibid., p. 73.

85. For the Western alchemical Latin nomenclature used here see Jung, *Psychology and Alchemy*, pp. 320, 449; and his *Mysterium*, pp. 514, 534.

86. Quoting from G. Heym's review of Jung's *Mysterium* in *Ambix* 6 (1957): 50; see also Jung, *Mysterium*, pp. 457–553.

87. Von Franz, *Myths*, p. 18 (emphasis in original).

88. Ibid., pp. 239–240.

89. Ibid. Figure 5 is slightly adapted from Von Franz, p. 240.

90. Jung, *Mysterium*, p. 534.

91. Von Franz, *Myths*, pp. 240–241.

92. Jung, *Mysterium*, p. 534.

93. Ibid., p. 537.

94. On the different kinds or stages of Chaos (inferior and superior) see R. Guénon, *Les états multiples de l'être* (Paris: Vega, 1947), chap. 12; and also his *Initiation et realisation spirituelle* (Paris: Edition Traditionnelles, 1952), p. 206. I am indebted to Prof. Robinet for these references.

95. Needham, *SCC*, 2: 91.

96. See Needham, *SCC*, vol. 5, pt. 2, p. xxxi–xxxii; and S. Mahdihassan, "The Genesis of Alchemy," *Indian Journal of the History of Science* 5 (1960): 41 ff; and his "Alchemy and its Chinese Origin as Revealed by its Etymology, Doctrines, and Symbols," *Iqbal Review* (1966): 22 ff.

97. On the significance of the "elixir" see Needham, *SCC*, vol. 5, pt. 2, pp. 8–126; and Gruman, *A History of Ideas about the Prolongation of Life*, pp. 28 ff.

98. Burckhardt, *Alchemy*, p. 73.

99. Welch quoting Eliade in "Bellagio Conference," p. 122.

100. See G. Scholem, *On the Kaballah and Its Symbolism* (New York: Schocken Books, 1965), p. 105. See also Carlo Suares, *The Cipher of Genesis* (Boulder: Shambhala, 1978).

101. Scholem, *Kaballah and Symbolism*, pp. 103–104. On the idea of an androgynous Adam in Jewish tradition see also Louis Ginzberg, *The Legends of the Jews* (Philadelphia: The Jewish Publication Society of America, 1955), vol. 5, pp. 88–89, n. 42.

102. On the *ṭumṭum* see *Encyclopedia Judaica* (Jerusalem: The Macmillan Co., 1971), vol. 2, p. 949 (under "Androgynos"); and *Encylopedia Talmudica* (Jerusalem: Talmudic Encylopedia Institute, 1974), pp. 386–399.

103. Scholem, *Kaballah and Symbolism*, pp. 159 ff; and see Jung, *Mysterium*, pp. 406–434.

104. G. Scholem, *Kabbalah* (New York: New American Library, 1978), pp. 128–135.

105. Ibid., pp. 128–135; and Jürgen Von Kempski, "Zimzum: Die Schöpfung aus dem Nichts," *Merkur* 14 (1960): pp. 1107–1126.

106. See especially David Hall, *The Uncertain Phoenix, Adventures Toward a Post-Cultural Sensibility*, passim.

107. See especially Hermann Hesse's discussion of Dostoevski, *In Sight of Chaos*, trans. Stephen Hudson (Zurich: Verlag Seldwyla, 1923), pp. 59–64.

108. Ibid., p. 60.

109. Ibid., p. 61.

110. See Turner, *Ritual Process*, pp. 94–203; and his *Dramas, Fields, and Metaphors* (Ithaca: Cornell University Press, 1974), pp. 14–17.

111. M. Carrouges, *La Mystique du Surhomme* (Paris: Galimard, 1948), p. 63.

112. Ibid., p. 64.

113. Ibid.

114. Ibid.

115. Ibid.

116. Ibid., p. 264.

117. Ibid., p. 67.

118. In general see Donald J. Munro, *The Concept of Man in Contemporary China* (Ann Arbor: University of Michigan Press, 1977); Frederick Wakeman, Jr., *History and Will: Philosophical Perspectives of Mao Tse-Tung's Thought* (Berkeley; Los Angeles, London: University of California Press, 1973); and also R. C. Zaehner, "A New Buddha and a New Tao," in *The Concise Encyclopedia of Living Faiths*, ed. R. C. Zaehner (Boston: Beacon Press, 1959), pp. 402–412.

119. See David C. Yu, "The Mythos of Chaos in Ancient Taoist and Contemporary Chinese Thought," paper delivered to the 1977 conference of the International Society for Chinese Philosophy in Hawaii. I am indebted to Prof. Yu for making this paper available to me. See also Bauer, *Search for Happiness*, pp. 392–418; and Paul V. Martinson, "From Reciprocity to Contradiction: Aspects of the Confucian-Maoist Transformation," in *Transitions and Transformations in The History of Religions*, ed. Frank E. Reynolds and Theodore M. Ludwig (Leiden: E. J. Brill, 1980), pp. 185–220.

120. Bauer, *Search for Happiness*, p. 413.

121. See Hall, *Uncertain Phoenix*, passim. See also the work of Robert Neville, "From Nothing to Being," pp. 21–34.

122. Hesse, *In Sight of Chaos*, pp. 63–64.

123. Ibid., p. 64.

124. Ibid.

125. Ibid.

126. Ibid.

127. *CCT*, 5/2/53–55; and Watson, p. 43.

128. *Chuang Tzu*, chapter 27 (*CCT*, 75/27/9–10; and Watson, pp. 304–305).

129. Willeford, *Fool and his Scepter*, p. xvii.

130. Quoting from Northrop Fry's introduction to G. Bachelard, *Psychoanalysis of Fire* (Boston: Beacon, 1964), p. vi.

131. Ibid.

132. See Plaks, *Archetype and Allegory*, p. 37.

133. See Stevens, *The Nursery Rhyme*, pp. 67–82; and William S. Baring-Gould, *The Annotated Mother Goose* (New York: Clarkson N. Potter, 1962), p. 268.

134. See A. W. Howitt, *The Native Tribes of South-East Australia* (London: Macmillan and Co., 1904), pp. 618–636.

135. Waley, *Three Ways of Thought*, p. 67.

136. See Delia Goetz and Sylvanus G. Morley, English version of Adrian Recinos' translation, *Popol Vuh, Sacred Book of the Ancient Quiche Maya* (Norman: University of Oklahoma Press, 1950), passim. See also Fontenrose, *Python*, pp. 504 ff; and Heiser, *Gourd Book*, p. 27.

137. Rene Guénon, "The Mysteries of the Letter Nun," in *Art and Thought*, ed. K. Bharatha Iyer (London: Luzac and Company, 1947), p. 166.

138. On the controversy over Jonah's "gourd" see Norrman and Haarberg, *Nature and Language*, pp. 27–32.

139. Guénon, "*Mysteries of Nun*," pp. 166–167.

140. Ibid., p. 167.

141. Ibid.

142. For a more positive, yet cautious, discussion of sound symbolism associated with cucurbits see Norrman and Haarberg, *Nature and Language*, pp. 141–144. They comment that "reduplication, which is widespread in the names of the cucurbits, may . . . carry some semic significance. A problem is that if phonosemic correlations exist, one does not know how far they extend geographically. Are they restricted to one language? Are they restricted to a family of languages?" (pp. 141–142).

143. Gardner, *Annotated Alice*, p. 263.

144. *Chuang Tzu*, chapter 3 (*CCT*, 7–8/3/2–10; and Watson pp. 50–51); see above, chapter 3.

145. *CCT*, 7/2/94–96; and Watson, p. 49.

146. T. Izutsu, "The Absolute and the Perfect Man in Taoism," *Eranos-Jahrbuch 1967* (Zurich: Rhein-Verlag, 1968), p. 420.

147. David L. Hall, "Process and Anarchy—A Taoist Vision of Creativity," *Philosophy East and West* 28 (1978): pp. 283–284.

148. *Chuang Tzu*, chapter 1 (*CCT*, 2–3/1/35–42; and Watson, p. 34–35).

149. James Legge, *The Religions of China* (New York: Charles Scribner's Sons, 1881), p. 167.

150. James Hillman, "Senex and Puer," *Eranos Jahrbuch 1967* (Zurich: Rhein-Verlag; 1968), pp. 349–350. For the "tailed" Adam motif in alchemy and Kabbala see Jung, *Mysterium*, pp. 408 ff. In China the tricksterlike thunder god frequently has the composite features of a bat, pig, and monkey. In Japan there are the important associations of the *kappa* figure with thunder, monkey, egg, gourd, and stone symbolism—see Ouwehand, *Namazu-e*, pp. 169–171, 203–219. Hun-tun may also be associated with the bat, dog, or monkeylike creatures known as the Mu-k'o and the Shan-hsiao, who were particularly linked to the Miao cultures in ancient China—see Eberhard, *LC*, pp. 439, 54–57. As noted in another chapter, there would also seem to be symbolic associations with the strange thunder animal Lei^c, the monkeylike, one-legged K'ui, and the legendary Wu-chih-hsi—Eberhard, *LC*, pp. 440, 57–60. With regard to the motif of the "closure of the holes of face" seen in the *hun-tun* theme, there is perhaps a connection with the Japanese monkey symbolism of "see, hear, speak no evil" (the *sambiki-zaru*)—on the problems of interpretation associated with this figure see V. A. Casal, "Far Eastern Monkey Lore," *Monumenta Nipponica* 12 (1956): 23.

151. Hillman, "Senex and Puer," p. 355.

152. Ibid.

153. Ibid.

GLOSSARY OF
CHINESE CHARACTERS

chai 齋
chan 湛
Chang Tao-ling 張道陵
ch'ang 猖
ch'ang-k'uang 猖狂
ch'ang-sheng 長生
ch'ang-tao 常道
chao-k'uang 照曠
che-hsien 謫仙
chen-i 真一
chen-jen 真人
ch'en 臣
ch'en-lun 沉淪
ch'eng 成
chi^a 紀
chi^b 幾(機)
chi^c 寂(宋)
chi^d 答
chi^e 稽
chi hsi liao hsi 寂兮寥兮
chi jan 寂然
chi-jen 畸人
ch'i^a 氣
ch'i^b 貟
ch'i ch'iao 七竅
ch'i chuan 氣專

ch'i-hsin 齊心
ch'i-tou 鬾頭
chiang shui 洚水
chiang yang 降揚
ch'iang-kung 絳宮
chiao^a 徼
chiao^b 醮
chiao ch'un san p'u 澆淳散朴
chien 繭
chih 知
chih chih 至治
chih-i^a 至一
chih i^b 志一
chih-jen 至人
chih-shen 至神
chih-tao 至道
chih-yen 巵言
ch'ih^a 癡
ch'ih/chih^b 治
ch'ih hua chih liu 治化之流
ch'ih-hsiao 鴟梟
ch'ih-jen 治人
ch'ih ts'ai 治才
ch'ih-tzu 赤子
chin yen 浸潭
ching 經

389

ching chi　經紀

ching shen　精神

ching-shih　靜室

ch'iu　丘

ch'iung-ch'i　窮奇

Chu-yin　燭陰

ch'u　出

ch'u ch'i i　處其一

ch'u-nü　處女

ch'u-tzu　處子

Chuan-hsü　顓頊（須）

chüeh-tui　絕對

chun　鈞

chün-tzu　君子

ch'un　純

ch'un ch'i
　chih shou　純氣之守

ch'un-ch'un　淳淳

chung　盅

chung hsin　忠信

chung ho ch'i　沖和氣

chung-kuo　中國

Chung-li　重黎

chung tung　蠢動

ch'unga　沖

ch'ungb　虫

ch'ung ch'i
　i wei ho　沖氣以為和

ch'ung-hsü　沖虛

ch'ung-ning　沖凝

chuo　濁

chuo-shih　濁世

chuo-ts'ai　濁才

chuo-wu　濁物

erh huang　二皇

erh shen　二神

fana　飯

fanb　反

fan lan　氾濫

fan te　反德

Fang-hu　方壺

fang-shih　方士

fei-jen　非人

fen　分

fen-hua　分化

feng-feng i-i　馮馮翼翼

Feng-ia (= P'ing-i)　馮夷

Feng-ib　馮翼

fua　復

fub　符

fu/fouc　浮

fu ch'i ch'u　復其初

fu ch'i ken　復其根

Fu-hsi　伏羲

fu-kuei　復歸

fu-kuei
　yü wu wu　復歸於無物

fu-kuei yü p'u　復歸於樸

fu pien erh wei i　復變而為一

Fu-po chiang chün　伏波將軍

fu p'u　復扑

fu te　復得

fu yu　浮游

han ho　合和

hao chih　好知

hao-hao han-han　浩浩瀚瀚

ho　合

ho-ch'i　合氣

ho chih chih　和之至

ho-ho　合和

ho hun-hun　合渾渾

ho li　和理

Hou-chi 后稷

hsi^a 習

hsi^b 襲

hsi^c 希

hsi^d 翕（歙）

hsi^e 狶

hsi^f 戲

hsi-ch'ang 習常

hsi-ching 襲精

hsi-hsi 歙歙

hsi-ming 襲明

hsi wei shih chih liu 狶韋氏之流

hsiang 象

hsiang-jen 象人

hsiao 孝

hsien^a 仙

hsien^b 僊（＝仙）

hsin 心

hsin-chai 心齋

hsin chih chuan yü nei 心志專於內

hsin-ning 心凝

hsin-yang 心養

hsing 性

hsing erh shang 形而上

hsing-ming 洔溟

hsiung-te 凶德

hsü^a 虛

hsü^b 墟

hsü-k'uo 虛霩

hsü-k'uo sheng yü-chou 虛霩生宇宙

hsü wu 虛無

hsüan 玄

hsüan-ming 玄冥

hsüan-p'in 玄牝

hsüan-ta 玄達

hsüan-te 玄德

hsüan-t'ung^a 玄通

hsüan-t'ung^b 玄同

hu^a 觳

hu^b 忽

hu^c 圓

hu^d 囵

hu^e 惚

hu^f 葫

hu^g 瓠

hu^h 壺

huⁱ 瓢

hu^j 蝴

hu^k 胡（糊）

hu^l 護

hu-li-hu-t'u 糊裏糊塗

hu-huang 惚恍

Hu-ling 壺領

hu-lu 葫蘆（壺盧）

hu-lun 囵圇

hu-t'u 糊塗

Hu Tzu 壺子

hua^a 化

hua^b 猾

hua ch'i tao 化其道

hua yu 化游

huai 懷

Huan-tou 讙兜

huang^a 恍（怳）

huang^b 宄（荒）

huang^c 簧

huang-ch'üan 黃泉

huang-hu 慌惚

huang-k'uang 恍狂

huang nang 黃囊
Huang Ti 黃帝
huang-t'ing 黃庭
hui feng hun ho 廻風混合
hun[a] 昏(昬)
hun[b] 婚
hun[c] 惛(涽)
hun[d] 混(渾)
hun[e] 睧
hun[f] 㥵(慁)
hun[g] 溷
hun[h] 圂
hun[i] 諢
hun[j] 魂
hun-chen 混嫃
hun-ch'i 混氣
hun ch'i hsin 渾其心
hun chu ts'ung sheng 混逐叢生
hun ch'üan 渾全
hun erh wei i 混而為一
hun fen 混分
hun-han 混瀚
hun-ho 混合
hun-hua 混化
hun-hui 混潰
hun-hun[a] 昏昏
hun-hun[b] 涽涽
hun-hun[c] 混混
hun-hun ku-ku 混混滑滑
hun-hun mo-mo 昏昏默默
hun-hun ts'ang-ts'ang 渾渾蒼蒼
hun-hun tun-tun 渾渾沌沌
hun-i[a] 渾儀
hun-i[b] 混夷
hun-i[c] 諢衣
hun-i[d] 混一
hun-jen 渾人
hun-jan 惛然
hun-lun 渾淪(混淪)
hun-mang 混芒
hun-mang chih chung 混芒之中
hun-ming 混溟
hun-ming chih ch'ung 混冥之中
hun-ming ta-ming 混冥大冥
hun-sheng 混生
hun-t'ang 混堂
hun-t'i 渾體
Hun-t'ien[a] 渾天
Hun-t'ien[b] (tien, chen) 混填
hun-t'o[a] 渾脫
hun-t'o[b] 混橐
hun-tun (t'un) 混沌(渾沌, 混敦, 渾敦, 倱伅)
hun-tun chi-tzu shen-shih 混沌雞子神室
hun-tun shih chih shu 渾沌氏之術
hun-tun t'ai yüan ho tzu 混沌胎元合子
hun-tun ting 混沌鼎
hun-tun wei p'u 渾沌為樸
hun-tung 混洞
hun-tung hung-wen 混洞紅文
hun-t'ung 混同

hun-yen 譚言

hun-yin 昏陰

hun-yüan 渾元

hung[a] 鴻

hung[b] 洪

hung[c] 汞

hung[d] 紅

hung[e] 訌

hung[f] 灯（烘）

Hung-chün
 tao-jen 洪鈞道人

Hung-meng 鴻濛

hung-meng
 hung-tung 鴻濛鴻洞

hung-shui 洪水

hung yüan
 ming hsiang 洪源溟濛鴻

huo 惑

huo luan 惑亂

i[a] 一

i[b] 義

i[c] 夷

i[d] 羿

i ch'ih i luan 一治一亂

i-shih 疑始

i tan shih,
 i p'iao yin 一簞食,一瓢飲

i ti 夷狄

i yüan 一原

jang[a] 讓

jang[b] 攘

jen 仁

ju-su 入素

juan 蝡

juan tung 蝡動

Jung 戎

jung ti 戎狄

kang 綱

kao-mu 搞末

kau-tsu 高祖

keng 羹

ku[a] 滑

ku[b] 孤

ku[c] 鼓

ku[d] 汩

ku[e] 蠱

ku(hua) i 滑疑

ku fu 鼓腹

Ku-mang 古莽

ku t'ai-ch'u 古太初

kua 弧

kua-shih 弧時

kua-yüeh 弧月

k'uai 塊

k'uai jan tu 塊然獨

k'uai jan
 tu ch'u 塊然獨處

k'uai jan
 wu chih 塊然無知

k'uang[a] 曠

k'uang[b] 狂

k'uang-fu 狂夫

kuei[a] 鬼

kuei[b] 歸

kuei-hsü 歸墟

kuei shen ti 鬼神帝

k'uei 塊

k'ui 虁

Kun 鯀

kun-i 昆夷（混夷）

k'un[a] 壼

k'un[b] 昆

k'un[c] 鯤昆

k'un-ao 壼奧

K'un-lun 崑崙

k'un-tun 困敦

kung 洪

kung(kung fu) 功 (功夫)

Kung-kung 共工

kung-shui 洪水

K'ung-t'ung 崆峒

k'uo-lu 廓落

kuo-shih 裹尸

Lao Chün 老君

lei[a] 儽

lei[b] 雷

lei[c] 獝

Lei-kung 雷公

lei-lei 儽儽

li 禮

li-ho 離合

li-p'i 儷皮

li yü
chung yang 立於中央

liao[a] 寥

Liao[b] 僚 (獠)

liao-k'uo 嶚廓

lieh-ch'üeh 列缺

lien 臉

ling-fu 靈府

ling-pao 靈寶

Ling-pao
wu-fu 靈寶五符

Lolo 玀玀

lu[a] 鑪

lu[b] 簬

lu[c] 飆

lu[d] 盧

lu[e] 爐

luan[a] 亂

luan[b] 鸞

luan-ch'en 亂臣

luan...shen 亂...神

luan t'ien-hsia 亂天下

lun 淪

lung 龍

Man 蠻

man-t'ou 饅頭

mang[a] 芒

mang[b] 莽

mang jan 芒然

mang jan...
hao-hao 芒然,...浩浩蕩蕩
tang-tang

mang...mang 芒...芒

mang-mang
ch'en-ch'en 茫茫沉沉

mang...wu 芒...芴

Mao shan 茅山

mei-mei 每每

mei-mei
hui-hui 媒媒晦晦

men hu-lu 悶葫蘆

men-men 悶悶

miao 妙

Miao 苗

miao...ming 窈...冥

mien-tzu 面子

ming[a] 冥

ming[b] 溟

ming[c] 瞑

ming[d] 明

ming-men 命門

ming-ming 緡緡

ming-ming
chih chung 冥冥之中

mo 默

mo lang ch'ieh 莫朗切

mu 母

mu-k'o 木客

nang 囊

nei-kuan 內觀

nei p'ing
  wai ch'eng 內乎外成

nei-tan 內丹

ni-shih 擬始

ni-wan 泥丸

ning[a] 凝

ning[b] 寧

ning chi 凝寂

ning ssu
  mo hsiang 凝思默想

no 儺

Nü-kua 女媧

o 惡

pan 抓

p'an 判

P'an-hu 攀瓠

P'an-keng 盤庚

P'an-ku 盤古

pao[a] 報

pao[b] 包

pao[c] 胞

pao[d] 抱

pao ch'i
  t'ai-ch'ing 抱其太清之李
  chih pen

pao-i[a] 抱一

pao-i[b] 包衣

pao kuo 包裹

pao kuo
  t'ien-ti 包裹天地

pao-p'u 抱樸

pao-shen 抱神

pao yüan
  shou i 抱元守一

p'ao[a] 庖

p'ao[b] 匏

p'ao[c] 炮

p'ao-hu 匏瓠

p'ao-tou 咅斗

p'eng 鵬

pi 閉

pi chiu ch'iao 閉九竅

P'i pu-tai 皮布袋

p'iao 瓢

pieh wei yin-yang 別為陰陽

pien[a] 辡

pien[b] 變

pien[c] 蓬

pien erh wei i 變而為一

pien hua 變化

p'ien-i 偏衣（偏裼）

po 博

p'o[a] 泊

p'o[b] 魄

p'ou 剖

pu-chih 不知

pu-hsing 不形

pu-hua 不化

pu-jen 不仁

pu-sheng 不生

pu-tai 不殆

pu-ts'ai 不才

pu-wei 不偽

p'u[a] 樸（朴）

p'u[b] 僕

p'u-chien 僕鑒

P'u-niu 僕牛

san 散

san-ch'ing 三清

san-jen 散人

San-miao 三苗

san mu 散木

Sang lin 桑林

shan[a] 膳饍

shan[b] 善

shan-hsiao 山魈

shan hsing 饍性

Shang-p'ien 上骿

Shang Ti 上帝

Shao-hao 少暤

shen[a] 神

shen[b] 身

shen-chu 神主

shen-jen 神人

shen-ming 神明

shen-niao 神鳥

shen-ning 神凝

Shen-nung 神農

shen-wu 神巫

shen-yu 神游

sheng[a] 生

sheng[b] 笙

sheng-fan 生番

sheng-jen chih tao 聖人之道

sheng-jen yü tun 聖人愚芚

shih[a] 食

shih[b] 遰

shih[c] 尸

shih[d] 始

shih mu 食母

shih-shih meng-meng 湯湯夢夢

shou 守

shou-chung 守中

shu[a] 儵

shu[b] 束

shu-fan 熟番

shuai-shih 衰世

Shun 舜

shun-p'u 純樸

shun-p'u wei san 純樸未散

ssu 巳

ssu-hai 四海

su 素

su p'u 素樸

sui tung 遂洞

ta 大

ta-ch'ih 大治

ta-ch'üan 大全

ta-hai 大駭

ta-ho 大聲

ta-hsiang 大象

ta huang lo(lao) 大荒落

ta-hun 大軍

ta-hun chih p'u 大渾之樸

ta-jen 大人

ta-kua 大仙

ta-k'uai 大塊

ta-kuei 大歸

ta-luan 大亂

ta mang lo 大芒落

ta-ming 大明

Ta-ping 大丙

ta-shun 大順

ta-te pu t'ung 大德不同

ta-tung 大洞

ta-t'ung[a] 大同

ta-t'ung[b] 大通

ta-t'ung
   hun-ming[a] 大同混冥

ta-t'ung
   hun-ming[b] 大通混冥

ta-t'ung
   ming-ming 大通冥冥

ta-t'ung
   wei-ming 大通未名

tai chih
   shen shan 待之甚善

t'ai 胎

t'ai-chao 太昭

t'ai-chi 太極

t'ai-ch'ing 太清

t'ai-ch'u 太初

t'ai-ho 太和（合）

t'ai-hsi 胎息

t'ai-hsü 太虛

t'ai-i[a] 太一

t'ai-i[b] 太易

t'ai-ku 泰古

t'ai-p'ing 太平

t'ai-shih 太始

t'ai-su 太素

Tan-fu 亶父

tan-t'ien 丹田

tang-tang 蕩蕩

tao 道

tao-chia 道家

tao-chiao 道教

tao chih
   tzu-jan 道法自然

tao lun 道淪

tao-shih 道士

tao-shu[a] 道術

tao-shu[b] 道樞

tao-te chia 道德家

Tao-te
   t'ien-tsun 道德天尊

Tao Tsang 道藏

t'ao-hua 陶化

T'ao-t'ieh 饕餮

T'ao-wu 檮杌

te[a] 德

te[b] 得

te-i 得一

ti[a] 帝

Ti[b] 狄

Ti Chiang 帝江

Ti Hung 帝鴻

Ti I 帝一

ti p'ing
   t'ien ch'eng 地平天成

tieh 佚

tieh-tzu 疊字

tieh-yun 疊韻

t'ien-ch'ang 天常

t'ien-chün 天均

t'ien-hsia
   hun erh wei i 天下混而為一

t'ien-hsia luan 天下亂

t'ien-hsia mu 天下母

t'ien-shih 天師

t'o[a] 橐（囊）

t'o[b] 脫

tou 豆

t'ou-hu 投壺

ts'ai 菜

ts'an-liao 參寥

ts'ang 藏

tso 鑿

Tso-ch'ih 鑿齒

tso-wang 坐忘

ts'un 存

tsung[a] 縱

tsung[b] 糉

tsung[c] 宗

tu 獨

tu fu yu 獨浮游

tu-li 獨力

tu p'o 獨泊

tun[a] (t'un) 沌 (渾)

tun[b] 敦 (惇)

tun[c] 遁 (遯)

tun[d] 鈍

tun chih nieh 敦之歲

tun-lun 敦倫

tun-tun 沌沌

tun-tun...
  hun-hun 沌沌 昏昏

tung 洞

tung-chih 冬至

tung-fang 洞房

tung-hung 洞潢

tung-t'ien 洞天

tung-tung
  shu-shu 洞洞屬屬

tung-t'ung 洞同

t'ung[a] 同

t'ung[b] 通

t'ung hsing 同行

t'ung-t'i 同體

t'ung (tung)-
  t'ung t'ai hsü 迥同太虛

t'ung yü ch'u 同於初

tzu 子

tzu-jan 自然

tzu sheng 自生

tz'u 慈

tz'u-jang 辭 (辭、詞) 讓

wai-tan 外丹

wan 玩

wan-hsi 歡喜

wan-t'uan 丸團

wang[a] 忘

wang[b] 汪

wang[c] 枉

wang[d] 恇

wang ch'i chih 忘其知

wang jan 汪然

wang-mang 汪芒

wei[a] 微

wei[b] 韋

wei hsiang 為象

wei-hsing 未形

wei jen 為人

Wei-lei 畏壘

Wei-lu 尾閭

wei-miao 微妙

wei p'an 未判

wei p'ing 未乎

wei p'ou 未剖

wei she 委蛇

wei yu hsing 未有形

wen 文

wu[a] 物

wu[b] 無 (无)

wu-chi 無極

wu-chih 無知

wu-chih-hsi 無支祈

wu-hsin 無心

wu hsin ch'iao 無心竅

wu-hsing 無形

wu hua 物化

wu shih 無識

wu suo chih
  chih mao　無所知之貌

wu mien mu　無面目

wu-ming　無名

wu-ming jen　無名人

wu suo hua　無所化

wu yin chih men　無垠之門

wu-wei　無為

wu-wei wu-hsing　無為無形

wu-wu juan-juan　無無蜎蜎

yaᵃ　亞

yaᵇ　啞瘂

yang　煬

yang-ch'i　養氣

yang-hsing　養性

yang-sheng　養生

Yaoᵃ　堯

Yaoᵇ　姚

Yaoᶜ　僥

yao-yao
  ming-ming　窈窈冥冥

yao-yao ming-ming...　窈窈冥冥
  mang wen mo min　芒芠漠閔

yeh-jen　野人

yinᵃ　隱

yinᵇ　淫

yinᶜ　飲

yin-yang　陰陽

yin-yang-wu-hsing　陰陽五行

ying　攖

ying-ning　攖寧

yuᵃ　有

yuᵇ　游（遊）

yuᶜ　遊

yu hsin
  yü wu chih　遊心於物之初
  ch'u

yu-hun　幽昏

yu-mingᵃ　有名

yu-mingᵇ　幽冥

yu-wei
  chih tao　有為之道

yu wu
  hun ch'eng　有物混成

yun　運

Yüᵃ　禹

yüᵇ　愚

yü-chou　宇宙

yü-jen
  chih hsin　愚人之心

yüanᵃ　遠

yüanᵇ　元

yüanᶜ　淵

yüan-ch'i　元氣

Yüan-shih
  t'ien-tsun　元始天尊

Yüeh　越

yung-jen　傭人

SELECTED BIBLIOGRAPHY

Aijmer, Göran. *The Dragon Boat Festival on the Hupeh-Huhan Plain, Central China. A Study in the Ceremonialism of the Transplantation of Rice*. Stockholm: The Ethnographic Museum of Sweden.1964.

Baring-Gould, William S. *The Annotated Mother Goose*. New York: Clarkson N. Potter, 1952.

Bauer, Wolfgang. *China and the Search for Happiness*. New York: Seabury Press, 1976.

Baumann, Hermann. *Das Doppelte Geschlecht. Ethnologische Studien zur Bisexualität in Ritus und Mythos*. Berlin: D. Reimer, 1955.

Bernheimer, R. *Wild Men in the Middle Ages*. Cambridge: Harvard University Press, 1952.

Bodde, Derk. *Annual Customs and Festivals in Peking as Recorded in the Yen-ching Sui-shih-chi by Tun Li-ch'en*. Peping: Henri Vetch, 1936.

————. *Festivals in Classical China*. Princeton: Princeton University Press, 1975.

————. "Myths of Ancient China," in *Mythologies of the Ancient World*. Edited by S. N. Kramer. Garden City: Doubleday and Co., 1961.

Bolle, Kees. *The Freedom of Man in Myth*. Nashville: Vanderbilt University Press, 1968.

Boodberg, Peter A. "Philological Notes on Chapter One of the Lao Tzu." *Harvard Journal of Asiatic Studies* 20 (1957): 598–618.

————. "Some Proleptical Remarks on the Evolution of Archaic Chinese." *Harvard Journal of Asiatic Studies* 2 (1937): 329–372.

Burckhardt, Titus. *Alchemy*. Baltimore: Penguin Books, 1967.

Burkhardt, V. R. *Chinese Creeds and Customs*. Reprint ed., Hong Kong: South China Morning Post, 1953, 1955, 1958.

Carroll, Lewis. *The Annotated Alice*. Introduction and Notes by Martin Gardner. New York: Clarkson N. Potter, 1960.

Carrouges, Michel. *La Mystique du Surhomme*. Paris: Gallimard, 1948.

Chan Wing-tsit. *The Way of Lao Tzu*. Indianapolis: Bobbs-Merrill, 1963.

Chang Chung-yuan. *Tao: A New Way of Thinking*. New York: Harper Colophon Books, 1975.

Chang Hsüan, comp. *Chung Wen Ch'ang Yung San Ch'ien Tzu Hsing I Shih* [The Etymologies of 3000 Chinese Characters in Common Usage]. Hong Kong: Hong Kong University Press, 1968.

Chang Kwang-chih. "Chung-kuo ch'uang shih shen-hua chih fen-hsi yü shih yen-chiu" [Chinese Creation Myths: A Study in Method]. *Bulletin of the Institute of Ethnology, Academica Sinica*, no. 8 (1959): 47–79 (with English summary).

——. *Early Chinese Civilization: Anthropological Perspectives*. Cambridge: Harvard University Press, 1976.

——. "A Working Hypothesis For the Early Cultural History of South China." *Bulletin of the Institute of Ethnology, Academia Sinica*, no. 7 (1959): 75–103.

Chen, Ellen Marie. "The Meaning of *te* in the *Tao Te Ching*: An examination of the concept of nature in Chinese Taoism." *Philosophy East and West* 23 (1973): 457–470.

——. "Nothingness and the Mother Principle in Early Chinese Taoism." *International Philosophical Quarterly* 9 (1969): 391–405.

——. "Origin and Development of Being from Non-Being in the 'Tao Te Ching.'" *International Philosophical Quarterly* 13 (1973): 403–418.

Chen Ku-ying. *Lao Tzu, Text, Notes, and Comments*. San Francisco: Chinese Materials Center, 1977.

Ch'en Meng-chia. *Lao Tzu Fen Shih* [Lao Tzu Explained Analytically]. Chungking: n.p., 1945.

Chiang Hsi-ch'ang. *Lao Tzu Chiao Ku* [Lao Tzu Collated and Explained]. Taipei: Ming Lun, 1970.

Chuang Tzu Yin Te [A Concordance to the Chuang Tzu]. Harvard-Yenching Institute Sinological Index Series, Supplement no. 20. Cambridge: Harvard University Press, 1956.

Chung Hua Ta Tzu Tien. 2 vols. Shanghai: Chung Hua Book Company, 1932.

Couvreur, F. S. *Dictionnaire Classique de la langue Chinoise*. Reprint ed., Taipei: Kuangchi Press, 1966.

Creel, H. G. *What is Taoism*. Chicago: University of Chicago Press, 1970.

de Beauclair, Inez. *Tribal Cultures of Southwest China*. Taipei: Orient Cultural Service, 1974.

de Groot, J. J. M. *Les fêtes annuellement célébrees à emoui*. Paris: Ernest Leroux, 1886.

——. *The Religious System of China*. 6 vols. Reprint ed., Taipei: Ch'eng-Wen Publishing Company, 1969.

de Gubernatis, Angelo. *La Mythologies des plantes*. Reprint ed., New York: Arno Press, 1978.

de Harlez, C. *Textes taoistes*. Paris: Annales du Musee Guimet, 1891.

Delcourt, Marie. *Hermaphrodite*. London: Studio Books, 1961.

de Rola, Stanislas Klossowski. *The Secret Art of Alchemy*. New York: Avon Books, 1973.

de Visser, M. W. *The Dragon in China and Japan*. Reprint ed., Wiesbaden: Martin Sandig, 1969.

Diamond, Stanley. *In Search of the Primitive, a Critique of Civilization*. New Brunswick, N. J.: Transaction Books, 1974.

Doré, Henry. *Researches Into Chinese Superstitions*. Translated by M. Kennelly. 5 vols. Reprint ed., Taipei: Ch'eng-Wen Publishing Company, 1966.

Douglas, Mary. *Purity and Danger: An Analysis of Pollution and Taboo*. New York: Frederick A. Praeger, 1966.

Drake, F. S., ed. *Symposium on Historical Archaeological and Linguistic Studies on Southern China, South-East Asia and the Hong Kong Region*. Hong Kong: Hong Kong University Press, 1967.

Durkheim, Emile, and Mauss, Marcel. *Primitive Classification*. Translated by Rodney Needham. Chicago: University of Chicago Press, 1963.

Duyvendak, J. J. L. *Tao Te Ching, The Book of the Way and Its Virtue*. London: John Murray, 1954.

Eberhard, Wolfram. *Chinese Festivals*. New York: Henry Schuman, 1952.

———. *The Local Cultures of South and East China*. Leiden: E. J. Brill, 1968.

———. *Moral and Social Values of the Chinese, Collected Essays*. Taipei: Ch'eng-Wen Publishing Company, 1971.

———. Review of Karlgren's "Legends and Cults." *Artibus Asiae* 9 (1946): 356–364.

Eliade, Mircea. *The Forge and the Crucible*. New York: Harper Torchbooks, 1971.

———. *Mephistopheles and the Androgyne*. New York: Sheed and Ward, 1965.

———. *Myth and Reality*. New York: Harper Torchbooks, 1963.

———. *The Quest, History and Meaning in Religion*. Chicago: University of Chicago Press, 1969.

———. Review of Baumann's *Das Doppelte Geschlecht. Ethnologische Studien zur Bisexualität in Ritus and Mythos. Revue de l'histoire des religions* 153 (1958): 89–92.

———. *Rites and Symbols of Initiation*. New York: Harper Torchbooks, 1958.

———. *Shamanism: Archaic Techniques of Ecstacy*. New York: Pantheon Books, 1964.

Erkes, Eduard. "Eine P'an-ku Mythe der Hsia-Zeit?" *T'oung Pao* 37 (1942): 159–173.

———. "Some Remarks on Karlgren's 'Fecundity Symbols.' " *Bulletin of the Museum of Far Eastern Antiquities* (Stockholm) 3 (1931): 63–68.

———. "Spüren chinesischer Weltschöpfungsmythen." *T'oung Pao* 28 (1931): 335–368.

Fontenrose, Joseph. *Python: A Study of Delphic Myth and Its Origins*. Berkeley and Los Angeles: University of California Press, 1959.

Forke, A. *The World Conception of the Chinese*. London: Probsthain, 1925.

Foucault, Michel. *The Order of Things, An Archaeology of the Human Sciences*. New York: Vintage Books, 1970.

Fung Yu-lan. *A History of Chinese Philosophy*. Translated by Derek Bodde. 2 vols. Princeton: Princeton University Press, 1952.

Gates, J. "Model Emperors of the Golden Age in Chinese Lore." *Journal of the American Oriental Society* 56 (1936): 51–76.

Girardot, N. J. "Part of the Way: Four Studies on Taoism." *History of Religions* 11 (1972): 319–337.

———. "The Problem of Creation Mythology in the Study of Chinese Religion." *History of Religions* 15 (1976): 289–318.

Graham, A. C. "Being in Western Philosophy Compared with Shih/fei and Yu/wu in Chinese Philosophy." *Asia Major* 7 (1959): 79–112.

———. *Book of Lieh-tzu*. London: John Murray, 1960

———. "The Date and Composition of Lieh tzu." *Asia Major* 8 (1961): 139–198.

———. "How Much of *Chuang Tzu* Did Chuang Tzu Write?" *Journal of the American Academy of Religion Thematic Issue*. Edited by Henry Rosemont, Jr. and Benjamin I. Schwartz. 47 (1979): 459–502.

Graham, D. Crockett. *Songs and Stories of the Ch'uan Miao*. Smithsonian Miscellaneous Collections, vol. 123. Washington, D.C.: Smithsonian Institution, 1954.

Granet, Marcel. *Danses et légendes de la Chine ancienne*. Reprint ed., Paris: University of France, 1959.

———. *Études sociologiques sur la Chine*. Reprint ed., Paris: University of France, 1953.

———. *La Pensée Chinoise*. Reprint ed., Paris: Albin Michel, 1968.

Gruman, Gerald J. *A History of Ideas About the Prolongation of Life*. Transactions of the American Philosophical Society, vol. 56. Philadelphia: American Philosophical Society, 1966.

Gunkel, Herman, *Schöpfung und Chaos in Urzeit und Endzeit*. Gottingen: Vandenhoeck und Ruprecht, 1895.

Hall, David L. "Process and Anarchy—A Taoist Vision of Creativity." *Philosophy East and West* 28 (1978): 271–285.

———. *The Uncertain Phoenix, Adventures Toward a Post-Cultural Sensibility*. New York: Fordham University Press, 1979.

Hawkes, David. *Ch'u Tz'u, The Songs of the South*. Boston: Beacon, 1959.

Heiser, Charles B. *The Gourd Book*. Norman: University of Oklahoma Press, 1979.

Hellbom, Anna-Britta. "The Creation Egg." *Ethnos* (Stockholm) 28 (1963): 63–104.

Hentze, Karl. *Chinese Tomb Figures*. London: Edward Goldston, 1928.

Hertz, R. *Death and the Right Hand*. Translated by Rodney and Claudia Needham. Glencoe, Ill.: Free Press, 1960.

Hewes, Gordon W. Review of Eberhard's *Kultur und Siedlung*. *American Anthropologist* 49 (1947): 105–108.

Hildburgh, W. L. "Note on the Gourd as an Amulet in Japan." *Man* 19 (1919): 25–29.

Hillman, James. "Senex and Puer." *Eranos-Jahrbuch 1967*. Zurich: Rhein-Verlag, 1968: 301–367.

Hisamatsu Shinichi. "The Characteristics of Oriental Nothingness. *Philosophical Studies of Japan* 2 (1960): 65–97.

Ho Ping-ti. *The Cradle of the East*. Chicago: University of Chicago Press, 1975.

Ho Ping-yu, and Needham, Joseph. "The Laboratory Equipment of the Early Medieval Chinese Alchemist." *Ambix* 7 (1959): 57–115.

Ho Ting-jui. *A Comparative Study of Myths and Legends of Formosan Aborigines*. Taipei: The Orient Cultural Service, 1971.

Hou Wai-lu. *Chung Kuo Ku Tai Ssu Hsiang Hsüeh Shuo Shih* [Reflections on Ancient Chinese Philosophy]. Chunking: Wen-feng, 1944.

Hsu Sung-peng. "Lao Tzu's Conception of Ultimate Reality: A Comparative Study." *International Philosophical Quarterly* 16 (1976): 197–218.

Hsüan Chu. *Chung Kuo Shen Hua Yen Chiu* [Studies on Chinese Mythology]. Shanghai: World Book Company, 1928.

Huai Nan Tzu Chu Shih [Commentary and Explanation of the Huai Nan Tzu]. Annotated by Kao Yu. Taipei: Hua Lien Publishing Company, 1968.

Huai Nan Tzu T'ung Chien [Index to the Huai Nan Tzu]. Peking: Centre franco-chinois d'études sinologiques, 1944.

Huang Wen-shan. "The Artistic Representation of Totems in Ancient Chinese Culture." *Bulletin of the Institute of Ethnology, Academia Sinica* 21 (1966): 1–13.

Izutsu, Toshihiko. "The Absolute and the Perfect Man in Taoism." *Eranos-Jahrbuch 1967* Zurich: Rhein-Verlag, 1968: 379–441.

————. *The Key Philosophical Concepts in Sufism and Taoism*. 2 vols. Tokyo: Keio Institute, 1967.

Jan Yün-hua. "Problems of Tao and Tao Te Ching." *Numen* 22 (1975): 208–234.

Jensen, Adolf. *Myth and Cult Among Primitive Peoples*. Translated by Marianna Tax Cholden and Wolfgang Weissleder. Chicago: University of Chicago Press, 1963.

Kaltenmark, Max. "Le Dompteur des flots." *Han-huie* [Han Hsüeh] (Peking) 3 (1948): 1–112.

————. *Lao Tzu and Taoism*. Translated by Roger Greaves. Stanford: Stanford University Press, 1969.

————. *Le Lie-sien Tchouen, biographies légendaires des immortels taoistes de l'antiquité*. Peking: Centre d'études sinologiques de Pékin, 1953.

————. "La Naissance du Monde en Chine." *La Naissance du Monde*. Paris: Editons du Seuil, 1959.

Karlgren, Bernhard. *Analytical Dictionary of Chinese*. Paris: Paul Geuthner, 1923.

————. *Grammata Serica*. Gotenburg: Elauders Boktryckeri, 1940.

————. "Legends and Cults in Ancient China." *Bulletin of the Museum of Far Eastern Antiquities* (Stockholm) 18 (1946): 199–365.

————. "Some Fecundity Symbols in Ancient China." *Bulletin of the Museum of Far Eastern Antiquities* (Stockholm) 2 (1930): 1–66.

————. "Word Families in Chinese." *Bulletin of the Museum of Far Eastern Antiquities* (Stockholm) 5 (1933): 9–20.

Kleiber, Nancy. "The Controversy About the Austronesian Homeland." *Anthropologica* 11 (1969): 151–163.

Köppers, W. "Der Hund in der Mythologie der zirkumpazifischen Volker." *Wiener Beiträge für Kultergeschichte W. Linguistik* 1 (1930): 259–399.

————. "Die Frage des Mutterrechts und des Totemismus im alten China." *Anthropos* 25 (1930): 981–1002.

Ku Chieh-kang, ed. *Ku Shih Pien* (Symposium on Chinese Ancient History). Peiping: Pu She, 1927–1941.

Kuhn, Alfred. *Berichte über den Weltanfang beiden Indochinesen*. Leipzig: n.p., 1935.

Lao Han [pseud.]. "Hua hu-lu" [Talking about the Bottle Gourd]. *Jen Wen Shih Chiai* [Culture World, Taipei] 1 (1971): 26–28.

Lathrap, Donald W. "Our Father the Cayman, Our Mother the Gourd: Spinden Revisited, or a Unitary Mode for the Emergence of Agriculture in the New World" in *The Origins of Agriculture*. Edited by Charles A. Reed. The Hague: Mouton, 1977.

Laufer, Berthold. *Chinese Pottery of the Han Dynasty*. Leiden: E. J. Brill, 1909.
————. *Sino-Iranica*. Reprint ed., Taipei: Ch'eng-Wen, 1967.
Lebar, F. M., Hickey, G. C., and Musgrave, J. K. *Ethnic Groups of Mainland Southeast Asia*. New Haven: Human Relation Area Files, 1964.
Legge, James. *The Chinese Classics*. 5 vols. Reprint ed., Hong Kong: Hong Kong University Press, 1960.
Lessa, William, and Vogt, Evon Z., ed. *Reader In Comparative Religion*. New York: Harper and Row, 1965.
Lévi-Strauss, Claude. *The Raw and the Cooked*. New York: Harper Torchbooks, 1970.
Li Hui-lin. *The Garden Flowers of China*. New York: Ronald Press, 1959.
————. "The Origin of Cultivated Plants in Southeast Asia." *Economic Botany* 25 (1970): 3–19.
————. "The Vegetables of Ancient China." *Economic Botany* 23 (1969): 253–260.
Li Hwei, "T'ai-wan yü tung-nan-ya ti t'ung-pao-p'ei-ou-hsing hung-shui ch'uan-shuo" [The Deluge Legend of Sibling-Mating Type in Taiwan and Southeast Asia]. *Bulletin of the Ethnological Society of China* (Taipei) 1 (1955): 171–206.
Lin, Paul J. *A Translation of Lao Tzu's Tao Te Ching and Wang Pi's Commentary*. Ann Arbor: Center for Chinese Studies, University of Michigan, 1977.
Lin Yueh-hwa. "The Miao-Man Peoples of Kweichow." *Harvard Journal of Asiatic Studies* 5 (1941): 261–345.
Ling shun-sheng. "Shen-chu yü yin-yang hsing ch'i ch'ung-pai" [Ancestral Tablet and Genital Symbolism in Ancient China]. *Bulletin of the Institute of Ethnology, Academia Sinica* 8 (1959): 1–46 (with English summary).
Liu, C. H. "The Dog-ancestor Story of the Aboriginal Tribes of Southern China." *Journal of the Royal Anthropological Institute* 62 (1932): 361–368.
Liu Wen-tien, ed. *Huai Nan Hung Lieh Chi Chieh* [Collected Commentaries on the *Huai Nan Tzu*]. Shanghai: Commercial Press, 1923.
Lo Meng-ts'e. "Shuo hun-tun yü chu-tzu ching ch'uan chih yen ta-hsiang" [The Primeval State and Ideas of Creation in Early Chinese Philosophy and Classics]. *Journal of Oriental Studies* (Hong Kong) 9 (January 1971–July 1971): 15–57, 230–305 (with English summary).
Loewe, Michael. "Man and Beast, The Hybrid In Early Chinese Art and Literature." *Numen* 25 (1978): 97–117.
Long, Charles H. *Alpha: the Myths of Creation*. New York: George Braziller Inc., 1963.
Mabuchi Toichi. *The Ethnology of the Southwestern Pacific*. Taipei: Orient Cultural Service, 1974.
Major, John S. "Myth, Cosmology and the Origins of Chinese Science." *Journal of Chinese Philosophy* 5 (1978): 1–20.
Maspero, Henri. "Légendes mythologiques dans le Chou king." *Journal Asiatique* 205 (1924): 1–100.
————. "Les Procédés de 'nourir le principe vital' dans la religion taoiste ancienne." *Journal Asiatique* 228 (1937): 77–252, 353–430.
————. *Le Taoisme. Mélanges posthumes sur les religions et l'histoire de la Chine*, vol. 2. Paris: University of France, 1967.
Mathew's Chinese-English Dictionary. Cambridge: Harvard University Press, 1966.
Mauss, Marrel. *The Gift*. Glencoe, Ill.: Free Press, 1954.

Morgan, E. *Tao, the Great Luminant*. Reprint ed., Taipei: Ch'eng-Wen Publishing Co., 1966.

Munro, Donald J. *The Concept of Man in Early China*. Stanford: Stanford University Press, 1969.

Needham, Joseph. *Science and Civilization in China*, vols. 1–5. Cambridge: The University Press: 1954–1974.

Norrman, Ralf, and Haarberg, Jon. *Nature and Language; A Semiotic Study of Cucurbits In Literature*. London: Routledge & Kegan Paul, 1980.

Numazawa, Franz. "Background of Myths on the Separation of Sky and Earth from the Point of View of Cultural History." *Scientia* (Milan) 88 (1953): 28–35.

Obayashi Taro. "The Origins of Japanese Mythology." *Acta Asiatica* 31 (1977): 1–23.

Opitz, Peter-Joachim. *Lao-Tzu Die Ordnungsspekulation im Tao-te-ching*. München: Paul List Verlag, 1967.

Ouwehand, C. *Namazu-e and Their Themes*. Leiden: E. J. Brill, 1964.

Pelliot, P. Review of W. Köpper's "Der Hund in der Mythologie der zirkumpazifischen Volker." *T'oung Pao* 28 (1931) 463–470.

Plaks, Andrew H. *Archetype and Allegory in the Dream of the Red Chamber*. Princeton: Princeton University Press, 1976.

Porée-Maspero, Eveline. *Étude sur les rites agraires des Cambodgiens*. 3 vols. Paris: Mouton and Co., 1952, 1964, 1969.

Prusek, J. *Chinese statelets and the Northern Barbarians in the Period 1400–300* B.C. New York: Humanities Press, 1971.

Przyluski, J. "Les Unipedes." *Mélanges Chinois et Bouddhiques* 2 (1933): 307–332.

Robinet, Isabelle. *Les Commentaires du Tao To King Jusqu' un VII siècle*. Paris: College de France, 1977.

———. *Méditation taoiste*. Paris: Dervy Livres, 1979.

Ruey Yih-fu [Jui I-fu]. "Miao-tsu hung-shui ku-shih yü fu-hsi nü-wa ti ch'uan-shuo" [Stories of a Deluge in the Miao and the Legend Concerning Fu-hsi and Nü-wa]. *The Journal of Anthropology, Institute of History and Philology, Academia Sinica* 1 (1938): 155–203.

Saso, Michael. *Taoism and the Rite of Cosmic Renewal*. Pullman, Wash.: Washington State University Press, 1972.

———. *The Teachings of Taoist Master Chuang*. New Haven: Yale University Press, 1978.

Saso, Michael, and Chappell, David W., ed. *Buddhist and Taoist Studies*. Honolulu: University of Hawaii Press, 1977.

Sauer, Carl O. *Agricultural Origins and Dispersals, The Domestication of Animals and Foodstuffs*. Reprint ed., Cambridge: The MIT Press, 1969.

Saussure, Leopold De. "Le système cosmologique des Chinois," *Revue générale des sciences* 32 (1921): 729–736.

Schafer, Edward H. *The Divine Woman: Dragon Ladies and Rain Maidens in T'ang Literature*. Berkeley, Los Angeles, London: University of California Press, 1973.

———. "The Idea of Created Nature in T'ang Literature." *Philosophy East and West* 15 (1965): 543–550.

———. *Pacing the Void, T'ang Approaches to the Stars*. Berkeley, Los Angeles, London: University of California Press, 1977.

————. "Ritual Exposure in Ancient China." *Harvard Journal of Asiatic Studies* 14 (1951): 130–184.

————. *The Vermilion Bird, T'ang Images of the South.* Berkeley and Los Angeles: University of California Press, 1967.

Schärer, Hans. *Ngaju Religion.* The Hague: Martinus Nijhoff, 1963.

Schipper, Kristopher M. *L'emperour Wou des Han dans la légende taoiste. Han Wou-ti Nei-tchouan.* Paris: École francaise d'extrême-orient, 1965.

————. Review of A. C. Graham's *Book of Lieh-tzu. T'oung Pao* 51 (1964): 288–294.

————. "Taoism: The Liturgical Tradition," Unpublished paper given at the First International Conference on Taoist Studies, 1968.

————. "The Taoist Body." *History of Religions* 17 (1978): 355–386.

Scholem, G. *On the Kaballah and Its Symbolism.* New York: Schocken Books, 1965.

Seidel, Anna K. *La Divinisation de Lao tseu dans le taoisme des Han.* Paris: École francaise d'extrême-orient, 1969.

————. "The Image of the Perfect Ruler in Early Taoist Messianism: Lao-tzu and Li Hung." *History of Religions* 9 (1969–1970): 216–247.

Shan Hai Ching T'ung Chien [Index to the Shan Hai Ching]. Peking: Centre franco-chinois d'études sinologiques, 1948.

Sheppard, M. J. "Egg Symbolism in Alchemy." *Ambix* 6 (1958): 140–148.

Shih, Joseph. "The Ancient Chinese Cosmogony." *Studia Missionalia* 28 (1969): 111–130.

————. "Revelation in Chinese Religion." *Studia Missionalia* 20 (1971): 237–266.

Shime (kake) Suigan. *Hyōtan monogatari* [The Story of the gourd]. N.p., 1922.

Sivin, Nathan. "Chinese Alchemy and the Manipulation of Time." *Isis* 67 (1967): 513–526.

————. *Chinese Alchemy: Preliminary Studies.* Cambridge: Harvard University Press, 1968.

————. "On the Word 'Taoist' as a Source of Perplexity." *History of Religions* 17 (1978): 303–330.

Smith, Jonathan Z. *Map Is Not Territory.* Leiden: E. J. Brill, 1978.

Soymié, M. "Le Lo-feou Chan, étude de géographie réligieuse." *Bulletin de l'école francaise d'extreme orient* 48 (1956): 1–139.

Sproul, Barbara. *Primal Myths, Creating the World.* San Francisco: Harper and Row, 1979.

————. "Prolegomena to the Study of Creation Myths." Ph.D. dissertation, Columbia University, 1972.

Stein, Rolf. "Architecture et pensée religieuse en extrême-orient." *Arts Asiatiques* 4 (1957): 163–186.

————. "Jardins en minature d'extrême-orient." *Bulletin de l'école francoise de l'extrême-orient* 42 (1942): 1–104.

Strickmann, Michel. "History, Anthropology, and Chinese Religion," *Harvard Journal of Asiatic Studies* 40 (1980): 201–248.

Su Hsüeh-lin. *K'un Lun Chih Mi* [Riddle of Mt. K'un-lun]. Taipei: Chinese Cultural Press, 1956.

Sun Lung-kee. "The Mythical World-View and Cosmogonic Myths of the Ancient Chinese." Unpublished paper, 1977.

Tai Yüan-ch'ang, comp. *Hsien Hsüeh Tz'u Tien* [Dictionary of Terms for the Study of the Practices of Taoist Immortality]. Taipei: Chen Shan Mei Publishing Company, 1962.

———. *Tao Hsüeh Tz'u Tien* [Dictionary of Terms for Taoist Studies]. Taipei: Chen Shan Mei Publishing Company, 1971.

Theil, P. J. "Shamanismus im alten China." *Sinologica* 10 (1968–1969): 149–204.

Tjan Tjoe-som. trans. *Po Hu T'ung, The Comprehensive Discussions in the White Tiger Hall*. 2 vols. Leiden: E. J. Brill, 1949,1952.

Tu Er-wei. *Feng Lin Kuei Lung K'ao Shih* [The Four Divine Animals Examined and Explained]. Taipei: Taiwan Commercial Press, 1971.

Turner, Victor. *Dramas, Fields, and Metaphors*. Ithaca: Cornell University Press, 1974.

———. *The Ritual Process*. Ithaca: Cornell University Press, 1977.

Tz'u Hai. 2 vols. Shanghai: Chung Hua Book Company, 1937; reprint ed., Taipei: Taiwan Chung Hua Book Company, 1971.

van Gennep, Arnold. *The Rites of Passage*. Translated by Monika B. Vizedom and Gabrielle L. Caffee. Chicago: University of Chicago Press, 1960.

Von Franz, Mari-Louise. *Creation Myths*. Zurich: Spring Publications, 1972.

Wakeman, Mary. *God's Battle With the Monster*. Leiden: E. J. Brill, 1973.

Waley, Arthur. *The Way and Its Power*. New York: Grove Press, 1958.

Walk, Leopold. "Das Flut-Geschwisterpaar als Ur-und Stammiltempaar der Menschheit. Ein Beitrag zur Mythengeschichte Süd-und Südostasiens." *Mitteilungen der Anthropologischen Gesellschaft in Wien* 78–79 (1949): 60–115.

Wallacker, Benjamin. *The Huai-Nan-Tzu Book Eleven: Behavior, Culture and the Cosmos*. American Oriental Series, no. 48. New Haven: American Oriental Society, 1962.

Watson, Burton. *The Complete Works of Chuang Tzu*. New York: Columbia University Press, 1968.

———. *Early Chinese Literature*. New York: Columbia University Press, 1967.

Welch, Holmes, and Seidel, Anna. *Facets of Taoism*. New Haven: Yale University Press, 1979.

Welsford, Enid. *The Fool*. London: Faber and Faber, 1935.

Wen I-to. *Wen I-to Ch'üan Chi* [Collected Works of Wen I-to]. 4 vols. Shanghai: K'ai Ming Book Store, 1948.

Wheatley, Paul. *The Pivot of the Four Quarters*. Chicago: Aldine, 1971.

Wiens, H. J. *Han Chinese Expansion in South China*. N. p.: Shoe String Press, 1967.

Willeford, William. *The Fool and His Scepter*. Evanston: Northwestern University Press, 1969.

Wright, Arthur F. "A Historian's Reflections on the Taoist Tradition." *History of Religions* 9 (1969–1970): 248–255.

Yang Pai-ling, comp. *Lieh Tzu Chi Shih* [Collected Explanations of the Lieh Tzu]. Taipei: Ming Lun Publishing Company, 1971.

Yu, David C. "The Creation Myth and Its Symbolism in Classical Taoism," *Philosophy East and West* 31 (1981): 479–500.

Yüan K'o. *Chung Kuo Ku Tai Shen Hua* [Ancient Chinese Myths]. Shanghai: Commercial Press, 1957.

INDEX

Abyss, 82; and chaos, 5, 24, 93; great, 92, 158; in *Lieh Tzu*, 162
Adam Kadmon, 299, 310
Agriculture, 209; Chinese, 214-222; in myths, 211–212, 237
Alchemy, 132, 136, 197; and chaos theme, 292, 307; Chinese, 291–293, 294, 295, 297–298; and creation, 295–298; gourds in, 292, 293; internal, 285–290; purpose of, 294; religious implications of, 291–295; and salvation, 291, 292, 298; symbolism in, 292–293; in Taoism, 42–43, 97, 132, 198–199, 285–290, 291–293, 294, 295, 297–298; texts of, 292; as transformation, 198–199, 201; *unus mundus* in, 295–298; Western, 286, 288, 292, 294, 295–298, 300. *See also* Metallurgy; Separation and reunification (*solve et coagula*)
Amulets, 26, 37
Analects, 261
Ancestor, 52, 84, 85; in Taoism, 260–261; *tsung*, 66, 67. *See also* Animal ancestor
Ancestral tablet, 261, 262–264
Animal: ancestor, 13, 24, 67, 172, 173, 177, 178, 179, 181, 182, 184, 185, 186–191, 192, 197, 199, 200, 201–202, 203, 206, 207, 209, 210, 214, 232–235, 236, 238, 239, 261, 262, 268, 272, 275, 306, 309, 311–316 (*see also* Deluge myths; P'an-hu); five poisonous, 34; spouse, 189–190, 191, 232, 320–322; totem, 87
Arrows, 89, 92, 188
Austroasiatic cultures, 170–171, 175

Barbarian, 122, 130, 174, 198, 201; Emperor Hun-tun as, 190, 270; motif, 171–173, 188, 189–190, 191; myths, 172–173
Bats, 223, 372 n. 49
Bauer, Wolfgang, 41, 68, 141, 303; on caves, 147–148; on paradise, 162
Baumann, Hermann, 183

Beginning: great, 104, 105, 140, 275; return to, 49, 55, 63, 67, 68, 74–75, 76, 80, 81, 84, 87, 98, 104–106, 107, 116, 117, 129, 130, 133, 135–136, 137, 139–143, 145, 154, 155, 159–160, 205, 258, 261, 268, 278, 282–283, 289, 298, 309. *See also* Creation
Being, 2, 51–52. *See also* Non-being
Bellows, 87, 92–93
Berger, Peter, 280
Bird: Emperor Hun-tun as, 82, 86–87, 92, 200; luan, 131; symbolism, 34, 131, 200–201, 224–225
Birth, 73, 144, 150–151; and death, 84, 97, 98; of Lao Tzu, 284–285; of P'an-ku, 143, 176
Block, 123, 124. *See also* Rebels, four wicked
Boodberg, Peter A., 144, 149
Borges, Jorge, 1
Boring (*tso*), 63, 81, 83, 88, 92, 99, 112, 139, 150, 154, 156, 187, 237; of Emperor Hun-tun, 13, 53, 93–94, 95–97, 140, 195, 244, 286; as initiation ritual, 96, 347–348 n. 77, 78
Breath manipulation, 288. *See also* Meditation
Buddhism, 68, 192, 194, 196, 197; Ch'an, 260, 302
Burckhardt, Titus, 294
Burkert, Walter, 7–8, 10
Butterfly, 106; Way, 111, 160, 308–309

Calabash. *See* Gourd; Mountain, calabash
Carroll, Lewis, 11, 25, 308
Carrouges, Michel, 301, 302
Cave (*tung*) imagery, 24, 147–148, 183, 190, 203. *See also* Paradise
Center (*axis mundi*), 23, 93, 149, 154, 200, 201, 252; Emperor Hun-tun as, 90; P'an-ku as, 193
Chang Chung-yuan, 48, 101–102
Chang Heng, 23